3495

Xlib Reference
Manual

Books That Help People Get More Out of Computers

X Protocol Reference Manual, *516 pages*

Describes the X Network Protocol which underlies all software for Version 11 of the X Window System.

Xlib Programming Manual, *680 pages*
Xlib Reference Manual, *1144 pages*

Complete programming and reference guides to the X library (Xlib), the lowest level of programming interface to X.

X Window System User's Guide

Orients the new user to window system concepts, provides detailed tutorials for many client programs, and explains how to customize the X environment.

Standard Edition, 752 pages
Motif Edition, 734 pages

X Toolkit Intrinsics Programming Manual

Complete guide to programming with Xt Intrinsics, the library of C language routines that facilitate the design of user interfaces, with reusable components called widgets.

Standard Edition, 624 pages
Motif Edition, 672 pages

X Toolkit Intrinsics Reference Manual, *916 pages*

Complete programmer's reference for the X Toolkit.

Motif Programming Manual, *1032 pages*

Complete guide to programming for the Motif graphical user interface.

XView Programming Manual, *776 pages*
XView Reference Manual, *292 pages*

Complete information on programming with XView, an easy-to-use toolkit that is widely available.

The X Window System in a Nutshell, *380 pages*

A single-volume quick reference that is an indispensable companion to the series.

Contact us for a catalog of our books, for orders, or for more information.

O'Reilly & Associates, Inc.

103 Morris Street, Suite A, Sebastopol CA 95472
(800) 998-9938 US/Canada   707-829-0515 overseas/local   707-829-0104 Fax

Volume Two

Xlib Reference Manual

Third Edition for X11, Release 4 and Release 5

Edited by Adrian Nye

O'Reilly & Associates, Inc.

Xlib Reference Manual

Editor: Adrian Nye

Printing History:

August 1988:	First Edition.
November 1988:	Minor revisions.
May 1989:	Release 3 updates added. Minor revisions.
April 1990:	Second Edition covers Release 3 and Release 4.
July 1990:	Minor revisions.
October 1990:	Minor revisions.
December 1991	Minor revisions.
June 1992:	Third Edition covers Release 4 and Release 5.

Volume 2, Third Edition: ISBN 1-56592-006-6

Table of Contents

Tables

Preface

In This Chapter:

Preface

What's New in This Edition

This Third Edition of *Xlib Reference Manual* covers Release 4 and Release 5 versions of the Xlib specification. We have added over 100 new reference pages. Many of these new reference pages cover new Release 5 functions, providing support for internationalization and device-independent color. The remaining new reference pages cover the macros and their function versions; these have never had reference pages in this book before. Now macros are covered both on the reference pages and Appendix C where they have always been.

We have also meticulously compared this manual against the MIT X Consortium's Release 5 Xlib specification, to make sure this manual accurately reflects the Xlib standard.

Finally, we have added an appendix describing the various character sets that are referred to on the reference pages.

About This Manual

This manual describes the X library, the C Language programming interface to Version 11 of the X Window System. The X library, known as Xlib, is the lowest level of programming interface to X. This library enables a programmer to write applications with an advanced user interface based on windows on the screen, with complete network transparency, that will run without changes on many types of workstations and personal computers.

Xlib is powerful enough to write effective applications without additional programming tools and is necessary for certain tasks even in applications written with higher-level "toolkits."

There are a number of these toolkits for X programming, the most notable being the DEC/MIT toolkit Xt, the Xview toolkit developed by Sun, the Andrew toolkit developed by IBM and Carnegie-Mellon University, and the InterViews toolkit from Stanford. These toolkits are still evolving, and only Xt is currently part of the X standard. Toolkits simplify the process of application writing considerably, providing a number of *widgets* that implement menus, command buttons, and other common features of the user interface.

This manual does not describe Xt or any other toolkit. That is done in Volumes Four, Five, and Six of our X Window System series. Nonetheless, much of the material described in this book is helpful for understanding and using the toolkits, since the toolkits themselves are written using Xlib and allow Xlib code to be intermingled with toolkit code.

Summary of Contents

This manual is divided into two volumes. This is the second volume, the *Xlib Reference Manual*. It includes reference pages for each of the Xlib functions (organized alphabetically), a permuted index, and numerous appendices and quick reference aids.

The first volume, the *Xlib Programming Manual*, provides a conceptual introduction to Xlib, including tutorial material and numerous programming examples. Arranged by task or topic, each chapter brings together a group of Xlib functions, describes the conceptual foundation they are based on, and illustrates how they are most often used in writing applications (or, in the case of the last chapter, in writing window managers). Volume One is structured so as to be useful as a tutorial and also as a task-oriented reference.

Volume One and Volume Two are designed to be used together. To get the most out of the examples in Volume One, you will need the exact calling sequences of each function from Volume Two. To understand fully how to use each of the functions described in Volume Two, all but the most experienced X "hacker" will need the explanation and examples in Volume One.

Both volumes include material from the original Xlib and X11 Protocol documentation provided by MIT, as well as from other documents provided on the MIT release tape. We have done our best to incorporate all of the useful information from the MIT documentation, to correct references we found to be in error, to reorganize and present it in a more useful form, and to supplement it with conceptual material, tutorials, reference aids, and examples. In other words, this manual is not only a replacement but is a superset of the MIT documentation.

Those of you familiar with the MIT documentation will recognize that each reference page in Volume Two includes the detailed specification of the routine found in Gettys, Newman, and Scheifler's *Xlib–C Language X Interface*, plus, in many cases, additional text that clarifies ambiguities and describes the context in which the routine would be used. We have also added cross references to related reference pages and to where additional information can be found in Volume One.

How to Use This Manual

Volume Two is designed to make it as easy and fast as possible to look up virtually any fact about Xlib. It includes a permuted index, reference pages for each library function, appendices that cover macros, structures, function groups, events, fonts, colors, cursors, keysyms, and errors, and at-a-glance tables for the graphics context and window attributes.

The permuted index is the standard UNIX way of finding a particular function name given a keyword. By looking up a word in the second column that you think describes the function you are looking for, you can find the group of functions that have that word in their description lines. The description line also appears at the top of each reference page. Once you have found the routine you are looking for, you can look for its reference page.

The permuted index provides a standard UNIX permuted index for all reference pages.

The reference pages themselves provide all the details necessary for calling each routine, including its arguments, returned values, definitions of the structure types of arguments and returned values, and the errors it may generate. Many of the pages also give hints about how the routine is used in the context of other routines. This is the part of this volume you will use the most.

Appendix A, *Function Group Summary*, groups the routines according to function, and provides brief descriptions. You'll find it useful to have in one place a description of related routines, so their differences can be noted and the appropriate one chosen.

Appendix B, *Error Messages and Protocol Requests*, describes the errors that Xlib routines can generate. When an error is handled by the default error handler, one of these messages is printed. Also printed is the X Protocol request that caused the error. Since Protocol requests do not map directly to Xlib routines, this appendix provides a table with which you can find out which Xlib routine in your code caused the error.

Appendix C, *Macros*, describes the macros that access members of the **Display** structure, classify keysyms, and convert resource manager types.

Appendix D, *The Server-side Color Database*, presents the standard color database. The color names in this database should be available on all servers, though the corresponding RGB values may have been modified to account for screen variations.

Appendix E, *Event Reference*, describes each event type and structure, in a reference page format. This is an invaluable reference for event programming.

Appendix F, *Structure Reference*, describes all structures used by Xlib except the event structures described in Appendix E, including which routines use each structure.

Appendix G, *Symbol Reference*, lists in alphabetical order and describes all of the symbols defined in Xlib include files.

Appendix H, *Keysym Reference*, lists and describes each character in the standard keysym families, used for translating keyboard events. The characters for English and foreign language keysyms are shown where possible.

Appendix I, *The Cursor Font*, describes the standard cursor font, including a illustration of the font shapes.

Appendix J, *The Xmu Library*, provides reference pages for each function in the miscellaneous utilities library (Xmu). This library is provided with the standard X distribution and is very useful when programming with Xlib.

Appendix K, *Character Sets and Encodings*, describes the standard character sets that are referred to on various reference pages.

The *Index* should help you to find what you need to know.

Finally, Volume Two concludes with at-a-glance charts that help in setting the graphics context (GC) and the window attributes.

Assumptions

Readers should be proficient in the C programming language, and should have a basic understanding of X, which can be gained by reading a tutorial book such as Volume One, *Xlib Programming Manual*. In addition, general familiarity with the principles of raster graphics will be helpful.

Font Conventions Used in This Manual

Italic is used for:

- UNIX pathnames, filenames, program names, user command names, and options for user commands.
- New terms where they are defined.

`Typewriter Font` is used for:

- Anything that would be typed verbatim into code, such as examples of source code and text on the screen.
- The contents of include files, such as structure types, structure members, symbols (defined constants and bit flags), and macros.
- Xlib functions.
- Names of subroutines of the example programs.

`Italic Typewriter Font` is used for:

- Arguments to Xlib functions, since they could be typed in code as shown but are arbitrary.

Helvetica Italics are used for:

- Titles of examples, figures, and tables.

Boldface is used for:

- Chapter and section headings.

Related Documents

The following documents are included on the X11 source tape:

> *Xt Toolkit Intrinsics* by Joel McCormack, Paul Asente, and Ralph Swick
> *Xt Toolkit Widgets* by Chris Peterson
> *Xlib–C Language X Interface* by Jim Gettys, Ron Newman, and Robert Scheifler
> *X Window System Protocol, Version 11* by Robert Scheifler

The following books on the X Window System are available from O'Reilly and Associates, Inc.:

> Volume Zero — *X Protocol Reference Manual*
> Volume One — *Xlib Programming Manual*
> Volume Three — *X Window System User's Guide*
> Volume Four — *X Toolkit Intrinsics Programming Manual*
> Volume Five — *X Toolkit Intrinsics Reference Manual*
> Volume Six — *Motif Programming Manual*
> Volume Seven — *XView Programmer's Guide*
> *PHIGS Programming Manual*
> *PHIGS Reference Manual*
> Quick Reference — *The X Window System in a Nutshell*

Requests for Comments

Please write to tell us about any flaws you find in this manual or how you think it could be improved, to help us provide you with the best documentation possible.

Our U.S. mail address, e-mail address, and telephone number are as follows:

O'Reilly and Associates, Inc.
103 Morris Street
Sebastopol, CA 95472
(800) 338-6887

UUCP: uunet!ora!adrian   Internet: adrian@ora.com

Bulk Sales Information

This manual is being resold by many workstation manufacturers as their official X Window System documentation. For information on volume discounts for bulk purchase, call O'Reilly and Associates, Inc., at (800) 338-6887, (in CA 800-533-6887) or send e-mail to linda@ora.com (uunet!ora!linda).

For companies requiring extensive customization of the book, source licensing terms are also available.

Acknowledgements

The information contained in this manual is based in part on *Xlib–C Language X Interface*, written by Jim Gettys, Ron Newman, and Robert Scheifler, and the *X Window System Protocol, Version 11*, by Robert Scheifler (with many contributors). The X Window System software and these documents were written under the auspices of the X Consortium at MIT. In addition, this manual includes material from Oliver Jones' Xlib tutorial presentation, which was given at the MIT X Conference in January 1988, and from David Rosenthal's *Inter-Client Communication Conventions Manual*.

I would like to thank the authors of these documents, and the X Consortium, for the copyright policy that allows others to build upon their work. Their generosity of spirit not only has made this book possible, but is the basis for the unparallelled speed with which the X Window System has been adopted as a *de facto* standard.

I would also like to thank the people who helped this book come into being. It was Tim O'Reilly who originally sent me out on a contract to write a manual for X Version 10 for a workstation manufacturer and later to another company to write a manual for X Version 11, from which this book began. I have learned most of what I know about computers and technical writing while working for Tim. For this book, he acted as an editor, he helped me reorganize several chapters, he worked on the *Color* and *Managing User Preferences* chapters when time was too short for me to do it, and he kept my spirits up through this long project.

This book would not be as good (and we might still be working on it) had it not been for Daniel Gilly. Daniel was my production assistant for critical periods in the project. He dealt with formatting issues, checked for consistent usage of terms and noticed irregularities in content, and edited files from written corrections by me and by others. His job was to take as much of the work off me as possible, and with his technical skill and knowledge of UNIX, he did that very well.

For the Release 5 edition, I'd like to thank Paula Ferguson, who took on the thankless task of finding all the changes that had been made in the Xlib specification, Al Tabayoyon of Tektronix, for reviewing the Xcms manpages.

This manual has benefitted from the work and assistance of the entire staff of O'Reilly and Associates, Inc. David Flanagan and Daniel Gilly drafted the R5 manpages as originally printed in David's R5 Update book, Susan Willing was responsible for graphics and design, and she proofed many drafts of the book; Linda Mui tailored the troff macros to the design by Sue Willing and myself and was invaluable in the final production process; John Strang figured out the resource manager and wrote the original section on that topic; Karen Cakebread edited a draft of the manual and established some conventions for terms and format. Peter Mui executed the "at-a-glance" tables at the end of the volume; Valerie Quercia, Tom Van Raalte, and Linda Walsh all contributed in some small ways; and Cathy Brennan, Suzanne Van Hove, and Jill Berlin fielded many calls from people interested in the X manual and saved me all the time that would have taken. Ruth Terry, Lenny Muellner, and Donna Woonteiler produced the Second Edition, with graphics done by Chris Reilly. Kismet McDonough, Lenny Muellner, and Donna Woonteiler produced the Third Edition. Ellie Cutler wrote the index. A special thanks to everyone at O'Reilly and Associates.

I would also like to thank the people from other companies that reviewed the book or otherwise made this project possible: John Posner, Barry Kingsbury, Jeff MacMann and Jeffrey Vroom of Stellar Computer; Oliver Jones of Apollo Computer; Sam Black, Jeff Graber, and Janet Egan of Masscomp; Al Tabayoyon, Paul Shearer, and many others from Tektronix; Robert Scheifler and Jim Fulton of the X Consortium (who helped with the *Color* and *Managing User Preferences* chapters), and Peter Winston II and Aub Harden of Integrated Computer Solutions. Despite the efforts of the reviewers and everyone else, any errors that remain are my own.

— *Adrian Nye*

Permuted Index

A permuted index takes the brief descriptive string from the title of each command page and rotates (permutes) the string so that each keyword will at one point start the second, or center column of the line. To find the command you want, simply scan down the middle of the page, looking for a keyword of interest on the right side of the blank gutter.

Permuted Index

How to Use the Permuted Index

The permuted index takes the brief descriptive string from the title of each command page and rotates (permutes) the string so that each keyword will at one point start the *second*, or center, column of the line. The beginning and end of the original string are indicated by a slash when they are in other than their original position; if the string is too long, it is truncated.

To find the command you want, simply scan down the middle of the page, looking for a keyword of interest on the right side of the blank gutter. Once you find the keyword you want, you can read (with contortions) the brief description of the command that makes up the entry. If things still look promising, you can look all the way over to the right for the name of the relevant command page.

The Permuted Index

/return a value with all bits set to	1 suitable for plane argument	XAllPlanes,
for string and font metrics of a	16-bit character string /the server	XQueryTextExtents16
/get string and font metrics of a	16-bit character string, locally	XTextExtents16
/get the width in pixels of a	16-bit character string, locally	XTextWidth16
XDrawImageString16: draw	16-bit image text characters	XDrawImageString16
XDrawText16: draw	16-bit polytext strings	XDrawText16
/get the width in pixels of an	8-bit character string, locally	XTextWidth
XDrawImageString: draw	8-bit image text characters	XDrawImageString
XDrawText: draw	8-bit polytext strings	XDrawText
XDrawString: draw an	8-bit text string, foreground only	XDrawString
disable or enable	access control XSetAccessControl:	XSetAccessControl
XAddHost: add a host to the	access control list	XAddHost
add multiple hosts to the	access control list XAddHosts:	XAddHosts
XRemoveHost: remove a host from the	access control list	XRemoveHost
remove multiple hosts from the	access control list XRemoveHosts:	XRemoveHosts
deny/ XEnableAccessControl: use	access control list to allow or	XEnableAccessControl
XDisableAccessControl: allow	access from any host	XDisableAccessControl
obtain a list of hosts having	access to this display XListHosts:	XListHosts
XActivateScreenSaver:	activate screen blanking	XActivateScreenSaver
release the keyboard from an	active grab XUngrabKeyboard:	XUngrabKeyboard
release the pointer from an	active grab XUngrabPointer:	XUngrabPointer
/change the parameters of an	active pointer grab	XChangeActivePointerGrab
function set XcmsAddFunctionSet:	add a Color Characterization	XcmsAddFunctionSet
value in an image XAddPixel:	add a constant value to every pixel	XAddPixel

Permuted Index

XQueryExtension:	get extension information	XQueryExtension
load a font if not already loaded;	get font ID XLoadFont:	XLoadFont
XDefaultColormap,:	get information on server defaults	XDefaultColormap,
XEventMaskOfScreen,:	get initial root window event mask	XEventMaskOfScreen,
XGetICValues:	get input context attributes	XGetICValues
system independent routine to	get machine name /operating	XmuGetHostname
colormaps/ XMaxCmapsOfScreen,:	get maximum number of installed	XMaxCmapsOfScreen,
by server XMaxRequestSize:	get maximum request size supported	XMaxRequestSize
colormaps/ XMinCmapsOfScreen,:	get minimum number of installed	XMinCmapsOfScreen,
XDisplayMotionBufferSize:	get motion history buffer size	XDisplayMotionBufferSize
screen XDisplayPlanes,:	get number of planes of specified	XDisplayPlanes,
XGetIconSizes:	get preferred icon sizes	XGetIconSizes
ScreenNumberOfScreen,:	get screen information	ScreenNumberOfScreen,
XLastKnownRequestProcessed,:	get serial number of last request/	XLastKnownRequestProcessed,
XImageByteOrder,:	get server's byte order	XImageByteOrder,
XTextExtents:	get string and font metrics locally	XTextExtents
16-bit character/ XTextExtents16:	get string and font metrics of a	XTextExtents16
XDisplayString,:	get string passed to XOpenDisplay()	XDisplayString,
name strings XmuInternStrings:	get the atoms for several property	XmuInternStrings
set XBaseFontNameListOfFontSet:	get the base font list of a font	XBaseFontNameListOfFontSet
XBlackPixel,:	get the black pixel value	XBlackPixel,
sizes XQueryBestCursor:	get the closest supported cursor	XQueryBestCursor
(CCC) of a/ XcmsCCCOfColormap:	get the Color Conversion Context	XcmsCCCOfColormap
XGetFontPath:	get the current font search path	XGetFontPath
XQueryPointer:	get the current pointer location	XQueryPointer
XGetPointerControl:	get the current pointer preferences	XGetPointerControl
parameters XGetScreenSaver:	get the current screen saver	XGetScreenSaver
Context (CCC) for/ XcmsDefaultCCC:	get the default Color Conversion	XcmsDefaultCCC
XDisplayOfIM:	get the display of an input method	XDisplayOfIM
keycode in/ XLookupKeysym:	get the keysym corresponding to a	XLookupKeysym
font set XFontsOfFontSet:	get the list of fonts used by a	XFontsOfFontSet
XLocaleOfFontSet:	get the locale of a font set	XLocaleOfFontSet
XLocaleOfIM:	get the locale of an input method	XLocaleOfIM
icon XGetIconName:	get the name to be displayed in an	XGetIconName
window XNextEvent:	get the next event of any type or	XNextEvent
XGetPointerMapping:	get the pointer button mapping	XGetPointerMapping
XListProperties:	get the property list for a window	XListProperties
window in normal/ XGetNormalHints:	get the size hints property of a	XGetNormalHints
XGetStandardColormap:	get the standard colormap property	XGetStandardColormap
XWhitePixel,:	get the white pixel value	XWhitePixel,
character string,/ XTextWidth16:	get the width in pixels of a 16-bit	XTextWidth16
character string,/ XTextWidth:	get the width in pixels of an 8-bit	XTextWidth
window XGetClassHint:	get the XA_WM_CLASS property of a	XGetClassHint
(command line/ XGetCommand:	get the XA_WM_COMMAND property	XGetCommand
property of/ XGetTransientForHint:	get the XA_WM_TRANSIENT_FOR	XGetTransientForHint
millimeters XWidthOfScreen,:	get width of screen in pixels or	XWidthOfScreen,
create a cursor from font	glyphs XCreateGlyphCursor:	XCreateGlyphCursor
the parameters of an active pointer	grab /change	XChangeActivePointerGrab
release a button from a passive	grab XUngrabButton:	XUngrabButton
release a key from a passive	grab XUngrabKey:	XUngrabKey
release the keyboard from an active	grab XUngrabKeyboard:	XUngrabKeyboard
release the pointer from an active	grab XUngrabPointer:	XUngrabPointer
release the server from	grab XUngrabServer:	XUngrabServer
XGrabKey:	grab a key	XGrabKey
XGrabButton:	grab a pointer button	XGrabButton
XGrabKeyboard:	grab the keyboard	XGrabKeyboard
XGrabPointer:	grab the pointer	XGrabPointer
XGrabServer:	grab the server	XGrabServer

and/ XLookupString: map a key event to ASCII string, keysym, ... XLookupString
XUngrabKey: release a key from a passive grab .... XUngrabKey
quark list /convert a key string to a binding list and a .... XrmStringToBindingQuarkList
XrmStringToQuarkList: convert a key string to a quark list .... XrmStringToQuarkList
XGrabKeyboard: grab the keyboard .... XGrabKeyboard
vector for the current state of the keyboard /obtain a bit .... XQueryKeymap
these/ /control the behavior of keyboard and pointer events when .... XAllowEvents
XAutoRepeatOff: turn off the keyboard auto-repeat keys .... XAutoRepeatOff
XAutoRepeatOn: turn on the keyboard auto-repeat keys .... XAutoRepeatOn
XGetInputFocus: return the current keyboard focus window .... XGetInputFocus
XSetInputFocus: set the keyboard focus window .... XSetInputFocus
XUngrabKeyboard: release the keyboard from an active grab .... XUngrabKeyboard
XChangeKeyboardMapping: change the keyboard mapping .... XChangeKeyboardMapping
/destroy and free a keyboard modifier mapping structure .... XFreeModifiermap
XNewModifiermap: create a keyboard modifier mapping structure .... XNewModifiermap
/obtain a list of the current keyboard preferences .... XGetKeyboardControl
XChangeKeyboardControl: change the keyboard preferences such as key/ .... XChangeKeyboardControl
convert a keysym to the appropriate keycode XKeysymToKeycode: .... XKeysymToKeycode
/get the keysym corresponding to a keycode in structure .... XLookupKeysym
XKeycodeToKeysym: convert a keycode to a keysym .... XKeycodeToKeysym
into/ XRefreshKeyboardMapping: read keycode-keysym mapping from server .... XRefreshKeyboardMapping
return symbols for keycodes XGetKeyboardMapping: .... XGetKeyboardMapping
/obtain the range of legal keycodes for a server .... XDisplayKeycodes
(Shift,/ XSetModifierMapping: set keycodes to be used as modifiers .... XSetModifierMapping
turn off the keyboard auto-repeat keys XAutoRepeatOff: .... XAutoRepeatOff
turn on the keyboard auto-repeat keys XAutoRepeatOn: .... XAutoRepeatOn
/obtain the mapping of modifier keys (Shift, Control, etc.) .... XGetModifierMapping
convert a keycode to a keysym XKeycodeToKeysym: .... XKeycodeToKeysym
convert a keysym name string to a keysym XStringToKeysym: .... XStringToKeysym
/map a key event to ASCII string, keysym, and ComposeStatus .... XLookupString
/translate a key event into a keysym and string, using various/ .... XmuLookup*
in/ XLookupKeysym: get the keysym corresponding to a keycode .... XLookupKeysym
XStringToKeysym: convert a keysym name string to a keysym .... XStringToKeysym
a keysym and string, using various keysym sets /a key event into .... XmuLookup*
XKeysymToString: convert a keysym symbol to a string .... XKeysymToString
XRebindKeysym: rebind a keysym to a string for client .... XRebindKeysym
XKeysymToKeycode: convert a keysym to the appropriate keycode .... XKeysymToKeycode
color gamut in terms of CIE L*a*b* coordinates /target screen's .... XcmsCIELabQueryMaxC,
/get serial number of last request processed by server .... XLastKnownRequestProcessed,
/obtain the range of legal keycodes for a server .... XDisplayKeycodes
return a list of database levels XrmQGetSearchList: .... XrmQGetSearchList
the XA_WM_COMMAND property (command line arguments) XGetCommand: get .... XGetCommand
a resource database from command line arguments /load .... XrmParseCommand
set the XA_WM_COMMAND atom (command line arguments) XSetCommand: .... XSetCommand
XDrawLine: draw a line between two points .... XDrawLine
XSetDashes: set a pattern of line dashes in a graphics context .... XSetDashes
XSetLineAttributes: set the line drawing components in a/ .... XSetLineAttributes
XDrawLines: draw multiple connected lines .... XDrawLines
draw multiple disjoint lines XDrawSegments: .... XDrawSegments
add a host to the access control list XAddHost: .... XAddHost
hosts to the access control list XAddHosts: add multiple .... XAddHosts
with the specified string list /the in-memory data associated .... XFreeStringList
a host from the access control list XRemoveHost: remove .... XRemoveHost
hosts from the access control list XRemoveHosts: remove multiple .... XRemoveHosts
to a binding list and a quark list /convert a key string .... XrmStringToBindingQuarkList
convert a key string to a quark list XrmStringToQuarkList: .... XrmStringToQuarkList
allocate a nested variable argument list XVaCreateNestedList: .... XVaCreateNestedList
/convert a key string to a binding list and a quark list .... XrmStringToBindingQuarkList

Permuted Index

the memory allocated for a font name array XFreeFontNames: free .... XFreeFontNames
XGetAtomName: get a string name for a property given its atom .... XGetAtomName
/look up RGB values from ASCII color name or translate hexadecimal value .... XParseColor
return an atom for a given property name string XInternAtom: .... XInternAtom
to hold atom list for a property name string /create AtomPtr .... XmuMakeAtom
specified/ /returns the property name string corresponding to the .... XmuGetAtomName
XmuNameOfAtom: return property name string represented by an/ .... XmuNameOfAtom
XStringToKeysym: convert a keysym name string to a keysym .... XStringToKeysym
get the atoms for several property name strings XmuInternStrings: .... XmuInternStrings
manager XStoreName: assign a name to a window for the window .... XStoreName
icon XSetIconName: set the name to be displayed in a window's .... XSetIconName
XGetIconName: get the name to be displayed in an icon .... XGetIconName
XDisplayName: report the display name (when connection to a display/ .... XDisplayName
XFetchName: get a window's name (XA_WM_NAME property) .... XFetchName
return a list of the available font names XListFonts: .... XListFonts
XListFontsWithInfo: obtain the names and information about/ .... XListFontsWithInfo
XVaCreateNestedList: allocate a nested variable argument list .... XVaCreateNestedList
Xpermalloc: allocate memory never to be freed .... Xpermalloc
XCreateAssocTable: create a new association table (X10) .... XCreateAssocTable
/copy a colormap and return a new colormap ID .... XCopyColormapAndFree
context) XUniqueContext: create a new context ID (not graphics .... XUniqueContext
XCreateRegion: create a new empty region .... XCreateRegion
XInsertModifiermapEntry: add a new entry to an XModifierKeymap/ .... XInsertModifiermapEntry
screen with/ XCreateGC: create a new graphics context for a given .... XCreateGC
XrmUniqueQuark: allocate a new quark .... XrmUniqueQuark
XCheckTypedWindowEvent: return the next event in queue matching type/ .... XCheckTypedWindowEvent
event/ XCheckTypedEvent: return the next event in queue that matches .... XCheckTypedEvent
XCheckWindowEvent: remove the next event matching both passed/ .... XCheckWindowEvent
XNextEvent: get the next event of any type or window .... XNextEvent
XMaskEvent: remove the next event that matches mask .... XMaskEvent
wait XCheckMaskEvent: remove the next event that matches mask; don't .... XCheckMaskEvent
specified/ XWindowEvent: remove the next event that matches the .... XWindowEvent
XctNextItem: parse the next item in a Compound Text string .... XctNextItem
return serial number of next request XNextRequest,: .... XNextRequest,
XSetErrorHandler: set a nonfatal error event handler .... XSetErrorHandler
XSetIOErrorHandler: set a nonfatal error event handler .... XSetIOErrorHandler
/allocate read/write (nonshareable) color planes .... XAllocColorPlanes
/allocate read/write (nonshared) colorcells .... XAllocColorCells
the server XNoOp: send a NoOp to exercise connection with .... XNoOp
size hints property of a window in normal state (not zoomed or/ /the .... XGetNormalHints
size hints property of a window in normal state (not zoomed or/ /the .... XSetNormalHints
/create a standard colormap if not already created .... XmuLookupStandardColormap
a colormap; install default if not already installed /uninstall .... XUninstallColormap
XLoadFont: load a font if not already loaded; get font ID .... XLoadFont
/get data from the context manager (not graphics context) .... XFindContext
/to a resource ID and context type (not graphics context) .... XSaveContext
/create a new context ID (not graphics context) .... XUniqueContext
of a window in normal state (not zoomed or iconified) /property .... XGetNormalHints
of a window in normal state (not zoomed or iconified) /property .... XSetNormalHints
return vendor release number XVendorRelease,: .... XVendorRelease,
XcmsScreenNumberOfCCC,: screen number associated with the/ .... XcmsScreenNumberOfCCC,
of screen XDisplayCells,: query number of cells in default colormap .... XDisplayCells,
display/ XmuDQNDisplays: return the number of display connections in a .... XmuDQNDisplays
XEventsQueued: check the number of events in the event queue .... XEventsQueued
XQLength,: return the number of events on the queue .... XQLength,
XMaxCmapsOfScreen,: get maximum number of installed colormaps/ .... XMaxCmapsOfScreen,
XMinCmapsOfScreen,: get minimum number of installed colormaps/ .... XMinCmapsOfScreen,
server /get serial number of last request processed by .... XLastKnownRequestProcessed,

XNextRequest,: return serial number of next request .... XNextRequest,
XPending: return the number of pending events .... XPending
screen XDisplayPlanes,: get number of planes of specified .... XDisplayPlanes,
XConnectionNumber,: get connection number or file descriptor .... XConnectionNumber,
state of the/ XQueryKeymap: obtain a bit vector for the current .... XQueryKeymap
screen black XcmsQueryBlack: obtain a color specification for .... XcmsQueryBlack
screen blue XcmsQueryBlue: obtain a color specification for .... XcmsQueryBlue
screen green XcmsQueryGreen: obtain a color specification for .... XcmsQueryGreen
screen red XcmsQueryRed: obtain a color specification for .... XcmsQueryRed
screen white XcmsQueryWhite: obtain a color specification for .... XcmsQueryWhite
XGetErrorText: obtain a description of error code .... XGetErrorText
access to this display XListHosts: obtain a list of hosts having .... XListHosts
XTextPropertyToStringList: obtain a list of strings from a/ .... XTextPropertyToStringList
keyboard/ XGetKeyboardControl: obtain a list of the current .... XGetKeyboardControl
image XGetPixel: obtain a single pixel value from an .... XGetPixel
information XWMGeometry: obtain a window's geometry .... XWMGeometry
XcmsLookupColor: obtain color values from a string .... XcmsLookupColor
from Xlib's GC cache XGetGCValues: obtain components of a given GC .... XGetGCValues
from an input/ XmbLookupString: obtain composed multi-byte input .... XmbLookupString
input from an/ XwcLookupString: obtain composed wide-character .... XwcLookupString
table XLookUpAssoc: obtain data from an association .... XLookUpAssoc
error/ XGetErrorDatabaseText: obtain error messages from the .... XGetErrorDatabaseText
XGetIMValues: obtain input method information .... XGetIMValues
of an XwcTextPerCharExtents: obtain per-character measurements .... XwcTextPerCharExtents
of an/ XmbTextPerCharExtents: obtain per-character measurements .... XmbTextPerCharExtents
colorcells XQueryColors: obtain RGB values for an array of .... XQueryColors
format for a/ XGetWindowProperty: obtain the atom type and property .... XGetWindowProperty
cursor, tile, or/ XQueryBestSize: obtain the "best" supported .... XQueryBestSize
screen's/ XcmsCIELabQueryMaxC,: obtain the bounds of the target .... XcmsCIELabQueryMaxC,
screen's/ XcmsCIELuvQueryMaxC,: obtain the bounds of the target .... XcmsCIELuvQueryMaxC,
specified/ XcmsQueryColor: obtain the color specification of a .... XcmsQueryColor
the specified/ XcmsQueryColors: obtain the color specifications of .... XcmsQueryColors
associated/ XcmsPrefixOfFormat: obtain the color string prefix .... XcmsPrefixOfFormat
window XGetWindowAttributes: obtain the current attributes of .... XGetWindowAttributes
drawable XGetGeometry: obtain the current geometry of .... XGetGeometry
tile shape XQueryBestTile: obtain the fastest supported fill .... XQueryBestTile
stipple shape XQueryBestStipple: obtain the fastest supported .... XQueryBestStipple
space/ XcmsFormatOfPrefix: obtain the format ID of the color .... XcmsFormatOfPrefix
associated with/ XGContextFromGC: obtain the GContext (resource ID) .... XGContextFromGC
context XIMOfIC: obtain the input method of an input .... XIMOfIC
(Shift,/ XGetModifierMapping: obtain the mapping of modifier keys .... XGetModifierMapping
structure for a/ XExtentsOfFontSet: obtain the maximum extents .... XExtentsOfFontSet
about/ XListFontsWithInfo: obtain the names and information .... XListFontsWithInfo
for a server XDisplayKeycodes: obtain the range of legal keycodes .... XDisplayKeycodes
a specified colorcell XQueryColor: obtain the RGB values and flags for .... XQueryColor
for a given/ XListPixmapFormats: obtain the supported pixmap formats .... XListPixmapFormats
XVisualIDFromVisual: obtain the visual ID from a Visual .... XVisualIDFromVisual
matches the/ XMatchVisualInfo: obtain the visual information that .... XMatchVisualInfo
XcmsScreenWhitePointOfCCC,: obtain the white .... XcmsScreenWhitePointOfCCC,
XmbTextEscapement: obtain the width of/ .... XmbTextEscapement
XwcTextEscapement: obtain the width of/ .... XwcTextEscapement
structure/ XGetRGBColormaps: obtain the XStandardColormap .... XGetRGBColormaps
/for the Function Set routine that obtains and initializes per-screen/ .... XcmsScreenInitProc
turn the screen saver on or off XForceScreenSaver: .... XForceScreenSaver
XAutoRepeatOff: turn off the keyboard auto-repeat keys .... XAutoRepeatOff
if two regions have the same size, offset, and shape /determine .... XEqualRegion
XOffsetRegion: change offset of a region .... XOffsetRegion
pixmap and copy data from one-plane pixmap. /multi-plane .... XmuCreatePixmapFromBitmap

set a window's XA_WM_SIZE_HINTS	property XSetWMSizeHints:	XSetWMSizeHints
XChangeProperty: change a	property associated with a window	XChangeProperty
XGetCommand: get the XA_WM_COMMAND	property (command line arguments)	XGetCommand
/set the XA_WM_TRANSIENT_FOR	property for a window	XSetTransientForHint
/obtain the atom type and	property format for a window	XGetWindowProperty
/get a string name for a	property given its atom	XGetAtomName
XGetFontProperty: get a font	property given its atom	XGetFontProperty
XListProperties: get the	property list for a window	XListProperties
return an atom for a given	property name string XInternAtom:	XInternAtom
AtomPtr to hold atom list for a	property name string /create	XmuMakeAtom
to the/ XmuGetAtomName: returns the	property name string corresponding	XmuGetAtomName
an AtomPtr XmuNameOfAtom: return	property name string represented by	XmuNameOfAtom
/get the atoms for several	property name strings	XmuInternStrings
XGetClassHint: get the XA_WM_CLASS	property of a window	XGetClassHint
/get the XA_WM_TRANSIENT_FOR	property of a window	XGetTransientForHint
XSetClassHint: set the XA_WM_CLASS	property of a window	XSetClassHint
XGetNormalHints: get the size hints	property of a window in normal/	XGetNormalHints
XSetNormalHints: set the size hints	property of a window in normal/	XSetNormalHints
XGetZoomHints: read the size hints	property of a zoomed window	XGetZoomHints
XSetZoomHints: set the size hints	property of a zoomed window	XSetZoomHints
XGetSizeHints: read any	property of type XA_WM_SIZE_HINTS	XGetSizeHints
XSetSizeHints: set the value of any	property of type XA_WM_SIZE_HINTS	XSetSizeHints
/multi-byte text list to a text	property structure	XmbTextListToTextProperty
/wide-character text list to a text	property structure	XwcTextListToTextProperty
/print the standard	protocol error message	XmuPrintDefaultErrorMessage
XProtocolRevision,: return	protocol release or version	XProtocolRevision,
queue XPutBackEvent:	push an event back on the input	XPutBackEvent
convert a string to a	quark XrmStringToQuark,:	XrmStringToQuark,
XrmUniqueQuark: allocate a new	quark	XrmUniqueQuark
XrmPermStringToQuark: allocate	quark for permanently allocated/	XrmPermStringToQuark
key string to a binding list and a	quark list /convert a	XrmStringToBindingQuarkList
convert a key string to a	quark list XrmStringToQuarkList:	XrmStringToQuarkList
/specification to a database using a	quark resource name and string/	XrmQPutStringResource
XrmClassToString: convert a	quark to a string	XrmClassToString
XrmNameToString: convert a	quark to a string	XrmNameToString
XrmQuarkToString: convert a	quark to a string	XrmQuarkToString
/convert a	quark to a string	XrmRepresentationToString
value using name and class as	quarks /get a resource	XrmQGetResource
specification into a database using	quarks /store a resource	XrmQPutResource
XDisplayHeight,:	query	XDisplayHeight,
XDoesBackingStore,:	query	XDoesBackingStore,
colormap of screen XDisplayCells,:	query number of cells in default	XDisplayCells,
display XBitmapBitOrder,:	query the bitmap format of a	XBitmapBitOrder,
font metrics XQueryTextExtents:	query the server for string and	XQueryTextExtents
font metrics/ XQueryTextExtents16:	query the server for string and	XQueryTextExtents16
millimeters XDisplayWidth,:	query width of screen in pixels or	XDisplayWidth,
the number of events in the event	queue XEventsQueued: check	XEventsQueued
a display connection to a display	queue XmuDQAddDisplay: add	XmuDQAddDisplay
creates an empty display	queue XmuDQCreate:	XmuDQCreate
of display connections in a display	queue /return the number	XmuDQNDisplays
a display connection from a display	queue XmuDQRemoveDisplay: remove	XmuDQRemoveDisplay
event without removing it from the	queue XPeekEvent: get an	XPeekEvent
without removing it from the	queue /by predicate procedure	XPeekIfEvent
push an event back on the input	queue XPutBackEvent:	XPutBackEvent
return the number of events on the	queue XQLength,:	XQLength,
XmuDQDestroy: destroy a display	queue, and optionally call/	XmuDQDestroy
connection /determine display	queue entry for specified display	XmuDQLookupDisplay
XCheckIfEvent: check the event	queue for a matching event; don't/	XCheckIfEvent

don't/ /return the next event in	queue matching type and window;	XCheckTypedWindowEvent
don't/ /return the next event in	queue that matches event type;	XCheckTypedEvent
XFlush: send all	queued requests to the server	XFlush
stacking order XRaiseWindow:	raise a window to the top of the	XRaiseWindow
XDisplayKeycodes: obtain the	range of legal keycodes for a/	XDisplayKeycodes
XReadBitmapFile:	read a bitmap from disk	XReadBitmapFile
property XGetWMIconName:	read a window's XA_WM_ICON_NAME	XGetWMIconName
XGetWMName:	read a window's XA_WM_NAME property	XGetWMName
property XGetWMNormalHints:	read a window's XA_WM_NORMAL_HINTS	XGetWMNormalHints
property XGetWMSizeHints:	read a window's XA_WM_SIZE_HINTS	XGetWMSizeHints
file XmuReadBitmapDataFromFile:	read and check bitmap data from a	XmuReadBitmapDataFromFile
stream source XmuReadBitmapData:	read and check bitmap data from any	XmuReadBitmapData
XA_WM_SIZE_HINTS XGetSizeHints:	read any property of type	XGetSizeHints
server/ XRefreshKeyboardMapping:	read keycode-keysym mapping from	XRefreshKeyboardMapping
properties XGetTextProperty:	read one of a window's text	XGetTextProperty
zoomed window XGetZoomHints:	read the size hints property of a	XGetZoomHints
property XGetWMHints:	read the window manager hints	XGetWMHints
XAllocNamedColor: allocate a	read-only colorcell from color name	XAllocNamedColor
closest/ XAllocColor: allocate a	read-only colormap cell with	XAllocColor
/set RGB values of a	read/write colorcell by color name	XStoreNamedColor
/set or change the RGB values of	read/write colorcells to the/	XStoreColors
/store a specified color into a	read/write colormap cell	XcmsStoreColor
/store the specified colors in	read/write colormap cells	XcmsStoreColors
/set or change the RGB values of a	read/write colormap entry to the/	XStoreColor
planes XAllocColorPlanes: allocate	read/write (nonshareable) color	XAllocColorPlanes
XAllocColorCells: allocate	read/write (nonshared) colorcells	XAllocColorCells
client XRebindKeysym:	rebind a keysym to a string for	XRebindKeysym
request that a top-level window be	reconfigured XReconfigureWMWindow:	XReconfigureWMWindow
draw an arc fitting inside a	rectangle XDrawArc:	XDrawArc
draw an outline of a	rectangle XDrawRectangle:	XDrawRectangle
XClipBox: generate the smallest	rectangle enclosing a region	XClipBox
XGetImage: place contents of a	rectangle from drawable into an/	XGetImage
within the/ XGetSubImage: copy a	rectangle in drawable to a location	XGetSubImage
XRectInRegion: determine if a	rectangle resides in a region	XRectInRegion
XUnionRectWithRegion: add a	rectangle to a region	XUnionRectWithRegion
XmuDrawRoundedRectangle: draws a	rectangle with rounded corners	XmuDrawRoundedRectangle
XmuFillRoundedRectangle: fill a	rectangle with rounded corners	XmuFillRoundedRectangle
draw the outlines of multiple	rectangles XDrawRectangles:	XDrawRectangles
in a graphics context to a list of	rectangles /change clip_mask	XSetClipRectangles
XFillRectangle: fill a	rectangular area	XFillRectangle
XClearArea: clear a	rectangular area in a window	XClearArea
XFillRectangles: fill multiple	rectangular areas	XFillRectangles
a color specification for screen	red XcmsQueryRed: obtain	XcmsQueryRed
/determine best allocation of	reds, greens, and blues in a/	XmuGetColormapAllocation
region XShrinkRegion:	reduce or expand the size of a	XShrinkRegion
/In CIELAB color space,	reduces or increases	XcmsCIELabClipL
/In CIELUV color space,	reduces or increases	XcmsCIELuvClipL
/In TekHVC color space,	reduces or increases	XcmsTekHVCClipV
the smallest rectangle enclosing a	region XClipBox: generate	XClipBox
XCreateRegion: create a new empty	region	XCreateRegion
deallocate memory associated with a	region XDestroyRegion:	XDestroyRegion
XOffsetRegion: change offset of a	region	XOffsetRegion
determine if a point is inside a	region XPointInRegion:	XPointInRegion
if a rectangle resides in a	region XRectInRegion: determine	XRectInRegion
graphics context to the specified	region /set clip_mask of the	XSetRegion
reduce or expand the size of a	region XShrinkRegion:	XShrinkRegion
add a rectangle to a	region XUnionRectWithRegion:	XUnionRectWithRegion
XSubtractRegion: subtract one	region from another	XSubtractRegion

Permuted Index

XcmsTekHVCToCIEuvY: Converts color specifications from .... XcmsTekHVCToCIEuvY
XcmsConvertColors: convert color specifications in XcmsColor/ .... XcmsConvertColors
XcmsQueryColors: obtain the color specifications of the specified/ .... XcmsQueryColors
the bottom child to the top of the stacking order /circulate .... XCirculateSubwindowsDown
the top child to the bottom of the stacking order /circulate .... XCirculateSubwindowsUp
position, size, border width, or stacking order /change the window .... XConfigureWindow
XLowerWindow: lower a window in the stacking order .... XLowerWindow
raise a window to the top of the stacking order XRaiseWindow: .... XRaiseWindow
XCirculateSubwindows: circulate the stacking order of children up or/ .... XCirculateSubwindows
XRestackWindows: change the stacking order of siblings .... XRestackWindows
of reds, greens, and blues in a standard colormap /best allocation .... XmuGetColormapAllocation
XmuStandardColormap: create one standard colormap .... XmuStandardColormap
in an/ XmuCreateColormap: create a standard colormap from information .... XmuCreateColormap
XmuLookupStandardColormap: create a standard colormap if not already/ .... XmuLookupStandardColormap
/standard colormaps and set standard colormap properties .... XmuAllStandardColormaps
XGetStandardColormap: get the standard colormap property .... XGetStandardColormap
/remove any standard colormap property .... XmuDeleteStandardColormap
XSetStandardColormap: change the standard colormap property .... XSetStandardColormap
colormap/ /create all supported standard colormaps and set standard .... XmuAllStandardColormaps
and screen /create all standard colormaps for given visual .... XmuVisualStandardColormaps
/create a cursor from the standard cursor font .... XCreateFontCursor
pixmap from a bitmap file in a standard location /a one-plane .... XmuLocateBitmapFile
/create a pixmap from a file in a standard location .... XmuLocatePixmapFile
/print the standard protocol error message .... XmuPrintDefaultErrorMessage
/generate position and size from standard window geometry string .... XParseGeometry
XSetWMProperties: set a window's standard window manager properties .... XSetWMProperties
XmuDrawLogo: draws the standard X logo .... XmuDrawLogo
/property of a window in normal state (not zoomed or iconified) .... XGetNormalHints
/property of a window in normal state (not zoomed or iconified) .... XSetNormalHints
XmbResetIC: reset the state of an input context .... XmbResetIC
XwcResetIC: reset the state of an input context .... XwcResetIC
/obtain a bit vector for the current state of the keyboard .... XQueryKeymap
XSetStipple: set the stipple in a graphics context .... XSetStipple
obtain the fastest supported stipple shape XQueryBestStipple: .... XQueryBestStipple
"best" supported cursor, tile, or stipple size /obtain the .... XQueryBestSize
XFreeFont: unload a font and free storage for the font structure .... XFreeFont
XrmPutFileDatabase: store a resource database in a file .... XrmPutFileDatabase
a database using/ XrmQPutResource: store a resource specification into .... XrmQPutResource
a resource/ XrmPutResource: store a resource specification into .... XrmPutResource
read/write/ XcmsStoreColor: store a specified color into a .... XcmsStoreColor
XStoreBuffer: store data in a cut buffer .... XStoreBuffer
XStoreBytes: store data in cut buffer 0 .... XStoreBytes
read/write/ XcmsStoreColors: store the specified colors in .... XcmsStoreColors
read and check bitmap data from any stream source XmuReadBitmapData: .... XmuReadBitmapData
allocate a color specified as a string XcmsAllocNamedColor: .... XcmsAllocNamedColor
obtain color values from a string XcmsLookupColor: .... XcmsLookupColor
for parsing a Compound Text string /create a XctData structure .... XctCreate
the next item in a Compound Text string XctNextItem: parse .... XctNextItem
for reparsing a Compound Text string /reset an XctData structure .... XctReset
an atom for a given property name string XInternAtom: return .... XInternAtom
convert a keysym symbol to a string XKeysymToString: .... XKeysymToString
internationalized multi-byte text string /measurements of an .... XmbTextPerCharExtents
hold atom list for a property name string /create AtomPtr to .... XmuMakeAtom
size from standard window geometry string /generate position and .... XParseGeometry
font metrics of a 16-bit character string /the server for string and XQueryTextExtents16
convert a quark to a string XrmClassToString: .... XrmClassToString
create a database from a string XrmGetStringDatabase: .... XrmGetStringDatabase
convert a quark to a string XrmNameToString: .... XrmNameToString

quark for permanently allocated	string /allocate	XrmPermStringToQuark
convert a quark to a	string XrmQuarkToString:	XrmQuarkToString
convert a quark to a	string XrmRepresentationToString:	XrmRepresentationToString
/window geometry given user geometry	string and default geometry	XGeometry
/query the server for	string and font metrics	XQueryTextExtents
XTextExtents: get	string and font metrics locally	XTextExtents
character/ /query the server for	string and font metrics of a 16-bit	XQueryTextExtents16
character/ XTextExtents16: get	string and font metrics of a 16-bit	XTextExtents16
XmuCopyISOLatin1Uppered: copy	string, changing lower case to/	XmuCopyISOLatin1Uppered
XmuCopyISOLatin1Lowered: copy	string, changing upper case to/	XmuCopyISOLatin1Lowered
/returns the property name	string corresponding to the/	XmuGetAtomName
XRebindKeysym: rebind a keysym to a	string for client	XRebindKeysym
XDrawString: draw an 8-bit text	string, foreground only	XDrawString
/map a key event to ASCII	string, keysym, and ComposeStatus	XLookupString
data associated with the specified	string list /free the in-memory	XFreeStringList
font metrics of a 16-bit character	string, locally /get string and	XTextExtents16
in pixels of an 8-bit character	string, locally /get the width	XTextWidth
in pixels of a 16-bit character	string, locally /get the width	XTextWidth16
return index in cursor font given	string name XmuCursorNameToIndex:	XmuCursorNameToIndex
its atom XGetAtomName: get	string name for a property given	XGetAtomName
/interface definition for color	string parsing procedure	XcmsParseStringProc
XDisplayString,: get	string passed to XOpenDisplay()	XDisplayString,
associated with a specified color	string prefix /of the color space	XcmsFormatOfPrefix
color space/ /obtain the color	string prefix associated with the	XcmsPrefixOfFormat
XmuNameOfAtom: return property name	string represented by an AtomPtr	XmuNameOfAtom
quark list /convert a key	string to a binding list and a	XrmStringToBindingQuarkList
/convert a keysym name	string to a keysym	XStringToKeysym
XrmStringToQuark,: convert a	string to a quark	XrmStringToQuark,
XrmStringToQuarkList: convert a key	string to a quark list	XrmStringToQuarkList
XDefaultString: return the default	string used for text conversion	XDefaultString
/a key event into a keysym and	string, using various keysym sets	XmuLookup*
using a quark resource name and	string value /to a database	XrmQPutStringResource
XDrawString16: draw two-byte text	strings	XDrawString16
XDrawText: draw 8-bit polytext	strings	XDrawText
XDrawText16: draw 16-bit polytext	strings	XDrawText16
the atoms for several property name	strings XmuInternStrings: get	XmuInternStrings
a resource from name and class as	strings XrmGetResource: get	XrmGetResource
XTextProperty/ /obtain a list of	strings from a specified	XTextPropertyToStringList
/compare and determine order of two	strings, ignoring case	XmuCompareISOLatin1
/set the specified list of	strings to an XTextProperty/	XStringListToTextProperty
allocate an XClassHint	structure XAllocClassHint:	XAllocClassHint
allocate an XIconSize	structure XAllocIconSize:	XAllocIconSize
allocate an XSizeHints	structure XAllocSizeHints:	XAllocSizeHints
allocate an XStandardColormap	structure XAllocStandardColormap:	XAllocStandardColormap
XAllocWMHints: allocate an XWMHints	structure	XAllocWMHints
XcmsColor: Xcms color	structure	XcmsColor
XcmsColorSpace: Xcms color space	structure	XcmsColorSpace
Color Characterization Function Set	structure XcmsFunctionSet: Xcms	XcmsFunctionSet
allocate memory for an XImage	structure XCreateImage:	XCreateImage
XctFree: free an XctData	structure	XctFree
an entry from an XModifierKeymap	structure /delete	XDeleteModifiermapEntry
structure of specified Screen	structure /get Display	XDisplayOfScreen,
XFontSetExtents: XFontSetExtents	structure	XFontSetExtents
font and free storage for the font	structure XFreeFont: unload a	XFreeFont
free a keyboard modifier mapping	structure /destroy and	XFreeModifiermap
a new entry to an XModifierKeymap	structure /add	XInsertModifiermapEntry
load a font and fill information	structure XLoadQueryFont:	XLoadQueryFont
corresponding to a keycode in	structure /get the keysym	XLookupKeysym

```
          supported cursor sizes  XQueryBestCursor: get the closest ............... XQueryBestCursor
     supported cursor, tile, or stipple/  XQueryBestSize: obtain the "best" ............... XQueryBestSize
        fastest supported stipple shape  XQueryBestStipple: obtain the ..................... XQueryBestStipple
              supported fill tile shape  XQueryBestTile: obtain the fastest ................ XQueryBestTile
              and flags for a specified/  XQueryColor: obtain the RGB values ............ XQueryColor
               an array of colorcells  XQueryColors: obtain RGB values for ........... XQueryColors
                      information  XQueryExtension: get extension ................... XQueryExtension
                 about a loaded font  XQueryFont: return information ..................... XQueryFont
             for the current state of the/  XQueryKeymap: obtain a bit vector ............... XQueryKeymap
                    pointer location  XQueryPointer: get the current ..................... XQueryPointer
            for string and font metrics  XQueryTextExtents: query the server .......... XQueryTextExtents
      server for string and font metrics/  XQueryTextExtents16: query the .................. XQueryTextExtents16
            children, parent, and root  XQueryTree: return a list of ........................... XQueryTree
           top of the stacking order  XRaiseWindow: raise a window to the ........... XRaiseWindow
                         disk  XReadBitmapFile: read a bitmap from ........... XReadBitmapFile
                 string for client  XRebindKeysym: rebind a keysym to a ......... XRebindKeysym
                    a cursor  XRecolorCursor: change the color of ............ XRecolorCursor
        a top-level window be reconfigured  XReconfigureWMWindow: request that ......... XReconfigureWMWindow
           rectangle resides in a region  XRectInRegion: determine if a ..................... XRectInRegion
    keycode-keysym mapping from server/  XRefreshKeyboardMapping: read .................. XRefreshKeyboardMapping
           from the client's save-set  XRemoveFromSaveSet: remove a window ... XRemoveFromSaveSet
                access control list  XRemoveHost: remove a host from the ........ XRemoveHost
         from the access control list  XRemoveHosts: remove multiple hosts ......... XRemoveHosts
      between another window and its/  XReparentWindow: insert a window .............. XReparentWindow
                      saver  XResetScreenSaver: reset the screen .......... XResetScreenSaver
                       size  XResizeWindow: change a window's ............ XResizeWindow
        RESOURCE_MANAGER property  XResourceManagerString: return the ............ XResourceManagerString
            stacking order of siblings  XRestackWindows: change the ..................... XRestackWindows
                   to a string  XrmClassToString: convert a quark .............. XrmClassToString
     contents of two resource databases  XrmCombineDatabase: combine the ............. XrmCombineDatabase
    contents of a resource file and  XrmCombineFileDatabase: combine the ....... XrmCombineFileDatabase
              resource database  XrmDestroyDatabase: destroy a .................... XrmDestroyDatabase
           resource database entries  XrmEnumerateDatabase: enumerate ............ XrmEnumerateDatabase
      resource database associated with/  XrmGetDatabase: retrieve the ....................... XrmGetDatabase
              database from a file  XrmGetFileDatabase: retrieve a .................... XrmGetFileDatabase
          name and class as strings  XrmGetResource: get a resource from .......... XrmGetResource
            database from a string  XrmGetStringDatabase: create a .................. XrmGetStringDatabase
                 resource manager  XrmInitialize: initialize the ............................ XrmInitialize
         locale of a resource database  XrmLocaleOfDatabase: return the ................. XrmLocaleOfDatabase
       contents of one database into/  XrmMergeDatabases: merge the .................. XrmMergeDatabases
                    a string  XrmNameToString: convert a quark to .......... XrmNameToString
        database from command line/  XrmParseCommand: load a resource ............ XrmParseCommand
     quark for permanently allocated/  XrmPermStringToQuark:  allocate ................. XrmPermStringToQuark
          resource database in a file  XrmPutFileDatabase: store a ........................ XrmPutFileDatabase
         specification to a resource/  XrmPutLineResource: add a resource ........... XrmPutLineResource
        specification into a resource/  XrmPutResource: store a resource ............... XrmPutResource
         resource specification with/  XrmPutStringResource: add a ...................... XrmPutStringResource
         value using name and class as/  XrmQGetResource: get a resource .............. XrmQGetResource
                  database levels  XrmQGetSearchList: return a list of ............... XrmQGetSearchList
     prepared list for a given resource  XrmQGetSearchResource: search ................ XrmQGetSearchResource
       specification into a database/  XrmQPutResource: store a resource ............ XrmQPutResource
         resource specification to a/  XrmQPutStringResource: add a .................... XrmQPutStringResource
                   to a string  XrmQuarkToString: convert a quark .............. XrmQuarkToString
             a quark to a string  XrmRepresentationToString: convert ........... XrmRepresentationToString
     resource database with a display  XrmSetDatabase: associate a ........................ XrmSetDatabase
   convert a key string to a binding/  XrmStringToBindingQuarkList: ...................... XrmStringToBindingQuarkList
                  to a quark  XrmStringToQuark,: convert a string ............ XrmStringToQuark,
          string to a quark list  XrmStringToQuarkList: convert a key ........... XrmStringToQuarkList
```

Xlib Functions

This section contains alphabetically organized reference pages for each Xlib function and their macro versions. The first reference page, Introduction, explains the format and contents of each of the following pages.

Introduction

This page describes the format of each reference page in this volume.

Name

XFunctionName – brief description of the function, interface definition or structure.

Synopsis

The Synopsis section presents the calling syntax for the routine, including the declarations of the arguments and return type. For example:

```
returntype XFunctionName(arg1, arg2, arg3);
      type1 arg1;
      type2 *arg2_return;
      type3 *arg3_in_out;
```

Arguments

The Arguments section describes each of the arguments used by the function. There are three sorts of arguments: arguments that specify data to the function, arguments that return data from the function, and arguments that do both. An example of each type is shown below:

arg1   Specifies information for `XFunctionName`. The description of arguments that pass data to the function always begins with the word "Specifies," as shown in this example.

arg2_return
      Returns a pointer to data to be filled in by `XFunctionName`. The description of arguments that return data from the function normally begins with the word "Returns."

arg3_in_out
      Specifies information for `XFunctionName`, and also returns data from the function. The description of arguments that both pass data to the function and return data from the function normally uses both the words "Specifies" and "Returns."

Returns

This section describes what the function returns (as the return value, not in its arguments).

Availability

The Availability section describes which specification releases include this function. They say either that a given function is available in Release 5 and later releases, or Release 4 and later releases. If there is no Availability section, the function is available in Release 3 and later.

Description

The Description section describes what the function does, what it returns, and what events or side-effects it causes. It also contains miscellaneous information such as examples of usage, special error cases, and pointers to related information in both volumes of this manual.

Structures

The Structures section contains the C definitions of the X-specific data types used by `FunctionName` as arguments or return values. It also contains definitions of important constants used by the function. Additional structures not shown can be found in Appendix F, *Structure Reference*.

Errors

The general description of the error types is contained in Appendix B, *Error Messages and Protocol Requests*. Some functions generate errors due to function-specific interpretation of arguments. Where appropriate, these function-specific causes have been listed along with the error event types they generate.

See Also

The "See Also" section lists other reference pages that contain information related to *XFunctionName*.

XActivateScreenSaver

Name

XActivateScreenSaver – activate screen blanking.

Synopsis

```
XActivateScreenSaver(display)
    Display *display;
```

Arguments

display   Specifies a connection to an X server; returned from `XOpenDisplay()`.

Description

`XActivateScreenSaver()` turns on the screen saver using the parameters set with `XSetScreenSaver()`. The screen saver blanks the screen or makes random changes to the display in order to save the phosphors from burnout when the screen is left unattended for an extended period of time. The interval that the server will wait before starting screen save activity can be set with `XSetScreenSaver()`. Exactly how the screen saver works is server-dependent.

For more information on the screen saver, see Volume One, Chapter 13, *Other Programming Techniques*.

See Also

XForceScreenSaver(), *XGetScreenSaver()*, *XResetScreenSaver()*, *XSetScreenSaver()*.

XAddHost

Name

XAddHost – add a host to the access control list.

Synopsis

```
XAddHost(display, host)
    Display *display;
    XHostAddress *host;
```

Arguments

display   Specifies a connection to an X server; returned from XOpenDisplay().

host   Specifies the network address of the host machine to be added.

Description

XAddHost() adds the specified host to the access control list for the server specified by *display*. The access control list is a primitive security feature that allows access to the server only by other machines listed in a file on the machine running the server. On UNIX-based systems, this file is called */etc/X?.hosts*, where *?* is the number of the server.

The application that calls XAddHost() and the server whose list is being updated must be running on the same host machine.

The **address** data must be a valid address for the type of network in which the server operates, as specified in the **family** member. Internet, DECnet and ChaosNet networks are currently supported.

For TCP/IP, the address should be in network byte order. For the DECnet family, the server performs no automatic swapping on the address bytes. A Phase IV address is two bytes long. The first byte contains the least significant eight bits of the node number. The second byte contains the most significant two bits of the node number in the least significant two bits of the byte, and the area in the most significant six bits of the byte.

For more information on access control, see Volume One, Chapter 13, *Other Programming Techniques*.

Structures

```
typedef struct {
    int family;            /* for example FamilyInternet */
    int length;            /* length of address, in bytes */
    char *address;         /* pointer to where to find the bytes */
} XHostAddress;

/* The following constants for family member */
#define FamilyInternet        0
#define FamilyDECnet          1
#define FamilyChaos           2
```

Errors

```
BadAccess
BadValue
```

See Also

XAddHosts(), XDisableAccessControl(), XEnableAccessControl(), XListHosts(), XRemoveHost(), XRemoveHosts(), XSetAccessControl().

XAddHosts

Name

XAddHosts – add multiple hosts to the access control list.

Synopsis

```
XAddHosts(display, hosts, num_hosts)
    Display *display;
    XHostAddress *hosts;
    int num_hosts;
```

Arguments

display   Specifies a connection to an X server; returned from XOpenDisplay().

hosts   Specifies each host that is to be added.

num_hosts   Specifies the number of hosts that are to be added.

Description

XAddHosts() adds each specified host to the access control list for the server specified by *display*. The access control list is a primitive security feature that allows access to the server only by other machines listed in a file on the machine running the server. On UNIX systems, this file is */etc/X?.hosts*, where *?* is the number of the display.

The application that calls XAddHosts() and the server whose list is being updated must be running on the same host machine.

The address data must be a valid address for the type of network in which the server operates, as specified by the family member. Internet, DECnet and ChaosNet networks are currently supported.

For TCP/IP, the address should be in network byte order. For the DECnet family, the server performs no automatic swapping on the address bytes. A Phase IV address is two bytes long. The first byte contains the least significant eight bits of the node number. The second byte contains the most significant two bits of the node number in the least significant two bits of the byte, and the area in the most significant six bits of the byte.

For more information on access control, see Volume One, Chapter 13, *Other Programming Techniques*.

Structures

```
typedef struct {
    int family;             /* for example Family Internet */
    int length;             /* length of address, in bytes */
    char *address;          /* pointer to where to find the bytes */
} XHostAddress;

/* The following constants for family member */
```

```
#define FamilyInternet      0
#define FamilyDECnet        1
#define FamilyChaos         2
```

Errors

```
BadAccess
BadValue
```

See Also

XAddHost(), *XDisableAccessControl()*, *XEnableAccessControl()*, *XListHosts()*, *XRemoveHost()*, *XRemoveHosts()*, *XSetAccessControl()*.

XAddPixel

Name

XAddPixel – add a constant value to every pixel value in an image.

Synopsis

```
XAddPixel(ximage, value)
    XImage *ximage;
    long value;
```

Arguments

ximage   Specifies a pointer to the image to be modified.

value   Specifies the constant value that is to be added. Valid pixel value ranges
                depend on the visual used to create the image. If this value added to the
                existing value causes an overflow, extra bits in the result are truncated.

Description

XAddPixel() adds a constant value to every pixel value in an image. This function is useful when you have a base pixel value derived from the allocation of color resources and need
to manipulate an image so that the pixel values are in the same range.

For more information on images, see Volume One, Chapter 6, *Drawing Graphics and Text*.

Structures

```
typedef struct _XImage {
    int width, height;      /* size of image */
    int xoffset;            /* number of pixels offset in X direction */
    int format;             /* XYBitmap, XYPixmap, ZPixmap */
    char *data;             /* pointer to image data */
    int byte_order;         /* data byte order, LSBFirst, MSBFirst */
    int bitmap_unit;        /* quantity of scan line 8, 16, 32 */
    int bitmap_bit_order;   /* LSBFirst, MSBFirst */
    int bitmap_pad;         /* 8, 16, 32 either XY or ZPixmap */
    int depth;              /* depth of image */
    int bytes_per_line;     /* accelerator to next line */
    int bits_per_pixel;     /* bits per pixel (ZPixmap) */
    unsigned long red_mask; /* bits in z arrangment */
    unsigned long green_mask;
    unsigned long blue_mask;
    char *obdata;           /* hook for object routines to hang on */
    struct funcs {          /* image manipulation routines */
    struct _XImage *(*create_image)();
    int (*destroy_image)();
    unsigned long (*get_pixel)();
    int (*put_pixel)();
    struct _XImage *(*sub_image)();
```

```
     int (*add_pixel)();
     } f;
} XImage;
```

See Also

XImageByteOrder(), *XCreateImage()*, *XDestroyImage()*, *XGetImage()*, *XGetPixel()*, *XGetSubImage()*, *XPutImage()*, *XPutPixel()*, *XSubImage()*.

XAddToSaveSet

Name

XAddToSaveSet – add a window to the client's save-set.

Synopsis

```
XAddToSaveSet(display, w)
    Display *display;
    Window w;
```

Arguments

display   Specifies a connection to an X server; returned from XOpenDisplay().

w   Specifies the ID of the window you want to add to the client's save-set.

Description

XAddToSaveSet() adds the specified window to the client's save-set.

The save-set is a safety net for windows that have been reparented by the window manager, usually to provide a titlebar or other decorations for each application. When the window manager dies unexpectedly, the windows in the save-set are reparented to their closest living ancestor, so that they remain alive. See Volume One, Chapter 13, *Other Programming Techniques*, for more information about save-sets.

Use XRemoveFromSaveSet() to remove a window from the client's save-set.

Errors

BadMatch   *w* not created by some other client.
BadWindow

See Also

XChangeSaveSet(), XRemoveFromSaveSet().

XAllocClassHint

Name

XAllocClassHint – allocate an XClassHint structure.

Synopsis

```
XClassHint *XAllocClassHint( )
```

Returns

The allocated structure.

Availability

Release 4 and later.

Description

XAllocClassHint() allocates and returns a pointer to an XClassHint structure, for use in calling XSetWMProperties(), XGetClassHint(), or XSetClassHint(). Note that the pointer fields in the XClassHint structure are initially set to NULL. If insufficient memory is available, XAllocClassHint() returns NULL. To free the memory allocated to this structure, use XFree().

The purpose of this function is to avoid compiled-in structure sizes, so that object files will be binary compatible with later releases that may have new members added to structures.

For more information, see Volume One, Chapter 10, *Interclient Communication*.

Structures

```
typedef struct {
    char *res_name;
    char *res_class;
} XClassHint;
```

See Also

XGetClassHint(), XSetClassHint(), XSetWMProperties().

XAllocColor

Name

XAllocColor – allocate a read-only colormap cell with closest hardware-supported color.

Synopsis

```
Status XAllocColor(display, colormap, colorcell_in_out)
    Display *display;
    Colormap colormap;
    XColor *colorcell_in_out;
```

Arguments

display   Specifies a connection to an X server; returned from XOpenDisplay().

colormap   Specifies the ID of the colormap in which the colorcell is to be allocated.

colorcell_in_out
                Specifies desired RGB values, and also returns the pixel value and the RGB
                values actually used in the colormap.

Returns

Zero on failure, non-zero on success.

Description

XAllocColor() returns the pixel value of a read-only (shareable) colorcell. The
requested RGB values are placed in colorcell_in_out, which is also used to return the
allocated pixel value and the actual RGB values of that colorcell. If XAllocColor() succeeds, it returns non-zero. If it fails, it returns zero.

XAllocColor() acts differently on static and dynamic visuals. On PseudoColor,
DirectColor, and GrayScale visuals, XAllocColor() fails if there are no unallocated colorcells and no allocated read-only cell exactly matches the requested RGB values.
On StaticColor, TrueColor, and StaticGray visuals, XAllocColor() returns
the closest RGB values available in the colormap. The colorcell_in_out structure
returns the actual RGB values allocated.

XAllocColor() does not use or affect the flags member of the XColor structure.

For more information, see Volume One, Chapter 7, *Color*.

Structures

```
typedef struct {
    unsigned long pixel;
    unsigned short red, green, blue;
```

```
    char flags;      /* DoRed, DoGreen, DoBlue */
    char pad;
} XColor;
```

Errors

BadColor   `colormap` is invalid.

See Also

XBlackPixel(), XWhitePixel(), XAllocColorCells(), XAllocColorPlanes(), XAllocNamedColor(), XFree-Colors(), XLookupColor(), XParseColor(), XQueryColor(), XQueryColors(), XStoreColor(), XStore-Colors(), XStoreNamedColor().

XAllocColorCells

Name

XAllocColorCells – allocate read/write (nonshared) colorcells.

Synopsis

```
Status XAllocColorCells(display, colormap, contig, plane_masks_return,
        nplanes, pixels_return, npixels_return)
    Display *display;
    Colormap colormap;
    Bool contig;
    unsigned long plane_masks_return[nplanes];
    unsigned int nplanes;
    unsigned long pixels_return[npixels_return];
    unsigned int npixels_return;
```

Arguments

display   Specifies a connection to an X server; returned from XOpenDisplay().

colormap   Specifies the ID of the colormap in which the colorcell is to be allocated.

contig   Specifies a boolean value. Pass True if the planes must be contiguous or False if the planes need not be contiguous.

plane_mask   Returns an array of plane masks.

nplanes   Specifies the number of plane masks returned in the plane masks array. Must be nonnegative.

pixels_return   Returns an array of pixel values.

npixels_return   Specifies the number of pixel values returned in the *pixels_return* array. Must be positive.

Returns

Zero on failure, non-zero on success.

Description

XAllocColorCells() allocates read/write colorcells in a read/write colormap. If npixels_return and nplanes are requested, then npixels_return base values and nplanes plane masks are returned. No mask will have any bits in common with any other mask, or with any of the pixels. By ORing together each of the pixels_return with any combination of the plane_masks_return, npixels_return*2$^{(nplanes)}$ distinct pixel values can be produced. For GrayScale or PseudoColor, each mask will have exactly one bit, and for DirectColor each will have exactly three bits. If *contig* is True, then if all plane masks are ORed together, a single contiguous set of bits will be formed for subfield) for `DirectColor`. The RGB values of the allocated entries are undefined until set with `XStoreColor`, `XStoreColors()`, or `XStoreNamedColor()`.

`Status` is zero on failure, and non-zero on success.

For more information, see Volume One, Chapter 7, *Color*.

Errors

`BadColor`

`BadValue`   `nplanes` is negative.

                  `npixels_return` is not positive.

See Also

XBlackPixel(), XWhitePixel(), XAllocColor(), XAllocColorPlanes(), XAllocNamedColor(), XFree-Colors(), XLookupColor(), XParseColor(), XQueryColor(), XQueryColors(), XStoreColor(), XStore-Colors(), XStoreNamedColor().

XAllocColorPlanes

Name

XAllocColorPlanes – allocate read/write (nonshareable) color planes.

Synopsis

```
Status XAllocColorPlanes(display, colormap, contig, pixels_return,
            npixels_return,
    nreds, ngreens, nblues, rmask_return, gmask_return, bmask_return)
    Display *display;
    Colormap colormap;
    Bool contig;
    unsigned long pixels_return[npixels];
    int npixels;
    int nreds, ngreens, nblues;
    unsigned long *rmask_return, *gmask_return, *bmask_return;
```

Arguments

display	Specifies a connection to an X server; returned from XOpen-Display().
colormap	Specifies the ID of the colormap to be used.
contig	Specifies a boolean value. Pass True if the planes must be contiguous or False if the planes do not need to be contiguous.
pixels_return	Returns an array of pixel values.
npixels	Specifies the number of pixel values returned in the pixels array. Must be positive.
nreds ngreens nblues	Specify the number of red, green, and blue planes (shades). Must be nonnegative.
rmask_return gmask_return bmask_return	Return bit masks for the red, green, and blue planes.

Returns

Zero on failure, non-zero on success.

Description

If npixels colors, nreds reds, ngreens greens, and nblues blues are requested, then npixels base values are returned, and the masks have nreds, ngreens, and nblues bits set to 1 respectively. No mask will have any bits in common with any other mask, or with any of the pixels_return. Unique pixel values are generated by by ORing together subsets of masks with each item in the pixels_return list (pixels_return does not by itself contain pixel values). In doing this, note that $npixels*(2^{(nreds+ngreens+nblues)})$ distinct pixel values are allocated.

If $contig$ is True, then each mask will have a contiguous set of bits. For DirectColor, each mask will lie within the corresponding pixel subfield.

Note, however, that there are actually only $npixels*(2^{nreds})$ independent red entries, $npixels*(2^{ngreens})$ independent green entries, and $npixels*(2^{nblues})$ independent blue entries in the colormap. This is true even for PseudoColor. When the pixel value of a colormap entry is changed using XStoreColors() or XStoreNamedColor(), the pixel is decomposed according to $rmask\_return$, $gmask\_return$, and $bmask\_return$ and the corresponding pixel subfield entries are updated.

Status is zero on failure, and non-zero on success.

For more information, see Volume One, Chapter 7, *Color*.

Errors

BadColor   colormap is invalid.

BadValue $npixels\_return$ is not positive.
                At least one of $nreds$, $ngreens$, $nblues$ is negative.

See Also

XBlackPixel(), *XWhitePixel()*, *XAllocColor()*, *XAllocColorCells()*, *XAllocNamedColor()*, *XFreeColors()*, *XLookupColor()*, *XParseColor()*, *XQueryColor()*, *XQueryColors()*, *XStoreColor()*, *XStoreColors()*, *XStoreNamedColor()*.

XAllocIconSize

Name

XAllocIconSize – allocate an `XIconSize` structure.

Synopsis

```
XIconSize *XAllocIconSize()
```

Returns

The allocated structure.

Availability

Release 4 and later.

Description

`XAllocIconSize()` allocates and returns a pointer to an `XIconSize` structure, for use in calling `XGetIconSizes()` or `XSetIconSizes()`. Note that all fields in the `XIconSize` structure are initially set to zero. If insufficient memory is available, `XAlloc-IconSize()` returns `NULL`. To free the memory allocated to this structure, use `XFree()`.

The purpose of this function is to avoid compiled-in structure sizes, so that object files will be binary compatible with later releases that may have new members added to structures.

For more information, see Volume One, Chapter 10, *Interclient Communication*.

Structures

```
typedef struct {
    int min_width, min_height;
    int max_width, max_height;
    int width_inc, height_inc;
} XIconSize;
```

See Also

XGetIconSizes(), XSetIconSizes().

XAllocNamedColor

Name

XAllocNamedColor – allocate a read-only colorcell from color name.

Synopsis

```
Status XAllocNamedColor(display, colormap, color_name, screen_def_return,
        exact_def_return)
    Display *display;
    Colormap colormap;
    char *color_name;
    XColor *screen_def_return;
    XColor *exact_def_return;
```

Arguments

display   Specifies a connection to an X server; returned from XOpenDisplay().

colormap   Specifies the ID of the colormap in which the colorcell will be allocated.

color_name   Specifies the color name string (for example, "red") you want. Uppercase or lowercase does not matter. If the color name is not in the Host Portable Character Encoding, the result is implementation-dependent.

screen_def_return
        Returns the pixel value and RGB values actually used in the colormap. This is the closest color supported by the hardware.

exact_def_return
        Returns the exact RGB values from the database corresponding to the *color_name* supplied.

Returns

Zero on failure, non-zero on success.

Description

XAllocNamedColor() determines the RGB values for the specified *color_name* from the color database, and then allocates a read-only colorcell with the closest color available, as described under XAllocColor().

Like XAllocColor, XAllocNamedColor() acts differently on static and dynamic visuals. On PseudoColor, DirectColor, and GrayScale visuals, XAllocNamedColor() fails if there are no unallocated colorcells and no allocated read-only colorcell exactly matches the database definition of the requested color. On StaticColor, True-Color, and StaticGray visuals, XAllocNamedColor() returns the closest RGB values (to the database definition of the requested color) available in the colormap. Both the database definition of the color, and the color actually allocated are returned.

XAllocNamedColor() returns a `Status` of zero if *color_name* was not found in the database or if the color could not be allocated. The function returns non-zero when it succeeds.

For more information, see Volume One, Chapter 7, *Color*.

Errors

`BadColor`   `colormap` is invalid.

Structures

```
typedef struct {
    unsigned long pixel;
    unsigned short red, green, blue;
    char flags;     /* DoRed, DoGreen, DoBlue */
    char pad;
} XColor;
```

See Also

XBlackPixel(), XWhitePixel(), XAllocColor(), XAllocColorCells(), XAllocColorPlanes(), XFreeColors(), XLookupColor(), XParseColor(), XQueryColor(), XQueryColors(), XStoreColor(), XStoreColors(), XStoreNamedColor().

XAllocSizeHints

Name

XAllocSizeHints – allocate an `XSizeHints` structure.

Synopsis

```
XSizeHints *XAllocSizeHints()
```

Returns

The allocated structure.

Availability

Release 4 and later.

Description

`XAllocSizeHints()` allocates and returns a pointer to an `XSizeHints` structure, for use in calling `XSetWMProperties()`, `XSetWMNormalHints()`, or `XGetWMNormal-Hints()`. Note that all fields in the `XSizeHints` structure are initially set to zero. If insufficient memory is available, `XAllocSizeHints()` returns `NULL`. To free the memory allocated to this structure, use `XFree()`.

The purpose of this function is to avoid compiled-in structure sizes, so that object files will be binary compatible with later releases that may have new members added to structures.

For more information, see Volume One, Chapter 10, *Interclient Communication*.

Structures

```
typedef struct {
    long flags;         /* marks which fields in this structure are defined */
    int x, y;           /* Obsolete */
    int width, height;  /* Obsolete */
    int min_width, min_height;
    int max_width, max_height;
    int width_inc, height_inc;
    struct {
        int x;          /* numerator */
        int y;          /* denominator */
    } min_aspect, max_aspect;
    int base_width, base_height;
    int win_gravity;
} XSizeHints;
```

See Also

XGetWMNormalHints(), *XSetWMNormalHints()*, *XSetWMProperties()*.

XAllocStandardColormap

Name

XAllocStandardColormap – allocate an `XStandardColormap` structure.

Synopsis

```
XStandardColormap *XAllocStandardColormap( )
```

Returns

The allocated structure.

Availability

Release 4 and later.

Description

`XAllocStandardColormap()` allocates and returns a pointer to an `XStandard-Colormap` structure for use in calling `XGetRGBColormaps()` or `XSet-RGBColormaps()`. Note that all fields in the `XStandardColormap` structure are initially set to zero. If insufficient memory is available, `XAllocStandardColormap()` returns NULL. To free the memory allocated to this structure, use `XFree()`.

The purpose of this function is to avoid compiled-in structure sizes, so that object files will be binary compatible with later releases that may have new members added to structures.

For more information, see Volume One, Chapter 7, *Color*.

Structures

```
/* value for killid field */

#define    ReleaseByFreeingColormap       ( (XID) 1L)

typedef struct {
    Colormap colormap;
    unsigned long red_max;
    unsigned long red_mult;
    unsigned long green_max;
    unsigned long green_mult;
    unsigned long blue_max;
    unsigned long blue_mult;
    unsigned long base_pixel;
    VisualID visualid;
    XID killid;
} XStandardColormap;
```

See Also

XGetRGBColormaps(), XSetRGBColormaps().

XAllocWMHints

Name

XAllocWMHints – allocate an XWMHints structure.

Synopsis

```
XWMHints *XAllocWMHints( )
```

Returns

The allocated structure.

Availability

Release 4 and later.

Description

The XAllocWMHints() function allocates and returns a pointer to an XWMHints structure, for use in calling XSetWMProperties(), XSetWMHints(), or XGetWMHints(). Note that all fields in the XWMHints structure are initially set to zero. If insufficient memory is available, XAllocWMHints() returns NULL. To free the memory allocated to this structure, use XFree().

The purpose of this function is to avoid compiled-in structure sizes, so that object files will be binary compatible with later releases that may have new members added to structures.

For more information, see Volume One, Chapter 10, *Interclient Communication*.

Structures

```
typedef struct {
    long flags;             /* marks which fields in this structure are defined */
    Bool input;             /* does this application rely on the window manager
                                   to get keyboard input? */
    int initial_state;      /* see below */
    Pixmap icon_pixmap;     /* pixmap to be used as icon */
    Window icon_window;     /* window to be used as icon */
    int icon_x, icon_y;     /* initial position of icon */
    Pixmap icon_mask;       /* pixmap to be used as mask for icon_pixmap */
    XID window_group;       /* id of related window group */
    /* this structure may be extended in the future */
} XWMHints;
```

See Also

XGetWMHints(), *XSetWMHints()*, *XSetWMProperties()*.

XAllowEvents

Name

XAllowEvents – control the behavior of keyboard and pointer events when these resources are grabbed.

Synopsis

```
XAllowEvents(display, event_mode, time)
    Display *display;
    int event_mode;
    Time time;
```

Arguments

display   Specifies a connection to an X server; returned from XOpenDisplay().

event_mode   Specifies the event mode. Pass one of these constants: AsyncPointer, SyncPointer, AsyncKeyboard, SyncKeyboard, Replay-Pointer, ReplayKeyboard, AsyncBoth, or SyncBoth.

time   Specifies the time when the grab should take place. Pass either a time-stamp, expressed in milliseconds, or the constant CurrentTime.

Description

XAllowEvents() releases the events queued in the server since the last XAllow-Events() call for the same device and by the same client. Events are queued in the server (not released to Xlib to propagate into Xlib's queues) only when the client has caused a device to "freeze" (by grabbing the device with mode GrabModeSync). The request has no effect if *time* is earlier than the last-grab time or later than the current server time.

The *event_mode* argument controls what device events are released for and just how and when they are released. The *event_mode* is interpreted as follows:

AsyncPointer   If XAllowEvents() is called with AsyncPointer while the pointer is frozen by the client, pointer event processing resumes normally, even if the pointer is frozen twice by the client on behalf of two separate grabs. AsyncPointer has no effect if the pointer is not frozen by the client, but the pointer need not be grabbed by the client.

AsyncKeyboard   If XAllowEvents() is called with AsyncKeyboard while the keyboard is frozen by the client, keyboard event processing resumes normally, even if the keyboard is frozen twice by the client on behalf of two separate grabs. AsyncKeyboard has no effect if the keyboard is not frozen by the client, but the keyboard need not be grabbed by the client.

SyncPointer   If XAllowEvents() is called with SyncPointer while the pointer is frozen by the client, normal pointer event processing continues until the next `ButtonPress` or `ButtonRelease` event is reported to the client. At this time, the pointer again appears to freeze. However, if the reported event causes the pointer grab to be released, then the pointer does not freeze, which is the case when an automatic grab is released by a `Button-Release` or when `XGrabButton()` or `XGrabKey()` has been called and the specified key or button is released. `SyncPointer` has no effect if the pointer is not frozen or not grabbed by the client.

SyncKeyboard   If `XAllowEvents()` is called with `SyncKeyboard` while the keyboard is frozen by the client, normal keyboard event processing continues until the next `KeyPress` or `KeyRelease` event is reported to the client. At this time, the keyboard again appears to freeze. However, if the reported event causes the keyboard grab to be released, then the keyboard does not freeze, which is the case when an automatic grab is released by a `ButtonRelease` or when `XGrabButton()` or `XGrabKey()` has been called and the specified key or button is released. `SyncKeyboard` has no effect if the keyboard is not frozen or not grabbed by the client.

ReplayPointer   This symbol has an effect only if the pointer is grabbed by the client and thereby frozen as the result of an event. In other words, `XGrabButton()` must have been called and the selected button/key combination pressed, or an automatic grab (initiated by a `ButtonPress`) must be in effect, or a previous `XAllow-Events()` must have been called with mode `SyncPointer`. If the `pointer_mode` of the `XGrabPointer()` was `Grab-ModeSync`, then the grab is released and the releasing event is processed as if it had occurred after the release, ignoring any passive grabs at or above in the hierarchy (towards the root) on the grab-window of the grab just released.

ReplayKeyboard   This symbol has an effect only if the keyboard is grabbed by the client and if the keyboard is frozen as the result of an event. In other words, `XGrabKey()` must have been called and the selected key combination pressed, or a previous `XAllow-Events()` must have been called with mode `SyncKeyboard`. If the `pointer_mode` or `keyboard_mode` of the `XGrab-Key()` was `GrabModeSync`, then the grab is released and the releasing event is processed as if it had occurred after the release, ignoring any passive grabs at or above in the hierarchy (towards the root).

SyncBoth   `SyncBoth` has the effect described for both `SyncKeyboard` and `SyncPointer`. `SyncBoth` has no effect unless both pointer and keyboard are frozen by the client. If the pointer or keyboard is frozen twice by the client on behalf of two separate grabs, `SyncBoth` "thaws" for both (but a subsequent freeze for `SyncBoth` will only freeze each device once).

AsyncBoth
    `AsyncBoth` has the effect described for both `AsyncKeyboard` and `AsyncPointer`. `AsyncBoth` has no effect unless both pointer and keyboard are frozen by the client. If the pointer and the keyboard were frozen by the client, or if both are frozen twice by two separate grabs, event processing (for both devices) continues normally. If a device is frozen twice by the client on behalf of the two separate grabs, `AsyncBoth` releases events for both.

`AsyncPointer`, `SyncPointer`, and `ReplayPointer` have no effect on the processing of keyboard events. `AsyncKeyboard`, `SyncKeyboard`, and `ReplayKeyboard` have no effect on the processing of pointer events.

It is possible for both a pointer grab and a keyboard grab (by the same or different clients) to be active simultaneously. If a device is frozen on behalf of either grab, no event processing is performed for the device. It is also possible for a single device to be frozen because of both grabs. In this case, the freeze must be released on behalf of both grabs before events will be released.

For more information on event handling, see Volume One, Chapter 9, *The Keyboard and Pointer*.

Errors

`BadValue`   Invalid mode constant.

See Also

XQLength(), XCheckIfEvent(), XCheckMaskEvent(), XCheckTypedEvent(), XCheckTypedWindow-Event(), XCheckWindowEvent(), XEventsQueued(), XGetInputFocus(), XGetMotionEvents(), XIfEvent(), XMaskEvent(), XNextEvent(), XPeekEvent(), XPeekIfEvent(), XPending(), XPutBackEvent(), XSelect-Input(), XSendEvent(), XSetInputFocus(), XSynchronize(), XWindowEvent().

XAllPlanes

Name

XAllPlanes, AllPlanes – return a value with all bits set to 1 suitable for plane argument.

Synopsis

```
unsigned long XAllPlanes()
```

Arguments

None.

Returns

A plane mask that includes all planes.

Description

XAllPlanes() returns a value with all bits set to 1 suitable for use in a plane mask in a GC, color allocation procedure, or in image handling.

The C language macro AllPlanes() is equivalent and slightly more efficient.

See Also

XAllocColorCells(), XChangeGC(), XCopyGC(), XCreateGC(), XGetGCValues(), XGetImage(), XGet-SubImage(), XSetPlaneMask(), XSetState().

XAutoRepeatOff

Name

XAutoRepeatOff – turn off the keyboard auto-repeat keys.

Synopsis

```
XAutoRepeatOff(display)
    Display *display;
```

Arguments

display   Specifies a connection to an X server; returned from XOpenDisplay().

Description

XAutoRepeatOff() turns off auto-repeat for the keyboard. It sets the keyboard so that holding any non-modal key down will not result in multiple events.

See Also

XAutoRepeatOn(), XBell(), XChangeKeyboardControl(), XGetDefault(), XGetKeyboardControl(), XGetPointerControl().

XAutoRepeatOn

Name

XAutoRepeatOn – turn on the keyboard auto-repeat keys.

Synopsis

```
XAutoRepeatOn(display)
    Display *display;
```

Arguments

display   Specifies a connection to an X server; returned from XOpenDisplay().

Description

XAutoRepeatOn() sets the keyboard to auto-repeat; that is, holding any non-modal key down will result in multiple KeyPress and KeyRelease event pairs with the same key-code member. Keys such as Shift Lock will still not repeat.

See Also

XAutoRepeatOff(), XBell(), XChangeKeyboardControl(), XGetDefault(), XGetKeyboardControl(), XGet-PointerControl().

XBaseFontNameListOfFontSet

Name

XBaseFontNameListOfFontSet – get the base font list of a font set.

Synopsis

```
char *XBaseFontNameListOfFontSet(font_set)
    XFontSet font_set;
```

Arguments

font_set   Specifies the font set.

Returns

The base font list string.

Availability

Release 5 and later.

Description

XBaseFontNameListOfFontSet() returns the original base font name list supplied by the client when the XFontSet was created. A NULL-terminated string containing a list of comma-separated font names is returned as the value of the function. Whitespace may appear immediately on either side of separating commas.

If XCreateFontSet() obtained an XLFD (X Logical Font Description) name from the font properties for the font specified by a non-XLFD base name, the XBaseFontName-ListOfFontSet() function will return the XLFD name instead of the non-XLFD base name.

The base font name list is owned by Xlib and should not be modified or freed by the client. It will be freed by a call to XFreeFontSet() on the associated XFontSet. Until freed, its contents will not be modified by Xlib.

See Also

XCreateFontSet(), XExtentsOfFontSet(), XFontsOfFontSet(), XLocaleOfFontSet().

XBell

Name

XBell – ring the bell.

Synopsis

```
XBell(display, percent)
    Display *display;
    int percent;
```

Arguments

display   Specifies a connection to an X server; returned from XOpenDisplay().

percent   Specifies the volume for the bell, relative to the base volume set with XChangeKeyboardControl(). Possible values are –100 (off), through 0 (base volume), to 100 (loudest) inclusive.

Description

Rings the bell on the keyboard at a volume relative to the base volume, if possible. *percent* can range from –100 to 100 inclusive (else a BadValue error). The volume at which the bell is rung when *percent* is nonnegative is:

```
volume = base - [(base * percent) / 100] + percent
```

and when *percent* is negative:

```
volume = base + [(base * percent) / 100]
```

To change the base volume of the bell, set the bell_percent variable of XChangeKeyboardControl().

Errors

BadValue   *percent* < –100 or *percent* > 100.

See Also

XAutoRepeatOff(), XAutoRepeatOn(), XChangeKeyboardControl(), XGetDefault(), XGetKeyboardControl(), XGetPointerControl().

XBitmap*

Name

XBitmapBitOrder, XBitmapPad, XBitmapUnit – query the bitmap format of a display.

Synopsis

```
int XBitmapUnit(display)
    Display *display;

int XBitmapBitOrder(display)
    Display *display;

int XBitmapPad(display)
    Display *display;
```

Arguments

display   Specifies a connection to an X Server; returned from XOpenDisplay().

Returns

XBitmapUnit() and XBitmapPad() return a number of bits. XBitmapBitOrder() returns LSBFirst or MSBFirst.

Description

These functions are used in connection with manipulating image data.

XBitmapUnit() returns the size of a bitmap's scanline unit in bits. The scanline is calculated in multiples of this value.

Within each bitmap unit, the left-most bit in the bitmap as displayed on the screen is either the least-significant or most-significant bit in the unit. XBitmapBitOrder() returns LSBFirst or MSBFirst to indicate the server's bit order.

Each scanline must be padded to a multiple of bits returned by XBitmapPad().

The C language macros BitmapUnit(), BitmapBitOrder(), and BitmapPad() are equivalent and slightly more efficient.

See Also

XImageByteOrder(), XGetImage(), XPutImage().

XBlackPixel*

Name

XBlackPixel, XBlackPixelOfScreen, BlackPixel, BlackPixelOfScreen – get the black pixel value.

Synopsis

```
unsigned long XBlackPixelOfScreen(screen)
     Screen *screen;

unsigned long XBlackPixel(display, screen_number)
     Display *display;
     int screen_number;
```

Arguments

screen   Specifies the appropriate `Screen` structure.

display   Specifies a connection to an X server; returned from `XOpenDisplay()`.

screen_number
         Specifies the appropriate screen number.

Returns

A pixel value.

Description

Each screen has a default colormap which has pixel values for black and white already allocated. These functions return the black pixel value. Note that this pixel value only represents black in a screen's default colormap.

`XBlackPixel()` and `XBlackPixelOfScreen()` are equivalent except that they require different arguments. One requires a pointer to a `Screen` structure, while the other requires a screen number. Unless you already have the pointer to a `Screen` structure in a variable, `XBlackPixel*()` is more convenient.

The C language macros `BlackPixel()` and `BlackPixelOfScreen()` are equivalent and slightly more efficient.

See Also

XWhitePixel(), *XWhitePixelOfScreen*(), *XDefaultColormap*().*

XCellsOfScreen

Name

XCellsOfScreen, CellsOfScreen – return size of default colormap.

Synopsis

```
int XCellsOfScreen(screen)
     Screen *screen;
```

Arguments

screen   Specifies the appropriate Screen structure.

Returns

The number of colorcells in the colormap.

Description

XCellsOfScreen() returns the number of colormap cells in the default colormap of the specified screen.

The C language macro CellsOfScreen() is equivalent and slightly more efficient.

See Also

XDefaultColormap(), *XDefaultDepthOfScreen*(), *XDefaultVisualOfScreen*().

XChangeActivePointerGrab

Name

XChangeActivePointerGrab – change the parameters of an active pointer grab.

Synopsis

```
XChangeActivePointerGrab(display, event_mask, cursor, time)
      Display *display;
      unsigned int event_mask;
      Cursor cursor;
      Time time;
```

Arguments

display   Specifies a connection to an X server; returned from `XOpenDisplay()`.

event_mask   Specifies which pointer events are reported to the client. This mask is the bitwise OR of one or more of these pointer event masks: `ButtonPress-Mask`, `ButtonReleaseMask`, `EnterWindowMask`, `LeaveWindow-Mask`, `PointerMotionMask`, `PointerMotionHintMask`, `Button1MotionMask`, `Button2MotionMask`, `Button3MotionMask`, `Button4MotionMask`, `Button5MotionMask`, `ButtonMotion-Mask`, `KeymapStateMask`.

cursor   Specifies the cursor that is displayed. A value of `None` will keep the current cursor.

time   Specifies the time when the grab should take place. Pass either a timestamp, expressed in milliseconds, or the constant `CurrentTime`.

Description

`XChangeActivePointerGrab()` changes the characteristics of an active pointer grab, if the specified time is no earlier than the last pointer grab time and no later than the current X server time. `XChangeActivePointerGrab()` has no effect on the passive parameters of `XGrabButton()`.

For more information on pointer grabbing, see Volume One, Chapter 9, *The Keyboard and Pointer*.

Errors

```
BadCursor
BadValue     The event_mask argument is invalid.
```

See Also

XChangePointerControl(), XGetPointerControl(), XGetPointerMapping(), XGrabPointer(), XQueryPointer(), XSetPointerMapping(), XUngrabPointer(), XWarpPointer().

Name

XChangeGC – change the components of a given graphics context.

Synopsis

```
XChangeGC(display, gc, valuemask, values)
    Display *display;
    GC gc;
    unsigned long valuemask;
    XGCValues *values;
```

Arguments

display   Specifies a connection to an X server; returned from XOpenDisplay().

gc   Specifies the graphics context.

valuemask   Specifies the components in the graphics context that you want to change. This argument is the bitwise OR of one or more of the GC component masks.

values   Specifies a pointer to the XGCValues structure.

Description

XChangeGC() changes any or all of the components of a GC. The valuemask specifies which components are to be changed; it is made by combining any number of the mask symbols listed in the Structures section using bitwise OR (|). The values structure contains the values to be set. These two arguments operate just like they do in XCreateGC(). Changing the clip_mask overrides any previous XSetClipRectangles() request for this GC. Changing the dash_offset or dashes overrides any previous XSetDashes() request on this GC.

Since consecutive changes to the same GC are buffered, there is no performance advantage to using this routine over the routines that set individual members of the GC.

Even if an error occurs, a subset of the components may have already been altered. The order in which components are altered and verified is server-dependent.

For more information, see Volume One, Chapter 5, *The Graphics Context*, and Chapter 6, *Drawing Graphics and Text*.

Structures

```
typedef struct {
    int function;                 /* logical operation */
    unsigned long plane_mask;     /* plane mask */
    unsigned long foreground;     /* foreground pixel */
    unsigned long background;     /* background pixel */
    int line_width;               /* line width */
```

```
    int line_style;      /* LineSolid, LineOnOffDash, LineDoubleDash */
    int cap_style;       /* CapNotLast, CapButt, CapRound, CapProjecting */
    int join_style;      /* JoinMiter, JoinRound, JoinBevel */
    int fill_style;      /* FillSolid, FillTiled, FillStippled */
    int fill_rule;       /* EvenOddRule, WindingRule */
    int arc_mode;        /* ArcChord, ArcPieSlice */
    Pixmap tile;         /* tile pixmap for tiling operations */
    Pixmap stipple;      /* stipple 1 plane pixmap for stipping */
    int ts_x_origin;     /* offset for tile or stipple operations */
    int ts_y_origin;
    Font font;                   /* default text font for text operations */
    int subwindow_mode;          /* ClipByChildren, IncludeInferiors */
    Bool graphics_exposures; /* generate events on XCopy, Area, XCopyPlane*/
    int clip_x_origin;           /* origin for clipping */
    int clip_y_origin;
    Pixmap clip_mask;    /* bitmap clipping; other calls for rects */
    int dash_offset;     /* patterned/dashed line information */
    char dashes;
} XGCValues;

#define GCFunction           (1L<<0)
#define GCPlaneMask          (1L<<1)
#define GCForeground         (1L<<2)
#define GCBackground         (1L<<3)
#define GCLineWidth          (1L<<4)
#define GCLineStyle          (1L<<5)
#define GCCapStyle           (1L<<6)
#define GCJoinStyle          (1L<<7)
#define GCFillStyle          (1L<<8)
#define GCFillRule           (1L<<9)
#define GCTile               (1L<<10)
#define GCStipple            (1L<<11)
#define GCTileStipXOrigin    (1L<<12)
#define GCTileStipYOrigin    (1L<<13)
#define GCFont               (1L<<14)
#define GCSubwindowMode      (1L<<15)
#define GCGraphicsExposures  (1L<<16)
#define GCClipXOrigin        (1L<<17)
#define GCClipYOrigin        (1L<<18)
#define GCClipMask           (1L<<19)
#define GCDashOffset         (1L<<20)
#define GCDashList           (1L<<21)
#define GCArcMode            (1L<<22)
```

Errors

```
BadAlloc
BadFont
BadGC
BadMatch
BadPixmap
BadValue
```

See Also

XDefaultGC(), XCopyGC(), XCreateGC(), XFreeGC(), XGContextFromGC(), XGetGCValues(), XSet-ArcMode(), XSetBackground(), XSetClipMask(), XSetClipOrigin(), XSetClipRectangles(), XSetDashes(), XSetFillRule(), XSetFillStyle(), XSetForeground(), XSetFunction(), XSetGraphicsExposures(), XSet-LineAttributes(), XSetPlaneMask(), XSetRegion(), XSetState(), XSetStipple(), XSetSubwindowMode(), XSetTSOrigin().

XChangeKeyboardControl

Name

XChangeKeyboardControl – change the keyboard preferences such as key click.

Synopsis

```
XChangeKeyboardControl(display, value_mask, values)
    Display *display;
    unsigned long value_mask;
    XKeyboardControl *values;
```

Arguments

display   Specifies a connection to an X server; returned from XOpenDisplay().

value_mask   Specifies a mask composed of ORed symbols from the table shown in the Structures section below, specifying which fields to set.

values   Specifies the settings for the keyboard preferences.

Description

XChangeKeyboardControl() sets user preferences such as key click, bell volume and duration, light state, and keyboard auto-repeat. Changing some or all these settings may not be possible on all servers.

The value_mask argument specifies which values are to be changed; it is made by combining any number of the mask symbols

The values structure contains the values to be set, as follows:

key_click_percent sets the volume for key clicks between 0 (off) and 100 (loud) inclusive. Setting to –1 restores the default.

bell_percent sets the base volume for the bell between 0 (off) and 100 (loud) inclusive. Setting to –1 restores the default.

bell_pitch sets the pitch (specified in Hz) of the bell. Setting to –1 restores the default.

bell_duration sets the duration (specified in milliseconds) of the bell. Setting to -1 restores the default.

led_mode is either LedModeOn or LedModeOff. led is a number between 1 and 32 inclusive that specifies which light's state is to be changed. If both led_mode and led are specified, then the state of the LED specified in led is changed to the state specified in led_mode. If only led_mode is specified, then all the LEDs assume the value specified by led_mode.

auto_repeat_mode is either AutoRepeatModeOn, AutoRepeatModeOff, or AutoRepeatModeDefault. key is a keycode between 7 and 255 inclusive. If both auto_repeat_mode and key are specified, then the auto-repeat mode of the key specified by key is set as specified by auto_repeat_mode. If only auto_repeat_mode is specified, then the global auto repeat mode for the entire keyboard is changed, without affecting the settings for each key. If the `auto_repeat_mode` is `AutoRepeatModeDefault` for either case, the key or the entire keyboard is returned to its default setting for the server, which is normally to have all non-modal keys repeat.

When a key is being used as a modifier key, it does not repeat regardless of the individual or global auto repeat mode.

The order in which the changes are performed is server-dependent, and some may be completed when another causes an error.

For more information on user preferences, see Volume One, Chapter 9, *The Keyboard and Pointer*.

Structures

```
/* masks for ChangeKeyboardControl */

#define KBKeyClickPercent      (1L<<0)
#define KBBellPercent          (1L<<1)
#define KBBellPitch            (1L<<2)
#define KBBellDuration         (1L<<3)
#define KBLed                  (1L<<4)
#define KBLedMode              (1L<<5)
#define KBKey                  (1L<<6)
#define KBAutoRepeatMode       (1L<<7)

/* structure for ChangeKeyboardControl */

typedef struct {
    int key_click_percent;
    int bell_percent;
    int bell_pitch;
    int bell_duration;
    int led;
    int led_mode;              /* LedModeOn or LedModeOff */
    int key;
    int auto_repeat_mode;      /* AutoRepeatModeOff, AutoRepeatModeOn,
                                  AutoRepeatModeDefault */
} XKeyboardControl;
```

Errors

BadMatch   *values*.`key` specified but *values*.`auto.repeat.mode` not specified.

                   values.`led` specified but *values*.`led_mode` not specified.

BadValue   *values*.key_click_percent < *−1*.
                values.bell_percent < *−1*.
                values.bell_pitch < *−1*.
                values.bell_duration < *−1*.

See Also

XAutoRepeatOff(), *XAutoRepeatOn()*, *XBell()*, *XGetDefault()*, *XGetKeyboardControl()*, *XGetPointer-Control()*.

XChangeKeyboardMapping

Name

XChangeKeyboardMapping – change the keyboard mapping.

Synopsis

```
XChangeKeyboardMapping(display, first_keycode,
        keysyms_per_keycode, keysyms, num_codes)
    Display *display;
    int first_keycode;
    int keysyms_per_keycode;
    KeySym *keysyms;
    int num_keycodes;
```

Arguments

display   Specifies a connection to an X server; returned from XOpenDisplay().

first_keycode
     Specifies the first keycode that is to be changed.

keysyms_per_keycode
     Specifies the number of keysyms that the caller is supplying for each keycode.

keysyms   Specifies a pointer to the list of keysyms.

num_keycodes
     Specifies the number of keycodes that are to be changed.

Description

Starting with *first_keycode*, XChangeKeyboardMapping() defines the keysyms for the specified number of keycodes. The symbols for keycodes outside this range remain unchanged. The number of elements in the *keysyms* list must be *keysyms_per_keycode* * num_keycodes (else a BadValue error). The specified *first_keycode* must be greater than or equal to min_keycode returned by XDisplayKeycodes() (see Appendix C, *Macros*) or a BadValue error results. In addition, the following expression must be less than or equal to max_keycode as returned by XDisplayKeycodes(), or a BadValue error results:

> *first_keycode* + *num_keycodes* − 1

The keysym number *N* (counting from 0) for keycode *K* has the following index in the *keysyms* array (counting from 0):

> (K − *first_keycode*) * *keysyms_per_keycode* + N

The specified *keysyms_per_keycode* can be chosen arbitrarily by the client to be large enough to hold all desired symbols. A special keysym value of NoSymbol should be used to fill in unused elements for individual keycodes. It is legal for `NoSymbol` to appear in non-trailing positions of the effective list for a keycode.

`XChangeKeyboardMapping()` generates a `MappingNotify` event, sent to this and all other clients, since the keycode to keysym mapping is global to all clients.

Errors

`BadAlloc`

`BadValue`   *first.keycode* less than *display*->`min_keycode`.
                  display->`max_keycode` exceeded (see above).

See Also

XDeleteModifiermapEntry(), *XFreeModifiermap()*, *XGetKeyboardMapping()*, *XGetModifierMapping()*, *XInsertModifiermapEntry()*, *XKeycodeToKeysym()*, *XKeysymToKeycode()*, *XKeysymToString()*, *XLookupKeysym()*, *XLookupString()*, *XNewModifierMap*, *XQueryKeymap()*, *XRebindKeySym*, *XRefreshKeyboardMapping()*, *XSetModifierMapping()*, *XStringToKeysym()*.

XChangePointerControl

Name

XChangePointerControl – change the pointer preferences.

Synopsis

```
XChangePointerControl(display, do_accel, do_threshold, accel_numerator,
        accel_denominator, threshold)
    Display *display;
    Bool do_accel, do_threshold;
    int accel_numerator, accel_denominator;
    int threshold;
```

Arguments

display   Specifies a connection to an X server; returned from XOpenDisplay().

do_accel   Specifies a boolean value that controls whether the values for the accel_numerator or accel_denominator are set. You can pass one of these constants: True or False.

do_threshold
                Specifies a boolean value that controls whether the value for the threshold is set. You can pass one of these constants: True or False.

accel_numerator
                Specifies the numerator for the acceleration multiplier.

accel_denominator
                Specifies the denominator for the acceleration multiplier.

threshold   Specifies the acceleration threshold. True or False.

Description

XChangePointerControl() defines how the pointing device functions. The acceleration is a fraction (accel_numerator/accel_denominator) which specifies how many times faster than normal the sprite on the screen moves for a given pointer movement. Acceleration takes effect only when a particular pointer motion is greater than threshold pixels at once, and only applies to the motion beyond threshold pixels. The values for do_accel and do_threshold must be True for the pointer values to be set; otherwise, the parameters will be unchanged. Setting any of the last three arguments to −1 restores the default for that argument.

The fraction may be rounded arbitrarily by the server.

Errors

BadValue   accel_denominator is 0.
                Negative value for do_accel or do_threshold.

See Also

XChangeActivePointerGrab(), *XGetPointerControl()*, *XGetPointerMapping()*, *XGrabPointer()*, *XQueryPointer()*, *XSetPointerMapping()*, *XUngrabPointer()*, *XWarpPointer()*.

XChangeProperty

Name

XChangeProperty – change a property associated with a window.

Synopsis

```
XChangeProperty(display, w, property, type, format, mode, data, nele-
        ments)
    Display *display;
    Window w;
    Atom property, type;
    int format;
    int mode;
    unsigned char *data;
    int nelements;
```

Arguments

display	Specifies a connection to an X server; returned from XOpenDisplay().
w	Specifies the ID of the window whose property you want to change.
property	Specifies the property atom.
type	Specifies the type of the property. X does not interpret the type, but simply passes it back to an application that later calls XGetWindowProperty.
format	Specifies whether the data should be viewed as a list of 8-bit, 16-bit, or 32-bit quantities. This information allows the X server to correctly perform byte-swap operations as necessary. If the format is 16-bit or 32-bit, you must explicitly cast your data pointer to a (char *) in the call to XChangeProperty(). Possible values are 8, 16, and 32.
mode	Specifies the mode of the operation. Possible values are PropMode-Replace, PropModePrepend, PropModeAppend.
data	Specifies the property data.
nelements	Specifies the number of elements in the property.

Description

XChangeProperty() changes a property and generates PropertyNotify events if they have been selected.

XChangeProperty() does the following according to the *mode* argument:

- PropModeReplace
  Discards the previous property value and stores the new data.

- PropModePrepend
  Inserts the data before the beginning of the existing data. If the property is undefined, it is treated as defined with the correct type and format with zero-length data. *type*

and *format* arguments must match the existing property value; otherwise a Bad-Match error occurs.

• PropModeAppend

Appends the data onto the end of the existing data. If the property is undefined, it is treated as defined with the correct type and format with zero-length data. *type* and *format* arguments must match the existing property value; otherwise a BadMatch error occurs.

The property may remain defined even after the client which defined it exits. The property becomes undefined only if the application calls XDeleteProperty(), destroys the specified window, or closes the last connection to the X server.

The maximum size of a property is server-dependent and can vary dynamically if the server has insufficient memory.

For more information, see Volume One, Chapter 10, *Interclient Communication*.

Errors

BadAlloc
BadAtom
BadMatch
BadValue
BadWindow

See Also

XDeleteProperty(), XGetAtomName(), XGetFontProperty(), XGetWindowProperty(), XInternAtom(), XListProperties(), XRotateWindowProperties(), XSetStandardProperties().

XChangeSaveSet

Name

XChangeSaveSet – add or remove a subwindow from the client's save-set.

Synopsis

```
XChangeSaveSet(display, w, change_mode)
    Display *display;
    Window w;
    int change_mode;
```

Arguments

display   Specifies a connection to an X server; returned from XOpenDisplay().

w   Specifies the ID of the window whose children you want to add or remove from the client's save-set; it must have been created by some other client.

change_mode   Specifies the mode. Pass one of these constants: SetModeInsert (adds the window to this client's save-set) or SetModeDelete (deletes the window from this client's save-set).

Description

XChangeSaveSet() adds or deletes windows from a client's save-set. This client is usually the window manager.

The save-set of the window manager is a list of other client's top-level windows which have been reparented. If the window manager dies unexpectedly, these top-level application windows are children of a window manager window and therefore would normally be destroyed. The save-set prevents this by automatically reparenting the windows listed in the save-set to their closest existing ancestor, and then remapping them.

Windows are removed automatically from the save-set by the server when they are destroyed.

For more information on save-sets, see Volume One, Chapter 13, *Other Programming Techniques*.

Errors

BadMatch   *w* not created by some other client.

BadValue

BadWindow

See Also

XAddToSaveSet(), XRemoveFromSaveSet().

XChangeWindowAttributes

Name

XChangeWindowAttributes – set window attributes.

Synopsis

```
XChangeWindowAttributes(display, w, valuemask, attributes)
    Display *display;
    Window w;
    unsigned long valuemask;
    XSetWindowAttributes *attributes;
```

Arguments

display   Specifies a connection to an X server; returned from XOpenDisplay().

w   Specifies the window ID.

valuemask   Specifies which window attributes are defined in the attributes argument. The mask is made by combining the appropriate mask symbols listed in the Structures section using bitwise OR (|). If valuemask is zero, the rest is ignored, and attributes is not referenced. The values and restrictions are the same as for XCreateWindow().

attributes   Window attributes to be changed. The valuemask indicates which members in this structure are referenced.

Description

XChangeWindowAttributes() changes any or all of the window attributes that can be changed. For descriptions of the window attributes, see Volume One, Chapter 4, *Window Attributes*.

Changing the background does not cause the window contents to be changed until the next Expose event or XClearWindow() call. Setting the border causes the border to be repainted immediately. Changing the background of a root window to None or Parent-Relative restores the default background pixmap. Changing the border of a root window to CopyFromParent restores the default border pixmap. Drawing into the pixmap that was set as the background pixmap or border pixmap attribute has an undefined effect, because the server may or may not make copies of these pixmaps.

Changing the win_gravity does not affect the current position of the window. Changing the backing_store of an obscured window to WhenMapped or Always may have no immediate effect. Also changing the backing_planes, backing_pixel, or save_under of a mapped window may have no immediate effect.

Multiple clients can select input on the same window; the event_mask attributes passed are disjoint. When an event is generated it will be reported to all interested clients. Therefore, the setting of the event_mask attribute by one client will not affect the event_mask of others on the same window. However, at most, one client at a time can select each of SubstructureRedirectMask, ResizeRedirectMask, and ButtonPressMask on any one window. If a client attempts to select on Substructure-RedirectMask, ResizeRedirectMask, or ButtonPressMask and some other client has already selected it on the same window, the X server generates a BadAccess error.

There is only one do_not_propagate_mask for a window, not one per client.

Changing the colormap attribute of a window generates a ColormapNotify event. Changing the colormap attribute of a visible window may have no immediate effect on the screen (because the colormap may not be installed until the window manager calls XInstallColormap( )).

Changing the cursor of a root window to None restores the default cursor.

For more information, see Volume One, Chapter 2, *X Concepts*, and Chapter 4, *Window Attributes*.

Structures

```
/*
 * Data structure for setting window attributes.
 */
typedef struct {
    Pixmap background_pixmap;       /* pixmap, None, or ParentRelative */
    unsigned long background_pixel; /* background pixel */
    Pixmap border_pixmap;           /* pixmap, None, or CopyFromParent */
    unsigned long border_pixel;     /* border pixel value */
    int bit_gravity;                /* one of bit gravity values */
    int win_gravity;                /* one of the window gravity values */
    int backing_store;              /* NotUseful, WhenMapped, Always */
    unsigned long backing_planes;   /* planes to be preseved if possible */
    unsigned long backing_pixel;    /* value to use in restoring planes */
    Bool save_under;                /* should bits under be saved (popups) */
    long event_mask;                /* set of events that should be saved */
    long do_not_propagate_mask;     /* set of events that should not
                                       propagate */
    Bool override_redirect;         /* override redirected config request */
    Colormap colormap;              /* colormap to be associated with window */
    Cursor cursor;                  /* cursor to be displayed (or None) */
} XSetWindowAttributes;

/* Definitions for valuemask argument of CreateWindow and
       ChangeWindowAttributes */

#define CWBackPixmap        (1L<<0)
#define CWBackPixel         (1L<<1)
#define CWBorderPixmap      (1L<<2)
#define CWBorderPixel       (1L<<3)
#define CWBitGravity        (1L<<4)
#define CWWinGravity        (1L<<5)
```

```
#define CWBackingStore       (1L<<6)
#define CWBackingPlanes      (1L<<7)
#define CWBackingPixel       (1L<<8)
#define CWOverrideRedirect   (1L<<9)
#define CWSaveUnder          (1L<<10)
#define CWEventMask          (1L<<11)
#define CWDontPropagate      (1L<<12)
#define CWColormap           (1L<<13)
#define CWCursor             (1L<<14)
```

Errors

```
BadAccess
```

```
BadColor          Specified colormap is invalid.
```

```
BadCursor
```

```
BadMatch
```

```
BadPixmap
```

```
BadValue
```

```
BadWindow
```

See Also

XGetGeometry(), XGetWindowAttributes(), XSetWindowBackground(), XSetWindowBackground-Pixmap(), XSetWindowBorder(), XSetWindowBorderPixmap().

XCheckIfEvent

Name

XCheckIfEvent – check the event queue for a matching event; don't wait.

Synopsis

```
Bool XCheckIfEvent(display, event_return, predicate, arg)
    Display *display;
    XEvent *event_return;
    Bool (*predicate)();
    char *arg;
```

Arguments

display   Specifies a connection to an X server; returned from `XOpenDisplay()`.

event_return

      Returns the matched event structure.

predicate   Specifies the procedure that is called to determine if the next event in the queue matches your criteria.

arg   Specifies the user-specified argument that will be passed to the predicate procedure.

Returns

`True` if a matching event is found, else `False`.

Description

`XCheckIfEvent()` returns the next event in the queue that is matched by the specified predicate procedure. If found, that event is removed from the queue, its structure is copied into the client-supplied `XEvent`, and `True` is returned. If no match is found, `XCheck-IfEvent()` returns `False` and flushes the request buffer. No other events are removed from the queue. Later events in the queue are not searched.

The predicate procedure is called with the arguments *display*, *event*, and *arg*.

For more information, see Volume One, Chapter 8, *Events*.

See Also

XQLength(), XAllowEvents(), XCheckMaskEvent(), XCheckTypedEvent(), XCheckTypedWindowEvent(), XCheckWindowEvent(), XEventsQueued(), XGetInputFocus(), XGetMotionEvents(), XIfEvent(), XMaskEvent(), XNextEvent(), XPeekEvent(), XPeekIfEvent(), XPending(), XPutBackEvent(), XSelectInput(), XSendEvent(), XSetInputFocus(), XSynchronize(), XWindowEvent().

XCheckMaskEvent

Name

XCheckMaskEvent – remove the next event that matches mask; don't wait.

Synopsis

```
Bool XCheckMaskEvent(display, event_mask, event_return)
    Display *display;
    long event_mask;
    XEvent *event_return;
```

Arguments

display   Specifies a connection to an X server; returned from XOpenDisplay().

event_mask   Specifies the event types to be returned. See list under XSelect-Input().

event_return
                 Returns a copy of the matched event's XEvent structure.

Returns

True if a matching event is found, else False.

Description

XCheckMaskEvent() removes the next event in the queue that matches the passed mask. The event is copied into an XEvent supplied by the caller and XCheckMaskEvent() returns True. Other events earlier in the queue are not discarded. If no such event has been queued, XCheckMaskEvent() flushes the request buffer and immediately returns False, without waiting.

For more information, see Volume One, Chapter 8, *Events*.

See Also

XQLength(), XAllowEvents(), XCheckIfEvent(), XCheckTypedEvent(), XCheckTypedWindowEvent(), XCheckWindowEvent(), XEventsQueued(), XGetInputFocus(), XGetMotionEvents(), XIfEvent(), XMaskEvent(), XNextEvent(), XPeekEvent(), XPeekIfEvent(), XPending(), XPutBackEvent(), XSelectInput(), XSendEvent(), XSetInputFocus(), XSynchronize(), XWindowEvent().

XCheckTypedEvent

Name

XCheckTypedEvent – return the next event in queue that matches event type; don't wait.

Synopsis

```
Bool XCheckTypedEvent(display, event_type, event_return)
    Display *display;
    int event_type;
    XEvent *event_return;
```

Arguments

display   Specifies a connection to an X server; returned from XOpenDisplay().

event_type   Specifies the event type to be compared.

event_return
                Returns a copy of the matched event structure.

Returns

True if a matching event is found, else False.

Description

XCheckTypedEvent() searches first the event queue, then the events available on the server connection, for the specified *event_type*. If there is a match, it returns the associated event structure. Events searched but not matched are not discarded. XCheckTypedEvent() returns True if the event is found. If the event is not found, XCheckTypedEvent() flushes the request buffer and returns False.

This command is similar to XCheckMaskEvent(), but it searches through the queue and any events available on the server connection instead of inspecting only the last item on the queue. It also matches only a single event type instead of multiple event types as specified by a mask.

For more information, see Volume One, Chapter 8, *Events*.

See Also

XQLength(), XAllowEvents(), XCheckIfEvent(), XCheckMaskEvent(), XCheckTypedWindowEvent(), XCheckWindowEvent(), XEventsQueued(), XGetInputFocus(), XGetMotionEvents(), XIfEvent(), XMaskEvent(), XNextEvent(), XPeekEvent(), XPeekIfEvent(), XPending(), XPutBackEvent(), XSelectInput(), XSendEvent(), XSetInputFocus(), XSynchronize(), XWindowEvent().

XCheckTypedWindowEvent

Name

XCheckTypedWindowEvent – return the next event in queue matching type and window; don't wait.

Synopsis

```
Bool XCheckTypedWindowEvent(display, w, event_type, event_return)
    Display *display;
    Window w;
    int event_type;
    XEvent *event_return;
```

Arguments

display	Specifies a connection to an X server; returned from XOpen-Display().
w	Specifies the window ID.
event_type	Specifies the event type to be compared.
event_return	Returns the matched event's associated structure into this client-supplied structure.

Returns

True if a matching event is found, else False.

Description

XCheckTypedWindowEvent() searches first the event queue, then any events available on the server connection, for an event that matches the specified window and the specified event type. Events searched but not matched are not discarded.

XCheckTypedWindowEvent(), if the event is found, removes the event from the queue, copies it into the specified XEvent structure, and returns True. It flushes the request buffer and returns False if the event is not found.

For more information, see Volume One, Chapter 8, *Events*.

See Also

XQLength(), *XAllowEvents()*, *XCheckIfEvent()*, *XCheckMaskEvent()*, *XCheckTypedEvent()*, *XCheckWindowEvent()*, *XEventsQueued()*, *XGetInputFocus()*, *XGetMotionEvents()*, *XIfEvent()*, *XMaskEvent()*, *XNextEvent()*, *XPeekEvent()*, *XPeekIfEvent()*, *XPending()*, *XPutBackEvent()*, *XSelectInput()*, *XSendEvent()*, *XSetInputFocus()*, *XSynchronize()*, *XWindowEvent()*.

XCheckWindowEvent

Name

XCheckWindowEvent – remove the next event matching both passed window and passed mask; don't wait.

Synopsis

```
Bool XCheckWindowEvent(display, w, event_mask, event_return)
    Display *display;
    Window w;
    long event_mask;
    XEvent *event_return;
```

Arguments

display   Specifies a connection to an X server; returned from XOpenDisplay().

w   Specifies the window ID. The event must match both the passed window and the passed event mask.

event_mask   Specifies the event mask. See XSelectInput() for a list of mask elements.

event_return
                Returns the XEvent structure.

Returns

True if a matching event is found, else False.

Description

XCheckWindowEvent() removes the next event in the queue that matches both the passed window and the passed mask. If such an event exists, it is copied into an XEvent supplied by the caller. Other events earlier in the queue are not discarded.

If a matching event is found, XCheckWindowEvent() returns True. If no such event has been queued, it flushes the request buffer and returns False, without waiting.

For more information, see Volume One, Chapter 8, *Events*.

See Also

XQLength(), XAllowEvents(), XCheckIfEvent(), XCheckMaskEvent(), XCheckTypedEvent(), XCheck-TypedWindowEvent(), XEventsQueued(), XGetInputFocus(), XGetMotionEvents(), XIfEvent(), XMask-Event(), XNextEvent(), XPeekEvent(), XPeekIfEvent(), XPending(), XPutBackEvent(), XSelectInput(), XSendEvent(), XSetInputFocus(), XSynchronize(), XWindowEvent().

XCirculateSubwindows

Name

XCirculateSubwindows – circulate the stacking order of children up or down.

Synopsis

```
XCirculateSubwindows(display, w, direction)
    Display *display;
    Window w;
    int direction;
```

Arguments

display	Specifies a connection to an X server; returned from XOpenDisplay().
w	Specifies the window ID of the parent of the subwindows to be circulated.
direction	Specifies the direction (up or down) that you want to circulate the children. Pass either RaiseLowest or LowerHighest.

Description

XCirculateSubwindows() circulates the children of the specified window in the specified direction, either RaiseLowest or LowerHighest. If some other client has selected SubstructureRedirectMask on the specified window, then a CirculateRequest event is generated, and no further processing is performed. If you specify RaiseLowest, this function raises the lowest mapped child (if any) that is occluded by another child to the top of the stack. If you specify LowerHighest, this function lowers the highest mapped child (if any) that occludes another child to the bottom of the stack. Exposure processing is performed on formerly obscured windows. If a child is actually restacked, the X server generates a CirculateNotify event.

For more information, see Volume One, Chapter 14, *Window Management*.

Errors

```
BadValue
BadWindow
```

See Also

XCirculateSubwindowsDown(), XCirculateSubwindowsUp(), XConfigureWindow(), XLowerWindow(), XMoveResizeWindow(), XMoveWindow(), XQueryTree(), XRaiseWindow(), XReparentWindow(), XResizeWindow(), XRestackWindows().

XCirculateSubwindowsDown

Name

XCirculateSubwindowsDown – circulate the bottom child to the top of the stacking order.

Synopsis

```
XCirculateSubwindowsDown(display, w)
    Display *display;
    Window w;
```

Arguments

display   Specifies a connection to an X server; returned from XOpenDisplay().

w   Specifies the window ID of the parent of the windows to be circulated.

Description

XCirculateSubwindowsDown() lowers the highest mapped child of the specified window that partially or completely obscures another child. The lowered child goes to the bottom of the stack. Completely unobscured children are not affected.

This function generates exposure events on any window formerly obscured. Repeated executions lead to round-robin lowering. XCirculateSubwindowsDown() is equivalent to XCirculateSubwindows(display, w, LowerHighest).

If some other client has selected SubstructureRedirectMask on the window, then a CirculateRequest event is sent to that client, and no further processing is performed. This allows the window manager to intercept this request when w is the root window. Normally, only the window manager should call XCirculateSubwindowsDown() on the root window.

For more information, see Volume One, Chapter 14, *Window Management*.

Errors

BadWindow

See Also

XCirculateSubwindows(), XCirculateSubwindowsUp(), XConfigureWindow(), XLowerWindow(), XMoveResizeWindow(), XMoveWindow(), XQueryTree(), XRaiseWindow(), XReparentWindow(), XResizeWindow(), XRestackWindows().

XCirculateSubwindowsUp

Name

XCirculateSubwindowsUp – circulate the top child to the bottom of the stacking order.

Synopsis

```
XCirculateSubwindowsUp(display, w)
    Display *display;
    Window w;
```

Arguments

display   Specifies a connection to an X server; returned from XOpenDisplay().

w   Specifies the window ID of the parent of the windows to be circulated.

Description

XCirculateSubwindowsUp() raises the lowest mapped child of the specified window that is partially or completely obscured by another child. The raised child goes to the top of the stack. This generates exposure events on the raised child (and its descendents, if any). Repeated executions lead to round robin-raising. Completely unobscured children are not affected.

XCirculateSubwindowsUp() is equivalent to XCirculateSubwindows(*display*, w, RaiseLowest).

If some other client has selected SubstructureRedirectMask on the window, then a CirculateRequest event is sent to that client, and no further processing is performed. This allows the window manager to intercept this request when w is the root window. Normally, only the window manager will call XCirculateSubwindowsUp() on the root window.

For more information, see Volume One, Chapter 14, *Window Management*.

Errors

BadWindow

See Also

XCirculateSubwindows(), XCirculateSubwindowsDown(), XConfigureWindow(), XLowerWindow(), XMoveResizeWindow(), XMoveWindow(), XQueryTree(), XRaiseWindow(), XReparentWindow(), XResizeWindow(), XRestackWindows().

XClearArea

Name

XClearArea – clear a rectangular area in a window.

Synopsis

```
XClearArea(display, w, x, y, width, height, exposures)
    Display *display;
    Window w;
    int x, y;
    unsigned int width, height;
    Bool exposures;
```

Arguments

display   Specifies a connection to an X server; returned from XOpenDisplay().

w   Specifies the ID of an InputOutput window.

x   Specify the x and y coordinates of the upper-left corner of the rectangle to be
y   cleared, relative to the origin of the window.

width   Specify the dimensions in pixels of the rectangle to be cleared.
height

exposures   Specifies whether exposure events are generated. Must be either True or
False.

Description

XClearArea() clears a rectangular area in a window.

If width is zero, the window is cleared from x to the right edge of the window. If height
is zero, the window is cleared from y to the bottom of the window. See the figure on the next
page..

If the window has a defined background tile or it is ParentRelative, the rectangle is
tiled with a plane_mask of all 1's, a function of GXcopy, and a subwindow_mode
of ClipByChildren. If the window has background None, the contents of the window
are not changed. In either case, if exposures is True, then one or more exposure events
are generated for regions of the rectangle that are either visible or are being retained in a
backing store.

For more information, see Volume One, Chapter 6, *Drawing Graphics and Text*.

Errors

BadMatch   Window is an `InputOnly` class window.

BadValue

BadWindow

See Also

XClearWindow(), XCopyArea(), XCopyPlane(), XDraw, XDrawArc(), XDrawArcs(), XDrawFilled(), XDrawLine(), XDrawLines(), XDrawPoint(), XDrawPoints(), XDrawRectangle(), XDrawRectangles(), XDrawSegments(), XFillArc(), XFillArcs(), XFillPolygon(), XFillRectangle(), XFillRectangles().

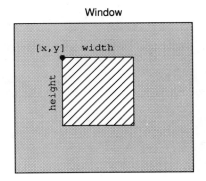

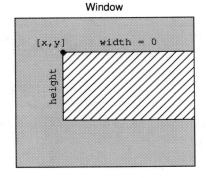

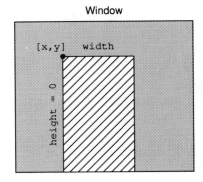

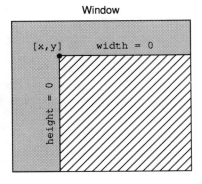

XClearWindow

Name

XClearWindow – clear an entire window.

Synopsis

```
XClearWindow(display, w)
    Display *display;
    Window w;
```

Arguments

display   Specifies a connection to an X server; returned from XOpenDisplay().

w   Specifies the ID of the window to be cleared.

Description

XClearWindow() clears a window, but does not cause exposure events. This function is equivalent to XClearArea(display, w, 0, 0, 0, 0, False).

If the window has a defined background tile or it is ParentRelative, the rectangle is tiled with a plane_mask of all 1's and function of GXcopy. If the window has background None, the contents of the window are not changed.

For more information, see Volume One, Chapter 6, *Drawing Graphics and Text*.

Errors

BadMatch   If w is an InputOnly class window.

BadWindow

See Also

XClearArea(), XCopyArea(), XCopyPlane(), XDraw, XDrawArc(), XDrawArcs(), XDrawFilled(), XDrawLine(), XDrawLines(), XDrawPoint(), XDrawPoints(), XDrawRectangle(), XDrawRectangles(), XDrawSegments(), XFillArc(), XFillArcs(), XFillPolygon(), XFillRectangle(), XFillRectangles().

XClipBox

Name

XClipBox – generate the smallest rectangle enclosing a region.

Synopsis

```
XClipBox(r, rect_return)
    Region r;
    XRectangle *rect_return;
```

Arguments

r   Specifies the region.

rect_return   Returns the smallest rectangle enclosing region r.

Description

XClipBox() returns the smallest rectangle that encloses the given region.

For more information, see Volume One, Chapter 6, *Drawing Graphics and Text*.

Structures

Region is a pointer to an opaque structure type.

See Also

XCreateRegion(), XDestroyRegion(), XEmptyRegion(), XEqualRegion(), XIntersectRegion(), XOffset-Region(), XPointInRegion(), XPolygonRegion(), XRectInRegion(), XSetRegion(), XShrinkRegion(), XSubtractRegion(), XUnionRectWithRegion(), XUnionRegion(), XXorRegion().

XCloseDisplay

Name

XCloseDisplay – disconnect a client program from an X server and display.

Synopsis

```
XCloseDisplay(display)
    Display *display;
```

Arguments

display   Specifies a connection to an X server; returned from XOpenDisplay().

Description

XCloseDisplay() closes the connection between the current client and the X server specified by the Display argument.

The XCloseDisplay() routine destroys all windows, resource IDs (Window, Font, Pixmap, Colormap, Cursor, and GContext), or other resources (GCs) that the client application has created on this display, unless the close down mode of the client's resources has been changed by XSetCloseDownMode(). Therefore, these windows, resource IDs, and other resources should not be referenced again. In addition, this routine discards any requests that have been buffered but not yet sent to the server.

Although these operations automatically (implicitly) occur when a process exits under UNIX, you should call XCloseDisplay() anyway so that any pending errors are reported as XCloseDisplay() performs a final XSync() operation.

For more information, see Volume One, Chapter 3, *Basic Window Program*.

Errors

BadGC   Default GC already freed.

See Also

XDefaultScreen(), XFree(), XNoOp(), XOpenDisplay().

XCloseIM

Name

XCloseIM – close an input method.

Synopsis

```
Status XCloseIM(im)
    XIM im;
```

Arguments

im   Specifies the input method.

Returns

Zero on failure, non-zero on success.

Availability

Release 5 and later.

Description

XCloseIM( ) closes the connection to an input method opened with XOpenIM( ). Once an input method is closed, none of the input contexts associated with that input method may be used.

See Also

XCreateIC(), XSetICFocus(), XSetICValues(), XmbResetIC(), XOpenIM(), XGetIMValues(), XDisplay-OfIM(), XLocaleOfIM().

XcmsAddColorSpace

Name

XcmsAddColorSpace – add a device-independent color space.

Synopsis

```
Status XcmsAddColorSpace(color_space)
    XcmsColorSpace *color_space;
```

Arguments

color_space   Specifies the device-independent color space to add.

Returns

Zero on failure, non-zero on success.

Availability

Release 5 and later.

Description

XcmsAddColorSpace() makes a device-independent color space (actually an Xcms-
ColorSpace structure) accessible by the color management system. Because format values for unregistered color spaces are assigned at run-time, they should be treated as private to
the client. If references to an unregistered color space must be made outside the client (for
example, storing color specifications in a file using the unregistered color space), then reference should be made by color space prefix (see XcmsFormatOfPrefix() and Xcms-
PrefixOfFormat()).

If the XcmsColorSpace structure is already accessible in the color management system,
XcmsAddColorSpace() returns XcmsSuccess.

Note that added XcmsColorSpace structures must be retained for reference by Xlib.

Structures

Refer to the XcmsColorSpace reference page.

See Also

XcmsColorSpace().

XcmsAddFunctionSet

Name

XcmsAddFunctionSet – add a Color Characterization function set.

Synopsis

```
Status XcmsAddFunctionSet(function_set)
    XcmsFunctionSet *function_set;
```

Arguments

function_set   Specifies the Color Characterization Function Set to add.

Returns

Zero on failure, non-zero on success.

Availability

Release 5 and later.

Description

XcmsAddFunctionSet() adds a Color Characterization Function Set to the color management system. If the function set contains device-dependent XcmsColorSpace structures not previously available in the color management system, XcmsAddFunctionSet() performs the internal registration necessary to make them accessible to the client. If an added XcmsColorSpace structure is for a device-dependent color space not registered with the X Consortium, because format values for unregistered color spaces are assigned at run-time they should be treated as private to the client. If references to an unregistered color space must be made outside the client (for example, storing color specifications in a file using the unregistered color space), then reference should be made by color space prefix (see XcmsFormatOfPrefix() and XcmsPrefixOfFormat()).

Additional function sets should be added before any calls to other Xlib routines are made. If not, the XcmsPerScrnInfo member of a previously created XcmsCCC will not have been initialized with the added function set.

Note that added XcmsFunctionSet structures must be retained for reference by Xlib.

Structures

Refer to the XcmsFunctionSet reference page.

See Also

XcmsFunctionSet().

XcmsAllocColor

Name

XcmsAllocColor – allocate a color specified in device-independent or device-dependent form.

Synopsis

```
Status XcmsAllocColor(display, colormap, color_in_out, result_format)
    Display *display;
    Colormap colormap;
    XcmsColor *color_in_out;
    XcmsColorFormat result_format;
```

Arguments

display   Specifies the connection to the X server.

colormap   Specifies the colormap.

color_in_out
                   Specifies the color to allocate and returns the pixel and color that is actually used in the colormap.

result_format
                   Specifies the desired color format for the returned color specification.

Returns

Zero on failure, non-zero on success.

Availability

Release 5 and later.

Description

The XcmsAllocColor() function is similar to XAllocColor() except the color can be specified in any format supported by the color management system (e.g., CIEXYZ, CIELUV, RGB). The XcmsAllocColor() function ultimately calls XAllocColor() to allocate a read-only color cell (colormap entry) with the specified color. XcmsAllocColor() first converts the color specified to an RGB value and then passes this to XAllocColor. XcmsAllocColor() returns the pixel value of the color cell and the color specification actually allocated. This returned color specification is the result of converting the RGB value returned by XAllocColor() into the format specified by the result_format argument. If there is no interest in a returned color specification, unnecessary computation can be bypassed if result_format is set to XcmsRGBFormat. If this routine returns Xcms-Failure, the color_in_out color specification is left unchanged.

Structures

The `XcmsColor` and `XcmsColorFormat` structures are shown on the `XcmsColor` reference page.

Errors

BadColor   The *colormap* argument does not name a defined Colormap.

See Also

XcmsAllocNamedColor(), XcmsLookupColor(), XcmsQueryColor(), XcmsQueryColors(), XcmsStoreNamedColor.

XcmsAllocNamedColor

Name

XcmsAllocNamedColor – allocate a color specified as a string.

Synopsis

```
Status XcmsAllocNamedColor(display, colormap, color_string,
       color_screen_return, color_exact_return,result_format)
   Display *display;
   Colormap colormap;
   char *color_string;
   XcmsColor *color_screen_return;
   XcmsColor *color_exact_return;
   XcmsColorFormat result_format;
```

Arguments

display   Specifies the connection to the X server.

colormap   Specifies the colormap.

color_string
                 Specifies the color string whose color definition structure is to be returned.

color_screen_return
                 Returns the pixel value of the color cell and color specification that actu-
                 ally is stored for that cell.

color_exact_return
                 Returns the color specification parsed from the color string or parsed from
                 the corresponding string found in a color name database.

result_format
                 Specifies the desired color format for the returned color specification.

Returns

Zero on failure, non-zero on success.

Description

The XcmsAllocNamedColor() function is similar to XAllocNamedColor() except
the color specification returned can be specified to be in any format supported by the color
management system. This function ultimately calls XAllocColor() to allocate a read-
only color cell with the color specified by a color string. The color string is parsed into an
XcmsColor structure, converted to an RGB value, then finally passed to XAlloc-
Color().

The color string may contain a color name that appears in the client-side or X server's color database; or a numerical color specification for any color management supported color spaces such that the string conforms to the uniform syntax:

<color_space>:<color_space_specific_encoding>

For example:

RGB:*red/green/blue*
RGBi:*R/G/B*
CIEXYZ:*X/Y/Z*
CIEuvY:*u/v/Y*
CIExyY:*x/y/Y*
CIELab:*L/a/b*
CIELuv:*L/u/v*
TekHVC:*H/V/C*

For the RGB color space, the *red*, *green*, and *blue* parameters are hexidecimal strings of one to four digits. For each of the other color spaces, each parameter is a floating-point number in standard string format. In each case, each number specifies a value for one of the parameters of the color space. Old-style RGB color strings beginning with a "#" remain supported for backwards compatibility. If the color name is not in the Host Portable Character Encoding the result is implementation-dependent. Color names are case-insensitive.

This function returns both the color specification as a result of parsing (exact specification) and the actual color specification stored (screen specification). This screen specification is the result of converting the RGB value returned by **XAllocColor()** into the format specified by *result_format*. If there is no interest in a returned color specification, unnecessary computation can be bypassed if *result_format* is set to **XcmsRGBFormat**.

Errors

BadColor   The *colormap* argument does not name a defined Colormap.

Structures

The **XcmsColor** and **XcmsColorFormat** structures are shown on the **XcmsColor** reference page.

See Also

XcmsAllocColor(), *XcmsLookupColor()*, *XcmsQueryColor()*, *XcmsQueryColors()*, *XcmsStoreColor()*, *XcmsStoreColors()*, *XcmsStoreNamedColor*, *XAllocColor()*, *XAllocNamedColor()*, *XLookupColor()*, *XParseColor()*, *XQueryColor()*, *XQueryColors()*, *XStoreColor()*, *XStoreColors()*.

XcmsCCCOfColormap

Name

XcmsCCCOfColormap – get the Color Conversion Context of a colormap.

Synopsis

```
XcmsCCC XcmsCCCOfColormap(display, colormap)
    Display *display;
    Colormap colormap;
```

Arguments

display   Specifies the connection to the X server.

colormap   Specifies the colormap for which the CCC is to be returned.

Returns

The Color Conversion Context.

Availability

Release 5 and later.

Description

XcmsCCCOfColormap() returns the CCC associated with the specified colormap. This CCC is used implicitly when the specified colormap is used as an argument to many Xcms device-independent color functions. XcmsCCCOfColormap() returns the CCC so that its contents can be modified and/or so it can be passed explicitly to color conversion functions that do not take a colormap argument (e.g., XcmsConvertColors()).

See Also

XcmsCreateCCC(), XcmsClientWhitePointOfCCC(), XcmsConvertColors(), XcmsDefaultCCC(), XcmsDisplayOfCCC(), XcmsFreeCCC(), XcmsScreenNumberOfCCC(), XcmsScreenWhitePointOfCCC(), XcmsSetCCCOfColormap(), XcmsSetCompressionProc(), XcmsSetWhiteAdjustProc(), XcmsSetWhitePoint(), XcmsVisualOfCCC().

XcmsCIELabQueryMax

Name

XcmsCIELabQueryMaxC, XcmsCIELabQueryMaxL, XcmsCIELabQueryMaxLC, Xcms-
CIELabQueryMinL – obtain the bounds of the target screen's
color gamut in terms of CIE L*a*b* coordinates.

Synopsis

```
Status XcmsCIELabQueryMaxC(ccc, hue_angle, L_star, color_return)
    XcmsCCC ccc;
    XcmsFloat hue_angle;
    XcmsFloat L_star;
    XcmsColor *color_return;

Status XcmsCIELabQueryMaxL(ccc, hue_angle, chroma, color_return)
    XcmsCCC ccc;
    XcmsFloat hue_angle;
    XcmsFloat chroma;
    XcmsColor *color_return;

Status XcmsCIELabQueryMaxLC(ccc, hue_angle, color_return)
    XcmsCCC ccc;
    XcmsFloat hue_angle;
    XcmsColor *color_return;

Status XcmsCIELabQueryMinL(ccc, hue_angle, chroma, color_return)
    XcmsCCC ccc;
    XcmsFloat hue_angle;
    XcmsFloat chroma;
    XcmsColor *color_return;
```

Arguments

ccc   Specifies the color conversion context. Note that the CCC's Client White
Point and White Point Adjustment procedures are ignored.

chroma   Specifies the CIELAB psychometric chroma at which to find maximum
lightness (MaxL) or minimum lightness (MinL).

color_return

Returns the CIE L*a*b* coordinates of maximum chroma (MaxC and
MaxLC), maximum lightness (MaxL), or minimum lightness (MinL) displayable by the screen for the given CC. The white point associated with
the returned color specification is the Screen White Point. The value
returned in the pixel member is undefined.

hue_angle   Specifies the CIELAB psychometric hue angle in degrees at which to find maximum chroma (MaxC and MaxLC), maximum lightness (MaxL), or minimum lightness (MinL).

L_star   Specifies the lightness (L*) at which to find maximum chroma (MaxC).

Returns

Zero on failure, non-zero on success.

Availability

Release 5 and later.

Description

XcmsCIELabQueryMaxC() finds the point of maximum chroma displayable by the screen at the given hue angle and lightness.

XcmsCIELabQueryMaxL() finds the point in CIELAB color space of maximum lightness (L*) displayable by the screen at the given hue angle and chroma. An XcmsFailure return value usually indicates that the given chroma is beyond maximum for the given hue angle.

XcmsCIELabQueryMaxLC() finds the point of maximum chroma displayable by the screen at the given hue angle.

XcmsCIELabQueryMinL() finds the point of minimum lightness (L*) displayable by the screen at the given hue angle and chroma. An XcmsFailure return value usually indicates that the given chroma is beyond maximum for the given hue angle.

All these functions return a point in CIE L*a*b* color space coordinates.

See Also

XcmsCIELuvQueryMaxC(), XcmsCIELuvQueryMaxL(), XcmsCIELuvQueryMaxLC(), XcmsCIELuv-QueryMinL(), XcmsTekHVCQueryMaxC(), XcmsTekHVCQueryMaxL, XcmsTekHVCQueryMaxLC, XcmsTekHVCQueryMinL, XcmsQueryBlack(), XcmsQueryBlue(), XcmsQueryGreen(), XcmsQuery-Red(), XcmsQueryWhite().

Name

XcmsCIELuvQueryMaxC, XcmsCIELuvQueryMaxL, XcmsCIELuvQueryMaxLC, Xcms-
CIELuvQueryMinL – obtain the bounds of the target screen's
color gamut in terms of CIE L*u*v* coordinates.

Synopsis

```
Status XcmsCIELuvQueryMaxC(ccc, hue_angle, L_star, color_return)
    XcmsCCC ccc;
    XcmsFloat hue_angle;
    XcmsFloat L_star;
    XcmsColor *color_return;

Status XcmsCIELuvQueryMaxL(ccc, hue_angle, chroma, color_return)
    XcmsCCC ccc;
    XcmsFloat hue_angle;
    XcmsFloat chroma;
    XcmsColor *color_return;

Status XcmsCIELuvQueryMaxLC(ccc, hue_angle, color_return)
    XcmsCCC ccc;
    XcmsFloat hue_angle;
    XcmsColor *color_return;

Status XcmsCIELuvQueryMinL(ccc, hue_angle, chroma, color_return)
    XcmsCCC ccc;
    XcmsFloat hue_angle;
    XcmsFloat chroma;
    XcmsColor *color_return;
```

Arguments

ccc
Specifies the color conversion context. Note that the CCC's Client White Point and White Point Adjustment procedures are ignored.

chroma
Specifies the CIELUV psychometric chroma at which to find maximum lightness (MaxL) or minimum lightness (MinL).

color_return
Returns the CIE L*u*v* coordinates of maximum chroma (MaxC and MaxLC), maximum lightness (MaxL), or minimum lightness (MinL) displayable by the screen for the given CC. The white point associated with the returned color specification is the Screen White Point. The value returned in the pixel member is undefined.

hue_angle   Specifies the CIELUV psychometric hue angle in degrees at which to find
maximum chroma (MaxC and MaxLC), maximum lightness (MaxL), or
minimum lightness (MinL).

L_star   Specifies the lightness (L*) at which to find maximum chroma (MaxC) or
maximum lightness (MaxL).

Returns

Zero on failure, non-zero on success.

Availability

Release 5 and later.

Description

XcmsCIELuvQueryMaxC() finds the point of maximum chroma displayable by the screen
at the given hue angle and lightness.

XcmsCIELuvQueryMaxL() finds the point in CIE L*u*v* color space of maximum lightness (L*) displayable by the screen at the given hue angle and chroma. An XcmsFailure
return value usually indicates that the given chroma is beyond maximum for the given hue
angle.

XcmsCIELuvQueryMaxLC() finds the point of maximum chroma displayable by the
screen at the given hue angle.

XcmsCIELuvQueryMinL() finds the point of minimum lightness (L*) displayable by the
screen at the given hue angle and chroma. An XcmsFailure return value usually indicates
that the given chroma is beyond maximum for the given hue angle.

All these functions return a point in CIE L*u*v* color space coordinates.

See Also

*XcmsCIELabQueryMaxC(), XcmsCIELabQueryMaxL(), XcmsCIELabQueryMaxLC(), XcmsCIELab-
QueryMinL(), XcmsTekHVCQueryMaxC(), XcmsTekHVCQueryMaxL, XcmsTekHVCQueryMaxLC,
XcmsTekHVCQueryMinL, XcmsQueryBlack(), XcmsQueryBlue(), XcmsQueryGreen(), XcmsQuery-
Red(), XcmsQueryWhite().*

XcmsClientWhitePointOfCCC

Name

XcmsClientWhitePointOfCCC – return the client white point associated with the specified Color Conversion Context.

Synopsis

```
XcmsColor *XcmsClientWhitePointOfCCC(ccc)
    XcmsCCC ccc;

ClientWhitePointOfCCC(ccc)
    XcmsCCC ccc;
```

Arguments

ccc   Specifies the color conversion context.

Returns

The XcmsColor structure containing the white point. See the XcmsColor reference page.

Availability

Release 5 and later.

Description

XcmsClientWhitePointOfCCC() and the macro ClientWhitePointOfCCC both return the Client White Point of the specified CCC. The Client White Point attribute of the CCC specifies the white point the client assumes to be associated with color specifications. If different from the Screen White Point, adjustments are specified by the CCC's white adjustment procedure.

See Also

XcmsCCCOfColormap(), XcmsCreateCCC(), XcmsConvertColors(), XcmsDefaultCCC(), XcmsDisplay-OfCCC(), XcmsScreenNumberOfCCC(), XcmsScreenWhitePointOfCCC(), XcmsSetCompressionProc(), XcmsSetWhiteAdjustProc(), XcmsSetWhitePoint(), XcmsVisualOfCCC().

XcmsColor

Name

XcmsColor – Xcms color structure.

Availability

Release 5 and later.

Description

The XcmsColor structure contains a union of substructures, each supporting a color space specific encoding.

The XcmsColorFormat type is used to identify the color space associated with the values in the XcmsColor structure. It is also used as an argument to some Xcms functions to indicate the desired format of returned color specifications.

Structures

The XcmsColor structure contains:

```
typedef unsigned long XcmsColorFormat;   /* Color Specification Format */

#define XcmsUndefinedFormat     (XcmsColorFormat)0x00000000
#define XcmsCIEXYZFormat        (XcmsColorFormat)0x00000001
#define XcmsCIEuvYFormat        (XcmsColorFormat)0x00000002
#define XcmsCIExyYFormat        (XcmsColorFormat)0x00000003
#define XcmsCIELabFormat        (XcmsColorFormat)0x00000004
#define XcmsCIELuvFormat        (XcmsColorFormat)0x00000005
#define XcmsTekHVCFormat        (XcmsColorFormat)0x00000006
#define XcmsRGBFormat           (XcmsColorFormat)0x80000000
#define XcmsRGBiFormat          (XcmsColorFormat)0x80000001

typedef struct {
    union {
        XcmsRGB RGB;
        XcmsRGBi RGBi;
        XcmsCIEXYZ CIEXYZ;
        XcmsCIEuvY CIEuvY;
        XcmsCIExyY CIExyY;
        XcmsCIELab CIELab;
        XcmsCIELuv CIELuv;
        XcmsTekHVC TekHVC;
        XcmsPad Pad;
    } spec;
    XcmsColorFormat format;
    unsigned long pixel;
} XcmsColor;                           /* Xcms Color Structure */

typedef double XcmsFloat;

typedef struct {
```

```
    unsigned short red;          /* 0x0000 to 0xffff */
    unsigned short green;        /* 0x0000 to 0xffff */
    unsigned short blue;         /* 0x0000 to 0xffff */
} XcmsRGB;                       /* RGB Device */

typedef struct {
    XcmsFloat red;               /* 0.0 to 1.0 */
    XcmsFloat green;             /* 0.0 to 1.0 */
    XcmsFloat blue;              /* 0.0 to 1.0 */
} XcmsRGBi;                      /* RGB Intensity */

typedef struct {
    XcmsFloat X;
    XcmsFloat Y;                 /* 0.0 to 1.0 */
    XcmsFloat Z;
} XcmsCIEXYZ;                    /* CIE XYZ */

typedef struct {
    XcmsFloat u_prime;           /* 0.0 to ~0.6 */
    XcmsFloat v_prime;           /* 0.0 to ~0.6 */
    XcmsFloat Y;                 /* 0.0 to 1.0 */
} XcmsCIEuvY;                    /* CIE u'v'Y */

typedef struct {
    XcmsFloat x;                 /* 0.0 to ~.75 */
    XcmsFloat y;                 /* 0.0 to ~.85 */
    XcmsFloat Y;                 /* 0.0 to 1.0 */
} XcmsCIExyY;                    /* CIE xyY */

typedef struct {
    XcmsFloat L_star;            /* 0.0 to 100.0 */
    XcmsFloat a_star;
    XcmsFloat b_star;
} XcmsCIELab;                    /* CIE L*a*b* */

typedef struct {
    XcmsFloat L_star;            /* 0.0 to 100.0 */
    XcmsFloat u_star;
    XcmsFloat v_star;
} XcmsCIELuv;                    /* CIE L*u*v* */

typedef struct {
    XcmsFloat H;                 /* 0.0 to 360.0 */
    XcmsFloat V;                 /* 0.0 to 100.0 */
    XcmsFloat C;                 /* 0.0 to 100.0 */
} XcmsTekHVC;                    /* TekHVC */

typedef struct {
    XcmsFloat pad0;
    XcmsFloat pad1;
    XcmsFloat pad2;
    XcmsFloat pad3;
```

```
} XcmsPad;        /* padded to 4 floats for future or   */
                  /* user-defined color space encodings */
                  /* that require more space than what  */
                  /* 3 floats can provide               */
```

See Also

XcmsAllocColor(), XcmsAllocNamedColor(), XcmsConvertColors(), XcmsLookupColor(), XcmsQuery-Color(), XcmsQueryColors(), XcmsStoreColor(), XcmsStoreColors(), XcmsStoreNamedColor, Xcms-ClientWhitePointOfCCC(), XcmsSetWhitePoint(), XcmsScreenWhitePointOfCCC(), XcmsCIELabQuery-MaxC(), XcmsCIELabQueryMaxL(), XcmsCIELabQueryMaxLC(), XcmsCIELabQueryMinL(), Xcms-CIELuvQueryMaxC(), XcmsCIELuvQueryMaxL(), XcmsCIELuvQueryMaxLC(), XcmsCIELuvQuery-MinL(), XcmsTekHVCQueryMaxC(), XcmsTekHVCQueryMaxL, XcmsTekHVCQueryMaxLC, XcmsTek-HVCQueryMinL, XcmsQueryBlack(), XcmsQueryBlue(), XcmsQueryGreen(), XcmsQueryRed(), Xcms-QueryWhite(), XcmsCompressionProc, XcmsWhiteAdjustProc, XcmsConversionProc, XcmsParse-StringProc.

XcmsColorSpace

Name

XcmsColorSpace – Xcms color space structure.

Availability

Release 5 and later.

Description

The XcmsColorSpace structure contain the information necessary to convert the encoding of color specifications to other color spaces, and to parse a color string encoded specifically for this color space.

The prefix member points to a string that identifies that a color strings encoding is for this particular color space.

> <color_space>:<color_space_specific_encoding>

For example, the prefix "cieuvy:" for the color string "CIEuvY:0.119/0.545/0.254". Although the prefix in the color string may be entered in uppercase or lowercase, all characters of the prefix specified in the XcmsColorSpace must be in lowercase.

The id member is predefined if the color space is registered with the X Consortium; otherwise assigned at run-time (see XcmsAddColorSpace()).

The parseString member points to the color space specific string parsing function.

The to_CIEXYZ member is pointer to an array of functions that, when executed in sequence, will convert a XcmsColor structure encoded for this color space to the CIEXYZ encoding.

The from_CIEXYZ member is pointer to an array of functions that, when executed in sequence, will convert a XcmsColor structure encoded for CIEXYZ to this color space's encoding.

The inverse_flag member if set (i.e., 1) indicates that for each function in the to_CIEXYZ list, there is an inverse function in the from_CIEXYZ list. Note however that the corresponding order is reversed—the inverse of the first function in to_CIEXYZ will be the last function in from_CIEXYZ.

Structures

The XcmsColorSpace structure contains:

```
typedef XcmsConversionProc *XcmsFuncListPtr;

typedef struct _XcmsColorSpace {
    char *prefix;
    XcmsColorFormat id;
    XcmsParseStringProc parseString;
    XcmsFuncListPtr to_CIEXYZ;
    XcmsFuncListPtr from_CIEXYZ;
```

```
        int inverse_flag;
} XcmsColorSpace;
```

See Also

XcmsAddColorSpace(), *XcmsAddFunctionSet()*, *XcmsFunctionSet*, *XcmsConversionProc*, *XcmsParse-StringProc*.

XcmsCompressionProc

Name

XcmsCompressionProc – interface definition for gamut compression procedure.

Synopsis

```
typedef Status (*XcmsCompressionProc)(ccc, colors_in_out, ncolors, index,
        compression_flags_return)
    XcmsCCC ccc;
    XcmsColor colors_in_out[];
    unsigned int ncolors;
    unsigned int index;
    Bool compression_flags_return[];
```

Arguments

ccc   Specifies the color conversion context.

colors_in_out
                Specifies an array of color specifications. Pixel members are ignored and
                remain unchanged upon return.

ncolors   Specifies the number of **XcmsColor** structures in the color specification
                array.

index   Specifies the index into the array of **XcmsColor** structures for the encoun-
                tered color specification that lies outside the **Screen**'s color gamut. Valid
                values are 0 (for the first element) to ncolors–1.

compression_flags_return
                Specifies an array of Boolean values (or **NULL**) for returned information
                that indicates if the color was compressed. For example, if this routine
                returns   **XcmsSuccessWithCompression**   and   compres-
                sion_flags_return[3] is **True**, this indicates that the fourth color
                specified in the color specification array was compressed. If you are not
                interested in knowing which color was compressed when the return value is
                XcmsSuccessWithCompression, then pass a **NULL**. Otherwise, allo-
                cate an array of Boolean values for each element in the color definition
                array and pass its address.

Returns

Zero on failure, non-zero on success.

Availability

Release 5 and later.

Description

A gamut compression procedure maps a range of colors in a device-independent color space into a range of colors displayable on a physical device.

When implementing a gamut compression procedure, consider the following rules and assumptions:

- The gamut compression procedure can attempt to compress one or multiple specifications at a time.

- When called, elements 0 to index–1 in the array of color specification array can be assumed to fall within the screen's color gamut. In addition these color specifications are already in some device-dependent format (typically XcmsRGBi). If any modifications are made to these color specifications, they must upon return be in their initial device-dependent format.

- When called, the element in the color specification array specified by the index argument contains the color specification outside the screen's color gamut encountered by the calling routine. In addition this color specification can be assumed to be in XcmsCIEXYZ. Upon return, this color specification must be in XcmsCIEXYZ.

- When called, elements from index to ncolors–1 in the color specification array may or may not fall within the screen's color gamut. In addition these color specifications can be assumed to be in XcmsCIEXYZ. If any modifications are made to these color specifications, they must upon return be in XcmsCIEXYZ.

- The color specifications passed to the gamut compression procedure have already been adjusted to the Screen White Point. This means that at this point the color specification's white point is the Screen White Point.

- If the gamut compression procedure uses a device-independent color space not initially accessible for use in the color management system, use XcmsAddColorSpace() to insure that it is added.

See Also

XcmsCCCOfColormap(), XcmsCreateCCC(), XcmsClientWhitePointOfCCC(), XcmsDefaultCCC(), XcmsSetCCCOfColormap(), XcmsSetCompressionProc(), XcmsSetWhiteAdjustProc(), XcmsSetWhitePoint().

XcmsConversionProc

Name

XcmsConversionProc – interface definition for the procedure for color conversion between device-independent color spaces.

Synopsis

For conversion between device-independent color spaces:
```
typedef Status (*XcmsConversionProc)(ccc, white_point, colors, ncolors)
    XcmsCCC ccc;
    XcmsColor *white_point[];
    XcmsColor colors[];
    unsigned int ncolors;
```

For conversion between CIEXYZ and device-dependent color spaces:
```
typedef Status (*XcmsConversionProc)(ccc, colors, ncolors, CIcompres-
    sion_flags_return)
    XcmsCCC ccc;
    XcmsColor colors[];
    unsigned int ncolors;
    Bool compression_flags_return[];
```

Arguments

ccc   Specifies the color conversion context.

white_point   Specifies the white point associated with the color specifications. Pixel member is ignored and the color specification is left unchanged upon return.

colors   Specifies an array of color specifications. Pixel members are ignored and remain unchanged upon return.

ncolors   Specifies the number of XcmsColor structures in the color specification array.

compression_flags_return
                Specifies an array of Boolean values (or NULL) for returned information that indicates if the color was compressed. During conversion, when a color is found to out of gamut, this argument is passed in the gamut compression function call. For an example, refer to the source code for Xcms-CIEXYZToRGBi.

Returns

Zero on failure, non-zero on success.

Availability

Release 5 and later.

Description

An XcmsConversionProc procedure converts XcmsColor between device-independent color space encodings.

Procedures provided and accessible in Xlib for conversion between device-independent color spaces are:

- XcmsCIELabToCIEXYZ – Converts color specifications from XcmsCIELab to Xcms-CIELab.

- XcmsCIELuvToCIEuvY – Converts color specifications from XcmsCIELuv to Xcms-CIEuvY.

- XcmsCIEXYZToCIELab – Converts color specifications from XcmsCIEXYZ to Xcms-CIELab.

- XcmsCIEXYZToCIEuvY – Converts color specifications from XcmsCIEXYZ to Xcms-CIEuvY.

- XcmsCIEXYZToCIExyY – Converts color specifications from XcmsCIEXYZ to Xcms-CIExyY.

- XcmsCIEuvYToCIELuv – Converts color specifications from XcmsCIEuvY to Xcms-CIELuv.

- XcmsCIEuvYToCIEXYZ – Converts color specifications from XcmsCIEuvY to Xcms-CIEXYZ.

- XcmsCIEuvYToCIETekHVC – Converts color specifications from XcmsCIEuvY to XcmsCIETekHVC.

- XcmsCIExyYToCIEXYZ – Converts color specifications from XcmsCIExyY to Xcms-CIEXYZ.

- XcmsTekHVCToCIEuvY – Converts color specifications from XcmsTekHVC to Xcms-CIEuvY.

Procedures provided and accessible in Xlib for conversion between CIEXYZ and device–dependent color spaces are:

- XcmsCIEXYZToRGBi – Converts color specifications from XcmsCIEXYZ to Xcms-RGBi.

- XcmsRGBToRGBi – Converts color specifications from XcmsRGB to XcmsRGBi.

- XcmsRGBiToCIEXYZ – Converts color specifications from XcmsRGBi to Xcms-CIEXYZ.

- XcmsRGBiToRGB – Converts color specifications from XcmsRGBi to XcmsRGB.

Structures

The XcmsColor structure and XcmsColorFormat type are shown on the XcmsColor reference page. Refer also to the XcmsColorSpace reference page.

See Also

XcmsColorSpace.

XcmsConvertColors

Name

XcmsConvertColors – convert color specifications in XcmsColor structures to another color space specific encoding.

Synopsis

```
Status XcmsConvertColors(ccc, colors_in_out, ncolors, target_format,
       compression_flags_return)
    XcmsCCC ccc;
    XcmsColor colors_in_out[ ];
    unsigned int ncolors;
    XcmsColorFormat target_format;
    Bool compression_flags_return[ ];
```

Arguments

ccc   Specifies the color conversion context. If conversion is between device-independent color spaces only (for example, TekHVC to CIELuv), the CCC is necessary only to specify the Client White Point.

colors_in_out

                Specifies an array of color specifications. Pixel members are ignored and remain unchanged upon return.

ncolors   Specifies the number of XcmsColor structures in the color specification array.

target_format

                Specifies the target color specification format.

compression_flags_return

                Specifies an array of ncolors Boolean values for returning compression status of each color conversion. If a non-NULL pointer is supplied, each element in the array is set to True if the corresponding color in the color specification array was compressed, and False otherwise. Pass NULL if the compression status is not useful.

Returns

Zero on failure, non-zero on success.

Availability

Release 5 and later.

Description

The XcmsConvertColors() function converts the color specifications in the specified array of XcmsColor structures from their current format (which may vary from element to element of the array) to a single target format using the specified CCC. If all the conversions succeed without gamut compression, `XcmsConvertColors()` returns `XcmsSuccess`. If one or more of the conversions required gamut compression, the function returns `Xcms-SuccessWithCompression`, and sets the appropriate flags in *compression_flags_return* array. If any of the conversions fail, the function returns `Xcms-Failure` and the contents of the color specification array are left unchanged.

Structures

The `XcmsColor` and `XcmsColorFormat` structures are shown on the `XcmsColor` reference page.

See Also

XcmsCCCOfColormap(), XcmsCreateCCC(), XcmsClientWhitePointOfCCC(), XcmsDefaultCCC(), XcmsScreenWhitePointOfCCC(), XcmsSetCompressionProc(), XcmsSetWhiteAdjustProc(), XcmsSet-WhitePoint().

Name

XcmsCreateCCC – create a Color Conversion Context.

Synopsis

```
XcmsCCC XcmsCreateCCC(display, screen_number, visual, client_white_point,
      compression_proc, compression_client_data, white_adjust_proc,
      white_adjust_client_data)
    Display *display;
    int screen_number;
    Visual *visual;
    XcmsColor *client_white_point;
    XcmsCompressionProc compression_proc;
    XPointer compression_client_data;
    XcmsWhiteAdjustProc white_adjust_proc;
    XPointer white_adjust_client_data;
```

Arguments

display   Specifies the connection to the X server.

screen_number
                 Specifies the appropriate screen number on the host server.

visual   Specifies the visual type.

client_white_point
                 Specifies the Client White Point. If NULL, the Client White Point is to be
                 assumed to be the same as the Screen White Point. Note that the pixel
                 member is ignored.

compression_proc
                 Specifies the gamut compression procedure that is to be applied when a
                 color lies outside the screen's color gamut. If NULL and when functions
                 using this CCC must convert a color specification to a device-dependent
                 format and encounters a color that lies outside the screen's color gamut,
                 that function will return XcmsFailure.

compression_client_data
                 Specifies client data for use by the gamut compression procedure or NULL.

white_adjust_proc
                 Specifies the white adjustment procedure that is to be applied when the Cli-
                 ent White Point differs from the Screen White Point. NULL indicates that
                 no white point adjustment is desired.

white_adjust_client_data
                 Specifies client data for use with the white point adjustment procedure or
                 NULL.

Returns

The Color Conversion Context.

Availability

Release 5 and later.

Description

XcmsCreateCCC() creates a color conversion context for the specified display, screen, and visual.

See Also

XcmsCCCOfColormap(), XcmsClientWhitePointOfCCC(), XcmsConvertColors(), XcmsDefaultCCC(), XcmsDisplayOfCCC(), XcmsFreeCCC(), XcmsScreenNumberOfCCC(), XcmsScreenWhitePoint-OfCCC(), XcmsSetCCCOfColormap(), XcmsSetCompressionProc(), XcmsSetWhiteAdjustProc(), Xcms-SetWhitePoint(), XcmsVisualOfCCC(), XcmsCompressionProc, XcmsWhiteAdjustProc.

XcmsDefaultCCC

Name

XcmsDefaultCCC – get the default Color Conversion Context for a screen.

Synopsis

```
XcmsCCC XcmsDefaultCCC(display, screen_number)
    Display *display;
    int screen_number;
```

Arguments

display   Specifies the connection to the X server.

screen_number   Specifies the screen number.

Returns

The Color Conversion Context.

Availability

Release 5 and later.

Description

XcmsDefaultCCC() returns the default CCC for the specified screen.

Xcms creates and associates a special CCC to each Screen before any other CCCs are created. This special per-Screen CCC is called a default CCC. At creation, per-Screen information like the device color characterization data (device profile) is obtained (refer to the ICCCM). Subsequent CCCs created for this Screen will use its device characterization data. In addition, CCC attributes (e.g., Client White Point) not explicitly specified in Xcms-CreateCCC() default to the values in the Screen's default CCC.

See Also

XcmsCCCOfColormap(), *XcmsCreateCCC()*, *XcmsClientWhitePointOfCCC()*, *XcmsConvertColors()*, *XcmsDisplayOfCCC()*, *XcmsFreeCCC()*, *XcmsScreenNumberOfCCC()*, *XcmsScreenWhitePoint-OfCCC()*, *XcmsSetCCCOfColormap()*, *XcmsSetCompressionProc()*, *XcmsSetWhiteAdjustProc()*, *Xcms-SetWhitePoint()*, *XcmsVisualOfCCC()*.

XcmsDisplayOfCCC

Name

XcmsDisplayOfCCC, DisplayOfCCC – return the display associated with a Color Conversion Context (CCC).

Synopsis

```
Display *XcmsDisplayOfCCC(ccc)
     XcmsCCC ccc;

DisplayOfCCC(ccc)
     XcmsCCC ccc;
```

Arguments

ccc   Specifies the color conversion context.

Returns

The display structure.

Availability

Release 5 and later.

Description

XcmsDisplayOfCCC() and DisplayOfCCC both return the display associated with the specified CCC.

See Also

XcmsCCCOfColormap(), XcmsCreateCCC(), XcmsClientWhitePointOfCCC(), XcmsConvertColors(), XcmsDefaultCCC(), XcmsDisplayOfCCC(), XcmsScreenNumberOfCCC(), XcmsScreenWhitePointOfCCC(), XcmsSetCompressionProc(), XcmsSetWhiteAdjustProc(), XcmsSetWhitePoint(), XcmsVisualOfCCC().

XcmsFormatOfPrefix

Name

XcmsFormatOfPrefix – obtain the format ID of the color space associated with a specified color string prefix.

Synopsis

```
XcmsColorFormat XcmsFormatOfPrefix(prefix)
    char *prefix;
```

Arguments

prefix   Specifies the string containing the color space prefix.

Returns

The color space format ID.

Availability

Release 5 and later.

Description

XcmsFormatOfPrefix() returns the format ID for the specified color space prefix. For example, XcmsCIEXYZFormat is returned for the prefix "CIEXYZ". Note that the prefix is case-insensitive. If the color space is not accessible in the color management system, Xcms-FormatOfPrefix() returns XcmsUndefinedFormat.

Structures

The XcmsColor structure and XcmsColorFormat type are shown on the XcmsColor reference page.

See Also

XcmsPrefixOfFormat().

XcmsFreeCCC

Name

XcmsFreeCCC – free a Color Conversion Context (CCC).

Synopsis

```
void XcmsFreeCCC(ccc)
     XcmsCCC ccc;
```

Arguments

ccc   Specifies the color conversion context.

Availability

Release 5 and later.

Description

XcmsFreeCCC() frees the memory used for the specified CCC. Note that calls to free default CCCs or to free CCCs currently associated with colormaps are ignored.

See Also

XcmsCreateCCC(), *XcmsCCCOfColormap()*, *XcmsDefaultCCC()*.

XcmsFunctionSet

Name

XcmsFunctionSet – Xcms Color Characterization Function Set structure.

Availability

Release 5 and later.

Description

The XcmsFunctionSet structure contains the information necessary to convert the encoding of color specifications between CIEXYZ, RGB Intensity, and RGB Device encodings; and how to obtain and free Screen Color Characterization Data (also known as the device profile) necessary for color specification conversion.

The DDColorSpaces member points to an array of pointers to XcmsColorSpace structures for device-dependent color spaces—the information necessary to convert the encoding of color specifications between CIEXYZ, RGB Intensity, and RGB Device encodings.

The screenInitProc member identifies the function that obtains the device profile.

The screenFreeProc member identifies the function that frees the function set specific device profile obtained with screenInitProc.

Structures

The XcmsFunctionSet structure contains:

```
typedef struct _XcmsFunctionSet {
    XcmsColorSpace **DDColorSpaces;
    XcmsScreenInitProc screenInitProc;
    XcmsScreenFreeProc screenFreeProc;
} XcmsFunctionSet;
```

See Also

XcmsAddFunctionSet(), *XcmsColorSpace*, *XcmsScreenInitProc*, *XcmsScreenFreeProc*.

XcmsLookupColor

Name

XcmsLookupColor – obtain color values from a string.

Synopsis

```
Status XcmsLookupColor(display, colormap, color_string,
        color_exact_return, color_screen_return, result_format)
    Display *display;
    Colormap colormap;
    char *color_string;
    XcmsColor *color_exact_return;
    XcmsColor *color_screen_return;
    XcmsColorFormat result_format;
```

Arguments

display   Specifies the connection to the X server.

colormap   Specifies the colormap.

color_string
                Specifies the color string.

color_exact_return
                Returns the color specification parsed from the color string or parsed from
                the corresponding string found in a color name database.

color_screen_return
                Returns the color that can be reproduced on the screen.

result_format
                Specifies the desired color format for the returned color specifications.

Returns

Zero on failure, non-zero on success.

Availability

Release 5 and later.

Description

The XcmsLookupColor() function looks up the string name of a color with respect to the
screen associated with the specified colormap, but does not store the color into any color cell
in the color map. It returns both the exact color values and the closest values provided by the
screen with respect to the visual type of the specified colormap. The values are returned in
the format specified by result_format.

The color string may contain a color name that appears in the client-side or X server's color database; or a numerical color specification for any color management supported color spaces such that the string conforms to the uniform syntax:

```
<color_space>:<color_space_specific_encoding>
```

For example:

```
RGB:red/green/blue
RGBi:R/G/B
CIEXYZ:X/Y/Z
CIEuvY:u/v/Y
CIExyY:x/y/Y
CIELab:L/a/b
CIELuv:L/u/v
TekHVC:H/V/C
```

For the RGB color space, the *red*, *green*, and *blue* parameters are hexadecimal strings of one to four digits. For each of the other color spaces, each parameter is a floating-point number in standard string format. In each case, each number specifies a value for one of the parameters of the color space. Old-style RGB color strings beginning with a "#" remain supported for backwards compatibility. If the color name is not in the Host Portable Character Encoding the result is implementation-dependent. Color names are case-insensitive.

If *format* is XcmsUndefinedFormat and the color string contains a numerical color specification, the specification is returned in the format used in that numerical color specification. If *format* is XcmsUndefinedFormat and the color string contains a color name, the specification is returned in the format used in the color name database entry for that color name.

XcmsLookupColor() returns XcmsSuccess or XcmsSuccessWithCompression if the name is resolved, otherwise it returns XcmsFailure. If XcmsSuccessWith-Compression is returned, then the color specification in *color_screen_return* is the result of gamut compression.

Structures

The XcmsColor and XcmsColorFormat structures are shown on the XcmsColor reference page.

See Also

XcmsAllocColor(), XcmsAllocNamedColor(), XcmsLookupColor(), XcmsQueryColor(), XcmsQueryColors(), XcmsStoreColor(), XcmsStoreColors(), XcmsStoreNamedColor, XAllocColor(), XAllocNamedColor(), XLookupColor(), XParseColor(), XQueryColor(), XQueryColors(), XStoreColor(), XStoreColors().

XcmsParseStringProc

Name

XcmsParseStringProc – interface definition for color string parsing procedure.

Synopsis

```
typedef int (*XcmsParseStringProc)(color_string, color_return)
    char *color_string;
    XcmsColor *color_return;
```

Arguments

color_string   Specifies the color string to parse.

color_return   Returns the color specification in the color space's encoding.

Returns

Zero on failure, non-zero on success.

Availability

Release 5 and later.

Description

XcmsParseStringProc is the type for a function whose pointer is placed in the parse-String field of an XcmsColorSpace structure. This function parses a color string into an XcmsColor structure, returning non-zero if it succeeded and zero otherwise.

See Also

XcmsColorSpace.

XcmsPrefixOfFormat

Name

XcmsPrefixOfFormat – obtain the color string prefix associated with the color space specified by a color format.

Synopsis

```
char *XcmsPrefixOfFormat(format)
    XcmsColorFormat format;
```

Arguments

format   Specifies the color specification format.

Returns

The color string prefix.

Availability

Release 5 and later.

Description

XcmsPrefixOfFormat() returns the string prefix associated with the color specification encoding specified by format. Otherwise, if none is found, it returns NULL. Note that the returned string must be treated as read-only.

Structures

The XcmsColor structure and XcmsColorFormat type are shown on the XcmsColor reference page.

See Also

XcmsFormatOfPrefix().

XcmsQueryBlack

Name

XcmsQueryBlack – obtain a color specification for screen black.

Synopsis

```
Status XcmsQueryBlack(ccc, target_format, color_return)
    XcmsCCC ccc;
    XcmsColorFormat target_format;
    XcmsColor *color_return;
```

Arguments

ccc   Specifies the color conversion context. Note that the CCC's Client White Point and White Point Adjustment procedures are ignored.

target_format
          Specifies the target color specification format.

color_return
          Returns the color specification in the specified target format. The white point associated with the returned color specification is the Screen White Point. The value returned in the pixel member is undefined.

Returns

Zero on failure, non-zero on success.

Availability

Release 5 and later.

Description

The XcmsQueryBlack() function returns the color specification in the format specified by *target_format* for screen black (i.e., zero intensity red, green, and blue on the target Screen).

Structures

The XcmsColor and XcmsColorFormat structures are shown on the XcmsColor reference page.

See Also

XcmsQueryBlue(), XcmsQueryGreen(), XcmsQueryRed(), XcmsQueryWhite().

XcmsQueryBlue

Name

XcmsQueryBlue – obtain a color specification for screen blue.

Synopsis

```
Status XcmsQueryBlue(ccc, target_format, color_return)
    XcmsCCC ccc;
    XcmsColorFormat target_format;
    XcmsColor *color_return;
```

Arguments

ccc   Specifies the color conversion context. Note that the CCC's Client White
                Point and White Point Adjustment procedures are ignored.

target_format
                Specifies the target color specification format.

color_return
                Returns the color specification in the specified target format. The white
                point associated with the returned color specification is the Screen White
                Point. The value returned in the pixel member is undefined.

Returns

Zero on failure, non-zero on success.

Availability

Release 5 and later.

Description

The XcmsQueryBlue() function returns the color specification in the format specified by
target_format for screen blue (i.e., full intensity blue and zero intensity red and green
on the target Screen).

Structures

The XcmsColor and XcmsColorFormat structures are shown on the XcmsColor reference page.

See Also

XcmsQueryBlack(), XcmsQueryGreen(), XcmsQueryRed(), XcmsQueryWhite().

XcmsQueryColor

Name

XcmsQueryColor – obtain the color specification of a specified colorcell.

Synopsis

```
Status XcmsQueryColor(display, colormap, color_in_out, result_format)
    Display *display;
    Colormap colormap;
    XcmsColor *color_in_out;
    XcmsColorFormat result_format;
```

Arguments

display   Specifies the connection to the X server.

colormap   Specifies the colormap.

color_in_out

Specifies the pixel of the color cell to query, and returns the color specification stored for that color cell.

result_format

Specifies the desired color format for the returned color specifications.

Returns

Zero on failure, non-zero on success.

Availability

Release 5 and later.

Description

XcmsQueryColor() obtains the RGB value for the colormap cell specified by the *pixel* field of the specified XcmsColor structure, and then converts the value to the target format specified by the *result_format* argument. If the pixel is not a valid index into the specified colormap, a BadValue error results.

Errors

BadColor   The *colormap* argument does not name a defined Colormap.

BadValue   The specified pixel does not represent a valid color cell in the specified colormap.

Structures

The XcmsColor structure and XcmsColorFormat type are shown on the XcmsColor reference page.

See Also

XcmsAllocColor(), XcmsAllocNamedColor(), XcmsStoreColor(), XcmsStoreColors(), XcmsStoreNamed-Color, XcmsQueryColors(), XcmsLookupColor(), XAllocColor(), XAllocNamedColor(), XQueryColor(), XQueryColors(), XStoreColor(), XStoreColors().

Name

XcmsQueryColors – obtain the color specifications of the specified colorcells.

Synopsis

```
Status XcmsQueryColors(display, colormap, colors_in_out, ncolors,
       result_format)
   Display *display;
   Colormap colormap;
   XcmsColor *colors_in_out[];
   unsigned int ncolors;
   XcmsColorFormat result_format;
```

Arguments

display   Specifies the connection to the X server.

colormap   Specifies the colormap.

colors_in_out
              Specifies an array of **XcmsColor** structures, each pixel member indicating the color cell to query. The color specifications for the color cells are returned in these structures.

ncolors   Specifies the number of **XcmsColor** structures in the *colors_in_out* array.

result_format
              Specifies the desired color format for the returned color specifications.

Returns

Zero on failure, non-zero on success.

Availability

Release 5 and later.

Description

XcmsQueryColors() obtains the RGB values for the colors stored in the colormap cells specified by the *pixel* fields of the specified **XcmsColor** structures, and then converts the values to the target format specified by the *result_format* argument. If a pixel is not a valid index into the specified colormap, a **BadValue** error results. If more than one pixel is in error, the one that gets reported is arbitrary.

Errors

BadColor   The *colormap* argument does not name a defined Colormap.

BadValue   A specified pixel does not represent a valid color cell in the specified color-map.

Structures

The XcmsColor structure and XcmsColorFormat type are shown on the XcmsColor reference page.

See Also

XcmsAllocColor(), XcmsAllocNamedColor(), XcmsStoreColor(), XcmsStoreColors(), XcmsStoreNamed-Color, XcmsQueryColor(), XcmsLookupColor(), XAllocColor(), XAllocNamedColor(), XQueryColor(), XQueryColors(), XStoreColor(), XStoreColors().

XcmsQueryGreen

Name

XcmsQueryGreen – obtain a color specification for screen green.

Synopsis

```
Status XcmsQueryGreen(ccc, target_format, color_return)
    XcmsCCC ccc;
    XcmsColorFormat target_format;
    XcmsColor *color_return;
```

Arguments

ccc
: Specifies the color conversion context. Note that the CCC's Client White Point and White Point Adjustment procedures are ignored.

target_format
: Specifies the target color specification format.

color_return
: Returns the color specification in the specified target format. The white point associated with the returned color specification is the Screen White Point. The value returned in the pixel member is undefined.

Returns

Zero on failure, non-zero on success.

Availability

Release 5 and later.

Description

The XcmsQueryGreen() function returns the color specification in the specified target format for full intensity green and zero intensity red and blue. The XcmsQueryGreen() function returns the color specification in the format specified by *target_format* for screen green (i.e., full intensity green and zero intensity red and blue on the target Screen).

Structures

The XcmsColor and XcmsColorFormat structures are shown on the XcmsColor reference page.

See Also

XcmsQueryBlack(), XcmsQueryBlue(), XcmsQueryRed(), XcmsQueryWhite().

XcmsQueryRed

Name

XcmsQueryRed – obtain a color specification for screen red.

Synopsis

```
Status XcmsQueryRed(ccc, target_format, color_return)
    XcmsCCC ccc;
    XcmsColorFormat target_format;
    XcmsColor *color_return;
```

Arguments

ccc   Specifies the color conversion context. Note that the CCC's Client White Point and White Point Adjustment procedures are ignored.

target_format
                 Specifies the target color specification format.

color_return
                 Returns the color specification in the specified target format. The white point associated with the returned color specification is the Screen White Point. The value returned in the pixel member is undefined.

Returns

Zero on failure, non-zero on success.

Availability

Release 5 and later.

Description

The XcmsQueryRed() function returns the color specification in the specified target format for full intensity red and zero intensity green and blue. The XcmsQueryRed() function returns the color specification in the format specified by *target_format* for screen red (i.e., full intensity red and zero intensity green and blue on the target Screen).

Structures

The XcmsColor and XcmsColorFormat structures are shown on the XcmsColor reference page.

See Also

XcmsQueryBlack(), XcmsQueryBlue(), XcmsQueryGreen(), XcmsQueryWhite().

XcmsQueryWhite

Name

XcmsQueryWhite – obtain a color specification for screen white.

Synopsis

```
Status XcmsQueryWhite(ccc, target_format, color_return)
    XcmsCCC ccc;
    XcmsColorFormat target_format;
    XcmsColor *color_return;
```

Arguments

ccc   Specifies the color conversion context. Note that the CCC's Client White
                Point and White Point Adjustment procedures are ignored.

target_format
                Specifies the target color specification format.

color_return
                Returns the color specification in the specified target format. The white
                point associated with the returned color specification is the Screen White
                Point. The value returned in the pixel member is undefined.

Returns

Zero on failure, non-zero on success.

Availability

Release 5 and later.

Description

The XcmsQueryWhite() function returns the color specification in the specified target
format for full intensity red, green, and blue. The XcmsQueryWhite() function returns
the color specification in the format specified by *target_format* for screen white (i.e.,
full intensity red, green, and blue on the target Screen).

Structures

The XcmsColor and XcmsColorFormat structures are shown on the XcmsColor reference page.

See Also

XcmsQueryBlack(), XcmsQueryBlue(), XcmsQueryGreen(), XcmsQueryRed().

XcmsScreenFreeProc

Name

XcmsScreenFreeProc – interface definition for the Function Set routine that frees the per-screen data.

Synopsis

```
typedef void (*XcmsScreenFreeProc)(screenData)
    XPointer screenData;
```

Arguments

screenData   Specifies the data to be freed.

Availability

Release 5 and later.

Description

XcmsScreenFreeProc is the definition for a procedure to be called to free the Function Set specific screenData field stored in an XcmsPerScrnInfo structure.

See Also

XcmsFunctionSet, *XcmsScreenInitProc*.

XcmsScreenInitProc

Name

XcmsScreenInitProc – interface specification for the Function Set routine that obtains and initializes per-screen information.

Synopsis

```
typedef Status (*XcmsScreenInitProc)(display, screen_number, screen_info)
    Display *display;
    int screen_number;
    XcmsPerScrnInfo *screen_info;
```

Arguments

display   Specifies the connection to the X server.

screen_number

        Specifies the appropriate screen number on the host server.

screen_info   Specifies the `XcmsPerScrnInfo` structure, which contains the per-screen information.

Returns

Zero on failure, non-zero on success.

Availability

Release 5 and later.

Description

The screen initialization function in the `XcmsFunctionSet` structure fetches the Color Characterization Data (device profile) for the specified screen, typically off properties on the screen's root window; then it initializes the specified `XcmsPerScrnInfo` structure. If successful, the procedure fills in the `XcmsPerScrnInfo` structure as follows:

- It sets the `screenData` member to the address of the created device profile data structure (contents known only by the function set).

- It next sets the `screenWhitePoint` member.

- It next sets the `functionSet` member to the address of the `XcmsFunctionSet` structure.

- It then sets the state member to `XcmsInitSuccess` and finally returns `Xcms-Success`.

If unsuccessful, the procedure sets the state member to `XcmsInitFailure` and returns `XcmsFailure`.

Structures

The XcmsPerScrnInfo structure contains:

```
typedef struct _XcmsPerScrnInfo {
    XcmsColor screenWhitePoint;
    XPointer functionSet;
    XPointer screenData;
    unsigned char state;
    char pad[3];
} XcmsPerScrnInfo;
```

The screenWhitePoint member specifies the white point inherent to the screen. The functionSet member specifies the appropriate Function Set. The screenData member specifies the device profile. The state member is set to one of the following:

- XcmsInitNone indicates initialization has not been previously attempted.

- XcmsInitFailure indicates initialization has been previously attempted but failed.

- XcmsInitSuccess indicates initialization has been previously attempted and suc-ceeded.

See Also

XcmsFunctionSet, XcmsScreenFreeProc.

XcmsScreenNumberOfCCC

Name

XcmsScreenNumberOfCCC, ScreenNumberOfCCC – screen number associated with the specified Color Conversion Context (CCC).

Synopsis

```
int XcmsScreenNumberOfCCC(ccc)
    XcmsCCC ccc;
ScreenNumberOfCCC(ccc)
    XcmsCCC ccc;
```

Arguments

ccc   Specifies the color conversion context.

Returns

The screen number.

Availability

Release 5 and later.

Description

XcmsScreenNumberOfCCC() and ScreenNumberOfCCC both return the number of the screen associated with the specified CCC.

See Also

XcmsCCCOfColormap(), XcmsCreateCCC(), XcmsClientWhitePointOfCCC(), XcmsConvertColors(), XcmsDefaultCCC(), XcmsDisplayOfCCC(), XcmsScreenWhitePointOfCCC(), XcmsSetCCCOfColormap(), XcmsSetCompressionProc(), XcmsSetWhiteAdjustProc(), XcmsSetWhitePoint(), XcmsVisualOfCCC().

XcmsScreenWhitePointOfCCC

Name

XcmsScreenWhitePointOfCCC, ScreenWhitePointOfCCC – obtain the white point of the screen associated with a specified Color Conversion Context.

Synopsis

```
XcmsColor *XcmsScreenWhitePointOfCCC(ccc)
    XcmsCCC ccc;

ScreenWhitePointOfCCC(ccc)
    XcmsCCC ccc;
```

Arguments

ccc   Specifies the color conversion context.

Returns

The white point in an XcmsColor structure. See the XcmsColor reference page.

Availability

Release 5 and later.

Description

XcmsScreenWhitePointOfCCC() and ScreenWhitePointOfCCC both return the white point of the screen associated with the specified CCC. The returned XcmsColor structure must be treated as read-only.

See Also

XcmsCCCOfColormap(), XcmsCreateCCC(), XcmsClientWhitePointOfCCC(), XcmsConvertColors(), XcmsDefaultCCC(), XcmsDisplayOfCCC(), XcmsScreenNumberOfCCC(), XcmsSetCompressionProc(), XcmsSetWhiteAdjustProc(), XcmsSetWhitePoint(), XcmsVisualOfCCC().

XcmsSetCCCOfColormap

Name

XcmsSetCCCOfColormap – change the Color Conversion Context (CCC) associated with a colormap.

Synopsis

```
XcmsCCC XcmsSetCCCOfColormap(display, colormap, ccc)
      Display *display;
      Colormap colormap;
      XcmsCCC ccc;
```

Arguments

display   Specifies the connection to the X server.

colormap   Specifies the colormap.

ccc   Specifies the color conversion context.

Returns

The previous Color Conversion Context.

Availability

Release 5 and later.

Description

XcmsSetCCCOfColormap() changes the CCC associated with the specified colormap. It returns the CCC previously associated with the colormap.

If the previous CCC is not used again in the application, it should be freed by calling Xcms-FreeCCC().

See Also

XcmsCCCOfColormap(), XcmsCreateCCC(), XcmsFreeCCC().

Name

XcmsSetCompressionProc – change the gamut compression procedure in a specified Color Conversion Context.

Synopsis

```
XcmsCompressionProc XcmsSetCompressionProc(ccc, compression_proc,
        client_data)
    XcmsCCC ccc;
    XcmsCompressionProc compression_proc;
    XPointer client_data;
```

Arguments

ccc   Specifies the color conversion context.

compression_proc

Specifies the gamut compression procedure to apply when a color lies outside the screen's color gamut. If NULL, when functions using this CCC must convert a color specification to a device-dependent format and they encounter a color that lies outside the screen's color gamut, the functions will return XcmsFailure.

client_data Specifies client data for the gamut compression procedure or NULL.

Returns

The previous compression procedure.

Availability

Release 5 and later.

Description

XcmsSetCompressionProc() function sets the gamut compression procedure and client data in the specified CCC with the newly specified procedure and client data, and returns the old procedure.

Gamut compression procedures provided with Xlib and intended for use with XcmsSetCompressionProc() are:

• XcmsCIELabClipL – In CIELAB color space, reduces or increases the CIE metric lightness (L*) of the color specification until it is within the screen's color gamut. No client data is necessary.

• XcmsCIELabClipab – In CIELAB color space while maintaining Psychometric Hue Angle, reduces the Psychometric Chroma of the color specification until it is within the screen's color gamut. No client data is necessary.

- `XcmsCIELabClipLab` – In CIELAB color space while maintaining Psychometric Hue Angle, replaces the color specification with the CIELAB coordinate that falls within the screen's color gamut and whose vector to the original coordinates is the shortest attainable. No client data is necessary.

- `XcmsCIELuvClipL` – In CIELUV color space, reduces or increases the CIE metric lightness (L*) of the color specification until it is within the screen's color gamut. No client data is necessary.

- `XcmsCIELuvClipuv` – In CIELUV color space while maintaining Psychometric Hue Angle, reduces the Psychometric Chroma of the color specification until it is within the screen's color gamut. No client data is necessary.

- `XcmsCIELuvClipLuv` – In CIELUV color space while maintaining Psychometric Hue Angle, replaces the color specification with the CIELuv coordinate that falls within the screen's color gamut and whose vector to the original coordinates is the shortest attainable. No client data is necessary.

- `XcmsTekHVCClipV` – In TekHVC color space, reduces or increases the Value of the color specification until it is within the screen's color gamut. No client data is necessary.

- `XcmsTekHVCClipC` – In TekHVC color space while maintaining Hue, reduces the Chroma of the color specification until it is within the screen's color gamut. No client data is necessary.

- `XcmsTekHVCClipVC` – In TekHVC color space while maintaining Hue, replaces the color specification with the TekHVC coordinate that falls within the screen's color gamut and whose vector to the original coordinates is the shortest attainable. No client data is necessary.

See Also

XcmsCCCOfColormap(), *XcmsCreateCCC()*, *XcmsConvertColors()*, *XcmsDefaultCCC()*, *XcmsScreenNumberOfCCC()*, *XcmsScreenWhitePointOfCCC()*, *XcmsSetWhiteAdjustProc()*, *XcmsSetWhitePoint()*.

XcmsSetWhiteAdjustProc

Name

XcmsSetWhiteAdjustProc – change the white point adjustment procedure in a specified Color Conversion Context.

Synopsis

```
XcmsWhiteAdjustProc XcmsSetWhiteAdjustProc(ccc, white_adjust_proc,
        client_data)
    XcmsCCC ccc;
    XcmsWhiteAdjustProc white_adjust_proc;
    XPointer client_data;
```

Arguments

ccc   Specifies the color conversion context.

client_data   Specifies client data for the white point adjustment procedure or NULL.

white_adjust_proc
                Specifies the white point adjustment procedure.

Returns

The previous white point adjust procedure.

Availability

Release 5 and later.

Description

XcmsSetWhiteAdjustProc() sets a new white point adjustment procedure and client data in the specified CCC, and returns the old procedure.

White adustment procedures provided with Xlib and intended for use with XcmsSet-WhiteAdjustProc() are:

- XcmsCIELabWhiteShiftColors – Uses the CIELAB color space to shift the chromatic character of colors by the chromatic displacement between the initial and target white point. No client data is necessary.

- XcmsCIELuvWhiteShiftColors – Uses the CIELUV color space to shift the chromatic character of colors by the chromatic displacement between the initial and target white point. No client data is necessary.

- XcmsTekHVCWhiteShiftColors – Uses the TekHVC color space to shift the chromatic character of colors by the chromatic displacement between the initial and target white point. No client data is necessary.

See Also

XcmsCCCOfColormap(), *XcmsCreateCCC()*, *XcmsClientWhitePointOfCCC()*, *XcmsConvertColors()*, *XcmsDefaultCCC()*, *XcmsScreenWhitePointOfCCC()*, *XcmsSetCompressionProc()*, *XcmsSetWhite-Point()*.

XcmsSetWhitePoint

Name

XcmsSetWhitePoint – set the Client White Point of a Color Conversion Context.

Synopsis

```
Status XcmsSetWhitePoint(ccc, color)
    XcmsCCC ccc;
    XcmsColor *color;
```

Arguments

ccc   Specifies the color conversion context.

color   Specifies the new Client White Point.

Returns

Zero on failure, non-zero on success.

Availability

Release 5 and later.

Description

XcmsSetWhitePoint() changes the Client White Point in the specified CCC. Note that the pixel member is ignored and that the color specification is left unchanged upon return. The format for the new white point must be XcmsCIEXYZFormat, XcmsCIEuvYFormat, XcmsCIExyYFormat, or XcmsUndefinedFormat. If color is NULL, this function sets the format component of the CCC's Client White Point specification to XcmsUndefined-Format, indicating that the Client White Point is assumed to be the same as the Screen White Point.

See Also

XcmsCCCOfColormap(), XcmsCreateCCC(), XcmsClientWhitePointOfCCC(), XcmsConvertColors(), XcmsDefaultCCC(), XcmsScreenWhitePointOfCCC(), XcmsSetCompressionProc(), XcmsSetWhite-AdjustProc().

XcmsStoreColor

Name

XcmsStoreColor – store a specified color into a read/write colormap cell.

Synopsis

```
Status XcmsStoreColor(display, colormap, color)
    Display *display;
    Colormap colormap;
    XcmsColor *color;
```

Arguments

display   Specifies the connection to the X server.

colormap   Specifies the colormap.

color   Specifies the color cell and the color to store. Values specified in this
             XcmsColor structure remain unchanged upon return.

Returns

Zero on failure, non-zero on success.

Availability

Release 5 and later.

Description

XcmsStoreColor() converts the color specified in the XcmsColor structure into RGB
values and then uses this RGB specification in an XColor structure, whose three flags (Do-
Red, DoGreen, and DoBlue) are set, in a call to XStoreColor() to change the color
cell specified by the pixel member of the XcmsColor structure. This pixel value must be a
valid index for the specified colormap, and the color cell specified by the pixel value must be
a read/write cell. If the pixel value is not a valid index, a BadValue error results. If the
color cell is unallocated or is allocated read-only, a BadAccess error results. If the colormap is an installed map for its screen, the changes are visible immediately.

Note that XStoreColor() does not return a Status therefore this function's return status
can only indicate if a color conversion was successful and the call to XStoreColor() was
made. XcmsStoreColor() returns XcmsSuccess if it succeeded in converting the
color specification and called XStoreColor(). It returns XcmsSuccessWith-
Compression if it converted the requested device-independent color to the device RGB
color space with gamut compression and completed the call to XStoreColor(). It returns
XcmsFailure if it could not convert the specified color at all. To obtain the actual color
stored, use XcmsQueryColor(). Due to the screen's hardware limitations or gamut compression, the color stored in the colormap may not be identical to the color specified.

Errors

BadAccess   The specified colormap cell was read-only.

BadColor   The *colormap* argument does not name a defined colormap.

BadValue   The specified pixel does not represent a valid color cell in the specified colormap.

Structures

The XcmsColor structure and XcmsColorFormat type are shown on the XcmsColor reference page.

See Also

XcmsAllocColor(), XcmsAllocNamedColor(), XcmsLookupColor(), XcmsQueryColor(), XcmsQueryColors(), XcmsStoreColors(), XcmsStoreNamedColor, XAllocColor(), XAllocNamedColor(), XLookupColor(), XParseColor(), XQueryColor(), XQueryColors(), XStoreColor(), XStoreColors().

XcmsStoreColors

Name

XcmsStoreColors – store the specified colors in read/write colormap cells.

Synopsis

```
Status XcmsStoreColors(display, colormap, colors, ncolors,
        compression_flags_return)
    Display *display;
    Colormap colormap;
    XcmsColor colors[];
    int ncolors;
    Bool compression_flags_return[];
```

Arguments

display   Specifies the connection to the X server.

colormap   Specifies the colormap.

colors   Specifies an array of XcmsColor structures, each specifying a color cell and the color to store in that cell. Values specified in the array remain unchanged upon return.

ncolors   Specifies the number of XcmsColor structures in the color specification array.

compression_flags_return
        Specifies an array of *ncolors* Boolean values for returning compression status. If a non-NULL pointer is supplied, each element of the array is set to True if the corresponding color was compressed, and False otherwise. Pass NULL if the compression status is not useful.

Returns

Zero on failure, non-zero on success.

Availability

Release 5 and later.

Description

The XcmsStoreColors() function converts the colors specified in the array of Xcms-Color structures into RGB values and then uses these RGB specifications in an XColor structures, whose three flags (DoRed, DoGreen, and DoBlue) are set, in a call to XStore-Colors() to change the color cells specified by the pixel member of the corresponding XcmsColor structure. Each pixel value must be a valid index for the specified colormap, and the color cell specified by each pixel value must be a read/write cell. If a pixel value is not a valid index, a BadValue error results. If a color cell is unallocated or is allocated read-only, a `BadAccess` error results. If more than one pixel is in error, the one that gets reported is arbitrary. If the colormap is an installed map for its screen, the changes are visible immediately.

`XcmsStoreColors()` returns `XcmsSuccess` if it succeeded in converting the color specificatons and called `XStoreColors()`. It returns `XcmsSuccessWith-Compression` if one or more of the requested device-independent colors required gamut compression during conversion to the device RGB color space, and it returns `Xcms-Failure` if it could not convert one or more of the specified colors at all. Note that `XStoreColors()` has no return value; therefore, a `XcmsSuccess` return value from this function indicates that conversions to RGB succeeded and the call to `XStoreColors()` was made. To obtain the actual colors stored, use `XcmsQueryColors()`. Due to the screen's hardware limitations or gamut compression, the colors stored in the colormap may not be identical to the colors specified.

Errors

`BadAccess`	A specified colormap cell was read-only.
`BadColor`	The *colormap* argument does not name a defined Colormap.
`BadValue`	The specified pixel does not represent a valid color cell in the specified colormap.

Structures

The `XcmsColor` and `XcmsColorFormat` structures are shown on the `XcmsColor` reference page.

See Also

XcmsAllocColor(), XcmsAllocNamedColor(), XcmsLookupColor(), XcmsQueryColor(), XcmsQuery-Colors(), XcmsStoreColor(), XcmsStoreNamedColor, XAllocColor(), XAllocNamedColor(), XLookup-Color(), XParseColor(), XQueryColor(), XQueryColors(), XStoreColor(), XStoreColors().

XcmsTekHVCQueryMaxC

Name

XcmsTekHVCQueryMaxC – find the maximum Chroma for a given TekHVC Hue and Value.

Synopsis

```
Status XcmsTekHVCQueryMaxC(ccc, hue, value, color_return)
    XcmsCCC ccc;
    XcmsFloat hue;
    XcmsFloat value;
    XcmsColor *color_return;
```

Arguments

ccc   Specifies the color conversion context. Note that the CCC's Client White
               Point and White Point Adjustment procedures are ignored.

hue   Specifies the Hue at which to find the maximum Chroma.

value   Specifies the Value at which to find the maximum Chroma.

color_return
               Returns the maximum Chroma along with the actual Hue and Value. The
               white point associated with the returned color specification is the Screen
               White Point. The value returned in the pixel member is undefined.

Returns

Zero on failure, non-zero on success.

Availability

Release 5 and later.

Description

XcmsTekHVCQueryMaxC() determines the maximum displayable Chroma for a given
Hue and Value. The maximum Chroma is returned in the color_return argument, along
with the actual Hue and Value at which it occurs. Note that because of gamut compression or
hardware limitations, the returned Hue and Value may differ from those specified by the hue
and value arguments.

Structures

The XcmsColor structure and XcmsColorFormat type are shown on the XcmsColor
reference page.

See Also

XcmsTekHVCQueryMaxV(), *XcmsTekHVCQueryMaxVC()*, *XcmsTekHVCQueryMaxVSamples()*, *XcmsTekHVCQueryMinV()*.

XcmsTekHVCQueryMaxV

Name

XcmsTekHVCQueryMaxV – find the maximum Value for a given TekHVC Hue and Chroma.

Synopsis

```
Status XcmsTekHVCQueryMaxV(ccc, hue, chroma, color_return)
    XcmsCCC ccc;
    XcmsFloat hue;
    XcmsFloat chroma;
    XcmsColor *color_return;
```

Arguments

ccc   Specifies the color conversion context. Note that the CCC's Client White Point and White Point Adjustment procedures are ignored.

hue   Specifies the Hue at which to find the maximum Value.

chroma   Specifies the chroma at which to find maximum Value.

color_return
               Returns the maximum Value along with the Hue and Chroma. The white point associated with the returned color specification is the Screen White Point. The value returned in the pixel member is undefined.

Returns

Zero on failure, non-zero on success.

Availability

Release 5 and later.

Description

XcmsTekHVCQueryMaxV() determines the maximum displayable Value for a given Hue and Chroma. The maximum Value is returned in the *color_return* argument along with the actual Hue and Chroma at which it occurs. Note that because of gamut compression or hardware limitations, the returned Hue and Chroma may differ from those specified by the *hue* and *chroma* arguments.

Structures

The XcmsColor structure and XcmsColorFormat type are shown on the XcmsColor reference page.

See Also

XcmsTekHVCQueryMaxC(), XcmsTekHVCQueryMaxVC(), XcmsTekHVCQueryMaxVSamples(), Xcms-TekHVCQueryMinV().

Name

XcmsTekHVCQueryMaxVC – find the maximum Chroma and the Value at which it occurs given a TekHVC Hue.

Synopsis

```
Status XcmsTekHVCQueryMaxVC(ccc, hue, color_return)
    XcmsCCC ccc;
    XcmsFloat hue;
    XcmsColor *color_return;
```

Arguments

ccc
Specifies the color conversion context. Note that the CCC's Client White Point and White Point Adjustment procedures are ignored.

hue
Specifies the Hue at which to find the maximum Chroma.

color_return
Returns the maximum Chroma, the Value at which that maximum Chroma is reached and actual Hue. The white point associated with the returned color specification is the Screen White Point. The value returned in the pixel member is undefined.

Returns

Zero on failure, non-zero on success.

Availability

Release 5 and later.

Description

XcmsTekHVCQueryMaxVC() determines the maximum displayable Chroma for a given Hue, and the Value at which that Chroma is reached. The Chroma and Value are returned in the color_return argument along with the actual Hue at which they occur. Note that because of gamut compression or hardware limitations, the returned Hue may differ from that specified by the hue argument.

Structures

The XcmsColor structure and XcmsColorFormat type are shown on the XcmsColor reference page.

See Also

XcmsTekHVCQueryMaxC(), *XcmsTekHVCQueryMaxV()*, *XcmsTekHVCQueryMaxVSamples()*, *Xcms-TekHVCQueryMinV()*.

XcmsTekHVCQueryMaxVSamples

Name

XcmsTekHVCQueryMaxVSamples – return the boundaries of the TekHVC gamut for a given Hue.

Synopsis

```
Status XcmsTekHVCQueryMaxVSamples(ccc, hue, colors_return, nsamples)
    XcmsCCC ccc;
    XcmsFloat hue;
    XcmsColor colors_return[];
    unsigned int nsamples;
```

Arguments

ccc   Specifies the color conversion context. Note that the CCC's Client White Point and White Point Adjustment procedures are ignored.

hue   Specifies the Hue at which to find the maximum Chroma/Value samples.

colors_return

                Specifies an array of nsamples XcmsColor structures into which the returned color specifications will be stored.

nsamples   Specifies the number of samples.

Returns

Zero on failure, non-zero on success.

Availability

Release 5 and later.

Description

For the specified Hue, XcmsTekHVCQueryMaxVSamples() partitions the legal values of Chroma into nsamples samples, and queries the maximum Value for the Hue and each Chroma sample. The resulting values are stored into the elements of the colors_return array. This function can be used to plot the upper boundary of the TekHVC device gamut for a given Hue.

Structures

The XcmsColor structure and XcmsColorFormat type are shown on the XcmsColor reference page.

See Also

XcmsTekHVCQueryMaxC(), *XcmsTekHVCQueryMaxV()*, *XcmsTekHVCQueryMaxVC()*, *XcmsTek-HVCQueryMinV()*.

XcmsTekHVCQueryMinV

Name

XcmsTekHVCQueryMinV – find the minimum Value for a given TekHVC Hue and Chroma.

Synopsis

```
Status XcmsTekHVCQueryMinV(ccc, hue, chroma, color_return)
    XcmsCCC ccc;
    XcmsFloat hue;
    XcmsFloat chroma;
    XcmsColor *color_return;
```

Arguments

ccc   Specifies the color conversion context. Note that the CCC's Client White Point and White Point Adjustment procedures are ignored.

hue   Specifies the Hue at which to find the minimum Value.

chroma   Specifies the chroma at which to find the minimum Value.

color_return
                Returns the minimum Value and the actual Hue and Chroma. The white point associated with the returned color specification is the Screen White Point. The value returned in the pixel member is undefined.

Returns

Zero on failure, non-zero on success.

Availability

Release 5 and later.

Description

XcmsTekHVCQueryMinV() determines the minimum displayable Value for a given Hue and Chroma. The minimum Value is returned in the color_return argument along with the actual Hue and Chroma at which it occurs. Note that because of gamut compression or hardware limitations, the returned Hue and Chroma may differ from those specified by the hue and chroma arguments.

Structures

The XcmsColor structure and XcmsColorFormat type are shown on the XcmsColor reference page.

See Also

XcmsTekHVCQueryMaxC(),   *XcmsTekHVCQueryMaxV()*,   *XcmsTekHVCQueryMaxVC()*,   *XcmsTek-HVCQueryMaxVSamples()*.

XcmsVisualOfCCC

Name

XcmsVisualOfCCC, VisualOfCCC – return the visual associated with a specified Color Conversion Context (CCC).

Synopsis

```
Visual *XcmsVisualOfCCC(ccc)
      XcmsCCC ccc;

VisualOfCCC(ccc)
      XcmsCCC ccc;
```

Arguments

ccc   Specifies the color conversion context.

Returns

The visual.

Availability

Release 5 and later.

Description

XcmsVisualOfCCC() and VisualOfCCC both return the visual associated with the specified CCC.

See Also

XcmsCreateCCC(), XcmsDefaultCCC(), XcmsClientWhitePointOfCCC(), XcmsCCCOfColormap(), XcmsCreateCCC(), XcmsClientWhitePointOfCCC(), XcmsDefaultCCC(), XcmsDisplayOfCCC(), XcmsScreenNumberOfCCC(), XcmsScreenWhitePointOfCCC().

XcmsWhiteAdjustProc

Name

XcmsWhiteAdjustProc – interface definition for the white point adjustment procedure.

Synopsis

```
typedef Status (*XcmsWhiteAdjustProc)(ccc, initial_white_point,
        target_white_point, target_format, colors_in_out, ncolors,
        compression_flags_return)
    XcmsCCC ccc;
    XcmsColor *initial_white_point;
    XcmsColor *target_white_point;
    XcmsColorFormat target_format;
    XcmsColor colors_in_out[];
    unsigned int ncolors;
    Bool compression_flags_return[];
```

Arguments

ccc   Specifies the color conversion context.

initial_white_point
                Specifies the initial white point.

target_white_point
                Specifies the target white point.

target_format
                Specifies the target color specification format.

colors_in_out
                Specifies an array of color specifications. Pixel members are ignored and
                remain unchanged upon return.

ncolors   Specifies the number of XcmsColor structures in the color specification
                array.

compression_flags_return
                Specifies an array of Boolean values (or NULL) for returned information
                that indicates if the color was compressed. For example, if this routine
                returns   XcmsSuccessWithCompression   and   compres-
                sion_flags_return[3] is True, this indicates that the fourth color
                specified in the color specification array was compressed. If the calling
                routine is not interested in knowing which color was compressed when the
                return value is XcmsSuccessWithCompression, it is allowed to pass
                a NULL for this argument.

Returns

Zero on failure, non-zero on success.

Availability

Release 5 and later.

Description

XcmsWhiteAdjustProc is a function that takes the color specifications, whose associated white point is *initial_white_point*, and modifies them for the *target_white_point*; returning the color specifications in the format specified by *target_format*.

See Also

XcmsSetWhiteAdjustProc().

XConfigureWindow

Name

XConfigureWindow – change the window position, size, border width, or stacking order.

Synopsis

```
XConfigureWindow(display, w, value_mask, values)
    Display *display;
    Window w;
    unsigned int value_mask;
    XWindowChanges *values;
```

Arguments

display	Specifies a connection to an X server; returned from XOpenDisplay().
w	Specifies the ID of the window to be reconfigured.
value_mask	Specifies which values are to be set using information in the values structure. value_mask is the bitwise OR of any number of symbols listed in the Structures section below.
values	Specifies a pointer to the XWindowChanges structure containing new configuration information. See the "Structures" section below.

Description

XConfigureWindow() changes the window position, size, border width, and/or the stacking order. If selected, a ConfigureNotify event is generated to announce any changes.

If the window to be reconfigured is a top-level window, there will be interaction with the window manager if the override_redirect attribute of the window is False. In this case, the X server sends a ConfigureRequest event to the window manager and does not reconfigure the window. The window manager receives this event and then makes the decision whether to allow the application to reconfigure its window. The client should wait for the ConfigureNotify event to find out the size and position of the window.

In Release 4, XReconfigureWMWindow() should be used instead of XConfigure-Window() for top-level windows. This routine properly handles restacking of top-level windows.

If a window's size actually changes, the window's subwindows may move according to their window gravity. If they do, GravityNotify events will be generated for them. Depending on the window's bit gravity, the contents of the window also may be moved. See Volume One, Chapter 4, *Window Attributes*, for further information.

Exposure processing is performed on formerly obscured windows, including the window itself and its inferiors, if regions of them were obscured but afterward are not. As a result of increasing the width or height, exposure processing is also performed on any new regions of the window and any regions where window contents are lost.

The members of XWindowChanges that you specify in *values* are:

x *y*	Specify the x and y coordinates of the upper-left outer corner of the window relative to the parent's origin.
width *height*	Specify the inside size of the window in pixels, not including the border. These arguments must be positive.
border_width	Specifies the width of the border in pixels.
sibling	Specifies the sibling window for stacking operations. If not specified, no change in the stacking order will be made. If specified, stack_mode must also be specified.
stack_mode	The stack mode can be any of these constants: Above, Below, TopIf, BottomIf, or Opposite.

The computation for the BottomIf, TopIf, and Opposite stacking modes is performed with respect to window *w*'s final size and position (as controlled by the other arguments to XConfigureWindow(), not its initial position.) It is an error if *sibling* is specified without *stack_mode*. If *sibling* and *stack_mode* are specified, the window is restacked as follows:

Stacking Flag	Position
Above	*w* is placed just above *sibling*.
Below	*w* is placed just below *sibling*.
TopIf	if *sibling* obscures *w*, then *w* is placed at the top of the stack.
BottomIf	if *w* obscures *sibling*, then *w* is placed at the bottom of the stack.
Opposite	if *sibling* occludes *w*, then *w* is placed at the top of the stack. If *w* occludes *sibling*, then *w* is placed at the bottom of the stack. If *w* and *sibling* do not overlap, no change is made.

If a stack_mode is specified but no sibling is specified, the window is restacked as follows:

Stacking Flag	Position
Above	*w* is placed at the top of the stack.
Below	*w* is placed at the bottom of the stack.
TopIf	if any sibling obscures *w*, then *w* is placed at the top of the stack.

Stacking Flag	Position
BottomIf	if *w* obscures any sibling, then window is placed at the bottom of the stack.
Opposite	if any sibling occludes *w*, then *w* is placed at the top of the stack, else if *w* occludes any sibling, then *w* is placed at the bottom of the stack.

Under Release 4, use XReconfigureWMWindow() to configure a top-level window.

Structures

```
typedef struct {
    int x, y;
    int width, height;
    int border_width;
    Window sibling;
    int stack_mode;
} XWindowChanges;

/* ConfigureWindow structure */
/* ChangeWindow value bits definitions for valuemask */
#define CWX              (1<<0)
#define CWY              (1<<1)
#define CWWidth          (1<<2)
#define CWHeight         (1<<3)
#define CWBorderWidth    (1<<4)
#define CWSibling        (1<<5)
#define CWStackMode      (1<<6)
```

Errors

BadMatch   Attempt to set any invalid attribute of InputOnly window.
sibling specified without a *stack_mode*.
The *sibling* window is not actually a sibling.

BadValue   *width* or *height* is 0.

BadWindow

See Also

XCirculateSubwindows(), XCirculateSubwindowsDown(), XCirculateSubwindowsUp(), XLower-Window(), XMoveResizeWindow(), XMoveWindow(), XQueryTree(), XReconfigureWMWindow(), XRaiseWindow(), XReparentWindow(), XResizeWindow(), XRestackWindows().

XConnectionNumber

Name

XConnectionNumber, ConnectionNumber – get connection number or file descriptor.

Synopsis

```
int XConnectionNumber(display)
      Display *display;
```

Arguments

display Specifies a connection to an X server; returned from `XOpenDisplay()`.

Returns

The connection number.

Description

`XConnectionNumber()` returns the connection number for the specified display. On a POSIX-conformant system, this is the file descriptor of the connection.

The C language macro `ConnectionNumber()` is equivalent and slightly more efficient.

XContextDependentDrawing

Name

XContextDependentDrawing – get a hint about context dependencies in the text of the locale.

Synopsis

```
Bool XContextDependentDrawing(font_set)
    XFontSet font_set;
```

Arguments

font_set   Specifies the font set.

Returns

True or False as described below.

Availability

Release 5 and later.

Description

If XContextDependentDrawing() returns True, then text in the locale of the specified font set may contain context dependencies. If it returns False, then text drawn with the font set does not contain context dependencies.

When text contains context dependencies, a character may be rendered with different glyphs in different locations in the string, a single character may be rendered with multiple font glyphs, and multiple characters may be rendered with a single glyph. When there are context dependencies, drawing the characters of a string individually may have different results than drawing the string with a single call to one of the internationalized text drawing functions. When changing or inserting characters into an already drawn string, the characters surrounding the change may also need to be redrawn.

See Also

XCreateFontSet(), XExtentsOfFontSet(), XFontsOfFontSet(), XBaseFontNameListOfFontSet(), XLocale-OfFontSet().

XConvertSelection

Name

XConvertSelection – request conversion of the selection.

Synopsis

```
XConvertSelection(display, selection, target, property,
                  requestor, time)
    Display *display;
    Atom selection, target;
    Atom property;
    Window requestor;
    Time time;
```

Arguments

display   Specifies a connection to an X server; returned from XOpenDisplay().

selection   Specifies the selection atom. XA_PRIMARY and XA_SECONDARY are the standard selection atoms.

target   Specifies the atom describing the desired format for the data.

property   Specifies the property in which the requested data is to be placed. None is also valid, but current conventions specify that the requestor is in a better position to select a property than the selection owner.

requestor   Specifies the requesting window.

time   Specifies the time when the conversion should take place. Pass the timestamp from the event that triggered the selection request.

Description

XConvertSelection() causes a SelectionRequest event to be sent to the current selection owner if there is one. This event specifies the selection property (*selection*), the format into which to convert that data before storing it (*target*), the property in which the owner will place the information (*property*), the window that wants the information (*requestor*), and the time of the conversion request (*time*).

The selection owner responds by sending a SelectionNotify event, which confirms the selected atom and type. If no owner for the specified selection exists, or if the owner could not convert to the type specified by requestor, the X server generates or the owner sends a SelectionNotify event to the *requestor* with property None. Whether or not the owner exists, the arguments are passed unchanged. See Volume One, Chapter 10, *Interclient Communication*, for a description of selection events and selection conventions.

Errors

```
BadAtom
BadWindow
```

See Also

XGetSelectionOwner(), XSetSelectionOwner().

XCopyArea

Name

XCopyArea – copy an area of a drawable.

Synopsis

```
XCopyArea(display, src, dest, gc, src_x, src_y, width,
                  height,  dest_x, dest_y)
    Display *display;
    Drawable src, dest;
    GC gc;
    int src_x, src_y;
    unsigned int width, height;
    int dest_x, dest_y;
```

Arguments

display	Specifies a connection to an X server; returned from XOpenDisplay().
src dest	Specify the source and destination rectangles to be combined. src and dest must have the same root and depth.
gc	Specifies the graphics context.
src_x src_y	Specify the x and y coordinates of the upper-left corner of the source rectangle relative to the origin of the source drawable.
width height	Specify the dimensions in pixels of both the source and destination rectangles.
dest_x dest_y	Specify the x and y coordinates within the destination window.

Description

XCopyArea() combines the specified rectangle of src with the specified rectangle of dest. src and dest must have the same root and depth.

If regions of the source rectangle are obscured and have not been retained in backing_store, or if regions outside the boundaries of the source drawable are specified, then those regions are not copied. Instead, the following occurs on all corresponding destination regions that are either visible or are retained in backing_store. If dest is a window with a background other than None, the corresponding regions of the destination are tiled (with plane_mask of all 1's and function GXcopy) with that background. Regardless of tiling, if the destination is a window and graphics_exposures in gc is True, then GraphicsExpose events for all corresponding destination regions are generated. If graphics_exposures is True but no regions are exposed, then a NoExpose event is generated.

If regions of the source rectangle are not obscured and graphics_exposures is False, one NoExpose event is generated on the destination.

XCopyArea() uses these graphics context components: function, plane_mask, subwindow_mode, graphics_exposures, clip_x_origin, clip_y_origin, and clip_mask.

Errors

BadDrawable

BadGC

BadMatch   The *src* and *dest* rectangles do not have the same root and depth.

See Also

XClearArea(), XClearWindow(), XCopyPlane(), XDraw, XDrawArc(), XDrawArcs(), XDrawFilled(), XDrawLine(), XDrawLines(), XDrawPoint(), XDrawPoints(), XDrawRectangle(), XDrawRectangles(), XDrawSegments(), XFillArc(), XFillArcs(), XFillPolygon(), XFillRectangle(), XFillRectangles().

XCopyColormapAndFree

Name

XCopyColormapAndFree – copy a colormap and return a new colormap ID.

Synopsis

```
Colormap XCopyColormapAndFree(display, colormap)
    Display *display;
    Colormap colormap;
```

Arguments

display   Specifies a connection to an X server; returned from XOpenDisplay().

colormap   Specifies the colormap you are moving out of.

Returns

The created colormap.

Description

XCopyColormapAndFree() is used to obtain a new virtual colormap when allocating colorcells out of a previous colormap has failed due to resource exhaustion (that is, too many cells or planes were in use in the original colormap). The visual and screen for the new colormap is the same as for the old.

XCopyColormapAndFree() moves all of the client's existing allocations from *colormap* to the returned Colormap. The read/write or read-only characteristics of each cell moved are preserved in the new colormap.

If *colormap* was created by the client with the *alloc* argument set to AllocAll, the new colormap is also created with AllocAll, all color values for all entries are copied from *colormap*, and then all entries in *colormap* are freed.

If *colormap* was created by the client with AllocNone, or not created by the client, the allocations to be moved are all those pixels and planes that have been allocated by the client using XAllocColor, XAllocNamedColor(), XAllocColorCells(), or XAlloc-ColorPlanes() and that have not been freed since they were allocated. Values in other entries of the new Colormap are undefined.

For more information, see Volume One, Chapter 7, *Color*.

Errors

BadAlloc

BadColor   colormap is invalid.

See Also

XDefaultColormap(), *XDisplayCells()*, *XCreateColormap()*, *XFreeColormap()*, *XGetStandard-Colormap()*, *XInstallColormap()*, *XListInstalledColormaps()*, *XSetStandardColormap()*, *XSetWindow-Colormap()*, *XUninstallColormap()*.

XCopyGC

Name

XCopyGC – copy a graphics context.

Synopsis

```
XCopyGC(display, src, valuemask, dest)
    Display *display;
    GC src;
    unsigned long valuemask;
    GC dest;
```

Arguments

display   Specifies a connection to an X server; returned from XOpenDisplay().

src   Specifies the components of the source graphics context.

valuemask Specifies the components in the source GC structure to be copied into the destination GC. valuemask is made by combining any number of the mask symbols listed in the Structures section using bitwise OR (|).

dest   Specifies the destination graphics context.

Description

XCopyGC() copies the selected elements of one graphics context to another. The source and destination GC's must have the same root and depth. XCopyGC() requires that both GC's exist before the call is made. See Volume One, Chapter 5, *The Graphics Context*, for a description of the graphics context.

Structures

The GC structure contains the following elements:

```
/*
 * Data structure for setting graphics context.
 */
typedef struct {
    int function;                   /* logical operation */
    unsigned long plane_mask;       /* plane mask */
    unsigned long foreground;       /* foreground pixel */
    unsigned long background;       /* background pixel */
    int line_width;                 /* line width */
    int line_style;                 /* Solid, OnOffDash, DoubleDash */
    int cap_style;                  /* NotLast, Butt, Round, Projecting */
    int join_style;                 /* Miter, Round, Bevel */
    int fill_style;                 /* Solid, Tiled, Stippled */
    int fill_rule;                  /* EvenOdd, Winding */
    int arc_mode;                   /* PieSlice */
    Pixmap tile;                    /* tile pixmap for tiling operations */
```

```
        Pixmap stipple;                  /* stipple 1 plane pixmap for stipping */
        int ts_x_origin;                 /* offset for tile or stipple operations */
        int ts_y_origin;
        Font font;                       /* default text font for text operations */
        int subwindow_mode;              /* ClipByChildren, IncludeInferiors */
        Bool graphics_exposures;         /* boolean, should exposures be generated */
        int clip_x_origin;               /* origin for clipping */
        int clip_y_origin;
        Pixmap clip_mask;                /* bitmap clipping; other calls for rects */
        int dash_offset;                 /* patterned/dashed line information */
        char dashes;
} XGCValues;

#define GCFunction              (1L<<0)
#define GCPlaneMask             (1L<<1)
#define GCForeground            (1L<<2)
#define GCBackground            (1L<<3)
#define GCLineWidth             (1L<<4)
#define GCLineStyle             (1L<<5)
#define GCCapStyle              (1L<<6)
#define GCJoinStyle             (1L<<7)
#define GCFillStyle             (1L<<8)
#define GCFillRule              (1L<<9)
#define GCTile                  (1L<<10)
#define GCStipple               (1L<<11)
#define GCTileStipXOrigin       (1L<<12)
#define GCTileStipYOrigin       (1L<<13)
#define GCFont                  (1L<<14)
#define GCSubwindowMode         (1L<<15)
#define GCGraphicsExposures     (1L<<16)
#define GCClipXOrigin           (1L<<17)
#define GCClipYOrigin           (1L<<18)
#define GCClipMask              (1L<<19)
#define GCDashOffset            (1L<<20)
#define GCDashList              (1L<<21)
#define GCArcMode               (1L<<22)
```

Errors

BadAlloc

BadGC

BadMatch   *src* and *dest* do not have the same root and depth.

See Also

XDefaultGC(), XChangeGC(), XCreateGC(), XFreeGC(), XGContextFromGC(), XGetGCValues(), XSetArcMode(), XSetBackground(), XSetClipMask(), XSetClipOrigin(), XSetClipRectangles(), XSet-Dashes(), XSetFillRule(), XSetFillStyle(), XSetForeground(), XSetFunction(), XSetGraphicsExposures(), XSetLineAttributes(), XSetPlaneMask(), XSetState(), XSetStipple(), XSetSubwindowMode(), XSet-TSOrigin().

XCopyPlane

Name

XCopyPlane – copy a single plane of a drawable into a drawable with depth, applying pixel values.

Synopsis

```
XCopyPlane(display, src, dest, gc, src_x, src_y, width, height,
                dest_x, dest_y, plane)
    Display *display;
    Drawable src, dest;
    GC gc;
    int src_x, src_y;
    unsigned int width, height;
    int dest_x, dest_y;
    unsigned long plane;
```

Arguments

display	Specifies a connection to an X server; returned from XOpenDisplay().
src dest	Specify the source and destination drawables.
gc	Specifies the graphics context.
src_x src_y	Specify the x and y coordinates of the upper-left corner of the source rectangle relative to the origin of the drawable.
width height	Specify the width and height in pixels. These are the dimensions of both the source and destination rectangles.
dest_x dest_y	Specify the x and y coordinates at which the copied area will be placed relative to the origin of the destination drawable.
plane	Specifies the source bit-plane. You must set exactly one bit, and the bit must specify a plane that exists in src.

Description

XCopyPlane() copies a single plane of a rectangle in the source into the entire depth of a corresponding rectangle in the destination. The plane of the source drawable and the foreground/background pixel values in gc are combined to form a pixmap of the same depth as the destination drawable, and the equivalent of an XCopyArea() is performed, with all the same exposure semantics.

XCopyPlane() uses these graphics context components: function, plane_mask, foreground, background, subwindow_mode, graphics_exposures, clip_x_origin, clip_y_origin, and clip_mask.

The *src* and *dest* drawables must have the same root, but need not have the same depth.

For more information, see Volume One, Chapter 5, *The Graphics Context*.

Errors

BadDrawable

BadGC

BadMatch   *src* and *dest* do not have the same root.

BadValue   *plane* does not have exactly one bit set, or bit specified in *plane* is not a plane in *src*.

See Also

XClearArea(), XClearWindow(), XCopyArea(), XDraw, XDrawArc(), XDrawArcs(), XDrawFilled(), XDrawLine(), XDrawLines(), XDrawPoint(), XDrawPoints(), XDrawRectangle(), XDrawRectangles(), XDrawSegments(), XFillArc(), XFillArcs(), XFillPolygon(), XFillRectangle(), XFillRectangles().

XCreateAssocTable

Name

XCreateAssocTable – create a new association table (X10).

Synopsis

```
XAssocTable *XCreateAssocTable(size)
    int size;
```

Arguments

size   Specifies the number of buckets in the hashed association table.

Returns

The created association table.

Description

XCreateAssocTable() creates an association table, which allows you to associate your own structures with X resources in a fast lookup table. This function is provided for compatibility with X Version 10. To use it you must include the file *<X11/X10.h>* and link with the library *-loldX*.

The *size* argument specifies the number of buckets in the hash system of XAssocTable. For reasons of efficiency the number of buckets should be a power of two. Some size suggestions might be: use 32 buckets per 100 objects; a reasonable maximum number of object per buckets is 8.

If there is an error allocating memory for the XAssocTable, a NULL pointer is returned.

For more information on association tables, see Volume One, Appendix B, *X10 Compatibility*.

Structures

```
typedef struct {
    XAssoc *buckets;    /* pointer to first bucket in array */
    int size;           /* table size (number of buckets) */
} XAssocTable;
```

See Also

XDeleteAssoc(), XDestroyAssocTable(), XLookUpAssoc(), XMakeAssoc().

XCreateBitmapFromData

Name

XCreateBitmapFromData – create a bitmap from X11 bitmap format data.

Synopsis

```
Pixmap XCreateBitmapFromData(display, drawable, data,
                    width, height)
    Display *display;
    Drawable drawable;
    char *data;
    unsigned int width, height;
```

Arguments

display   Specifies a connection to an X server; returned from XOpenDisplay().

drawable   Specifies a drawable. This determines which screen to create the bitmap on.

data   Specifies the bitmap data, in X11 bitmap file format.

width   Specify the dimensions in pixels of the created bitmap. If smaller than the
height   bitmap data, the upper-left corner of the data is used.

Returns

The created Pixmap.

Description

XCreateBitmapFromData() creates a single-plane pixmap from an array of hexadecimal data. This data may be defined in the program or included (using #include). The bitmap data must be in X version 11 format as shown below (it cannot be in X10 format). The following format is assumed for the data, where the variables are members of the XImage structure described in Volume One, Chapter 6, *Drawing Graphics and Text*:

```
format=XYPixmap
bit_order=LSBFirst
byte_order=LSBFirst
bitmap_unit=8
bitmap_pad=8
xoffset=0
no extra bytes per line
```

XCreateBitmapFromData() creates an image with the specified data and copies it into the created pixmap. The following is an example of creating a bitmap:

```
#define gray_width 16
#define gray_height 16
#define gray_x_hot 8
```

```
#define gray_y_hot 8
static char gray_bits[] = {
    0xf8, 0x1f, 0xe3, 0xc7, 0xcf, 0xf3, 0x9f, 0xf9,
    0xbf, 0xfd, 0x33, 0xcc, 0x7f, 0xfe, 0x7f, 0xfe,
    0x7e, 0x7e, 0x7f, 0xfe, 0x37, 0xec, 0xbb, 0xdd,
    0x9c, 0x39, 0xcf, 0xf3, 0xe3, 0xc7, 0xf8, 0x1f};

Pixmap XCreateBitmapFromData(display, window, gray_bits,
        gray_width, gray_height);
```

If the call could not create a pixmap of the requested size on the server, XCreateBitmap-
FromData() returns None, and the server generates a BadAlloc error. If the requested
depth is not supported on the screen of the specified drawable, the server generates a Bad-
Match error.

The user should free the bitmap using XFreePixmap() when it is no longer needed.

For more information, see Volume One, Chapter 6, *Drawing Graphics and Text.*

Errors

BadAlloc   Server has insufficient memory to create bitmap.

BadDrawable

BadValue   Specified bitmap dimensions are zero.

See Also

*XCreatePixmap(), XCreatePixmapFromBitmapData(), XCreatePixmapFromBitmapData(), XFree-
Pixmap(), XQueryBestSize(), XQueryBestStipple(), XQueryBestTile(), XReadBitmapFile(), XSetTile(),
XSetWindowBackgroundPixmap(), XSetWindowBorderPixmap(), XWriteBitmapFile().*

XCreateColormap

Name

XCreateColormap – create a colormap.

Synopsis

```
Colormap XCreateColormap(display, w, visual, alloc)
    Display *display;
    Window w;
    Visual *visual;
    int alloc;
```

Arguments

display	Specifies a connection to an X server; returned from XOpenDisplay().
w	Specifies a window ID. The colormap created will be associated with the same screen as the window.
visual	Specifies a pointer to the Visual structure for the colormap. The visual class and depth must be supported by the screen.
alloc	Specifies how many colormap entries to allocate. Pass either AllocNone or AllocAll.

Returns

The created colormap.

Description

XCreateColormap() creates a colormap of the specified visual type and allocates either none or all of its entries, and returns the colormap ID.

It is legal to specify any visual class in the structure pointed to by the *visual* argument. If the class is StaticColor, StaticGray, or TrueColor, the colorcells will have pre-allocated read-only values defined by the individual server but unspecified by the X11 protocol. In these cases, *alloc* must be specified as AllocNone (else a BadMatch error).

For the other visual classes, PseudoColor, DirectColor, and GrayScale, you can pass either AllocAll or AllocNone to the *alloc* argument. If you pass AllocNone, the colormap has no allocated entries. This allows your client programs to allocate read-only colorcells with XAllocColor or read/write cells with XAllocColorCells(), Alloc-ColorPlanes and XStoreColors(). If you pass the constant AllocAll, the entire colormap is allocated writable (all the entries are read/write, nonshareable and have undefined initial RGB values), and the colors can be set with XStoreColors(). However, you cannot free these entries with XFreeColors(), and no relationships between the entries are defined.

If the visual class is PseudoColor or GrayScale and *alloc* is AllocAll, this function simulates a call to the function XAllocColor() cells returning all pixel values from 1 to (map_entries - 1). For a visual class of DirectColor, the processing for AllocAll simulates a call to the function XAllocColorPlanes(), returning a pixel value of 0 and mask values the same as the red_mask, green_mask, and blue_mask members in *visual*.

The *visual* argument should be as returned from the DefaultVisual macro, XMatch-VisualInfo(), or XGetVisualInfo().

If the hardware colormap on the server is immutable, and therefore there is no possibility that a virtual colormap could ever be installed, XCreateColormap() returns the default colormap. Code should check the returned ID against the default colormap to catch this situation.

For more information on creating colormaps, see Volume One, Chapter 7, *Color*.

Errors

BadAlloc

BadMatch   Didn't use AllocNone for StaticColor, StaticGray, or True-Color.
visual type not supported on screen.

BadValue

BadWindow

See Also

XDefaultColormap(), XDisplayCells(), XCopyColormapAndFree(), XFreeColormap(), XGetStandard-Colormap(), XInstallColormap(), XListInstalledColormaps(), XSetStandardColormap(), XSetWindow-Colormap(), XUninstallColormap().

XCreateFontCursor

Name

XCreateFontCursor – create a cursor from the standard cursor font.

Synopsis

```
#include <X11/cursorfont.h>
Cursor XCreateFontCursor(display, shape)
    Display *display;
    unsigned int shape;
```

Arguments

display   Specifies a connection to an X server; returned from XOpenDisplay().

shape   Specifies which character in the standard cursor font should be used for the cursor.

Returns

The created cursor.

Description

X provides a set of standard cursor shapes in a special font named "cursor." Programs are encouraged to use this interface for their cursors, since the font can be customized for the individual display type and shared between clients.

The hotspot comes from the information stored in the font. The initial colors of the cursor are black for the foreground and white for the background. XRecolorCursor() can be used to change the colors of the cursor to those desired.

For more information about cursors and their shapes in fonts, see Appendix I, *The Cursor Font*.

Errors

```
BadAlloc
```

```
BadFont
```

```
BadValue
```
The *shape* argument does not specify a character in the standard cursor font.

See Also

XCreateGlyphCursor(), XCreatePixmapCursor(), XDefineCursor(), XFreeCursor(), XQueryBest-Cursor(), XQueryBestSize(), XRecolorCursor(), XUndefineCursor().

Name

XCreateFontSet – create a font set.

Synopsis

```
XFontSet XCreateFontSet(display, base_font_name_list,
        missing_charset_list_return, missing_charset_count_return,
        def_string_return)
    Display *display;
    char *base_font_name_list;
    char ***missing_charset_list_return;
    int *missing_charset_count_return;
    char **def_string_return;
```

Arguments

display   Specifies the connection to the X server.

base_font_name_list
                Specifies the base font names.

missing_charset_list_return
                Returns the missing charsets.

missing_charset_count_return
                Returns the number of missing charsets.

def_string_return
                Returns the string drawn for missing charsets.

Returns

The created font set.

Availability

Release 5 and later.

Description

XCreateFontSet() creates a font set for the specified display. The font set is bound to the current locale when XCreateFontSet() is called. The *font_set* may be used in subsequent calls to obtain font and character information, and to image text in the locale of the *font_set*.

The *base_font_name_list* argument is a comma-separated list of base font names which Xlib uses to load the fonts needed for the locale. The string is NULL-terminated, and is assumed to be in the Host Portable Character Encoding; otherwise, the result is implementation-dependent. Whitespace immediately on either side of a separating comma is ignored.

Use of XLFD font names permits Xlib to obtain the fonts needed for a variety of locales from a single locale-independent base font name. When used, this single base font name should name a family of fonts whose members are encoded in the various charsets needed by the locales of interest.

Alternatively, an XLFD base font name can explicitly name a charset needed for the locale. This allows the user to specify an exact font for use with a charset required by a locale, fully controlling the font selection.

If a base font name is not an XLFD name, Xlib will attempt to obtain an XLFD name from the font properties for the font. If this action is successful in obtaining an XLFD name, the `XBaseFontNameListOfFontSet()` function will return this XLFD name instead of the client-supplied name.

The following algorithm is used to select the fonts that will be used to display text with the `XFontSet`:

For each font charset required by the locale, the base font name list is searched for the first one of the following cases that names a set of fonts that exist at the server:

1. The first XLFD-conforming base font name that specifies the required charset or a super-set of the required charset in its `CharSetRegistry` and `CharSetEncoding` fields. The implementation may use a base font name whose specified charset is a superset of the required charset, for example, an ISO8859-1 font for an ASCII charset.

2. The first set of one or more XLFD-conforming base font names that specify one or more charsets that can be remapped to support the required charset. The Xlib implementation may recognize various mappings from a required charset to one or more other charsets, and use the fonts for those charsets. For example, JIS Roman is ASCII with tilde and backslash replaced by yen and overbar; Xlib may load an ISO8859-1 font to support this character set, if a JIS Roman font is not available.

3. The first XLFD-conforming font name, or the first non-XLFD font name for which an XLFD font name can be obtained, combined with the required charset (replacing the `CharSetRegistry` and `CharSetEncoding` fields in the XLFD font name). As in case 1, the implementation may use a charset which is a superset of the required charset.

4. The first font name that can be mapped in some implementation-dependent manner to one or more fonts that support imaging text in the charset.

For example, assume a locale required the charsets:

```
ISO8859-1
JISX0208.1983
JISX0201.1976
GB2312-1980.0
```

Users could supply a *base_font_name_list* which explicitly specifies the charsets, insuring that specific fonts get used if they exist:

```
"-JIS-Fixed-Medium-R-Normal—26-180-100-100-C-240-JISX0208.1983-0,\
-JIS-Fixed-Medium-R-Normal—26-180-100-100-C-120-JISX0201.1976-0,\
-GB-Fixed-Medium-R-Normal—26-180-100-100-C-240-GB2312-1980.0,\
-Adobe-Courier-Bold-R-Normal—25-180-75-75-M-150-ISO8859-1"
```

Or they could supply a *base_font_name_list* which omits the charsets, letting Xlib select font charsets required for the locale:

```
"-JIS-Fixed-Medium-R-Normal—26-180-100-100-C-240,\
-JIS-Fixed-Medium-R-Normal—26-180-100-100-C-120,\
-GB-Fixed-Medium-R-Normal—26-180-100-100-C-240,\
-Adobe-Courier-Bold-R-Normal—25-180-100-100-M-150"
```

Or they could simply supply a single base font name which allows Xlib to select from all available fonts which meet certain minimum XLFD property requirements:

```
"-*-*-*-R-Normal—*-180-100-100-*-*"
```

If XCreateFontSet() is unable to create the font set, either because there is insufficient memory or because the current locale is not supported, XCreateFontSet() returns NULL, *missing_charset_list_return* is set to NULL, and *missing_charset_count_return* is set to zero. If fonts exist for all of the charsets required by the current locale, XCreateFontSet() returns a valid XFontSet, *missing_charset_list_return* is set to NULL, and *missing_charset_count_return* is set to zero.

If no font exists for one or more of the required charsets, XCreateFontSet() sets *missing_charset_list_return* to a list of one or more NULL-terminated charset names for which no font exists, and sets *missing_charset_count_return* to the number of missing fonts. The charsets are from the list of the required charsets for the encoding of the locale, and do not include any charsets to which Xlib may be able to remap a required charset.

If no font exists for any of the required charsets, or if the locale definition in Xlib requires that a font exist for a particular charset and a font is not found for that charset, XCreateFontSet() returns NULL. Otherwise, XCreateFontSet() returns a valid XFontSet to *font_set*.

When an Xmb/wc drawing or measuring function is called with an XFontSet that has missing charsets, some characters in the locale will not be drawable. If *def_string_return* is non-NULL, XCreateFontSet() returns a pointer to a string which represents the glyph(s) which are drawn with this XFontSet when the charsets of the available fonts do not include all font glyph(s) required to draw a codepoint. The string does not necessarily consist of valid characters in the current locale and is not necessarily drawn with the fonts loaded for the font set, but the client can draw and measure the "default glyphs" by including this string in a string being drawn or measured with the XFontSet.

If the string returned to *def_string_return* is the empty string (""), no glyphs are drawn, and the escapement is zero. The returned string is NULL-terminated. It is owned by Xlib and should not be modified or freed by the client. It will be freed by a call to XFree-FontSet() with the associated XFontSet. Until freed, its contents will not be modified by Xlib.

The client is responsible for constructing an error message from the missing charset and default string information, and may choose to continue operation in the case that some fonts did not exist.

The returned XFontSet and missing charset list should be freed with XFreeFontSet() and XFreeStringList(), respectively. The client-supplied *base_font_name_list* may be freed by the client after calling XCreateFontSet().

See Also

XExtentsOfFontSet(), XFontsOfFontSet(), XFreeFontSet().

Name

XCreateGC – create a new graphics context for a given screen with the depth of the specified drawable.

Synopsis

```
GC XCreateGC(display, drawable, valuemask, values)
    Display *display;
    Drawable drawable;
    unsigned long valuemask;
    XGCValues *values;
```

Arguments

display	Specifies a connection to an X server; returned from XOpenDisplay().
drawable	Specifies a drawable. The created GC can only be used to draw in drawables of the same depth as this drawable.
valuemask	Specifies which members of the GC are to be set using information in the values structure. valuemask is made by combining any number of the mask symbols listed in the Structures section.
values	Specifies a pointer to an XGCValues structure which will provide components for the new GC.

Returns

The created GC.

Description

XCreateGC() creates a new graphics context resource in the server. The returned GC can be used in subsequent drawing requests, but only on drawables on the same screen and of the same depth as the drawable specified in the drawable argument.

The specified components of the new graphics context in valuemask are set to the values passed in the values argument. Unset components default as follows:

Component	Value
function	GX copy
plane_mask	all 1's
foreground	0
background	1
line_width	0
line_style	LineSolid
cap_style	CapButt

Component	Value
join_style	JoinMiter
fill_style	FillSolid
fill_rule	EvenOddRule
arc_mode	ArcPieSlice
tile	Pixmap filled with foreground pixel
stipple	Pixmap filled with 1's
ts_x_origin	0
ts_y_origin	0
font	(implementation-dependent)
subwindow_mode	ClipByChildren
graphics_exposures	True
clip_x_origin	0
clip_y_origin	0
clip_mask	None
dash_offset	0
dashes	4 (i.e., the list [4, 4])

An application should minimize the number of GCs it creates, because some servers cache a limited number of GCs in the display hardware, and can attain better performance with a small number of GCs.

For more information, see Volume One, Chapter 5, *The Graphics Context*.

Errors

BadAlloc   Server could not allocate memory for GC.

BadDrawable   Specified drawable is invalid.

BadFont   Font specified for *font* component of GC has not been loaded.

BadMatch   Pixmap specified for *tile* component has different depth or is on different screen from the specified drawable. Or pixmap specified for stipple or clip_mask component has depth other than 1.

BadPixmap   Pixmap specified for *tile*, *stipple*, or clip_mask components is invalid.

BadValue   Values specified for *function*, line_style, cap_style, join_style, fill_style, fill_rule, subwindow_mode, graphics_exposures, dashes, or arc_mode are invalid, or invalid mask specified for *valuemask* argument.

Structures

```
typedef struct {
    int function;              /* logical operation */
    unsigned long plane_mask;  /* plane mask */
    unsigned long foreground;  /* foreground pixel */
    unsigned long background;  /* background pixel */
    int line_width;            /* line width */
    int line_style;            /* LineSolid, LineOnOffDash, LineDoubleDash */
    int cap_style;             /* CapNotLast, CapButt, CapRound, CapProjecting */
    int join_style;            /* JoinMiter, JoinRound, JoinBevel */
    int fill_style;            /* FillSolid, FillTiled, FillStippled */
    int fill_rule;             /* EvenOddRule, WindingRule */
    int arc_mode;              /* ArcPieSlice, ArcChord */
    Pixmap tile;               /* tile pixmap for tiling operations */
    Pixmap stipple;            /* stipple 1 plane pixmap for stipping */
    int ts_x_origin;           /* offset for tile or stipple operations */
    int ts_y_origin;
    Font font;                 /* default text font for text operations */
    int subwindow_mode;        /* ClipByChildren, IncludeInferiors */
    Bool graphics_exposures;   /* generate events on XCopyArea, XCopyPlane */
    int clip_x_origin;         /* origin for clipping */
    int clip_y_origin;
    Pixmap clip_mask;          /* bitmap clipping; other calls for rects */
    int dash_offset;           /* patterned/dashed line information */
    char dashes;
} XGCValues;

#define GCFunction           (1L<<0)
#define GCPlaneMask          (1L<<1)
#define GCForeground         (1L<<2)
#define GCBackground         (1L<<3)
#define GCLineWidth          (1L<<4)
#define GCLineStyle          (1L<<5)
#define GCCapStyle           (1L<<6)
#define GCJoinStyle          (1L<<7)
#define GCFillStyle          (1L<<8)
#define GCFillRule           (1L<<9)
#define GCTile               (1L<<10)
#define GCStipple            (1L<<11)
#define GCTileStipXOrigin    (1L<<12)
#define GCTileStipYOrigin    (1L<<13)
#define GCFont               (1L<<14)
#define GCSubwindowMode      (1L<<15)
#define GCGraphicsExposures  (1L<<16)
#define GCClipXOrigin        (1L<<17)
#define GCClipYOrigin        (1L<<18)
#define GCClipMask           (1L<<19)
#define GCDashOffset         (1L<<20)
```

```
#define GCDashList          (1L<<21)
#define GCArcMode           (1L<<22)
```

See Also

XDefaultGC(), XChangeGC(), XCopyGC(), XFreeGC(), XGContextFromGC(), XGetGCValues(), XSet-ArcMode(), XSetBackground(), XSetClipMask(), XSetClipOrigin(), XSetClipRectangles(), XSetDashes(), XSetFillRule(), XSetFillStyle(), XSetForeground(), XSetFunction(), XSetGraphicsExposures(), XSet-LineAttributes(), XSetPlaneMask(), XSetState(), XSetStipple(), XSetSubwindowMode(), XSetTSOrigin().

XCreateGlyphCursor

Name

XCreateGlyphCursor – create a cursor from font glyphs.

Synopsis

```
Cursor XCreateGlyphCursor(display, source_font, mask_font, source_char,
        mask_char, foreground_color, background_color)
    Display *display;
    Font source_font, mask_font;
    unsigned int source_char, mask_char;
    XColor *foreground_color;
    XColor *background_color;
```

Arguments

display   Specifies a connection to an X server; returned from XOpenDisplay().

source_font   Specifies the font from which a character is to be used for the cursor.

mask_font   Specifies the mask font or None.

source_char   Specifies the index into the cursor shape font.

mask_char ·   Specifies the index into the mask shape font. Optional; specify 0 if not needed.

foreground_color
                Specifies the red, green, and blue (RGB) values for the foreground.

background_color
                Specifies the red, green, and blue (RGB) values for the background.

Returns

The created cursor.

Description

XCreateGlyphCursor() is similar to XCreatePixmapCursor(), but the source and mask bitmaps are obtained from separate font characters, perhaps in separate fonts. The mask font and character are optional. If mask_char is not specified, all pixels of the source are displayed.

The x offset for the hotspot of the created cursor is the left-bearing for the source character, and the y offset is the ascent, each measured from the upper-left corner of the bounding rectangle of the character.

The origins of the source and mask (if it is defined) characters are positioned coincidently and define the hotspot. The source and mask need not have the same bounding box metrics, and there is no restriction on the placement of the hotspot relative to the bounding boxes.

Note that *source_char* and *mask_char* are of type `unsigned int`, not of type `XChar2b`. For two-byte matrix fonts, *source_char* and *mask_char* should be formed with the `byte1` member in the most significant byte and the `byte2` member in the least significant byte.

You can free the fonts with `XFreeFont()` if they are no longer needed after creating the glyph cursor.

For more information on fonts and cursors, see Volume One, Chapter 6, *Drawing Graphics and Text*.

Structures

```
typedef struct {
    unsigned long pixel;
    unsigned short red, green, blue;
    char flags;             /* DoRed, DoGreen, DoBlue */
    char pad;
} XColor;
```

Errors

BadAlloc

BadFont

BadValue   *source_char* not defined in *source_font*.
                mask_char not defined in *mask_font* (if *mask_font* defined).

See Also

XCreateFontCursor(), XCreatePixmapCursor(), XDefineCursor(), XFreeCursor(), XQueryBestCursor(), XQueryBestSize(), XRecolorCursor(), XUndefineCursor().

XCreateIC

Name

XCreateIC – create an input context.

Synopsis

```
XIC XCreateIC(im, ...)
    XIM im;
```

Arguments

im   Specifies the input method.

...   Specifies the variable length argument list to set XIC values.

Returns

The created input context.

Availability

Release 5 and later.

Description

XCreateIC() creates an input context associated with the specified input method. The first argument to this function is the "parent" input method, and it is followed by a NULL-terminated variable-length argument list of input context attribute name/value pairs. The tables below list the standard attribute names and their types. Note that the XNInputStyle attribute and XNFontSet sub-attribute for the Preedit and Status areas must be specified when the IC is created. XNSpotLocation must be specified for the Preedit area if the pre-edit interaction style is XIMPreeditPosition. All the Preedit and Status callbacks must be specified in the call to XCreateIC() if the interaction style is XIMPreeditCallbacks or XIMStatusCallbacks. Any other attributes may be set with XCreateIC(), but are not required.

Input Context Attributes

Name	Type	Notes
XNInputStyle	XIMStyle	Required at IC creation; may not be changed.
XNClientWindow	Window	Must be set before IC use; may not be changed.
XNFocusWindow	Window	Changes may cause geometry negotiation.
XNResourceName	char *	
XNResourceClass	char *	
XNGeometryCallback	XIMCallback *	

Name	Type	Notes
XNFilterEvents	unsigned long	Read-only attribute; may not be set.
XNPreeditAttributes	XVaNestedList	See sub-attributes below.
XNStatusAttributes	XVaNestedList	See sub-attributes below.

Preedit and Status Area Sub-attributes

Name	Type	Notes
XNArea	XRectangle *	
XNAreaNeeded	XRectangle *	
XNSpotLocation	XPoint *	Required at IC creation for XIMPreeditPosition style.
XNColormap	Colormap	
XNStdColormap	Atom	
XNForeground	unsigned long	
XNBackground	unsigned long	
XNBackgroundPixmap	Pixmap	
XNFontSet	XFontSet	Required at IC creation; changes may cause geometry negotiation.
XNLineSpacing	int	Changes may cause geometry negotiation.
XNCursor	Cursor	
XNPreeditStartCallback	XIMCallback *	Required at IC creation for XIMPreeditCallbacks style.
XNPreeditDoneCallback	XIMCallback *	Required at IC creation for XIMPreeditCallbacks style.
XNPreeditDrawCallback	XIMCallback *	Required at IC creation for XIMPreeditCallbacks style.
XNPreeditCaretCallback	XIMCallback *	Required at IC creation for XIMPreeditCallbacks style.
XNStatusStartCallback	XIMCallback *	Required at IC creation for XIMStatusCallbacks style.
XNStatusDoneCallback	XIMCallback *	Required at IC creation for XIMStatusCallbacks style.
XNStatusDrawCallback	XIMCallback *	Required at IC creation for XIMStatusCallbacks style.

In addition to the attribute names above, the special name `XNVaNestedList` indicates that the following argument is a `XVaNestedList` of attribute name/value pairs. When a nested list is encountered in an argument list, the contents of the nested list are processed as if they appeared in the original argument list at that point.

`XCreateIC()` returns a `NULL` value if no input context could be created. A `NULL` value could be returned for any of the following reasons:

*   A required argument was not set.

*   A read-only argument was set (for example, `XNFilterEvents`).

*   The argument name is not recognized.

*   The input method encountered an implementation-dependent error.

Errors

`BadAtom`	A value for an Atom argument does not name a defined Atom.
`BadColor`	A value for a Colormap argument does not name a defined Colormap.
`BadPixmap`	A value for a Pixmap argument does not name a defined Pixmap.
`BadWindow`	A value for a Window argument does not name a defined Window.

See Also

XOpenIM(), XSetICFocus(), XSetICValues(), XDestroyIC(), XIMOfIC(), XmbResetIC(), XwcResetIC.

XCreateImage

Name

XCreateImage – allocate memory for an **XImage** structure.

Synopsis

```
XImage *XCreateImage(display, visual, depth, format, offset,
                     data, width, height, bitmap_pad, bytes_per_line)
    Display *display;
    Visual *visual;
    unsigned int depth;
    int format;
    int offset;
    char *data;
    unsigned int width;
    unsigned int height;
    int bitmap_pad;
    int bytes_per_line;
```

Arguments

display
: Specifies a connection to an X server; returned from **XOpenDisplay()**.

visual
: Specifies a pointer to a visual that should match the visual of the window the image is to be displayed in.

depth
: Specifies the depth of the image.

format
: Specifies the format for the image. Pass one of these constants: **XYBitmap**, **XYPixmap**, or **ZPixmap**.

offset
: Specifies the number of pixels beyond the beginning of the data (pointed to by *data*) where the image actually begins. This is useful if the image is not aligned on an even addressable boundary.

data
: Specifies a pointer to the image data.

width
height
: Specify the width and height in pixels of the image.

bitmap_pad
: Specifies the quantum of a scan line. In other words, the start of one scan line is separated in client memory from the start of the next scan line by an integer multiple of this many bits. You must pass one of these values: 8, 16, or 32.

bytes_per_line
: Specifies the number of bytes in the client image between the start of one scan line and the start of the next. If you pass a value of 0 here, Xlib assumes that the scan lines are contiguous in memory and thus calculates the value of **bytes_per_line** itself.

Returns

The image structure.

Description

XCreateImage() allocates the memory needed for an XImage structure for the specified display and visual.

This function does not allocate space for the image itself. It initializes the structure with byte order, bit order, and bitmap unit values, and returns a pointer to the XImage structure. The red, green, and blue mask values are defined for ZPixmap format images only and are derived from the Visual structure passed in.

Note that when the image is created using XCreateImage(), XGetImage(), or XSub-Image(), the destroy procedure that XDestroyImage() calls frees both the image structure and the data pointed to by the image structure. For a description of images, see Volume One, Chapter 6, *Drawing Graphics and Text*.

See Also

XImageByteOrder(), XAddPixel(), XDestroyImage(), XGetImage(), XGetPixel(), XGetSubImage(), XPut-Image(), XPutPixel(), XSubImage().

Name

XCreatePixmap – create a pixmap.

Synopsis

```
Pixmap XCreatePixmap(display, drawable, width, height, depth)
    Display *display;
    Drawable drawable;
    unsigned int width, height;
    unsigned int depth;
```

Arguments

display	Specifies a connection to an X server; returned from XOpenDisplay().
drawable	Specifies the drawable. May be an InputOnly window.
width height	Specify the width and height in pixels of the pixmap. The values must be non-zero.
depth	Specifies the depth of the pixmap. The depth must be supported by the screen of the specified drawable. (Use XListDepths() if in doubt.)

Returns

The created Pixmap.

Description

XCreatePixmap() creates a *pixmap* resource and returns its pixmap ID. The initial contents of the pixmap are undefined.

The server uses the *drawable* argument to determine which screen the pixmap is stored on. The pixmap can only be used on this screen. The pixmap can only be drawn drawn into with GCs of the same depth, and can only be copied to drawables of the same depth, except in XCopyPlane().

A bitmap is a single-plane pixmap. There is no separate bitmap type in X Version 11.

Pixmaps should be considered a precious resource, since many servers have limits on the amount of off-screen memory available.

If you are creating a pixmap for use in XCreatePixmapCursor(), specify depth = 1, fg = 1, and bg = 0.

For more information, see Volume One, Chapter 6, *Drawing Graphics and Text*.

Errors

`BadAlloc`

`BadDrawable`

`BadValue` *width* or *height* is 0.
depth is not supported on screen.

See Also

XCreateBitmapFromData(), *XCreatePixmapFromBitmapData()*, *XFreePixmap()*, *XListDepths()*, *XList-PixmapFormat*, *XQueryBestCursor()*, *XQueryBestSize()*, *XQueryBestStipple()*, *XQueryBestTile()*, *XReadBitmapFile()*, *XSetTile()*, *XSetWindowBackgroundPixmap()*, *XSetWindowBorderPixmap()*, *XWriteBitmapFile()*.

XCreatePixmapCursor

Name

XCreatePixmapCursor – create a cursor from two bitmaps.

Synopsis

```
Cursor XCreatePixmapCursor(display, source, mask, foreground_color,
        background_color, x, y)
    Display *display;
    Pixmap source;
    Pixmap mask;
    XColor *foreground_color;
    XColor *background_color;
    unsigned int x, y;
```

Arguments

display   Specifies a connection to an X server; returned from XOpenDisplay().

source   Specifies the shape of the source cursor. A pixmap of depth 1.

mask   Specifies the bits of the cursor that are to be displayed (the mask or stipple). A pixmap of depth 1. May be None.

foreground_color
            Specifies the red, green, and blue (RGB) values for the foreground.

background_color
            Specifies the red, green, and blue (RGB) values for the background.

x   Specify the coordinates of the cursor's hotspot relative to the source's ori-
y   gin. Must be a point within the source.

Returns

The created cursor.

Description

XCreatePixmapCursor() creates a cursor and returns a cursor ID. Foreground and background RGB values must be specified using *foreground_color* and *background_color*, even if the server only has a monochrome screen. The *foreground_color* is used for the 1 bits in the source, and the background is used for the 0 bits. Both source and mask (if specified) must have depth 1, but can have any root. The mask pixmap defines the shape of the cursor; that is, the 1 bits in the mask define which source pixels will be displayed. If no mask is given, all pixels of the source are displayed. The mask, if present, must be the same size as the source.

The pixmaps can be freed immediately if no further explicit references to them are to be made.

For more information on cursors, see Volume One, Chapter 6, *Drawing Graphics and Text*.

Structures

```
typedef struct {
    unsigned long pixel;
    unsigned short red, green, blue;
    char flags;     /* DoRed, DoGreen, DoBlue */
    char pad;
} XColor;
```

Errors

BadAlloc

BadMatch   Mask bitmap must be the same size as source bitmap.

BadPixmap

See Also

XCreateBitmapFromData(), XDefineCursor(), XCreateFontCursor(), XCreatePixmap(), XCreate-PixmapCursor(), XFreeCursor(), XFreePixmap(), XQueryBestCursor(), XQueryBestCursor(), XQuery-BestSize(), XQueryBestSize(), XReadBitmapFile(), XRecolorCursor(), XUndefineCursor().

Name

XCreatePixmapFromBitmapData – create a pixmap with depth from bitmap data.

Synopsis

```
Pixmap XCreatePixmapFromBitmapData(display, drawable, data,
                width, height, fg, bg, depth)
    Display *display;
    Drawable drawable;
    char *data;
    unsigned int width, height;
    unsigned long fg, bg;
    unsigned int depth;
```

Arguments

display   Specifies a connection to an Display structure, returned from XOpen-
             Display().

drawable   Specifies a drawable ID which indicates which screen the pixmap is to be
             used on.

data   Specifies the data in bitmap format.

width   Specify the width and height in pixels of the pixmap to create.
height

fg   Specify the foreground and background pixel values to use.
bg

depth   Specifies the depth of the pixmap. Must be valid on the screen specified by
             drawable.

Returns

The created Pixmap.

Description

XCreatePixmapFromBitmapData() creates a pixmap of the given depth using bitmap
data and foreground and background pixel values.

The following format for the data is assigned, where the variables are members of the
XImage structure described in Volume One, Chapter 6, *Drawing Graphics and Text*:

```
format=XYPixmap
bit_order=LSBFirst
byte_order=LSBFirst
bitmap_unit=8
```

```
bitmap_pad=8
xoffset=0
no extra bytes per line
```

`XCreatePixmapFromBitmapData( )` creates an image from the data and uses `XPut-Image( )` to place the data into the pixmap. For example:

```
#define gray_width 16
#define gray_height 16
#define gray_x_hot 8
#define gray_y_hot 8
static char gray_bits[] = {
    0xf8, 0x1f, 0xe3, 0xc7, 0xcf, 0xf3, 0x9f, 0xf9, 0xbf,
    0xfd, 0x33, 0xcc, 0x7f, 0xfe, 0x7f, 0xfe, 0x7e, 0x7e,
    0x7f, 0xfe, 0x37, 0xec, 0xbb, 0xdd, 0x9c, 0x39, 0xcf,
    0xf3, 0xe3, 0xc7, 0xf8, 0x1f};
unsigned long foreground, background;
unsigned int depth;

/* open display, determine colors and depth */

Pixmap XCreatePixmapFromBitmapData(display, window, gray_bits,
        gray_width, gray_height, foreground, background, depth);
```

If you want to use data of a different format, it is straightforward to write a routine that does this yourself, using images.

Pixmaps should be considered a precious resource, since many servers have limits on the amount of off-screen memory available.

If you are creating a pixmap for use in `XCreatePixmapCursor( )`, specify `depth=1`, `fg=1`, and `bg=0`.

Errors

`BadAlloc`

`BadDrawable`

`BadGC`

`BadValue`   *depth* is not a valid depth on the screen specified by `drawable`.

See Also

XCreateBitmapFromData(), XCreateFontCursor(), XCreatePixmap(), XCreatePixmapCursor(), XDefineCursor(), XFreeCursor(), XFreePixmap(), XListPixmapFormats(), XQueryBestCursor(), XQueryBestSize(), XReadBitmapFile(), XRecolorCursor(), XUndefineCursor().

XCreateRegion

Name

XCreateRegion – create a new empty region.

Synopsis

```
Region XCreateRegion()
```

Returns

The created region.

Description

XCreateRegion() creates a new region of undefined size. XPolygonRegion() can be used to create a region with a defined shape and size. Many of the functions that perform operations on regions can also create regions.

For a description of regions, see Volume One, Chapter 6, *Drawing Graphics and Text*.

Structures

Region is a pointer to an opaque structure type.

See Also

XClipBox(), XDestroyRegion(), XEmptyRegion(), XEqualRegion(), XIntersectRegion(), XOffsetRegion(), XPointInRegion(), XPolygonRegion(), XRectInRegion(), XSetRegion(), XShrinkRegion(), XSubtractRegion(), XUnionRectWithRegion(), XUnionRegion(), XXorRegion().

XCreateSimpleWindow

Name

XCreateSimpleWindow – create an unmapped `InputOutput` window.

Synopsis

```
Window XCreateSimpleWindow(display, parent, x, y, width, height, bor-
        der_width, border, background)
    Display *display;
    Window parent;
    int x, y;
    unsigned int width, height, border_width;
    unsigned long border;
    unsigned long background;
```

Arguments

display	Specifies a pointer to the *Display* structure; returned from `XOpen-Display()`.
parent	Specifies the parent window ID. Must be an *InputOutput* window.
x *y*	Specify the x and y coordinates of the upper-left pixel of the new window's border relative to the origin of the parent (inside the parent window's border).
width *height*	Specify the width and height, in pixels, of the new window. These are the inside dimensions, not including the new window's borders, which are entirely outside of the window. Must be non-zero. Any part of the window that extends outside its parent window is clipped.
border_width	Specifies the width, in pixels, of the new window's border.
border	Specifies the pixel value for the border of the window.
background	Specifies the pixel value for the background of the window.

Returns

The window.

Description

XCreateSimpleWindow() creates an unmapped `InputOutput` subwindow of the specified parent window. Use `XCreateWindow()` if you want to set the window attributes while creating a window. (After creation, `XChangeWindowAttributes()` can be used.)

XCreateSimpleWindow() returns the ID of the created window. The new window is placed on top of the stacking order relative to its siblings. Note that the window is unmapped when it is created—use `MapWindow` to display it. This function generates a `Create-Notify` event.

The initial conditions of the window are as follows:

The window inherits its depth, class, and visual from its parent. All other window attributes have their default values.

All properties have undefined values.

The new window will not have a cursor defined; the cursor will be that of the window's parent until the cursor attribute is set with `XDefineCursor()` or `XChangeWindow-Attributes()`.

If no background or border is specified, `CopyFromParent` is implied.

For more information, see Volume One, Chapter 2, *X Concepts*, and Volume One, Chapter 3, *Basic Window Program*.

Errors

`BadAlloc`

`BadMatch`

`BadValue`   *width* or *height* is zero.

`BadWindow`   Specified parent is an `InputOnly` window.

See Also

XCreateWindow(), XDestroySubwindows(), XDestroyWindow().

XCreateWindow

Name

XCreateWindow – create a window and set attributes.

Synopsis

```
Window XCreateWindow(display, parent, x, y, width, height, border_width,
        depth, class, visual, valuemask, attributes)
    Display *display;
    Window parent;
    int x, y;
    unsigned int width, height;
    unsigned int border_width;
    int depth;
    unsigned int class;
    Visual *visual
    unsigned long valuemask;
    XSetWindowAttributes *attributes;
```

Arguments

display	Specifies a connection to an X server; returned from XOpenDisplay().
parent	Specifies the parent window. Parent must be InputOutput if class of window created is to be InputOutput.
x y	Specify the x and y coordinates of the upper-left pixel of the new window's border relative to the origin of the parent (upper-left inside the parent's border).
width height	Specify the width and height, in pixels, of the window. These are the new window's inside dimensions. These dimensions do not include the new window's borders, which are entirely outside of the window. Must be non-zero, otherwise the server generates a BadValue error.
border_width	
	Specifies the width, in pixels, of the new window's border. Must be 0 for InputOnly windows, otherwise a BadMatch error is generated.
depth	Specifies the depth of the window, which can be different from the parent's depth. A depth of CopyFromParent means the depth is taken from the parent. Use XListDepths() if choosing an unusual depth. The specified depth paired with the visual argument must be supported on the screen.
class	Specifies the new window's class. Pass one of these constants: Input-Output, InputOnly, or CopyFromParent.
visual	Specifies a connection to an visual structure describing the style of color-map to be used with this window. CopyFromParent is valid.

    valuemask   Specifies which window attributes are defined in the *attributes* argument. If *valuemask* is 0, *attributes* is not referenced. This mask is the bitwise OR of the valid attribute mask bits listed in the Structures section below.

    attributes   Attributes of the window to be set at creation time should be set in this structure. The *valuemask* should have the appropriate bits set to indicate which attributes have been set in the structure.

Returns

The window.

Description

To create an unmapped subwindow for a specified parent window use XCreateWindow() or XCreateSimpleWindow(). XCreateWindow() is a more general function that allows you to set specific window attributes when you create the window. If you do not want to set specific attributes when you create a window, use XCreateSimpleWindow(), which creates a window that inherits its attributes from its parent. XCreateSimple-Window() creates only InputOutput windows that use the default depth and visual.

XCreateWindow() returns the ID of the created window. XCreateWindow() causes the X server to generate a CreateNotify event. The newly created window is placed on top of its siblings in the stacking order.

Extension packages may define other classes of windows.

The visual should be DefaultVisual() or one returned by XGetVisualInfo() or XMatchVisualInfo(). The depth should be DefaultDepth(), 1, or a depth returned by XListDepths(). In current implementations of Xlib, if you specify a visual other than the one used by the parent, you must first find (using XGetRGBColormaps()) or create a colormap matching this visual and then set the colormap window attribute in the *attributes* and *valuemask* arguments. Otherwise, you will get a BadMatch error.

The created window is not yet displayed (mapped) on the user's display. To display the window, call XMapWindow. The new window initially uses the same cursor as its parent. A new cursor can be defined for the new window by calling XDefineCursor(). The window will not be visible on the screen unless it and all of its ancestors are mapped and it is not obscured by any of its ancestors.

For more information, see Volume One, Chapter 4, *Window Attributes*.

Errors

`BadAlloc`

`BadColor`   Invalid colormap in attributes.

`BadCursor`

`BadMatch`   Any invalid setting of a window attribute.

Attribute besides `win_gravity`, `event_mask`, `do_not_propa-gate_mask`, `override_redirect`, or `cursor` specified for `Input-Only` window.

depth non-zero for `InputOnly`.

Parent of `InputOutput` is `InputOnly`.

border_width is non-zero for `InputOnly`, or depth or visual invalid for screen.

depth not supported on screen for `InputOutput`.

width or *height* is 0.

visual not supported on screen.

`BadPixmap`

`BadValue`

Structures

```
/*
 * Data structure for setting window attributes.
 */
typedef struct {
    Pixmap background_pixmap;       /* background or None or ParentRelative */
    unsigned long background_pixel; /* background pixel */
    Pixmap border_pixmap;           /* border of the window */
    unsigned long border_pixel;     /* border pixel value */
    int bit_gravity;                /* one of bit gravity values */
    int win_gravity;                /* one of the window gravity values */
    int backing_store;              /* NotUseful, WhenMapped, Always */
    unsigned long backing_planes;   /* planes to be preseved if possible */
    unsigned long backing_pixel;    /* value to use in restoring planes */
    Bool save_under;                /* should bits under be saved (popups) */
    long event_mask;                /* set of events that should be saved */
    long do_not_propagate_mask;     /* set of events that should not
                                           propagate */
    Bool override_redirect;         /* boolean value for override-redirect */
    Colormap colormap;              /* colormap to be associated with window */
    Cursor cursor;                  /* cursor to be displayed (or None) */
} XSetWindowAttributes;
```

```
/* Definitions for valuemask argument */

#define CWBackPixmap          (1L<<0)
#define CWBackPixel           (1L<<1)
#define CWBorderPixmap        (1L<<2)
#define CWBorderPixel         (1L<<3)
#define CWBitGravity          (1L<<4)
#define CWWinGravity          (1L<<5)
#define CWBackingStore        (1L<<6)
#define CWBackingPlanes       (1L<<7)
#define CWBackingPixel        (1L<<8)
#define CWOverrideRedirect    (1L<<9)
#define CWSaveUnder           (1L<<10)
#define CWEventMask           (1L<<11)
#define CWDontPropagate       (1L<<12)
#define CWColormap            (1L<<13)
#define CWCursor              (1L<<14)
```

Errors

```
BadWindow
```

See Also

XCreateSimpleWindow(), XDestroySubwindows(), XDestroyWindow(), XListDepths().

XDefault*

Name

XDefaultColormap, XDefaultColormapOfScreen, XDefaultDepth, XDefaultDepthOfScreen, XDefaultGC, XDefaultGCOfScreen, XDefaultRootWindow, XDefaultScreen, XDefaultScreenOfDisplay, XDefaultVisual, XDefaultVisualOfScreen, DefaultColormap, DefaultColormapOfScreen, DefaultDepth, DefaultDepth-OfScreen, DefaultGC, DefaultGCOfScreen, DefaultRootWindow, Default-Screen, DefaultScreenOfDisplay, DefaultVisual, DefaultVisualOfScreen – get information on server defaults.

Synopsis

```
Colormap XDefaultColormap(display, screen_number)
     Display *display;
     int screen_number;

Colormap XDefaultColormapOfScreen(screen)
     Screen *screen;

int XDefaultDepth(display, screen_number)
     Display *display;
     int screen_number;

int XDefaultDepthOfScreen(screen)
     Screen *screen;

GC XDefaultGC(display, screen_number)
     Display *display;
     int screen_number;

GC XDefaultGCOfScreen(screen)
     Screen *screen;

Window XDefaultRootWindow(display)
     Display *display;

int XDefaultScreen(display)
     Display *display;

Screen *XDefaultScreenOfDisplay(display)
     Display *display;

Visual *XDefaultVisual(display, screen_number)
     Display *display;
     int screen_number;

Visual *XDefaultVisualOfScreen(screen)
     Screen *screen;
```

Arguments

display   Specifies a connection to an X server; returned from XOpenDisplay().

screen_number
                    Specifies the appropriate screen number on the host server.

screen   Specifies the appropriate Screen structure.

Description

This page describes several pairs of functions such as such as XDefaultColormap*()
and XDefaultColormapOfScreen(). The only difference is the arguments: one takes
a Display pointer and integer screen number, while the other takes a Screen pointer.

XDefaultScreen*() returns the default screen number referenced by the XOpen-
Display() function. XDefaultScreenOfDisplay() return a pointer to the Screen
structure of the default screen.

XDefaultColormap() and XDefaultColormapOfScreen() return the default
colormap ID on the specified screen. Most routine allocations of color should be made out of
this colormap.

XDefaultDepth() and XDefaultDepthOfScreen() return the depth (number of
planes) of the root window of the specified screen. Other depths may also be supported on
this screen (see XMatchVisualInfo()).

XDefaultGC() and XDefaultGCOfScreen() return the default graphics context of
the specified screen, which has the same depth as the root window of the screen. The GC
must never be freed.

XDefaultRootWindow*() returns the root window of the default screen.

XDefaultVisual*() and XDefaultVisualOfScreen() return the default visual of
the specified screen.

The C language macros DefaultColormap(), DefaultColormapOfScreen(),
DefaultDepth(), DefaultDepthOfScreen(), DefaultGC(), Default-
GCOfScreen(), DefaultRootWindow*(), DefaultScreen(), Default-
ScreenOfDisplay(), DefaultVisual(), and DefaultVisualOfScreen() are
equivalent and slightly more efficient.

See Also

XOpenDisplay().

Name

XDefaultString – return the default string used for text conversion.

Synopsis

```
char *XDefaultString()
```

Returns

The string used for unconvertible characters.

Availability

Release 5 and later.

Description

XDefaultString() returns the default string used by Xlib for text conversion (for example, in XmbTextListToTextProperty()). The default string is the string in the current locale which is output when an unconvertible character is found during text conversion. If the string returned by XDefaultString() is the empty string (""), no character is output in the converted text. XDefaultString() does not return NULL.

The string returned by XDefaultString() is independent of the default string for text drawing; see XCreateFontSet() to obtain the default string for an XFontSet.

The returned string is NULL-terminated. It is owned by Xlib and should not be modified or freed by the client. It may be freed after the current locale is changed. Until freed, it will not be modified by Xlib.

See Also

XmbTextListToTextProperty(), XwcTextListToTextProperty(), XmbTextPropertyToTextList(), XwcTextPropertyToTextList(), XwcFreeStringList().

XDefineCursor

Name

XDefineCursor – assign a cursor to a window.

Synopsis

```
XDefineCursor(display, w, cursor)
    Display *display;
    Window w;
    Cursor cursor;
```

Arguments

display   Specifies a connection to an X server; returned from XOpenDisplay().

w   Specifies the ID of the window in which the cursor is to be displayed.

cursor   Specifies the cursor to be displayed when the pointer is in the specified window. Pass None to have the parent's cursor displayed in the window, or for the root window, to have the default cursor displayed.

Description

Sets the cursor attribute of a window, so that the specified cursor is shown whenever this window is visible and the pointer is inside. If XDefineCursor() is not called, the parent's cursor is used by default.

For more information on available cursors, see Appendix I, *The Cursor Font*.

Errors

BadCursor
BadWindow

See Also

XCreateFontCursor(), XCreateGlyphCursor(), XCreatePixmapCursor(), XFreeCursor(), XQueryBest-Cursor(), XQueryBestSize(), XRecolorCursor(), XUndefineCursor().

XDeleteAssoc

Name

XDeleteAssoc – delete an entry from an association table.

Synopsis

```
XDeleteAssoc(display, table, x_id)
    Display *display;
    XAssocTable *table;
    XID x_id;
```

Arguments

display   Specifies a connection to an X server; returned from `XOpenDisplay()`.

table   Specifies one of the association tables created by `XCreateAssocTable`.

x_id   Specifies the X resource ID of the association to be deleted.

Description

This function is provided for compatibility with X Version 10. To use it you must include the file *<X11/X10.h>* and link with the library *-loldX*.

`XDeleteAssoc()` deletes an association in an `XAssocTable` keyed on its `XID`. Redundant deletes (and deletes of nonexistent `XID`'s) are meaningless and cause no problems. Deleting associations in no way impairs the performance of an `XAssocTable`.

For more information on association tables, see Volume One, Appendix B, *X10 Compatibility*.

Structures

```
typedef struct {
    XAssoc *buckets;    /* pointer to first bucket in array */
    int size;           /* table size (number of buckets) */
} XAssocTable;
```

See Also

XCreateAssocTable(), XDestroyAssocTable(), XLookUpAssoc(), XMakeAssoc().

XDeleteContext

Name

XDeleteContext – delete a context entry for a given window and type.

Synopsis

```
int XDeleteContext(display, rid, context)
    Display *display;
    XID rid;
    XContext context;
```

Arguments

display   Specifies a connection to an X server; returned from XOpenDisplay().

rid   Specifies the resource ID with which the data is associated.

context   Specifies the context type to which the data belongs.

Returns

XCNOENT if the context could not be found, or zero if it succeeds.

Description

XDeleteContext() deletes the entry for the given resource ID and type from the context data structure defined in *<X11/Xutil.h>*. This function returns XCNOENT if the context could not be found, or zero if it succeeds. XDeleteContext() does not free the memory allocated for the data whose address was saved.

See Volume One, Chapter 13, *Other Programming Techniques*, for a description of context management.

Structures

```
typedef int XContext;
```

See Also

XFindContext(), XSaveContext(), XUniqueContext().

XDeleteModifiermapEntry

Name

XDeleteModifiermapEntry – delete an entry from an `XModifierKeymap` structure.

Synopsis

```
XModifierKeymap *XDeleteModifiermapEntry(modmap,
               keycode_entry, modifier)
    XModifierKeymap *modmap;
    KeyCode keycode_entry;
    int modifier;
```

Arguments

modmap   Specifies a pointer to an `XModifierKeymap()` structure.

keycode_entry
                    Specifies the keycode of the key to be deleted from *modmap*.

modifier   Specifies the modifier you no longer want mapped to the keycode specified
                    in *keycode_entry*. This should be one of the constants: `ShiftMap-
                    Index`, `LockMapIndex`, `ControlMapIndex`, `Mod1MapIndex`,
                    `Mod2MapIndex`, `Mod3MapIndex`, `Mod4MapIndex`, or `Mod5Map-
                    Index`.

Returns

The modified structure.

Description

XDeleteModifiermapEntry() returns an `XModifierKeymap()` structure suitable
for calling `XSetModifierMapping()`, in which the specified keycode is deleted from the
set of keycodes that is mapped to the specified modifier (like Shift or Control). `XDelete-
ModifiermapEntry()` itself does not change the mapping.

This function is normally used by calling `XGetModifierMapping()` to get a pointer to
the current `XModifierKeymap()` structure for use as the *modmap* argument to
`XDeleteModifiermapEntry()`.

For a description of the modifier map, see `XSetModifierMapping()`.

Structures

```
typedef struct {
    int max_keypermod;      /* server's max number of keys per modifier */
    KeyCode *modifiermap;   /* an 8 by max_keypermod array of
          * keycodes to be used as modifiers */
} XModifierKeymap;

#define ShiftMapIndex    0
```

```
#define LockMapIndex      1
#define ControlMapIndex   2
#define Mod1MapIndex      3
#define Mod2MapIndex      4
#define Mod3MapIndex      5
#define Mod4MapIndex      6
#define Mod5MapIndex      7
```

See Also

XFreeModifiermap(), XGetKeyboardMapping(), XGetModifierMapping(), XKeycodeToKeysym(), XKeysymToKeycode(), XKeysymToString(), XLookupKeysym(), XLookupString(), XNewModifiermap(), XQueryKeymap(), XRebindKeySym, XRefreshKeyboardMapping(), XSetModifierMapping(), XStringTo-Keysym(), XInsertModifiermapEntry.

XDeleteProperty

Name

XDeleteProperty – delete a window property.

Synopsis

```
XDeleteProperty(display, w, property)
    Display *display;
    Window w;
    Atom property;
```

Arguments

display   Specifies a connection to an X server; returned from XOpenDisplay().

w   Specifies the ID of the window whose property you want to delete.

property   Specifies the atom of the property to be deleted.

Description

XDeleteProperty() deletes a window property, so that it no longer contains any data. Its atom, specified by property, still exists after the call so that it can be used again later by any application to set the property once again. If the property was defined on the specified window, XDeleteProperty() generates a PropertyNotify event.

See the introduction to properties in Volume One, Chapter 2, *X Concepts*, or more detailed information in Volume One, Chapter 10, *Interclient Communication*.

Errors

```
BadAtom
BadWindow
```

See Also

XChangeProperty(), XGetAtomName(), XGetFontProperty(), XGetWindowProperty(), XInternAtom(), XListProperties(), XRotateWindowProperties(), XSetStandardProperties().

XDestroyAssocTable

Name

XDestroyAssocTable – free the memory allocated for an association table.

Synopsis

```
XDestroyAssocTable(table)
    XAssocTable *table;
```

Arguments

table   Specifies the association table whose memory is to be freed.

Description

This function is provided for compatibility with X Version 10. To use it you must include the file *<X11/X10.h>* and link with the library *-loldX*.

Using an `XAssocTable` after it has been destroyed will have unpredictable consequences.

For more information on association tables, see Volume One, Appendix B, *X10 Compatibility*.

Structures

```
typedef struct {
    XAssoc *buckets;      /* pointer to first bucket in array */
    int size;             /* table size (number of buckets) */
} XAssocTable;
```

See Also

XCreateAssocTable(), XDeleteAssoc(), XLookUpAssoc(), XMakeAssoc().

XDestroyIC

Name

XDestroyIC – destroy an input context.

Synopsis

```
void XDestroyIC(ic)
    XIC ic;
```

Arguments

ic   Specifies the input context.

Availability

Release 5 and later.

Description

XDestroyIC() destroys the specified input context. Once destroyed, the input context should no longer be used.

See Also

XSetICFocus(), XSetICValues(), XCreateIC(), XIMOfIC(), XmbResetIC(), XwcResetIC.

XDestroyImage

Name

XDestroyImage – deallocate memory associated with an image.

Synopsis

```
XDestroyImage(ximage)
     XImage *ximage;
```

Arguments

ximage   Specifies a pointer to the image.

Description

XDestroyImage() deallocates the memory associated with an XImage structure. This memory includes both the memory holding the XImage structure, and the memory holding the actual image data. (If the image data is statically allocated, the pointer to the data in the XImage structure must be set to zero before calling XDestroyImage().)

For more information on images, see Volume One, Chapter 6, *Drawing Graphics and Text*.

See Also

XImageByteOrder(), XAddPixel(), XCreateImage(), XGetImage(), XGetPixel(), XGetSubImage(), XPutImage(), XPutPixel(), XSubImage().

XDestroyRegion

Name

XDestroyRegion – deallocate memory associated with a region.

Synopsis

```
XDestroyRegion(r)
    Region r;
```

Arguments

r   Specifies the region to be destroyed.

Description

XDestroyRegion() frees the memory associated with a region and invalidates pointer r.

See Volume One, Chapter 6, *Drawing Graphics and Text*, for a description of regions.

See Also

XClipBox(), *XCreateRegion()*, *XEmptyRegion()*, *XEqualRegion()*, *XIntersectRegion()*, *XOffsetRegion()*, *XPointInRegion()*, *XPolygonRegion()*, *XRectInRegion()*, *XSetRegion()*, *XShrinkRegion()*, *XSubtractRegion()*, *XUnionRectWithRegion()*, *XUnionRegion()*, *XXorRegion()*.

XDestroySubwindows

Name

XDestroySubwindows – destroy all subwindows of a window.

Synopsis

```
XDestroySubwindows(display, w)
    Display *display;
    Window w;
```

Arguments

display   Specifies a connection to an X server; returned from `XOpenDisplay()`.

w   Specifies the ID of the window whose subwindows are to be destroyed.

Description

This function destroys all descendants of the specified window (recursively), in bottom to top stacking order.

`XDestroySubwindows()` generates exposure events on window w, if any mapped subwindows were actually destroyed. This is much more efficient than deleting many subwindows one at a time, since much of the work need only be performed once for all of the windows rather than for each window. It also saves multiple exposure events on the windows about to be destroyed. The subwindows should never again be referenced. The X server generates a `DestroyNotify` event for each window destroyed.

`XCloseDisplay()` automatically destroys all windows that have been created by that client on the specified display (unless called after a `fork` system call).

Never call `XDestroySubwindows()` with the window argument set to the root window! This will destroy all the applications on the screen, and if there is only one screen, often the server as well.

Errors

`BadWindow`

See Also

XCreateSimpleWindow(), *XCreateWindow()*, *XDestroyWindow()*.

XDestroyWindow

Name

XDestroyWindow – unmap and destroy a window and all subwindows.

Synopsis

```
XDestroyWindow(display, w)
    Display *display;
    Window w;
```

Arguments

display   Specifies a connection to an X server; returned from `XOpenDisplay()`.

w   Specifies the ID of the window to be destroyed.

Description

If *w* is mapped, an `UnmapWindow` request is performed automatically. The window and all inferiors (recursively) are then destroyed, and a `DestroyNotify` event is generated for each window. The ordering of the `DestroyNotify` events is such that for any given window, `DestroyNotify` is generated on all inferiors of the window before being generated on the window itself. The ordering among siblings and across subhierarchies is not otherwise constrained.

The windows should never again be referenced.

Destroying a mapped window will generate exposure events on other windows that were obscured by the windows being destroyed. `XDestroyWindow()` may also generate `EnterNotify` events if *w* was mapped and contained the pointer.

No windows are destroyed if you try to destroy the root window.

Errors

`BadWindow`

See Also

XCreateSimpleWindow(), *XCreateWindow()*, *XDestroySubwindows()*.

XDisableAccessControl

Name

XDisableAccessControl – allow access from any host.

Synopsis

```
XDisableAccessControl(display)
    Display *display;
```

Arguments

display   Specifies a connection to an X server; returned from `XOpenDisplay()`.

Description

`XDisableAccessControl()` instructs the server to allow access from clients on any host. This disables use of the host access list.

This routine can only be called from a client running on the same host as the server.

For more information on access control, see Volume One, Chapter 13, *Other Programming Techniques*.

Errors

`BadAccess`

See Also

XAddHost(), *XAddHosts()*, *XEnableAccessControl()*, *XListHosts()*, *XRemoveHost()*, *XRemoveHosts()*, *XSetAccessControl()*.

XDisplayCells

Name

XDisplayCells, DisplayCells – query number of cells in default colormap of screen.

Synopsis

```
int XDisplayCells(display, screen_number)
      Display *display;
      int screen_number;
```

Arguments

display   Specifies a connection to an X server; returned from `XOpenDisplay()`.

screen_number
                 Specifies the appropriate screen number on the host server.

Returns

The number of colorcells in a colormap.

Description

`XDisplayCells()` returns the number of entries in the default colormap of the specified screen.

The C language macro `DisplayCells()` is equivalent and slightly more efficient.

This function is misnamed; it should really be XScreenCells().

See Also

XDisplayPlanes(), XDefaultColormap().*

XDisplayHeight*

Name

XDisplayHeight, XDisplayHeightMM, DisplayHeight, DisplayHeightMM – query height of screen in pixels or millimeters.

Synopsis

```
int XDisplayHeight(display, screen_number)
    Display *display;
    int screen_number;

int XDisplayHeightMM(display, screen_number)
    Display *display;
    int screen_number;
```

Arguments

display   Specifies a connection to an X server; returned from `XOpenDisplay()`.

screen_number
   Specifies the appropriate screen number on the server.

Returns

The height in pixels or millimeters.

Description

`XDisplayHeight*()` returns an integer that describes the height of the screen in pixels. `XDisplayHeightMM()` returns the height of the specified screen in millimeters.

The C language macros `DisplayHeight()` and `DisplayHeightMM()` are equivalent and slightly more efficient.

These functions are misnamed; they should really be `XScreenHeight()` and `XScreenHeightMM()`.

See Also

XDisplayWidth(), *XDisplayWidthMM*(), *XGetWindowAttributes*(), *XGetGeometry*().

XDisplayKeycodes

Name

XDisplayKeycodes – obtain the range of legal keycodes for a server.

Synopsis

```
XDisplayKeycodes(display, min_keycodes_return, max_keycodes_return)
    Display *display;
    int *min_keycodes_return, *max_keycodes_return;
```

Arguments

display   Specifies a connection to an X server; returned from XOpen-Display().

min_keycodes_return
          Returns the minimum keycode.

max_keycodes_return
          Returns the maximum keycode.

Description

XDisplayKeycodes() returns the *min_keycodes_return* and *max_keycodes_return* supported by the specified server. The minimum keycode returned is never less than 8, and the maximum keycode returned is never greater than 255. Not all keycodes in this range are required to have corresponding keys.

For more information, see Volume One, Chapter 9, *The Keyboard and Pointer*.

See Also

XKeycodeToKeysym(), *XKeysymToKeycode()*, *XLookupString()*.

XDisplayMotionBufferSize

Name

XDisplayMotionBufferSize – get motion history buffer size.

Synopsis

```
unsigned long XDisplayMotionBufferSize(display)
      Display *display;
```

Arguments

display   Specifies a connection to an X server; returned from `XOpenDisplay()`.

Returns

The size in events of the buffer.

Description

`XDisplayMotionBufferSize()` queries the approximate maximum number of elements in the motion history buffer.

The X server may, but is not required to, retain the recent history of the pointer motion in a motion history buffer. If there is no motion history buffer, `XDisplayMotionBuffer-Size()` returns zero.

Motion history buffers were implemented for the first time in MIT's sample servers in Release 5, but some earlier releases of commercial servers may provide support.

An application gains access to the motion history buffer with `XGetMotionEvents()`. This buffer may contain a finer granularity of events than is reported by `MotionNotify` events.

There is no such macro as `DisplayMotionBufferSize()`.

See Also

XGetMotionEvents().

XDisplayName

Name

XDisplayName – report the display name (when connection to a display fails).

Synopsis

```
char *XDisplayName(string)
    char *string;
```

Arguments

string   Specifies the character string.

Returns

The display name string.

Description

XDisplayName() is normally used to report the name of the display the program attempted to open with XOpenDisplay(). This is necessary because X error handling begins only after the connection to the server succeeds.

If a NULL string is specified, XDisplayName() looks in the DISPLAY environment variable and returns the display name that the user was requesting. Otherwise, XDisplayName() returns its own argument.

For more information, see Volume One, Chapter 3, *Basic Window Program*.

See Also

XGetErrorDatabaseText(), XGetErrorText(), XSetAfterFunction(), XSetErrorHandler(), XSetIOError-Handler(), XSynchronize().

XDisplayOfIM

Name

XDisplayOfIM – get the display of an input method.

Synopsis

```
Display *XDisplayOfIM(im)
    XIM im;
```

Arguments

im   Specifies the input method.

Returns

The display structure.

Availability

Release 5 and later.

Description

XDisplayOfIM() returns the display associated with the specified input method.

See Also

XOpenIM(), XCloseIM(), XGetIMValues(), XLocaleOfIM().

XDisplayOfScreen

Name

XDisplayOfScreen, DisplayOfScreen – get Display structure of specified Screen structure.

Synopsis

```
Display *XDisplayOfScreen(screen)
      Screen *screen;
```

Arguments

screen   Specifies the appropriate Screen structure.

Returns

The display structure.

Description

XDisplayOfScreen() returns the display of the specified screen.

The C language macro DisplayOfScreen() is equivalent and slightly more efficient.

See Also

XScreenNumberOfScreen(), XScreenOfDisplay().

XDisplayPlanes

Name

XDisplayPlanes, DisplayPlanes – get number of planes of specified screen.

Synopsis

```
int XDisplayPlanes(display, screen_number)
    Display *display;
    int screen_number;
```

Arguments

display   Specifies a connection to an X server; returned from XOpenDisplay().

screen_number
               Specifies the appropriate screen number on the host server.

Returns

The number of planes.

Description

XDisplayPlanes() returns the depth (number of planes or number of bits per pixel) of the root window of the specified screen.

The C language macro DisplayPlanes() is equivalent and slightly more efficient.

This function is misnamed; it should really be XScreenPlanes().

See Also

XDefaultDepth(), XDefaultDepthOfScreen().*

XDisplayString

Name

XDisplayString, DisplayString – get string passed to `XOpenDisplay()`.

Synopsis

```
char *XDisplayString(display)
      Display *display;
```

Arguments

display   Specifies a connection to an X server; returned from `XOpenDisplay()`.

Returns

The display name string.

Description

`XDisplayString()` returns the string that was passed to `XOpenDisplay()` when the current display was opened. On POSIX-conformant systems, if the passed string was NULL, it returns the value of the DISPLAY environment variable when the current display was opened.

`XDisplayString()` is useful for printing error messages when `XOpenDisplay()` fails, and for applications that invoke the *fork* system call and want to open a new connection to the same display from the child process.

The C language macro `DisplayString()` is equivalent and slightly more efficient. `XDisplayName()` is also a similar function.

See Also

XOpenDisplay().

XDisplayWidth*

Name

XDisplayWidth, XDisplayWidthMM, DisplayWidth, DisplayWidthMM – query width of screen in pixels or millimeters.

Synopsis

```
int XDisplayWidth(display, screen_number)
    Display *display;
    int screen_number;

int XDisplayWidthMM(display, screen_number)
    Display *display;
    int screen_number;
```

Arguments

display   Specifies a connection to an X server; returned from `XOpenDisplay()`.

screen_number
                 Specifies the appropriate screen number on the server.

Returns

The width in pixels or millimeters.

Description

`XDisplayWidth*()` returns an integer that describes the width of the screen in pixels. `XDisplayWidthMM()` returns the width of the specified screen in millimeters.

The C language macros `DisplayWidth()` and `DisplayWidthMM()` are equivalent and slightly more efficient.

These functions are misnamed; they should really be `XScreenWidth()` and `XScreenWidthMM()`.

See Also

XDisplayHeight(), *XDisplayHeightMM*(), *XGetWindowAttributes*(), *XGetGeometry*().

XDoes*

Name

XDoesBackingStore, XDoesSaveUnders, DoesBackingStore, DoesSaveValues – query server support for backing store or save unders.

Synopsis

```
int XDoesBackingStore(screen)
    Screen *screen;

Bool XDoesSaveUnders(screen)
    Screen *screen;
```

Arguments

screen   Specifies the appropriate Screen structure.

Returns

XDoesSaveUnders() returns True or False. XDoesBackingStore() returns WhenMapped, NotUseful, or Always.

Description

XDoesSaveUnders() returns a boolean value indicating whether the screen supports save unders. If True, the screen supports save unders. If False, the screen does not support save unders.

XDoesBackingStore() returns a value indicating whether the screen supports backing stores. The value returned can be one of WhenMapped, NotUseful, or Always.

Save unders and backing stores are optional server features controlled with window attributes. These macros tell you whether the server supports them. A "save under" is an area beneath a window (usually a menu or dialog box) that the server saves, so that when the window is removed from the screen, the underlying applications do not need to redraw their windows. This speeds up user response with a slight cost in increased server memory consumption. A "backing store" is an off-screen copy of a window, maintained even when the window is not visible or not mapped. The server uses the copy to redraw the window whenever that window would otherwise have received an Expose event. This reduces the load on applications at the expense of a possibly great increase in server memory usage.

The C language macros DoesSaveUnders() and DoesBackingStore() are equivalent and slightly more efficient.

See Also

XChangeWindowAttributes(), *XGetWindowAttributes()*.

XDraw

Name

XDraw – draw a polyline or curve between vertex list (from X10).

Synopsis

```
Status XDraw(display, drawable, gc, vlist, vcount)
    Display *display;
    Drawable drawable;
    GC gc;
    Vertex *vlist;
    int vcount;
```

Arguments

display	Specifies a connection to an X server; returned from XOpenDisplay().
drawable	Specifies the drawable.
gc	Specifies the graphics context.
vlist	Specifies a pointer to the list of vertices that indicates what to draw.
vcount	Specifies how many vertices are in vlist.

Returns

Zero on failure, non-zero on success.

Description

This function is provided for compatibility with X Version 10. To use it you must include the file *<X11/X10.h>* and link with the library *-loldX*. Its performance is likely to be low.

XDraw draws an arbitrary polygon or curve. The figure drawn is defined by the specified list of vertices (*vlist*). The points are connected by lines as specified in the flags member of each of the Vertex structures.

The Vertex structure contains an x,y coordinate and a bitmask called flags that specifies the drawing parameters.

The x and y elements of Vertex are the coordinates of the vertex that are relative to either the previous vertex (if VertexRelative is 1) or the upper-left inside corner of the drawable (if VertexRelative is 0). If VertexRelative is 0 the coordinates are said to be absolute. The first vertex must be an absolute vertex.

If the VertexDontDraw bit is 1, no line or curve is drawn from the previous vertex to this one. This is analogous to picking up the pen and moving to another place before drawing another line.

If the VertexCurved bit is 1, a spline algorithm is used to draw a smooth curve from the previous vertex, through this one, to the next vertex. Otherwise, a straight line is drawn from the previous vertex to this one. It makes sense to set VertexCurved to 1 only if a previous and next vertex are both defined (either explicitly in the array, or through the definition of a closed curve—see below.)

It is permissible for `VertexDontDraw` bits and `VertexCurved` bits to both be 1. This is useful if you want to define the previous point for the smooth curve, but you do not want an actual curve drawing to start until this point.

If `VertexStartClosed` bit is 1, then this point marks the beginning of a closed curve. This vertex must be followed later in the array by another vertex whose absolute coordinates are identical and which has `VertexEndClosed` bit of 1. The points in between form a cycle for the purpose of determining predecessor and successor vertices for the spline algorithm.

XDraw achieves the effects of the X10 `XDraw`, `XDrawDashed`, and `XDrawPatterned` functions.

XDraw uses the following graphics context components: `function, plane_mask, line_width, line_style, cap_style, join_style, fill_style, subwindow_ mode, clip_x_origin, clip_y_origin,` and `clip_mask`. This function also uses these graphics context mode-dependent components: `foreground, background, tile, stipple, ts_x_origin, ts_y_origin, dash_offset,` and `dashes`.

A `Status` of zero is returned on failure, and non-zero on success.

For more information, see Volume One, Appendix B, *X10 Compatibility*.

Structures

```
typedef struct _Vertex {
    short x,y;
    unsigned short flags;
} Vertex;

/* defined constants for use as flags */

#define VertexRelative        0x0001     /* else absolute */
#define VertexDontDraw        0x0002     /* else draw */
#define VertexCurved          0x0004     /* else straight */
#define VertexStartClosed     0x0008     /* else not */
#define VertexEndClosed       0x0010     /* else not */
```

See Also

XClearArea(), XClearWindow(), XCopyArea(), XCopyPlane(), XDrawArc(), XDrawArcs(), XDraw-Filled(), XDrawLine(), XDrawLines(), XDrawPoint(), XDrawPoints(), XDrawRectangle(), XDraw-Rectangles(), XDrawSegments(), XFillArc(), XFillArcs(), XFillPolygon(), XFillRectangle(), XFill-Rectangles().

XDrawArc

Name

XDrawArc – draw an arc fitting inside a rectangle.

Synopsis

```
XDrawArc(display, drawable, gc, x, y, width, height,
              angle1, angle2)
    Display *display;
    Drawable drawable;
    GC gc;
    int x, y;
    unsigned int width, height;
    int angle1, angle2;
```

Arguments

display	Specifies a connection to an X server; returned from XOpenDisplay().
drawable	Specifies the drawable.
gc	Specifies the graphics context.
x y	Specify the x and y coordinates of the upper-left corner of the rectangle that contains the arc, relative to the origin of the specified drawable.
width height	Specify the width and height in pixels of the major and minor axes of the arc.
angle1	Specifies the start of the arc relative to the three-o'clock position from the center. Angles are specified in 64ths of a degree (360 * 64 is a complete circle).
angle2	Specifies the end of the arc relative to the start of the arc. Angles are specified in 64ths of a degree (360 * 64 is a complete circle).

Description

XDrawArc() draws a circular or elliptical arc. An arc is specified by a rectangle and two angles. The x and y coordinates are relative to the origin of the drawable, and define the upper-left corner of the rectangle. The center of the circle or ellipse is the center of the rectangle, and the major and minor axes are specified by the width and height, respectively. The angles are signed integers in 64ths of a degree, with positive values indicating counterclockwise motion and negative values indicating clockwise motion, truncated to a maximum of 360 degrees. The start of the arc is specified by angle1 relative to the three-o'clock position from the center, and the path and extent of the arc is specified by angle2 relative to the start of the arc.

By specifying one axis to be zero, a horizontal or vertical line is drawn (inefficiently).

Angles are computed based solely on the coordinate system and ignore the aspect ratio. In other words, if the bounding rectangle of the arc is not square and *angle1* is zero and *angle2* is (45x64), a point drawn from the center of the bounding box through the end-point of the arc will not pass through the corner of the rectangle.

For any given arc, no pixel is drawn more than once, even if *angle2* is greater than *angle1* by more than 360 degrees. See XDrawArcs() for a detailed description of the pixels drawn by XDrawArc().

XDrawArc() uses these graphics context components: function, plane_mask, line_width, line_style, cap_style, join_style, fill_style, subwindow_mode, clip_x_origin, clip_y_origin, and clip_mask. This function also uses these graphics context mode-dependent components: foreground, background, tile, stipple, ts_x_origin, ts_y_origin, dash_offset, and dashes.

For more information, see Volume One, Chapter 6, *Drawing Graphics and Text*.

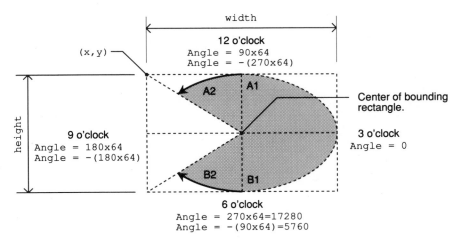

Example 1:
Arc from A1 to A2, Counterclockwise
A1 = 90 X 64
A2 = 45 X 64

Example 2:
Arc from B1 to B2, Clockwise
B1 = 270 X 64
B2 = -(45 X 64)

Errors

```
BadDrawable
BadGC
BadMatch
```

See Also

XClearArea(), XClearWindow(), XCopyArea(), XCopyPlane(), XDraw, XDrawArcs(), XDrawFilled(),
XDrawLine(), XDrawLines(), XDrawPoint(), XDrawPoints(), XDrawRectangle(), XDrawRectangles(),
XDrawSegments(), XFillArc(), XFillArcs(), XFillPolygon(), XFillRectangle(), XFillRectangles().

XDrawArcs

Name

XDrawArcs – draw multiple arcs.

Synopsis

```
XDrawArcs(display, drawable, gc, arcs, narcs)
    Display *display;
    Drawable drawable;
    GC gc;
    XArc *arcs;
    int narcs;
```

Arguments

display   Specifies a connection to an X server; returned from XOpenDisplay().

drawable   Specifies the drawable.

gc   Specifies the graphics context.

arcs   Specifies a pointer to an array of arcs.

narcs   Specifies the number of arcs in the array.

Description

This is the plural version of XDrawArc(). See XDrawArc() for details of drawing a single arc.

There is a limit to the number of arcs that can be drawn in a single call. It varies according to the server. To determine how many arcs you can draw in a single call, find out your server's maximum request size using XMaxRequestSize(). Subtract three and divide by three: this is the maximum number of arcs you can draw in a single XDrawArcs() call.

The arcs are drawn in the order listed in the arcs array.

By specifying one axis to be zero, a horizontal or vertical line can be drawn. Angles are computed based solely on the coordinate system, ignoring the aspect ratio.

For any given arc, no pixel is drawn more than once. If the last point in one arc coincides with the first point in the following arc, the two arcs will join correctly. If the first point in the first arc coincides with the last point in the last arc, the two arcs will join correctly. If two arcs join correctly and if line_width is greater than 0 and the arcs intersect, no pixel is drawn more than once. Otherwise, the intersecting pixels of intersecting arcs are drawn multiple times. Specifying an arc with one endpoint and a clockwise extent draws the same pixels as specifying the other endpoint and an equivalent counterclockwise extent, except as it affects joins.

XDrawArcs() uses these graphics context components: function, plane_mask, line_width, line_style, cap_style, join_style, fill_style, subwindow_ mode, clip_x_origin, clip_y_origin, and clip_mask. This function also uses these graphics context mode-dependent components: `foreground`, `background`, `tile`, `stipple`, `ts_x_origin`, `ts_y_origin`, `dash_offset`, and `dashes`.

The following is a technical explanation of the points drawn by `XDrawArcs()`. For an arc specified as [`x`, `y`, `width`, `height`, `angle1`, `angle2`], the origin of the major and minor axes is at [`x+(width/2)`, `y+(height/2)`], and the infinitely thin path describing the entire circle or ellipse intersects the horizontal axis at [`x`, `y+(height/2)`] and [`x+width`, `y+(height/2)`] and intersects the vertical axis at [`x+(width/2)`,`y`] and [`x+(width/2)`, `y+height`]. These coordinates can be fractional. That is, they are not truncated to discrete coordinates. The path should be defined by the ideal mathematical path. For a wide line with line width `line_width`, the bounding outlines for filling are given by the infinitely thin paths describing the arcs:

```
[x+dx/2, y+dy/2, width-dx, height-dy, angle1, angle2]
```

and

```
[x-line_width/2, y-line_width/2, width+line_width, height+line_width,
angle1, angle2]
```

where

```
dx=min(line_width,width)
dy=min(line_width,height)
```

If (`height != width`) the angles must be specified in the effectively skewed coordinate system of the ellipse (for a circle, the angles and coordinate systems are identical). The relationship between these angles and angles expressed in the normal coordinate system of the screen (as measured with a protractor) is as follows:

```
skewed-angle = atan(tan(normal-angle) * width/height) + adjust
```

The skewed-angle and normal-angle are expressed in radians (rather than in 64ths of a degree) in the range [`0,2*PI`], and where `atan` returns a value in the range [`-PI/2,PI/2`], and where `adjust` is:

```
0        for normal-angle in the range [0,PI/2]
PI       for normal-angle in the range [PI/2,(3*PI)/2]
2*PI     for normal-angle in the range [(3*PI)/2,2*PI]
```

For more information, see Volume One, Chapter 6, *Drawing Graphics and Text*.

Structures

```
typedef struct {
    short x, y;
    unsigned short width, height;
    short angle1, angle2;    /* Start and end of arc, in */
                             /* 64ths of degrees */
} XArc;
```

Errors

```
BadDrawable
BadGC
BadMatch
```

See Also

XClearArea(), XClearWindow(), XCopyArea(), XCopyPlane(), XDraw, XDrawArc(), XDrawFilled(),
XDrawLine(), XDrawLines(), XDrawPoint(), XDrawPoints(), XDrawRectangle(), XDrawRectangles(),
XDrawSegments(), XFillArc(), XFillArcs(), XFillPolygon(), XFillRectangle(), XFillRectangles().

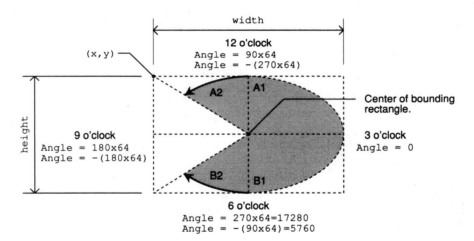

Example 1:
Arc from A1 to A2, Counterclockwise
A1 = 90 X 64
A2 = 45 X 64

Example 2:
Arc from B1 to B2, Clockwise
B1 = 270 X 64
B2 = −(45 X 64)

XDrawFilled

Name

XDrawFilled – draw a filled polygon or curve from vertex list (from X10).

Synopsis

```
Status XDrawFilled(display, drawable, gc, vlist, vcount)
    Display *display;
    Drawable drawable;
    GC gc;
    Vertex *vlist;
    int vcount;
```

Arguments

display   Specifies a connection to an X server; returned from XOpenDisplay().

drawable   Specifies the drawable.

gc   Specifies the graphics context.

vlist   Specifies a pointer to the list of vertices.

vcount   Specifies how many vertices are in vlist.

Returns

Zero on failure, non-zero on success.

Description

This function is provided for compatibility with X Version 10. To use it you must include the file *<X11/X10.h>* and link with the library *-loldX*. XDrawFilled() achieves the effects of the X Version 10 XDrawTiled and XDrawFilled() functions.

XDrawFilled() draws arbitrary polygons or curves, according to the same rules as XDraw, and then fills them.

XDrawFilled() uses the following graphics context components: function, plane_mask, line_width, line_style, cap_style, join_style, fill_style, subwindow_mode, clip_x_origin, clip_y_origin, and clip_mask. This function also uses these graphics context mode-dependent components: foreground, background, tile, stipple, ts_x_origin, ts_y_origin, dash_offset, dashes, fill_style and fill_rule.

XDrawFilled() returns a Status of zero on failure, and non-zero on success.

For more information, see Volume One, Appendix B, *X10 Compatibility*.

See Also

XClearArea(), XClearWindow(), XCopyArea(), XCopyPlane(), XDraw, XDrawArc(), XDrawArcs(), XDrawLine(), XDrawLines(), XDrawPoint(), XDrawPoints(), XDrawRectangle(), XDrawRectangles(), XDrawSegments(), XFillArc(), XFillArcs(), XFillPolygon(), XFillRectangle(), XFillRectangles().

XDrawImageString

Name

XDrawImageString – draw 8-bit image text characters.

Synopsis

```
XDrawImageString(display, drawable, gc, x, y, string, length)
    Display *display;
    Drawable drawable;
    GC gc;
    int x, y;
    char *string;
    int length;
```

Arguments

display	Specifies a connection to an X server; returned from XOpenDisplay().
drawable	Specifies the drawable.
gc	Specifies the graphics context.
x	Specify the x and y coordinates of the baseline starting position for the
y	image text character, relative to the origin of the specified drawable.
string	Specifies the character string.
length	Specifies the number of characters in the string argument.

Description

XDrawImageString draws a string, but unlike XDrawString() it draws both the foreground and the background of the characters. It draws the characters in the foreground and fills the bounding box with the background.

XDrawImageString() uses these graphics context components: plane_mask, foreground, background, font, subwindow_mode, clip_x_origin, clip_y_origin, and clip_mask. The function and fill_style defined in gc are ignored; the effective function is GXcopy and the effective fill_style is FillSolid.

XDrawImageString() first fills a destination rectangle with the background pixel defined in gc, and then paints the text with the foreground pixel. The upper-left corner of the filled rectangle is at [x, y - font_ascent], the width is overall->width and the height is ascent + descent, where overall->width, ascent, and descent are as would be returned by XQueryTextExtents() using gc and string.

For fonts defined with 2-byte matrix indexing and used with XDrawImageString(), each byte is used as a byte2 with a byte1 of zero. For more information, see Volume One, Chapter 6, *Drawing Graphics and Text*, and Chapter 5, *The Graphics Context*.

Errors

```
BadDrawable
BadGC
BadMatch
```

See Also

XDrawImageString16(), XDrawString(), XDrawString16(), XDrawText(), XDrawText16(), XQueryText-Extents(), XQueryTextExtents16(), XTextExtents(), XTextExtents16(), XTextWidth(), XTextWidth16().

XDrawImageString16

Name

XDrawImageString16 – draw 16-bit image text characters.

Synopsis

```
XDrawImageString16(display, drawable, gc, x, y, string, length)
 Display *display;
 Drawable drawable;
 GC gc;
 int x, y;
 XChar2b *string;
 int length;
```

Arguments

display   Specifies a connection to an X server; returned from XOpenDisplay().

drawable   Specifies the drawable.

gc   Specifies the graphics context.

x   Specify the x and y coordinates of the baseline starting position for the
y   image text character, relative to the origin of the specified drawable.

string   Specifies the character string.

length   Specifies the number of characters in the string argument.

Description

XDrawImageString16() draws a string, but unlike XDrawString16() it draws both
the foreground and the background of the characters. It draws the characters in the foreground and fills the bounding box with the background.

XDrawImageString16() uses these graphics context components: plane_mask,
foreground, background, font, subwindow_mode, clip_x_origin, clip_y_
origin, and clip_mask. The function and fill_style defined in gc are ignored;
the effective function is GXcopy and the effective fill_style is FillSolid.

XDrawImageString16() first fills a destination rectangle with the background pixel
defined in gc, and then paints the text with the foreground pixel. The upper-left corner of
the filled rectangle is at [x, y - font_ascent], the width is overall->width and
the height is ascent + descent, where overall->width, ascent, and descent
are as would be returned by XQueryTextExtents16() using gc and string.

For more information, see Volume One, Chapter 6, *Drawing Graphics and Text*, and Chapter
5, *The Graphics Context*.

Structures

```
typedef struct {
    unsigned char byte1;
    unsigned char byte2;
} XChar2b;
```

Errors

```
BadDrawable
BadGC
BadMatch
```

See Also

XDrawImageString(), XDrawString(), XDrawString16(), XDrawText(), XDrawText16(), XQueryText-Extents(), XQueryTextExtents16(), XTextExtents(), XTextExtents16(), XTextWidth(), XTextWidth16().

XDrawLine

Name

XDrawLine – draw a line between two points.

Synopsis

```
XDrawLine(display, drawable, gc, x1, y1, x2, y2)
    Display *display;
    Drawable drawable;
    GC gc;
    int x1, y1, x2, y2;
```

Arguments

display   Specifies a connection to an X server; returned from XOpenDisplay().

drawable   Specifies the drawable.

gc   Specifies the graphics context.

x1, y1,   Specify the coordinates of the endpoints of the line relative to the drawable
x2, y2   origin. XDrawLine() connects point (x1, y1) to point (x2, y2).

Description

XDrawLine() uses the components of the specified graphics context to draw a line between two points in the specified drawable. No pixel is drawn more than once.

XDrawLine() uses these graphics context components: function, plane_mask, line_width, line_style, cap_style, fill_style, subwindow_mode, clip_x_origin, clip_y_origin, and clip_mask. XDrawLine() also uses these graphics context mode-dependent components: foreground, background, tile, stipple, ts_x_origin, ts_y_origin, dash_offset, and dashes.

For more information, see Volume One, Chapter 6, *Drawing Graphics and Text*, and Chapter 5, *The Graphics Context*.

Errors

BadDrawable   Specified drawable is invalid.

BadGC   Specified GC is invalid, or does not match the depth of drawable.

BadMatch   Specified drawable is an InputOnly window.

See Also

XClearArea(), XClearWindow(), XCopyArea(), XCopyPlane(), XDraw, XDrawArc(), XDrawArcs(), XDrawFilled(), XDrawLines(), XDrawPoint(), XDrawPoints(), XDrawRectangle(), XDrawRectangles(), XDrawSegments(), XFillArc(), XFillArcs(), XFillPolygon(), XFillRectangle(), XFillRectangles().

XDrawLines

Name

XDrawLines – draw multiple connected lines.

Synopsis

```
XDrawLines(display, drawable, gc, points, npoints, mode)
    Display *display;
    Drawable drawable;
    GC gc;
    XPoint *points;
    int npoints;
    int mode;
```

Arguments

display   Specifies a connection to an X server; returned from XOpenDisplay().

drawable   Specifies the drawable.

gc   Specifies the graphics context.

points   Specifies a pointer to an array of points.

npoints   Specifies the number of points in the array.

mode   Specifies the coordinate mode. Pass either CoordModeOrigin or CoordModePrevious.

Description

XDrawLines() draws a series of lines joined end-to-end.

It draws lines connecting each point in the list (points array) to the next point in the list. The lines are drawn in the order listed in the points array. For any given line, no pixel is drawn more than once. If thin (zero line width) lines intersect, pixels will be drawn multiple times. If the first and last points coincide, the first and last lines will join correctly. If wide lines intersect, the intersecting pixels are drawn only once, as though the entire multiline request were a single filled shape.

There is a limit to the number of lines that can be drawn in a single call, which varies according to the server. To determine how many lines you can draw in a single call, find out your server's maximum request size using XMaxRequestSize(). Subtract three and divide by two, and this is the maximum number of lines you can draw in a single XDrawLines() call.

The mode argument may have two values:

• CoordModeOrigin indicates that all points are relative to the drawable's origin.

• CoordModePrevious indicates that all points after the first are relative to the previous point. (The first point is always relative to the drawable's origin.)

XDrawLines() uses the following components of the specified graphics context to draw multiple connected lines in the specified drawable: function, plane_mask, line_width, line_style, cap_style, join_style, fill_style, subwindow_mode, clip_x_origin, clip_y_ origin, and clip_mask. This function also uses these graphics context mode-dependent components: foreground, background, tile, stipple, ts_x_origin, ts_y_origin, dash_offset, and dashes.

For more information, see Volume One, Chapter 6, *Drawing Graphics and Text*, and Chapter 5, *The Graphics Context*.

Structures

```
typedef struct {
    short x, y;
} XPoint;
```

Errors

BadDrawable   Specified drawable is invalid.

BadGC   Specified GC is invalid, or does not match the depth of drawable.

BadMatch   Specified drawable is an InputOnly window.

BadValue   Invalid coordinate_mode.

See Also

XClearArea(), XClearWindow(), XCopyArea(), XCopyPlane(), XDraw, XDrawArc(), XDrawArcs(), XDrawFilled(), XDrawLine(), XDrawPoint(), XDrawPoints(), XDrawRectangle(), XDrawRectangles(), XDrawSegments(), XFillArc(), XFillArcs(), XFillPolygon(), XFillRectangle(), XFillRectangles().

XDrawPoint

Name

XDrawPoint – draw a point.

Synopsis

```
XDrawPoint(display, drawable, gc, x, y)
    Display *display;
    Drawable drawable;
    GC gc;
    int x, y;
```

Arguments

display   Specifies a connection to an X server; returned from XOpenDisplay().

drawable   Specifies the drawable.

gc   Specifies the graphics context.

x   Specify the x and y coordinates of the point, relative to the origin of the
y   drawable.

Description

XDrawPoint() draws a single point into the specified drawable. XDrawPoint() uses these graphics context components: function, plane_mask, foreground, subwindow_mode, clip_x_origin, clip_y_origin, and clip_mask. Use XDrawPoints() to draw multiple points.

For more information, see Volume One, Chapter 6, *Drawing Graphics and Text*, and Chapter 5, *The Graphics Context*.

Errors

```
BadDrawable
BadGC
BadMatch
```

See Also

XClearArea(), XClearWindow(), XCopyArea(), XCopyPlane(), XDraw, XDrawArc(), XDrawArcs(), XDrawFilled(), XDrawLine(), XDrawLines(), XDrawPoints(), XDrawRectangle(), XDrawRectangles(), XDrawSegments(), XFillArc(), XFillArcs(), XFillPolygon(), XFillRectangle(), XFillRectangles().

XDrawPoints

Name

XDrawPoints – draw multiple points.

Synopsis

```
XDrawPoints(display, drawable, gc, points, npoints, mode)
    Display *display;
    Drawable drawable;
    GC gc;
    XPoint *points;
    int npoints;
    int mode;
```

Arguments

display   Specifies a connection to an X server; returned from XOpenDisplay().

drawable   Specifies the drawable.

gc   Specifies the graphics context.

points   Specifies a pointer to an array of XPoint structures containing the positions of the points.

npoints   Specifies the number of points to be drawn.

mode   Specifies the coordinate mode. CoordModeOrigin treats all coordinates as relative to the origin, while CoordModePrevious treats all coordinates after the first as relative to the previous point, while the first is still relative to the origin.

Description

XDrawPoints() draws one or more points into the specified drawable. XDraw-Points() draws the points in the order listed in the array.

In R4 and earlier, because of the maximum request size, there is a limit to the number of points that can be drawn in a single XDrawPoints() call, that varies according to the server. In R5, Xlib breaks the call up into as many requests as required. To determine how many points you can draw in a single call in R4, you find out your server's maximum request size using XMaxRequestSize(). Subtract three and this is the maximum number of points you can draw in a single XDrawPoints() call.

XDrawPoints() uses these graphics context components: function, plane_mask, foreground, subwindow_mode, clip_x_origin, clip_y_origin, and clip_mask.

For more information, see Volume One, Chapter 6, *Drawing Graphics and Text*, and Chapter 5, *The Graphics Context*.

Structures

```
typedef struct {
    short x, y;
} XPoint;
```

Errors

```
BadDrawable
BadGC
BadMatch
BadValue
```

See Also

XClearArea(), *XClearWindow()*, *XCopyArea()*, *XCopyPlane()*, *XDraw*, *XDrawArc()*, *XDrawArcs()*, *XDrawFilled()*, *XDrawLine()*, *XDrawLines()*, *XDrawPoints()*, *XDrawRectangle()*, *XDrawRectangles()*, *XDrawSegments()*, *XFillArc()*, *XFillArcs()*, *XFillPolygon()*, *XFillRectangle()*, *XFillRectangles()*.

XDrawRectangle

Name

XDrawRectangle – draw an outline of a rectangle.

Synopsis

```
XDrawRectangle(display, drawable, gc, x, y, width, height)
    Display *display;
    Drawable drawable;
    GC gc;
    int x, y;
    unsigned int width, height;
```

Arguments

display   Specifies a connection to an X server; returned from XOpenDisplay().

drawable   Specifies the drawable.

gc   Specifies the graphics context.

x   Specify the x and y coordinates of the upper-left corner of the rectangle,
y   relative to the drawable's origin.

width   Specify the width and height in pixels. These dimensions define the outline
height   of the rectangle.

Description

XDrawRectangle() draws the outline of the rectangle by using the x and y coordinates, width and height, and graphics context you specify. Specifically, XDraw-Rectangle() uses these graphics context components: function, plane_mask, line_width, line_style, join_style, fill_style, subwindow_mode, clip_x_origin, clip_y_origin, and clip_mask. This function also uses these graphics context mode-dependent components: foreground, background, tile, stipple, ts_x_origin, ts_y_origin, dash_offset, and dashes.

For the specified rectangle, no pixel is drawn more than once.

For more information, see Volume One, Chapter 6, *Drawing Graphics and Text*, and Chapter 5, *The Graphics Context*.

Errors

BadDrawable
BadGC
BadMatch

See Also

XClearArea(), XClearWindow(), XCopyArea(), XCopyPlane(), XDraw, XDrawArc(), XDrawArcs(), XDrawFilled(), XDrawLine(), XDrawLines(), XDrawPoint(), XDrawPoints(), XDrawRectangles(), XDrawSegments(), XFillArc(), XFillArcs(), XFillPolygon(), XFillRectangle(), XFillRectangles().

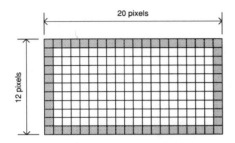

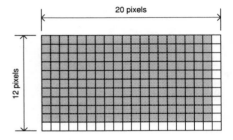

`XDrawRectangle (display, drawable, gc, 0, 0, 19, 11);`   `XFillRectangle (display, drawable, gc, 0, 0, 19, 11);`

XDrawRectangles

Name

XDrawRectangles – draw the outlines of multiple rectangles.

Synopsis

```
XDrawRectangles(display, drawable, gc, rectangles, nrectangles)
 Display *display;
 Drawable drawable;
 GC gc;
 XRectangle rectangles[];
 int nrectangles;
```

Arguments

display	Specifies a connection to an X server; returned from XOpenDisplay().
drawable	Specifies the drawable.
gc	Specifies the graphics context.
rectangles	Specifies a pointer to an array of rectangles containing position and size information.
nrectangles	Specifies the number of rectangles in the array.

Description

XDrawRectangles() draws the outlines of the specified rectangles by using the position and size values in the array of rectangles. The x and y coordinates of each rectangle are relative to the drawable's origin, and define the upper-left corner of the rectangle.

The rectangles are drawn in the order listed. For any given rectangle, no pixel is drawn more than once. If rectangles intersect, pixels are drawn multiple times.

In R4 and earlier there is a limit to the number of rectangles that can be drawn in a single XDrawRectangles() call, based on the maximum request size, which varies according to the server. In R5, Xlib chops your call into as many protocol requests as required. To determine how many rectangles you can draw in a single call in R4, find out your server's maximum request size using XMaxRequestSize(). Subtract three and divide by two. This is the maximum number of rectangles you can draw in a single XDrawRectangles() call.

This function uses these graphics context components: function, plane_mask, line_width, line_style, join_style, fill_style, subwindow_mode, clip_x_origin, clip_y_origin, and clip_mask. XDrawRectangles() also uses these graphics context mode-dependent components: foreground, background, tile, stipple, ts_x_origin, ts_y_origin, dash_offset, and dashes.

For more information, see Volume One, Chapter 6, *Drawing Graphics and Text*, and Chapter 5, *The Graphics Context*.

Structures

```
typedef struct {
    short x, y;
    unsigned short width, height;
} XRectangle;
```

Errors

```
BadDrawable
BadGC
BadMatch
```

See Also

XClearArea(), XClearWindow(), XCopyArea(), XCopyPlane(), XDraw, XDrawArc(), XDrawArcs(),
XDrawFilled(), XDrawLine(), XDrawLines(), XDrawPoint(), XDrawPoints(), XDrawRectangle(),
XDrawSegments(), XFillArc(), XFillArcs(), XFillPolygon(), XFillRectangle(), XFillRectangles().

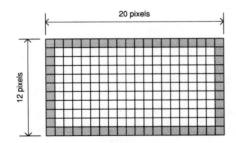

XDrawRectangle (display, drawable, gc, 0, 0, 19, 11);

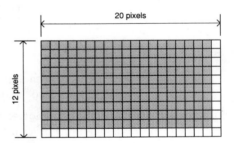

XFillRectangle (display, drawable, gc, 0, 0, 19, 11);

XDrawSegments

Name

XDrawSegments – draw multiple disjoint lines.

Synopsis

```
XDrawSegments(display, drawable, gc, segments, nsegments)
    Display *display;
    Drawable drawable;
    GC gc;
    XSegment *segments;
    int nsegments;
```

Arguments

display   Specifies a connection to an X server; returned from XOpenDisplay().

drawable   Specifies the drawable.

gc   Specifies the graphics context.

segments   Specifies a pointer to an array of line segments.

nsegments   Specifies the number of segments in the array.

Description

XDrawSegments() draws multiple line segments into the specified drawable. Each line is specified by a pair of points, so the line may be connected or disjoint.

For each segment, XDrawSegments() draws a line between $(x1, y1)$ and $(x2, y2)$. The lines are drawn in the order listed in *segments*. For any given line, no pixel is drawn more than once. If lines intersect, pixels will be drawn multiple times. The lines will be drawn separately, without regard to the join_style.

In R4 and earlier there is a limit to the number of rectangles that can be drawn in a single XDrawSegments() call, based on the maximum request size, which varies according to the server. In R5, Xlib chops your call into as many protocol requests as required. To determine how many rectangles you can draw in a single call in R4, find out your server's maximum request size using XMaxRequestSize(). Subtract three and divide by two. This is the maximum number of segments you can draw in a single XDrawSegments() call.

XDrawSegments() uses these graphics context components: function, plane_mask, line_width, line_style, cap_style, fill_style, subwindow_mode, clip_x_origin, clip_y_origin, and clip_mask. XDrawSegments() also uses these graphics context mode-dependent components: foreground, background, tile, stipple, ts_x_origin, ts_y_origin, dash_offset, and dashes.

For more information, see Volume One, Chapter 6, *Drawing Graphics and Text*, and Chapter 5, *The Graphics Context*.

Structures

```
typedef struct {
    short x1, y1, x2, y2;
} XSegment;
```

Errors

BadDrawable   Specified drawable is invalid.

BadGC   Specified GC is invalid, or does not match the depth of drawable.

BadMatch   Specified *drawable* is an InputOnly window.

See Also

XClearArea(), XClearWindow(), XCopyArea(), XCopyPlane(), XDraw, XDrawArc(), XDrawArcs(), XDrawFilled(), XDrawLine(), XDrawLines(), XDrawPoint(), XDrawPoints(), XDrawRectangle(), XDrawRectangles(), XFillArc(), XFillArcs(), XFillPolygon(), XFillRectangle(), XFillRectangles().

XDrawString

Name

XDrawString – draw an 8-bit text string, foreground only.

Synopsis

```
XDrawString(display, drawable, gc, x, y, string, length)
    Display *display;
    Drawable drawable;
    GC gc;
    int x, y;
    char *string;
    int length;
```

Arguments

display	Specifies a connection to an X server; returned from XOpenDisplay().
drawable	Specifies the drawable.
gc	Specifies the graphics context.
x	Specify the x and y coordinates of the baseline starting position for the
y	character, relative to the origin of the specified drawable.
string	Specifies the character string.
length	Specifies the number of characters in *string*.

Description

XDrawString() draws the given string into a drawable using the foreground only to draw set bits in the font. It does not affect any other pixels in the bounding box for each character.

The *y* coordinate defines the baseline row of pixels while the *x* coordinate is the point from which lbearing, rbearing, and width are measured.

XDrawString() uses these graphics context components: function, plane_mask, fill_style, font, subwindow_mode, clip_x_origin, clip_y_origin, and clip_mask. This function also uses these graphics context mode-dependent components: foreground, background, tile, stipple, ts_x_origin, and ts_y_origin. Each character image, as defined by the font in *gc*, is treated as an additional mask for a fill operation on the drawable.

For more information, see Volume One, Chapter 6, *Drawing Graphics and Text*, and Chapter 5, *The Graphics Context*.

Errors

```
BadDrawable
BadGC
BadMatch
```

See Also

XDrawImageString(), XDrawImageString16(), XDrawString16(), XDrawText(), XDrawText16(), XQueryTextExtents(), XQueryTextExtents16(), XTextExtents(), XTextExtents16(), XTextWidth(), XText-Width16().

XDrawString16

Name

XDrawString16 – draw two-byte text strings.

Synopsis

```
XDrawString16(display, drawable, gc, x, y, string, length)
    Display *display;
    Drawable drawable;
    GC gc;
    int x, y;
    XChar2b *string;
    int length;
```

Arguments

display   Specifies a connection to an X server; returned from XOpenDisplay().

drawable   Specifies the drawable.

gc   Specifies the graphics context.

x   Specify the x and y coordinates of the baseline starting position for the
y   character, relative to the origin of the specified drawable.

string   Specifies the character string. Characters are two bytes wide.

length   Specifies the number of characters in string.

Description

XDrawString16() draws a string in the foreground pixel value without drawing the surrounding pixels.

The y coordinate defines the baseline row of pixels while the x coordinate is the point from which lbearing, rbearing, and width are measured. For more information on text placement, see Volume One, Chapter 6, *Drawing Graphics and Text*.

XDrawString16() uses these graphics context components: function, plane_mask, fill_style, font, subwindow_mode, clip_x_origin, clip_y_origin, and clip_mask. This function also uses these graphics context mode-dependent components: foreground, background, tile, stipple, ts_x_origin, and ts_y_origin. Each character image, as defined by the font in gc, is treated as an additional mask for a fill operation on the drawable. For fonts defined with 2-byte matrix indexing and used with XDrawString16(), each byte is used as a byte2 with a byte1 of zero.

For more information, see Volume One, Chapter 6, *Drawing Graphics and Text*, and Chapter 5, *The Graphics Context*.

Structures

```
typedef struct {
    unsigned char byte1;
    unsigned char byte2;
} XChar2b;
```

Errors

BadDrawable BadFont
BadGC
BadMatch

See Also

XDrawImageString(), *XDrawImageString16()*, *XDrawString()*, *XDrawText()*, *XDrawText16()*, *XQuery-TextExtents()*, *XQueryTextExtents16()*, *XTextExtents()*, *XTextExtents16()*, *XTextWidth()*, *XTextWidth16()*.

XDrawText

Name

XDrawText – draw 8-bit polytext strings.

Synopsis

```
XDrawText(display, drawable, gc, x, y, items, nitems)
    Display *display;
    Drawable drawable;
    GC gc;
    int x, y;
    XTextItem *items;
    int nitems;
```

Arguments

display	Specifies a connection to an X server; returned from XOpenDisplay().
drawable	Specifies the drawable.
gc	Specifies the graphics context.
x	Specify the x and y coordinates of the baseline starting position for the ini-
y	tial string, relative to the origin of the specified drawable.
items	Specifies a pointer to an array of text items.
nitems	Specifies the number of text items in the items array.

Description

XDrawText() is capable of drawing multiple strings on the same horizontal line and changing fonts between strings. Each XTextItem structure contains a string, the number of characters in the string, the delta offset from the starting position for the string, and the font. Each text item is processed in turn. The font in each XTextItem is stored in the specified GC and used for subsequent text. If the XTextItem.font is None, the font in the GC is used for drawing and is not changed. Switching between fonts with different drawing directions is permitted.

The delta in each XTextItem specifies the change in horizontal position before the string is drawn. The delta is always added to the character origin and is not dependent on the draw direction of the font. For example, if x = 40, y = 20, and items[0].delta = 8, the string specified by items[0].chars would be drawn starting at x = 48, y = 20. The delta for the second string begins at the rbearing of the last character in the first string. A negative delta would tend to overlay subsequent strings on the end of the previous string.

Only the pixels selected in the font are drawn (the background member of the GC is not used to fill the bounding box).

In all X releases, there is a limit to the number and size of strings that can be drawn in a single `XDrawText()` call, that varies according to the server. To determine how much text you can draw in a single call, you find out your server's maximum request size using `XMaxRequestSize()`. Subtract four, and then subtract `((strlen(string) + 2) / 4)` for each string. This is the maximum amount of text you can draw in a single `XDrawText()` call.

`XDrawText()` uses the following elements in the specified GC: function, `plane_mask`, `fill_style`, font, `subwindow_mode`, `clip_x_origin`, `clip_y_origin`, and `clip_mask`. This function also uses these graphics context mode-dependent components: foreground, background, tile, stipple, `ts_x_origin`, and `ts_y_origin`.

For more information, see Volume One, Chapter 6, *Drawing Graphics and Text*, and Chapter 5, *The Graphics Context*.

Structures

```
typedef struct {
    char *chars;      /* pointer to string */
    int nchars;       /* number of characters */
    int delta;        /* delta between strings */
    Font font;        /* font to print it in, None don't change */
} XTextItem;
```

Errors

BadDrawable
BadFont
BadGC
BadMatch

See Also

XDrawImageString(), *XDrawImageString16()*, *XDrawString()*, *XDrawString16()*, *XDrawText16()*, *XQueryTextExtents()*, *XQueryTextExtents16()*, *XTextExtents()*, *XTextExtents16()*, *XTextWidth()*, *XTextWidth16()*.

XDrawText16

Name

XDrawText16 – draw 16-bit polytext strings.

Synopsis

```
XDrawText16(display, drawable, gc, x, y, items, nitems)
    Display *display;
    Drawable drawable;
    GC gc;
    int x, y;
    XTextItem16 *items;
    int nitems;
```

Arguments

display   Specifies a connection to an X server; returned from XOpenDisplay().

drawable   Specifies the drawable.

gc   Specifies the graphics context.

x   Specify the x and y coordinates of the baseline starting position for the ini-
y   tial string, relative to the origin of the specified drawable.

items   Specifies a pointer to an array of text items using two-byte characters.

nitems   Specifies the number of text items in the array.

Description

XDrawText16() is capable of drawing multiple strings on the same horizontal line and changing fonts between strings. Each XTextItem structure contains a string, the number of characters in the string, the delta offset from the starting position for the string, and the font. Each text item is processed in turn. The font in each XTextItem is stored in the specified GC and used for subsequent text. If the XTextItem16.font is None, the font in the GC is used for drawing and is not changed. Switching between fonts with different drawing directions is permitted.

The delta in each XTextItem specifies the change in horizontal position before the string is drawn. The delta is always added to the character origin and is not dependent on the draw-ing direction of the font. For example, if $x = 40, y = 20,$ and items[0].delta = 8, the string specified by items[0].chars would be drawn starting at $x = 48, y = 20.$ The delta for the second string begins at the rbearing of the last character in the first string. A negative delta would tend to overlay subsequent strings on the end of the previ-ous string.

Only the pixels selected in the font are drawn (the background member of the GC is not used to fill the bounding box).

310   Xlib Reference Manual

In all X releases there is a limit to the number and size of strings that can be drawn in a single XDrawText16() call, that varies according to the server. To determine how much text you can draw in a single call, you find out your server's maximum request size using XMax-RequestSize(). Subtract four, and then subtract ((strlen(string) + 2) / 4) for each string. This is the maximum amount of text you can draw in a single XDraw-Text16() call.

XDrawText16() uses the following elements in the specified GC: function, plane_mask, fill_style, font, subwindow_mode, clip_x_origin, clip_y_origin, and clip_mask. This function also uses these graphics context mode-dependent components: foreground, background, tile, stipple, ts_x_origin, and ts_y_origin.

Note that the chars member of the XTextItem16 structure is of type XChar2b, rather than of type char as it is in the XTextItem structure. For fonts defined with linear indexing rather than two-byte matrix indexing, the X server will interpret each member of the XChar2b structure as a 16-bit number that has been transmitted most significant byte first. In other words, the byte1 member of the XChar2b structure is taken as the most significant byte.

For more information, see Volume One, Chapter 6, *Drawing Graphics and Text*, and Chapter 5, *The Graphics Context*.

Structures

```
typedef struct {
    XChar2b *chars;      /* 2 byte characters */
    int nchars;          /* number of characters */
    int delta;           /* delta between strings */
    Font font;           /* font to print it in, None don't change */
} XTextItem16;

typedef struct {         /* normal 16 bit characters are two bytes */
    unsigned char byte1;
    unsigned char byte2;
} XChar2b;
```

Errors

BadDrawable
BadFont
BadGC
BadMatch

See Also

XDrawImageString(), XDrawImageString16(), XDrawString(), XDrawString16(), XDrawText(), XQueryTextExtents(), XQueryTextExtents16(), XTextExtents(), XTextExtents16(), XTextWidth(), XText-Width16().

XEmptyRegion

Name

XEmptyRegion – determine if a region is empty.

Synopsis

```
Bool XEmptyRegion(r)
    Region r;
```

Arguments

r   Specifies the region to be checked.

Returns

True if it's empty, else False.

Description

XEmptyRegion() will return True if the specified region is empty, or False otherwise.

Structures

Region is a pointer to an opaque structure type.

See Also

XClipBox(), *XCreateRegion()*, *XDestroyRegion()*, *XEqualRegion()*, *XIntersectRegion()*, *XOffset-Region()*, *XPointInRegion()*, *XPolygonRegion()*, *XRectInRegion()*, *XSetRegion()*, *XShrinkRegion()*, *XSubtractRegion()*, *XUnionRectWithRegion()*, *XUnionRegion()*, *XXorRegion()*.

XEnableAccessControl

Name

XEnableAccessControl – use access control list to allow or deny connection requests.

Synopsis

```
XEnableAccessControl(display)
    Display *display;
```

Arguments

display   Specifies a connection to an X server; returned from XOpenDisplay().

Description

XEnableAccessControl() instructs the server to use the host access list to determine whether access should be granted to clients seeking a connection with the server.

By default, the host access list is used. If access has not been disabled with XDisable-AccessControl() or XSetAccessControl(), this routine does nothing.

This routine can only be called by clients running on the same host as the server.

For more information, see Volume One, Chapter 13, *Other Programming Techniques*.

Errors

BadAccess

See Also

XAddHost(), XAddHosts(), XDisableAccessControl(), XListHosts(), XRemoveHost(), XRemoveHosts(), XSetAccessControl().

XEqualRegion

Name

XEqualRegion – determine if two regions have the same size, offset, and shape.

Synopsis

```
Bool XEqualRegion(r1, r2)
    Region r1, r2;
```

Arguments

r1
r2   Specify the two regions you want to compare.

Returns

True or False.

Description

XEqualRegion() returns True if the two regions are identical; i.e., they have the same offset, size and shape, or False otherwise.

Regions are located using an offset from a point (the *region origin*) which is common to all regions. It is up to the application to interpret the location of the region relative to a drawable.

For more information, see Volume One, Chapter 6, *Drawing Graphics and Text*.

Structures

Region is a pointer to an opaque structure type.

See Also

XClipBox(), XCreateRegion(), XDestroyRegion(), XEmptyRegion(), XIntersectRegion(), XOffsetRegion(), XPointInRegion(), XPolygonRegion(), XRectInRegion(), XSetRegion(), XShrinkRegion(), XSubtractRegion(), XUnionRectWithRegion(), XUnionRegion(), XXorRegion().

XEventMaskOfScreen

Name

XEventMaskOfScreen, EventMaskOfScreen – get initial root window event mask.

Synopsis

```
long XEventMaskOfScreen(screen)
    Screen *screen;
```

Arguments

screen   Specifies the appropriate Screen structure.

Returns

An event mask.

Description

XEventMaskOfScreen() returns the event mask at connection setup time of the root window for the specified screen.

The C language macro EventMaskOfScreen() is equivalent and slightly more efficient.

See Also

XSelectEvents().

Name

XEventsQueued – check the number of events in the event queue.

Synopsis

```
int XEventsQueued(display, mode)
    Display *display;
    int mode;
```

Arguments

display   Specifies a connection to a Display structure, returned from XOpen-
            Display().

mode   Specifies whether the request buffer is flushed if there are no events in
            Xlib's queue. You can specify one of these constants: QueuedAlready,
            QueuedAfterFlush, QueuedAfterReading.

Returns

The number of events.

Description

XEventsQueued() checks whether events are queued. If there are events in Xlib's queue,
the routine returns immediately to the calling routine. Its return value is the number of
events regardless of mode.

mode specifies what happens if no events are found on Xlib's queue.

- If mode is QueuedAlready, and there are no events in the queue, XEvents-
  Queued() returns zero (it does not flush the request buffer or attempt to read more
  events from the connection).

- If mode is QueuedAfterFlush, and there are no events in the queue, XEvents-
  Queued() flushes the request buffer, attempts to read more events out of the application's connection, and returns the number read.

- If mode is QueuedAfterReading, and there are no events in the queue, XEvents-
  Queued() attempts to read more events out of the application's connection without
  flushing the request buffer and returns the number read.

Note that XEventsQueued() always returns immediately without I/O if there are events
already in the queue.

XEventsQueued() with mode QueuedAfterFlush is identical in behavior to XPend-
ing(). XEventsQueued() with mode QueuedAlready is identical to the
QLength() macro (see Appendix C, Macros).

For more information, see Volume One, Chapter 8, Events.

See Also

XQLength(), XAllowEvents(), XCheckIfEvent(), XCheckMaskEvent(), XCheckTypedEvent(), XCheck-TypedWindowEvent(), XCheckWindowEvent(), XGetInputFocus(), XGetMotionEvents(), XIfEvent(), XMaskEvent(), XNextEvent(), XPeekEvent(), XPeekIfEvent(), XPending(), XPutBackEvent(), XSelect-Input(), XSendEvent(), XSetInputFocus(), XSynchronize(), XWindowEvent().

XExtentsOfFontSet

Name

XExtentsOfFontSet – obtain the maximum extents structure for a font set.

Synopsis

```
XFontSetExtents *XExtentsOfFontSet(font_set)
      XFontSet font_set;
```

Arguments

font_set   Specifies the font set.

Returns

A structure containing the extents.

Availability

Release 5 and later.

Description

XExtentsOfFontSet() returns an XFontSetExtents() structure for the given font set.

The XFontSetExtents() structure is owned by Xlib and should not be modified or freed by the client. It will be freed by a call to XFreeFontSet() with the associated XFontSet. Until freed, its contents will not be modified by Xlib.

Structures

The XFontSetExtents structure contains:

```
typedef struct {
    XRectangle max_ink_extent;     /*over all drawable characters*/
    XRectangle max_logical_extent; /*over all drawable characters*/
} XFontSetExtents;
```

The XRectangles used to return font set metrics are the usual Xlib screen-oriented XRectangles, with x, y giving the upper-left corner, and width and height always positive.

The max_ink_extent member gives the maximum extent, over all drawable characters, of the rectangles which bound the character glyph image drawn in the foreground color, relative to a constant origin. See XmbTextExtents and XwcTextExtents for detailed semantics.

The max_logical_extent member gives the maximum extent, over all drawable characters, of the rectangles which specify minimum spacing to other graphical features, relative to a constant origin. Other graphical features drawn by the client, for example, a border surrounding the text, should not intersect this rectangle. The max_logical_extent member should be used to compute minimum interline spacing and the minimum area which must be allowed in a text field to draw a given number of arbitrary characters.

Due to context-dependent rendering, appending a given character to a string may increase the string's extent by an amount which exceeds the font's max extent:

```
max possible added extent = (max_extent * <total # chars>)—prev_string_extent
```

See Also

XCreateFontSet(), *XFontsOfFontSet()*.

XFetchBuffer

Name

XFetchBuffer – return data from a cut buffer.

Synopsis

```
char *XFetchBuffer(display, nbytes_return, buffer)
    Display *display;
    int *nbytes_return;
    int buffer;
```

Arguments

display   Specifies a connection to an X server; returned from XOpenDisplay().

nbytes_return
      Returns the number of bytes in *buffer* returned by XFetchBuffer().
If there is no data in the buffer, *nbytes_return* is set to 0.

buffer   Specifies which buffer you want data from. Specify an integer from 0 to 7 inclusive.

Returns

The buffer data.

Description

XFetchBuffer() returns data from one of the eight buffers provided for interclient communication. If the buffer contains data, XFetchBuffer() returns the number of bytes in *nbytes_return*, otherwise it returns NULL and sets *nbytes_return* to 0. The appropriate amount of storage is allocated and the pointer returned; the client must free this storage when finished with it by calling XFree(). Note that the cut buffer does not necessarily contain text, so it may contain embedded null bytes and may not terminate with a null byte.

Selections are preferred over cut buffers as a communication scheme.

For more information on cut buffers, see Volume One, Chapter 13, *Other Programming Techniques*.

Errors

BadValue   *buffer* not an integer between 0 and 7 inclusive.

See Also

XFetchBytes(), XRotateBuffers(), XStoreBuffer(), XStoreBytes().

XFetchBytes

Name

XFetchBytes – return data from cut buffer 0.

Synopsis

```
char *XFetchBytes(display, nbytes_return)
    Display *display;
    int *nbytes_return;
```

Arguments

display   Specifies a connection to an X server; returned from XOpenDisplay().

nbytes_return
                Returns the number of bytes in the string returned by XFetchBytes().
                If there is no data in the buffer, *nbytes_return is set to 0.

Returns

The buffer data.

Description

XFetchBytes() returns data from cut buffer 0 of the eight buffers provided for interclient communication. If the buffer contains data, XFetchBytes() returns the number of bytes in nbytes_return, otherwise it returns NULL and sets *nbytes_return to 0. The appropriate amount of storage is allocated and the pointer returned; the client must free this storage when finished with it by calling XFree(). Note that the cut buffer does not necessarily contain text, so it may contain embedded null bytes and may not terminate with a null byte.

Use XFetchBuffer() to fetch data from any specified cut buffer.

Selections are preferred over cut buffers as a communication method.

For more information on cut buffers, see Volume One, Chapter 13, *Other Programming Techniques*.

See Also

XFetchBuffer(), XRotateBuffers(), XStoreBuffer(), XStoreBytes().

XFetchName

Name

XFetchName – get a window's name (XA_WM_NAME property).

Synopsis

```
Status XFetchName(display, w, window_name_return)
    Display *display;
    Window w;
    char **window_name_return;
```

Arguments

display   Specifies a connection to an X server; returned from XOpenDisplay().

w   Specifies the ID of the window whose name you want a pointer set to.

window_name_return
               Returns a pointer to the window name, which will be a NULL-terminated
               string. If the XA_WM_NAME property has not been set for this window,
               XFetchName() sets window_name_return to NULL. When finished
               with it, a client must free the name string using XFree().

Returns

Zero on failure, non-zero on success.

Description

XFetchName() is superseded by XGetWMName() in Release 4. XFetchName() returns
the current value of the XA_WM_NAME property for the specified window. XFetchName()
returns non-zero if it succeeds, and zero if the property has not been set for the argument
window.

If the data returned by the server is in the Latin Portable Character Encoding, then the
returned string is in the Host Portable Character Encoding. Otherwise, the result is implementation-dependent.

For more information, see Volume One, Chapter 10, *Interclient Communication*, and Chapter
14, *Window Management*.

Errors

BadWindow

See Also

XGetClassHint(), XGetIconName(), XGetIconSizes(), XGetNormalHints(), XGetSizeHints(), XGet-TransientForHint(), XGetWMHints(), XGetZoomHints(), XSetClassHint(), XSetCommand(), XSetIcon-Name(), XSetIconSizes(), XSetNormalHints(), XSetSizeHints(), XSetTransientForHint(), XSetWMHints(), XSetZoomHints(), XStoreName().

XFillArc

Name

XFillArc – fill an arc.

Synopsis

```
XFillArc(display, drawable, gc,  x, y, width, height, angle1, angle2)
    Display *display;
    Drawable drawable;
    GC gc;
    int x, y;
    unsigned int width, height;
    int angle1, angle2;
```

Arguments

display	Specifies a connection to an X server; returned from XOpenDisplay().
drawable	Specifies the drawable.
gc	Specifies the graphics context.
x y	Specify the x and y coordinates of the upper-left corner of the bounding box containing the arc, relative to the origin of the drawable.
width height	Specify the width and height in pixels. These are the major and minor axes of the arc.
angle1	Specifies the start of the arc relative to the three-o'clock position from the center. Angles are specified in 64ths of degrees.
angle2	Specifies the path and extent of the arc relative to the start of the arc. Angles are specified in 64ths of degrees.

Description

XFillArc() draws a filled arc. The x, y, width, and height arguments specify the bounding box for the arc. See XDrawArc() for the description of how this bounding box is used to compute the arc. Some, but not all, of the pixels drawn with XDrawArc() will be drawn by XFillArc() with the same arguments. See XFillRectangle() for an example of the differences in pixels drawn by the draw and fill routines.

The arc forms one boundary of the area to be filled. The other boundary is determined by the arc_mode in the GC. If the arc_mode in the GC is ArcChord, the single line segment joining the endpoints of the arc is used. If ArcPieSlice, the two line segments joining the endpoints of the arc with the center point are used.

XFillArc() uses these graphics context components: function, plane_mask, fill_style, arc_mode, subwindow_mode, clip_x_origin, clip_y_origin, and `clip_mask`. This function also uses these graphics context mode-dependent components: `foreground`, `background`, `tile`, `stipple`, `ts_x_origin`, and `ts_y_origin`.

For more information, see Volume One, Chapter 6, *Drawing Graphics and Text*, and Chapter 5, *The Graphics Context*.

Errors

```
BadDrawable
BadGC
BadMatch
```

See Also

XClearArea(), XClearWindow(), XCopyArea(), XCopyPlane(), XDraw, XDrawArc(), XDrawArcs(), XDrawFilled(), XDrawLine(), XDrawLines(), XDrawPoint(), XDrawPoints(), XDrawRectangle(), XDrawRectangles(), XDrawSegments(), XFillArcs(), XFillPolygon(), XFillRectangle(), XFillRectangles().

XFillArcs

Name

XFillArcs – fill multiple arcs.

Synopsis

```
XFillArcs(display, drawable, gc, arcs, narcs)
    Display *display;
    Drawable drawable;
    GC gc;
    XArc *arcs;
    int narcs;
```

Arguments

display   Specifies a connection to an X server; returned from XOpenDisplay().

drawable   Specifies the drawable.

gc   Specifies the graphics context.

arcs   Specifies a pointer to an array of arc definitions.

narcs   Specifies the number of arcs in the array.

Description

For each arc, XFillArcs() fills the region closed by the specified arc and one or two line segments, depending on the arc_mode specified in the GC. It does not draw the complete outlines of the arcs, but some pixels may overlap.

The arc forms one boundary of the area to be filled. The other boundary is determined by the arc_mode in the GC. If the arc_mode in the GC is ArcChord, the single line segment joining the endpoints of the arc is used. If ArcPieSlice, the two line segments joining the endpoints of the arc with the center point are used. The arcs are filled in the order listed in the array. For any given arc, no pixel is drawn more than once. If filled arcs intersect, pixels will be drawn multiple times.

In R4 and earlier there is a limit to the number of rectangles that can be drawn in a single call, based on the maximum request size, which varies according to the server. In R5, Xlib chops your call into as many protocol requests as required. To determine how many rectangles you can draw in a single call in R4, you find out your server's maximum request size using XMaxRequestSize(). Subtract three and divide by three, and this is the maximum number of arcs you can fill in a single XFillArcs() call.

XFillArcs() use these graphics context components: function, plane_mask, fill_style, arc_mode, subwindow_mode, clip_x_origin, clip_y_origin, and clip_mask. This function also uses these graphics context mode-dependent components: foreground, background, tile, stipple, ts_x_origin, and ts_y_ origin.

For more information, see Volume One, Chapter 6, *Drawing Graphics and Text*, and Chapter 5, *The Graphics Context*.

Structures

```
typedef struct {
    short x, y;
    unsigned short width, height;
    short angle1, angle2;           /*  64ths of Degrees */
} XArc;
```

Errors

```
BadDrawable
BadGC
BadMatch
```

See Also

XClearArea(), XClearWindow(), XCopyArea(), XCopyPlane(), XDraw, XDrawArc(), XDrawArcs(), XDrawFilled(), XDrawLine(), XDrawLines(), XDrawPoint(), XDrawPoints(), XDrawRectangle(), XDrawRectangles(), XDrawSegments(), XFillArc(), XFillPolygon(), XFillRectangle(), XFillRectangles().

XFillPolygon

Name

XFillPolygon – fill a polygon.

Synopsis

```
XFillPolygon(display, drawable, gc, points, npoints, shape, mode)
    Display *display;
    Drawable drawable;
    GC gc;
    XPoint *points;
    int npoints;
    int shape;
    int mode;
```

Arguments

display	Specifies a connection to an X server; returned from `XOpenDisplay()`.
drawable	Specifies the drawable.
gc	Specifies the graphics context.
points	Specifies a pointer to an array of points.
npoints	Specifies the number of points in the array.
shape	Specifies an argument that helps the server to improve performance. Pass the last constant in this list that is valid for the polygon to be filled: `Complex`, `Nonconvex`, or `Convex`.
mode	Specifies the coordinate mode. Pass either `CoordModeOrigin` or `CoordModePrevious`.

Description

`XFillPolygon()` fills the region closed by the specified path. Some but not all of the path itself will be drawn. The path is closed automatically if the last point in the list does not coincide with the first point. No pixel of the region is drawn more than once.

The *mode* argument affects the interpretation of the points that define the polygon:

- `CoordModeOrigin` indicates that all points are relative to the drawable's origin.
- `CoordModePrevious` indicates that all points after the first are relative to the previous point. (The first point is always relative to the drawable's origin.)

The *shape* argument allows the fill routine to optimize its performance given tips on the configuration of the area.

- `Complex` indicates the path may self-intersect. The `fill_rule` of the GC must be consulted to determine which areas are filled. See Volume One, Chapter 5, *The Graphics Context*, for a discussion of the fill rules `EvenOddRule` and `WindingRule`.

- Nonconvex indicates the path does not self-intersect, but the shape is not wholly convex. If known by the client, specifying Nonconvex instead of Complex may improve performance. If you specify Nonconvex for a self-intersecting path, the graphics results are undefined.

- Convex means that for every pair of points inside the polygon, the line segment connecting them does not intersect the path. Convex can improve performance even more than Nonconvex, but if the path is not convex, the graphics results are undefined.

Contiguous coincident points in the path are not treated as self-intersection.

XFillPolygon() uses these graphics context components when filling the polygon area: function, plane_mask, fill_style, fill_rule, subwindow_mode, clip_x_origin, clip_y_origin, and clip_mask. This function also uses these mode-dependent components of the GC: foreground, background, tile, stipple, ts_x_origin, and ts_y_origin.

For more information, see Volume One, Chapter 6, *Drawing Graphics and Text*, and Chapter 5, *The Graphics Context*.

Structures

```
typedef struct {
    short x, y;
} XPoint;
```

Errors

```
BadDrawable
BadGC
BadMatch
BadValue
```

See Also

XClearArea(), XClearWindow(), XCopyArea(), XCopyPlane(), XDraw, XDrawArc(), XDrawArcs(), XDrawFilled(), XDrawLine(), XDrawLines(), XDrawPoint(), XDrawPoints(), XDrawRectangle(), XDrawRectangles(), XDrawSegments(), XFillArc(), XFillArcs(), XFillRectangle(), XFillRectangles().

XFillRectangle

Name

XFillRectangle – fill a rectangular area.

Synopsis

```
XFillRectangle(display, drawable, gc, x, y, width, height)
    Display *display;
    Drawable drawable;
    GC gc;
    int x, y;
    unsigned int width, height;
```

Arguments

display   Specifies a connection to an X server; returned from XOpenDisplay().

drawable   Specifies the drawable.

gc   Specifies the graphics context.

x
y   Specify the x and y coordinates of the upper-left corner of the rectangle, relative to the origin of the drawable.

width
height   Specify the dimensions in pixels of the rectangle to be filled.

Description

XFillRectangle() fills the rectangular area in the specified drawable using the x and y coordinates, width and height dimensions, and graphics context you specify. XFill-Rectangle() draws some but not all of the path drawn by XDrawRectangle() with the same arguments.

XFillRectangle() uses these graphics context components: function, plane_mask, fill_style, subwindow_mode, clip_x_origin, clip_y_origin, and clip_ mask. This function also uses these graphics context components depending on the fill_style: foreground, background tile, stipple, ts_x_origin, and ts_y_origin.

For more information, see Volume One, Chapter 6, *Drawing Graphics and Text*, and Chapter 5, *The Graphics Context*.

Errors

BadDrawable
BadGC
BadMatch

See Also

XClearArea(), XClearWindow(), XCopyArea(), XCopyPlane(), XDraw, XDrawArc(), XDrawArcs(), XDrawFilled(), XDrawLine(), XDrawLines(), XDrawPoint(), XDrawPoints(), XDrawRectangle(), XDrawRectangles(), XDrawSegments(), XFillArc(), XFillArcs(), XFillPolygon(), XFillRectangles().

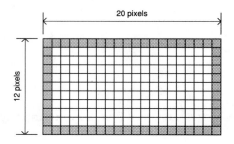

XDrawRectangle (display, drawable, gc, 0, 0, 19, 11);

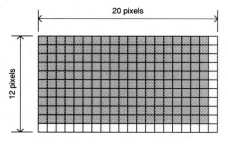

XFillRectangle (display, drawable, gc, 0, 0, 19, 11);

XFillRectangles

Name

XFillRectangles – fill multiple rectangular areas.

Synopsis

```
XFillRectangles(display, drawable, gc, rectangles, nrectangles)
 Display *display;
 Drawable drawable;
 GC gc;
 XRectangle *rectangles;
 int nrectangles;
```

Arguments

display   Specifies a connection to an X server; returned from XOpenDisplay().

drawable   Specifies the drawable.

gc   Specifies the graphics context.

rectangles   Specifies a pointer to an array of rectangles.

nrectangles   Specifies the number of rectangles in the array.

Description

XFillRectangles() fills multiple rectangular areas in the specified drawable using the graphics context.

The x and y coordinates of each rectangle are relative to the drawable's origin, and define the upper left corner of the rectangle. The rectangles are drawn in the order listed. For any given rectangle, no pixel is drawn more than once. If rectangles intersect, the intersecting pixels will be drawn multiple times.

In R4 and earlier there is a limit to the number of rectangles that can be drawn in a single call, based on the maximum request size, which varies according to the server. In R5, Xlib chops your call into as many protocol requests as required. To determine how many rectangles you can draw in a single call in R4, find out your server's maximum request size using XMaxRequestSize(). Subtract three and divide by two, and this is the maximum number of rectangles you can fill in a single XDrawRectangles() call.

XFillRectangles() uses these graphics context components: function, plane_mask, fill_style, subwindow_mode, clip_x_origin, clip_y_ origin, and clip_ mask. This function also uses these graphics context components depending on the fill_ style: foreground, background, tile, stipple, ts_x_origin, and ts_y_ origin.

For more information, see Volume One, Chapter 6, *Drawing Graphics and Text*, and Chapter 5, *The Graphics Context*.

Structures

```
typedef struct {
    short x, y;
    unsigned short width, height;
} XRectangle;
```

Errors

```
BadDrawable
BadGC
BadMatch
```

See Also

XClearArea(), XClearWindow(), XCopyArea(), XCopyPlane(), XDraw, XDrawArc(), XDrawArcs(), XDrawFilled(), XDrawLine(), XDrawLines(), XDrawPoint(), XDrawPoints(), XDrawRectangle(), XDrawRectangles(), XDrawSegments(), XFillArc(), XFillArcs(), XFillPolygon(), XFillRectangle(), XFillRectangles().

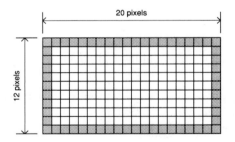

XDrawRectangle (display, drawable, gc, 0, 0, 19, 11);

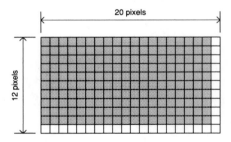

XFillRectangle (display, drawable, gc, 0, 0, 19, 11);

XFilterEvent

Name

XFilterEvent – filter X events for an input method.

Synopsis

```
Bool XFilterEvent(event, w)
    XEvent *event;
    Window w;
```

Arguments

event   Specifies the event to filter.

w   Specifies the window for which the filter is to be applied.

Returns

`True` if the event was filtered, else `False`.

Availability

Release 5 and later.

Description

`XFilterEvent()` passes the specified event to any event filters registered for the specified window. This allows input methods to intercept and respond to events that they are interested in. Internationalized clients should call `XFilterEvent()` from their event loops, generally directly after calling `XNextEvent()`. If `XFilterEvent()` returns `True`, then some input method has filtered the event, and the client should not dispatch it any further. If `XFilterEvent()` returns `False`, the client should continue processing it.

If the window argument is `None`, `XFilterEvent()` applies the filter to the window specified in the `XEvent` structure. The window argument is provided so that layers above Xlib that do event redirection can indicate to which window an event has been redirected.

If a grab has occurred in the client, and `XFilterEvent()` returns `True`, the client should ungrab the keyboard.

Input methods register event filters using a non-public mechanism internal to Xlib.

See Also

XNextEvent().

XFindContext

Name

XFindContext – get data from the context manager (not graphics context).

Synopsis

```
int XFindContext(display, rid, context, data_return)
    Display *display;
    XID rid;
    XContext context;
    XPointer *data_return;
```

Arguments

display   Specifies a connection to an X server; returned from XOpenDisplay().

rid   Specifies the resource ID with which the data is associated.

context   Specifies the context type to which the data corresponds.

data_return   Returns the data.

Returns

XCNOENT (a non-zero error code) if the context could not be found, or zero on success.

Description

XFindContext() gets data that has been assigned to the specified resource ID. The context manager is used to associate data with windows for use within an application.

This application should have called XUniqueContext() to get a unique ID, and then XSaveContext() to save the data into the array. The meaning of the data is indicated by the context ID, but is completely up to the client.

XFindContext() returns XCNOENT (a non-zero error code) if the context could not be found and zero (0) otherwise.

For more information on the context manager, see Volume One, Chapter 13, *Other Programming Techniques*.

Structures

```
typedef int XContext;
```

See Also

XDeleteContext(), XSaveContext(), XUniqueContext().

XFlush

Name

XFlush – send all queued requests to the server.

Synopsis

```
XFlush(display)
    Display *display;
```

Arguments

display   Specifies a connection to an X server; returned from XOpenDisplay().

Description

XFlush() sends to the server ("flushes") all requests that have been buffered but not yet sent.

Flushing is done automatically when input is read if no matching events are in Xlib's queue (with XPending(), XNextEvent(), or XWindowEvent(), etc.), or when a call is made that gets information from the server (such as XQueryPointer(), XGetFontInfo) so XFlush() is seldom needed. It is used when the buffer must be flushed before any of these calls are reached.

For more information, see Volume One, Chapter 2, *X Concepts*, and Chapter 3, *Basic Window Program*.

See Also

XSync().

XFlushGC

Name

XFlushGC – force cached GC changes to the server.

Synopsis

```
void XFlushGC(display, gc)
    Display *display;
    GC gc;
```

Arguments

display   Specifies the connection to the X server.

gc   Specifies the graphics context.

Availability

Release 5 and later.

Description

Xlib normally defers sending changes to the components of a GC to the server until a graphics function is actually called with that GC. This permits batching of component changes into a single server request. In some circumstances, however, it may be necessary for the client to explicitly force sending of the changes to the server. An example might be when a protocol extension uses the GC indirectly, in such a way that the extension interface cannot know what GC will be used. In a case like this, the extension library could use XFlush-GC ( ) to force any cached changes to the GC it will use to be flushed to the server.

See Also

XChangeGC(), XSetForeground().

XFontSetExtents

Name

XFontSetExtents – XFontSetExtents structure.

Structures

The XFontSetExtents structure contains:

```
typedef struct {
    XRectangle max_ink_extent;      /*over all drawable characters*/
    XRectangle max_logical_extent;  /*over all drawable characters*/
} XFontSetExtents;
```

The XRectangles used to return font set metrics are the usual Xlib screen-oriented XRectangles, with x, y giving the upper-left corner, and width and height always positive.

The max_ink_extent member gives the maximum extent, over all drawable characters, of the rectangles which bound the character glyph image drawn in the foreground color, relative to a constant origin. See XmbTextExtents and XwcTextExtents for detailed semantics.

The max_logical_extent member gives the maximum extent, over all drawable characters, of the rectangles which specify minimum spacing to other graphical features, relative to a constant origin. Other graphical features drawn by the client, for example, a border surrounding the text, should not intersect this rectangle. The max_logical_extent member should be used to compute minimum interline spacing and the minimum area which must be allowed in a text field to draw a given number of arbitrary characters.

Due to context-dependent rendering, appending a given character to a string may increase the string's extent by an amount which exceeds the font's max extent:

```
max possible added extent = (max_extent * <total # chars>)—prev_string_extent
```

See Also

XCreateFontSet(), *XExtentsOfFontSet()*, *XFontsOfFontSet()*.

Name

XFontsOfFontSet – get the list of fonts used by a font set.

Synopsis

```
int XFontsOfFontSet(font_set, font_struct_list_return,
        font_name_list_return)
    XFontSet font_set;
    XFontStruct ***font_struct_list_return;
    char ***font_name_list_return;
```

Arguments

font_set   Specifies the font set.

font_struct_list_return
> Returns the list of font structs.

font_name_list_return
> Returns the list of font names.

Returns

The number of fonts in the list (which is also the number of elements in the lists of structures).

Availability

Release 5 and later.

Description

XFontsOfFontSet() returns a list of one or more **XFontStructs** and font names for the fonts used by the given font set. A list of pointers to the **XFontStruct** structures is returned to *font_struct_list_return*. A list of pointers to NULL-terminated, fully specified, font name strings in the locale of the font set is returned to *font_name_list_return*. The number of elements in each array is returned as the value of the function. The arrays are in the same order, and their elements correspond to one another.

Because it is not guaranteed that a given character will be imaged using a single font glyph, there is no provision for mapping a character or default string to the font properties, font ID, or direction hint for the font for the character. The client may access the **XFontStruct** list to obtain these values for all the fonts currently in use.

It is not required that fonts be loaded from the server at the creation of an **XFontSet**. Xlib may choose to cache font data, loading it only as needed to draw text or compute text dimensions. Therefore, existence of the per-char metrics in the **XFontStruct** structures in the

XFontStructSet is undefined. Also, note that all properties in the XFontStruct structures are in the STRING encoding.

The XFontStruct and font name lists are owned by Xlib and should not be modified or freed by the client. They will be freed by a call to XFreeFontSet() on the associated XFontSet. Until freed, their contents will not be modified by Xlib.

See Also

XCreateFontSet(), XExtentsOfFontSet(), XBaseFontNameListOfFontSet(), XLocaleOfFontSet().

XForceScreenSaver

Name

XForceScreenSaver – turn the screen saver on or off.

Synopsis

```
XForceScreenSaver(display, mode)
    Display *display;
    int mode;
```

Arguments

display   Specifies a connection to an X server; returned from `XOpenDisplay()`.

mode   Specifies whether the screen saver is active or reset. The possible modes are: `ScreenSaverActive` or `ScreenSaverReset`.

Description

`XForceScreenSaver()` resets or activates the screen saver.

If the specified mode is `ScreenSaverActive` and the screen saver currently is disabled, the screen saver is activated, even if the screen saver had been disabled by calling `XSet-ScreenSaver()` with a timeout of zero (0). This means that the screen may go blank or have some random change take place to save the phosphors.

If the specified mode is `ScreenSaverReset` and the screen saver currently is enabled, the screen is returned to normal, the screen saver is deactivated and the activation timer is reset to its initial state (as if device input had been received). `Expose` events may be generated on all visible windows if the server cannot save the entire screen contents.

For more information on the screen saver, see Volume One, Chapter 13, *Other Programming Techniques*.

Errors

BadValue

See Also

XActivateScreenSaver(), XGetScreenSaver(), XResetScreenSaver(), XSetScreenSaver().

XFree

Name

XFree – free specified memory allocated by an Xlib function.

Synopsis

```
XFree(data)
    void *data;
```

Arguments

data   Specifies a pointer to the data that is to be freed.

Description

XFree() is a general purpose routine for freeing memory allocated by Xlib calls. You must use it to free any objects that were allocated by Xlib, unless an alternate function is explicitly specified for the object.

See Also

XDefaultScreen(), XCloseDisplay(), XNoOp(), XOpenDisplay().

XFreeColormap

Name

XFreeColormap – delete a colormap and install the default colormap.

Synopsis

```
XFreeColormap(display, colormap)
    Display *display;
    Colormap colormap;
```

Arguments

display   Specifies a connection to an X server; returned from XOpenDisplay().

colormap   Specifies the colormap to delete.

Description

XFreeColormap() destroys the specified colormap, unless it is the default colormap for a screen. That is, it not only uninstalls colormap from the hardware colormap if it is installed, but also frees the associated memory including the colormap ID.

XFreeColormap() performs the following processing:

* If colormap is an installed map for a screen, it uninstalls the colormap (see XUninstallColormap()).

* If colormap is defined as the colormap attribute for a window (by XCreate-Window() or XChangeWindowAttributes()), it changes the colormap attribute for the window to the constant None, generates a ColormapNotify event, and frees the colormap. The colors displayed with a colormap of None are server-dependent, since the default colormap is normally used.

For more information, see Volume One, Chapter 7, *Color*.

Errors

BadColor   Invalid colormap.

See Also

XDefaultColormap(), XDisplayCells(), XCopyColormapAndFree(), XCreateColormap(), XGetStandard-Colormap(), XInstallColormap(), XListInstalledColormaps(), XSetStandardColormap(), XSetWindow-Colormap(), XUninstallColormap().

XFreeColors

Name

XFreeColors – free colormap cells or planes.

Synopsis

```
XFreeColors(display, colormap, pixels, npixels, planes)
    Display *display;
    Colormap colormap;
    unsigned long pixels[];
    int npixels;
    unsigned long planes;
```

Arguments

display   Specifies a connection to an X server; returned from `XOpenDisplay()`.

colormap   Specifies the colormap.

pixels   Specifies an array of pixel values.

npixels   Specifies the number of pixels.

planes   Specifies the planes you want to free.

Description

`XFreeColors()` frees the cells whose values are computed by ORing together subsets of the planes argument with each pixel value in the pixels array.

If the cells are read/write, they become available for reuse, unless they were allocated with `XAllocColorPlanes()`, in which case all the related pixels may need to be freed before any become available.

If the cells were read-only, they become available only if this is the last client to have allocated those shared cells.

For more information, see Volume One, Chapter 7, *Color*.

Errors

BadAccess   Attempt to free a colorcell not allocated by this client (either unallocated or allocated by another client).

BadColor   colormap is invalid.

BadValue   A pixel value is not a valid index into colormap.

Note: if more than one pixel value is in error, the one reported is arbitrary.

See Also

XBlackPixel(), *XWhitePixel()*, *XAllocColor()*, *XAllocColorCells()*, *XAllocColorPlanes()*, *XAllocNamed-Color()*, *XLookupColor()*, *XParseColor()*, *XQueryColor()*, *XQueryColors()*, *XStoreColor()*, *XStore-Colors()*, *XStoreNamedColor()*.

XFreeCursor

Name

XFreeCursor – release a cursor.

Synopsis

```
XFreeCursor(display, cursor)
    Display *display;
    Cursor cursor;
```

Arguments

display   Specifies a connection to an X server; returned from XOpenDisplay().

cursor   Specifies the ID of the cursor to be affected.

Description

XFreeCursor() deletes the association between the cursor ID and the specified cursor. The cursor storage is freed when all other clients have freed it. Windows with their cursor attribute set to this cursor will have this attribute set to None (which implies CopyFrom-Parent). The specified cursor ID should not be referred to again.

Errors

BadCursor

See Also

XCreateFontCursor(), XCreateGlyphCursor(), XCreatePixmapCursor(), XDefineCursor(), XQueryBestCursor(), XQueryBestSize(), XRecolorCursor(), XUndefineCursor().

XFreeExtensionList

Name

XFreeExtensionList – free memory allocated for a list of installed extensions.

Synopsis

```
XFreeExtensionList(list)
    char **list;
```

Arguments

list   Specifies a pointer to the list of extensions returned from XList-
                Extensions().

Description

XFreeExtensionList() frees the memory allocated by XListExtensions().

For more information, see Volume One, Chapter 13, *Other Programming Techniques*.

See Also

XListExtensions(), *XQueryExtension()*.

XFreeFont

Name

XFreeFont – unload a font and free storage for the font structure.

Synopsis

```
XFreeFont(display, font_struct)
    Display *display;
    XFontStruct *font_struct;
```

Arguments

display   Specifies a connection to an X server; returned from XOpenDisplay().

font_struct   Specifies the storage associated with the font.

Description

XFreeFont() frees the memory allocated for the *font_struct* font information structure (XFontStruct) filled by XQueryFont() or XLoadQueryFont(). XFreeFont() frees all storage associated with the *font_struct* argument. Neither the data nor the font should be referenced again.

The server unloads and frees the font itself if no other client has loaded it.

For more information, see Volume One, Chapter 6, *Drawing Graphics and Text*.

Structures

```
typedef struct {
    XExtData *ext_data;             /* hook for extension to hang data */
    Font fid;                       /* Font ID for this font */
    unsigned direction;             /* hint about direction the font is painted */
    unsigned min_char_or_byte2;     /* first character */
    unsigned max_char_or_byte2;     /* last character */
    unsigned min_byte1;             /* first row that exists */
    unsigned max_byte1;             /* last row that exists */
    Bool all_chars_exist;           /* flag if all characters have non-zero size*/
    unsigned default_char;          /* char to print for undefined character */
    int n_properties;               /* how many properties there are */
    XFontProp *properties;          /* pointer to array of additional properties*/
    XCharStruct min_bounds;         /* minimum bounds over all existing char*/
    XCharStruct max_bounds;         /* minimum bounds over all existing char*/
    XCharStruct *per_char;          /* first_char to last_char information */
    int ascent;                     /* logical extent above baseline for spacing */
    int descent;                    /* logical descent below baseline for spacing */
} XFontStruct;
```

Errors

    BadFont

See Also

XCreateFontCursor(), *XFreeFontInfo()*, *XFreeFontNames()*, *XFreeFontPath()*, *XGetFontPath()*, *XGet-FontProperty()*, *XListFonts()*, *XListFontsWithInfo()*, *XLoadFont()*, *XLoadQueryFont()*, *XQueryFont()*, *XSetFont()*, *XSetFontPath()*, *XUnloadFont()*.

Name

XFreeFontInfo – free the memory allocated by `XListFontsWithInfo`.

Synopsis

```
XFreeFontInfo(names, info, actual_count)
    char **names;
    XFontStruct *info;
    int actual_count;
```

Arguments

names
Specifies a pointer to the list of font names that were returned by `XList-FontsWithInfo()`.

info
Specifies a pointer to the list of font information that was returned by `XListFontsWithInfo()`.

actual_count
Specifies the number of matched font names returned by `XListFonts-WithInfo()`.

Description

`XFreeFontInfo()` frees the list of font information structures allocated by `XList-FontsWithInfo()`. It does not unload the specified fonts themselves. To free an `XFontStruct` structure without closing the font, call `XFreeFontInfo()` with the names argument specified as NULL.

Structures

```
typedef struct {
    XExtData *ext_data;            /* hook for extension to hang data */
    Font fid;                      /* Font ID for this font */
    unsigned direction;            /* hint about direction the font is painted */
    unsigned min_char_or_byte2;    /* first character */
    unsigned max_char_or_byte2;    /* last character */
    unsigned min_byte1;            /* first row that exists */
    unsigned max_byte1;            /* last row that exists */
    Bool all_chars_exist;          /* flag if all characters have non-zero size */
    unsigned default_char;         /* char to print for undefined character */
    int n_properties;              /* how many properties there are */
    XFontProp *properties;         /* pointer to array of additional properties */
    XCharStruct min_bounds;        /* minimum bounds over all existing char */
    XCharStruct max_bounds;        /* minimum bounds over all existing char */
    XCharStruct *per_char;         /* first_char to last_char information */
```

```
    int ascent;      /* logical extent above baseline for spacing */
    int descent;     /* logical descent below baseline for spacing */
} XFontStruct;
```

See Also

XCreateFontCursor(), XFreeFont(), XFreeFontNames(), XGetFontPath(), XGetFontProperty(), XList-Fonts(), XListFontsWithInfo(), XLoadFont(), XLoadQueryFont(), XQueryFont(), XSetFont(), XSetFont-Path(), XUnloadFont().

XFreeFontNames

Name

XFreeFontNames – free the memory allocated for a font name array.

Synopsis

```
XFreeFontNames(list)
    char *list[];
```

Arguments

list   Specifies the array of font name strings to be freed.

Description

XFreeFontNames() frees the array of strings returned by XListFonts() or XList-FontsWithInfo().

See Also

XCreateFontCursor(), *XFreeFont()*, *XFreeFontInfo()*, *XFreeFontPath()*, *XGetFontPath()*, *XGetFont-Property()*, *XListFonts()*, *XListFontsWithInfo()*, *XLoadFont()*, *XLoadQueryFont()*, *XQueryFont()*, *XSet-Font()*, *XSetFontPath()*, *XUnloadFont()*.

XFreeFontPath

Name

XFreeFontPath – free the memory allocated by XGetFontPath.

Synopsis

```
XFreeFontPath(list)
    char **list;
```

Arguments

list   Specifies an array of strings allocated by XGetFontPath().

Description

XFreeFontPath() frees the array of pathnames returned by XGetFontPath().

For more information, see Volume One, Chapter 6, *Drawing Graphics and Text*.

See Also

XCreateFontCursor(), XFreeFont(), XFreeFontInfo(), XFreeFontNames(), XGetFontPath(), XGetFont-Property(), XListFonts(), XListFontsWithInfo(), XLoadFont(), XLoadQueryFont(), XQueryFont(), XSet-Font(), XSetFontPath(), XUnloadFont().

XFreeFontSet

Name

XFreeFontSet – free a font set.

Synopsis

```
void XFreeFontSet(display, font_set)
    Display *display;
    XFontSet font_set;
```

Arguments

display   Specifies the connection to the X server.

font_set   Specifies the font set.

Availability

Release 5 and later.

Description

XFreeFontSet() frees the specified font set. The associated base font name list, font name list, XFontStruct list, and XFontSetExtents(), if any, are freed.

See Also

XExtentsofFontSet, *XFontsOfFontSet()*, *XCreateFontSet()*.

XFreeGC

Name

XFreeGC – free a graphics context.

Synopsis

```
XFreeGC(display, gc)
    Display *display;
    GC gc;
```

Arguments

display   Specifies a connection to an X server; returned from XOpenDisplay().

gc   Specifies the graphics context to be freed.

Description

XFreeGC() frees all memory associated with a graphics context, and removes the GC from the server and display hardware.

For more information, see Volume One, Chapter 5, *The Graphics Context*.

Errors

BadGC

See Also

XDefaultGC(), XChangeGC(), XCopyGC(), XCreateGC(), XGContextFromGC(), XSetArcMode(), XSet-Background(), XSetClipMask(), XSetClipOrigin(), XSetClipRectangles(), XSetDashes(), XSetFillRule(), XSetFillStyle(), XSetForeground(), XSetFunction(), XSetGraphicsExposures(), XSetLineAttributes(), XSetPlaneMask(), XSetState(), XSetStipple(), XSetSubwindowMode(), XSetTSOrigin().

XFreeModifiermap

Name

XFreeModifiermap – destroy and free a keyboard modifier mapping structure.

Synopsis

```
XFreeModifiermap(modmap)
    XModifierKeymap *modmap;
```

Arguments

modmap   Specifies a pointer to the `XModifierKeymap()` structure to be freed.

Description

`XFreeModifiermap()` frees an `XModifierKeymap()` structure originally allocated by `XNewModifierMap` or `XGetModifierMapping()`.

For more information, see Volume One, Chapter 9, *The Keyboard and Pointer*.

Structures

```
typedef struct {
    int max_keypermod;      /* server's max number of keys per modifier */
    KeyCode *modifiermap;   /* an 8 by max_keypermod array of
                             * keycodes to be used as modifiers */
} XModifierKeymap;
```

See Also

XChangeKeyboardMapping(), XDeleteModifiermapEntry(), XGetKeyboardMapping(), XGetModifier-Mapping(), XInsertModifiermapEntry(), XKeycodeToKeysym(), XKeysymToKeycode(), XKeysymTo-String(), XLookupKeysym(), XLookupString(), XNewModifierMap, XQueryKeymap(), XRebindKeySym, XRefreshKeyboardMapping(), XSetModifierMapping(), XStringToKeysym().

XFreePixmap

Name

XFreePixmap – free a pixmap ID.

Synopsis

```
XFreePixmap(display, pixmap)
    Display *display;
    Pixmap pixmap;
```

Arguments

display   Specifies a connection to an X server; returned from XOpenDisplay().

pixmap   Specifies the pixmap whose ID should be freed.

Description

XFreePixmap() disassociates a pixmap ID from its resource. If no other client has an ID for that resource, it is freed by the server. The Pixmap should never be referenced again by this client. If it is, the ID will be unknown and a BadPixmap error will result.

Errors

BadPixmap

See Also

XCreateBitmapFromData(), XCreatePixmap(), XCreatePixmapFromBitmapData(), XQueryBestSize(), XQueryBestStipple(), XQueryBestTile(), XReadBitmapFile(), XSetTile(), XSetWindowBackground-Pixmap(), XSetWindowBorderPixmap(), XWriteBitmapFile().

XFreeStringList

Name

XFreeStringList – free the in-memory data associated with the specified string list.

Synopsis

```
void XFreeStringList(list)
    char **list;
```

Arguments

list   Specifies the list of strings to be freed.

Availability

Release 4 and later.

Description

XFreeStringList() releases memory allocated by **XTextPropertyToString-List()**, **XmbTextPropertyToTextList()**, and the missing charset allocated by **XCreateFontSet()**.

See Also

XGetTextProperty(), *XSetTextProperty()*, *XStringListToTextProperty()*, *XTextPropertytoStringList*.

XGContextFromGC

Name

XGContextFromGC – obtain the GContext (resource ID) associated with the specified graphics context.

Synopsis

```
GContext XGContextFromGC (gc)
    GC gc;
```

Arguments

gc   Specifies the graphics context of the desired resource ID.

Returns

The GContext.

Description

XGContextFromGC() extracts the resource ID from the GC structure. The GC structure is Xlib's local cache of GC values and contains a field for the GContext ID. This function is essentially a macro that accesses this field, since the GC structure is intended to be opaque.

A GContext is needed to set a field of the XVisualInfo structure prior to calling XGet-VisualInfo().

See Also

XDefaultGC(), XChangeGC(), XCopyGC(), XCreateGC(), XFreeGC(), XSetArcMode(), XSet-Background(), XSetClipMask(), XSetClipOrigin(), XSetClipRectangles(), XSetDashes(), XSetFillRule(), XSetFillStyle(), XSetForeground(), XSetFunction(), XSetGraphicsExposures(), XSetLineAttributes(), XSetPlaneMask(), XSetState(), XSetStipple(), XSetSubwindowMode(), XSetTSOrigin().

XGeometry

Name

XGeometry – calculate window geometry given user geometry string and default geometry.

Synopsis

```
int XGeometry(display, screen, position, default_position, bwidth,
              fwidth, fheight, xadder, yadder, x_return, y_return,
          height_return, width_return, height_return)
    Display *display;
    int screen;
    char *position, *default_position;
    unsigned int bwidth;
    unsigned int fwidth, fheight;
    int xadder, yadder;
    int *x_return, *y_return, *width_return, *height_return;
```

Arguments

display	Specifies a connection to an X server; returned from XOpen-Display().
screen	Specifies which screen the window is on.
position	Specifies the user- or program-supplied geometry string, perhaps incomplete.
default_position	Specifies the default geometry string and must be complete.
bwidth	Specifies the border width.
fheight fwidth	Specify the font height and width in pixels (increment size).
xadder yadder	Specify additional interior padding in pixels needed in the window.
x_return y_return	Return the user-specified or default coordinates of the window.
width_return height_return	Return the window dimensions in pixels.

Returns

A bitmask composed of the symbols XValue, YValue, WidthValue, HeightValue, XNegative, and/or YNegative.

Description

XGeometry has been superseded by XWMGeometry as of Release 4.

XGeometry returns the position and size of a window given a user-supplied geometry (allowed to be partial) and a default geometry. Each user-supplied specification is copied into the appropriate returned argument, unless it is not present, in which case the default specification is used. The default geometry should be complete while the user-supplied one may not be.

XGeometry is useful for processing command-line options and user preferences. These geometry strings are of the form:

```
=<width>x<height>{+-}<xoffset>{+-}<yoffset>
```

The "=" at the beginning of the string is now optional. (Items enclosed in <> are integers, and items enclosed in {} are a set from which one item is to be chosen. Note that the brackets should not appear in the actual string.)

The XGeometry return value is a bitmask that indicates which values were present in *user_position*. This bitmask is composed of the exclusive OR of the symbols XValue, YValue, WidthValue, HeightValue, XNegative, or YNegative.

If the function returns either XValue or YValue, you should place the window at the requested position. The border width (*bwidth*), size of the width and height increments (typically *fwidth* and *fheight*), and any additional interior space (*xadder* and *yadder*) are passed in to make it easy to compute the resulting size.

See Also

XParseGeometry(), XTranslateCoordinates(), XWMGeometry.

XGetAtomName

Name

XGetAtomName – get a string name for a property given its atom.

Synopsis

```
char *XGetAtomName(display, atom)
    Display *display;
    Atom atom;
```

Arguments

display   Specifies a connection to an X server; returned from XOpenDisplay().

atom   Specifies the atom whose string name you want returned.

Returns

The atom name string.

Description

An atom is a number identifying a property. Properties also have a string name. XGet-AtomName() returns the string name that was specified in the original call to XIntern-Atom() that returned this atom, or, for predefined atoms, a string version of the symbolic constant without the XA_ is returned. If the data returned by the server is in the Latin Portable Character Encoding, then the returned string is in the Host Portable Character Encoding. Otherwise, the result is implementation-dependent. If the specified atom is not defined, XGetAtomName() returns NULL, and generates a BadAtom error.

For example, XGetAtomName() returns "XA_WM_CLASS" (a string) when passed the predefined atom XA_WM_CLASS (a defined constant).

You should free the resulting string with XFree() when it is no longer needed.

XInternAtom() performs the inverse function, returning the atom given the string.

Errors

BadAtom

See Also

XChangeProperty(), XDeleteProperty(), XGetFontProperty(), XGetWindowProperty(), XInternAtom(), XListProperties(), XRotateWindowProperties(), XSetStandardProperties().

XGetClassHint

Name

XGetClassHint – get the XA_WM_CLASS property of a window.

Synopsis

```
Status XGetClassHint(display, w, class_hints_return)
    Display *display;
    Window w;
    XClassHint *class_hints_return;
```

Arguments

display   Specifies a connection to an X server; returned from XOpenDisplay().

w   Specifies the ID of the window for which the property is desired.

class_hints_return
      Returns the XClassHints structure.

Returns

Zero on failure, non-zero on success.

Description

XGetClassHint() obtains the XA_WM_CLASS property for the specified window. This property stores the resource class and instance name, that the window manager uses to get any resource settings that may control how the window manager manages the application that set this property. If the data returned by the server is in the Latin Portable Character Encoding, then the returned strings are in the Host Portable Character Encoding. Otherwise, the result is implementation-dependent. XGetClassHint() returns a Status of zero on failure, non-zero on success.

The XClassHint structure returned contains res_class, which is the name of the client such as "emacs", and res_name, which should be the first of the following that applies:

- Command-line option (*–rn name*)

- A specific environment variable (e.g., RESOURCE_NAME)

- The trailing component of argv [0] (after the last /)

To free res_name and res_class when finished with the strings, use XFree().

For more information on using hints, see Volume One, Chapter 10, *Interclient Communication*.

Structures

```
typedef struct {
    char *res_name;
    char *res_class;
} XClassHint;
```

Errors

```
BadWindow
```

See Also

XAllocClassHint(), XFetchName(), XGetIconName(), XGetIconSizes(), XGetNormalHints(), XGetSize-Hints(), XGetTransientForHint(), XGetWMHints(), XGetZoomHints(), XSetClassHint(), XSet-Command(), XSetIconName(), XSetIconSizes(), XSetNormalHints(), XSetSizeHints(), XSetTransientFor-Hint(), XSetWMHints(), XSetZoomHints(), XStoreName(), XSetWMProperties(), XSetWMProperties().

XGetCommand

Name

XGetCommand – get the XA_WM_COMMAND property (command-line arguments).

Synopsis

```
Status XGetCommand(display, w, argv_return, argc_return)
    Display *display;
    Window w;
    char ***argv_return;
    int *argc_return;
```

Arguments

display   Specifies a connection to an X server; returned from XOpenDisplay().

w   Specifies the window.

argv_return   Returns the application's argument list.

argc_return   Returns the number of arguments returned.

Returns

Zero on failure, non-zero on success.

Description

XGetCommand() reads the XA_WM_COMMAND property from the specified window and returns a string list. If the XA_WM_COMMAND property exists, it is of type XA_STRING and format 8. If sufficient memory can be allocated to contain the string list, XGetCommand() fills in the *argv_return* and *argc_return* arguments and returns a non-zero status. If the data returned by the server is in the Latin Portable Character Encoding, then the returned strings are in the Host Portable Character Encoding. Otherwise, the result is implementation-dependent. Otherwise, it returns a zero status. If the data returned by the server is in the Latin Portable Character Encoding, then the returned strings are in the Host Portable Character Encoding. Otherwise, the result is implementation-dependent. To free the memory allocated to the string list, use XFreeStringList().

Errors

BadWindow

See Also

XFetchName(), XGetClassHint(), XGetIconName(), XGetIconSizes(), XGetNormalHints(), XGetSizeHints(), XGetTransientForHint(), XGetWMHints(), XGetZoomHints(), XSetClassHint(), XSetIconName(), XSetIconSizes(), XSetNormalHints(), XSetSizeHints(), XSetTransientForHint(), XSetWMHints(), XSetZoomHints(), XStoreName().

XGetDefault

Name

XGetDefault – extract an option value from the resource database.

Synopsis

```
char *XGetDefault(display, program, option)
    Display *display;
    char *program;
    char *option;
```

Arguments

display   Specifies a connection to an X server; returned from `XOpenDisplay()`.

program   Specifies the program name to be looked for in the resource database. The program name is usually `argv[0]`, the first argument on the UNIX command line.

option   Specifies the option name or keyword. Lines containing both the *program* name and the *option* name, separated only by a period or asterisk, will be matched.

Returns

The resource value.

Description

`XGetDefault()` returns a character string containing the user's default value for the specified *program* name and *option* name. `XGetDefault()` returns NULL if no key can be found that matches *option* and *program*. For a description of the matching rules, see `XrmGetResource()`.

The strings returned by `XGetDefault()` are owned by Xlib and should not be modified or freed by the client.

Lines in the user's resource database look like this:

```
xterm.foreground:       #c0c0ff
xterm.geometry:         =81x28
xterm.saveLines:        256
xterm.font:             8x13
xterm.keyMapFile:       /usr/black/.keymap
xterm.activeIcon:       on
xmh.header.font         9x15
```

The portion on the left is known as a key; the portion on the right is the value. Uppercase or lowercase is important in keys. The convention is to capitalize only the second and successive words in each option, if any.

Resource specifications are usually loaded into the XA_RESOURCE_MANAGER property on the root window at login. If no such property exists, a resource file in the user's home directory is loaded. On a UNIX-based system, this file is *$HOME/.Xdefaults*. After loading these defaults, XGetDefault() merges additional defaults specified by the XENVIRONMENT environment variable. If XENVIRONMENT is defined, it contains a full path name for the additional resource file. If XENVIRONMENT is not defined, XGetDefault() looks for *$HOME/.Xdefaults*-name, where *name* specifies the name of the machine on which the application is running.

The first invocation of XGetDefault() reads and merges the various resource files into Xlib so that subsequent requests are fast. Therefore, changes to the resource files from the program will not be felt until the next invocation of the application.

For more information, see Volume One, Chapter 11, *Managing User Preferences*.

See Also

XAutoRepeatOff(), XAutoRepeatOn(), XBell(), XChangeKeyboardControl(), XGetKeyboardControl(), XGetPointerControl().

XGetErrorDatabaseText

Name

XGetErrorDatabaseText – obtain error messages from the error database.

Synopsis

```
XGetErrorDatabaseText(display, name, message,
                  default_string, buffer_return, length)
    Display display;
    char *name, *message;
    char *default_string;
    char *buffer_return;
    int length;
```

Arguments

display	Specifies a connection to an X server; returned from XOpen-Display().
name	Specifies the name of the application.
message	Specifies the type of the error message. One of XProtoError, XlibMessage, or XRequest (see the "Description" section below).
default_string	Specifies the default error message.
buffer	Returns the error description.
length	Specifies the size of the return buffer.

Description

XGetErrorDatabaseText() returns a message from the error message database. Given *name* and *message* as keys, XGetErrorDatabaseText() uses the resource manager to look up a string and returns it in the buffer argument. Xlib uses this function internally to look up its error messages. On a UNIX-based system, the error message database is usually */usr/lib/X11/XErrorDB*.

The *name* argument should generally be the name of your application. The *message* argument should indicate which type of error message you want. If the name and message are not in the Host Portable Character Encoding, then the result is implementation-dependent. Three predefined *message* types are used by Xlib to report errors:

XProtoError	The protocol error number is used as a string for the message argument.
XlibMessage	These are the message strings that are used internally by Xlib.
XRequest	For a core protocol request, the major request protocol number is used for the message argument. For an extension request, the extension name (as given by InitExtension) followed by a period (.) and the minor request protocol number is used for the message argument.

If no string is found in the error database, `XGetErrorDatabaseText()` returns the `default_string` that you specify to the buffer. The string in *buffer* will be of length *length*. The `default_string` is assumed to be in the encoding of the current locale. The `buffer_return` text is in the encoding of the current locale.

See Also

XDisplayName(), *XGetErrorText()*, *XSetAfterFunction()*, *XSetErrorHandler()*, *XSetIOErrorHandler()*, *XSynchronize()*.

XGetErrorText

Name

XGetErrorText – obtain a description of error code.

Synopsis

```
XGetErrorText(display, code, buffer_return, length)
    Display *display;
    int code;
    char *buffer_return;
    int length;
```

Arguments

display   Specifies a connection to an X server; returned from XOpenDisplay().

code   Specifies the error code for which you want to obtain a description.

buffer_return
                Returns a pointer to the error description text.

length   Specifies the size of the buffer.

Description

XGetErrorText() obtains textual descriptions of errors. XGetErrorText() returns a pointer to a NULL-terminated string describing the specified error code with length *length*. The returned text is in the encoding of the current locale. This string is copied from static data and therefore may be freed. This routine allows extensions to the Xlib library to define their own error codes and error strings that can be accessed easily.

For more information, see Volume One, Chapter 3, *Basic Window Program*.

See Also

XDisplayName(), *XGetErrorDatabaseText()*, *XSetAfterFunction()*, *XSetErrorHandler()*, *XSetIOError-Handler()*, *XSynchronize()*.

XGetFontPath

Name

XGetFontPath – get the current font search path.

Synopsis

```
char **XGetFontPath(display, npaths_return)
    Display *display;
    int *npaths_return;
```

Arguments

display   Specifies a connection to an X server; returned from XOpenDisplay().

npaths_return
                 Returns the number of strings in the font path array.

Returns

A list of strings comprising the font search path.

Description

XGetFontPath() allocates and returns an array of strings containing the search path for fonts. The contents of these strings are implementation-dependent and are not intended to be interpreted by client applications. The data in the font path should be freed, using XFree-FontPath(), when no longer needed.

See Also

XCreateFontCursor(), XFreeFont(), XFreeFontInfo(), XFreeFontNames(), XFreeFontPath(), XGet-FontProperty(), XListFonts(), XListFontsWithInfo(), XLoadFont(), XLoadQueryFont(), XQueryFont(), XSetFont(), XSetFontPath(), XUnloadFont().

XGetFontProperty

Name

XGetFontProperty – get a font property given its atom.

Synopsis

```
Bool XGetFontProperty(font_struct, atom, value_return)
    XFontStruct *font_struct;
    Atom atom;
    unsigned long *value_return;
```

Arguments

font_struct   Specifies the storage associated with the font.

atom   Specifies the atom associated with the property name you want returned.

value_return
               Returns the value of the font property.

Returns

True if the atom was defined, else False.

Description

XGetFontProperty() returns the value of the specified font property, given the atom for that property. The function returns False if the atom was not defined, or True if was defined.

There are a set of predefined atoms for font properties which can be found in *<X11/Xatom.h>*. These atoms are listed and described in Volume One, Chapter 6, *Drawing Graphics and Text*. This set contains the standard properties associated with a font. The predefined font properties are likely but not guaranteed to be present for any given font.

See Volume One, Appendix I, *Logical Font Description Conventions*, for more information on font properties.

Structures

```
typedef struct {
    XExtData *ext_data;          /* hook for extension to hang data */
    Font fid;                    /* Font ID for this font */
    unsigned direction;          /* hint about direction the font is painted */
    unsigned min_char_or_byte2;  /* first character */
    unsigned max_char_or_byte2;  /* last character */
    unsigned min_byte1;          /* first row that exists */
    unsigned max_byte1;          /* last row that exists */
    Bool all_chars_exist;        /* flag if all characters have non-zero size*/
    unsigned default_char;       /* char to print for undefined character */
    int n_properties;            /* how many properties there are */
    XFontProp *properties;       /* pointer to array of additional properties*/
```

```
        XCharStruct min_bounds;      /* minimum bounds over all existing char*/
        XCharStruct max_bounds;      /* minimum bounds over all existing char*/
        XCharStruct *per_char;       /* first_char to last_char information */
        int ascent;                  /* logical extent above baseline for spacing */
        int descent;                 /* logical descent below baseline for spacing */
} XFontStruct;
```

See Also

XChangeProperty(), XDeleteProperty(), XGetAtomName(), XGetWindowProperty(), XInternAtom(), XListProperties(), XRotateWindowProperties(), XSetStandardProperties().

XGetGCValues

Name

XGetGCValues – obtain components of a given GC from Xlib's GC cache.

Synopsis

```
Status XGetGCValues(display, gc, valuemask, values_return)
    Display *display;
    GC gc;
    unsigned long valuemask;
    XGCValues *values_return;
```

Arguments

display   Specifies a connection to an X server; returned from XOpenDisplay().

gc   Specifies the graphics context.

valuemask   Specifies which components in the GC are to be returned in the values_return argument. This argument is the bitwise inclusive OR of zero or more of the valid GC component mask bits.

values_return
                 Returns the GC values in the specified XGCValues structure.

Returns

Zero on failure, non-zero on success.

Availability

Release 4 and later.

Description

XGetGCValues() returns the components specified by valuemask for the specified GC. Note that the clip mask and dash list (represented by the GCClipMask and GCDashList bits, respectively, in the valuemask) cannot be requested. Also note that an invalid resource ID (with one or more of the three most-significant bits set to one) will be returned for GCFont, GCTile, and GCStipple if the component has never been explicitly set by the client. If the valuemask contains a valid set of GC mask bits (any of those listed in the Structures section with the exception of GCClipMask and GCDashList) and no error occur, XGetGCValues() sets the requested components in values_return and returns a non-zero status. Otherwise, it returns a zero status.

For more information, see Volume One, Chapter 5, *The Graphics Context*.

Structures

```
typedef struct {
    int function;              /* logical operation */
    unsigned long plane_mask;  /* plane mask */
    unsigned long foreground;  /* foreground pixel */
    unsigned long background;  /* background pixel */
    int line_width;            /* line width */
    int line_style;            /* LineSolid, LineOnOffDash, LineDoubleDash */
    int cap_style;             /* CapNotLast, CapButt, CapRound, CapProjecting */
    int join_style;            /* JoinMiter, JoinRound, JoinBevel */
    int fill_style;            /* FillSolid, FillTiled, FillStippled */
    int fill_rule;             /* EvenOddRule, WindingRule */
    int arc_mode;              /* ArcPieSlice, ArcChord */
    Pixmap tile;               /* tile pixmap for tiling operations */
    Pixmap stipple;            /* stipple 1 plane pixmap for stipping */
    int ts_x_origin;           /* offset for tile or stipple operations */
    int ts_y_origin;
    Font font;                 /* default text font for text operations */
    int subwindow_mode;        /* ClipByChildren, IncludeInferiors */
    Bool graphics_exposures;   /* generate events on XCopyArea, XCopyPlane */
    int clip_x_origin;         /* origin for clipping */
    int clip_y_origin;
    Pixmap clip_mask;          /* bitmap clipping; other calls for rects */
    int dash_offset;           /* patterned/dashed line information */
    char dashes;
} XGCValues;

#define GCFunction           (1L<<0)
#define GCPlaneMask          (1L<<1)
#define GCForeground         (1L<<2)
#define GCBackground         (1L<<3)
#define GCLineWidth          (1L<<4)
#define GCLineStyle          (1L<<5)
#define GCCapStyle           (1L<<6)
#define GCJoinStyle          (1L<<7)
#define GCFillStyle          (1L<<8)
#define GCFillRule           (1L<<9)
#define GCTile               (1L<<10)
#define GCStipple            (1L<<11)
#define GCTileStipXOrigin    (1L<<12)
#define GCTileStipYOrigin    (1L<<13)
#define GCFont               (1L<<14)
#define GCSubwindowMode      (1L<<15)
#define GCGraphicsExposures  (1L<<16)
#define GCClipXOrigin        (1L<<17)
#define GCClipYOrigin        (1L<<18)
#define GCClipMask           (1L<<19)    /* not valid in this call */
#define GCDashOffset         (1L<<20)
```

```
#define GCDashList        (1L<<21)    /* not valid in this call */
#define GCArcMode         (1L<<22)
```

See Also

XChangeGC(), XCopyGC(), XCreateGC().

XGetGeometry

Name

XGetGeometry – obtain the current geometry of drawable.

Synopsis

```
Status XGetGeometry(display, drawable, root_return, x_return, y_return,
        width_return, height_return, border_width_return, depth_return)
    Display *display;
    Drawable drawable;
    Window *root_return;
    int *x_return, *y_return;
    unsigned int *width_return, *height_return;
    unsigned int *border_width_return;
    unsigned int *depth_return;
```

Arguments

display	Specifies a connection to an X server; returned from XOpenDisplay().
drawable	Specifies the drawable, either a window or a pixmap.
root_return	Returns the root window ID of the specified window.
x_return y_return	Return the coordinates of the upper-left pixel of the window's border, relative to its parent's origin. For pixmaps, these coordinates are always zero.
width_return height_return	Return the dimensions of the drawable. For a window, these return the inside size (not including the border).
border_width_return	Returns the borderwidth, in pixels, of the window's border, if the drawable is a window. Returns zero if the drawable is a pixmap.
depth_return	Returns the depth of the pixmap or window (bits per pixel for the object).

Returns

Zero on failure, non-zero on success.

Description

This function gets the current geometry of a drawable, plus the ID of the root window of the screen the window is on. It is legal to pass to this function on InputOnly window.

XGetGeometry() returns a Status of zero on failure, or non-zero on success.

Errors

```
BadDrawable
```

See Also

XConfigureWindow(), XGetWindowAttributes(), XMoveResizeWindow(), XMoveWindow(), XResize-Window().

XGetIconName

Name

XGetIconName – get the name to be displayed in an icon.

Synopsis

```
Status XGetIconName(display, w, icon_name_return)
    Display *display;
    Window w;
    char **icon_name_return;
```

Arguments

display   Specifies a connection to an X server; returned from XOpenDisplay().

w   Specifies the ID of the window whose icon name you want to learn.

icon_name_return

     Returns a pointer to the name to be displayed in the window's icon. The name is a NULL-terminated string. If the data returned by the server is in the Latin Portable Character Encoding, then the returned string is in the Host Portable Character Encoding. Otherwise, the result is implementation-dependent. If a name hasn't been assigned to the window, XGet-IconName() sets this argument to NULL. When finished with it, a client must free the icon name string using XFree().

Returns

Zero on failure, non-zero on success.

Description

XGetIconName() is superseded by XGetWMIconName() in Release 4. XGetIcon-Name() reads the icon name property of a window. This function is primarily used by window managers to get the name to be written in a window's icon when they need to display that icon. XGetIconName() returns a non-zero Status if it succeeds, and zero if no icon name has been set for the argument window.

For more information, see Volume One, Chapter 10, *Interclient Communication*.

Errors

BadWindow

See Also

XFetchName(), XGetClassHint(), XGetIconSizes(), XGetNormalHints(), XGetSizeHints(), XGet-TransientForHint(), XGetWMHints(), XGetZoomHints(), XSetClassHint(), XSetCommand(), XSetIcon-Name(), XSetIconSizes(), XSetNormalHints(), XSetSizeHints(), XSetTransientForHint(), XSetWMHints(), XSetZoomHints(), XStoreName().

XGetIconSizes

Name

XGetIconSizes – get preferred icon sizes.

Synopsis

```
Status XGetIconSizes(display, w, size_list_return, count_return)
    Display *display;
    Window w;
    XIconSize **size_list_return;
    int *count_return;
```

Arguments

display   Specifies a connection to an X server; returned from XOpenDisplay().

w   Specifies the window ID (usually of the root window).

size_list_return
                   Returns a pointer to the size list.

count_return
                   Returns the number of items in the size list.

Returns

Zero on failure, non-zero on success.

Description

XGetIconSizes() reads the XA_WM_ICON_SIZE property that should be set by the window manager to specify its desired icon sizes. XGetIconSizes() returns a Status of zero if a window manager has not set icon sizes, and a non-zero Status otherwise. This function should be called by all programs to find out what icon sizes are preferred by the window manager. The application should then use XSetWMHints() to supply the window manager with an icon pixmap or window in one of the supported sizes. To free the data allocated in size_list_return, use XFree().

For more information, see Volume One, Chapter 10, *Interclient Communication*.

Structures

```
typedef struct {
    int min_width, min_height;
    int max_width, max_height;
    int width_inc, height_inc;
} XIconSize;
/* width_inc and height_inc provide the preferred increment of sizes in the
 * range from min_width to max_width and min_height to max_height. */
```

Errors

    BadWindow

See Also

XAllocIconSize(), XFetchName(), XGetClassHint(), XGetIconName(), XGetNormalHints(), XGetSize-Hints(), XGetTransientForHint(), XGetWMHints(), XGetZoomHints(), XSetClassHint(), XSet-Command(), XSetIconSizes(), XSetNormalHints(), XSetSizeHints(), XSetTransientForHint(), XSet-WMHints(), XSetZoomHints(), XStoreName().*

XGetICValues

Name

XGetICValues – get input context attributes.

Synopsis

```
char *XGetICValues(ic, ... )
   XIC ic;
```

Arguments

ic   Specifies the input context.

...   Specifies the variable length argument list to set or get XIC values.

Returns

NULL if no error occurred; otherwise, the name of the first attribute that could not be obtained.

Availability

Release 5 and later.

Description

XGetICValues() queries the values of input context attributes. The first argument is the input context, and it is followed by a NULL-terminated variable-length argument list of attribute name/value pairs. The standard attributes and their types are listed in the tables below.

Input Context Attributes

Name	Type	Notes
XNInputStyle	XIMStyle	Required at IC creation; may not be changed.
XNClientWindow	Window	Must be set before IC use; may not be changed.
XNFocusWindow	Window	Changes may cause geometry negotiation.
XNResourceName	char *	
XNResourceClass	char *	
XNGeometryCallback	XIMCallback *	
XNFilterEvents	unsigned long	Read-only attribute; may not be set.
XNPreeditAttributes	XVaNestedList	See sub-attributes below.
XNStatusAttributes	XVaNestedList	See sub-attributes below.

Preedit and Status Area Sub-attributes

Name	Type	Notes
XNArea	XRectangle *	
XNAreaNeeded	XRectangle *	
XNSpotLocation	XPoint *	Required at IC creation for XIMPreeditPosition style.
XNColormap	Colormap	
XNStdColormap	Atom	
XNForeground	unsigned long	
XNBackground	unsigned long	
XNBackgroundPixmap	Pixmap	
XNFontSet	XFontSet	Required at IC creation; changes may cause geometry negotiation.
XNLineSpacing	int	Changes may cause geometry negotiation.
XNCursor	Cursor	
XNPreeditStartCallback	XIMCallback *	Required at IC creation for XIMPreeditCallbacks style.
XNPreeditDoneCallback	XIMCallback *	Required at IC creation for XIMPreeditCallbacks style.
XNPreeditDrawCallback	XIMCallback *	Required at IC creation for XIMPreeditCallbacks style.
XNPreeditCaretCallback	XIMCallback *	Required at IC creation for XIMPreeditCallbacks style.
XNStatusStartCallback	XIMCallback *	Required at IC creation for XIMStatusCallbacks style.
XNStatusDoneCallback	XIMCallback *	Required at IC creation for XIMStatusCallbacks style.
XNStatusDrawCallback	XIMCallback *	Required at IC creation for XIMStatusCallbacks style.

In addition to the attribute names above, the special name XNVaNestedList indicates that the following argument is a XVaNestedList of attribute name/value pairs. When a nested list is encountered in an argument list, the contents of the nested list are processed as if they appeared in the original argument list at that point.

The XGetICValues() function returns NULL if no error occurred; otherwise, it returns the name of the first attribute that could not be obtained. An attribute could be not obtained for any of the following reasons:

• The attribute name is not recognized.

• The input method encountered an implementation-dependent error.

Each attribute value argument to `XGetICValues()` (the argument that follows the attribute name) must be the address of a location into which the value is to be stored. For attributes that are pointer types (`XNArea`, for example), `XGetICValues()` returns a pointer to a copy of the attribute value. In this case, the client must free the memory allocated for that copy with `XFree()`.

See Also

XCreateIC(), *XOpenIM()*, *XSetICFocus()*, *XSetICValues()*, *XmbResetIC()*, *XwcResetIC.*

XGetImage

Name

XGetImage – place contents of a rectangle from drawable into an image.

Synopsis

```
XImage *XGetImage(display, drawable, x, y, width, height,
                  plane_mask, format)
    Display *display;
    Drawable drawable;
    int x, y;
    unsigned int width, height;
    unsigned long plane_mask;
    int format;
```

Arguments

display	Specifies a connection to an X server; returned from XOpenDisplay().
drawable	Specifies the drawable to get the data from.
x y	Specify the x and y coordinates of the upper-left corner of the rectangle, relative to the origin of the drawable.
width height	Specify the width and height in pixels of the image.
plane_mask	Specifies a plane mask that indicates which planes are represented in the image.
format	Specifies the format for the image. Pass either XYPixmap or ZPixmap.

Returns

The created image.

Description

XGetImage() dumps the contents of the specified rectangle, a drawable, into a client-side XImage structure, in the format you specify. Depending on which format you pass to the format argument, the function does the following:

- If the format is XYPixmap, the function gets only the bit planes you passed to the plane_mask argument.

- If the format is ZPixmap, the function sets to 0 the bits in all planes not specified in the plane_mask argument. The function performs no range checking on the values in plane_mask, and ignores extraneous bits.

XGetImage() returns the depth of the image to the depth member of the XImage structure. This depth is as specified when the drawable was created.

XGetImage

If the drawable is a pixmap, the specified rectangle must be completely inside the pixmap, or a `BadMatch` error will occur, and the `visual` field in the image will be `None`. If `XGet-Image()` fails, it returns `NULL`. If the drawable is a window, the window must be viewable, and the specified rectangle must not go off the edge of the screen. Otherwise, a `BadMatch` error will occur. If the drawable is a window, the *visual* argument will return the visual specified when the drawable was created.

The returned image will include any visible portions of inferiors contained in the rectangle. The image will not include the cursor. The specified area can include the borders. The returned contents of visible regions of inferiors of different depth than the specified window are undefined.

If the window has a backing-store, the backing-store contents are returned for regions of the window that are obscured by noninferior windows. Otherwise, the return contents of such obscured regions are undefined.

The data in the image structure is stored in the server's natural byte- and bit-order.

For more information, see Volume One, Chapter 6, *Drawing Graphics and Text*.

Errors

`BadDrawable`

`BadMatch`   See the "Description" section above.

`BadValue`

See Also

XImageByteOrder(), XAddPixel(), XCreateImage(), XDestroyImage(), XGetPixel(), XGetSubImage(), XPutImage(), XPutPixel(), XSubImage().

XGetIMValues

Name

XGetIMValues – obtain input method information.

Synopsis

```
char * XGetIMValues(im, ...)
    XIM im;
```

Arguments

im   Specifies the input method.

...   Specifies the variable length argument list to get XIM values.

Returns

NULL if no error occurred; otherwise, the name of the first attribute that could not be obtained.

Availability

Release 5 and later.

Description

XGetIMValues() queries the values of input method attributes. The first argument is the input method, and it is followed by a NULL-terminated variable-length argument list of attribute name/value pairs. Only one standard attribute is defined by Xlib: XNQueryInput-Style. It is of type XIMStyles * (shown below) and is used to query the input styles supported by the input method. A client should always query the input method to determine which styles are supported. The client should then find an input style it is capable of supporting, and use that style when creating input contexts. If the client cannot find an input style that it can support it should negotiate with the user the continuation of the program (exit, choose another input method, and so on).

The attribute value argument (which follows the attribute name argument) must be the address of a location where the returned value will be stored. For the XNQueryInput-Style attribute, the client must pass the address of a variable of type XIMStyles*, and is responsible for freeing the memory allocated for the XIMStyles data structure with XFree().

XGetIMValues() returns NULL if it succeeds. Otherwise it returns the name of the first attribute for which a value could not be obtained.

Structures

```
#define XIMPreeditArea       0x0001L
#define XIMPreeditCallbacks  0x0002L
#define XIMPreeditPosition   0x0004L
```

```
#define XIMPreeditNothing      0x0008L
#define XIMPreeditNone         0x0010L
#define XIMStatusArea          0x0100L
#define XIMStatusCallbacks     0x0200L
#define XIMStatusNothing       0x0400L
#define XIMStatusNone          0x0800L

typedef unsigned long XIMStyle;

typedef struct {
    unsigned short count_styles;
    XIMStyle *supported_styles;
} XIMStyles;
```

See Also

XOpenIM(), *XCloseIM()*, *XDisplayOfIM()*, *XLocaleOfIM()*.

XGetInputFocus

Name

XGetInputFocus – return the current keyboard focus window.

Synopsis

```
XGetInputFocus(display, focus_return, revert_to_return)
    Display *display;
    Window *focus_return;
    int *revert_to_return;
```

Arguments

display   Specifies a connection to an X server; returned from XOpenDisplay().

focus_return

     Returns the ID of the focus window, or one of the constants Pointer-Root or None.

revert_to_return

     Returns the window to which the focus would revert if the focus window became invisible. This is one of these constants: RevertToParent, RevertToPointerRoot, or RevertToNone. Must not be a window ID.

Description

XGetInputFocus() returns the current keyboard focus window and the window to which the focus would revert if the focus window became invisible.

XGetInputFocus() does not report the last focus change time. This is available only from FocusIn and FocusOut events.

See Also

XQLength(), XAllowEvents(), XCheckIfEvent(), XCheckMaskEvent(), XCheckTypedEvent(), XCheck-TypedWindowEvent(), XCheckWindowEvent(), XEventsQueued(), XGetMotionEvents(), XIfEvent(), XMaskEvent(), XNextEvent(), XPeekEvent(), XPeekIfEvent(), XPending(), XPutBackEvent(), XSelect-Input(), XSendEvent(), XSetInputFocus(), XSynchronize(), XWindowEvent().

XGetKeyboardControl

Name

XGetKeyboardControl – obtain a list of the current keyboard preferences.

Synopsis

```
XGetKeyboardControl(display, values_return)
    Display *display;
    XKeyboardState *values_return;
```

Arguments

display   Specifies a connection to an X server; returned from XOpenDisplay().

values_return
            Returns filled XKeyboardState() structure.

Description

XGetKeyboardControl() returns the current control values for the keyboard. For the LEDs (light emitting diodes), the least significant bit of *led_mask* corresponds to LED 1, and each bit that is set to 1 in *led_mask* indicates an LED that is lit. auto_repeats is a bit vector; each bit that is set to 1 indicates that auto-repeat is enabled for the corresponding key. The vector is represented as 32 bytes. Byte N (from 0) contains the bits for keys 8N to 8N+7, with the least significant bit in the byte representing key 8N. *global_auto_repeat* is either AutoRepeatModeOn or AutoRepeatModeOff.

For the ranges of each member of XKeyboardState(), see the description of XChange-PointerControl().

For more information, see Volume One, Chapter 9, *The Keyboard and Pointer*.

Structures

```
typedef struct {
    int key_click_percent;
    int bell_percent;
    unsigned int bell_pitch, bell_duration;
    unsigned long led_mask;
    int global_auto_repeat;
    char auto_repeats[32];
} XKeyboardState;
```

See Also

XAutoRepeatOff(), XAutoRepeatOn(), XBell(), XChangeKeyboardControl(), XGetDefault(), XGet-PointerControl().

XGetKeyboardMapping

Name

XGetKeyboardMapping – return symbols for keycodes.

Synopsis

```
KeySym *XGetKeyboardMapping(display, first_keycode, keycode_count,
                keysyms_per_keycode_return)
    Display *display;
    KeyCode first_keycode;
    int keycode_count;
    int *keysyms_per_keycode_return;
```

Arguments

display   Specifies a connection to an X server; returned from XOpenDisplay().

first_keycode
      Specifies the first keycode that is to be returned.

keycode_count
      Specifies the number of keycodes that are to be returned.

keysyms_per_keycode_return
      Returns the number of keysyms per keycode.

Returns

The list of KeySyms.

Description

Starting with *first_keycode*, XGetKeyboardMapping() returns the symbols for the specified number of keycodes. The specified *first_keycode* must be greater than or equal to min_keycode as returned by XDisplayKeycodes(), otherwise a BadValue error occurs. In addition, the following expression must be less than or equal to max_keycode (also returned by XDisplayKeycodes()) as returned in the Display structure, otherwise a BadValue error occurs:

```
first_keycode + keycode_count - 1
```

The number of elements in the keysyms list is:

```
keycode_count * keysyms_per_keycode_return
```

Then, keysym number N (counting from 0) for keycode K has an index (counting from 0) of the following (in keysyms):

```
(K - first_keycode) * keysyms_per_keycode_return + N
```

The `keysyms_per_keycode_return` value is chosen arbitrarily by the server to be large enough to report all requested symbols. A special `KeySym` value of `NoSymbol` is used to fill in unused elements for individual keycodes.

Use `XFree()` to free the returned keysym list when you no longer need it.

For more information, see Volume One, Chapter 9, *The Keyboard and Pointer*.

Errors

BadValue   *first_keycode* less than *display->*min_keycode.

                       *display->*max_keycode exceeded.

See Also

XChangeKeyboardMapping(), XDeleteModifiermapEntry(), XFreeModifiermap(), XGetModifier-Mapping(), XInsertModifiermapEntry(), XKeycodeToKeysym(), XKeysymToKeycode(), XKeysymTo-String(), XLookupKeysym(), XLookupString(), XNewModifierMap, XQueryKeymap(), XRebindKeySym, XRefreshKeyboardMapping(), XSetModifierMapping(), XStringToKeysym().

XGetModifierMapping

Name

XGetModifierMapping – obtain the mapping of modifier keys (Shift, Control, etc.).

Synopsis

```
XModifierKeymap *XGetModifierMapping(display)
    Display *display;
```

Arguments

display   Specifies a connection to an X server; returned from XOpenDisplay().

Returns

The current modifier mapping.

Description

XGetModifierMapping() returns the keycodes of the keys being used as modifiers.

There are eight modifiers, represented by the symbols ShiftMapIndex, LockMapIndex, ControlMapIndex, Mod1MapIndex, Mod2MapIndex, Mod3MapIndex, Mod4Map-Index, and Mod5MapIndex. The modifiermap member of the XModifier-Keymap() structure contains eight sets of keycodes, each set containing max_keypermod keycodes. Zero keycodes are not meaningful. If an entire modifiermap is filled with zero's, the corresponding modifier is disabled. No keycode will appear twice anywhere in the map.

Structures

```
typedef struct {
    int max_keypermod;          /* server's max number of keys per modifier */
    KeyCode *modifiermap;       /* an 8 by max_keypermod array of
                                 * keycodes to be used as modifiers */
} XModifierKeymap;

/* modifier names.  Used to build a SetModifierMapping request or
   to read a GetModifierMapping request. */
#define ShiftMapIndex        0
#define LockMapIndex         1
#define ControlMapIndex      2
#define Mod1MapIndex         3
#define Mod2MapIndex         4
#define Mod3MapIndex         5
#define Mod4MapIndex         6
#define Mod5MapIndex         7
```

See Also

XChangeKeyboardMapping(), XDeleteModifiermapEntry(), XFreeModifiermap(), XGetKeyboard-Mapping(), XInsertModifiermapEntry(), XKeycodeToKeysym(), XKeysymToKeycode(), XKeysymTo-String(), XLookupKeysym(), XLookupString(), XNewModifierMap, XQueryKeymap(), XRebindKeySym, XRefreshKeyboardMapping(), XSetModifierMapping(), XStringToKeysym().

XGetMotionEvents

Name

XGetMotionEvents – get events from pointer motion history buffer.

Synopsis

```
XTimeCoord *XGetMotionEvents(display, w, start, stop, nevents_return)
    Display *display;
    Window w;
    Time start, stop;
    int *nevents_return;
```

Arguments

display   Specifies a connection to an X server; returned from XOpenDisplay().

w   Specifies the ID of the window whose associated pointer motion events will be returned.

start   Specify the time interval for which the events are returned from the motion
stop   history buffer. Pass a time stamp (in milliseconds) or CurrentTime.

nevents_return
                 Returns the number of events returned from the motion history buffer.

Returns

The list of pointer positions.

Description

XGetMotionEvents() returns all events in the motion history buffer that fall between the specified start and stop times (inclusive) and that have coordinates that lie within (including borders) the specified window at its present placement. The x and y coordinates of the XTimeCoord return structure are reported relative to the origin of *w*.

XGetMotionEvent returns NULL if the server does not support a motion history buffer (which is common), or if the start time is after the stop time, or if the start time is in the future. If the stop time is in the future, it is equivalent to specifying the constant Current-Time, since the server does not wait to report future events. A motion history buffer is supported if XDisplayMotionBufferSize() (display) > 0. The pointer position at each pointer hardware interrupt is then stored for later retrieval.

Use XFree() to free the returned XTimeCoord structures when they are no longer needed.

For more information, see Volume One, Chapter 9, *The Keyboard and Pointer*.

Structures

```
typedef struct _XTimeCoord {
    Time time;
    short x, y;
} XTimeCoord;
```

Errors

```
BadWindow
```

See Also

XQLength(), XAllowEvents(), XCheckIfEvent(), XCheckMaskEvent(), XCheckTypedEvent(), XCheck-
TypedWindowEvent(), XCheckWindowEvent(), XEventsQueued(), XGetInputFocus(), XIfEvent(),
XMaskEvent(), XNextEvent(), XPeekEvent(), XPeekIfEvent(), XPending(), XPutBackEvent(), XSelect-
Input(), XSendEvent(), XSetInputFocus(), XSynchronize(), XWindowEvent().

XGetNormalHints

Name

XGetNormalHints – get the size hints property of a window in normal state (not zoomed or iconified).

Synopsis

```
Status XGetNormalHints(display, w, hints_return)
    Display *display;
    Window w;
    XSizeHints *hints_return;
```

Arguments

display   Specifies a connection to an X server; returned from XOpenDisplay().

w   Specifies the ID of the window to be queried.

hints_return

Returns the sizing hints for the window in its normal state.

Returns

Zero on failure, non-zero on success.

Description

XGetNormalHints() has been superseded by XGetWMNormalHints() as of Release 4, because new interclient communication conventions are now standard.

XGetNormalHints() returns the size hints for a window in its normal state by reading the XA_WM_NORMAL_HINTS property. This function is normally used only by a window manager. It returns a non-zero Status if it succeeds, and zero if it fails (e.g., the application specified no normal size hints for this window.)

For more information on using hints, see Volume One, Chapter 10, *Interclient Communication*.

Structures

```
typedef struct {
    long flags;    /* which fields in structure are defined */
    int x, y;
    int width, height;
    int min_width, min_height;
    int max_width, max_height;
    int width_inc, height_inc;
    struct {
        int x;     /* numerator */
        int y;     /* denominator */
    } min_aspect, max_aspect;
```

```
} XSizeHints;

/* flags argument in size hints */
#define USPosition   (1L << 0)    /* user specified x, y */
#define USSize       (1L << 1)    /* user specified width, height */

#define PPosition    (1L << 2)    /* program specified position */
#define PSize        (1L << 3)    /* program specified size */
#define PMinSize     (1L << 4)    /* program specified minimum size */
#define PMaxSize     (1L << 5)    /* program specified maximum size */
#define PResizeInc   (1L << 6)    /* program specified resize increments */
#define PAspect      (1L << 7)    /* program specified min/max aspect ratios */
#define PAllHints (PPosition|PSize|PMinSize|PMaxSize|PResizeInc|PAspect)
```

Errors

BadWindow

See Also

XFetchName(), XGetClassHint(), XGetIconName(), XGetIconSizes(), XGetSizeHints(), XGetTransient-ForHint(), XGetWMHints(), XGetZoomHints(), XSetClassHint(), XSetCommand(), XSetIconName(), XSetIconSizes(), XSetNormalHints(), XSetSizeHints(), XSetTransientForHint(), XSetWMHints(), XSetZoomHints(), XStoreName().

XGetPixel

Name

XGetPixel – obtain a single pixel value from an image.

Synopsis

```
unsigned long XGetPixel(ximage, x, y)
    XImage *ximage;
    int x;
    int y;
```

Arguments

ximage   Specifies a pointer to the image.

x   Specify the x and y coordinates of the pixel whose value is to be returned.
y

Returns

The pixel value.

Description

XGetPixel() returns the specified pixel from the named image. The x and y coordinates are relative to the origin (upper-left [0,0]) of the image). The pixel value is returned in the normalized format (that is, the least-significant byte of the long is the least-significant byte of the pixel). The x and y coordinates must be contained in the image.

For more information, see Volume One, Chapter 6, *Drawing Graphics and Text*.

Structures

```
typedef struct _XImage {
    int width, height;       /* size of image */
    int xoffset;             /* number of pixels offset in X direction */
    int format;              /* XYBitmap, XYPixmap, ZPixmap */
    char *data;              /* pointer to image data */
    int byte_order;          /* data byte order, LSBFirst, MSBFirst */
    int bitmap_unit;         /* quant. of scan line 8, 16, 32 */
    int bitmap_bit_order;    /* LSBFirst, MSBFirst */
    int bitmap_pad;          /* 8, 16, 32 either XY or ZPixmap */
    int depth;               /* depth of image */
    int bytes_per_line;      /* accelerator to next line */
    int bits_per_pixel;      /* bits per pixel (ZPixmap) */
    unsigned long red_mask;  /* bits in z arrangment */
    unsigned long green_mask;
    unsigned long blue_mask;
    char *obdata;            /* hook for the object routines to hang on */
    struct funcs {           /* image manipulation routines */
        struct _XImage *(*create_image)();
```

```
        int (*destroy_image)();
        unsigned long (*get_pixel)();
        int (*put_pixel)();
        struct _XImage *(*sub_image)();
        int (*add_pixel)();
    } f;
} XImage;
```

See Also

XImageByteOrder(), *XAddPixel()*, *XCreateImage()*, *XDestroyImage()*, *XGetImage()*, *XGetSubImage()*, *XPutImage()*, *XPutPixel()*, *XSubImage()*.

XGetPointerControl

Name

XGetPointerControl – get the current pointer preferences.

Synopsis

```
XGetPointerControl(display, accel_numerator_return,
        accel_denominator_return, threshold_return)
            Display *display;
    int *accel_numerator_return, *accel_denominator_return;
    int *threshold_return;
```

Arguments

display   Specifies a connection to an X server; returned from XOpenDisplay().

accel_numerator_return
      Returns the numerator for the acceleration multiplier.

accel_denominator_return
      Returns the denominator for the acceleration multiplier.

threshold_return
      Returns the acceleration threshold in pixels. The pointer must move more than this amount before acceleration takes effect.

Description

XGetPointerControl() gets the pointer's current acceleration parameters.

accel_numerator_return divided by *accel_denominator_return* is the number of pixels the cursor moves per unit of motion of the pointer, applied only to the amount of movement over *threshold_return*.

See Also

XChangeActivePointerGrab(), *XChangePointerControl()*, *XGetPointerMapping()*, *XGrabPointer()*, *XQueryPointer()*, *XSetPointerMapping()*, *XUngrabPointer()*, *XWarpPointer()*.

XGetPointerMapping

Name

XGetPointerMapping – get the pointer button mapping.

Synopsis

```
int XGetPointerMapping(display, map_return, nmap)
    Display *display;
    unsigned char map_return[];
    int nmap;
```

Arguments

display   Specifies a connection to an X server; returned from XOpenDisplay().

map_return   Returns the mapping list. Array begins with map_return[].

nmap   Specifies the number of items in mapping list.

Returns

The number of elements in the pointer list.

Description

XGetPointerMapping() returns the current mapping of the pointer buttons. Information is returned in both the arguments and the function's return value. *map_return* is an array of the numbers of the buttons as they are currently mapped. Elements of the list are indexed starting from 1. The nominal mapping for a pointer is the identity mapping: map_return[i]=i+1. If map[2]=2, it means that the third physical button triggers the second logical button.

nmap indicates the desired number of button mappings.

The return value of the function is the actual number of elements in the pointer list, which may be greater or less than *nmap*.

See Also

XChangeActivePointerGrab(), *XChangePointerControl()*, *XGetPointerControl()*, *XGrabPointer()*, *XQueryPointer()*, *XSetPointerMapping()*, *XUngrabPointer()*, *XWarpPointer()*.

XGetRGBColormaps

Name

XGetRGBColormaps – obtain the `XStandardColormap` structure associated with the specified property.

Synopsis

```
Status XGetRGBColormaps(display, w, std_colormap_return, count_return,
        property)
    Display *display;
    Window w;
    XStandardColormap **std_colormap_return;
    int *count_return;
    Atom property;
```

Arguments

display　　　Specifies a connection to an X server; returned from `XOpenDisplay()`.

w　　　　　　Specifies the window.

std_colormap_return
　　　　　　Returns the `XStandardColormap` structure.

count_return
　　　　　　Returns the number of colormaps.

property　　Specifies the property name.

Returns

Zero on failure, non-zero on success.

Availability

Release 4 and later.

Description

`XGetRGBColormaps()` returns the RGB colormap definitions stored in the specified property on the named window. If the property exists, is of type `RGB_COLOR_MAP`, is of format 32, and is long enough to contain a colormap definition, `XGetRGBColormaps()` allocates and fills in space for the returned colormaps, and returns a non-zero status. Otherwise, none of the fields are set, and `XGetRGBColormaps()` returns a zero status. If the `visualid` field is not present, `XGetRGBColormaps()` assumes the default visual for the screen on which the window is located; if the `killid` field is not present, it is assumed to have a value of `None`, which indicates that the resources cannot be released. Note that it is the caller's responsibility to honor the ICCCM restriction that only `RGB_DEFAULT_MAP` contain more than one definition.

XGetRGBColormaps() does not install the colormaps into the hardware colormap, it does not allocate entries, and it does not even create virtual colormaps. It just provides information about designs of colormap and the IDs of the colormaps if some other client has already created them. The application can otherwise attempt to create a virtual colormap of the appropriate type, and allocate its entries according to the information in the XStandard-Colormap structure. Installing the colormap must then be done with XInstall-Colormap(), in cooperation with the window manager. Any of these steps could fail, and the application should be prepared.

If the server or another client has already created a standard colormap of this type, then its ID will be returned in the colormap member of the XStandardColormap structure. Some servers and window managers, particular on high-performance workstations, will create some or all of the standard colormaps so they can be quickly installed when needed by applications.

An application should go through the standard colormap creation process only if it needs the special qualities of the standard colormaps and if another client has not already created them. For one, they allow the application to convert RGB values into pixel values quickly because the mapping is predictable. Given an XStandardColormap structure for an XA_RGB_BEST_MAP colormap, and floating point RGB coefficients in the range 0.0 to 1.0, you can compose pixel values with the following C expression:

```
pixel = base_pixel
    + ((unsigned long) (0.5 + r * red_max)) * red_mult
    + ((unsigned long) (0.5 + g * green_max)) * green_mult
    + ((unsigned long) (0.5 + b * blue_max)) * blue_mult;
```

The use of addition rather than logical-OR for composing pixel values permits allocations where the RGB value is not aligned to bit boundaries.

XGetRGBColormaps() supersedes XGetStandardColormap().

For more information, see Volume One, Chapter 7, *Color*.

Structures

```
typedef struct {
    Colormap colormap;
    unsigned long red_max;
    unsigned long red_mult;
    unsigned long green_max;
    unsigned long green_mult;
    unsigned long blue_max;
    unsigned long blue_mult;
    unsigned long base_pixel;
    VisualID visualid;              /* added by ICCCM version 1 */
    XID killid;                     /* added by ICCCM version 1 */
} XStandardColormap;
```

Errors

    BadAtom
    BadWindow

See Also

XAllocStandardColormap(), XSetRGBColormaps().

XGetScreenSaver

Name

XGetScreenSaver – get the current screen saver parameters.

Synopsis

```
XGetScreenSaver(display, timeout_return, interval_return,
        prefer_blanking_return, allow_exposures_return)
            Display *display;
    int *timeout_return, *interval_return;
    int *prefer_blanking_return;
    int *allow_exposures_return;
```

Arguments

display   Specifies a connection to an X server; returned from XOpenDisplay().

timeout_return
            Returns the idle time, in seconds, until the screen saver turns on.

interval_return
            Returns the interval between screen saver invocations, in seconds.

prefer_blanking_return
            Returns the current screen blanking preference, one of these constants: DontPreferBlanking, PreferBlanking, or DefaultBlanking.

allow_exposures_return
            Returns the current screen save control value, either DontAllow-Exposures, AllowExposures, or DefaultExposures.

Description

XGetScreenSaver() returns the current settings of the screen saver, which may be set with XSetScreenSaver().

A positive *timeout_return* indicates that the screen saver is enabled. A *timeout_return* of zero indicates that the screen saver is disabled.

If the server-dependent screen saver method supports periodic change, *interval_return* serves as a hint about the length of the change period, and zero serves as a hint that no periodic change will be made. An *interval_return* of zero indicates that random pattern motion is disabled.

For more information on the screen saver, see Volume One, Chapter 13, *Other Programming Techniques*.

See Also

XActivateScreenSaver(), XForceScreenSaver(), XResetScreenSaver(), XSetScreenSaver().

XGetSelectionOwner

Name

XGetSelectionOwner – return the owner of a selection.

Synopsis

```
Window XGetSelectionOwner(display, selection)
    Display *display;
    Atom selection;
```

Arguments

display   Specifies a connection to an X server; returned from `XOpenDisplay()`.

selection   Specifies the selection atom whose owner you want returned.

Returns

The window associated with the selection owner.

Description

`XGetSelectionOwner()` returns the window ID of the current owner of the specified selection. If no selection was specified, or there is no owner, the function returns the constant `None`.

For more information on selections, see Volume One, Chapter 10, *Interclient Communication*.

Errors

`BadAtom`

See Also

XConvertSelection(), XSetSelectionOwner().

XGetSizeHints

Name

XGetSizeHints – read any property of type XA_WM_SIZE_HINTS.

Synopsis

```
Status XGetSizeHints(display, w, hints_return, property)
    Display *display;
    Window w;
    XSizeHints *hints_return;
    Atom property;
```

Arguments

display   Specifies a connection to an X server; returned from XOpenDisplay().

w   Specifies the ID of the window for which size hints will be returned.

hints_return
      Returns the size hints structure.

property   Specifies a property atom of type XA_WM_SIZE_HINTS. May be XA_WM_NORMAL_HINTS, XA_WM_ZOOM_HINTS (in Release 3), or a property defined by an application.

Returns

Zero on failure, non-zero on success.

Description

XGetSizeHints() has been superseded by XGetWMSizeHints() as of Release 4, because the interclient communication conventions are now standard.

XGetSizeHints() returns the XSizeHints structure for the named property and the specified window. XGetSizeHints() is used by XGetNormalHints() and XGet-ZoomHints(), and can be used to retrieve the value of any property of type XA_WM_SIZE_HINTS; thus, it is useful if other properties of that type get defined. This function is used almost exclusively by window managers.

XGetSizeHints() returns a non-zero Status if a size hint was defined, and zero otherwise.

For more information on using hints, see Volume One, Chapter 10, *Interclient Communication*.

Structures

```
typedef struct {
    long flags;     /* which fields in structure are defined */
    int x, y;
```

```
            int width, height;
            int min_width, min_height;
            int max_width, max_height;
            int width_inc, height_inc;
            struct {
                int x;      /* numerator */
                int y;      /* denominator */
            } min_aspect, max_aspect;
            int base_width, base_height;
            int win_gravity
        } XSizeHints;

        /* flags argument in size hints */
        #define USPosition  (1L << 0)    /* user specified x, y */
        #define USSize      (1L << 1)    /* user specified width, height */

        #define PPosition   (1L << 2)    /* program specified position */
        #define PSize       (1L << 3)    /* program specified size */
        #define PMinSize    (1L << 4)    /* program specified minimum size */
        #define PMaxSize    (1L << 5)    /* program specified maximum size */
        #define PResizeInc  (1L << 6)    /* program specified resize increments */
        #define PAspect     (1L << 7)    /* program specified min/max aspect ratios */
        #define PAllHints (PPosition|PSize|PMinSize|PMaxSize|PResizeInc|PAspect)
        #define PBaseSize   (1L << 8)
        #define PWinGravity (1L << 9)
```

Errors

    BadAtom
    BadWindow

See Also

XFetchName(), XGetClassHint(), XGetIconName(), XGetIconSizes(), XGetNormalHints(), XGet-
TransientForHint(), XGetWMHints(), XGetZoomHints(), XSetClassHint(), XSetCommand(), XSetIcon-
Name(), XSetIconSizes(), XSetNormalHints(), XSetSizeHints(), XSetTransientForHint(), XSetWMHints(),
XSetZoomHints(), XStoreName().

XGetStandardColormap

Name

XGetStandardColormap – get the standard colormap property.

Synopsis

```
Status XGetStandardColormap(display, w, cmap_info_return, property)
    Display *display;
    Window w;
    XStandardColormap *colormap_return;
    Atom property;
```

Arguments

display   Specifies a connection to an X server; returned from XOpenDisplay().

w   Specifies the ID of the window on which the property is set. This is normally the root window.

colormap_return
        Returns the filled colormap information structure.

property   Specifies the atom indicating the type of standard colormap desired. The predefined standard colormap atoms are XA_RGB_BEST_MAP, XA_RGB_RED_MAP, XA_RGB_GREEN_MAP, XA_RGB_BLUE_MAP, XA_RGB_DEFAULT_MAP, and XA_RGB_GRAY_MAP.

Returns

Zero on failure, non-zero on success.

Description

XGetStandardColormap() is superseded by XGetRGBColormaps() in Release 4. XGetStandardColormap() gets a property on the root window that describes a standard colormap. XGetStandardColormap() returns zero if it fails, or non-zero if it succeeds.

See Volume One, Chapter 7, *Color*, for a complete description of standard colormaps.

Structures

```
typedef struct {
    Colormap colormap;    /* ID of colormap created by XCreateColormap */
    unsigned long red_max;
    unsigned long red_mult;
    unsigned long green_max;
    unsigned long green_mult;
    unsigned long blue_max;
    unsigned long blue_mult;
    unsigned long base_pixel;
```

```
        VisualID visualid;
        XID killid;
} XStandardColormap;
```

Errors

```
BadAtom
BadWindow
```

See Also

XDefaultColormap(), XDisplayCells(), XCopyColormapAndFree(), XCreateColormap(), XFree-Colormap(), XInstallColormap(), XListInstalledColormaps(), XSetStandardColormap(), XSetWindow-Colormap(), XUninstallColormap().

XGetSubImage

Name

XGetSubImage – copy a rectangle in drawable to a location within the pre-existing image.

Synopsis

```
XImage *XGetSubImage(display, drawable, x, y, width, height,
                  plane_mask, format, dest_image, dest_x, dest_y)
    Display *display;
    Drawable drawable;
    int x, y;
    unsigned int width, height;
    unsigned long plane_mask;
    int format;
    XImage *dest_image;
    int dest_x, dest_y;
```

Arguments

display	Specifies a connection to an X server; returned from XOpenDisplay().
drawable	Specifies the drawable from which the rectangle is to be copied.
x y	Specify the x and y coordinates of the upper-left corner of the rectangle, relative to the origin of the drawable.
width height	Specify the width and height in pixels of the subimage taken.
plane_mask	Specifies which planes of the drawable are transferred to the image.
format	Specifies the format for the image. Either XYPixmap or ZPixmap.
dest_image	Specifies the destination image.
dest_x dest_y	Specify the x and y coordinates of the destination rectangle's upper-left corner, relative to the image's origin.

Returns

The same image specified by dest_image.

Description

XGetSubImage() updates the dest_image with the specified subimage in the same manner as XGetImage(), except that it does not create the image or necessarily fill the entire image. If format is XYPixmap, the function transmits only the bit planes you specify in plane_mask. If format is ZPixmap, the function transmits as zero the bits in all planes not specified in plane_mask. The function performs no range checking on the values in plane_mask and ignores extraneous bits.

The depth of the destination `XImage` structure must be the same as that of the drawable. Otherwise, a `BadMatch` error is generated. If the specified subimage does not fit at the specified location on the destination image, the right and bottom edges are clipped. If the drawable is a window, the window must be mapped or held in backing store, and it must be the case that, if there were no inferiors or overlapping windows, the specified rectangle of the window would be fully visible on the screen. Otherwise, a `BadMatch` error is generated.

If the window has a backing store, the backing store contents are returned for regions of the window that are obscured by noninferior windows. Otherwise, the return contents of such obscured regions are undefined. Also undefined are the returned contents of visible regions of inferiors of different depth than the specified window.

`XSubImage()` extracts a subimage from an image, instead of from a drawable like `XGet-SubImage()`.

If a problem occurs, `XGetSubImage()` returns `NULL`.

For more information on images, see Volume One, Chapter 6, *Drawing Graphics and Text*.

Errors

`BadDrawable`

`BadGC`

`BadMatch`   Depth of *dest_image* is not the same as depth of *drawable*.

`BadValue`

See Also

XImageByteOrder(), XAddPixel(), XCreateImage(), XDestroyImage(), XGetImage(), XGetPixel(), XPut-Image(), XPutPixel(), XSubImage().

XGetTextProperty

Name

XGetTextProperty – read one of a window's text properties.

Synopsis

```
Status XGetTextProperty(display, w, text_prop_return, property)
    Display *display;
    Window w;
    XTextProperty *text_prop_return;
    Atom property;
```

Arguments

display   Specifies a connection to an X server; returned from XOpenDisplay().

w   Specifies the window.

text_prop_return
              Returns the XTextProperty structure.

property   Specifies the property name.

Returns

Zero on failure, non-zero on success.

Availability

Release 4 and later.

Description

XGetTextProperty() reads the specified property from the window and stores the data in the returned XTextProperty structure. It stores the data in the value field, the type of the data in the encoding field, the format of the data in the format field, and the number of items of data in the nitems field. An extra byte containing null (which is not included in the nitems number) is stored at the end of the value field of text_prop_return. The particular interpretation of the property's encoding and data as "text" is left to the calling application. If the specified property does not exist on the window, XGetText-Property() sets the value field to NULL, the encoding field to None, the format field to zero, and the nitems field to zero.

If it was able to set these files in the XTextProperty structure, XGetTextProperty() returns a non-zero status; otherwise, it returns a zero status.

For more information, see Volume One, Chapter 10, *Interclient Communication*.

Structures

```
typedef struct {
    unsigned char *value;          /* same as Property routines */
    Atom encoding;                 /* prop type */
    int format;                    /* prop data format: 8, 16, or 32 */
    unsigned long nitems;          /* number of data items in value */
} XTextProperty;
```

Errors

```
BadAtom
BadWindow
```

See Also

XFreeStringList(), XSetTextProperty(), XStringListToTextProperty(), XTextPropertytoStringList.

XGetTransientForHint

Name

XGetTransientForHint – get the XA_WM_TRANSIENT_FOR property of a window.

Synopsis

```
Status XGetTransientForHint(display, w, prop_window_return)
    Display *display;
    Window w;
    Window *prop_window_return;
```

Arguments

display   Specifies a connection to an X server; returned from XOpenDisplay().

w   Specifies the ID of the window to be queried.

prop_window_return
              Returns the window contained in the XA_WM_TRANSIENT_FOR property of
              the specified window.

Returns

Zero on failure, non-zero on success.

Description

XGetTransientForHint() obtains the XA_WM_TRANSIENT_FOR property for the specified window. XGetTransientForHint() is normally used by a window manager. This property should be set for windows that are to appear only temporarily on the screen, such as pop-up dialog boxes. The window returned is the main window to which this popup window is related. This lets the window manager decorate the popup window appropriately.

XGetTransientForHint() returns a Status of zero on failure, and non-zero on success.

For more information on using hints, see Volume One, Chapter 10, *Interclient Communication*.

Errors

BadWindow

See Also

XFetchName(), XGetClassHint(), XGetIconName(), XGetIconSizes(), XGetNormalHints(), XGetSizeHints(), XGetWMHints(), XGetZoomHints(), XSetClassHint(), XSetCommand(), XSetIconName(), XSetIconSizes(), XSetNormalHints(), XSetSizeHints(), XSetTransientForHint(), XSetWMHints(), XSetZoomHints(), XStoreName().

XGetVisualInfo

Name

XGetVisualInfo – find the visual information structures that match the specified template.

Synopsis

```
XVisualInfo *XGetVisualInfo(display, vinfo_mask, vinfo_template,
        nitems_return)
    Display *display;
    long vinfo_mask;
    XVisualInfo *vinfo_template;
    int *nitems_return;
```

Arguments

display   Specifies a connection to an X server; returned from XOpenDisplay().

vinfo_mask   Specifies the visual mask value. Indicates which elements in template are to be matched.

vinfo_template
                Specifies the visual attributes that are to be used in matching the visual structures.

nitems_return
                Returns the number of matching visual structures.

Returns

The visual information structure.

Description

XGetVisualInfo() returns a list of visual structures that describe visuals supported by the server and that match the attributes specified by the *vinfo_template* argument. If no visual structures match the template fields specified in Vinfo_mask, XGetVisual-Info() returns a NULL. To free the data returned by this function, use XFree().

For more information, see Volume One, Chapter 7, *Color*.

Structures

```
typedef struct {
    Visual *visual;
    VisualID visualid;
    int screen;
    unsigned int depth;
    int class;
    unsigned long red_mask;
    unsigned long green_mask;
    unsigned long blue_mask;
```

```
        int colormap_size;
        int bits_per_rgb;
} XVisualInfo;

/* The symbols for the vinfo_mask argument are: */

#define VisualNoMask            0x0
#define VisualIDMask            0x1
#define VisualScreenMask        0x2
#define VisualDepthMask         0x4
#define VisualClassMask         0x8
#define VisualRedMaskMask       0x10
#define VisualGreenMaskMask     0x20
#define VisualBlueMaskMask      0x40
#define VisualColormapSizeMask  0x80
#define VisualBitsPerRGBMask    0x100
#define VisualAllMask           0x1FF
```

See Also

XDefaultVisual(), *XVisualIDFromVisual()*, *XMatchVisualInfo()*, *XListDepths()*.

XGetWindowAttributes

Name

XGetWindowAttributes – obtain the current attributes of window.

Synopsis

```
Status XGetWindowAttributes(display, w, window_attributes_return)
    Display *display;
    Window w;
    XWindowAttributes *window_attributes_return;
```

Arguments

display   Specifies a connection to an X server; returned from XOpenDisplay().

w   Specifies the window whose current attributes you want.

window_attributes_return
     Returns a filled XWindowAttributes structure, containing the current attributes for the specified window.

Returns

Zero on failure, non-zero on success.

Description

XGetWindowAttributes() returns the XWindowAttributes structure containing the current window attributes.

XGetWindowAttributes() returns a Status of zero on failure, or non-zero on success. However, it will only return zero if you have defined an error handler that does not exit, using XSetErrorHandler(). The default error handler exits, and therefore XGetWindowAttributes() never gets a chance to return. (Such error handling is relevant only if you are writing a window manager or other application that deals with windows that might have been destroyed.)

The following list briefly describes each member of the XWindowAttributes structure. For more information, see Volume One, Chapter 4, *Window Attributes*.

x, y   The current position of the upper-left pixel of the window's border, relative to the origin of its parent.

width, height   The current dimensions in pixels of this window, not including the border.

border_width   The current border width of the window.

depth   The number of bits per pixel in this window.

visual   The visual structure.

root   The root window ID of the screen containing the window.

class   The window class. One of these constants: `InputOutput` or `Input-Only`.

bit_gravity   The new position for existing contents after resize. One of the constants `ForgetGravity`, `StaticGravity`, or `CenterGravity`, or one of the compass constants (`NorthWestGravity`, `NorthGravity`, etc.).

win_gravity   The new position for this window after its parent is resized. One of the constants `CenterGravity`, `UnmapGravity`, `StaticGravity`, or one of the compass constants.

backing_store   When to maintain contents of the window. One of these constants: `NotUseful`, `WhenMapped`, or `Always`.

backing_planes
                The bit planes to be preserved in a backing store.

backing_pixel   The pixel value used when restoring planes from a partial backing store.

save_under   A boolean value, indicating whether saving bits under this window would be useful.

colormap   The colormap ID being used in this window, or `None`.

map_installed   A boolean value, indicating whether the colormap is currently installed. If `True`, the window is being displayed in its chosen colors.

map_state   The window's map state. One of these constants: `IsUnmapped`, `Is-Unviewable`, or `IsViewable`. `IsUnviewable` indicates that the specified window is mapped but some ancestor is unmapped.

all_event_masks
                The set of events any client have selected. This member is the bitwise inclusive OR of all event masks selected on the window by all clients.

your_event_mask
                The bitwise inclusive OR of all event mask symbols selected by the querying client.

do_not_propagate_mask
                The bitwise inclusive OR of the event mask symbols that specify the set of events that should not propagate. This is global across all clients.

override_redirect
                A boolean value, indicating whether this window will override structure control facilities. This is usually only used for temporary pop-up windows such as menus. Either `True` or `False`.

screen   A pointer to the `Screen` structure for the screen containing this window.

Errors

```
BadDrawable
BadWindow
```

Structures

The XWindowAttributes structure contains:

```
typedef struct {
    int x, y;                        /* location of window */
    int width, height;               /* width and height of window */
    int border_width;                /* border width of window */
    int depth;                       /* depth of window */
    Visual *visual;                  /* the associated visual structure */
    Window root;                     /* root of screen containing window */
    int class;                       /* InputOutput, InputOnly*/
    int bit_gravity;                 /* one of bit gravity values */
    int win_gravity;                 /* one of the window gravity values */
    int backing_store;               /* NotUseful, WhenMapped, Always */
    unsigned long backing_planes;    /* planes to be preserved if possible */
    unsigned long backing_pixel;     /* value to be used when restoring planes */
    Bool save_under;                 /* boolean, should bits under be saved */
    Colormap colormap;               /* colormap to be associated with window */
    Bool map_installed;              /* boolean, is colormap currently
                                        installed */
    int map_state;                   /* IsUnmapped, IsUnviewable, IsViewable */
    long all_event_masks;            /* set of events all people have interest
                                        in */
    long your_event_mask;            /* my event mask */
    long do_not_propagate_mask;      /* set of events that should not
                                        propagate */
    Bool override_redirect;          /* boolean value for override-redirect */
    Screen *screen;                  /* pointer to correct screen */
} XWindowAttributes;
```

See Also

XChangeWindowAttributes(), XGetGeometry(), XSetWindowBackground(), XSetWindowBackground-Pixmap(), XSetWindowBorder(), XSetWindowBorderPixmap().

XGetWindowProperty

Name

XGetWindowProperty – obtain the atom type and property format for a window.

Synopsis

```
int XGetWindowProperty(display, w, property, long_offset, long_length,
            delete, req_type, actual_type_return, actual_format_return,
            nitems_return, bytes_after_return, prop_return)
    Display *display;
    Window w;
    Atom property;
    long long_offset, long_length;
    Bool delete;
    Atom req_type;
    Atom *actual_type_return;
    int *actual_format_return;
    unsigned long *nitems_return;
    unsigned long *bytes_after_return;
    unsigned char **prop_return;
```

Arguments

display   Specifies a connection to an X server; returned from XOpenDisplay().

w   Specifies the ID of the window whose atom type and property format you want to obtain.

property   Specifies the atom of the desired property.

long_offset   Specifies the offset in 32-bit quantities where data will be retrieved.

long_length   Specifies the length in 32-bit multiples of the data to be retrieved.

delete   Specifies a boolean value of True or False. If you pass True and a property is returned, the property is deleted from the window after being read and a PropertyNotify event is generated on the window.

req_type   Specifies an atom describing the desired format of the data. If AnyPropertyType is specified, returns the property from the specified window regardless of its type. If a type is specified, the function returns the property only if its type equals the specified type.

actual_type_return
                Returns the actual type of the property.

actual_format_return
                Returns the actual data type of the returned data.

nitems_return
> Returns the actual number of 8-, 16-, or 32-bit items returned in *prop_return*.

bytes_after_return
> Returns the number of bytes remaining to be read in the property if a partial read was performed.

prop_return Returns a pointer to the data actually returned, in the specified format. XGetWindowProperty() always allocates one extra byte after the data and sets it to NULL. This byte is not counted in *nitems_return*.

Returns

Success on success. The failure return value is undefined.

Description

XGetWindowProperty() gets the value of a property if it is the desired type. XGet-WindowProperty() sets the return arguments acccording to the following rules:

- If the specified property does not exist for the specified window, then: *actual_type_return* is None; *actual_format_return* = 0; and *bytes_after_return* = 0. *delete* is ignored in this case, and *nitems_return* is empty.

- If the specified property exists, but its type does not match *req_type*, then: *actual_type_return* is the actual property type; *actual_format_return* is the actual property format (never zero); and *bytes_after_return* is the property length in bytes (even if *actual_format_return* is 16 or 32). *delete* is ignored in this case, and *nitems_return* is empty.

- If the specified property exists, and either *req_type* is AnyPropertyType or the specified type matches the actual property type, then: *actual_type_return* is the actual property type; and *actual_format_return* is the actual property format (never zero). *bytes_after_return* and *nitems_return* are defined by combining the following values:

  > N = actual length of stored property in bytes (even if *actual_format_return* is 16 or 32)
  > I = 4 * *long_offset* (convert offset from *longs* into bytes)
  > L = MINIMUM((N - I), 4 * *long_length*) (BadValue if L < 0)
  > bytes_after = N - (I + L) (number of trailing unread bytes in stored property)

The returned data (in *prop_return*) starts at byte index *I* in the property (indexing from 0). The actual length of the returned data in bytes is *L*. *L* is converted into the number of 8-, 16-, or 32-bit items returned by dividing by 1, 2, or 4 respectively and this value is returned in *nitems_return*. The number of trailing unread bytes is returned in *bytes_after_return*.

If *delete* == True and *bytes_after_return* == 0 the function deletes the property from the window and generates a PropertyNotify event on the window.

When XGetWindowProperty() executes successfully, it returns Success. The Success return value and the undocumented value returned on failure are the opposite of all other routines that return int or Status. The value of Success is undocumented, but is zero (0) in the current sample implementation from MIT. The failure value, also undocumented, is currently one (1). Therefore, comparing either value to True or False, or using the syntax "if (!XGetWindowProperty(. . .))" is incorrect.

To free the resulting data, use XFree().

For more information, see Volume One, Chapter 10, *Interclient Communication*.

Errors

BadAtom

BadValue   Value of *long_offset* caused *L* to be negative above.

BadWindow

See Also

XChangeProperty(), XGetAtomName(), XGetFontProperty(), XListProperties(), XRotateWindow-Properties(), XSetStandardProperties().

XGetWMClientMachine

Name

XGetWMClientMachine – get a window's XA_WM_CLIENT_MACHINE property.

Synopsis

```
Status XGetWMClientMachine(display, w, text_prop_return)
    Display *display;
    Window w;
    XTextProperty *text_prop_return;
```

Arguments

display   Specifies a connection to an X server; returned from XOpenDisplay().

w   Specifies the window.

text_prop_return
               Returns the XTextProperty structure that describes the machine the client is running on.

Returns

Zero on failure, non-zero on success.

Availability

Release 4 and later.

Description

XGetWMClientMachine() performs an XGetTextProperty() to get the WM_CLIENT_MACHINE property of the specified window. This property should contain the name of the host machine on which this client is being run, as seen from the server. This function returns non-zero status in success; otherwise it returns a zero status.

This function is normally used along with XGetCommand() by a session manager or window manager to get complete information on how to reinvoke an application.

For more information, see Volume One, Chapter 10, *Interclient Communication*.

Structures

```
typedef struct {
    unsigned char *value;        /* same as Property routines */
    Atom encoding;               /* prop type */
    int format;                  /* prop data format: 8, 16, or 32 */
    unsigned long nitems;        /* number of data items in value */
} XTextProperty;
```

See Also

XSetWMClientMachine(), *XGetCommand()*.

XGetWMColormapWindows

Name

XGetWMColormapWindows – get a window's WM_COLORMAP_WINDOWS property.

Synopsis

```
Status XGetWMColormapWindows(display, w, colormap_windows_return,
        count_return)
    Display *display;
    Window w;
    Window *colormap_windows_return;
    int count_return;
```

Arguments

display   Specifies a connection to an X server; returned from XOpenDisplay().

w   Specifies the top-level window of an application.

colormap_windows_return
                Returns the list of windows that have custom colormaps.

count_return
                Returns the number of windows in the list.

Returns

Zero on failure, non-zero on success.

Availability

Release 4 and later.

Description

XGetWMColormapWindows() gets the WM_COLORMAP_WINDOWS property on the specified window. This property contains a list of windows that have custom colomaps that need to be installed. The XGetWMColormapWindows() function stores the list in its colormap_windows_return argument.

If the property exists, if it is of type WINDOW, if it is of format 32, and if the atom WM_COLORMAP_WINDOWS can be interned, XGetWMColormapWindows() sets the colormap_windows_return argument to a list of window identifiers, sets the count_return argument to the number of elements in list, and returns a non-zero status. Otherwise, it sets neither of the return arguments and returns a zero status. To release the list of window identifiers, use XFree().

This function is called by window managers to find out what colormaps to install and when to install them.

For more information, see Volume One, Chapter 10, *Interclient Communication*.

Errors

```
BadWindow
```

See Also

XSetWMColormapWindows().

XGetWMHints

Name

XGetWMHints – read the window manager hints property.

Synopsis

```
XWMHints *XGetWMHints(display, w)
    Display *display;
    Window w;
```

Arguments

display   Specifies a connection to an X server; returned from XOpenDisplay().

w   Specifies the ID of the window to be queried.

Returns

The window manager hints structure.

Description

This function is primarily for window managers. XGetWMHints() returns NULL if no XA_WM_HINTS property was set on window *w*, and returns a pointer to an XWMHints structure if it succeeds. Programs must free the space used for that structure by calling XFree().

For more information on using hints, see Volume One, Chapter 10, *Interclient Communication*.

Structures

```
typedef struct {
    long flags;         /* marks which fields in this structure are defined */
    Bool input;         /* does application need window manager for input */
    int initial_state;  /* see below */
    Pixmap icon_pixmap; /* pixmap to be used as icon */
    Window icon_window; /* window to be used as icon */
    int icon_x, icon_y; /* initial position of icon */
    Pixmap icon_mask;   /* icon mask bitmap */
    XID window_group;   /* ID of related window group */
    /* this structure may be extended in the future */
} XWMHints;

/* initial state flag: */
#define DontCareState   0
#define NormalState     1
#define ZoomState       2
#define IconicState     3
#define InactiveState   4
```

Errors

    BadWindow

See Also

XAllocWMHints(), *XFetchName()*, *XGetClassHint()*, *XGetIconName()*, *XGetIconSizes()*, *XGetNormal-Hints()*, *XGetSizeHints()*, *XGetTransientForHint()*, *XGetZoomHints()*, *XSetClassHint()*, *XSet-Command()*, *XSetIconName()*, *XSetIconSizes()*, *XSetNormalHints()*, *XSetSizeHints()*, *XSetTransientFor-Hint()*, *XSetWMHints()*, *XSetZoomHints()*, *XStoreName()*, *XSetWMProperties()*.

XGetWMIconName

Name

XGetWMIconName – read a window's XA_WM_ICON_NAME property.

Synopsis

```
Status XGetWMIconName(display, w, text_prop_return)
   Display *display;
   Window w;
   XTextProperty *text_prop_return;
```

Arguments

display   Specifies a connection to an X server; returned from XOpenDisplay().

w   Specifies the window.

text_prop_return
               Returns the XTextProperty structure.

Returns

Zero on failure, non-zero on success.

Availability

Release 4 and later.

Description

XGetWMIconName() performs an XGetTextProperty() on the XA_WM_ICON_NAME property of the specified window. XGetWMIconName() supersedes XGetIconName().

This function is primarily used by window managers to get the name to be written in a window's icon when they need to display that icon.

For more information, see Volume One, Chapter 10, *Interclient Communication*.

Structures

```
typedef struct {
    unsigned char *value;        /* same as Property routines */
    Atom encoding;               /* prop type */
    int format;                  /* prop data format: 8, 16, or 32 */
    unsigned long nitems;        /* number of data items in value */
} XTextProperty;
```

See Also

XGetWMName(), XSetWMIconName(), XSetWMName(), XSetWMProperties().

XGetWMName

Name

XGetWMName – read a window's XA_WM_NAME property.

Synopsis

```
Status XGetWMName(display, w, text_prop_return)
    Display *display;
    Window w;
    XTextProperty *text_prop_return;
```

Arguments

display   Specifies a connection to an X server; returned from XOpenDisplay().

w   Specifies the window.

text_prop_return
                Returns the XTextProperty structure.

Returns

Zero on failure, non-zero on success.

Availability

Release 4 and later.

Description

XGetWMName() performs an XGetTextProperty() on the XA_WM_NAME property of the specified window. XGetWMName() supersedes XFetchName().

XGetWMName() returns non-zero if it succeeds, and zero if the property has not been set for the argument window.

For more information, see Volume One, Chapter 10, *Interclient Communication*.

Structures

```
typedef struct {
    unsigned char *value;       /* same as Property routines */
    Atom encoding;              /* prop type */
    int format;                 /* prop data format: 8, 16, or 32 */
    unsigned long nitems;       /* number of data items in value */
} XTextProperty;
```

See Also

XGetWMIconName(), *XSetWMIconName()*, *XSetWMName()*, *XSetWMProperties()*.

XGetWMNormalHints

Xlib – Window Manager Hints

Name

XGetWMNormalHints – read a window's XA_WM_NORMAL_HINTS property.

Synopsis

```
Status XGetWMNormalHints(display, w, hints_return, supplied_return)
    Display *display;
    Window w;
    XSizeHints *hints_return;
    long *supplied_return;
```

Arguments

display   Specifies a connection to an X server; returned from XOpenDisplay().

w   Specifies the window.

hints_return
      Returns the size hints for the window in its normal state.

supplied_return
      Returns the hints that were supplied by the user.

Returns

Zero on failure, non-zero on success.

Availability

Release 4 and later.

Description

XGetWMNormalHints() returns the size hints stored in the XA_WM_NORMAL_HINTS property on the specified window. If the property is of type XA_WM_SIZE_HINTS, of format 32, and is long enough to contain either an old (pre-ICCCM) or new size hints structure, XGetWMNormalHints() sets the various fields of the XSizeHints structure, sets the *supplied_return* argument to the list of fields that were supplied by the user (whether or not they contained defined values) and returns a non-zero status. XGetWMNormalHints() returns a zero status if the application specified no normal size hints for this window.

XGetWMNormalHints() supersedes XGetNormalHints().

If XGetWMNormalHints() returns successfully and a pre-ICCCM size hints property is read, the *supplied_return* argument will contain the following bits:

(USPosition|USSize|PPosition|PSize|PMinSize|PMaxSize|PResizeInc|PAspect)

436   Xlib Reference Manual

If the property is large enough to contain the base size and window gravity fields as well, the `supplied` argument will also contain the following bits:

`(PBaseSize|PWinGravity)`

This function is normally used only by a window manager.

For more information, see Volume One, Chapter 10, *Interclient Communication*.

Structures

```
typedef struct {
    long flags;          /* marks which fields in this structure are defined */
    int x, y;            /* obsolete for new window mgrs, but clients */
    int width, height;   /* should set so old wm's don't mess up */
    int min_width, min_height;
    int max_width, max_height;
    int width_inc, height_inc;
    struct {
            int x;       /* numerator */
            int y;       /* denominator */
    } min_aspect, max_aspect;
    int base_width, base_height;     /* added by ICCCM version 1 */
    int win_gravity;                 /* added by ICCCM version 1 */
} XSizeHints;
```

Errors

`BadWindow`

See Also

XAllocSizeHints(), *XGetWMSizeHints()*, *XSetWMNormalHints()*, *XSetWMProperties()*, *XSetWMSize-Hints()*.

XGetWMProtocols

Name

XGetWMProtocols – get a window's WM_PROTOCOLS property.

Synopsis

```
Status XGetWMProtocols(display, w, protocols_return, count_return)
    Display *display;
    Window w;
    Atom **protocols_return;
    int *count_return;
```

Arguments

display   Specifies a connection to an X server; returned from XOpenDisplay().

w   Specifies the window.

protocols_return
                Returns the list of protocols.

count_return
                Returns the number of protocols in the list.

Returns

Zero on failure, non-zero on success.

Availability

Release 4 and later.

Description

XGetWMProtocols() gets the list of atoms stored in the WM_PROTOCOLS property of the specified window. These atoms describe window manager protocols in which the owner of this window is willing to participate.

If the property exists, is of type ATOM, is of format 32, and the atom WM_PROTOCOLS can be interned, XGetWMProtocols() sets the protocols_return argument to a list of atoms, sets the count_return argument to the number of elements in list, and returns a a non-zero status. Otherwise, it sets neither of the return arguments and returns a zero status.

The list of standard protocols at present is as follows:

WM_TAKE_FOCUS   Assignment of keyboard focus.

WM_SAVE_YOURSELF   Save client state warning.

WM_DELETE_UNKNOWN   Request to delete top-level window.

For more information, see Volume One, Chapter 10, *Interclient Communication*.

Errors

    BadWindow

See Also

XSetWMProtocols().

XGetWMSizeHints

Name

XGetWMSizeHints – read a window's XA_WM_SIZE_HINTS property.

Synopsis

```
Status XGetWMSizeHints(display, w, hints_return, supplied_return,
        property)
    Display *display;
    Window w;
    XSizeHints *hints_return;
    long *supplied_return;
    Atom property;
```

Arguments

display   Specifies a connection to an X server; returned from XOpenDisplay().

w   Specifies the window.

hints_return
               Returns the XSizeHints structure.

supplied_return
               Returns the hints that were supplied by the user.

property   Specifies the property name.

Returns

Zero on failure, non-zero on success.

Availability

Release 4 and later.

Description

XGetWMSizeHints() returns the size hints stored in the specified property on the named window. If the property is of type XA_WM_SIZE_HINTS, of format 32, and is long enough to contain either an old (pre-ICCCM) or new size hints structure, XGetWMSizeHints() sets the various fields of the XSizeHints structure, sets the supplied_return argument to the list of fields that were supplied by the user (whether or not they contained defined values), and returns a non-zero status. If the hint was not set, it returns a zero status. To get a window's normal size hints, you can use the XGetWMNormalHints() function instead.

XGetWMSizeHints() supersedes XGetSizeHints().

If XGetWMSizeHints() returns successfully and a pre-ICCCM size hints property is read, the supplied_return argument will contain the following bits:

(USPosition|USSize|PPosition|PSize|PMinSize|PMaxSize|PResizeInc|PAspect)

If the property is large enough to contain the base size and window gravity fields as well, the `supplied` argument will also contain the following bits:

`(PBaseSize|PWinGravity)`

This function is used almost exclusively by window managers.

For more information, see Volume One, Chapter 10, *Interclient Communication*.

Structures

```
typedef struct {
    long flags;            /* marks which fields in this structure are defined */
    int x, y;              /* obsolete for new window mgrs, but clients */
    int width, height;     /* should set so old wm's don't mess up */
    int min_width, min_height;
    int max_width, max_height;
    int width_inc, height_inc;
    struct {
            int x;         /* numerator */
            int y;         /* denominator */
    } min_aspect, max_aspect;
    int base_width, base_height;   /* added by ICCCM version 1 */
    int win_gravity;               /* added by ICCCM version 1 */
} XSizeHints;
```

Errors

```
BadAtom
BadWindow
```

See Also

XAllocSizeHints(), *XGetWMNormalHints()*, *XSetWMNormalHints()*, *XSetWMSizeHints()*.

XGetZoomHints

Name

XGetZoomHints – read the size hints property of a zoomed window.

Synopsis

```
Status XGetZoomHints(display, w, zhints_return)
    Display *display;
    Window w;
    XSizeHints *zhints_return;
```

Arguments

display   Specifies a connection to an X server; returned from XOpenDisplay().

w   Specifies the ID of the window to be queried.

zhints_return
             Returns a pointer to the zoom hints.

Returns

Zero on failure, non-zero on success.

Description

XGetZoomHints() is obsolete beginning in Release 4, because zoom hints are no longer defined in the ICCCM.

XGetZoomHints() is primarily for window managers. XGetZoomHints() returns the size hints for a window in its zoomed state (not normal or iconified) read from the XA_WM_ZOOM_HINTS property. It returns a non-zero Status if it succeeds, and zero if the application did not specify zoom size hints for this window.

For more information on using hints, see Volume One, Chapter 10, *Interclient Communication*.

Structures

```
typedef struct {
    long flags;     /* which fields in structure are defined */
    int x, y;
    int width, height;
    int min_width, min_height;
    int max_width, max_height;
    int width_inc, height_inc;
    struct {
        int x;      /* numerator */
        int y;      /* denominator */
    } min_aspect, max_aspect;
} XSizeHints;
```

```
/* flags argument in size hints */
#define USPosition  (1L << 0)    /* user specified x, y */
#define USSize      (1L << 1)    /* user specified width, height */

#define PPosition   (1L << 2)    /* program specified position */
#define PSize       (1L << 3)    /* program specified size */
#define PMinSize    (1L << 4)    /* program specified minimum size */
#define PMaxSize    (1L << 5)    /* program specified maximum size */
#define PResizeInc  (1L << 6)    /* program specified resize increments */
#define PAspect     (1L << 7)    /* program specified min/max aspect ratios */
#define PAllHints (PPosition|PSize|PMinSize|PMaxSize|PResizeInc|PAspect)
```

Errors

```
BadWindow
```

See Also

XFetchName(), XGetClassHint(), XGetIconName(), XGetIconSizes(), XGetNormalHints(), XGetSize-Hints(), XGetTransientForHint(), XGetWMHints(), XSetClassHint(), XSetCommand(), XSetIconName(), XSetIconSizes(), XSetNormalHints(), XSetSizeHints(), XSetTransientForHint(), XSetWMHints(), XSet-ZoomHints(), XStoreName().

XGrabButton

Name

XGrabButton – grab a pointer button.

Synopsis

```
XGrabButton(display, button, modifiers, grab_window, owner_events,
        event_mask, pointer_mode, keyboard_mode, confine_to, cursor)
Display *display;
unsigned int button;
unsigned int modifiers;
Window grab_window;
Bool owner_events;
unsigned int event_mask;
int pointer_mode, keyboard_mode;
Window confine_to;
Cursor cursor;
```

Arguments

display   Specifies a connection to an X server; returned from XOpenDisplay().

button   Specifies the mouse button. May be Button1, Button2, Button3, Button4, Button5, or AnyButton. The constant AnyButton is equivalent to issuing the grab request for all possible buttons. The button symbols cannot be ORed.

modifiers   Specifies a set of keymasks. This is a bitwise OR of one or more of the following symbols: ShiftMask, LockMask, ControlMask, Mod1Mask, Mod2Mask, Mod3Mask, Mod4Mask, Mod5Mask, or AnyModifier. AnyModifier is equivalent to issuing the grab key request for all possible modifier combinations (including no modifiers).

grab_window   Specifies the ID of the window you want to the grab to occur in.

owner_events
                Specifies a boolean value of either True or False. See the "Description" section below.

event_mask   Specifies the event mask to take effect during the grab. This mask is the bitwise OR of one or more of the event masks listed on the reference page for XSelectInput().

pointer_mode
                Controls processing of pointer events during the grab. Pass one of these constants: GrabModeSync or GrabModeAsync.

keyboard_mode
: Controls processing of keyboard events during the grab. Pass one of these constants: GrabModeSync or GrabModeAsync.

confine_to
: Specifies the ID of the window to confine the pointer. One possible value is the constant None, in which case the pointer is not confined to any window.

cursor
: Specifies the cursor to be displayed during the grab. One possible value you can pass is the constant None, in which case the existing cursor is used.

Description

XGrabButton() establishes a passive grab, such that an active grab may take place when the specified key/button combination is pressed in the specified window. After this call:

- IF the specified button is pressed when the specified modifier keys are down (and no other buttons or modifier keys are down),
- AND *grab_window* contains the pointer,
- AND the *confine_to* window (if any) is viewable,
- AND these constraints are not satisfied for any ancestor,
- THEN the pointer is actively grabbed as described in XGrabPointer(), the last pointer grab time is set to the time at which the button was pressed, and the ButtonPress event is reported.

The interpretation of the remaining arguments is as for XGrabPointer(). The active grab is terminated automatically when all buttons are released (independent of the state of modifier keys).

A modifier of AnyModifier is equivalent to issuing the grab request for all possible modifier combinations (including no modifiers). A button of AnyButton is equivalent to issuing the request for all possible buttons (but at least one).

XGrabButton() overrides all previous passive grabs by the same client on the same key/button combination on the same window, but has no effect on an active grab. The request fails if some other client has already issued an XGrabButton() with the same button/key combination on the same window. When using AnyModifier or AnyButton, the request fails completely (no grabs are established) if there is a conflicting grab for any combination.

The *owner_events* argument specifies whether the grab window should receive all events (False) or whether the grabbing application should receive all events normally (True).

The *pointer_mode* and *keyboard_mode* control the processing of events during the grab. If either is GrabModeSync, events for that device are not sent from the server to Xlib until XAllowEvents() is called to release the events. If either is GrabModeAsync, events for that device are sent normally.

An automatic grab takes place between a `ButtonPress` event and the corresponding `ButtonRelease` event, so this call is not necessary in some of the most common situations. But this call is necessary for certain styles of menus.

For more information on grabbing, see Volume One, Chapter 9, *The Keyboard and Pointer*.

Errors

BadAccess   When using `AnyModifier` or `AnyButton` and there is a conflicting grab by another client. No grabs are established.

                Another client has already issued an `XGrabButton()` request with the same key/button combination on the same window.

BadCursor

BadValue

BadWindow

See Also

XChangeActivePointerGrab(), *XGrabKey()*, *XGrabKeyboard()*, *XGrabPointer()*, *XGrabServer()*, *XUngrabButton()*, *XUngrabKey()*, *XUngrabKeyboard()*, *XUngrabPointer()*, *XUngrabServer()*.

Name

XGrabKey – grab a key.

Synopsis

```
XGrabKey(display, keycode, modifiers, grab_window, owner_events,
              pointer_mode, keyboard_mode)
    Display *display;
    int keycode;
    unsigned int modifiers;
    Window grab_window;
    Bool owner_events;
    int pointer_mode, keyboard_mode;
```

Arguments

display
: Specifies a connection to an X server; returned from XOpenDisplay().

keycode
: Specifies the keycode to be grabbed. It may be a modifier key. Specifying AnyKey is equivalent to issuing the request for all key codes.

modifiers
: Specifies a set of keymasks. This is a bitwise OR of one or more of the following symbols: ShiftMask, LockMask, ControlMask, Mod1Mask, Mod2Mask, Mod3Mask, Mod4Mask, Mod5Mask, or AnyModifier. AnyModifier is equivalent to issuing the grab key request for all possible modifier combinations (including no modifiers). All specified modifiers do not need to have currently assigned keycodes.

grab_window
: Specifies the window in which the specified key combination will initiate an active grab.

owner_events
: Specifies whether the grab window should receive all events (False) or whether the grabbing application should receive all events normally (True).

pointer_mode
: Controls processing of pointer events during the grab. Pass one of these constants: GrabModeSync or GrabModeAsync.

keyboard_mode
: Controls processing of keyboard events during the grab. Pass one of these constants: GrabModeSync or GrabModeAsync.

Description

XGrabKey() establishes a passive grab on the specified keys, such that when the specified key/modifier combination is pressed, the keyboard may be grabbed, and all keyboard events sent to this application. More formally, once an XGrabKey() call has been issued on a particular key/button combination:

- IF the keyboard is not already actively grabbed,

- AND the specified key, which itself can be a modifier key, is logically pressed when the specified modifier keys are logically down,

- AND no other keys or modifier keys are logically down,

- AND EITHER the grab window is an ancestor of (or is) the focus window OR the grab window is a descendent of the focus window and contains the pointer,

- AND a passive grab on the same key combination does not exist on any ancestor of the grab window,

- THEN the keyboard is actively grabbed, as for XGrabKeyboard(), the last keyboard grab time is set to the time at which the key was pressed (as transmitted in the Key-Press event), and the KeyPress event is reported.

The active grab is terminated automatically when the specified key is released (independent of the state of the modifier keys).

The *pointer_mode* and *keyboard_mode* control the processing of events during the grab. If either is GrabModeSync, events for that device are not sent from the server to Xlib until XAllowEvents() is called to send the events. If either is GrabModeAsync, events for that device are sent normally.

For more information on grabbing, see Volume One, Chapter 9, *The Keyboard and Pointer*.

Errors

BadAccess   When using AnyModifier or AnyKey and another client has grabbed any overlapping combinations. In this case, no grabs are established.

                               Another client has issued XGrabKey() for the same key combination in *grab_window*.

BadValue   *keycode* is not in the range between min_keycode and max_ keycode as returned by XDisplayKeycodes().

BadWindow

See Also

XChangeActivePointerGrab(), XGrabButton(), XGrabKeyboard(), XGrabPointer(), XGrabServer(), XUngrabButton(), XUngrabKey(), XUngrabKeyboard(), XUngrabPointer(), XUngrabServer().

XGrabKeyboard

Name

XGrabKeyboard – grab the keyboard.

Synopsis

```
int XGrabKeyboard(display, grab_window, owner_events, pointer_mode,
                  keyboard_mode, time)
    Display *display;
    Window grab_window;
    Bool owner_events;
    int pointer_mode, keyboard_mode;
    Time time;
```

Arguments

display   Specifies a connection to an X server; returned from XOpenDisplay().

grab_window Specifies the ID of the window that requires continuous keyboard input.

owner_events
        Specifies a boolean value of either True or False. See the "Description" section below.

pointer_mode
        Controls processing of pointer events during the grab. Pass either Grab-ModeSync or GrabModeAsync.

keyboard_mode
        Controls processing of keyboard events during the grab. Pass either GrabModeSync or GrabModeAsync.

time   Specifies the time when the grab should take place. Pass either a time-stamp, expressed in milliseconds, or the constant CurrentTime.

Returns

GrabSuccess on success. AlreadyGrabbed, GrabNotViewable, GrabInvalid-Time, or GrabFrozen on failure.

Description

XGrabKeyboard() actively grabs control of the main keyboard. Further key events are reported only to the grabbing client. This request generates FocusIn and FocusOut events.

XGrabKeyboard() processing is controlled by the value in the *owner_events* argument:

• If *owner_events* is False, all generated key events are reported to *grab_window*.

- If *owner_events* is True, then if a generated key event would normally be reported to this client, it is reported normally. Otherwise the event is reported to *grab_window*.

Both KeyPress and KeyRelease events are always reported, independent of any event selection made by the client.

XGrabKeyboard() processing of pointer events and keyboard events are controlled by *pointer_mode* and *keyboard_mode*:

- If the *pointer_mode* or *keyboard_mode* is GrabModeAsync, event processing for the respective device continues normally.

- For *keyboard_mode* GrabModeAsync only: if the keyboard was currently frozen by this client, then processing of keyboard events is resumed.

- If the *pointer_mode* or *keyboard_mode* is GrabModeSync, events for the respective device are queued by the server until a releasing XAllowEvents() request occurs or until the keyboard grab is released as described above.

If the grab is successful, XGrabKeyboard() returns the constant GrabSuccess. XGrabKeyboard() fails under the following conditions and returns the following:

- If the keyboard is actively grabbed by some other client, it returns AlreadyGrabbed.

- If *grab_window* is not viewable, it returns GrabNotViewable.

- If *time* is earlier than the last keyboard grab time or later than the current server time, it returns GrabInvalidTime.

- If the pointer is frozen by an active grab of another client, the request fails with a status GrabFrozen.

If the grab succeeds, the last keyboard grab time is set to the specified time, with Current-Time replaced by the current X server time.

For more information on grabbing, see Volume One, Chapter 9, *The Keyboard and Pointer*.

Errors

```
BadValue
BadWindow
```

See Also

XChangeActivePointerGrab(), XGrabButton(), XGrabKey(), XGrabPointer(), XGrabServer(), XUngrabButton(), XUngrabKey(), XUngrabKeyboard(), XUngrabPointer(), XUngrabServer().

Name

XGrabPointer – grab the pointer.

Synopsis

```
int XGrabPointer(display, grab_window, owner_events, event_mask,
                 pointer_mode, keyboard_mode, confine_to, cursor, time)
    Display *display;
    Window grab_window;
    Bool owner_events;
    unsigned int event_mask;
    int pointer_mode, keyboard_mode;
    Window confine_to;
    Cursor cursor;
    Time time;
```

Arguments

display   Specifies a connection to an X server; returned from XOpenDisplay().

grab_window   Specifies the ID of the window that should grab the pointer input independent of pointer location.

owner_events
                   Specifies if the pointer events are to be reported normally within this application (pass True) or only to the grab window (pass False).

event_mask   Specifies the event mask symbols that can be ORed together. Only events selected by this mask, plus ButtonPress and ButtonRelease, will be delivered during the grab. See XSelectInput() for a complete list of event masks.

pointer_mode
                   Controls further processing of pointer events. Pass either GrabModeSync or GrabModeAsync.

keyboard_mode
                   Controls further processing of keyboard events. Pass either GrabMode-Sync or GrabModeAsync.

confine_to   Specifies the ID of the window to confine the pointer. One option is None, in which case the pointer is not confined to any window.

cursor   Specifies the ID of the cursor that is displayed with the pointer during the grab. One option is None, which causes the cursor to keep its current pattern.

time   Specifies the time when the grab request took place. Pass either a timestamp, expressed in milliseconds (from an event), or the constant CurrentTime.

Returns

`GrabSuccess` on success. `GrabNotViewable`, `AlreadyGrabbed`, `GrabInvalid-Time`, or `GrabFrozen` on failure.

Description

`XGrabPointer()` actively grabs control of the pointer. Further pointer events are only reported to the grabbing client until `XUngrabPointer()` is called.

event_mask is always augmented to include `ButtonPressMask` and `Button-ReleaseMask`. If *owner_events* is `False`, all generated pointer events are reported to *grab_window*, and are only reported if selected by *event_mask*. If *owner_events* is `True`, then if a generated pointer event would normally be reported to this client, it is reported normally; otherwise the event is reported with respect to the *grab_window*, and is only reported if selected by *event_mask*. For either value of *owner_events*, unreported events are discarded.

pointer_mode controls processing of pointer events during the grab, and *keyboard_mode* controls further processing of main keyboard events. If the mode is `GrabModeAsync`, event processing continues normally. If the mode is `GrabModeSync`, events for the device are queued by the server but not sent to clients until the grabbing client issues a releasing `XAllowEvents()` request or an `XUngrabPointer()` request.

If a cursor is specified, then it is displayed regardless of which window the pointer is in. If no cursor is specified, then when the pointer is in *grab_window* or one of its subwindows, the normal cursor for that window is displayed. When the pointer is outside `grab_window`, the cursor for *grab_window* is displayed.

If a *confine_to* window is specified, then the pointer will be restricted to that window. The *confine_to* window need have no relationship to the *grab_window*. If the pointer is not initially in the *confine_to* window, then it is warped automatically to the closest edge (and enter/leave events generated normally) just before the grab activates. If the *confine_to* window is subsequently reconfigured, the pointer will be warped automatically as necessary to keep it contained in the window.

The *time* argument lets you avoid certain circumstances that come up if applications take a long while to respond or if there are long network delays. Consider a situation where you have two applications, both of which normally grab the pointer when clicked on. If both applications specify the timestamp from the `ButtonPress` event, the second application will successfully grab the pointer, while the first will get a return value of `Already-Grabbed`, indicating that the other application grabbed the pointer before its request was processed. This is the desired response because the latest user action is most important in this case.

`XGrabPointer()` generates `EnterNotify` and `LeaveNotify` events.

If the grab is successful, it returns the constant `GrabSuccess`. The `XGrabPointer()` function fails under the following conditions, with the following return values:

- If *grab_window* or *confine_to* window is not viewable, or if the `confine_to` window is completely off the screen, `GrabNotViewable` is returned.

- If the pointer is actively grabbed by some other client, the constant `AlreadyGrabbed` is returned.

- If the pointer is frozen by an active grab of another client, `GrabFrozen` is returned.

- If the specified time is earlier than the last-pointer-grab time or later than the current X server time, `GrabInvalidTime` is returned. (If the call succeeds, the last pointer grab time is set to the specified time, with the constant `CurrentTime` replaced by the current X server time.)

For more information on grabbing, see Volume One, Chapter 9, *The Keyboard and Pointer*.

Errors

```
BadCursor
BadValue
BadWindow
```

See Also

XChangeActivePointerGrab(), XGrabButton(), XGrabKey(), XGrabKeyboard(), XGrabServer(), XUngrabButton(), XUngrabKey(), XUngrabKeyboard(), XUngrabPointer(), XUngrabServer().

XGrabServer

Name

XGrabServer – grab the server.

Synopsis

```
XGrabServer(display)
    Display *display;
```

Arguments

display   Specifies a connection to an X server; returned from XOpenDisplay().

Description

Grabbing the server means that only requests by the calling client will be acted on. All others will be queued in the server until the next XUngrabServer() call. The X server should not be grabbed any more than is absolutely necessary.

See Also

XChangeActivePointerGrab(), XGrabButton(), XGrabKey(), XGrabKeyboard(), XGrabPointer(), XUngrabButton(), XUngrabKey(), XUngrabKeyboard(), XUngrabPointer(), XUngrabServer().

XHeight*OfScreen

Name

XHeightOfScreen, XHeightMMOfScreen, HeightOfScreen, HeightMMOfScreen – get height of screen in pixels or millimeters

Synopsis

```
int XHeightOfScreen(screen)
      Screen *screen;

int XHeightMMOfScreen(screen)
      Screen *screen;
```

Arguments

screen   Specifies the appropriate Screen structure.

Returns

Height in pixels or millimeters.

Description

XHeightOfScreen() returns the height of the specified screen in pixels. XHeight-MMOfScreen() returns the height of the specified screen in millimeters.

The C language macros HeightOfScreen() and HeightMMOfScreen() are equivalent and slightly more efficient.

These functions are equivalent to XDisplayHeight*() and XDisplayHeightMM() except that they take different arguments.

See Also

XDisplayHeight()*, *XDisplayHeightMM()*.

XIconifyWindow

Name

XIconifyWindow – request that a top-level window be iconified.

Synopsis

```
Status XIconifyWindow(display, w, screen_number)
    Display *display;
    Window w;
    int screen_number;
```

Arguments

display   Specifies a connection to an X server; returned from XOpenDisplay().

w   Specifies the window.

screen_number

Specifies the appropriate screen number on the server.

Returns

Zero on failure, non-zero on success.

Availability

Release 4 and later.

Description

XIconifyWindow() sends a WM_CHANGE_STATE ClientMessage event with a format of 32 and a first data element of IconicState (as described in Section 4.1.4 of the *Inter-Client Communication Conventions Manual* in Volume Zero, *X Protocol Reference Manual*), to the root window of the specified screen. Window managers may elect to receive this message and, if the window is in its normal state, may treat it as a request to change the window's state from normal to iconic. If the WM_CHANGE_STATE property cannot be interned, XIconifyWindow() does not send a message and returns a zero status. It returns a non-zero status if the client message is sent successfully; otherwise, it returns a zero status.

For more information, see Volume One, Chapter 10, *Interclient Communication*.

Errors

BadWindow

See Also

XReconfigureWindow, XWithdrawWindow().

XIfEvent

Name

XIfEvent – wait for event matched in predicate procedure.

Synopsis

```
XIfEvent(display, event_return, predicate, args)
    Display *display;
    XEvent *event_return;
    Bool (*predicate)();
    char *args;
```

Arguments

display   Specifies a connection to an X server; returned from XOpenDisplay().

event_return
                 Returns the matched event.

predicate   Specifies the procedure to be called to determine if the next event satisfies
                 your criteria.

args   Specifies the user-specified arguments to be passed to the predicate proce-
                 dure.

Description

XIfEvent() checks the event queue for events, uses the user-supplied routine to check if
one meets certain criteria, and removes the matching event from the input queue.
XIfEvent() returns only when the specified predicate procedure returns True for an
event. The specified predicate is called once for each event on the queue until a match is
made, and each time an event is added to the queue, with the arguments display,
event_return, and arg.

If no matching events exist on the queue, XIfEvent() flushes the request buffer and waits
for an appropriate event to arrive. Use XCheckIfEvent() if you don't want to wait for an
event.

For more information, see Volume One, Chapter 8, *Events*.

See Also

*XQLength(), XAllowEvents(), XCheckIfEvent(), XCheckMaskEvent(), XCheckTypedEvent(), XCheck-
TypedWindowEvent(), XCheckWindowEvent(), XEventsQueued(), XGetInputFocus(), XGetMotion-
Events(), XMaskEvent(), XNextEvent(), XPeekEvent(), XPeekIfEvent(), XPending(), XPutBackEvent(),
XSelectInput(), XSendEvent(), XSetInputFocus(), XSynchronize(), XWindowEvent().*

XImageByteOrder

Name

XImageByteOrder, ImageByteOrder – get server's byte order.

Synopsis

```
int XImageByteOrder(display)
    Display *display;
```

Arguments

display   Specifies a connection to an X server; returned from XOpenDisplay().

Returns

LSBFirst or MSBFirst.

Description

XImageByteOrder() specifies the required byte order for images for each scanline unit in XY format (bitmap) or for each pixel value in Z format. It can return either LSBFirst or MSBFirst.

The C language macro ImageByteOrder() is equivalent and slightly more efficient.

See Also

XGetImage(), XPutImage().

XIMOfIC

Name

XIMOfIC – obtain the input method of an input context.

Synopsis

```
XIM XIMOfIC(ic)
    XIC ic;
```

Arguments

ic   Specifies the input context.

Returns

The input method.

Availability

Release 5 and later.

Description

XIMOfIC() returns the input method associated with a given input context.

See Also

XSetICFocus(), XSetICValues(), XCreateIC(), XDestroyIC(), XmbResetIC(), XwcResetIC.

XInsertModifiermapEntry

Name

XInsertModifiermapEntry – add a new entry to an `XModifierKeymap` structure.

Synopsis

```
XModifierKeymap *XInsertModifiermapEntry(modmap,
                keycode_entry, modifier)
    XModifierKeymap *modmap;
    KeyCode keycode_entry;
    int modifier;
```

Arguments

modmap   Specifies a pointer to an `XModifierKeymap()` structure.

keycode_entry
      Specifies the keycode of the key to be added to *modmap*.

modifier   Specifies the modifier you want mapped to the keycode specified in *key-code_entry*. This should be one of the constants: `ShiftMapIndex`, `LockMapIndex`, `ControlMapIndex`, `Mod1MapIndex`, `Mod2MapIndex`, `Mod3MapIndex`, `Mod4MapIndex`, or `Mod5MapIndex`.

Returns

The modifier map structure with the keycode added.

Description

`XInsertModifiermapEntry()` returns an `XModifierKeymap` structure suitable for calling `XSetModifierMapping()`, in which the specified keycode is added to the set of keycodes that is mapped to the specified modifier (like Shift or Control). `XInsertModifiermapEntry()` does not change the mapping itself.

This function is normally used by calling `XGetModifierMapping()` to get a pointer to the current `XModifierKeymap` structure for use as the *modmap* argument to `XInsertModifiermapEntry()`.

Note that the structure pointed to by *modmap* is freed by `XInsertModifiermapEntry()`. It should not be freed or otherwise used by applications.

For a description of the modifier map, see `XSetModifierMapping()`.

Structures

```
typedef struct {
    int max_keypermod;        /* server's max number of keys per modifier */
    KeyCode *modifiermap;     /* an 8 by max_keypermod array of
                               * keycodes to be used as modifiers */
} XModifierKeymap;
```

```
#define ShiftMapIndex      0
#define LockMapIndex       1
#define ControlMapIndex    2
#define Mod1MapIndex       3
#define Mod2MapIndex       4
#define Mod3MapIndex       5
#define Mod4MapIndex       6
#define Mod5MapIndex       7
```

See Also

XDeleteModifiermapEntry(), *XFreeModifiermap()*, *XGetKeyboardMapping()*, *XGetModifierMapping()*, *XKeycodeToKeysym()*, *XKeysymToKeycode()*, *XKeysymToString()*, *XLookupKeysym()*, *XLookupString()*, *XNewModifierMap*, *XQueryKeymap()*, *XRebindKeySym*, *XRefreshKeyboardMapping()*, *XSetModifierMapping()*, *XStringToKeysym()*.

XInstallColormap

Name

XInstallColormap – install a colormap.

Synopsis

```
XInstallColormap(display, colormap_return)
    Display *display;
    Colormap colormap_return;
```

Arguments

display   Specifies a connection to an X server; returned from XOpenDisplay().

colormap_return
                 Specifies the colormap to install.

Description

XInstallColormap() installs a virtual colormap into a hardware colormap. If there is only one hardware colormap, XInstallColormap() loads a virtual colormap into the hardware colormap. All windows associated with this colormap immediately display with their chosen colors. Other windows associated with the old colormap will display with false colors. If additional hardware colormaps are possible, XInstallColormap() loads the new hardware map and keeps the existing ones. Other windows will then remain in their true colors unless the limit for colormaps has been reached. If the maximum number of allowed hardware colormaps is already installed, an old colormap is swapped out. The MinCmaps-OfScreen(*screen*) and MaxCmapsOfScreen(*screen*) macros can be used to determine how many hardware colormaps are supported.

If *colormap_return* is not already an installed map, a ColormapNotify event is generated on every window having *colormap_return* as an attribute. If a colormap is uninstalled as a result of the install, a ColormapNotify event is generated on every window having that colormap as an attribute.

Colormaps are usually installed and uninstalled by the window manager, not by clients. At any time, there is a subset of the installed colormaps, viewed as an ordered list, called the "required list." The length of the required list is at most the min_maps specified for each screen in the Display structure. When a colormap is installed with XInstall-Colormap() it is added to the head of the required list and the last colormap in the list is removed if necessary to keep the length of the list at min_maps. When a colormap is uninstalled with XUninstallColormap() and it is in the required list, it is removed from the list. No other actions by the server or the client change the required list. It is important to realize that on all but high-performance workstations, min_maps is likely to be 1. If the hardware colormap is immutable, and therefore installing any colormap is impossible, XInstallColormap() will work but not do anything.

For more information, see Volume One, Chapter 7, *Color*.

Errors

`BadColor`   Invalid colormap.

See Also

XDefaultColormap(), *XDisplayCells()*, *XCopyColormapAndFree()*, *XCreateColormap()*, *XFree-Colormap()*, *XGetStandardColormap()*, *XListInstalledColormaps()*, *XSetStandardColormap()*, *XSet-WindowColormap()*, *XUninstallColormap()*.

XInternAtom

Name

XInternAtom – return an atom for a given property name string.

Synopsis

```
Atom XInternAtom(display, property_name, only_if_exists)
    Display *display;
    char *property_name;
    Bool only_if_exists;
```

Arguments

display   Specifies a connection to an X server; returned from XOpenDisplay().

property_name
                 Specifies the string name of the property for which you want the atom.
                 Uppercase or lowercase is important. If the property name is not in the
                 Host Portable Character Encoding, then the result is implementation-
                 dependent.

only_if_exists
                 Specifies a boolean value: if no such property_name exists XIntern-
                 Atom() will return None if this argument is set to True or will create the
                 atom if it is set to False.

Returns

The atom.

Description

XInternAtom() returns the atom identifier corresponding to string property_name. If
the atom does not exist, then XInternAtom() either returns None (if only_if_exists
is True) or creates the atom and returns its ID (if only_if_exists is False). The
string name should be a NULL-terminated. Case matters: the strings "thing," "Thing," and
"thinG" all designate different atoms. The atom will remain defined even after the client that
defined it has exited. It will become undefined only when the last connection to the X server
closes. Therefore, the number of atoms interned should be kept to a minimum.

This function is the opposite of XGetAtomName(), which returns the atom name when
given an atom ID.

Predefined atoms require no call to XInternAtom(). Predefined atoms are defined in
<X11/Xatom.h> and begin with the prefix XA_. Predefined atoms are the only ones that do
not require a call to XInternAtom().

Errors

```
BadAlloc
BadValue
```

See Also

XChangeProperty(), *XDeleteProperty()*, *XGetAtomName()*, *XGetFontProperty()*, *XGetWindow-Property()*, *XListProperties()*, *XRotateWindowProperties()*, *XSetStandardProperties()*.

XIntersectRegion

Name

XIntersectRegion – compute the intersection of two regions.

Synopsis

```
XIntersectRegion(sra, srb, dr_return)
    Region sra, srb;
    Region dr_return;
```

Arguments

sra   Specify the two regions with which to perform the computation.
srb

dr_return   Returns the result of the computation.

Description

XIntersectRegion() generates a region that is the intersection of two regions.

Structures

Region is a pointer to an opaque structure type.

See Also

XClipBox(), XCreateRegion(), XDestroyRegion(), XEmptyRegion(), XEqualRegion(), XOffsetRegion(), XPointInRegion(), XPolygonRegion(), XRectInRegion(), XSetRegion(), XShrinkRegion(), XSubtract-Region(), XUnionRectWithRegion(), XUnionRegion(), XXorRegion().

XKeycodeToKeysym

Name

XKeycodeToKeysym – convert a keycode to a keysym.

Synopsis

```
KeySym XKeycodeToKeysym(display, keycode, index)
    Display *display;
    KeyCode keycode;
    int index;
```

Arguments

display   Specifies a connection to an X server; returned from XOpenDisplay().

keycode   Specifies the keycode.

index   Specifies which keysym in the list for the keycode to return.

Returns

The KeySym.

Description

XKeycodeToKeysym() returns one of the keysyms defined for the specified keycode. XKeycodeToKeysym() uses internal Xlib tables. index specifies which keysym in the array of keysyms corresponding to a keycode should be returned. If no symbol is defined, XKeycodeToKeysym() returns NoSymbol.

See Also

IsCursorKey(), IsFunctionKey(), IsKeypadKey(), IsMiscFunctionKey(), IsModifierKey(), IsPFKey(), XChangeKeyboardMapping(), XDeleteModifiermapEntry(), XDisplayKeycodes(), XFreeModifiermap(), XGetKeyboardMapping(), XGetModifierMapping(), XInsertModifiermapEntry(), XKeysymToKeycode(), XKeysymToString(), XLookupKeysym(), XLookupString(), XNewModifiermap(), XQueryKeymap(), XRebindKeysym(), XRefreshKeyboardMapping(), XSetModifierMapping(), XStringToKeysym().

XKeysymToKeycode

Name

XKeysymToKeycode – convert a keysym to the appropriate keycode.

Synopsis

```
KeyCode XKeysymToKeycode(display, keysym)
    Display *display;
    Keysym keysym;
```

Arguments

display   Specifies a connection to an X server; returned from `XOpenDisplay()`.

keysym   Specifies the keysym that is to be searched for.

Returns

The keycode.

Description

`XKeysymToKeycode()` returns the keycode corresponding to the specified keysym in the current mapping. If the specified keysym is not defined for any keycode, `XKeysymToKeycode()` returns zero.

See Also

IsCursorKey(), IsFunctionKey(), IsKeypadKey(), IsMiscFunctionKey(), IsModifierKey(), IsPFKey(), XChangeKeyboardMapping(), XDeleteModifiermapEntry(), XDisplayKeycodes(), XFreeModifiermap(), XGetKeyboardMapping(), XGetModifierMapping(), XInsertModifiermapEntry(), XKeycodeToKeysym(), XKeysymToString(), XLookupKeysym(), XLookupString(), XNewModifiermap(), XQueryKeymap(), XRebindKeysym(), XRefreshKeyboardMapping(), XSetModifierMapping(), XStringToKeysym().

XKeysymToString

Name

XKeysymToString – convert a keysym symbol to a string.

Synopsis

```
char *XKeysymToString(keysym)
    KeySym keysym;
```

Arguments

keysym   Specifies the keysym that is to be converted.

Returns

The string mapped to the specified keysym.

Description

XKeysymToString() converts a keysym symbol (a number) into a character string. The returned string is in a static area and must not be modified. The returned string is in the Host Portable Character Encoding. If the specified keysym is not defined, XKeysymToString() returns NULL. For example, XKeysymToString() converts XK_Shift to "Shift".

Note that XKeysymString does not return the string that is mapped to the keysym, but only a string version of the keysym itself. In other words, even if the F1 key is mapped to the string "STOP" using XRebindKeysym(), XKeysymToString() still returns "F1". XLookupString(), however, would return "STOP".

In Release 4, XKeysymToString() can process keysyms that are not defined by the Xlib standard. Note that the set of keysyms that are available in this manner and the mechanisms by which Xlib obtains them is implementation-dependent. (In the MIT sample implementation, the resource file */usr/lib/X11/XKeysymDB* is used starting in Release 4. The keysym name is used as the resource name, and the resource value is the keysym value in uppercase hexadecimal.)

See Also

IsCursorKey(), IsFunctionKey(), IsKeypadKey(), IsMiscFunctionKey(), IsModifierKey(), IsPFKey(), XChangeKeyboardMapping(), XDeleteModifiermapEntry(), XFreeModifiermap(), XGetKeyboard-Mapping(), XGetModifierMapping(), XInsertModifiermapEntry(), XKeycodeToKeysym(), XKeysymTo-Keycode(), XLookupKeysym(), XLookupString(), XNewModifiermap(), XQueryKeymap(), XRebind-Keysym(), XRefreshKeyboardMapping(), XSetModifierMapping(), XStringToKeysym().

XKillClient

Name

XKillClient – destroy a client or its remaining resources.

Synopsis

```
XKillClient(display, resource)
    Display *display;
    XID resource;
```

Arguments

display   Specifies a connection to an X server; returned from XOpenDisplay().

resource   Specifies any resource created by the client you want to destroy, or the constant AllTemporary.

Description

If a valid resource is specified, XKillClient() forces a close-down of the client that created the resource. If the client has already terminated in either RetainPermanent or RetainTemporary mode, all of the client's resources are destroyed. If AllTemporary is specified in the *resource* argument, then the resources of all clients that have terminated in RetainTemporary are destroyed.

For more information, see Volume One, Chapter 13, *Other Programming Techniques*.

Errors

BadValue

See Also

XSetCloseDownMode().

XLastKnownRequestProcessed

Name

XLastKnownRequestProcessed, LastKnownRequestProcessed – get serial number of last request processed by server.

Synopsis

```
unsigned long XLastKnownRequestProcessed(display)
    Display *display;
```

Arguments

display   Specifies a connection to an X server; returned from XOpenDisplay().

Returns

The serial number.

Description

XLastKnownRequestProcessed() extracts the full serial number of the last request known by Xlib to have been processed by the X server. Xlib automatically sets this number when replies, events, and errors are received. This can be useful in error and warning handlers.

The C language macro LastKnownRequestProcessed() is equivalent and slightly more efficient.

See Also

XNextRequest().

XListDepths

Name

XListDepths – determine the depths available on a given screen.

Synopsis

```
int *XListDepths(display, screen_number, count_return)
    Display *display;
    int screen_number;
    int *count_return;
```

Arguments

display   Specifies a connection to an X server; returned from `XOpenDisplay()`.

screen_number
       Specifies the appropriate screen number on the host server.

count_return
       Returns the number of depths.

Returns

The list of depths, or NULL on failure.

Availability

Release 4 and later.

Description

`XListDepths()` returns the array of depths that are available on the specified screen. If the specified *screen_number* is valid and sufficient memory for the array can be allocated, `XListDepths()` sets *count_return* to the number of available depths. Otherwise, it does not set *count_return* and returns NULL. To release the memory allocated for the array of depths, use `XFree()`.

See Also

XDefaultDepthOfScreen(), XDefaultDepth(), XListPixmapFormats().

XListExtensions

Name

XListExtensions – return a list of all extensions to X supported by the server.

Synopsis

```
char **XListExtensions(display, nextensions_return)
    Display *display;
    int *nextensions_return;
```

Arguments

display   Specifies a connection to an X server; returned from XOpenDisplay().

nextensions_return
              Returns the number of extensions in the returned list.

Returns

The list of extension name strings.

Description

XListExtensions() lists all the X extensions supported by the current server. If the data returned by the server is in the Latin Portable Character Encoding, then the returned strings are in the Host Portable Character Encoding. Otherwise, the result is implementation-dependent.

For more information on extensions, see Volume One, Chapter 13, *Other Programming Techniques*.

See Also

XFreeExtensionList(), XQueryExtension().

XListFonts

Name

XListFonts – return a list of the available font names.

Synopsis

```
char **XListFonts(display, pattern, maxnames, actual_count_return)
    Display *display;
    char *pattern;
    int maxnames;
    int *actual_count_return;
```

Arguments

display   Specifies a connection to an X server; returned from XOpenDisplay().

pattern   Specifies the string associated with the font names you want returned. You
                can specify any string, including asterisks (*) and question marks (?). The
                asterisk indicates a wildcard for any number of characters and the question
                mark indicates a wildcard for a single character. Uppercase or lowercase is
                not important. If the pattern string is not in the Host Portable Character
                Encoding the result is implementation-dependent.

maxnames   Specifies the maximum number of names that are to be in the returned list.

actual_count_return
                Returns the actual number of font names in the list.

Returns

The list of font names.

Description

XListFonts() returns a list of font names that match the string *pattern*. Each returned
font name string is terminated by NULL. If the data returned by the server is in the Latin Portable Character Encoding, then the returned strings are in the Host Portable Character Encoding. Otherwise, the result is implementation-dependent. The maximum number of names
returned in the list is the value you passed to *maxnames*. The function returns the actual
number of font names in *actual_count_return*.

If no fonts match the specified names, XListFonts() returns NULL.

The client should call XFreeFontNames() when done with the font name list.

The font search path (the order in which font names in various directories are compared to
pattern) is set by XSetFontPath().

For more information on fonts, see Volume One, Chapter 6, *Drawing Graphics and Text*.

See Also

XCreateFontCursor(), XFreeFont(), XFreeFontInfo(), XFreeFontNames(), XFreeFontPath(), XGet-FontPath(), XGetFontProperty(), XListFontsWithInfo(), XLoadFont(), XLoadQueryFont(), XQuery-Font(), XSetFont(), XSetFontPath(), XUnloadFont().

XListFontsWithInfo

Name

XListFontsWithInfo – obtain the names and information about available fonts.

Synopsis

```
char **XListFontsWithInfo(display, pattern, maxnames,
                count_return, info_return)
    Display *display;
    char *pattern;    /* NULL-terminated */
    int maxnames;
    int *count_return;
    XFontStruct **info_return;
```

Arguments

display   Specifies a connection to an X server; returned from `XOpenDisplay()`.

pattern   Specifies the string associated with the font names you want returned. You can specify any string, including asterisks (*) and question marks (?). The asterisk indicates a wildcard on any number of characters and the question mark indicates a wildcard on a single character. Uppercase or lowercase is not important. If the pattern string is not in the Host Portable Character Encoding the result is implementation-dependent.

maxnames   Specifies the maximum number of names that are to be in the returned list.

count_return

Returns the actual number of matched font names.

info_return Returns a pointer to a list of font information structures. `XListFonts-WithInfo()` provides enough space for *maxnames* pointers.

Returns

The list of font names.

Description

`XListFontsWithInfo()` returns a list of font names that match the specified *pattern* and a also returns limited information about each font that matches. The list of names is limited to the size specified by the *maxnames* argument. If the data returned by the server is in the Latin Portable Character Encoding, then the returned strings are in the Host Portable Character Encoding. Otherwise, the result is implementation-dependent.

`XListFontsWithInfo()` returns NULL if no matches were found.

To free the allocated name array, the client should call `XFreeFontNames()`. To free the font information array, the client should call `XFreeFontInfo()`.

The information returned for each font is identical to what `XLoadQueryFont()` would return, except that the per-character metrics (`lbearing`, `rbearing`, `width`, `ascent`, `descent` for single characters) are not returned.

The font search path (the order in which font names in various directories are compared to *pattern*) is set by `XSetFontPath()`.

For more information on fonts, see Volume One, Chapter 6, *Drawing Graphics and Text*.

Structures

```
typedef struct {
    XExtData *ext_data;             /* hook for extension to hang data */
    Font fid;                       /* Font ID for this font */
    unsigned direction;             /* hint about direction the font is painted */
    unsigned min_char_or_byte2;     /* first character */
    unsigned max_char_or_byte2;     /* last character */
    unsigned min_byte1;             /* first row that exists */
    unsigned max_byte1;             /* last row that exists */
    Bool all_chars_exist;           /* flag if all characters have non-zero size */
    unsigned default_char;          /* char to print for undefined character */
    int n_properties;               /* how many properties there are */
    XFontProp *properties;          /* pointer to array of additional properties */
    XCharStruct min_bounds;         /* minimum bounds over all existing char */
    XCharStruct max_bounds;         /* minimum bounds over all existing char */
    XCharStruct *per_char;          /* first_char to last_char information */
    int ascent;                     /* logical extent above baseline for spacing */
    int descent;                    /* logical descent below baseline for spacing */
} XFontStruct;
```

See Also

XCreateFontCursor(), XFreeFont(), XFreeFontInfo(), XFreeFontNames(), XFreeFontPath(), XGetFontPath(), XGetFontProperty(), XListFonts(), XLoadFont(), XLoadQueryFont(), XQueryFont(), XSetFont(), XSetFontPath(), XUnloadFont().

Name

XListHosts – obtain a list of hosts having access to this display.

Synopsis

```
XHostAddress *XListHosts(display, nhosts_return, state_return)
    Display *display;
    int *nhosts_return;
    Bool *state_return;
```

Arguments

display   Specifies a connection to an X server; returned from `XOpenDisplay()`.

nhosts_return
        Returns the number of hosts currently in the access control list.

state_return
        Returns whether the access control list is currently being used by the server to process new connection requests from clients. `True` if enabled, `False` if disabled.

Returns

The list of structures describing each host.

Description

`XListHosts()` returns the current access control list as well as whether the use of the list is enabled or disabled. `XListHosts()` allows a program to find out what machines make connections, by looking at a list of host structures. This `XHostAddress` list should be freed when it is no longer needed.

For more information on access control lists, see Volume One, Chapter 13, *Other Programming Techniques*.

Structures

```
typedef struct {
    int family;
    int length;
    char *address;
} XHostAddress;
```

See Also

XAddHost(), *XAddHosts()*, *XDisableAccessControl()*, *XEnableAccessControl()*, *XRemoveHost()*, *XRemoveHosts()*, *XSetAccessControl()*.

XListInstalledColormaps

Name

XListInstalledColormaps – get a list of installed colormaps.

Synopsis

```
Colormap *XListInstalledColormaps(display, w, num_return)
    display *display;
    Window w;
    int *num_return;
```

Arguments

display	Specifies a connection to an X server; returned from XOpenDisplay().
w	Specifies the ID of the window for whose screen you want the list of currently installed colormaps.
num_return	Returns the number of currently installed colormaps in the returned list.

Returns

The list of colormaps.

Description

XListInstalledColormaps() returns a list of the currently installed colormaps for the screen containing the specified window. The order in the list is not significant. There is no distinction in the list between colormaps actually being used by windows and colormaps no longer in use which have not yet been freed or destroyed.

The allocated list should be freed using XFree() when it is no longer needed.

For more information on installing colormaps, see Volume One, Chapter 7, *Color*.

Errors

BadWindow

See Also

XDefaultColormap(), XDisplayCells(), XCopyColormapAndFree(), XCreateColormap(), XFreeColormap(), XGetStandardColormap(), XInstallColormap(), XSetStandardColormap(), XSetWindowColormap(), XUninstallColormap().

XListPixmapFormats

Name

XListPixmapFormats – obtain the supported pixmap formats for a given server.

Synopsis

```
XPixmapFormatValues *XListPixmapFormats(display, count_return)
    Display *display;
    int *count_return;
```

Arguments

display   Specifies a connection to an X server; returned from XOpenDisplay().

count_return
                Returns the number of pixmap formats that are supported by the server.

Returns

A list of structures describing pixmap formats.

Availability

Release 4 and later.

Description

XListPixmapFormats() returns an array of XPixmapFormatValues structures that describe the types of Z format images that are supported by the specified server. If insufficient memory is available, XListPixmapFormats() returns NULL. To free the allocated storage for the XPixmapFormatValues structures, use XFree().

Structures

```
typedef struct {
    int depth;
    int bits_per_pixel;
    int scanline_pad;
} XPixmapFormatValues;
```

See Also

XListDepths().

XListProperties

Name

XListProperties – get the property list for a window.

Synopsis

```
Atom *XListProperties(display, w, num_prop_return)
    Display *display;
    Window w;
    int *num_prop_return;
```

Arguments

display   Specifies a connection to an X server; returned from `XOpenDisplay()`.

w   Specifies the window whose property list you want.

num_prop_return
             Returns the length of the properties array.

Returns

The list of Atoms.

Description

`XListProperties()` returns a pointer to an array of atoms for properties that are defined for the specified window. `XListProperties()` returns NULL on failure (when window w is invalid or if no properties were found).

To free the memory allocated by this function, use `XFree()`.

For more information, see Volume One, Chapter 10, *Interclient Communication*.

Errors

`BadWindow`

See Also

XChangeProperty(), XDeleteProperty(), XGetAtomName(), XGetFontProperty(), XGetWindow-Property(), XInternAtom(), XRotateWindowProperties(), XSetStandardProperties().

XLoadFont

Name

XLoadFont – load a font if not already loaded; get font ID.

Synopsis

```
Font XLoadFont(display, name)
    Display *display;
    char *name;
```

Arguments

display   Specifies a connection to an X server; returned from XOpenDisplay().

name   Specifies the name of the font in a NULL-terminated string. As of Release 4, the * and ? wildcards are allowed and may be supported by the server. Uppercase or lowercase is not important. If the font name is not in the Host Portable Character Encoding, the result is implementation-dependent.

Returns

The Font ID.

Description

XLoadFont() loads a font into the server if it has not already been loaded by another client. XLoadFont() returns the font ID or, if it was unsuccessful, generates a BadName error. When the font is no longer needed, the client should call XUnloadFont(). Fonts are not associated with a particular screen. Once the font ID is available, it can be set in the font member of any GC, and thereby used in subsequent drawing requests.

Font information is usually necessary for locating the text. Call XLoadFontWithInfo() to get the info at the time you load the font, or call XQueryFont() if you used XLoadFont() to load the font.

For more information on fonts, see Volume One, Chapter 6, *Drawing Graphics and Text*.

Errors

BadAlloc   Server has insufficient memory to store font.

BadName   *name* specifies an unavailable font.

See Also

XCreateFontCursor(), XFreeFont(), XFreeFontInfo(), XFreeFontNames(), XFreeFontPath(), XGetFontPath(), XGetFontProperty(), XListFonts(), XListFontsWithInfo(), XLoadQueryFont(), XQueryFont(), XSetFont(), XSetFontPath(), XUnloadFont().

Name

XLoadQueryFont – load a font and fill information structure.

Synopsis

```
XFontStruct *XLoadQueryFont(display, name)
    Display *display;
    char *name;
```

Arguments

display   Specifies a connection to an X server; returned from `XOpenDisplay()`.

name   Specifies the name of the font. This name is a NULL-terminated string. As
             of Release 4, the * and ? wildcards are allowed and may be supported by
             the server. Uppercase or lowercase is not important. If the font name is not
             in the Host Portable Character Encoding, the result is implementation-
             dependent.

Returns

The font description structure.

Description

`XLoadQueryFont()` performs an `XLoadFont()` and `XQueryFont()` in a single
operation. `XLoadQueryFont()` provides the easiest way to get character-size tables for
placing a proportional font. That is, `XLoadQueryFont()` both opens (loads) the specified
font and returns a pointer to the appropriate `XFontStruct` structure. If the font does not
exist, `XLoadQueryFont()` returns NULL.

The `XFontStruct` structure consists of the font-specific information and a pointer to an
array of `XCharStruct` structures for each character in the font.

For more information on fonts, see Volume One, Chapter 6, *Drawing Graphics and Text*.

Errors

BadAlloc   Server has insufficient memory to store font.

BadName   name specifies an unavailable font.

Structures

```
typedef struct {
    XExtData *ext_data;          /* hook for extension to hang data */
    Font fid;                    /* Font ID for this font */
    unsigned direction;          /* hint about direction the font is painted */
    unsigned min_char_or_byte2;  /* first character */
```

```
          unsigned max_char_or_byte2;  /* last character */
          unsigned min_byte1;          /* first row that exists */
          unsigned max_byte1;          /* last row that exists */
          Bool all_chars_exist;        /* flag if all characters have non-zero size*/
          unsigned default_char;       /* char to print for undefined character */
          int n_properties;            /* how many properties there are */
          XFontProp *properties;       /* pointer to array of additional properties*/
          XCharStruct min_bounds;      /* minimum bounds over all existing char*/
          XCharStruct max_bounds;      /* minimum bounds over all existing char*/
          XCharStruct *per_char;       /* first_char to last_char information */
          int ascent;                  /* logical extent above baseline for spacing */
          int descent;                 /* logical descent below baseline for spacing */
} XFontStruct;

typedef struct {
          short lbearing;              /* origin to left edge of character */
          short rbearing;              /* origin to right edge of character */
          short width;                 /* advance to next char's origin */
          short ascent;                /* baseline to top edge of character */
          short descent;               /* baseline to bottom edge of character */
          unsigned short attributes;   /* per char flags (not predefined) */
} XCharStruct;
```

See Also

XCreateFontCursor(), XFreeFont(), XFreeFontInfo(), XFreeFontNames(), XFreeFontPath(), XGet-FontPath(), XGetFontProperty(), XListFonts(), XListFontsWithInfo(), XLoadFont(), XQueryFont(), XSetFont(), XSetFontPath(), XUnloadFont().

XLocaleOfFontSet

Name

XLocaleOfFontSet – get the locale of a font set.

Synopsis

```
char *XLocaleOfFontSet ( font_set )
    XFontSet font_set;
```

Arguments

font_set   Specifies the font set.

Returns

The locale name (NULL-terminated).

Availability

Release 5 and later.

Description

XLocaleOfFontSet() returns the name of the locale bound to the specified XFontSet, as a NULL-terminated string.

The returned locale name string is owned by Xlib and should not be modified or freed by the client. It may be freed by a call to XFreeFontSet() with the associated XFontSet. Until freed, it will not be modified by Xlib.

See Also

XCreateFontSet(), XExtentsOfFontSet(), XFontsOfFontSet(), XBaseFontNameListOfFontSet(), XContextDependentDrawing().

XLocaleOfIM

Name

XLocaleOfIM – get the locale of an input method.

Synopsis

```
char * XLocaleOfIM(im)
    XIM im;
```

Arguments

im   Specifies the input method.

Returns

The locale name.

Availability

Release 5 and later.

Description

XLocaleOfIM( ) returns the name of the locale associated with the specified input method. The returned string is owned by Xlib and should not be freed by the client.

See Also

XOpenIM(), *XCloseIM()*, *XGetIMValues()*, *XDisplayOfIM()*.

Name

XLookUpAssoc – obtain data from an association table.

Synopsis

```
char * XLookUpAssoc(display, table, x_id)
    Display *display;
    XAssocTable *table;
    XID x_id;
```

Arguments

display   Specifies a connection to an X server; returned from XOpenDisplay().

table   Specifies the association table.

x_id   Specifies the X resource ID.

Returns

The data from the association table.

Description

This function is provided for compatibility with X Version 10. To use it you must include the file *<X11/X10.h>* and link with the library *-loldX*.

Association tables provide a way of storing data locally and accessing by ID. XLookUp-Assoc() retrieves the data stored in an XAssocTable by its XID. If the matching XID can be found in the table, the routine returns the data associated with it. If the x_id cannot be found in the table the routine returns NULL.

For more information on association tables, see Volume One, Appendix B, *X10 Compatibility*.

Structures

```
typedef struct {
    XAssoc *buckets;          /* pointer to first bucket in bucket array */
    int size;                 /* table size (number of buckets) */
} XAssocTable;

typedef struct _XAssoc {
    struct _XAssoc *next;     /* next object in this bucket */
    struct _XAssoc *prev;     /* previous object in this bucket */
    Display *display;         /* display which owns the ID */
    XID x_id;                 /* X Window System ID */
    char *data;               /* pointer to untyped memory */
} XAssoc;
```

See Also

XCreateAssocTable(), XDeleteAssoc(), XDestroyAssocTable(), XMakeAssoc().

Name

XLookupColor – get database RGB values and closest hardware-supported RGB values from color name.

Synopsis

```
Status XLookupColor(display, colormap, colorname, exact_def_return,
      screen_def_return)
   Display *display;
   Colormap colormap;
   char *colorname;
   XColor *exact_def_return, *screen_def_return;
```

Arguments

display   Specifies a connection to an X server; returned from XOpen-Display().

colormap   Specifies the colormap.

colorname   Specifies a color name string (for example "red"). Uppercase or lowercase does not matter. If the color name is not in the Host Portable Character Encoding, the result is implementation-dependent.

exact_def_return
                 Returns the exact RGB values for the specified color name from the */usr/lib/X11/rgb* database.

screen_def_return
                 Returns the closest RGB values possible on the hardware.

Returns

Zero on failure, non-zero on success.

Description

XLookupColor() looks up RGB values for a color given the colorname string. It returns both the exact color values and the closest values possible on tthe screen specified by *colormap*.

XLookupColor() returns non-zero if *colorname* exists in the RGB database or zero if it does not exist.

To determine the exact RGB values, XLookupColor() uses a database on the X server. On UNIX, this database is */usr/lib/X11/rgb*. To read the colors provided by the database on a UNIX-based system, see */usr/lib/X11/rgb.txt*. The location, name, and contents of this file are server-dependent.

For more information see Volume One, Chapter 7, *Color*, and Appendix D, *The Color Database*, in this volume.

Errors

BadName   Color name not in database.

BadColor   Invalid colormap.

Structures

```
typedef struct {
    unsigned long pixel;
    unsigned short red, green, blue;
    char flags;          /* DoRed, DoGreen, DoBlue */
    char pad;
} XColor;
```

See Also

XBlackPixel(), XWhitePixel(), XAllocColor(), XAllocColorCells(), XAllocColorPlanes(), XAllocNamed-Color(), XFreeColors(), XParseColor(), XQueryColor(), XQueryColors(), XStoreColor(), XStore-Colors(), XStoreNamedColor().

XLookupKeysym

Name

XLookupKeysym – get the keysym corresponding to a keycode in structure.

Synopsis

```
KeySym XLookupKeysym(event, index)
    XKeyEvent *event;
    int index;
```

Arguments

event   Specifies the `KeyPress` or `KeyRelease` event that is to be used.

index   Specifies which keysym from the list associated with the keycode in the event to return. These correspond to the modifier keys, and the symbols `Shift-MapIndex`, `LockMapIndex`, `ControlMapIndex`, `Mod1MapIndex`, `Mod2MapIndex`, `Mod3MapIndex`, `Mod4MapIndex`, and `Mod5MapIndex` can be used.

Returns

The keysym.

Description

Given a keyboard event and the *index* into the list of keysyms for that keycode, `XLookup-Keysym()` returns the keysym from the list that corresponds to the keycode in the event. If no keysym is defined for the keycode of the event, `XLookupKeysym()` returns `No-Symbol`.

Each keycode may have a list of associated keysyms, which are portable symbols representing the meanings of the key. The *index* specifies which keysym in the list is desired, indicating the combination of modifier keys that are currently pressed. Therefore, the program must interpret the `state` member of the `XKeyEvent` structure to determine the *index* before calling this function. The exact mapping of modifier keys into the list of keysyms for each keycode is server-dependent beyond the fact that the first keysym corresponds to the keycode without modifier keys, and the second corresponds to the keycode with Shift pressed.

`XLookupKeysym()` simply calls `XKeycodeToKeysym()`, using arguments taken from the specified event structure.

Structures

```
typedef struct {
    int type;               /* of event */
    unsigned long serial;   /* # of last request processed by server */
    Bool send_event;        /* true if this came from a SendEvent request */
```

```
    Display *display;        /* display the event was read from */
    Window window;           /* "event" window it is reported relative to */
    Window root;             /* root window that the event occured on */
    Window subwindow;        /* child window */
    Time time;               /* milliseconds */
    int x, y;                /* pointer x, y coordinates in event window */
    int x_root, y_root;      /* coordinates relative to root */
    unsigned int state;      /* key or button mask */
    unsigned int keycode;    /* detail */
    Bool same_screen;        /* same screen flag */
} XKeyEvent;
```

See Also

XChangeKeyboardMapping(), XDeleteModifiermapEntry(), XFreeModifiermap(), XGetKeyboard-Mapping(), XGetModifierMapping(), XInsertModifiermapEntry(), XKeycodeToKeysym(), XKeysymTo-Keycode(), XKeysymToString(), XLookupString(), XNewModifiermap(), XQueryKeymap(), XRebind-Keysym(), XRefreshKeyboardMapping(), XSetModifierMapping(), XStringToKeysym().

XLookupString

Name

XLookupString – map a key event to ASCII string, keysym, and `ComposeStatus`.

Synopsis

```
int XLookupString(event_structure, buffer_return, bytes_buffer,
      keysym_return,
      status_in_out)
   XKeyEvent *event_structure;
   char *buffer_return;
   int bytes_buffer;
   KeySym *keysym_return;
   XComposeStatus *status_in_out;    /* may not be implemented */
```

Arguments

event_structure
>   Specifies the key event to be used.

buffer_return
>   Returns the resulting string (not NULL-terminated). Returned value of the function is the length of the string.

bytes_buffer
>   Specifies the length of the buffer. No more than *bytes_buffer* of translation are returned.

keysym_return
>   If this argument is not NULL, it specifies the keysym ID computed from the event.

status_in_out
>   Specifies the XComposeStatus structure that contains compose key state information and that allows the compose key processing to take place. This can be NULL if the caller is not interested in seeing compose key sequences. Not implemented in X Consortium Xlib through Release 5.

Returns

Length of string in *buffer_return* argument.

Description

XLookupString() gets an ASCII string and a keysym that are currently mapped to the keycode in a KeyPress or KeyRelease event, using the modifier bits in the key event to deal with shift, lock and control. The XLookupString() return value is the length of the translated string and the string's bytes are copied into *buffer_return*. The length may be greater than 1 if the event's keycode translates into a keysym that was rebound with XRebindKeysym( ).

Note that the string returned in *buffer* is not NULL-terminated. If you need a NULL-terminated string, copy *buffer* into another string as follows:

```
len = XLookupString((XKeyEvent *)event, buffer, 10, nil, nil);
if (len)
    (void) strncat (cmd_buf, buffer, len);
```

The compose *status.in.out* is not implemented in any release of the X Consortium version of Xlib through Release 5.

In Release 4, XLookupString( ) implements the new concept of keyboard groups. Keyboard groups support having two complete sets of keysyms for a keyboard. Which set will be used can be toggled using a particular key. This is implemented by using the first two keysyms in the list for a key as one set, and the next two keysyms as the second set. For more information on keyboard groups, see Volume One, Appendix G, *Release Notes*.

For more information on using XLookupString( ) in general, see Volume One, Chapter 9, *The Keyboard and Pointer*.

Structures

```
/*
 * Compose sequence status.in.out structure, used in calling XLookupString.
 */
typedef struct _XComposeStatus {
    char *compose_ptr;          /* state table pointer */
    int chars_matched;          /* match state */
} XComposeStatus;

typedef struct {
    int type;                   /* of event */
    unsigned long serial;       /* # of last request processed by server */
    Bool send_event;            /* true if this came from a SendEvent request */
    Display *display;           /* Display the event was read from */
    Window window;              /* "event" window it is reported relative to */
    Window root;                /* root window that the event occured on */
    Window subwindow;           /* child window */
    Time time;                  /* milliseconds */
    int x, y;                   /* pointer x, y coordinates in event window */
    int x_root, y_root;         /* coordinates relative to root */
    unsigned int state;         /* key or button mask */
    unsigned int keycode;       /* detail */
    Bool same_screen;           /* same screen flag */
} XKeyEvent;
```

See Also

XChangeKeyboardMapping(), XDeleteModifiermapEntry(), XFreeModifiermap(), XGetKeyboard-Mapping(), XGetModifierMapping(), XInsertModifiermapEntry(), XKeycodeToKeysym(), XKeysymTo-Keycode(), XKeysymToString(), XLookupKeysym(), XNewModifiermap(), XQueryKeymap(), XRebind-Keysym(), XRefreshKeyboardMapping(), XSetModifierMapping(), XStringToKeysym().

XLowerWindow

Name

XLowerWindow – lower a window in the stacking order.

Synopsis

```
XLowerWindow(display, w)
    Display *display;
    Window w;
```

Arguments

display   Specifies a connection to an X server; returned from XOpenDisplay().

w   Specifies the ID of the window to be lowered.

Description

XLowerWindow() lowers a window in the stacking order of its siblings so that it does not obscure any sibling windows. If the windows are regarded as overlapping sheets of paper stacked on a desk, then lowering a window is analogous to moving the sheet to the bottom of the stack, while leaving its x and y location on the desk constant. Lowering a mapped window will generate exposure events on any windows it formerly obscured.

If the override_redirect attribute of the window (see Chapter 4, *Window Attributes*) is False and the window manager has selected SubstructureRedirectMask on the parent, then a ConfigureRequest event is sent to the window manager, and no further processing is performed. Otherwise, the window is lowered to the bottom of the stack.

LeaveNotify events are sent to the lowered window if the pointer was inside it, and EnterNotify events are sent to the window which was immediately below the lowered window at the pointer position.

For more information, see Volume One, Chapter 14, *Window Management*.

Errors

BadWindow

See Also

XCirculateSubwindows(), XCirculateSubwindowsDown(), XCirculateSubwindowsUp(), XConfigure-Window(), XMoveResizeWindow(), XMoveWindow(), XQueryTree(), XRaiseWindow(), XReparent-Window(), XResizeWindow(), XRestackWindows().

XMakeAssoc

Name

XMakeAssoc – create an entry in an association table.

Synopsis

```
XMakeAssoc(display, table, x_id, data)
    Display *display;
    XAssocTable *table;
    XID x_id;
    char * data;
```

Arguments

display   Specifies a connection to an X server; returned from XOpenDisplay().

table   Specifies the association table in which an entry is to be made.

x_id   Specifies the X resource ID.

data   Specifies the data to be associated with the X resource ID.

Description

XMakeAssoc() inserts data into an XAssocTable keyed on an XID. Association tables allow you to easily associate data with resource ID's for later retrieval. Association tables are local, accessible only by this client.

This function is provided for compatibility with X Version 10. To use it you must include the file *<X11/X10.h>* and link with the library *-loldX*.

Data is inserted into the table only once. Redundant inserts are meaningless and cause no problems. The queue in each association bucket is sorted from the lowest XID to the highest XID.

For more information, see Volume One, Appendix B, *X10 Compatibility*.

Structure

```
typedef struct {
    XAssoc *buckets;         /* pointer to first bucket in bucket array */
    int size;                /* table size (number of buckets) */
} XAssocTable;

typedef struct _XAssoc {
    struct _XAssoc *next;    /* next object in this bucket */
    struct _XAssoc *prev;    /* previous object in this bucket */
    Display *display;        /* display which owns the ID */
    XID x_id;                /* X Window System ID */
    char *data;              /* pointer to untyped memory */
} XAssoc;
```

See Also

XCreateAssocTable(), XDeleteAssoc(), XDestroyAssocTable(), XLookUpAssoc().

XMapRaised

Name

XMapRaised – map a window on top of its siblings.

Synopsis

```
XMapRaised(display, w)
    Display *display;
    Window w;
```

Arguments

display   Specifies a connection to an X server; returned from XOpenDisplay().

w   Specifies the window ID of the window to be mapped and raised.

Description

XMapRaised() marks a window as eligible to be displayed, and positions the window at the top of the stack of its siblings. It will actually be displayed if its ancestors are mapped and it is not obscured by unrelated windows. XMapRaised() is similar to XMap-Window(), except it additionally raises the specified window to the top of the stack among its siblings. Mapping an already mapped window with XMapRaised() raises the window. See XMapWindow() for further details.

For more information, see Volume One, Chapter 14, *Window Management*.

Errors

BadWindow

See Also

XMapSubwindows(), XMapWindow(), XUnmapSubwindows(), XUnmapWindow().

XMapSubwindows

Name

XMapSubwindows – map all subwindows of window.

Synopsis

```
XMapSubwindows(display, w)
    Display *display;
    Window w;
```

Arguments

display   Specifies a connection to an X server; returned from XOpenDisplay().

w   Specifies the ID of the window whose subwindows are to be mapped.

Description

XMapSubwindows() maps all subwindows of a window in top-to-bottom stacking order. XMapSubwindows() also generates an Expose event on each newly displayed window. This is much more efficient than mapping many windows one at a time, as much of the work need only be performed once for all of the windows rather than for each window. XMapSubwindows() is not recursive—it does not map the subwindows of the subwindows.

For more information, see Volume One, Chapter 14, *Window Management*.

Errors

BadWindow

See Also

XMapRaised(), XMapWindow(), XUnmapSubwindows(), XUnmapWindow().

XMapWindow

Name

XMapWindow – map a window.

Synopsis

```
XMapWindow(display, w)
    Display *display;
    Window w;
```

Arguments

display   Specifies a connection to an X server; returned from XOpenDisplay().

w   Specifies the ID of the window to be mapped.

Description

XMapWindow() maps a window, making it eligible for display. Whether it becomes visible immediately depends on its stacking order among its siblings, the mapping status of its ancestors, and the placement of other visible windows. If all the ancestors are mapped, and it is not obscured by siblings higher in the stacking order, and it is not obscured by unrelated windows (children of ancestors), then the window and all of its mapped subwindows are displayed.

Mapping a window that has an unmapped ancestor does not display the window but marks it as eligible for display when its ancestors become mapped. Mapping an already mapped window has no effect (it does not raise the window).

If the window becomes viewable and no earlier contents for it are remembered (because of backing store), the X server tiles the window with its background. If the window's background is undefined, the existing screen contents are not altered, and the X server generates zero or more Expose events. If backing-store was maintained while the window was unmapped, no Expose events are generated. If backing-store will now be maintained, a full-window exposure is always generated. Otherwise, only visible regions may be reported. Similar tiling and exposure take place for any newly viewable inferiors.

Note that for a top-level window, the window manager is likely to intervene and delay the mapping of the window. The application must not draw until it has received an Expose event on the window. If the window is an InputOutput window, XMapWindow() generates Expose events on each opaque window that it causes to become displayed. The client should call XSelectInput() for exposure events, then map, and then process input events. The client's normal response to an Expose event should be to repaint the window. If you fail to wait for the Expose event before drawing, the drawing may not appear in the window.

Errors

```
BadWindow
```

See Also

XMapRaised(), XMapSubwindows(), XUnmapSubwindows(), XUnmapWindow().

XMaskEvent

Name

XMaskEvent – remove the next event that matches mask.

Synopsis

```
XMaskEvent(display, event_mask, event_return)
    Display *display;
    long event_mask;
    XEvent *event_return;
```

Arguments

display   Specifies a connection to an X server; returned from XOpenDisplay().

event_mask   Specifies the event mask. See XSelectInput() for a complete list of the event mask symbols that can be ORed together.

event_return
         Returns the event removed from the event queue.

Description

XMaskEvent() removes the next event in the queue which matches the passed mask. The event is copied into an XEvent supplied by the caller. Other events in the queue are not discarded. If no such event has been queued, XMaskEvent() flushes the request buffer and waits until one is received. Use XCheckMaskEvent() if you do not wish to wait.

XMaskEvent() cannot return MappingNotify, SelectionClear, Selection-Notify, or SelectionRequest events because these event types are by definition unmaskable.

See Also

XAllowEvents(), XCheckIfEvent(), XCheckMaskEvent(), XCheckTypedEvent(), XCheckTypedWindow-Event(), XCheckWindowEvent(), XEventsQueued(), XGetInputFocus(), XGetMotionEvents(), XIfEvent(), XNextEvent(), XPeekEvent(), XPeekIfEvent(), XPending(), XPutBackEvent(), XQLength(), XSelect-Input(), XSendEvent(), XSetInputFocus(), XSynchronize(), XWindowEvent().

XMatchVisualInfo

Name

XMatchVisualInfo – obtain the visual information that matches the desired depth and class.

Synopsis

```
Status XMatchVisualInfo(display, screen, depth, class, vinfo_return)
    Display *display;
    int screen;
    int depth;
    int class;
    XVisualInfo *vinfo_return;
```

Arguments

display   Specifies a connection to an X server; returned from XOpenDisplay().

screen   Specifies the screen.

depth   Specifies the desired depth of the visual.

class   Specifies the desired class of the visual, such as PseudoColor or True-
               Color.

vinfo_return
               Returns the matched visual information.

Returns

Zero on failure, non-zero on success.

Description

XMatchVisualInfo() returns the visual information for a visual supported on the screen
that matches the specified depth and class. Because multiple visuals that match the
specified depth and class may be supported, the exact visual chosen is undefined.

If a visual is found, this function returns a non-zero value and the information on the visual is
returned to vinfo_return. If a visual is not found, it returns zero.

For more information on visuals, see Volume One, Chapter 7, Color.

Structures

```
typedef struct {
    Visual *visual;
    VisualID visualid;
    int screen;
    unsigned int depth;
    int class;
    unsigned long red_mask;
    unsigned long green_mask;
```

```
        unsigned long blue_mask;
        int colormap_size;
        int bits_per_rgb;
} XVisualInfo;
```

See Also

XDefaultVisual(), *XGetVisualInfo()*.

XMaxCmapsOfScreen

Name

XMaxCmapsOfScreen, MaxCmapsOfScreen – get maximum number of installed colormaps supported by a screen.

Synopsis

```
int XMaxCmapsOfScreen(screen)
      Screen *screen;
```

Arguments

screen   Specifies the appropriate Screen structure.

Returns

The maximum number of colormaps.

Description

XMaxCmapsOfScreen() returns the maximum number of installed colormaps supported by the specified screen.

The C language macro MaxCmapsOfScreen() is equivalent and slightly more efficient.

See Also

XInstallColormap().

XMaxRequestSize

Name

XMaxRequestSize – get maximum request size supported by server.

Synopsis

```
long XMaxRequestSize(display)
    Display *display;
```

Arguments

display　　　　Specifies a connection to an X server; returned from XOpenDisplay().

Returns

The maximum request size in 4-byte units.

Description

XMaxRequestSize() returns the maximum request size (in 4-byte units) supported by the server. Single protocol requests to the server can be no longer than this size. The protocol guarantees the size to be no smaller than 4096 units (16384 bytes). Xlib automatically breaks data up into multiple protocol requests as necessary for the following functions: XDraw-Points(), XDrawRectangles(), XDrawSegments(), XFillArcs(), XFill-Rectangles(), and XPutImage(). Xlib does not break up data for XDrawArcs(), XDrawLines(), or XFillPolygon().

There is no macro MaxRequestSize().

See Also

XDrawArcs(), XDrawLines(), XFillPolygon().

XmbDrawImageString

Name

XmbDrawImageString – draw internationalized multi-byte image text.

Synopsis

```
void XmbDrawImageString(display, drawable, font_set, gc, x, y, string,
        num_bytes)
    Display *display;
    Drawable drawable;
    XFontSet font_set;
    GC gc;
    int x, y;
    char *string;
    int num_bytes;
```

Arguments

display	Specifies the connection to the X server.
drawable	Specifies the drawable.
font_set	Specifies the font set.
gc	Specifies the graphics context.
x, y	Specifies the starting position and baseline of the text, relative to the origin of the specified drawable.
string	Specifies the character string.
num_bytes	Specifies the number of bytes in the string argument.

Availability

Release 5 and later.

Description

XmbDrawImageString() fills a destination rectangle with the background pixel defined in the GC and then paints the specified multi-byte text with the foreground pixel. The filled rectangle is the rectangle returned to *overall_logical_return* by XmbText-Extents() for the same text and XFontSet.

When the XFontSet has missing charsets, each unavailable character is drawn with the default string returned by XCreateFontSet(). The behavior for an invalid codepoint is undefined.

XmbDrawImageString() draws with fonts from the font set rather than the font of the GC. For this reason, it may modify the font value of the GC. Except for the font, it uses the same GC components as its pre-X11R5 analog XDrawImageString().

See Also

XDrawImageString(), *XDrawString()*, *XDrawText()*, *XmbDrawString()*, *XmbDrawText()*, *XwcDraw-ImageString()*.

XmbDrawString

Name

XmbDrawString – draw internationalized multi-byte text.

Synopsis

```
void XmbDrawString(display, drawable, font_set, gc, x, y, string,
        num_bytes)
    Display *display;
    Drawable drawable;
    XFontSet font_set;
    GC gc;
    int x, y;
    char *string;
    int num_bytes;
```

Arguments

display	Specifies the connection to the X server.
drawable	Specifies the drawable.
font_set	Specifies the font set.
gc	Specifies the graphics context.
x, y	Specifies the starting position and baseline of the text, relative to the origin of the specified drawable.
string	Specifies the character string.
num_bytes	Specifies the number of bytes in the string argument.

Availability

Release 5 and later.

Description

XmbDrawString() draws the specified multi-byte text with the foreground pixel. When the XFontSet has missing charsets, each unavailable character is drawn with the default string returned by XCreateFontSet(). The behavior for an invalid codepoint is undefined.

XmbDrawString() draws with fonts from the font set rather than the font of the GC. For this reason, it may modify the font value of the GC. Except for the font, it uses the same GC components as its pre-X11R5 analog XDrawString().

See Also

XDrawImageString(), XDrawString(), XDrawText(), XmbDrawImageString(), XmbDrawText(), XwcDrawString().

XmbDrawText

Name

XmbDrawText – draw internationalized multi-byte text using multiple font sets.

Synopsis

```
void XmbDrawText(display, drawable, gc, x, y, items, nitems)
    Display *display;
    Drawable drawable;
    GC gc;
    int x, y;
    XmbTextItem *items;
    int nitems;
```

Arguments

display	Specifies the connection to the X server.
drawable	Specifies the drawable.
gc	Specifies the graphics context.
x, y	Specifies the starting position and baseline of the text, relative to the origin of the specified drawable.
items	Specifies an array of text items.
nitems	Specifies the number of text items in the array.

Description

XmbDrawText() allows complex spacing and font set shifts between internationalized multi-byte text strings. Each text item is processed in turn, with the origin of a text element advanced in the primary draw direction by the escapement of the previous text item. A text item delta specifies an additional escapement of the text item drawing origin in the primary draw direction. A font_set member other than None in an item causes the font set to be used for this and subsequent text items in the items list. Leading text items with font_set member set to None will not be drawn.

XmbDrawText() does not perform any context-dependent rendering between text segments. Clients may compute the drawing metrics by passing each text segment to XmbTextExtents() or XmbTextPerCharExtents(). When the XFontSet has missing charsets, each unavailable character is drawn with the default string returned by XCreateFontSet(). The behavior for an invalid codepoint is undefined.

XmbDrawText() draws with fonts from the font sets of the items list rather than the font of the GC. For this reason, it may modify the font value of the GC. Except for the font, it uses the same GC components as its pre-X11R5 analog XDrawText().

Structures

The `XmbTextItem` structure contains:

```
typedef struct {
        char *chars;            /* pointer to string */
        int nchars;             /* number of characters */
        int delta;              /* pixel delta between strings */
        XFontSet font_set;      /* fonts, None means don't change */
} XmbTextItem;
```

See Also

XDrawImageString(), *XDrawString()*, *XDrawText()*, *XmbDrawImageString()*, *XmbDrawString()*, *XwcDrawText()*.

XmbLookupString

Name

XmbLookupString – obtain composed multi-byte input from an input method.

Synopsis

```
int XmbLookupString(ic, event, buffer_return, bytes_buffer,
        keysym_return, status_return)
    XIC ic;
    XKeyPressedEvent *event;
    char *buffer_return;
    int bytes_buffer;
    KeySym *keysym_return;
    Status *status_return;
```

Arguments

ic   Specifies the input context.

event   Specifies the keypress event to be used.

buffer_return
            Returns a multibyte string (if any) from the input method.

bytes_buffer
            Specifies the number of bytes in the return buffer.

keysym_return
            Returns the KeySym computed from the event if this argument is not NULL.

status_return
            Returns a value indicating what kind of data is returned.

Returns

Number of characters in the string in *bytes_buffer*.

Availability

Release 5 and later.

Description

XmbLookupString() passes a KeyPress event to an input context, returns composed text in the encoding of the locale of the input context if any is ready, and may return a keysym corresponding to the KeyPress event as well.

There are several possible results of a call to XmbLookupString(), and a client should check the value returned in the *status_return* argument to determine which has occurred. The possible values are:

XBufferOverflow

> The input string to be returned is too large for the supplied *buffer_return*. The required size in bytes is returned as the value of the function, and the contents of *buffer_return* and *keysym_return* are not modified. The client should re-call the function with the same event and a buffer of adequate size in order to obtain the string.

XLookupNone

> No consistent input has been composed so far. The contents of *buffer_return* and *keysym_return* are not modified, and the function returns zero.

XLookupChars

> Some input characters have been composed. They are placed in the *buffer_return* argument, and the string length is returned as the value of the function. The string is encoded in the locale bound to the input context. The contents of the *keysym_return* argument is not modified.

XLookupKeySym

> A KeySym has been returned instead of a string and is returned in *keysym_return*. The contents of the *buffer_return* argument is not modified, and the function returns zero.

XLookupBoth

> Both a KeySym and a string are returned; XLookupChars and XLookupKeySym occur simultaneously.

When XmbLookupString() returns a string, the return value of the function is the length in bytes of that string. The returned string is a multi-byte string in the encoding of the locale of the input context. If that encoding is state-dependent, the string begins in the initial state of the encoding.

When both a keysym and a string are returned, the string does not necessarily correspond to the keysym. An application that is not interested in return keysyms can pass a NULL *keysym_return*.

Note that only KeyPress events should be passed to XmbLookupString(). When KeyRelease events are passed, the resulting behavior is undefined. It does not make any difference if the input context passed as an argument to XmbLookupString() is the one currently in possession of the focus or not. Input may have been composed within an input context before it lost the focus, and that input may be returned on subsequent calls to XmbLookupString() even though it no longer has any more keyboard focus.

See Also

XLookupKeysym(), XwcLookupString().

XmbResetIC

Name

XmbResetIC – reset the state of an input context.

Synopsis

```
char * XmbResetIC(ic)
    XIC ic;
```

Arguments

ic   Specifies the input context.

Returns

Availability

Release 5 and later. Implementation-dependent (see the "Description" section).

Description

XmbResetIC() resets an input context to its initial state. Any input pending on that context is deleted. The input method is required to clear the Preedit area, if any, and update the Status area accordingly. Calling this function does not change the input context focus.

The return value of XmbResetIC() is implementation-dependent. If there was input pending on the input context, XmbResetIC() may return composed multi-byte text in the encoding of the locale of the input context, or it may return NULL. If any string is returned, the client is responsible for freeing it by calling XFree().

See Also

XCreateIC(), XSetICFocus(), XSetICValues(), XwcResetIC.

Name

XmbSetWMProperties – set window manager properties using internationalized encoding.

Synopsis

```
void XmbSetWMProperties(display, w, window_name, icon_name, argv, argc,
                              normal_hints, wm_hints, class_hints)
      Display *display;
      Window w;
      char *window_name;
      char *icon_name;
      char *argv[];
      int argc;
      XSizeHints *normal_hints;
      XWMHints *wm_hints;
      XClassHint *class_hints;
```

Arguments

display	Specifies a connection to an X server; returned from XOpenDisplay().
w	Specifies the window. Should be a top-level window.
window_name	Specifies the window name, which should be a NULL-terminated string.
icon_name	Specifies the icon name, which should be a NULL-terminated string.
argv	Specifies the application's argument list.
argc	Specifies the number of arguments.
hints	Specifies the size hints for the window in its normal state.
wm_hints	Specifies the XWMHints structure to be used.
class_hints	Specifies the XClassHint structure to be used.

Availability

Release 5 and later.

Description

XmbSetWMProperties() stores the standard set of window manager properties, with text properties in standard encodings for internationalized text communication. The standard window manager properties for a given window are WM_NAME, WM_ICON_NAME, WM_HINTS, WM_NORMAL_HINTS, WM_CLASS, WM_COMMAND, WM_CLIENT_MACHINE, and WM_LOCALE_NAME.

If the *window_name* argument is non-NULL, XmbSetWMProperties() sets the WM_NAME property. If the *icon_name* argument is non-NULL, XmbSet-WMProperties() sets the WM_ICON_NAME property. The *window_name* and *icon_name* arguments are NULL-terminated strings in the encoding of the current locale. If the arguments can be fully converted to the XA_STRING encoding, the properties are created with type XA_STRING: otherwise, the arguments are converted to Compound Text, and the properties are created with type COMPOUND_TEXT.

If the *normal_hints* argument is non-NULL, XmbSetWMProperties() calls XSetWMNormalHints(), which sets the WM_NORMAL_HINTS property. If the *wm_hints* argument is non-NULL, XmbSetWMProperties() calls XSetWMHints(), which sets the WM_HINTS property.

If the *argv* argument is non-NULL, XmbSetWMProperties() sets the WM_COMMAND property from *argv* and *argc*. Note that an argc of 0 indicates a zero-length command.

The hostname of this machine is stored using XSetWMClientMachine().

If the *class_hints* argument is non-NULL, XmbSetWMProperties() sets the WM_CLASS property. If the res_name member in the XClassHint structure is set to the NULL pointer and the RESOURCE_NAME environment variable is set, the value of the environment variable is substituted for res_name. If the res_name member is NULL, the environment variable is not set, and *argv* and *argv[0]* are set, then the value of *argv[0]*, stripped of any directory prefixes, is substituted for res_name.

It is assumed that the supplied class_hints.res_name and argv, the RESOURCE_NAME environment variable, and the hostname of this machine are in the encoding of the locale announced for the LC_CTYPE category. (On POSIX-compliant systems, the LC_CTYPE, else LANG environment variable). The corresponding WM_CLASS, WM_COMMAND, and WM_CLIENT_MACHINE properties are typed according to the local host locale announcer. No encoding conversion is performed prior to storage in the properties.

For clients that need to process the property text in a locale, XmbSetWMProperties() sets the WM_LOCALE_NAME property to be the name of the current locale. The name is assumed to be in the Host Portable Character Encoding, and is converted to STRING for storage in the property.

Structures

```
typedef struct {
    long flags;         /* marks which fields in this structure */
                        /* are defined */
    int x, y;           /* obsolete for new window mgrs, but clients */
    int width, height;  /* should set so old wm's don't mess up */
    int min_width, min_height;
    int max_width, max_height;
    int width_inc, height_inc;
    struct {
            int x;      /* numerator */
            int y;      /* denominator */
    } min_aspect, max_aspect;
```

```
        int base_width, base_height; /* added by ICCCM version 1 */
        int win_gravity;              /* added by ICCCM version 1 */
    } XSizeHints;

    /* flags argument in size hints */
    #define USPosition (1L << 0)    /* user specified x, y */
    #define USSize     (1L << 1)    /* user specified width, height */
    #define PPosition  (1L << 2)    /* program specified position */
    #define PSize      (1L << 3)    /* program specified size */
    #define PMinSize   (1L << 4)    /* program specified minimum size */
    #define PMaxSize   (1L << 5)    /* program specified maximum size */
    #define PResizeInc (1L << 6)    /* program specified resize increments */
    #define PAspect    (1L << 7)    /* program specified min/max aspect ratios */
    #define PAllHints (PPosition|PSize|PMinSize|PMaxSize|PResizeInc|PAspect)

    typedef struct {
        long flags;     /* marks which fields in this structure */
                        /* are defined */
        Bool input;     /* does this application rely on the window */
                        /* manager to get keyboard input? */
        int initial_state;      /* see below */
        Pixmap icon_pixmap;     /* pixmap to be used as icon */
        Window icon_window;     /* window to be used as icon */
        int icon_x, icon_y;     /* initial position of icon */
        Pixmap icon_mask;       /* icon mask bitmap */
        XID window_group;       /* id of related window group */
        /* this structure may be extended in the future */
    } XWMHints;

    #define USPosition  (1L << 0)  /* user specified x, y */
    #define USSize      (1L << 1)  /* user specified width, height */
    #define PPosition   (1L << 2)  /* program specified position */
    #define PSize       (1L << 3)  /* program specified size */
    #define PMinSize    (1L << 4)  /* program specified minimum size */
    #define PMaxSize    (1L << 5)  /* program specified maximum size */
    #define PResizeInc  (1L << 6)  /* program specified resize increments * /
    #define PAspect     (1L << 7)  /* program specified min/max aspect ratios */
    #define PAllHints (PPosition|PSize|PMinSize|PMaxSize|PResizeInc|PAspect)
    #define PBaseSize   (1L << 8)  /* program specified base for incrementing */
    #define PWinGravity (1L << 9)  /* program specified window gravity */

    typedef struct {
        char *res_name;
        char *res_class;
    } XClassHint;
```

Errors

```
BadAlloc
BadWindow
```

See Also

XSetWMClientMachine(), *XSetWMColormapWindows()*, *XSetWMHints()*, *XSetWMNormalHints()*, *XSet-WMProperties()*, *XSetWMProtocols()*.

XmbTextEscapement

Name

XmbTextEscapement – obtain the width of internationalized multi-byte text.

Synopsis

```
int XmbTextEscapement(font_set, string, num_bytes)
    XFontSet font_set;
    char *string;
    int num_bytes;
```

Arguments

font_set   Specifies the font set.

string   Specifies the character string.

num_bytes   Specifies the number of bytes in the string argument.

Returns

Escapement in pixels.

Availability

Release 5 and later.

Description

XmbTextEscapement() returns the escapement in pixels of the specified multi-byte string using the fonts loaded for the specified font set. The escapement is the distance in pixels in the primary draw direction from the drawing origin to the origin of the next character to be drawn, assuming that the rendering of the next character is not dependent on the supplied string.

The escapement is always positive, regardless of the character-rendering order.

See Also

XmbTextExtents(), XmbTextPerCharExtents(), XwcTextEscapement().

XmbTextExtents

Name

XmbTextExtents – compute the extents of internationalized multi-byte text.

Synopsis

```
int XmbTextExtents(font_set, string, num_bytes, overall_ink_return,
       overall_logical_return)
   XFontSet font_set;
   char *string;
   int num_bytes;
   XRectangle *overall_ink_return;
   XRectangle *overall_logical_return;
```

Arguments

font_set   Specifies the font set.

string   Specifies the character string.

num_bytes   Specifies the number of bytes in the string argument.

overall_ink_return
                Returns the overall ink dimensions.

overall_logical_return
                Returns the overall logical dimensions.

Returns

Escapement in pixels.

Availability

Release 5 and later.

Description

XmbTextExtents() sets the components of the specified *overall_ink_return* and
overall_logical_return arguments to the overall bounding box of the string's
image, and the overall logical bounding box of the string's image plus inter-line and inter-
character spacing. It returns the value returned by XmbTextEscapement(). The
returned metrics are relative to the drawing origin of the string, using the fonts loaded for the
specified font set.

If the *overall_ink_return* argument is non-NULL, it is set to the bounding box of the
string's character ink. Note that the *overall_ink_return* for a non-descending horizontally drawn Latin character is conventionally entirely above the baseline, that is, *over-
all_ink_return.height* <= -overall_ink_return.y. The *over-
all_ink_return* for a nonkerned character is entirely at and to the right of the origin,
that is, *overall_ink_return.x* >= 0. A character consisting of a single pixel at the

origin would have *overall_ink_return* fields $y = 0$, $x = 0$, *width* = 1, and *height* = 1.

If the *overall_logical_return* argument is non-NULL, it is set to the bounding box which provides minimum spacing to other graphical features for the string. Other graphical features, for example, a border surrounding the text, should not intersect this rectangle.

When the XFontSet has missing charsets, metrics for each unavailable character are taken from the default string returned by XCreateFontSet() so that the metrics represent the text as it will actually be drawn. The behavior for an invalid codepoint is undefined.

Structures

```
typedef struct {
    short x, y;
    unsigned short width, height;
} XRectangle;
```

See Also

XmbTextEscapement(), XmbTextPerCharExtents(), XwcTextExtents().

XmbTextListToTextProperty

Name

XmbTextListToTextProperty – convert an internationalized multi-byte text list to a text property structure.

Synopsis

```
int XmbTextListToTextProperty(display, list, count, style,
        text_prop_return)
    Display *display;
    char **list;
    int count;
    XICCEncodingStyle style;
    XTextProperty *text_prop_return;
```

Arguments

display   Specifies the connection to the X server.

list   Specifies an array of NULL-terminated multi-byte strings.

count   Specifies the number of strings specified.

style   Specifies the manner in which the property is encoded.

text_prop_return
                   Returns the XTextProperty structure.

Returns

Success on success. XNoMemory or XLocaleNotSupported on failure.

Availability

Release 5 and later.

Description

XmbTextListToTextProperty() sets the specified XTextProperty value to a set of null-separated elements representing the concatenation of the specified list of NULL-terminated text strings. A final terminating null is stored at the end of the *value* field of *text_prop_return* but is not included in the *nitems* field.

XmbTextListToTextProperty() sets the encoding field of *text_prop_return* to an Atom (for the specified display), which names the encoding specified by *style*, and converts the specified text list to this encoding for storage in the value field of *text_prop_return*. If the style XStringStyle or XCompoundTextStyle is specified, this encoding is STRING or COMPOUND_TEXT, respectively. If the style XTextStyle is specified, this encoding is the encoding of the current locale. If the style XStdICCTextStyle is specified, this encoding is STRING if the text is fully convertible to STRING, otherwise it is COMPOUND_TEXT.

If insufficient memory is available for the new value string, XmbTextListToText-
Property() returns XNoMemory. If the current locale is not supported, it returns
XLocaleNotSupported. In both of these error cases, it does not set
text_prop_return. XmbTextListToTextProperty() will not return XLocale-
NotSupported if XSupportsLocale() has returned True for the current locale.

If the supplied text is not fully convertible to the specified encoding, XmbTextListTo-
TextProperty() returns the number of unconvertible characters. Each unconvertible
character is converted to an implementation-defined and encoding-specific default string. If
the text is fully convertible, XmbTextListToTextProperty() returns Success. Note
that full convertibility to all styles except XStringStyle is guaranteed. If the supplied
text contains bytes that are not valid characters in the encoding of the locale ("invalid
codepoints"), the result is undefined.

XmbTextListToTextProperty() allocates memory for the *value* field of the
XTextProperty. The client is responsible for freeing this memory by calling XFree().

Structures

The XTextProperty structure contains:

```
typedef struct {
    unsigned char *value;    /* property data */
    Atom encoding;           /* type of property */
    int format;              /* 8, 16, or 32 */
    unsigned long items;     /* number of items in value */
} XTextProperty;
```

The XICCEncodingStyle structure contains:

```
typedef enum   {
    XStringStyle,          /* STRING */
    XCompoundTextStyle,    /* COMPOUND_TEXT */
    XTextStyle,            /* text in owner's encoding (current locale) */
    XStdICCTextStyle       /* STRING, else COMPOUND_TEXT */
} XICCEncodingStyle;
```

The possible return values of this function are as follows:

```
#define    XNoMemory                    −1
#define    XLocaleNotSupported          −2
#define    XConverterNotFound           −3
```

See Also

*XSetTextProperty(), XStringListToTextProperty(), XwcTextListToTextProperty(), XmbTextPropertyTo-
TextList(), XwcTextPropertyToTextList(), XwcFreeStringList(), XDefaultString().*

XmbTextPerCharExtents

Name

XmbTextPerCharExtents – obtain per-character measurements of an internationalized multi-byte text string.

Synopsis

```
Status XmbTextPerCharExtents(font_set, string, num_bytes,
        ink_array_return, logical_array_return, array_size,
        num_chars_return, overall_ink_return, overall_logical_return)
    XFontSet font_set;
    char *string;
    int num_bytes;
    XRectangle *ink_array_return;
    XRectangle *logical_array_return;
    int array_size;
    int *num_chars_return;
    XRectangle *overall_ink_return;
    XRectangle *overall_logical_return;
```

Arguments

font_set   Specifies the font set.

string   Specifies the character string.

num_bytes   Specifies the number of bytes in the string argument.

ink_array_return
                Returns the ink dimensions for each character.

logical_array_return
                Returns the logical dimensions for each character.

array_size   Specifies the size of *ink_array_return* and *logical_array_return*. Note that the caller must pass in arrays of this size.

num_chars_return
                Returns the number characters in the string argument.

overall_ink_return
                Returns the overall ink extents of the entire string.

overall_logical_return
                Returns the overall logical extents of the entire string.

Returns

Zero on failure, non-zero on success.

Availability

Release 5 and later.

Description

`XmbTextPerCharExtents()` returns the text dimensions of each character of the specified text, using the fonts loaded for the specified font set. Each element of *ink_array_return* and *logical_array_return* is set to the corresponding character's drawn metrics, relative to the drawing origin of the string. The number of elements of *ink_array_return* and *logical_array_return* that have been set is returned in *num_chars_return*.

Each element of *ink_array_return* is set to the bounding box of the corresponding character's drawn foreground color. Each element of *logical_array_return* is set to the bounding box which provides minimum spacing to other graphical features for the corresponding character. Other graphical features should not intersect any of the *logical_array_return* rectangles.

Note that an `XRectangle` represents the effective drawing dimensions of the character, regardless of the number of font glyphs that are used to draw the character, or the direction in which the character is drawn. If multiple characters map to a single character glyph, the dimensions of all the `XRectangle`s of those characters are the same.

When the `XFontSet` has missing charsets, metrics for each unavailable character are taken from the default string returned by `XCreateFontSet()`, so that the metrics represent the text as it will actually be drawn. The behavior for an invalid codepoint is undefined.

If the *array_size* is too small for the number of characters in the supplied text, the function returns zero and *num_chars_return* is set to the number of rectangles required. Otherwise, it returns a non-zero value.

If the *overall_ink_return* or *overall_logical_return* argument is non-`NULL`, `XmbTextPerCharExtents()` returns the maximum extent of the string's metrics to *overall_ink_return* or *overall_logical_return*, as is done by `XmbTextExtents()`.

Structures

```
typedef struct {
    short x, y;
    unsigned short width, height;
} XRectangle;
```

See Also

XmbTextEscapement(), XmbTextExtents(), XwcTextPerCharExtents().

XmbTextPropertyToTextList

Name

XmbTextPropertyToTextList – convert an internationalized text property to a list of multi-byte strings.

Synopsis

```
int XmbTextPropertyToTextList(display, text_prop, list_return,
        count_return)
    Display *display;
    XTextProperty *text_prop;
    char ***list_return;
    int *count_return;
```

Arguments

display   Specifies the connection to the X server.

text_prop   Specifies the XTextProperty structure to be used.

list_return   Returns a list of NULL-terminated character strings.

count_return
                Returns the number of strings.

Returns

Success on success. XNoMemory, XLocaleNotSupported, or XConverterNot-Found on failure.

Availability

Release 5 and later.

Description

XmbTextPropertyToTextList() returns a list of multi-byte text strings encoded in the current locale representing the NULL-separated elements of the specified XText-Property structure. The data in *text_prop* must be format 8.

Multiple elements of the property (for example, the strings in a disjoint text selection) are separated by a null byte. The contents of the property are not required to be NULL-terminated; any terminating null should not be included in *text_prop.nitems*.

If insufficient memory is available for the list and its elements, XmbTextPropertyTo-TextList() returns XNoMemory. If the current locale is not supported, it returns XLocaleNotSupported. If the encoding field of *text_prop* is not convertible to the encoding of the current locale, it returns XConverterNotFound. For supported locales, existence of a converter from COMPOUND_TEXT, STRING, or the encoding of the current locale is guaranteed although the actual text may contain unconvertible characters. Conversion of other encodings is implementation-dependent. In all of these error cases, the function does not set any return values.

Otherwise, `XmbTextPropertyToTextList()` returns the list of NULL-terminated text strings to *list_return*, and the number of text strings to *count_return*.

If the *value* field of *text_prop* is not fully convertible to the encoding of the current locale, the function returns the number of unconvertible characters. Each unconvertible character is converted to a string in the current locale that is specific to the current locale. To obtain the value of this string, use `XDefaultString()`. If all characters are convertible, `XmbTextPropertyToTextList()` returns Success. If the text property contains "invalid codepoints" or bytes that are not valid characters in the encoding of the property, the result is undefined.

To free the storage for the list and its contents returned by `XmbTextPropertyToText-List()`, use `XFreeStringList()`.

Structures

The `XTextProperty` structure contains:

```
typedef struct          {
    unsigned char *value;      /* property data */
    Atom encoding;             /* type of property */
    int format;                /* 8, 16, or 32 */
    unsigned long nitems;      /* number of items in value */
} XTextProperty;
```

The possible return values of this function are as follows:

```
#define   XNoMemory              -1
#define   XLocaleNotSupported    -2
#define   XConverterNotFound     -3
```

See Also

XSetTextProperty(), XStringListToTextProperty(), XDefaultString(), XmbTextListToTextProperty(), XwcFreeStringList(), XwcTextListToTextProperty(), XwcTextPropertyToTextList().

XMinCmapsOfScreen

Name

XMinCmapsOfScreen, MinCmapsOfScreen – get minimum number of installed colormaps supported by a screen.

Synopsis

```
int XMinCmapsOfScreen(screen)
     Screen *screen;
```

Arguments

screen   Specifies the appropriate Screen structure.

Returns

The minimum number of colormaps.

Description

XMinCmapsOfScreen() returns the minimum number of installed colormaps supported by the specified screen.

The C language macro MinCmapsOfScreen() is equivalent and slightly more efficient.

See Also

XInstallColormap().

XMoveResizeWindow

Name

XMoveResizeWindow – change the size and position of a window.

Synopsis

```
XMoveResizeWindow(display, w, x, y, width, height)
    Display *display;
    Window w;
    int x, y;
    unsigned int width, height;
```

Arguments

display	Specifies a connection to an X server; returned from XOpenDisplay().
w	Specifies the ID of the window to be reconfigured.
x y	Specify the new x and y coordinates of the upper-left pixel of the window's border, relative to the window's parent.
width height	Specify the new width and height in pixels. These arguments define the interior size of the window.

Description

XMoveResizeWindow() moves or resizes a window or both. XMoveResizeWindow() does not raise the window. Resizing a mapped window may lose its contents and generate an Expose event on that window depending on the bit_gravity attribute. Configuring a window may generate exposure events on windows that the window formerly obscured, depending on the new size and location parameters.

If the override_redirect attribute of the window is False (see Volume One, Chapter 4, *Window Attributes*) and the window manager has selected SubstructureRedirect-Mask on the parent, then a ConfigureRequest event is sent to the window manager, and no further processing is performed.

If a client has selected StructureNotifyMask on the window, then a Configure-Notify event is generated after the move and resize takes place, and the event will contain the final position and size of the window. This is only useful in the case of top-level windows, since the window manager may modify or prevent them being moved or resized.

Errors

```
BadValue
BadWindow
```

See Also

XCirculateSubwindows(), *XCirculateSubwindowsDown()*, *XCirculateSubwindowsUp()*, *XConfigure-Window()*, *XLowerWindow()*, *XMoveWindow()*, *XQueryTree()*, *XRaiseWindow()*, *XReparentWindow()*, *XResizeWindow()*, *XRestackWindows()*.

XMoveWindow

Name

XMoveWindow – move a window.

Synopsis

```
XMoveWindow(display, w, x, y)
    Display *display;
    Window w;
    int x, y;
```

Arguments

display   Specifies a connection to an X server; returned from XOpenDisplay().

w   Specifies the ID of the window to be moved.

x   Specify the new x and y coordinates of the upper-left pixel of the window's
y   border (or of the window itself, if it has no border), relative to the window's
            parent.

Description

XMoveWindow() changes the position of the origin of the specified window relative to its parent. XMoveWindow() does not change the mapping state, size, or stacking order of the window, nor does it raise the window. Moving a mapped window will lose its contents if:

- Its background_pixmap attribute is ParentRelative.

- The window is obscured by nonchildren and no backing store exists.

If the contents are lost, exposure events will be generated for the window and any mapped subwindows. Moving a mapped window will generate exposure events on any formerly obscured windows.

If the override_redirect attribute of the window is False (see Volume One, Chapter 4, *Window Attributes*) and the window manager has selected SubstructureRedirect-Mask on the parent, then a ConfigureRequest event is sent to the window manager, and no further processing is performed.

If a client has selected StructureNotifyMask on the window, then a Configure-Notify event is generated after the move takes place, and the event will contain the final position of the window. This is only useful in the case of top-level windows, since the window manager may modify or disallow moves.

Errors

BadWindow

See Also

XCirculateSubwindows(), *XCirculateSubwindowsDown()*, *XCirculateSubwindowsUp()*, *XConfigure-Window()*, *XLowerWindow()*, *XMoveResizeWindow()*, *XQueryTree()*, *XRaiseWindow()*, *XReparent-Window()*, *XResizeWindow()*, *XRestackWindows()*.

XNewModifiermap

Xlib – Keyboard –

Name

XNewModifiermap – create a keyboard modifier mapping structure.

Synopsis

```
XModifierKeymap *XNewModifiermap(max_keys_per_mod)
    int max_keys_per_mod;
```

Arguments

max_keys_per_mod
Specifies the maximum number of keycodes assigned to any of the modifiers in the map.

Returns

The created modifier map structure.

Description

XNewModifiermap() allocates space for an XModifierKeymap() structure, sets its fields, and returns a pointer to the structure.

This function is used when more than one XModifierKeymap() structure is needed. max_keys_per_mod depends on the server and should be gotten from the XModifier-Keymap() structure returned by XGetModifierMapping().

For more information on keyboard preferences, see Volume One, Chapter 9, *The Keyboard and Pointer*.

Structures

```
typedef struct {
    int max_keypermod;          /* server's max number of keys per modifier */
    KeyCode *modifiermap;       /* An 8 by max_keypermod array of the
                                   modifiers */
} XModifierKeymap;
```

See Also

XChangeKeyboardMapping(), XDeleteModifiermapEntry(), XFreeModifiermap(), XGetKeyboard-Mapping(), XGetModifierMapping(), XInsertModifiermapEntry(), XKeycodeToKeysym(), XKeysymTo-Keycode(), XKeysymToString(), XLookupKeysym(), XLookupString(), XQueryKeymap(), XRebind-Keysym(), XRefreshKeyboardMapping(), XSetModifierMapping(), XStringToKeysym().

XNextEvent

Name

XNextEvent – get the next event of any type or window.

Synopsis

```
XNextEvent(display, event_return)
    Display *display;
    XEvent *event_return;
```

Arguments

display   Specifies a connection to an X server; returned from `XOpenDisplay()`.

event_return
                   Returns the event removed from the event queue.

Description

`XNextEvent()` removes an event from the head of the event queue and copies it into an `XEvent` structure supplied by the caller. If the event queue is empty, `XNextEvent()` flushes the request buffer and waits (blocks) until an event is received. Use `XCheckMask-Event()` or `XCheckIfEvent()` if you do not want to wait.

For more information, see Volume One, Chapter 8, *Events*.

See Also

XQLength(), XAllowEvents(), XCheckIfEvent(), XCheckMaskEvent(), XCheckTypedEvent(), XCheck-TypedWindowEvent(), XCheckWindowEvent(), XEventsQueued(), XGetInputFocus(), XGetMotion-Events(), XIfEvent(), XMaskEvent(), XPeekEvent(), XPeekIfEvent(), XPending(), XPutBackEvent(), XSelectInput(), XSendEvent(), XSetInputFocus(), XSynchronize(), XWindowEvent().

XNextRequest

Name

XNextRequest, NextRequest – return serial number of next request.

Synopsis

```
unsigned long XNextRequest(display)
    Display *display;
```

Arguments

display   Specifies a connection to an X server; returned from XOpenDisplay().

Returns

The serial number.

Description

XNextRequest() extracts the full serial number that Xlib will use for the next request. Serial numbers are maintained separately for each display connection.

The C language macro NextRequest() is equivalent and slightly more efficient.

See Also

XLastKnownRequestProcessed().

XNoOp

Name

XNoOp – send a NoOp to exercise connection with the server.

Synopsis

```
XNoOp(display)
    Display *display;
```

Arguments

display   Specifies a connection to an X server; returned from XOpenDisplay().

Description

XNoOp() sends a NoOperation request to the X server, thereby exercising the connection. This request can be used to measure the response time of the network connection. XNoOp() does not flush the request buffer.

See Also

XDefaultScreen(), XCloseDisplay(), XFree(), XOpenDisplay().

XOffsetRegion

Name

XOffsetRegion – change offset of a region.

Synopsis

```
XOffsetRegion(r, dx, dy)
    Region r;
    int dx, dy;
```

Arguments

r   Specifies the region.

dx   Specify the amount to move the specified region relative to the origin of all
dy   regions.

Description

XOffsetRegion() changes the offset of the region the specified amounts in the x and y
directions.

Regions are located using an offset from a point (the *region origin*) which is common to all
regions. It is up to the application to interpret the location of the region relative to a drawable. If the region is to be used as a clip_mask by calling XSetRegion(), the upper-left
corner of the region relative to the drawable used in the graphics request will be at
(xoffset + clip_x_origin, yoffset + clip_y_origin), where xoffset
and yoffset are the offset of the region and clip_x_origin and clip_y_origin are
components of the GC used in the graphics request.

Structures

Region is a pointer to an opaque structure type.

See Also

XClipBox(), XCreateRegion(), XDestroyRegion(), XEmptyRegion(), XEqualRegion(), XIntersect-
Region(), XPointInRegion(), XPolygonRegion(), XRectInRegion(), XSetRegion(), XShrinkRegion(),
XSubtractRegion(), XUnionRectWithRegion(), XUnionRegion(), XXorRegion().

XOpenDisplay

Name

XOpenDisplay – connect a client program to an X server.

Synopsis

```
Display *XOpenDisplay(display_name)
 char *display_name;
```

Arguments

display_name   Specifies the display name, which determines the server to connect
                      to and the communications domain to be used. See Description
                      below.

Returns

The display structure.

Description

The XOpenDisplay() routine connects the client to the server controlling the hardware
display through TCP or DECnet communication protocols, or through some local inter-pro-
cess communication protocol.

On a POSIX-conformant system, if display_name is NULL, the value defaults to the contents of the DISPLAY environment variable on UNIX-based systems. On non-UNIX-based systems, see that operating system's Xlib manual for the default display_name. The encoding and interpretation of the display name is implementation-dependent. Strings in the Host
Portable Character Encoding are supported; support for other characters is implementation-
dependent. The display_name or DISPLAY environment variable is a string that has the
format hostname:server or hostname:server.screen. For example,
frog:0.2 would specify screen 2 of server 0 on the machine frog.

hostname   Specifies the name of the host machine on which the display is physically con-
            nected. You follow the hostname with either a single colon (:) or a double
            colon (::), which determines the communications domain to use. Any or all of
            the communication protocols can be used simultaneously on a server built to
            support them (but only one per client).

   •   If hostname is a host machine name and a single colon (:) separates the
       hostname and display number, XOpenDisplay() connects to the server
       using TCP streams. If the hostname is not specified, Xlib uses what it
       believes is the fastest transport.

   •   If hostname is a host machine name and a double colon (::) separates
       the hostname and display number, XOpenDisplay() connects with the
       server using DECnet streams. To use DECnet, however, you must build all

software for DECnet. A single X server can accept both TCP and DECnet connections if it has been built for DECnet.

Note that support for use of the string "unix" in a display name is no longer part of the Xlib specification as of Release 4.

server   Specifies the number of the server on its host machine. This display number may be followed by a period (.). A single CPU can have more than one display; the displays are numbered starting from 0.

screen   Specifies the number of the default screen on *server*. Multiple screens can be connected to (controlled by) a single X server, but they are used as a single display by a single user. *screen* merely sets an internal variable that is returned by the DefaultScreen() macro. If *screen* is omitted, it defaults to 0.

If successful, XOpenDisplay() returns a pointer to a Display. This structure provides many of the specifications of the server and its screens. If XOpenDisplay() does not succeed, it returns NULL.

After a successful call to XOpenDisplay(), all of the screens on the server may be used by the application. The screen number specified in the *display_name* argument serves only to specify the value that will be returned by the DefaultScreen() macro. After opening the display, you can use the ScreenCount() macro to determine how many screens are available. Then you can reference each screen with integer values between 0 and the value returned by (ScreenCount() -1). You can access elements of the Display and Screen structures only using the information macros and functions listed in Appendix C, *Macros*.

For more information, see Volume One, Chapter 2, *X Concepts*, and Chapter 3, *Basic Window Program*.

See Also

XDefaultScreen(), XCloseDisplay(), XFree(), XNoOp().

XOpenIM

Name

XOpenIM – open input method.

Synopsis

```
XIM XOpenIM(display, db, res_name, res_class)
    Display *display;
    XrmDatabase db;
    char *res_name;
    char *res_class;
```

Arguments

display   Specifies the connection to the X server.

db   Specifies the resource database.

res_name   Specifies the full resource name of the application.

res_class   Specifies the full class name of the application.

Returns

The input method ID.

Availability

Release 5 and later.

Description

XOpenIM() opens an input method. The current locale and modifiers are bound to the input method when it is opened. The locale associated with an input method cannot be changed dynamically. This implies the strings returned by XmbLookupString() or XwcLookup-String(), for any input context affiliated with a given input method, will be encoded in the locale that was current at the time the input method was opened.

The specific input method to which this call will be routed is identified on the basis of the current locale. XOpenIM() will identify a default input method corresponding to the current locale. That default can be modified using XSetLocaleModifiers() with the input method ("im") modifier.

The db argument is the resource database to be used by the input method for looking up resources that are private to the input method. It is not intended that this database be used to look up values that can be set as IC values in an input context. If db is NULL, no data base is passed to the input method.

The res_name and res_class arguments specify the resource name and class of the application. They are intended to be used as prefixes by the input method when looking up resources that are common to all input contexts that may be created for this input method.

The characters used for resource names and classes must be in the X portable character set. The resources looked up are not fully specified if `res_name` or `res_class` is NULL.

The `res_name` and `res_class` arguments are not assumed to exist beyond the call to XOpenIM(). The specified resource database is assumed to exist for the lifetime of the input method.

XOpenIM() returns NULL if no input method could be opened.

See Also

XCloseIM(), XGetIMValues(), XDisplayOfIM(), XLocaleOfIM().

XParseColor

Name

XParseColor – look up RGB values from ASCII color name or translate hexadecimal value.

Synopsis

```
Status XParseColor(display, colormap, spec, exact_def_return)
    Display *display;
    Colormap colormap;
    char *spec;
    XColor *exact_def_return;
```

Arguments

display   Specifies a connection to an X server; returned from XOpenDisplay().

colormap   Specifies a colormap associated with the screen on which to look up the color. This argument is required, but is meaningful only with Xcms color specifications.

spec   Specifies the color string (see the "Description" section). Uppercase or lowercase does not matter. If the color name is not in the Host Portable Character Encoding, the result is implementation-dependent.

exact_def_return
                 Returns the RGB values corresponding to the specified color name or hexadecimal specification, and sets its DoRed, DoGreen, and DoBlue flags.

Returns

Zero on failure, non-zero on success.

Description

XParseColor() looks up the string name of a color with respect to the screen associated with the specified colormap. It returns the exact color value. It or hexadecimal values specified, or translating the hexadecimal code into separate RGB values.

XParseColor() takes a string specification of a color, typically from a user-specified command line or resource value, and returns the corresponding red, green, and blue values, suitable for a subsequent call to XAllocColor or XStoreColor(). *spec* can be given in several forms, and may be looked up in different ways depending on the form.

* Color name, such as "blue. This form is looked up in the server's RGB database, a sample of which is listed in Appendix D, *The Color Database*.

* Xcms color name, such as TekHVC:0.0/100.0/0.0. This form is looked up in the client-side database for the screen associated with the specified colormap. This form is supported starting in Release 5. For more information on this form of color specification, see the *Programmer's Supplement for Release 5*, or the Third Edition of Volume One.

Hexadecimal specification such as #3a7. This form consists of an initial sharp sign character followed by one of the following formats:

#RGB	(one character per color)
#RRGGBB	(two characters per color)
#RRRGGGBBB	(three characters per color)
#RRRRGGGGBBBB	(four characters per color)

where R, G, and B represent single hexadecimal digits (uppercase or lowercase). The hexadecimal strings must be NULL-terminated so that `XParseColor()` knows when it has reached the end. When fewer than 16 bits each are specified, they represent the most significant bits of the value. For example, #3a7 is the same as #3000a0007000. The hexadecimal style is discouraged in Release 5 and later.

Status is zero on failure, non-zero on success. This routine will fail if the initial character is a sharp sign but the string otherwise fails to fit one of the above formats, or if the initial character is not a sharp sign and the named color does not exist in the server's database.

For more information, see Volume One, Chapter 7, *Color* and in the Third Edition, the chapter on Device-Independent Color.

Structures

```
typedef struct {
    unsigned long pixel;
    unsigned short red, green, blue;
    char flags;     /* DoRed, DoGreen, DoBlue */
    char pad;
} XColor;
```

Errors

BadColor   Invalid colormap.

See Also

XBlackPixel(), XWhitePixel(), XAllocColor(), XcmsAllocColor(), XAllocColorCells(), XAllocColor-Planes(), XAllocNamedColor(), XcmsAllocNamedColor(), XFreeColors(), XLookupColor(), XQuery-Color(), XQueryColors(), XStoreColor(), XcmsStoreColor(), XStoreColors(), XcmsStoreColors(), XStoreNamedColor().

XParseGeometry

Name

XParseGeometry – generate position and size from standard window geometry string.

Synopsis

```
int XParseGeometry(parsestring, x_return, y_return, width_return,
        height_return)
    char *parsestring;
    int *x_return, *y_return;
    unsigned int *width_return, *height_return;
```

Arguments

parsestring   Specifies the string you want to parse.

x_return   Return the x and y coordinates (offsets) from the string.
y_return

width_return   Return the width and height in pixels from the string.
height_return

Returns

A bit mask composed of the OR of the symbols XValue, YValue, WidthValue, HeightValue, XNegative, and/or YNegative.

Description

By convention, X applications provide a geometry command-line option to indicate window size and placement. XParseGeometry() makes it easy to conform to this standard because it allows you to parse the standard window geometry string. Specifically, this function lets you parse strings of the form:

=<width_return>x<height_return>{+-}<xoffset>{+-}<yoffset>

The items in this string map into the arguments associated with this function. (Items enclosed in <> are integers and items enclosed in {} are a set from which one item is allowed. Note that the brackets should not appear in the actual string.) If the string is not in the Host Portable Character Encoding, the result is implementation-dependent.

XParseGeometry() returns a bitmask that indicates which of the four values (width_return, height_return, xoffset, and yoffset) were actually found in the string, and whether the x and y values are negative. The bits are represented by these constants: XValue, YValue, WidthValue, HeightValue, XNegative, and YNegative, and are defined in <X11/Xutil.h>. For each value found, the corresponding argument is updated and the corresponding bitmask element set; for each value not found, the argument is left unchanged, and the bitmask element is not set.

For more information, see Volume One, Chapter 11, *Managing User Preferences*.

See Also

XGeometry, XTranslateCoordinates(), XWMGeometry.

XPeekEvent

Name

XPeekEvent – get an event without removing it from the queue.

Synopsis

```
XPeekEvent(display, event_return)
    Display *display;
    XEvent *event_return;
```

Arguments

display   Specifies a connection to an X server; returned from XOpenDisplay().

report_return
                Returns the event peeked from the input queue.

Description

XPeekEvent() peeks at an input event from the head of the event queue and copies it into an XEvent supplied by the caller, without removing it from the input queue. If the queue is empty, XPeekEvent() flushes the request buffer and waits (blocks) until an event is received. If you do not want to wait, use the QLength() macro or XQLength() to determine if there are any events to peek at, or use XCheckIfEvent(). XEventsQueued() can perform the equivalent of either QLength() or XPending() and more.

For more information, see Volume One, Chapter 8, *Events*.

See Also

XQLength(), XAllowEvents(), XCheckIfEvent(), XCheckMaskEvent(), XCheckTypedEvent(), XCheck-TypedWindowEvent(), XCheckWindowEvent(), XEventsQueued(), XGetInputFocus(), XGetMotion-Events(), XIfEvent(), XMaskEvent(), XNextEvent(), XPeekIfEvent(), XPending(), XPutBackEvent(), XSelectInput(), XSendEvent(), XSetInputFocus(), XSynchronize(), XWindowEvent().

XPeekIfEvent

Name

XPeekIfEvent – get an event matched by predicate procedure without removing it from the queue.

Synopsis

```
XPeekIfEvent(display, event_return, predicate, arg)
    Display *display;
    XEvent *event_return;
    Bool (*predicate)();
    XPointer arg;
```

Arguments

display   Specifies a connection to an X server; returned from `XOpenDisplay()`.

event_return
                Returns a copy of the matched event.

predicate   Specifies the procedure to be called to determine if each event that arrives in the queue is the desired one.

arg   Specifies the user-specified argument that will be passed to the predicate procedure.

Description

`XPeekIfEvent()` returns an event only when the specified predicate procedure returns `True` for the event. The event is copied into *event_return* but not removed from the queue. The specified predicate is called each time an event is added to the queue, with the arguments *display*, *event_return*, and *arg*.

`XPeekIfEvent()` flushes the request buffer if no matching events could be found on the queue, and then waits for the next matching event.

For more information, see Volume One, Chapter 8, *Events*.

See Also

XQLength(), XAllowEvents(), XCheckIfEvent(), XCheckMaskEvent(), XCheckTypedEvent(), XCheck-TypedWindowEvent(), XCheckWindowEvent(), XEventsQueued(), XGetInputFocus(), XGetMotion-Events(), XIfEvent(), XMaskEvent(), XNextEvent(), XPeekEvent(), XPending(), XPutBackEvent(), XSelectInput(), XSendEvent(), XSetInputFocus(), XSynchronize(), XWindowEvent().

XPending

Name

XPending – return the number of pending events.

Synopsis

```
int XPending(display)
    Display *display;
```

Arguments

display   Specifies a connection to an X server; returned from XOpenDisplay().

Returns

The number of events.

Description

XPending() returns the number of events that have been received by Xlib from the server, but not yet removed from the queue. If there are no events on the queue, XPending() flushes the request buffer, and returns the number of events transferred to the input queue as a result of the flush.

The QLength macro or XQLength() returns the number of events on the queue, but without flushing the request buffer first.

For more information, see Volume One, Chapter 8, *Events*.

See Also

XQLength(), XAllowEvents(), XCheckIfEvent(), XCheckMaskEvent(), XCheckTypedEvent(), XCheckTypedWindowEvent(), XCheckWindowEvent(), XEventsQueued(), XGetInputFocus(), XGetMotionEvents(), XIfEvent(), XMaskEvent(), XNextEvent(), XPeekEvent(), XPeekIfEvent(), XPutBackEvent(), XSelectInput(), XSendEvent(), XSetInputFocus(), XSynchronize(), XWindowEvent().

Xpermalloc

Name

Xpermalloc – allocate memory never to be freed.

Synopsis

```
char *Xpermalloc(size)
    unsigned int size;
```

Arguments

size   Specifies the size in bytes of the space to be allocated. This specification is
                rounded to the nearest 4-byte boundary.

Returns

A pointer to the allocated memory.

Description

Xpermalloc() allocates some memory that will not be freed until the process exits.
Xpermalloc is used by some toolkits for permanently allocated storage and allows some
performance and space savings over the completely general memory allocator.

XPlanesOfScreen

Name

XPlanesOfScreen, PlanesOfScreen – return the depth of a root window.

Synopsis

```
int XPlanesOfScreen(screen)
    Screen *screen;
```

Arguments

screen   Specifies the appropriate Screen structure.

Returns

The number of planes.

Description

XPlanesOfScreen() returns the depth of the root window of the specified screen.

The C language macro PlanesOfScreen() is equivalent and slightly more efficient.

XPlanesOfScreen() and XDisplayPlanes() are equivalent except that they take different arguments.

See Also

XDisplayPlanes(), XDefaultDepth().*

XPointInRegion

Name

XPointInRegion – determine if a point is inside a region.

Synopsis

```
Bool XPointInRegion(r, x, y)
    Region r;
    int x, y;
```

Arguments

r   Specifies the region.

x   Specify the x and y coordinates of the point relative to the region's origin.

y

Returns

True if the point is inside the region, else False.

Description

XPointInRegion() returns True if the point x, y is contained in the region r. A point exactly on the boundary of the region is considered inside the region.

Regions are located using an offset from a point (the *region origin*) which is common to all regions. It is up to the application to interpret the location of the region relative to a drawable.

For more information on regions, see Volume One, Chapter 6, *Drawing Graphics and Text*.

Structures

Region is a pointer to an opaque structure type.

See Also

XClipBox(), XCreateRegion(), XDestroyRegion(), XEmptyRegion(), XEqualRegion(), XIntersectRegion(), XOffsetRegion(), XPolygonRegion(), XRectInRegion(), XSetRegion(), XShrinkRegion(), XSubtractRegion(), XUnionRectWithRegion(), XUnionRegion(), XXorRegion().

XPolygonRegion

Name

XPolygonRegion – generate a region from points in a polygon.

Synopsis

```
Region XPolygonRegion(points, n, fill_rule)
    XPoint points[];
    int n;
    int fill_rule;
```

Arguments

points   Specifies a pointer to an array of points.

n   Specifies the number of points in the polygon.

fill_rule   Specifies whether areas overlapping an odd number of times should be part
                of the region (WindingRule) or not part of the region (EvenOddRule).
                See Volume One, Chapter 5, *The Graphics Context*, for a description of the
                fill rule.

Returns

The created region.

Description

XPolygonRegion() creates a region defined by connecting the specified points, and
returns a pointer to be used to refer to the region.

Regions are located relative to a point (the *region origin*) which is common to all regions. In
XPolygonRegion(), the coordinates specified in points are relative to the region origin. By specifying all points relative to the drawable in which they will be used, the region
origin can be coincident with the drawable origin. It is up to the application whether to interpret the location of the region relative to a drawable or not.

If the region is to be used as a clip_mask by calling XSetRegion(), the upper-left corner of the region relative to the drawable used in the graphics request will be at (xoffset
+ clip_x_origin, yoffset + clip_y_origin), where xoffset and
yoffset are the offset of the region (if any) and clip_x_origin and
clip_y_origin are elements of the GC used in the graphics request. The fill_rule
can be either of these values:

EvenOddRule   Areas overlapping an odd number of times are *not* part of the
                region.

WindingRule   Overlapping areas are always filled.

For more information on structures, see Volume One, Chapter 6, *Drawing Graphics and Text*.

Structures

Region is a pointer to an opaque structure type.

See Also

XClipBox(), XCreateRegion(), XDestroyRegion(), XEmptyRegion(), XEqualRegion(), XIntersect-Region(), XOffsetRegion(), XPointInRegion(), XRectInRegion(), XSetRegion(), XShrinkRegion(), XSubtractRegion(), XUnionRectWithRegion(), XUnionRegion(), XXorRegion().

XProtocol*

Name

XProtocolRevision, XProtocolVersion, ProtocolRevision, ProtocolVersion – return protocol release or version.

Synopsis

```
int XProtocolRevision(display)
     Display *display;

int XProtocolVersion(display)
     Display *display;
```

Arguments

display   Specifies a connection to an X server; returned from XOpenDisplay().

Returns

The revision or version number.

Description

XProtocolRevision() returns the minor protocol revision number of the X server. XProtocolVersion() returns the major version number of the X protocol associated with the connected display. As of Release 4 and 5, the protocol revision level is zero, and the major version number is 11.

The C language macros ProtocolRevision() and ProtocolVersion() are equivalent and slightly more efficient.

See Also

XVendorRelease(), XServerVendor().

XPutBackEvent

Name

XPutBackEvent – push an event back on the input queue.

Synopsis

```
XPutBackEvent(display, event)
    Display *display;
    XEvent *event;
```

Arguments

display   Specifies a connection to an X server; returned from XOpenDisplay().

event   Specifies a pointer to the event to be requeued.

Description

XPutBackEvent() pushes an event back onto the head of the current display's input queue (so that it would become the one returned by the next XNextEvent() call). This can be useful if you have read an event and then decide that you'd rather deal with it later. There is no limit to how many times you can call XPutBackEvent() in succession.

For more information, see Volume One, Chapter 8, *Events*.

See Also

XQLength(), XAllowEvents(), XCheckIfEvent(), XCheckMaskEvent(), XCheckTypedEvent(), XCheck-TypedWindowEvent(), XCheckWindowEvent(), XEventsQueued(), XGetInputFocus(), XGetMotion-Events(), XIfEvent(), XMaskEvent(), XNextEvent(), XPeekEvent(), XPeekIfEvent(), XPending(), XSelect-Input(), XSendEvent(), XSetInputFocus(), XSynchronize(), XWindowEvent().

XPutImage

Name

XPutImage – draw an image on a window or pixmap.

Synopsis

```
XPutImage(display, d, gc, image, src_x, src_y, dest_x, dest_y, width,
                height)
    Display *display;
    Drawable d;
    GC gc;
    XImage *image;
    int src_x, src_y;
    int dest_x, dest_y;
    unsigned int width, height;
```

Arguments

display	Specifies a connection to an X server; returned from XOpenDisplay().
d	Specifies the drawable.
gc	Specifies the graphics context.
image	Specifies the image you want combined with the rectangle.
src_x src_y	Specify the coordinates of the upper-left corner of the rectangle to be copied, relative to the origin of the image.
dest_x dest_y	Specify the x and y coordinates, relative to the origin of the drawable, where the upper-left corner of the copied rectangle will be placed.
width height	Specify the width and height in pixels of the rectangular area to be copied.

Description

XPutImage() draws a section of an image on a rectangle in a window or pixmap. The section of the image is defined by src_x, src_y, $width$, and $height$.

There is no limit to the size of image that can be sent to the server using XPutImage(). XPutImage() automatically decomposes the call into multiple protocol requests to make sure that the maximum request size of the server is not exceeded.

XPutImage() uses these graphics context components: function, plane_mask, subwindow_mode, clip_x_origin, clip_y_origin, and clip_mask. This function also uses these graphics context mode-dependent components: foreground and background.

If an XYBitmap format image is used, then the depth of *d* must be 1, otherwise a Bad-Match error is generated. The foreground pixel in *gc* defines the source for bits set to one in the image, and the background pixel defines the source for the bits set to zero.

For XYPixmap and ZPixmap format images, the depth of the image must match the depth of drawable or a BadMatch error results.

Structures

```
typedef struct _XImage {
    int width, height;          /* size of image */
    int xoffset;                /* number of pixels offset in x direction */
    int format;                 /* XYBitmap, XYPixmap, ZPixmap */
    char *data;                 /* pointer to image data */
    int byte_order;             /* data byte order, LSBFirst, MSBFirst */
    int bitmap_unit;            /* quant. of scan line 8, 16, 32 */
    int bitmap_bit_order;       /* LSBFirst, MSBFirst */
    int bitmap_pad;             /* 8, 16, 32 either XY or ZPixmap */
    int depth;                  /* depth of image */
    int bytes_per_line;         /* accelerator to next line */
    int bits_per_pixel;         /* bits per pixel (ZPixmap) */
    char *obdata;               /* hook for the object routines to hang on */
    struct funcs {              /* image manipulation routines */
        struct _XImage *(*create_image)();
        int (*destroy_image)();
        unsigned long (*get_pixel)();
        int (*put_pixel)();
          struct _XImage *(*sub_image)();
        int (*add_pixel)();
    } f;
} XImage;
```

Errors

BadDrawable

BadGC

BadMatch   See Description above.

BadValue

See Also

XImageByteOrder(), XAddPixel(), XCreateImage(), XDestroyImage(), XGetImage(), XGetPixel(), XGetSubImage(), XPutPixel(), XSubImage().

Name

XPutPixel – set a pixel value in an image.

Synopsis

```
XPutPixel(ximage, x, y, pixel)
    XImage *ximage;
    int x;
    int y;
    unsigned long pixel;
```

Arguments

ximage   Specifies a pointer to the image to be modified.

x   Specify the x and y coordinates of the pixel to be set, relative to the origin
y   of the image.

pixel   Specifies the new pixel value.

Description

XPutPixel() overwrites the pixel in the named image with the specified pixel value. The
x and y coordinates are relative to the origin of the image. The input pixel value must be in
same bit- and byte-order as the machine in which the client is running (that is, the Least Significant Byte (LSB) of the long is the LSB of the pixel). The x and y coordinates must be
contained in the image.

Structures

```
typedef struct _XImage {
    int width, height;       /* size of image */
    int xoffset;             /* number of pixels offset in x direction */
    int format;              /* XYBitmap, XYPixmap, ZPixmap */
    char *data;              /* pointer to image data */
    int byte_order;          /* data byte order, LSBFirst, MSBFirst */
    int bitmap_unit;         /* quant. of scan line 8, 16, 32 */
    int bitmap_bit_order;    /* LSBFirst, MSBFirst */
    int bitmap_pad;          /* 8, 16, 32 either XY or ZPixmap */
    int depth;               /* depth of image */
    int bytes_per_line;      /* accelerator to next line */
    int bits_per_pixel;      /* bits per pixel (ZPixmap) */
    unsigned long red_mask;  /* bits in z arrangment */
    unsigned long green_mask;
    unsigned long blue_mask;
    char *obdata;            /* hook for the object routines to hang on */
    struct funcs {           /* image manipulation routines */
        struct _XImage *(*create_image)();
            int (*destroy_image)();
```

```
        unsigned long (*get_pixel)();
        int (*put_pixel)();
        struct _XImage *(*sub_image)();
        int (*add_pixel)();
    } f;
} XImage;
```

See Also

XImageByteOrder(), *XAddPixel()*, *XCreateImage()*, *XDestroyImage()*, *XGetImage()*, *XGetPixel()*, *XGet-SubImage()*, *XPutImage()*, *XSubImage()*.

XQLength

Name

XQLength, QLength – return the number of events on the queue.

Synopsis

```
int XQLength(display)
     Display *display;
```

Arguments

display   Specifies a connection to an X server; returned from XOpenDisplay().

Returns

The number of events on the queue.

Description

XQLength() returns the number of events currently on the queue for the connected display. Note that there may be more events that have not yet been read into the queue (see XEventsQueued()).

The C language macro QLength() is equivalent and slightly more efficient.

See Also

XEventsQueued(), XPending(), XPeekEvent().

XQueryBestCursor

Name

XQueryBestCursor – get the closest supported cursor sizes.

Synopsis

```
Status XQueryBestCursor(display, d, width, height,
                width_return, height_return)
    Display *display;
    Drawable d;
    unsigned int width, height;
    unsigned int *width_return, *height_return;
```

Arguments

display
: Specifies a connection to an X server; returned from XOpen-Display().

d
: Specifies a drawable that indicates which screen the cursor is to be used on. The best cursor may be different on different screens.

width
height
: Specify the preferred width and height, in pixels.

width_return
height_return
: Returns the closest supported cursor dimensions, in pixels, on the display hardware.

Returns

Zero on failure, non-zero on success.

Description

XQueryBestCursor() returns the closest cursor dimensions actually supported by the display hardware to the dimensions you specify.

Call this function if you wish to use a cursor size other than 16 by 16. XQueryBest-Cursor() provides a way to find out what size cursors are actually possible on the display. Applications should be prepared to use smaller cursors on displays which cannot support large ones.

XQueryBestCursor() returns non-zero if the call succeeded in getting a supported size (which may be the same or different from the specified size), or zero if the call failed.

Errors

BadDrawable

See Also

XCreateFontCursor(), XCreateGlyphCursor(), XCreatePixmapCursor(), XDefineCursor(), XFree-Cursor(), XQueryBestSize(), XRecolorCursor(), XUndefineCursor().

XQueryBestSize

Name

XQueryBestSize – obtain the "best" supported cursor, tile, or stipple size.

Synopsis

```
Status XQueryBestSize(display, class, which_screen, width,
                height, width_return, height_return)
    Display *display;
    int class;
    Drawable which_screen;
    unsigned int width, height;
    unsigned int *width_return, *height_return;
```

Arguments

display	Specifies a connection to an X server; returned from XOpenDisplay().
class	Specifies the class that you are interested in. Pass one of these constants: TileShape, CursorShape, or StippleShape.
which_screen	Specifies a drawable ID that tells the server which screen you want the best size for.
width *height*	Specify the preferred width and height in pixels.
width_return *height_return*	Return the closest supported width and height, in pixels, available for the object on the display hardware.

Returns

Zero on failure, non-zero on success.

Description

XQueryBestSize() returns the "fastest" or "closest" size to the specified size. For *class* of CursorShape, this is the closest size that can be fully displayed on the screen. For TileShape and StippleShape, this is the closest size that can be tiled or stippled "fastest."

For CursorShape, the drawable indicates the desired screen. For TileShape and StippleShape, the drawable indicates the screen and possibly the visual class and depth (server-dependent). An InputOnly window cannot be used as the drawable for TileShape or StippleShape (else a BadMatch error occurs).

XQueryBestSize() returns non-zero if the call succeeded in getting a supported size (may be the same or different from the specified size), or zero if the call failed.

Errors

BadDrawable

BadMatch   InputOnly drawable for *class* TileShape or StippleShape.

BadValue

See Also

XCreateBitmapFromData(), *XCreatePixmap()*, *XCreatePixmapFromBitmapData()*, *XFreePixmap()*, *XQueryBestStipple()*, *XQueryBestTile()*, *XReadBitmapFile()*, *XSetTile()*, *XSetWindowBackground-Pixmap()*, *XSetWindowBorderPixmap()*, *XWriteBitmapFile()*.

XQueryBestStipple

Name

XQueryBestStipple – obtain the fastest supported stipple shape.

Synopsis

```
Status XQueryBestStipple(display, which_screen, width, height,
                width_return, height_return)
    Display *display;
    Drawable which_screen;
    unsigned int width, height;
    unsigned int *width_return, *height_return;
```

Arguments

display	Specifies a connection to an X server; returned from XOpen-Display().
which_screen	Specifies a drawable that tells the server which screen you want the best size for.
width height	Specify the preferred width and height in pixels.
width_return height_return	Return the width and height, in pixels, of the stipple best supported by the display hardware.

Returns

Zero on failure, non-zero on success.

Description

XQueryBestStipple() returns the closest stipple size that can be stippled fastest. The drawable indicates the screen and possibly the visual class and depth. An InputOnly window cannot be used as the drawable (else a BadMatch error occurs).

XQueryBestStipple() returns non-zero if the call succeeded in getting a supported size (may be the same or different from the specified size), or zero if the call failed.

For more information on stipples, see Volume One, Chapter 5, *The Graphics Context*.

Errors

BadDrawable

BadMatch   InputOnly window.

See Also

XCreateBitmapFromData(), *XCreatePixmap()*, *XCreatePixmapFromBitmapData()*, *XFreePixmap()*, *XQueryBestSize()*, *XQueryBestTile()*, *XReadBitmapFile()*, *XSetTile()*, *XSetWindowBackground-Pixmap()*, *XSetWindowBorderPixmap()*, *XWriteBitmapFile()*.

XQueryBestTile

Name

XQueryBestTile – obtain the fastest supported fill tile shape.

Synopsis

```
Status XQueryBestTile(display, which_screen, width, height, width_return,
        height_return)
    Display *display;
    Drawable which_screen;
    unsigned int width, height;
    unsigned int *width_return, *height_return;
```

Arguments

display	Specifies a connection to an X server; returned from XOpen-Display().
which_screen	Specifies a drawable that tells the server which screen you want the best size for.
width height	Specify the preferred width and height in pixels.
width_return height_return	Return the width and height, in pixels, of the tile best supported by the display hardware.

Returns

Zero on failure, non-zero on success.

Description

XQueryBestTile( ) returns the closest size that can be tiled fastest. The drawable indicates the screen and possibly the visual class and depth. An InputOnly window cannot be used as the drawable.

XQueryBestTile( ) returns non-zero if the call succeeded in getting a supported size (may be the same or different from the specified size), or zero if the call failed.

For more information on tiles, see Volume One, Chapter 5, *The Graphics Context*.

Errors

BadDrawable

BadMatch   InputOnly drawable specified.

See Also

XCreateBitmapFromData(), *XCreatePixmap()*, *XCreatePixmapFromBitmapData()*, *XFreePixmap()*, *XQueryBestSize()*, *XQueryBestStipple()*, *XReadBitmapFile()*, *XSetTile()*, *XSetWindowBackground-Pixmap()*, *XSetWindowBorderPixmap()*, *XWriteBitmapFile()*.

XQueryColor

Name

XQueryColor – obtain the RGB values and flags for a specified colorcell.

Synopsis

```
XQueryColor(display, colormap, def_in_out)
    Display *display;
    Colormap colormap;
    XColor *def_in_out;
```

Arguments

display   Specifies a connection to an X server; returned from XOpenDisplay().

colormap   Specifies the ID of the colormap from which RGB values will be retrieved.

def_in_out   Specifies the pixel value and returns the RGB contents of that colorcell.

Description

XQueryColor() returns the RGB values in colormap colormap for the colorcell corresponding to the pixel value specified in the pixel member of the XColor structure def_in_out. The RGB values are returned in the red, green, and blue members of that structure, and the flags member of that structure is set to (DoRed | DoGreen | DoBlue). The values returned for an unallocated entry are undefined.

For more information, see Volume One, Chapter 7, *Color*.

Structures

```
typedef struct {
    unsigned long pixel;
    unsigned short red, green, blue;
    char flags;          /* DoRed, DoGreen, DoBlue */
    char pad;
} XColor;
```

Errors

BadColor   Invalid colormap.

BadValue   Pixel not valid index into colormap.

See Also

XBlackPixel(), XWhitePixel(), XAllocColor(), XAllocColorCells(), XAllocColorPlanes(), XAllocNamed-Color(), XFreeColors(), XLookupColor(), XParseColor(), XQueryColors(), XStoreColor(), XStore-Colors(), XStoreNamedColor().

XQueryColors

Name

XQueryColors – obtain RGB values for an array of colorcells.

Synopsis

```
XQueryColors(display, colormap, defs_in_out, ncolors)
    Display *display;
    Colormap colormap;
    XColor defs_in_out[ncolors];
    int ncolors;
```

Arguments

display   Specifies a connection to an X server; returned from XOpenDisplay().

colormap   Specifies the ID of the colormap from which RGB values will be retrieved.

defs_in_out   Specifies an array of XColor structures. In each one, pixel is set to indicate which colorcell in the colormap to return, and the RGB values in that colorcell are returned in red, green, and blue.

ncolors   Specifies the number of XColor structures in the color definition array.

Description

XQueryColors() is similar to XQueryColor(), but it returns an array of RGB values. It returns the RGB values in colormap *colormap* for each colorcell corresponding to the pixel value specified in the pixel member of each XColor structure in the color-cell_def array. The RGB values are returned in the red, green, and blue members of that same structure, and sets the flags member in each XColor structure to (DoRed | DoGreen | DoBlue).

For more information, see Volume One, Chapter 7, *Color*.

Structures

```
typedef struct {
    unsigned long pixel;
    unsigned short red, green, blue;
    char flags;         /* DoRed, DoGreen, DoBlue */
    char pad;
} XColor;
```

Errors

BadColor   Invalid colormap.

BadValue   Pixel not valid index into *colormap*.

Note: if more than one pixel value is in error, the one reported is arbitrary.

See Also

XBlackPixel(), XWhitePixel(), XAllocColor(), XAllocColorCells(), XAllocColorPlanes(), XAllocNamed-Color(), XFreeColors(), XLookupColor(), XParseColor(), XQueryColor(), XStoreColor(), XStore-Colors(), XStoreNamedColor().

XQueryExtension

Name

XQueryExtension – get extension information.

Synopsis

```
Bool XQueryExtension(display, name, major_opcode_return,
        first_event_return, first_error_return)
    Display *display;
    char *name;
    int *major_opcode_return;
    int *first_event_return;
    int *first_error_return;
```

Arguments

display   Specifies a connection to an X server; returned from XOpenDisplay().

name   Specifies the name of the desired extension. Uppercase or lowercase is important. If the extension name is not in the Host Portable Character Encoding, the result is implementation-dependent.

major_opcode_return
                 Returns the major opcode of the extension, for use in error handling routines.

first_event_return
                 Returns the code of the first custom event type created by the extension.

first_error_return
                 Returns the code of the first custom error defined by the extension.

Returns

True if the extension is present, else False.

Description

XQueryExtension() determines if the named extension is present, and returns True if it is. If so, the routines in the extension can be used just as if they were core Xlib requests, except that they may return new types of events or new error codes. The available extensions can be listed with XListExtensions().

The *major_opcode_return* for the extension is returned, if it has one. Otherwise, zero is returned. This opcode will appear in errors generated in the extension.

If the extension involves additional event types, the base event type code is returned in *first_event_return*. Otherwise, zero is returned in *first_event_return*. The format of the events is specific to the extension.

If the extension involves additional error codes, the base error code is returned in *first_error_return*. Otherwise, zero is returned. The format of additional data in the errors is specific to the extension.

See Volume One, Chapter 13, *Other Programming Techniques*, for more information on using extensions, and Volume One, Appendix C, *Writing Extensions to X*, for information on writing them.

See Also

XFreeExtensionList(), *XListExtensions()*.

XQueryFont

Name

XQueryFont – return information about a loaded font.

Synopsis

```
XFontStruct *XQueryFont(display, font_ID)
    Display *display;
    XID font_ID;
```

Arguments

display   Specifies a connection to an X server; returned from XOpenDisplay().

font_ID   Specifies either the font ID or the graphics context ID. You can declare the data type for this argument as either Font or GContext (both X IDs). If GContext, the font in that GC will be queried.

Returns

The font information structure.

Description

XQueryFont() returns a pointer to an XFontStruct structure containing information describing the specified font. This call is needed if you loaded the font with XLoadFont(), but need the font information for multiple calls to determine the extent of text. XLoad-QueryFont() combines these two operations.

If the font hasn't been loaded (or the font ID passed is invalid), XQueryFont() returns NULL.

If font_ID is declared as data type GContext (also a resource ID), this function queries the font specified by the font component of the GC specified by this ID. This is useful for getting information about the default font, whose ID is stored in the default GC. However, in this case the GContext ID will be the ID stored in the fid field of the returned XFont-Struct, and you can't use that ID in XSetFont() or XUnloadFont(), since it is not itself the ID of the font.

Use XFreeFont() to free this data.

For more information on fonts, see Volume One, Chapter 6, *Drawing Graphics and Text*.

Errors

BadFont

Structures

```
typedef struct {
    XExtData *ext_data;            /* hook for extension to hang data */
    Font fid;                      /* font ID for this font */
    unsigned direction;            /* hint about direction font is painted */
    unsigned min_char_or_byte2;    /* first character */
    unsigned max_char_or_byte2;    /* last character */
    unsigned min_byte1;            /* first row that exists */
    unsigned max_byte1;            /* last row that exists */
    Bool all_chars_exist;          /* flag if all characters have non-zero size*/
    unsigned default_char;         /* char to print for undefined character */
    int n_properties;              /* how many properties there are */
    XFontProp *properties;         /* pointer to array of additional properties*/
    XCharStruct min_bounds;        /* minimum bounds over all existing char*/
    XCharStruct max_bounds;        /* minimum bounds over all existing char*/
    XCharStruct *per_char;         /* first_char to last_char information */
    int ascent;                    /* logical extent above baseline for spacing */
    int descent;                   /* logical descent below baseline for spacing */
} XFontStruct;
```

See Also

XCreateFontCursor(), XFreeFont(), XFreeFontInfo(), XFreeFontNames(), XFreeFontPath(), XGetFontPath(), XGetFontProperty(), XListFonts(), XListFontsWithInfo(), XLoadFont(), XLoadQueryFont(), XSetFont(), XSetFontPath(), XUnloadFont().

XQueryKeymap

Name

XQueryKeymap – obtain a bit vector for the current state of the keyboard.

Synopsis

```
XQueryKeymap(display, keys_return)
    Display *display;
    char keys_return[32];
```

Arguments

display   Specifies a connection to an X server; returned from XOpenDisplay().

keys_return   Returns an array of bytes that identifies which keys are pressed down.
                 Each bit represents one key of the keyboard.

Description

XQueryKeymap() returns a bit vector for the logical state of the keyboard, where each bit set to 1 indicates that the corresponding key is currently pressed down. The vector is represented as 32 bytes. Byte N (from 0) contains the bits for keys $8N$ to $8N+7$ with the least significant bit in the byte representing key $8N$. Note that the logical state may lag the physical state if device event processing is frozen due to a grab.

See Also

XChangeKeyboardMapping(), XDeleteModifiermapEntry(), XFreeModifiermap(), XGetKeyboard-Mapping(), XGetModifierMapping(), XInsertModifiermapEntry(), XKeycodeToKeysym(), XKeysymTo-Keycode(), XKeysymToString(), XLookupKeysym(), XLookupString(), XNewModifiermap(), XRebind-Keysym(), XRefreshKeyboardMapping(), XSetModifierMapping(), XStringToKeysym().

Name

XQueryPointer – get the current pointer location.

Synopsis

```
Bool XQueryPointer(display, window, root_return, child_return,
        root_x_return, route_y_return, win_x_return, win_y_return,
        mask_return)
    Display *display;
    Window window;
    Window *root_return, *child_return;
    int *root_x_return, *route_y_return;
    int *win_x_return, *win_y_return;
    unsigned int *mask_return;
```

Arguments

display	Specifies a connection to an X server; returned from XOpen-Display().
window	Specifies a window which indicates which screen the pointer position is returned for, and child_return will be a child of this window if pointer is inside a child.
root_return	Returns the root window ID the pointer is currently on.
child_return	Returns the ID of the child of w the pointer is located in, or zero if it not in a child.
root_x_return route_y_return	Return the x and y coordinates of the pointer relative to the root's origin.
win_x_return win_y_return	Return the x and y coordinates of the pointer relative to the origin of window window.
mask_return	Returns the current state of the modifier keys and pointer buttons. This is a mask composed of the OR of any number of the following symbols: ShiftMask, LockMask, ControlMask, Mod1Mask, Mod2Mask, Mod3Mask, Mod4Mask, Mod5Mask, Button1Mask, Button2Mask, Button3Mask, Button4Mask, Button5Mask.

Returns

True if the pointer is on the same screen as the window argument, else False.

Description

XQueryPointer() gets the pointer coordinates relative to a window and relative to the root window, the *root_return* window ID and the *child_return* window ID (if any) the pointer is currently in, and the current state of modifier keys and buttons.

If XQueryPointer() returns False, then the pointer is not on the same screen as *window*, *child_return* is None, and *win_x_return* and *win_y_return* are zero. However, *root_return*, *root_x_return*, and *route_y_return* are still valid. If XQueryPointer() returns True, then the pointer is on the same screen as *window*, and all return values are valid.

The logical state of the pointer buttons and modifier keys can lag behind their physical state if device event processing is frozen due to a grab.

Errors

BadWindow

See Also

XChangeActivePointerGrab(), *XChangePointerControl()*, *XGetPointerControl()*, *XGetPointer-Mapping()*, *XGrabPointer()*, *XSetPointerMapping()*, *XUngrabPointer()*, *XWarpPointer()*.

XQueryTextExtents

Name

XQueryTextExtents – query the server for string and font metrics.

Synopsis

```
XQueryTextExtents(display, font_ID, string, nchars, direction_return,
        font_ascent_return, font_descent_return, overall_return)
    Display *display;
    XID font_ID;
    char *string;
    int nchars;
    int *direction_return;
    int *font_ascent_return, *font_descent_return;
    XCharStruct *overall_return;
```

Arguments

display	Specifies a connection to an X server; returned from XOpenDisplay().
font_ID	Specifies the appropriate font ID previously returned by XLoadFont(), or the GContext that specifies the font.
string	Specifies the character string for which metrics are to be returned.
nchars	Specifies the number of characters in string.

direction_return

Returns the direction the string would be drawn using the specified font. Either FontLeftToRight or FontRightToLeft.

font_ascent_return

Returns the maximum ascent for the specified font.

font_descent_return

Returns the maximum descent for the specified font.

overall_return

Returns the overall characteristics of the string. These are the sum of the width measurements for each character, the maximum font_ascent_return and font_descent_return, the minimum lbearing added to the width of all characters up to the character with the smallest lbearing, and the maximum rbearing added to the width of all characters up to the character with the largest rbearing.

Description

XQueryTextExtents() returns the dimensions in pixels that specify the bounding box of the specified string of characters in the named font, and the maximum ascent and descent for the entire font. This function queries the server and, therefore, suffers the round trip overhead that is avoided by XTextExtents(), but XQueryTextExtents() does not require a filled `XFontInfo` structure stored on the client side. Therefore, this function would be used when memory is precious, or when just a small number of text width calculations are to be done.

The returned *font_ascent_return* and *font_descent_return* should usually be used to calculate the line spacing, while the `width`, `rbearing`, and `lbearing` members of *overall_return* should be used for horizontal measures. The total height of the bounding rectangle, good for any string in this font, is *font_ascent_return* + *font_descent_return*.

overall_return.ascent is the maximum of the ascent metrics of all characters in the string. The *overall_return.descent* is the maximum of the descent metrics. The *overall_return.width* is the sum of the character-width metrics of all characters in the string. The *overall_return.lbearing* is usually the lbearing of the first character in the string, and *overall_return.rbearing* is the rbearing of the last character in the string plus the sum of the widths of all the characters up to but not including the last character. More technically, here is the X protocol definition: *For each character in the string, let W be the sum of the character-width metrics of all characters preceding it in the string, let L be the lbearing metric of the character plus W, and let R be the rbearing metric of the character plus W. The* overall_return.lbearing *is the minimum L of all characters in the string, and the* overall_return.rbearing *is the maximum R.*

For more information on drawing text, see Volume One, Chapter 6, *Drawing Graphics and Text*.

Structures

```
typedef struct {
    short lbearing;              /* origin to left edge of character */
    short rbearing;              /* origin to right edge of character */
    short width;                 /* advance to next char's origin */
    short ascent;                /* baseline to top edge of character */
    short descent;               /* baseline to bottom edge of character */
    unsigned short attributes;   /* per char flags (not predefined) */
} XCharStruct;
```

Errors

```
BadFont
BadGC
```

See Also

XDrawImageString(), XDrawImageString16(), XDrawString(), XDrawString16(), XDrawText(), XDrawText16(), XQueryTextExtents16(), XTextExtents(), XTextExtents16(), XTextWidth(), XTextWidth16().

XQueryTextExtents16

Name

XQueryTextExtents16 – query the server for string and font metrics of a 16-bit character
string.

Synopsis

```
XQueryTextExtents16(display, font_ID, string, nchars, direction_return,
        font_ascent_return, descent, overall_return\&)
    Display *display;
    XID font_ID;
    XChar2b *string;
    int nchars;
    int *direction_return;
    int *font_ascent_return, *font_descent_return;
    XCharStruct *overall_return\&;
```

Arguments

display   Specifies a connection to an X server; returned from XOpenDisplay().

font_ID   Specifies the appropriate font ID previously returned by XLoadFont(),
                    or the GContext that specifies the font.

string   Specifies the character string for which metrics are to be returned.

nchars   Specifies the number of characters in string.

direction_return
                    Returns the direction of painting in the specified font. Either Font-
                    LefttoRight or FontRighttoLeft.

font_ascent_return
                    Returns the maximum ascent in pixels for the specified font.

descent   Returns the maximum descent in pixels for the specified font.

overall_return
                    Returns the overall characteristics of the string. These are the sum of the
                    width measurements for each character, the maximum
                    font_ascent_return and descent, the minimum lbearing added
                    to the width of all characters up to the character with the smallest lbear-
                    ing, and the maximum rbearing added to the width of all characters up
                    to the character with the largest rbearing.

Description

XQueryTextExtents16() returns the dimensions in pixels that specify the bounding
box of the specified string of characters in the named font, and the maximum ascent and
descent for the entire font. This function queries the server and, therefore, suffers the round

trip overhead that is avoided by XTextExtents16(), but XQueryTextExtents() does not require a filled XFontInfo structure.

The returned *font_ascent_return* and *font_descent_return* should usually be used to calculate the line spacing, while the width, rbearing, and lbearing members of *overall_return* should be used for horizontal measures. The total height of the bounding rectangle, good for any string in this font, is *font_ascent_return* + *font_descent_return*.

overall_return.font_ascent_return is the maximum of the ascent metrics of all characters in the string. The *overall_return.descent* is the maximum of the descent metrics. The *overall_return.width* is the sum of the character-width metrics of all characters in the string. The *overall_return.lbearing* is usually the lbearing of the first character in the string, and *overall_return.rbearing* is the rbearing of the last character in the string plus the sum of the widths of all the characters up to but not including the last character. More technically, here is the X protocol definition: *For each character in the string, let W be the sum of the character-width metrics of all characters preceding it in the string, let L be the lbearing metric of the character plus W, and let R be the rbearing metric of the character plus W. The* overall_return.lbearing *is the minimum L of all characters in the string, and the* overall_return.rbearing *is the maximum R.*

For fonts defined with linear indexing rather than two-byte matrix indexing, the server interprets each XChar2b as a 16-bit number that has been transmitted with the most significant byte first. That is, byte one of the XChar2b is taken as the most significant byte.

If the font has no defined default character, then undefined characters in the string are taken to have all zero metrics.

Structures

```
typedef struct {              /* normal 16-bit characters are two bytes */
    unsigned char byte1;
    unsigned char byte2;
} XChar2b;

typedef struct {
    short lbearing;           /* origin to left edge of character */
    short rbearing;           /* origin to right edge of character */
    short width;              /* advance to next char's origin */
    short ascent;             /* baseline to top edge of character */
    short descent;            /* baseline to bottom edge of character */
    unsigned short attributes; /* per char flags (not predefined) */
} XCharStruct;
```

Errors

BadFont

BadGC

See Also

XDrawImageString(), XDrawImageString16(), XDrawString(), XDrawString16(), XDrawText(), XDraw-Text16(), XQueryTextExtents(), XTextExtents(), XTextExtents16(), XTextWidth(), XTextWidth16().

XQueryTree

Name

XQueryTree – return a list of children, parent, and root.

Synopsis

```
Status XQueryTree(display, w, root_return, parent_return, children_
          return, nchildren_return)
    Display *display;
    Window w;
    Window *root_return;
    Window *parent_return;
    Window **children_return;
    unsigned int *nchildren_return;
```

Arguments

display   Specifies a connection to an X server; returned from XOpenDisplay().

w   Specifies the ID of the window to be queried. For this window, XQuery-Tree() will list its children, its root, its parent, and the number of children.

root_return   Returns the root ID for the specified window.

parent_return
            Returns the parent window of the specified window.

children_return
            Returns the list of children associated with the specified window.

nchildren_return
            Returns the number of children associated with the specified window.

Returns

Zero on failure, non-zero on success.

Description

XQueryTree() uses its last four arguments to return the root ID, the parent ID, a pointer to a list of children and the number of children in that list, all for the specified window *w*. The *children_return* are listed in current stacking order, from bottommost (first) to topmost (last). XQueryTree() returns zero if it fails, non-zero if it succeeds.

You should deallocate the list of children with XFree() when it is no longer needed.

Errors

BadWindow.

See Also

XCirculateSubwindows(), XCirculateSubwindowsDown(), XCirculateSubwindowsUp(), XConfigure-Window(), XLowerWindow(), XMoveResizeWindow(), XMoveWindow(), XRaiseWindow(), XReparent-Window(), XResizeWindow(), XRestackWindows().

XRaiseWindow

Name

XRaiseWindow – raise a window to the top of the stacking order.

Synopsis

```
XRaiseWindow(display, w)
    Display *display;
    Window w;
```

Arguments

display   Specifies a connection to an X server; returned from XOpenDisplay().

w   Specifies the ID of the window to be raised to the top of the stack.

Description

XRaiseWindow() moves a window to the top of the stacking order among its siblings. If the windows are regarded as overlapping sheets of paper stacked on a desk, then raising a window is analogous to moving the sheet to the top of the stack, while leaving its x and y location on the desk constant.

Raising a mapped window may generate exposure events for that window and any mapped subwindows of that window that were formerly obscured.

If the override_redirect attribute of the window (see Volume One, Chapter 4, *Window Attributes*) is False and the window manager has selected SubstructureRedirect-Mask on the parent, then a ConfigureRequest event is sent to the window manager, and no further processing is performed.

Errors

BadWindow

See Also

XCirculateSubwindows(), *XCirculateSubwindowsDown()*, *XCirculateSubwindowsUp()*, *XConfigure-Window()*, *XLowerWindow()*, *XMoveResizeWindow()*, *XMoveWindow()*, *XQueryTree()*, *XReparent-Window()*, *XResizeWindow()*, *XRestackWindows()*.

XReadBitmapFile

Name

XReadBitmapFile – read a bitmap from disk.

Synopsis

```
int XReadBitmapFile(display, d, filename, width_return, height_return,
      bitmap_return, x_hot_return, y_hot_return)
   Display *display;
   Drawable d;
   char *filename;
   unsigned int *width_return, *height_return;
   Pixmap *bitmap_return;
   int *x_hot_return, *y_hot_return;
```

Arguments

display	Specifies a connection to an X server; returned from XOpen-Display().
d	Specifies the drawable.
filename	Specifies the filename to use. The format of the filename is operating system specific.
width_return height_return	Return the dimensions in pixels of the bitmap that is read.
bitmap_return	Returns the pixmap resource ID that is created.
x_hot_return y_hot_return	Return the hotspot coordinates in the file (or –1,–1 if none present).

Returns

BitmapSuccess on success. BitmapOpenFailed, BitmapFileInvalid, or BitmapNoMemory on failure.

Description

XReadBitmapFile() reads in a file containing a description of a pixmap of depth 1 (a bitmap) in X Version 11 bitmap format. The file is parsed in the encoding of the current locale. The ability to read other than the standard format is implementation-dependent.

XReadBitmapFile() creates a pixmap of the appropriate size and reads the bitmap data from the file into the pixmap. The caller should free the pixmap using XFreePixmap() when finished with it.

If the file cannot be opened, XReadBitmapFile() returns BitmapOpenFailed. If the file can be opened but does not contain valid bitmap data, XReadBitmapFile() returns

BitmapFileInvalid. If insufficient working storage is allocated, XReadBitmap-
File() returns BitmapNoMemory. If the file is readable and valid, XReadBitmap-
File() returns BitmapSuccess.

Here is an example X Version 11 bitmap file:

```
#define name_width_return 16
#define name_height_return 16
#define name_x_hot_return 8
#define name_y_hot_return 8
static char name_bits[] = {
  0xf8, 0x1f, 0xe3, 0xc7, 0xcf, 0xf3, 0x9f, 0xf9, 0xbf, 0xfd, 0x33, 0xcc,
  0x7f, 0xfe, 0x7f, 0xfe, 0x7e, 0x7e, 0x7f, 0xfe, 0x37, 0xec, 0xbb, 0xdd,
  0x9c, 0x39, 0xcf, 0xf3, 0xe3, 0xc7, 0xf8, 0x1f};
```

For more information, see Volume One, Chapter 6, *Drawing Graphtcs and Text*.

Errors

BadDrawable
BadMatch

See Also

*XCreateBitmapFromData(), XCreatePixmap(), XCreatePixmapFromBitmapData(), XFreePixmap(),
XQueryBestSize(), XQueryBestStipple(), XQueryBestTile(), XSetTile(), XSetWindowBackground-
Pixmap(), XSetWindowBorderPixmap(), XWriteBitmapFile().*

XRebindKeysym

Name

XRebindKeysym – rebind a keysym to a string for client.

Synopsis

```
XRebindKeysym(display, keysym, mod_list, mod_count, string,
              num_bytes)
    Display *display;
    KeySym keysym;
    KeySym *mod_list;
    int mod_count;
    unsigned char *string;
    int num_bytes;
```

Arguments

display   Specifies a connection to an X server; returned from `XOpenDisplay()`.

keysym   Specifies the keysym to be rebound.

mod_list   Specifies a pointer to an array of keysyms that are being used as modifiers.

mod_count   Specifies the number of modifiers in the modifier list.

string   Specifies a pointer to the string that is to be copied and returned by `XLookupString()` in response to later events.

num_bytes   Specifies the length of the string.

Description

XRebindKeysym() binds the *string* to the specified *keysym*, so that *string* and *keysym* are returned by `XLookukpString` when that key is pressed and the modifiers specified in *mod_list* are also being held down. This function rebinds the meaning of a keysym for a client. It does not redefine the keycode in the server but merely provides an easy way for long strings to be attached to keys. No text conversions are performed; the client is responsible for supplying appropriately encoded strings. Note that you are allowed to rebind a keysym that may not exist.

See Volume One, Chapter 9, *The Keyboard and Pointer*, for a description of keysyms and keyboard mapping.

See Also

XChangeKeyboardMapping(), XDeleteModifiermapEntry(), XFreeModifiermap(), XGetKeyboard-Mapping(), XGetModifierMapping(), XInsertModifiermapEntry(), XKeycodeToKeysym(), XKeysymTo-Keycode(), XKeysymToString(), XLookupKeysym(), XLookupString(), XNewModifiermap(), XQuery-Keymap(), XRefreshKeyboardMapping(), XSetModifierMapping(), XStringToKeysym().

XRecolorCursor

Name

XRecolorCursor – change the color of a cursor.

Synopsis

```
XRecolorCursor(display, cursor, foreground_color, background_color)
    Display *display;
    Cursor cursor;
    XColor *foreground_color, *background_color;
```

Arguments

display   Specifies a connection to an X server; returned from XOpenDisplay().

cursor   Specifies the cursor ID.

foreground_color
               Specifies the red, green, and blue (RGB) values for the foreground.

background_color
               Specifies the red, green, and blue (RGB) values for the background.

Description

XRecolorCursor() applies a foreground and background color to a cursor. Cursors are normally created using a single plane pixmap, composed of 0's and 1's, with one pixel value assigned to 1's and another assigned to 0's. XRecolorCursor() changes these pixel values. If the cursor is being displayed on a screen, the change is visible immediately. On some servers, these color selections are read/write cells from the colormap, and can't be shared by applications.

Structures

```
typedef struct {
    unsigned long pixel;
    unsigned short red, green, blue;
    char flags;      /* DoRed, DoGreen, DoBlue */
    char pad;
} XColor;
```

Errors

BadCursor

See Also

XCreateFontCursor(), XCreateGlyphCursor(), XCreatePixmapCursor(), XDefineCursor(), XFreeCursor(), XQueryBestCursor(), XQueryBestSize(), XUndefineCursor().

XReconfigureWMWindow

Name

XReconfigureWMWindow – request that a top-level window be reconfigured.

Synopsis

```
Status XReconfigureWMWindow(display, w, screen_number,  value_mask, val-
      ues)
   Display *display;
   Window w;
   int screen_number;
   unsigned int value_mask;
   XWindowChanges *values;
```

Arguments

display
: Specifies a connection to an X server; returned from XOpenDisplay().

w
: Specifies the window.

screen_number
: Specifies the appropriate screen number on the host server.

value_mask
: Specifies which values are to be set using information in the values struc-ture. This mask is the bitwise inclusive OR of the valid configure window values bits.

values
: Specifies a pointer to the XWindowChanges structure.

Returns

Zero on failure, non-zero on success.

Availability

Release 4 and later.

Description

XReconfigureWMWindow() issues a ConfigureWindow request on the specified top-level window. If the stacking mode is changed and the request fails with a BadMatch error, the error event is trapped and a synthetic ConfigureRequest event containing the same configuration parameters is sent to the root of the specified window. Window managers may elect to receive this event and treat it as a request to reconfigure the indicated window.

For more information, see Volume One, Chapter 10, *Interclient Communication*.

Structures

```
typedef struct {
    int x, y;
```

```
        int width, height;
        int border_width;
        Window sibling;
        int stack_mode;
} XWindowChanges;
```

Errors

```
BadValue
BadWindow
```

See Also

XIconifyWindow(), *XWithdrawWindow()*.

XRectInRegion

Name

XRectInRegion – determine if a rectangle resides in a region.

Synopsis

```
int XRectInRegion(r, x, y, width, height)
    Region r;
    int x, y;
    unsigned int width, height;
```

Arguments

r   Specifies the region.

x   Specify the x and y coordinates of the upper-left corner of the rectangle,
y   relative to the region's origin.

width   Specify the width and height in pixels of the rectangle.
height

Returns

RectangleIn, RectangleOut, or RectanglePart.

Description

XRectInRegion() returns RectangleIn if the rectangle is completely contained in the region r, RectangleOut if it is completely outside, and RectanglePart if it is partially inside.

Regions are located using an offset from a point (the *region origin*) which is common to all regions. It is up to the application to interpret the location of the region relative to a drawable. If the region is to be used as a clip_mask by calling XSetRegion(), the upper-left corner of region relative to the drawable used in the graphics request will be at (xoffset + clip_x_origin, yoffset + clip_y_origin), where xoffset and yoffset are the offset of the region and clip_x_origin and clip_y_origin are the clip origin in the GC used.

For this function, the x and y arguments are interpreted relative to the region origin; no drawable is involved.

Structures

Region is a pointer to an opaque structure type.

See Also

XClipBox(), XCreateRegion(), XDestroyRegion(), XEmptyRegion(), XEqualRegion(), XIntersect-Region(), XOffsetRegion(), XPointInRegion(), XPolygonRegion(), XSetRegion(), XShrinkRegion(), XSubtractRegion(), XUnionRectWithRegion(), XUnionRegion(), XXorRegion().

XRefreshKeyboardMapping

Name

XRefreshKeyboardMapping – read keycode-keysym mapping from server into Xlib.

Synopsis

```
XRefreshKeyboardMapping(map_event)
    XMappingEvent *map_event;
```

Arguments

map_event   Specifies the mapping event that triggered this call.

Description

XRefreshKeyboardMapping() causes Xlib to update its knowledge of the mapping between keycodes and keysyms. This updates the application's knowledge of the keyboard.

The application should call XRefreshKeyboardMapping() when a MappingNotify event occurs. MappingNotify events occur when some client has called XChange-KeyboardMapping().

For more information, see Volume One, Chapter 9, *The Keyboard and Pointer*.

Structures

```
typedef struct {
    int type;
    unsigned long serial;    /* # of last request processed by server */
    Bool send_event;         /* true if this came from a SendEvent request */
    Display *display;        /* display the event was read from */
    Window window;           /* unused */
    int request;             /* one of MappingModifier, MappingKeyboard, */
                             /* MappingPointer */
    int first_keycode;       /* first keycode */
    int count;               /* defines range of change with first_keycode*/
} XMappingEvent;
```

See Also

XChangeKeyboardMapping(), XDeleteModifiermapEntry(), XFreeModifiermap(), XGetKeyboard-Mapping(), XGetModifierMapping(), XInsertModifiermapEntry(), XKeycodeToKeysym(), XKeysymTo-Keycode(), XKeysymToString(), XLookupKeysym(), XLookupString(), XNewModifierMap, XQuery-Keymap(), XRebindKeysym(), XSetModifierMapping(), XStringToKeysym().

XRemoveFromSaveSet

Name

XRemoveFromSaveSet – remove a window from the client's save-set.

Synopsis

```
XRemoveFromSaveSet(display, w)
    Display *display;
    Window w;
```

Arguments

display   Specifies a connection to an X server; returned from XOpenDisplay().

w   Specifies the window you want to remove from this client's save-set. This window must have been created by a client other than the client making this call.

Description

XRemoveFromSaveSet() removes a window from the save-set of the calling application.

The save-set is a safety net for windows that have been reparented by the window manager, usually to provide a shadow or other background for each window. When the window manager dies unexpectedly, the windows in the save-set are reparented to their closest living ancestor, so that they remain alive.

This call is not necessary when a window is destroyed since destroyed windows are automatically removed from the save-set. Therefore, many window managers get away without ever calling XRemoveFromSaveSet(). See Volume One, Chapter 14, *Window Management*, for more information about save-sets.

Errors

BadMatch   *w* not created by some other client.

BadWindow

See Also

XAddToSaveSet(), XChangeSaveSet().

XRemoveHost

Name

XRemoveHost – remove a host from the access control list.

Synopsis

```
XRemoveHost(display, host)
    Display *display;
    XHostAddress *host;
```

Arguments

display   Specifies a connection to an X server; returned from XOpenDisplay().

host   Specifies the network address of the machine to be removed.

Description

XRemoveHost() removes the specified host from the access control list of the connected server. The server must be on the same host as the process that calls XRemoveHost() in order to change the access control list.

If you remove your own machine from the access control list, you can no longer connect to that server, and there is no way back from this call other than to log out, edit the access control file, and reset the server. The address data must be a valid address for the type of network in which the server operates, as specified in the family member.

For TCP/IP, the address should be in network byte order. For the DECnet family, the server performs no automatic swapping on the address bytes. A Phase IV address is two bytes long. The first byte contains the least significant eight bits of the node number. The second byte contains the most significant two bits of the node number in the least significant two bits of the byte, and the area in the most significant six bits of the byte.

For more information on access control lists, see Volume One, Chapter 13, *Other Programming Techniques*.

Structures

```
typedef struct {
    int family;        /* for example Family Internet */
    int length;        /* length of address, in bytes */
    char *address;     /* pointer to where to find the bytes */
} XHostAddress;

/* constants used for family member of XHostAddress */
#define FamilyInternet     0
#define FamilyDECnet       1
#define FamilyChaos        2
```

Errors

```
BadAccess
BadValue
```

See Also

XAddHost(), XAddHosts(), XDisableAccessControl(), XEnableAccessControl(), XListHosts(), XRemove-Hosts(), XSetAccessControl().

XRemoveHosts

Name

XRemoveHosts – remove multiple hosts from the access control list.

Synopsis

```
XRemoveHosts(display, hosts, num_hosts)
    Display *display;
    XHostAddress *hosts;
    int num_hosts;
```

Arguments

display   Specifies a connection to an X server; returned from XOpenDisplay().

hosts   Specifies the list of hosts that are to be removed.

num_hosts   Specifies the number of hosts that are to be removed.

Description

XRemoveHosts() removes each specified host from the access control list of the connected server. The server must be on the same host as the process that call XRemoveHosts(), in order to change the access control list.

If you remove your machine from the access control list, you can no longer connect to that server, and there is no way back from this call except to log out, edit the access control file, and reset the server.

The address data must be a valid address for the type of network in which the server operates, as specified in the family member.

For TCP/IP, the address should be in network byte order. For the DECnet family, the server performs no automatic swapping on the address bytes. A Phase IV address is two bytes long. The first byte contains the least significant eight bits of the node number. The second byte contains the most significant two bits of the node number in the least significant two bits of the byte, and the area in the most significant six bits of the byte.

For more information on access control lists, see Volume One, Chapter 13, *Other Programming Techniques*.

Structures

```
typedef struct {
    int family;          /* for example Family Internet */
    int length;          /* length of address, in bytes */
    char *address;       /* pointer to where to find the bytes */
} XHostAddress;

/* constants used for family member of XHostAddress */
#define FamilyInternet      0
```

```
#define FamilyDECnet        1
#define FamilyChaos         2
```

Errors

```
BadAccess
BadValue
```

See Also

XAddHost(), *XAddHosts()*, *XDisableAccessControl()*, *XEnableAccessControl()*, *XListHosts()*, *XRemove-Host()*, *XSetAccessControl()*.

XReparentWindow

Name

XReparentWindow – insert a window between another window and its parent.

Synopsis

```
XReparentWindow(display, win, parent, x, y)
    Display *display;
    Window win;
    Window parent;
    int x, y;
```

Arguments

display	Specifies a connection to an X server; returned from XOpenDisplay().
win	Specifies the ID of the window to be reparented.
parent	Specifies the window ID of the new parent window.
x y	Specify the coordinates of the window relative to the new parent.

Description

XReparentWindow() modifies the window hierarchy by placing window *win* as a child of window *parent*. This function is usually used by a window manager to put a decoration window behind each application window. In the case of the window manager, the new parent window must first be created as a child of the root window.

If *win* is mapped, an XUnmapWindow() request is performed on it automatically. *win* is then removed from its current position in the hierarchy, and is inserted as a child of the specified parent. *win* is placed on top in the stacking order with respect to siblings.

A ReparentNotify event is then generated. The override_redirect member of the structure returned by this event is set to either True or False. Window manager clients normally should ignore this event if this member is set to True.

Finally, if the window was originally mapped, an XMapWindow() request is performed automatically.

Descendants of *win* remain descendants of *win*; they are not reparented to the old parent of *win*.

Normal exposure processing on formerly obscured windows is performed. The server might not generate exposure events for regions from the initial unmap that are immediately obscured by the final map. The request fails if the new parent is not on the same screen as the old parent, or if the new parent is the window itself or an inferior of the window.

Errors

BadMatch   *parent* not on same screen as old parent of *win*.

                  win has a `ParentRelative` background and *parent* is not the same
                  depth as *win*.

                  parent is *win* or an inferior of *win*.

BadWindow   *parent* is `InputOnly` and *win* is not.

See Also

XCirculateSubwindows(), *XCirculateSubwindowsDown()*, *XCirculateSubwindowsUp()*, *XConfigure-Window()*, *XLowerWindow()*, *XMoveResizeWindow()*, *XMoveWindow()*, *XQueryTree()*, *XRaise-Window()*, *XResizeWindow()*, *XRestackWindows()*.

XResetScreenSaver

Name

XResetScreenSaver – reset the screen saver.

Synopsis

```
XResetScreenSaver(display)
    Display *display;
```

Arguments

display   Specifies a connection to an X server; returned from XOpenDisplay().

Description

XResetScreenSaver() redisplays the screen if the screen saver was activated. This may result in exposure events to all visible windows if the server cannot save the screen contents. If the screen is already active, nothing happens.

For more information on the screen saver, see Volume One, Chapter 13, *Other Programming Techniques*.

See Also

XActivateScreenSaver(), XForceScreenSaver(), XGetScreenSaver(), XSetScreenSaver().

XResizeWindow

Name

XResizeWindow – change a window's size.

Synopsis

```
XResizeWindow(display, w, width, height)
    Display *display;
    Window w;
    unsigned int width, height;
```

Arguments

display   Specifies a connection to an X server; returned from XOpenDisplay().

w   Specifies the ID of the window to be resized.

width   Specify the new dimensions of the window in pixels.
height

Description

XResizeWindow() changes the inside dimensions of the window. The border is resized to match but its border width is not changed. XResizeWindow() does not raise the window, or change its origin. Changing the size of a mapped window may lose its contents and generate an Expose event, depending on the bit_gravity attribute (see Volume One, Chapter 4, *Window Attributes*). If a mapped window is made smaller, exposure events will be generated on windows that it formerly obscured.

If the override_redirect attribute of the window is False and the window manager has selected SubstructureRedirectMask on the parent, then a ConfigureRequest event is sent to the window manager, and no further processing is performed.

If the client has selected StructureNotifyMask on the window, then a Configure-Notify event is generated after the move takes place, and the event will contain the final size of the window.

Errors

BadValue   Either width or height is zero.

BadWindow

See Also

XCirculateSubwindows(), XCirculateSubwindowsDown(), XCirculateSubwindowsUp(), XConfigure-Window(), XLowerWindow(), XMoveResizeWindow(), XMoveWindow(), XQueryTree(), XRaise-Window(), XReparentWindow(), XRestackWindows().

XResourceManagerString

Name

XResourceManagerString – return the RESOURCE_MANAGER property.

Synopsis

```
char *XResourceManagerString(display)
    Display *display;
```

Arguments

display   Specifies the connection to the X server.

Returns

The resource manager property string.

Description

XResourceManagerString() returns the RESOURCE_MANAGER property from the root window of screen zero, which was returned when the connection was opened using XOpenDisplay(). The property is converted from type STRING to the current locale. The conversion is identical to that produced by XmbTextPropertyToTextList() for a singleton STRING property. The returned string is owned by Xlib, and should not be freed by the client. Note that the property value must be in a format that is acceptable to XrmGet-StringDatabase(). If no property exists, NULL is returned.

See Also

XScreenResourceString().

XRestackWindows

Name

XRestackWindows – change the stacking order of siblings.

Synopsis

```
XRestackWindows(display, windows, nwindows);
    Display *display;
    Window windows[];
    int nwindows;
```

Arguments

display   Specifies a connection to an X server; returned from `XOpenDisplay()`.

windows   Specifies an array containing the windows to be restacked. All the windows must have a common parent.

nwindows   Specifies the number of windows in the `windows` array.

Description

`XRestackWindows()` restacks the windows in the order specified, from top to bottom. The stacking order of the first window in the `windows` array will be on top, and the other windows will be stacked underneath it in the order of the array. Note that you can exclude other siblings from the `windows` array so that the top window in the array will not move relative to these other siblings.

For each window in the window array that is not a child of the specified window, a `Bad-Match` error will be generated. If the `override_redirect` attribute of the window is `False` and the window manager has selected `SubstructureRedirectMask` on the parent, then `ConfigureRequest` events are sent to the window manager for each window whose `override_redirect` is not set, and no further processing is performed. Otherwise, the windows will be restacked in top to bottom order.

Errors

```
BadMatch
BadWindow
```

See Also

XCirculateSubwindows(), *XCirculateSubwindowsDown()*, *XCirculateSubwindowsUp()*, *XConfigure-Window()*, *XLowerWindow()*, *XMoveResizeWindow()*, *XMoveWindow()*, *XQueryTree()*, *XRaise-Window()*, *XReparentWindow()*, *XResizeWindow()*.

XrmClassToString

Name

XrmClassToString – convert a quark to a string.

Synopsis

```
#define XrmClassToString(class) XrmQuarkToString(class)
char *XrmQuarkToString(quark)
  XrmQuark quark;
```

Arguments

quark   Specifies the quark for which the equivalent string is desired.

Returns

The string.

Description

XrmClassToString is an alias for XrmQuarkToString(). It returns the string for which the specified quark is serving as a shorthand symbol. The quark was earlier set to represent the string by XrmStringToQuark() or XrmStringToClass(). The string pointed to by the return value must not be modified or freed, because that string is in the data structure used by the resource manager for assigning quarks. If no string exists for that quark, XrmClassToString returns NULL.

Since the resource manager needs to make many comparisons of strings when it gets data from the database, it is more efficient to convert these strings into quarks, and to compare quarks instead. Since quarks are represented by integers, comparing quarks is trivial.

For more information, see Volume One, Chapter 11, *Managing User Preferences*.

Structures

```
typedef int XrmQuark;
```

See Also

XrmDestroyDatabase(), XrmGetFileDatabase(), XrmGetResource(), XrmGetStringDatabase(), XrmInitialize(), XrmMergeDatabases(), XrmParseCommand(), XrmPutFileDatabase(), XrmPutLineResource(), XrmPutResource(), XrmPutStringResource(), XrmQGetResource(), XrmQGetSearchList(), XrmQGetSearchResource(), XrmQPutResource(), XrmQPutStringResource(), XrmStringToBindingQuarkList(), XrmStringToQuarkList(), XrmStringToQuark(), XrmUniqueQuark().

XrmCombineDatabase

Name

XrmCombineDatabase – combine the contents of two resource databases.

Synopsis

```
void XrmCombineDatabase(source_db, target_db, override)
    XrmDatabase source_db;
    XrmDatabase *target_db;
    Bool override;
```

Arguments

source_db   Specifies the resource database that is to be merged into the target database.

target_db   Specifies the address of the resource database with which the resource file is to be combined.

override   Specifies whether resources from source_db should override matching resources in target_db.

Availability

Release 5 and later.

Description

XrmCombineDatabase() merges the contents of one database into another. If the same resource specifier is used for an entry in both databases, the entry in source_db will replace the entry in target_db if override is True; otherwise, the entry in from source_db is discarded.

If target_db points to a NULL database, XrmCombineDatabase() simply stores source_db at the location pointed to by target_db. Otherwise, source_db is destroyed by the merge, and the database pointed to by target_db is not destroyed.

The database entries are merged without changing values or types, regardless of the locales of the databases. The locale of the target database is not modified.

See Also

XrmCombineFileDatabase(), XrmMergeDatabases().

XrmCombineFileDatabase

Name

XrmCombineFileDatabase – combine the contents of a resource file and a resource database.

Synopsis

```
Status XrmCombineFileDatabase(filename, target_db, override)
    char *filename;
    XrmDatabase *target_db;
    Bool override;
```

Arguments

filename   Specifies the name of the resource file.

target_db   Specifies the address of the resource database with which the resource file is to be combined.

override   Specifies whether resources from the file should override matching resources in the database.

Returns

Zero on failure, non-zero on success.

Availability

Release 5 and later.

Description

XrmCombineFileDatabase() merges the contents of a resource file into a database. If the same resource specifier is used for an entry in both the file and the database, the entry in the file will replace the entry in the database if *override* is True; otherwise, the entry in the file is discarded.

If *target_db* points to a NULL database, XrmCombineFileDatabase() creates a new database, reads the file into it and stores this new database at the location pointed to by *target_db*. Otherwise, the database pointed to by *target_db* is not destroyed by the merge.

If the file cannot be read a zero status is returned; otherwise a non-zero status is returned.

The file is parsed in the current locale. The database entries are merged without changing values or types, regardless of the locale of the database, and the locale of the target database is not modified.

See Also

XrmCombineDatabase(), *XrmMergeDatabases()*.

XrmDestroyDatabase

Name

XrmDestroyDatabase – destroy a resource database.

Synopsis

```
void XrmDestroyDatabase(database)
    XrmDatabase database;
```

Arguments

database   Specifies the resource database.

Availability

Release 4 and later.

Description

XrmDestroyDatabase() destroys a resource database and frees its allocated memory. The destroyed resource database should not be referenced again. If database is NULL, XrmDestroyDatabase() returns immediately.

For more information, see Volume One, Chapter 11, *Managing User Preferences*.

See Also

XrmMergeDatabases().

XrmEnumerateDatabase

Name

XrmEnumerateDatabase – enumerate resource database entries.

Synopsis

```
Bool XrmEnumerateDatabase(database, name_prefix, class_prefix, mode,
        proc, arg)
    XrmDatabase database;
    XrmNameList name_prefix;
    XrmClassList class_prefix;
    int mode;
    Bool (*proc)();
    XPointer arg;
```

Arguments

database   Specifies the resource database.

name_prefix Specifies the resource name prefix.

class_prefix
                Specifies the resource class prefix.

mode   Specifies the number of levels to enumerate.

proc   Specifies the procedure that is to be called for each matching entry.

arg   Specifies the user-supplied argument that will be passed to the procedure.

Returns

True or False, as returned by *proc*.

Availability

Release 5 and later.

Description

XrmEnumerateDatabase() calls the specified procedure for each resource in the database that would match some completion of the given name/class resource prefix. The order
in which resources are found is implementation-dependent. If *mode* is XrmEnumOne-
Level, then a resource must match the given name/class prefix with just a single name and
class appended. If *mode* is XrmEnumAllLevels, the resource must match the given
name/class prefix with one or more names and classes appended. If the procedure returns
True, the enumeration terminates and the function returns True. If the procedure always
returns False, all matching resources are enumerated and the function returns False.

The procedure is called with the following arguments:

```
(*proc)(database, bindings, quarks, type, value, arg)
        XrmDatabase() *database;
        XrmBindingList bindings;
        XrmQuarkList quarks;
        XrmRepresentation *type;
        XrmValue *value;
        XPointer closure;
```

The bindings and quarks lists are terminated by NULLQUARK. Note that pointers to the database and type are passed, but these values should not be modified.

Structures

The legal values for the *mode* argument are:

```
#define    XrmEnumAllLevels          0
#define    XrmEnumOneLevel           1
```

See Also

XrmGetResource(), XrmInitialize(), XrmPutResource().

XrmGetDatabase

Name

XrmGetDatabase – retrieve the resource database associated with a display.

Synopsis

```
XrmDatabase XrmGetDatabase(display)
    Display *display;
```

Arguments

display   Specifies the connection to the X server.

Returns

The database.

Availability

Release 5 and later.

Description

XrmGetDatabase() returns the database associated with the specified display. It returns NULL if a database has not yet been set with XrmSetDatabase().

See Also

XrmSetDatabase().

XrmGetFileDatabase

Name

XrmGetFileDatabase – retrieve a database from a file.

Synopsis

```
XrmDatabase XrmGetFileDatabase(filename)
    char *filename;
```

Arguments

filename   Specifies the resource database filename.

Returns

The database.

Description

`XrmGetFileDatabase()` opens the specified file, creates a new resource database, and loads the database with the data read in from the file. The return value of the function is as a pointer to the created database.

The specified file must contain lines in the format accepted by `XrmPutLineResource()`. The file is parsed in the current locale and the database is created in the current locale. If `XrmGetFileDatabase()` cannot open the specified file, it returns NULL.

For more information, see Volume One, Chapter 11, *Managing User Preferences*.

Structures

`XrmDatabase` is a pointer to an opaque data type.

See Also

XrmDestroyDatabase(), XrmGetResource(), XrmGetStringDatabase(), XrmInitialize(), XrmMerge-Databases(), XrmParseCommand(), XrmPutFileDatabase(), XrmPutLineResource(), XrmPut-Resource(), XrmPutStringResource(), XrmQGetResource(), XrmQGetSearchList(), XrmQGetSearch-Resource(), XrmQPutResource(), XrmQPutStringResource(), XrmQuarkToString(), XrmStringTo-BindingQuarkList(), XrmStringToQuarkList(), XrmStringToQuark(), XrmUniqueQuark().

XrmGetResource

Name

XrmGetResource – get a resource from name and class as strings.

Synopsis

```
Bool XrmGetResource(database, str_name, str_class, str_type_return,
        value_return)
    XrmDatabase database;
    char *str_name;
    char *str_class;
    char **str_type_return;
    XrmValue *value_return;
```

Arguments

database   Specifies the database that is to be used.

str_name   Specifies the fully qualified name of the value being retrieved.

str_class   Specifies the fully qualified class of the value being retrieved.

str_type_return
                Returns a pointer to the representation type of the destination. In this func-
                tion, the representation type is represented as a string, not as an Xrm-
                Representation.

value_return
                Returns the value in the database. Do not modify or free this data.

Returns

True if the resource was found, else False.

Description

XrmGetResource() retrieves a resource from the specified database. It takes a fully
qualified name/class pair, a destination resource representation, and the address of a value
(size/address pair). The value and returned type point into database memory; therefore, you
must not modify the data.

The database only frees or overwrites entries on XrmPutResource(), XrmQPut-
Resource(), or XrmMergeDatabases(). A client that is not storing new values into
the database or is not merging the database should be safe using the address passed back at
any time until it exits. If a resource was found, XrmGetResource() returns True; otherwise it returns False.

Most applications and toolkits do not make random probes into a resource database to fetch
resources. The X toolkit access pattern for a resource database is quite stylized. A series of
from 1 to 20 probes are made with only the last name/class differing in each probe. Xrm-
GetResource() uses at worst a 2^n algorithm, where n is the length of the name/class list.

This can be improved upon by the application programmer by prefetching a list of database levels that might match the first part of a name/class list.

Structures

`XrmDatabase` is a pointer to an opaque data type.

```
typedef struct {
    unsigned int    size;
    XPointer        addr;
} XrmValue;
```

See Also

XrmDestroyDatabase(), XrmGetFileDatabase(), XrmGetStringDatabase(), XrmInitialize(), XrmMerge-Databases(), XrmParseCommand(), XrmPutFileDatabase(), XrmPutLineResource(), XrmPut-Resource(), XrmPutStringResource(), XrmQGetResource(), XrmQGetSearchList(), XrmQGetSearch-Resource(), XrmQPutResource(), XrmQPutStringResource(), XrmQuarkToString(), XrmStringTo-BindingQuarkList(), XrmStringToQuarkList(), XrmStringToQuark(), XrmUniqueQuark().

XrmGetStringDatabase

Name

XrmGetStringDatabase – create a database from a string.

Synopsis

```
XrmDatabase XrmGetStringDatabase(data)
    char *data;
```

Arguments

data   Specifies the database contents using a string.

Returns

The created database.

Description

XrmGetStringDatabase() creates a new database and stores in it the resources specified in data. The return value is subsequently used to refer to the created database. Xrm-
GetStringDatabase() is similar to XrmGetFileDatabase(), except that it reads
the information out of a string instead of a file. Each line in the string is separated by a new
line character in the format accepted by XrmPutLineResource(). The string is parsed
in the current locale and the database is created in the current locale.

For more information, see Volume One, Chapter 11, *Managing User Preferences.*

Structures

XrmDatabase is a pointer to an opaque data type.

See Also

*XrmDestroyDatabase(), XrmGetFileDatabase(), XrmGetResource(), XrmInitialize(), XrmMerge-
Databases(), XrmParseCommand(), XrmPutFileDatabase(), XrmPutLineResource(), XrmPut-
Resource(), XrmPutStringResource(), XrmQGetResource(), XrmQGetSearchList(), XrmQGetSearch-
Resource(), XrmQPutResource(), XrmQPutStringResource(), XrmQuarkToString(), XrmStringTo-
BindingQuarkList(), XrmStringToQuarkList(), XrmStringToQuark(), XrmUniqueQuark().*

XrmInitialize

Name

XrmInitialize – initialize the resource manager.

Synopsis

```
void XrmInitialize( );
```

Description

`XrmInitialize()` initializes the resource manager, and should be called once before using any other resource manager functions. It just creates a representation type of "String" for values defined as strings. This representation type is used by `XrmPutString-Resource()` and `XrmQPutStringResource()`, which require a value as a string. See `XrmQPutResource()` for a description of representation types.

For more information, see Volume One, Chapter 11, *Managing User Preferences*.

See Also

XrmDestroyDatabase(), XrmGetFileDatabase(), XrmGetResource(), XrmGetStringDatabase(), XrmMergeDatabases(), XrmParseCommand(), XrmPutFileDatabase(), XrmPutLineResource(), XrmPutResource(), XrmPutStringResource(), XrmQGetResource(), XrmQGetSearchList(), XrmQGetSearchResource(), XrmQPutResource(), XrmQPutStringResource(), XrmQuarkToString(), XrmStringToBindingQuarkList(), XrmStringToQuarkList(), XrmStringToQuark(), XrmUniqueQuark().

XrmLocaleOfDatabase

Name

XrmLocaleOfDatabase – return the locale of a resource database.

Synopsis

```
char *XrmLocaleOfDatabase(database)
    XrmDatabase database;
```

Arguments

database   Specifies the database that is to be used.

Returns

The locale string.

Availability

Release 5 and later.

Description

XrmLocaleOfDatabase() returns the name of the locale bound to the specified database, as a NULL-terminated string. The returned locale name string is owned by Xlib and
should not be modified or freed by the client. Xlib is not permitted to free the string until the
database is destroyed. Until the string is freed, it will not be modified by Xlib.

See Also

XrmGetFileDatabase(), XrmGetStringDatabase(), XrmDestroyDatabase().

XrmMergeDatabases

Name

XrmMergeDatabases – merge the contents of one database into another.

Synopsis

```
void XrmMergeDatabases(source_db, target_db)
    XrmDatabase source_db, *target_db;
```

Arguments

source_db   Specifies the resource database to be merged into the existing database.

target_db   Specifies a pointer to the resource database into which the source_db
               database will be merged.

Description

XrmMergeDatabases() merges source_db into target_db. This procedure is used
to combine databases, for example, an application specific database of defaults and a database of user preferences. If the same specifier is used for an entry in both databases, the entry
in the source_db will replace the entry in the target_db (that is, it overrides
target_db). If target_db is NULL, XrmMergeDatabases() simply stores
source_db in it. Otherwise, source_db is destroyed by the merge, but the database
pointed to by target_db is not destroyed. The database entries are merged without changing values or types, regardless of the locales of the databases. The locale of the target database is not modified.

For more information, see Volume One, Chapter 11, *Managing User Preferences*.

Structures

XrmDatabase is a pointer to an opaque data type.

See Also

*XrmDestroyDatabase(), XrmGetFileDatabase(), XrmGetResource(), XrmGetStringDatabase(), Xrm-
Initialize(), XrmParseCommand(), XrmPutFileDatabase(), XrmPutLineResource(), XrmPutResource(),
XrmPutStringResource(), XrmQGetResource(), XrmQGetSearchList(), XrmQGetSearchResource(),
XrmQPutResource(), XrmQPutStringResource(), XrmQuarkToString(), XrmStringToBindingQuark-
List(), XrmStringToQuarkList(), XrmStringToQuark(), XrmUniqueQuark().*

XrmNameToString

Name

XrmNameToString – convert a quark to a string.

Synopsis

```
#define XrmNameToString(name) XrmQuarkToString(name)

char *XrmQuarkToString(quark)
    XrmQuark quark;
```

Arguments

quark   Specifies the quark for which the equivalent string is desired.

Returns

The string.

Description

XrmNameToString is an alias for XrmQuarkToString(). It returns the string for which the specified quark is serving as a shorthand symbol. The quark was determined earlier using XrmStringToQuark or XrmStringToName(). The string pointed to by the return value must not be modified or freed, because that string is in the data structure used by the resource manager for assigning quarks. If no string exists for that quark, XrmNameToString returns NULL.

Since the resource manager needs to make many comparisons of strings when it gets data from the database, it is more efficient to convert these strings into quarks, and to compare quarks instead. Since quarks are represented by integers, comparing quarks is trivial.

For more information, see Volume One, Chapter 11, *Managing User Preferences*.

Structures

```
typedef int XrmQuark;
```

See Also

XrmDestroyDatabase(), XrmGetFileDatabase(), XrmGetResource(), XrmGetStringDatabase(), XrmInitialize(), XrmMergeDatabases(), XrmParseCommand(), XrmPutFileDatabase(), XrmPutLineResource(), XrmPutResource(), XrmPutStringResource(), XrmQGetResource(), XrmQGetSearchList(), XrmQGetSearchResource(), XrmQPutResource(), XrmQPutStringResource(), XrmStringToBindingQuarkList(), XrmStringToQuarkList(), XrmStringToQuark(), XrmUniqueQuark().

XrmParseCommand

Name

XrmParseCommand – load a resource database from command-line arguments.

Synopsis

```
void XrmParseCommand(database, table, table_count, name, argc_in_out,
        argv_in_out)
    XrmDatabase *database;
    XrmOptionDescList table;
    int table_count;
    char *name;
    int *argc_in_out;
    char **argv_in_out;
```

Arguments

database   Specifies a pointer to the resource database. If *database* contains NULL, a new resource database is created and a pointer to it is returned in *database*. If a database is created, it is created in the current locale.

table   Specifies table of command-line arguments to be parsed.

table_count   Specifies the number of entries in the table.

name   Specifies the application name.

argc_in_out   Before the call, specifies the number of arguments. After the call, returns the number of arguments not parsed.

argv_in_out   Before the call, specifies a pointer to the command-line arguments. After the call, returns a pointer to a string containing the command-line arguments that could not be parsed.

Description

XrmParseCommand() parses an (*argc_in_out*, *argv_in_out*) pair according to the specified option table, loads recognized options into the specified database with the type "String" and modifies the (*argc_in_out*, *argv_in_out*) pair to remove all recognized options.

The specified table is used to parse the command line. Recognized entries in the table are removed from *argv_in_out*, and entries are made in the specified resource database. The table entries contain information on the option string, the option name, which style of option and a value to provide if the option kind is XrmoptionNoArg. See the example table below. The option names are compared byte-for-byte to arguments in *argv*, independent of any locale. The resource values given in the table are stored in the resource database without modification. All resource database entries are created using a "String" representation type.

argc_in_out specifies the number of arguments in *argv_in_out* and is set to the remaining number of arguments that were not parsed. *name* should be the name of your application for use in building the database entry. *name* is prepended to the `specifier` in the option table before storing the specification. No separating (binding) character is inserted. The table must contain either a dot (.) or an asterisk (*) as the first character in each `specifier` entry. The `specifier` entry can contain multiple components. If the name arguments and the specifiers are not in the Host Portable Character Encoding, the result is implementation-dependent.

The following is a typical options table:

```
static XrmOptionDescRec opTable[ ] = {
{"-background",   "*background",                  XrmoptionSepArg, (XPointer) NULL},
{"-bd",           "*borderColor",                 XrmoptionSepArg, (XPointer) NULL},
{"-bg",           "*background",                  XrmoptionSepArg, (XPointer) NULL},
{"-borderwidth",  "*TopLevelShell.borderWidth",   XrmoptionSepArg, (XPointer) NULL},
{"-bordercolor",  "*borderColor",                 XrmoptionSepArg, (XPointer) NULL},
{"-bw",           "*TopLevelShell.borderWidth",   XrmoptionSepArg, (XPointer) NULL},
{"-display",      ".display",                     XrmoptionSepArg, (XPointer) NULL},
{"-fg",           "*foreground",                  XrmoptionSepArg, (XPointer) NULL},
{"-fn",           "*font",                        XrmoptionSepArg, (XPointer) NULL},
{"-font",         "*font",                        XrmoptionSepArg, (XPointer) NULL},
{"-foreground",   "*foreground",                  XrmoptionSepArg, (XPointer) NULL},
{"-geometry",     ".TopLevelShell.geometry",      XrmoptionSepArg, (XPointer) NULL},
{"-iconic",       ".TopLevelShell.iconic",        XrmoptionNoArg,  (XPointer) "on"},
{"-name",         ".name",                        XrmoptionSepArg, (XPointer) NULL},
{"-reverse",      "*reverseVideo",                XrmoptionNoArg,  (XPointer) "on"},
{"-rv",           "*reverseVideo",                XrmoptionNoArg,  (XPointer) "on"},
{"-synchronous",  ".synchronous",                 XrmoptionNoArg,  (XPointer) "on"},
{"-title",        ".TopLevelShell.title",         XrmoptionSepArg, (XPointer) NULL},
{"-xrm",          NULL,                           XrmoptionResArg, (XPointer) NULL},
};
```

In this table, if the *-background* (or *-bg*) option is used to set background colors, the stored resource specifier will match all resources of attribute background. If the *-borderwidth* option is used, the stored resource specifier applies only to border width attributes of class `TopLevelShell` (that is, outermost windows, including pop-up windows). If the *-title* option is used to set a window name, only the topmost application windows receive the resource.

When parsing the command line, any unique unambiguous abbreviation for an option name in the table is considered a match for the option. Note that uppercase and lowercase matter.

For more information, see Volume One, Chapter 11, *Managing User Preferences*.

Structures

`XrmDatabase` is a pointer to an opaque data type.

```
typedef enum {
    XrmoptionNoArg,     /* value is specified in OptionDescRec.value */
    XrmoptionIsArg,     /* value is the option string itself */
    XrmoptionStickyArg, /* value is chars immediately following option */
    XrmoptionSepArg,    /* value is next argument in argv */
```

```
    XrmoptionResArg,      /* resource and value in next argument in argv */
    XrmoptionSkipArg,     /* ignore this option and next argument in argv */
    XrmoptionSkipLine,    /* ignore this option and the rest of argv */
    XrmoptionSkipNArgs    /* new in R4: ignore this option, skip */
                          /* number specified in next argument */
} XrmOptionKind;

typedef struct {
    char *option;          /* option specification string in argv */
    char *resourceName;    /* binding & resource name (w/out application name) */
    XrmOptionKind argKind; /* which style of option it is */
    XPointer value;        /* value to provide if XrmoptionNoArg */
} XrmOptionDescRec, *XrmOptionDescList;
```

See Also

XrmDestroyDatabase(), XrmGetFileDatabase(), XrmGetResource(), XrmGetStringDatabase(), XrmInitialize(), XrmMergeDatabases(), XrmPutFileDatabase(), XrmPutLineResource(), XrmPutResource(), XrmPutStringResource(), XrmQGetResource(), XrmQGetSearchList(), XrmQGetSearchResource(), XrmQPutResource(), XrmQPutStringResource(), XrmQuarkToString(), XrmStringToBindingQuarkList(), XrmStringToQuarkList(), XrmStringToQuark(), XrmUniqueQuark().

XrmPermStringToQuark

Name

XrmPermStringToQuark — allocate quark for permanently allocated string.

Synopsis

```
XrmQuark XrmPermStringToQuark(string)
    char *string;
```

Arguments

string   Specifies the string for which a quark is to be allocated.

Returns

The quark.

Description

XrmPermStringToQuark returns a quark which uniquely represents a string. If the string is not in the Host Portable Character Encoding the conversion is implementation-dependent. XrmPermStringToQuark is just like XrmStringToQuark except that Xlib is permitted to assume the string argument is permanently allocated, and hence that the string can be used as the value to be returned by XrmQuarkToString.

If you do not want to use permanently allocated storage, use XrmStringToQuark.

Structures

XrmDatabase is a pointer to an opaque data type.

See Also

XrmDestroyDatabase, XrmGetResource, XrmGetStringDatabase, XrmInitialize, XrmMergeDatabases, XrmParseCommand, XrmPutFileDatabase, XrmPutLineResource, XrmPutResource, XrmPutStringResource, XrmQGetResource, XrmQGetSearchList, XrmQGetSearchResource, XrmQPutResource, XrmQPutStringResource, XrmQuarkToString, XrmStringToBindingQuarkList, XrmStringToQuarkList, XrmStringToQuark, XrmUniqueQuark.

Name

XrmPutFileDatabase – store a resource database in a file.

Synopsis

```
void XrmPutFileDatabase(database, stored_db)
     XrmDatabase database;
     char *stored_db;
```

Arguments

database   Specifies the resource database that is to be saved.

stored_db   Specifies the filename for the stored database.

Description

XrmPutFileDatabase() stores a copy of the specified database in the specified file. The file is a text file that contains lines in the format that is accepted by XrmPutLine-Resource(). The file is written in the locale of the database. Entries containing resource names that are not in the Host Portable Character Encoding, or containing values that are not in the encoding of the database locale, are written in an implementation-dependent manner. The order in which entries are written is implementation-dependent. Entries with representation types other than "String" are ignored.

For more information, see Volume One, Chapter 11, *Managing User Preferences*.

Structures

XrmDatabase is a pointer to an opaque data type.

See Also

XrmDestroyDatabase(), XrmGetFileDatabase(), XrmGetResource(), XrmGetStringDatabase(), XrmInitialize(), XrmMergeDatabases(), XrmParseCommand(), XrmPutLineResource(), XrmPutResource(), XrmPutStringResource(), XrmQGetResource(), XrmQGetSearchList(), XrmQGetSearchResource(), XrmQPutResource(), XrmQPutStringResource(), XrmQuarkToString(), XrmStringToBindingQuarkList(), XrmStringToQuarkList(), XrmStringToQuark(), XrmUniqueQuark().

XrmPutLineResource

Name

XrmPutLineResource – add a resource specification to a resource database.

Synopsis

```
void XrmPutLineResource(database, line)
    XrmDatabase *database;
    char *line;
```

Arguments

database   Specifies a pointer to the resource database. If database contains NULL, a new resource database is created and a pointer to it is returned in database. If a database is created, it is created in the current locale.

line   Specifies the resource name (possibly with multiple components) and value pair as a single string, in the format resource:value.

Description

XrmPutLineResource() adds a single resource entry to the specified database. The line string is parsed in the locale of the database. If the resource name is not in the Host Portable Character Encoding the result is implementation-dependent. Note that comment lines are not stored.

XrmPutLineResource() is similar to XrmPutStringResource(), except that instead of having separate string arguments for the resource and its value, XrmPutLine-Resource() takes a single string argument (line) which consists of the resource name, a colon, then the value. Since the value is a string, it is stored into the database with representation type String.

Any whitespace before or after the name or colon in the line argument is ignored. The value is terminated by a new-line or a NULL character. The value may contain embedded new-line characters represented by the "\" and "n" two-character pair (not the single "\n" character), which are converted into a single linefeed character. In addition, the value may run over onto the next line; this is indicated by a "\" character at the end of each line to be continued.

Null-terminated strings without a new line are also permitted. XrmPutResource(), XrmQPutResource(), XrmPutStringResource(), XrmQPutString-Resource() and XrmPutLineResource() all store data into a database. See Xrm-QPutResource() for the most complete description of this process.

For more information, see Volume One, Chapter 11, *Managing User Preferences*.

Structures

`XrmDatabase` is a pointer to an opaque data type.

See Also

XrmDestroyDatabase(), XrmGetFileDatabase(), XrmGetResource(), XrmGetStringDatabase(), XrmInitialize(), XrmMergeDatabases(), XrmParseCommand(), XrmPutFileDatabase(), XrmPutResource(), XrmPutStringResource(), XrmQGetResource(), XrmQGetSearchList(), XrmQGetSearchResource(), XrmQPutResource(), XrmQPutStringResource(), XrmQuarkToString(), XrmStringToBindingQuarkList(), XrmStringToQuarkList(), XrmStringToQuark(), XrmUniqueQuark().

XrmPutResource

Name

XrmPutResource – store a resource specification into a resource database.

Synopsis

```
void XrmPutResource(database, specifier, type, value)
    XrmDatabase *database;
    char *specifier;
    char *type;
    XrmValue *value;
```

Arguments

database   Specifies a pointer to the resource database. If database contains NULL, a
                new resource database is created and a pointer to it is returned in *data-*
                base. If a database is created, it is created in the current locale.

specifier   Specifies a complete or partial specification of the resource.

type   Specifies the type of the resource.

value   Specifies the value of the resource.

Description

XrmPutResource() is one of several functions which store data into a database.

XrmPutResource() first converts *specifier* into a binding list and a quark list by calling XrmStringToBindingQuarkList(), and converts *type* into an Xrm-
Representation by calling XrmStringToRepresentation. Finally, it puts the
data into the database. If the specifier and type are not in the Host Portable Character encoding, the result is implementation-dependent. The value is stored in the database without
modification.

XrmPutResource(), XrmQPutResource(), XrmPutStringResource(), Xrm-
QPutStringResource() and XrmPutLineResource() all store data into a database. See the description of XrmQPutResource() for the most complete description of
this process.

For more information, see Volume One, Chapter 11, *Managing User Preferences*.

Structures

XrmDatabase is a pointer to an opaque data type.

```
typedef struct {
    unsigned int    size;
    XPointer        addr;
} XrmValue, *XrmValuePtr;
```

See Also

XrmDestroyDatabase(), XrmGetFileDatabase(), XrmGetResource(), XrmGetStringDatabase(), Xrm-Initialize(), XrmMergeDatabases(), XrmParseCommand(), XrmPutFileDatabase(), XrmPutLine-Resource(), XrmPutStringResource(), XrmQGetResource(), XrmQGetSearchList(), XrmQGetSearch-Resource(), XrmQPutResource(), XrmQPutStringResource(), XrmQuarkToString(), XrmStringTo-BindingQuarkList(), XrmStringToQuarkList(), XrmStringToQuark(), XrmUniqueQuark().

XrmPutStringResource

Name

XrmPutStringResource – add a resource specification with separate resource name and value.

Synopsis

```
void XrmPutStringResource(database, specifier, value)
    XrmDatabase *database;
    char *specifier;
    char *value;
```

Arguments

database   Specifies a pointer to the resource database. If *database* contains NULL, a new resource database is created and a pointer to it is returned in *database*.

specifier   Specifies the resource, as a string.

value   Specifies the value of the resource, as a string.

Description

XrmPutStringResource() adds a resource specification with the specified resource and value to the specified database. The *specifier* string may contain both names and classes, bound with either loose (*) or tight (.) bindings. See the description of XrmGet-Resource() for more information about bindings.

The representation type used in the database is String. If the specifier is not in the Host Portable Character Encoding, the result is implementation-dependent. The value is stored in the database without modification.

XrmPutResource(), XrmQPutResource(), XrmPutStringResource(), Xrm-QPutStringResource() and XrmPutLineResource() all store data into a database. See XrmQPutResource() for the most complete description of this process.

For more information, see Volume One, Chapter 11, *Managing User Preferences*.

Structures

XrmDatabase is a pointer to an opaque data type.

See Also

XrmDestroyDatabase(), XrmGetFileDatabase(), XrmGetResource(), XrmGetStringDatabase(), Xrm-Initialize(), XrmMergeDatabases(), XrmParseCommand(), XrmPutFileDatabase(), XrmPutLine-Resource(), XrmPutResource(), XrmQGetResource(), XrmQGetSearchList(), XrmQGetSearch-Resource(), XrmQPutResource(), XrmQPutStringResource(), XrmQuarkToString(), XrmStringTo-BindingQuarkList(), XrmStringToQuarkList(), XrmStringToQuark(), XrmUniqueQuark().

XrmQGetResource

Name

XrmQGetResource – get a resource value using name and class as quarks.

Synopsis

```
Bool XrmQGetResource(database, quark_name, quark_class, quark_type_
        return, value_return)
    XrmDatabase database;
    XrmNameList quark_name;
    XrmClassList quark_class;
    XrmRepresentation *quark_type_return;
    XrmValue *value_return;
```

Arguments

database   Specifies the database that is to be used.

quark_name   Specifies the fully qualified name of the value being retrieved (as a list of quarks).

quark_class   Specifies the fully qualified class of the value being retrieved (as a list of quarks).

quark_type_return
                  Returns a pointer to the representation type of the value. In this function, the representation type is represented as a quark.

value_return
                  Returns a pointer to the value in the database. Do not modify or free this data.

Returns

True if the resource was found, else False.

Description

XrmQGetResource() retrieves a resource from the specified database. It takes fully qualified name and class strings, and returns the representation and value of the matching resource. The value returned points into database memory; you must not modify that data. If a resource was found, XrmQGetResource() returns True. Otherwise, it returns False.

Currently, the database only frees or overwrites entries when new data is stored with XrmMergeDatabases(), or XrmPutResource() and related routines. A client that avoids these functions should be safe using the address passed back at any time until it exits.

XrmQGetResource() is very similar to XrmGetResource(), except that in XrmGetResource(), the equivalent arguments to *quark_name*, *quark_class*, and *quark_type_return* arguments are strings instead of quarks.

See `XrmGetResource()` for a full description of how data is looked up in the database.

For more information, see Volume One, Chapter 11, *Managing User Preferences*.

Structures

`XrmDatabase` is a pointer to an opaque data type.

```
typedef XrmQuarkList XrmNameList;
typedef XrmQuarkList XrmClassList;
typedef XrmQuark     XrmRepresentation;

typedef struct {
    unsigned int    size;
    XPointer        addr;
} XrmValue, *XrmValuePtr;
```

See Also

XrmDestroyDatabase(), XrmGetFileDatabase(), XrmGetResource(), XrmGetStringDatabase(), Xrm-Initialize(), XrmMergeDatabases(), XrmParseCommand(), XrmPutFileDatabase(), XrmPutLine-Resource(), XrmPutResource(), XrmPutStringResource(), XrmQGetSearchList(), XrmQGetSearch-Resource(), XrmQPutResource(), XrmQPutStringResource(), XrmQuarkToString(), XrmStringTo-BindingQuarkList(), XrmStringToQuarkList(), XrmStringToQuark(), XrmUniqueQuark().

XrmQGetSearchList

Name

XrmQGetSearchList – return a list of database levels.

Synopsis

```
Bool XrmQGetSearchList(database, names, classes,
                list_return, list_length)
    XrmDatabase database;
    XrmNameList names;
    XrmClassList classes;
    XrmSearchList list_return;
    int list_length;
```

Arguments

database   Specifies the database to be searched.

names   Specifies a list of resource names.

classes   Specifies a list of resource classes.

list_return   Returns a search list for further use. The caller must allocate sufficient space for the list before calling XrmQGetSearchList().

list_length   Specifies the number of entries (not the byte size) allocated for list_return.

Returns

True if list_return was large enough for the search list, else False.

Description

XrmQGetSearchList() is a tool for searching the database more efficiently. It is used in combination with XrmQGetSearchResource(). Often, one searches the database for many similar resources which differ only in their final component (e.g., xmh.toc.foreground, xmh.toc.background, etc). Rather than looking for each resource in its entirety, XrmGetSearchList searches the database for the common part of the resource name, returning a whole list of items in the database that match it. This list is called the *search list*. This search list is then used by XrmQGetSearchList(), which searches for the last components one at a time. In this way, the common work of searching for similar resources is done only once, and the specific part of the search is done on the much shorter search list.

XrmQGetSearchList() takes a list of names and classes and returns a list of database levels where a match might occur. The returned list is in best-to-worst order and uses the same algorithm as XrmGetResource() for determining precedence. If list_return was large enough for the search list, XrmQGetSearchList(-) returns True. Otherwise, it returns False.

The size of the search list that must be allocated by the caller is dependent upon the number of levels and wildcards in the resource specifiers that are stored in the database. The worst case length is 3^n , where n is the number of name or class components in `names` or `classes`.

Only the common prefix of a resource name should be specified in the name and class list to `XrmQGetSearchList()`. In the example above, the common prefix would be `xmh.toc`. However, note that `XrmQGetSearchResource()` requires that *name* represent a single component only. Therefore, the common prefix must be all but the last component of the name and class.

For more information, see Volume One, Chapter 11, *Managing User Preferences*.

Structures

`XrmDatabase` is a pointer to an opaque data type.

```
typedef XrmQuarkList XrmNameList;
typedef XrmQuarkList XrmClassList;
typedef XrmQuark     XrmRepresentation;
```

`XrmSearchList` is a pointer to an opaque data type.

See Also

XrmDestroyDatabase(), XrmGetFileDatabase(), XrmGetResource(), XrmGetStringDatabase(), XrmInitialize(), XrmMergeDatabases(), XrmParseCommand(), XrmPutFileDatabase(), XrmPutLineResource(), XrmPutResource(), XrmPutStringResource(), XrmQGetResource(), XrmQGetSearchResource(), XrmQPutResource(), XrmQPutStringResource(), XrmQuarkToString(), XrmStringToBindingQuarkList(), XrmStringToQuarkList(), XrmStringToQuark(), XrmUniqueQuark().

XrmQGetSearchResource

Name

XrmQGetSearchResource – search prepared list for a given resource.

Synopsis

```
Bool XrmQGetSearchResource(list, name, class, type_return,
                value_return)
    XrmSearchList list;
    XrmName name;
    XrmClass class;
    XrmRepresentation *type_return;
    XrmValue *value_return;
```

Arguments

list   Specifies the search list returned by `XrmQGetSearchList()`.

name   Specifies the resource name.

class   Specifies the resource class.

type_return   Returns the data representation type.

value_return
                Returns the value from the database.

Returns

`True` if the resource was found, else `False`.

Description

`XrmQGetSearchResource()` is a tool for searching the database more efficiently. It is used in combination with `XrmQGetSearchList()`. Often, one searches the database for many similar resources which differ only in their final component (e.g., xmh.toc.foreground, xmh.toc.background, etc). Rather than looking for each resource in its entirety, `XrmQGetSearchList()` searches the database for the common part of the resource name, returning a whole list of items in the database that match it. This list is called the *search list*. `XrmQGetSearchResource()` searches the search list for the resource that is fully identified by *name* and *class*. The search stops with the first match. `XrmQGetSearchResource()` returns `True` if the resource was found; otherwise, it returns `False`.

A call to `XrmQGetSearchList()` with a name and class list containing all but the last component of a resource name followed by a call to `XrmQGetSearchResource()` with the last component name and class returns the same database entry as `XrmQGetResource()` or `XrmQGetResource()` would with the fully qualified name and class.

For more information, see Volume One, Chapter 11, *Managing User Preferences*.

Structures

`XrmDatabase` is a pointer to an opaque data type.

```
typedef XrmQuark XrmName;
typedef XrmQuark XrmClass;
typedef XrmQuark XrmRepresentation;

typedef struct {
    unsigned int    size;
    XPointer        addr;
} XrmValue, *XrmValuePtr;
```

`XrmSearchList` is a pointer to an opaque data type.

See Also

XrmDestroyDatabase(), XrmGetFileDatabase(), XrmGetResource(), XrmGetStringDatabase(), XrmInitialize(), XrmMergeDatabases(), XrmParseCommand(), XrmPutFileDatabase(), XrmPutLineResource(), XrmPutResource(), XrmPutStringResource(), XrmQGetResource(), XrmQGetSearchList(), XrmQPutResource(), XrmQPutStringResource(), XrmQuarkToString(), XrmStringToBindingQuarkList(), XrmStringToQuarkList(), XrmStringToQuark(), XrmUniqueQuark().

XrmQPutResource

Name

XrmQPutResource – store a resource specification into a database using quarks.

Synopsis

```
void XrmQPutResource(database, bindings, quarks, type, value)
  XrmDatabase *database;
  XrmBindingList bindings;
  XrmQuarkList quarks;
  XrmRepresentation type;
  XrmValue *value;
```

Arguments

database   Specifies a pointer to the resource database. If database contains NULL, a new
            resource database is created and a pointer to it is returned in *database*. If a
            database is created, it is created in the current locale.

bindings   Specifies a list of bindings for binding together the *quarks* argument.

quarks   Specifies the complete or partial name or class list of the resource to be
            stored.

type   Specifies the type of the resource.

value   Specifies the value of the resource.

Description

XrmQPutResource() stores a resource specification into the database. If a resource entry
with the identical bindings and quarks already exists in the database, the previous value is
replaced by the new specified value. The value is stored in the database without modification.

database can be a previously defined database, as returned by XrmGetString-
Database(), XrmGetFileDatabase(), or from XrmMergeDatabases(). If
database is NULL, a new database is created and a pointer to it returned in *database*.

bindings and *quarks* together specify where the value should be stored in the database.
See XrmStringToBindingQuarkList() for a brief description of binding and quark
lists. See XrmGetResource() for a description of the resource manager naming conventions and lookup rules.

type is the representation type of *value*. This provides a way to distinguish between different representations of the same information. Representation types are user-defined character strings describing the way the data is represented. For example, a color may be specified
by a color name ("red"), or be coded in a hexadecimal string ("#4f6c84") (if it is to be used
as an argument to XParseColor().) The representation type would distinguish between
these two. Representation types are created from simple character strings by using the macro

XrmStringToRepresentation. The type XrmRepresentation is actually the same type as XrmQuark, since it is an ID for a string. The representation is stored along with the value in the database, and is returned when the database is accessed.

value specifies the value of the resource, specified as an XrmValue.

XrmGetResource() contains the complete description of how data is accessed from the database, and so provides a good perspective on how it is stored.

For more information, see Volume One, Chapter 11, *Managing User Preferences*.

Structures

XrmDatabase is a pointer to an opaque data type.

```
typedef enum {
    XrmBindTightly, XrmBindLoosely
} XrmBinding, *XrmBindingList;

typedef int XrmQuark, *XrmQuarkList;
typedef XrmQuarkList XrmNameList;
typedef XrmQuark XrmRepresentation;

typedef struct {
    unsigned int size;
    XPointer addr;
} XrmValue, *XrmValuePtr;
```

See Also

XrmDestroyDatabase(), XrmGetFileDatabase(), XrmGetResource(), XrmGetStringDatabase(), XrmInitialize(), XrmMergeDatabases(), XrmParseCommand(), XrmPutFileDatabase(), XrmPutLineResource(), XrmPutResource(), XrmPutStringResource(), XrmQGetResource(), XrmQGetSearchList(), XrmQGetSearchResource(), XrmQPutStringResource(), XrmQuarkToString(), XrmStringToBindingQuarkList(), XrmStringToQuarkList(), XrmStringToQuark(), XrmUniqueQuark().

XrmQPutStringResource

Name

XrmQPutStringResource – add a resource specification to a database using a quark resource name and string value.

Synopsis

```
void XrmQPutStringResource(database, bindings, quarks, value)
    XrmDatabase *database;
    XrmBindingList bindings;
    XrmQuarkList quarks;
    char *value;
```

Arguments

database   Specifies a pointer to the resource database. If database contains NULL, a new resource database is created and a pointer to it is returned in database. If a database is created, it is created in the current locale.

bindings   Specifies a list of bindings for binding together the quarks argument.

quarks   Specifies the complete or partial name or class list of the resource to be stored.

value   Specifies the value of the resource as a string.

Description

XrmQPutStringResource() stores a resource specification into the specified database.

XrmQPutStringResource() is a cross between XrmQPutResource() and XrmPutString-Resource(). Like XrmQPutResource(), it specifies the resource by quarks and bindings, two lists that together make a name/class list with loose and tight bindings. Like Xrm-PutStringResource(), it specifies the value to be stored as a string, that value is converted into an XrmValue, and the default representation type String is used. The value is stored in the database without modification.

XrmPutResource(), XrmQPutResource(), XrmPutStringResource(), XrmQPut-StringResource() and XrmPutLineResource() all store data into a database. See Xrm-QPutResource() for the most complete description of this process.

For more information, see Volume One, Chapter 11, *Managing User Preferences*.

Structures

XrmDatabase is a pointer to an opaque data type.

```
typedef enum {
    XrmBindTightly, XrmBindLoosely
} XrmBinding, *XrmBindingList;

typedef int XrmQuark, *XrmQuarkList;
```

See Also

XrmDestroyDatabase(), XrmGetFileDatabase(), XrmGetResource(), XrmGetStringDatabase(), Xrm-Initialize(), XrmMergeDatabases(), XrmParseCommand(), XrmPutFileDatabase(), XrmPutLine-Resource(), XrmPutResource(), XrmPutStringResource(), XrmQGetResource(), XrmQGetSearchList(), XrmQGetSearchResource(), XrmQPutResource(), XrmQuarkToString(), XrmStringToBindingQuark-List(), XrmStringToQuarkList(), XrmStringToQuark(), XrmUniqueQuark().

Name

XrmQuarkToString – convert a quark to a string.

Synopsis

```
char *XrmQuarkToString(quark)
    XrmQuark quark;
```

Arguments

quark   Specifies the quark for which the equivalent string is desired.

Returns

The string.

Description

XrmQuarkToString() returns the string for which the specified quark is serving as a shorthand symbol. The quark was earlier set to represent the string by XrmStringTo-Quark(). The string pointed to by the return value must not be modified or freed, because that string is in the data structure used by the resource manager for assigning quarks. If no string exists for that quark, XrmQuarkToString() returns NULL.

Since the resource manager needs to make many comparisons of strings when it gets data from the database, it is more efficient to convert these strings into quarks, and to compare quarks instead. Since quarks are represented by integers, comparing quarks is trivial.

The three #define statements in the Structures section provide an extra level of abstraction. They define macros so that names, classes and representations can also be represented as quarks.

For more information, see Volume One, Chapter 11, *Managing User Preferences*.

Structures

```
typedef int XrmQuark;

/* macro definitions from <X11/Xresource.h> */

#define XrmNameToString(name) XrmQuarkToString(name)
#define XrmClassToString(class) XrmQuarkToString(class)
#define XrmRepresentationToString(type) XrmQuarkToString(type)
```

See Also

XrmDestroyDatabase(), XrmGetFileDatabase(), XrmGetResource(), XrmGetStringDatabase(), Xrm-Initialize(), XrmMergeDatabases(), XrmParseCommand(), XrmPutFileDatabase(), XrmPutLine-Resource(), XrmPutResource(), XrmPutStringResource(), XrmQGetResource(), XrmQGetSearchList(), XrmQGetSearchResource(), XrmQPutResource(), XrmQPutStringResource(), XrmStringToBinding-QuarkList(), XrmStringToQuarkList(), XrmStringToQuark(), XrmUniqueQuark().

XrmRepresentationToString

Name

XrmRepresentationToString – convert a quark to a string.

Synopsis

```
#define XrmRepresentationToString(type) XrmQuarkToString(type)

char *XrmQuarkToString(quark)
    XrmQuark quark;
```

Arguments

quark   Specifies the quark for which the equivalent string is desired.

Returns

The string.

Description

XrmRepresentationToString is an alias for XrmQuarkToString(). It returns the string for which the specified quark is serving as a shorthand symbol. The quark was returned earlier by XrmStringToQuark or XrmStringToRepresentation(). The string pointed to by the return value must not be modified or freed, because that string is in the data structure used by the resource manager for assigning quarks. If no string exists for that quark, XrmRepresentationToString returns NULL.

Since the resource manager needs to make many comparisons of strings when it gets data from the database, it is more efficient to convert these strings into quarks, and to compare quarks instead. Since quarks are represented by integers, comparing quarks is trivial.

For more information, see Volume One, Chapter 11, *Managing User Preferences*.

Structures

```
typedef int XrmQuark;
```

See Also

XrmDestroyDatabase(), XrmGetFileDatabase(), XrmGetResource(), XrmGetStringDatabase(), XrmInitialize(), XrmMergeDatabases(), XrmParseCommand(), XrmPutFileDatabase(), XrmPutLineResource(), XrmPutResource(), XrmPutStringResource(), XrmQGetResource(), XrmQGetSearchList(), XrmQGetSearchResource(), XrmQPutResource(), XrmQPutStringResource(), XrmStringToBindingQuarkList(), XrmStringToQuarkList(), XrmStringToQuark(), XrmUniqueQuark().

XrmSetDatabase

Name

XrmSetDatabase – associate a resource database with a display.

Synopsis

```
void XrmSetDatabase(display, database)
    Display *display;
    XrmDatabase database;
```

Arguments

display   Specifies the connection to the X server.

database   Specifies the resource database.

Availability

Release 5 and later.

Description

XrmSetDatabase() associates the specified resource database (or NULL) with the specified display. The database previously associated with the display (if any) is not destroyed. A client or toolkit may find this function convenient for retaining a database once it is constructed.

See Also

XrmGetDatabase().

XrmStringToBindingQuarkList

Name

XrmStringToBindingQuarkList – convert a key string to a binding list and a quark list.

Synopsis

```
XrmStringToBindingQuarkList(string, bindings_return, quarks_return)
    char *string;
    XrmBindingList bindings_return;
    XrmQuarkList quarks_return;
```

Arguments

string　　　　Specifies the string for which the list of quarks and list of bindings_return are to be generated. Must be NULL-terminated.

bindings_return
　　　　　　　　Returns the binding list. The caller must allocate sufficient space for the binding list before the call.

quarks_return
　　　　　　　　Returns the list of quarks. The caller must allocate sufficient space for the quarks list before the call.

Description

XrmStringToBindingQuarkList() converts a resource specification string into two lists—one of quarks and one of bindings. Component names in the list are separated by a dot (.) indicating a tight binding or an asterisk (*) indicating a loose binding. If the string does not start with dot or asterisk, a dot (".") is assumed.

A tight binding means that the quarks on either side of the binding are consecutive in the key. A loose binding, on the other hand, is a wildcard that can match any number of unspecified components in between the two quarks separated by the binding. Tight and loose bindings are used in the match rules, which compare multicomponent strings to find matches and determine the best match. See XrmGetResource() for a full description of lookup rules.

For example, *a.b*c becomes:

quarks	bindings
a	XrmBindLoosely
b	XrmBindTightly
c	XrmBindLoosely

For more information, see Volume One, Chapter 11, *Managing User Preferences*.

Structures

```
typedef int XrmQuark, *XrmQuarkList;
typedef enum (
    XrmBindLoosely, XrmBindTightly
) XrmBinding, *XrmBindingList;
```

See Also

XrmDestroyDatabase(), XrmGetFileDatabase(), XrmGetResource(), XrmGetStringDatabase(), Xrm-Initialize(), XrmMergeDatabases(), XrmParseCommand(), XrmPutFileDatabase(), XrmPutLine-Resource(), XrmPutResource(), XrmPutStringResource(), XrmQGetResource(), XrmQGetSearchList(), XrmQGetSearchResource(), XrmQPutResource(), XrmQPutStringResource(), XrmQuarkToString(), XrmStringToQuarkList(), XrmStringToQuark(), XrmUniqueQuark().

Name

XrmStringToQuark, XrmStringToName, XrmStringToClass, XrmStringToRepresentation – convert a string to a quark.

Synopsis

```
XrmQuark XrmStringToQuark(string)
    char *string;

#define XrmStringToName(string) XrmStringToQuark(string)
#define XrmStringToClass(string) XrmStringToQuark(string)
#define XrmStringToRepresentation(string) XrmStringToQuark(string)
```

Arguments

string   Specifies the string for which a quark is to be allocated.

Returns

The quark.

Description

XrmStringToQuark() returns a quark that will represent the specified string. If the string is not in the Host Portable Character Encoding, the conversion is implementation-dependent. Since string is copied, it may be freed. XrmQuarkToString() performs the inverse function.

A quark is an integer representation of a string. Since the resource manager needs to make many comparisons of strings when it gets data from the database, it is more efficient to convert these strings into quarks, and to compare quarks instead. Since quarks are presently represented by integers, comparing quarks is trivial.

The macros XrmStringToName(), XrmStringToClass(), and XrmStringToRepresentation() provide alternate names for XrmStringToQuark(). They help document when a name, class, or representation (as opposed to some other type of string) is being converted into a quark.

For more information, see Volume One, Chapter 11, *Managing User Preferences*.

Structures

```
typedef int XrmQuark;
```

See Also

XrmQGetResource(), XrmQGetSearchList(), XrmQGetSearchResource(), XrmQPutResource(), XrmQPutStringResource(), XrmQuarkToString(), XrmStringToBindingQuarkList(), XrmStringToQuarkList(), XrmUniqueQuark().

XrmStringToQuarkList

Name

XrmStringToQuarkList – convert a key string to a quark list.

Synopsis

```
void XrmStringToQuarkList(string, quarks_return)
    char *string;
    XrmQuarkList quarks_return;
```

Arguments

string
Specifies the string for which a list of quarks is to be generated. Must be NULL-terminated. The components may be separated by the dot (.) character (tight binding) or the asterisk (*) character (loose binding).

quarks_return
Returns the list of quarks.

Description

XrmStringToQuarkList() converts *string* (generally a fully qualified name/class string) to a list of quarks. If the string is not in the Host Portable Character Encoding, the conversion is implementation-dependent. Components of the string may be separated by a tight binding (the "." character) or a loose binding ("*"). Use XrmStringToBinding-QuarkList() for lists which contain both tight and loose bindings. See XrmGet-Resource() for a description of tight and loose binding.

Each component of the string is individually converted into a quark. See XrmStringTo-Quark() for information about quarks and converting strings to quarks. *quarks_return* is a NULL-terminated list of quarks.

For example, xmh.toc.command.background is converted into a list of four quarks: the quarks for xmh, toc, command, and background, in that order. A NULLQUARK is appended to the end of the list.

Note that XrmStringToNameList and XrmStringToClassList are macros that perform exactly the same function as XrmStringToQuarkList(). These may be used in cases where they clarify the code.

For more information, see Volume One, Chapter 11, *Managing User Preferences*.

Structures

```
typedef int XrmQuark *XrmQuarkList;

#define XrmStringToNameList(str, name)  XrmStringToQuarkList((str), (name))
#define XrmStringToClassList(str,class) XrmStringToQuarkList((str), (class))
```

See Also

XrmDestroyDatabase(), XrmGetFileDatabase(), XrmGetResource(), XrmGetStringDatabase(), Xrm-
Initialize(), XrmMergeDatabases(), XrmParseCommand(), XrmPutFileDatabase(), XrmPutLine-
Resource(), XrmPutResource(), XrmPutStringResource(), XrmQGetResource(), XrmQGetSearchList(),
XrmQGetSearchResource(), XrmQPutResource(), XrmQPutStringResource(), XrmQuarkToString(),
XrmStringToBindingQuarkList(), XrmStringToQuark(), XrmStringToRepresentation, XrmUnique-
Quark().

XrmUniqueQuark

Name

XrmUniqueQuark – allocate a new quark.

Synopsis

```
XrmQuark XrmUniqueQuark()
```

Returns

The quark.

Description

XrmUniqueQuark() allocates a quark that is guaranteed not to represent any existing string. For most applications, XrmStringToQuark() is more useful, as it binds a quark to a string. However, on some occasions, you may want to allocate a quark that has no string equivalent.

The shorthand name for a string is called a *quark* and is the type XrmQuark. Quarks are used to improve performance of the resource manager, which must make many string comparisons. Quarks are presently represented as integers. Simple comparisons of quarks can be performed rather than lengthy string comparisons.

A quark is to a string what an atom is to a property name in the server, but its use is entirely local to your application.

For more information, see Volume One, Chapter 11, *Managing User Preferences*.

Structures

```
typedef int XrmQuark;
```

See Also

XrmDestroyDatabase(), XrmGetFileDatabase(), XrmGetResource(), XrmGetStringDatabase(), XrmInitialize(), XrmMergeDatabases(), XrmParseCommand(), XrmPutFileDatabase(), XrmPutLineResource(), XrmPutResource(), XrmPutStringResource(), XrmQGetResource(), XrmQGetSearchList(), XrmQGetSearchResource(), XrmQPutResource(), XrmQPutStringResource(), XrmQuarkToString(), XrmStringToBindingQuarkList(), XrmStringToQuarkList(), XrmStringToQuark().

Name

XRootWindow, XRootWindowOfScreen, RootWindow, RootWindowOfScreen – return root window ID.

Synopsis

```
Window XRootWindow(display, screen_number)
      Display *display;
      int screen_number;

Window XRootWindowOfScreen(screen)
      Screen *screen;
```

Arguments

display   Specifies a connection to an X server; returned from `XOpenDisplay()`.

screen_number
      Specifies the appropriate screen number on the host server.

screen   Specifies the appropriate `Screen` structure.

Returns

The window ID.

Description

`XRootWindow()` and `XRootWindowOfScreen()` return the root window of the specified screen. The only difference between them is their arguments. These are useful as arguments of functions that need a drawable of a particular screen (such as `XCreatePixmap()` or `XCreateGC()`), and for creating top-level windows.

The C language macros `RootWindow()` and `RootWindowOfScreen()` are equivalent and slightly more efficient.

See Also

XDefaultRootWindow().

XRotateBuffers

Name

XRotateBuffers – rotate the cut buffers.

Synopsis

```
XRotateBuffers(display, rotate)
    Display *display;
    int rotate;
```

Arguments

display   Specifies a connection to an X server; returned from XOpenDisplay().

rotate   Specifies how many positions to rotate the cut buffers.

Description

XRotateBuffers() rotates the 8 cut buffers the amount specified by rotate. The contents of buffer 0 moves to buffer rotate, contents of buffer 1 moves to buffer (rotate+1) mod 8, contents of buffer 2 moves to buffer (rotate+2) mod 8, and so on.

This routine will not work if any of the buffers have not been stored into with XStoreBuffer() or XStoreBytes().

This cut buffer numbering is global to the display.

See the description of cut buffers in Volume One, Chapter 13, *Other Programming Techniques*.

Errors

BadMatch

See Also

XFetchBuffer(), XFetchBytes(), XStoreBuffer(), XStoreBytes().

XRotateWindowProperties

Name

XRotateWindowProperties – rotate properties in the properties array.

Synopsis

```
XRotateWindowProperties(display, w, properties, num_prop, npositions)
    Display *display;
    Window w;
    Atom properties[];
    int num_prop;
    int npositions;
```

Arguments

display   Specifies a connection to an X server; returned from XOpenDisplay().

w   Specifies the ID of the window whose properties are to be rearranged.

properties   Specifies the list of properties to be rotated.

num_prop   Specifies the length of the properties array.

npositions   Specifies the number of positions to rotate the property list. The sign controls the direction of rotation.

Description

XRotateWindowProperties() rotates the contents of an array of properties on a window. If the property names in the *properties* array are viewed as if they were numbered starting from 0 and if there are *num_prop* property names in the list, then the value associated with property name *I* becomes the value associated with property name (*I* + *npositions*) mod *num_prop*, for all *I* from 0 to *num_prop* – 1. Therefore, the sign of *npositions* controls the direction of rotation. The effect is to rotate the states by *npositions* places around the virtual ring of property names (right for positive *npositions*, left for negative *nposition*).

If *npositions* mod *num_prop* is non-zero, a PropertyNotify event is generated for each property, in the order listed.

If a BadAtom, BadMatch, or BadWindow error is generated, no properties are changed.

Errors

BadAtom   Undefined atom in the property list.

BadMatch   An atom appears more that once in the list or no property with that name is
                 defined for the window.

BadWindow

See Also

XChangeProperty(), XDeleteProperty(), XGetAtomName(), XGetFontProperty(), XGetWindow-
Property(), XInternAtom(), XListProperties(), XSetStandardProperties().

XSaveContext

Name

XSaveContext – save a data value corresponding to a resource ID and context type (not graphics context).

Synopsis

```
int XSaveContext(display, rid, context, data)
    Display *display;
    XID rid;
    XContext context;
    caddr_t data;
```

Arguments

display   Specifies a connection to an X server; returned from XOpenDisplay().

rid   Specifies the ID of the resource with which the data is associated.

context   Specifies the context type to which the data corresponds.

data   Specifies the data to be associated with the resource and context.

Returns

XCNOMEM (a non-zero error code) if an error has occurred or zero (0) otherwise.

Description

XSaveContext() saves data to the context manager database, according to the specified resource and context ID. The context manager is used for associating data with windows within an application. The client must have called XUniqueContext() to get the context ID before calling this function. The meaning of the data is indicated by the context ID, but is completely up to the client.

If an entry with the specified resource and context ID already exists, XSaveContext() writes over it with the specified data.

The XSaveContext() function returns XCNOMEM (a non-zero error code) if an error has occurred and zero (0) otherwise. For more information, see the description of the context manager in Volume One, Chapter 13, *Other Programming Techniques*.

Structures

```
typedef int XContext;
```

See Also

XDeleteContext(), XFindContext(), XUniqueContext().

XScreen*

Name

XScreenCount, XScreenNumberOfScreen, XScreenOfDisplay, ScreenCount, ScreenNumber-OfScreen, ScreenOfDisplay – get screen information.

Synopsis

```
int XScreenCount(display)
    Display *display;

int XScreenNumberOfScreen(screen)
    Screen *screen;

Screen *XScreenOfDisplay(display, screen_number)
    Display *display;
    int screen_number;
```

Arguments

display   Specifies a connection to an X server; returned from XOpenDisplay().

screen   Specifies the appropriate Screen structure.

screen_number
                Specifies the appropriate screen number on the host server.

Returns

The number of screens, a screen number, or a Screen structure.

Description

XScreenCount() returns the number of screens on the specified display. XScreen-NumberOfScreen() returns a screen number given a pointer to a Screen structure. XScreenOfDisplay() returns pointer to a Screen structure given the screen number. XScreenNumberOfScreen() and XScreenOfDisplay() are opposites.

The C language macros ScreenCount(), ScreenNumberOfScreen(), and Screen-OfDisplay() are equivalent and slightly more efficient.

See Also

XDefaultScreenOfDisplay(), XDefaultScreen().*

XScreenResourceString

Name

XScreenResourceString – return the SCREEN_RESOURCES property.

Synopsis

```
char *XScreenResourceString(screen)
    Screen *screen;
```

Arguments

screen   Specifies the screen.

Returns

The property data string.

Availability

Release 5 and later.

Description

XScreenResourceString() returns the SCREEN_RESOURCES property from the root window of the specified screen. The property is converted from type STRING to the current locale. The conversion is identical to that produced by XmbTextPropertyToText-List() for a singleton STRING property. Note that the property value must be in a format that is acceptable to XrmGetStringDatabase(). If no property exists, NULL is returned. The caller is responsible for freeing the returned string, using XFree().

XScreenResourceString() reads the window property each time it is requested. This differs from the behavior of XResourceManagerString() which simply returns the value of the property as it was defined when the connection with the X server was established.

See Also

XResourceManagerString().

XSelectInput

Name

XSelectInput – select the event types to be sent to a window.

Synopsis

```
XSelectInput(display, w, event_mask)
    Display *display;
    Window w;
    long event_mask;
```

Arguments

display   Specifies a connection to an X server; returned from XOpenDisplay().

w   Specifies the ID of the window interested in the events.

event_mask   Specifies the event mask. This mask is the bitwise OR of one or more of
               the valid event mask bits (see below).

Description

XSelectInput() defines which input events the window is interested in. If a window is
not interested in a device event (button, key, motion, or border crossing), it propagates up to
the closest ancestor unless otherwise specified in the do_not_propagate_mask attribute.

The bits of the mask are defined in <X11/X.h> :

ButtonPressMask	NoEventMask
ButtonReleaseMask	KeyPressMask
EnterWindowMask	KeyReleaseMask
LeaveWindowMask	ExposureMask
PointerMotionMask	VisibilityChangeMask
PointerMotionHintMask	StructureNotifyMask
Button1MotionMask	ResizeRedirectMask
Button2MotionMask	SubstructureNotifyMask
Button3MotionMask	SubstructureRedirectMask
Button4MotionMask	FocusChangeMask
Button5MotionMask	PropertyChangeMask
ButtonMotionMask	ColormapChangeMask
KeymapStateMask	OwnerGrabButtonMask

A call on XSelectInput() overrides any previous call on XSelectInput() for the
same window from the same client but not for other clients. Multiple clients can select input
on the same window; their event_mask window attributes are disjoint. When an event is
generated it will be reported to all interested clients. However, only one client at a time can
select for each of SubstructureRedirectMask, ResizeRedirectMask, and
ButtonPress.

If a window has both `ButtonPressMask` and `ButtonReleaseMask` selected, then a `ButtonPress` event in that window will automatically grab the mouse until all buttons are released, with events sent to windows as described for `XGrabPointer()`. This ensures that a window will see the `ButtonRelease` event corresponding to the `ButtonPress` event, even though the mouse may have exited the window in the meantime.

If `PointerMotionMask` is selected, events will be sent independent of the state of the mouse buttons. If instead, one or more of `Button1MotionMask`, `Button2Motion-Mask`, `Button3MotionMask`, `Button4MotionMask`, or `Button5MotionMask` is selected, `MotionNotify` events will be generated only when one or more of the specified buttons is depressed.

`XCreateWindow()` and `XChangeWindowAttributes()` can also set the *event_mask* attribute.

For more information, see Volume One, Chapter 8, *Events*.

Errors

`BadValue`   Specified event mask invalid.

`BadWindow`

See Also

XQLength(), XAllowEvents(), XCheckIfEvent(), XCheckMaskEvent(), XCheckTypedEvent(), XCheck-TypedWindowEvent(), XCheckWindowEvent(), XEventsQueued(), XGetInputFocus(), XGetMotion-Events(), XIfEvent(), XMaskEvent(), XNextEvent(), XPeekEvent(), XPeekIfEvent(), XPending(), XPut-BackEvent(), XSendEvent(), XSetInputFocus(), XSynchronize(), XWindowEvent().

XSendEvent

Name

XSendEvent – send an event.

Synopsis

```
Status XSendEvent(display, w, propagate, event_mask, event_send)
    Display *display;
    Window w;
    Bool propagate;
    long event_mask;
    XEvent *event_send;
```

Arguments

display   Specifies a connection to an X server; returned from `XOpenDisplay()`.

w   Specifies the ID of the window where you want to send the event. Pass the window resource ID, `PointerWindow`, or `InputFocus`.

propagate   Specifies how the sent event should propagate depending on *event_mask*. See description below. May be `True` or `False`.

event_mask   Specifies the event mask. See `XSelectInput()` for a detailed list of the event masks.

event_send   Specifies a pointer to the event to be sent.

Returns

Zero on failure, non-zero on success.

Description

`XSendEvent()` sends an event from one client to another (or conceivably to itself). This function is used for communication between clients using selections, for simulating user actions in demos, and for other purposes.

The specified event is sent to the window indicated by *w* regardless of active grabs.

If *w* is set to `PointerWindow`, the destination of the event will be the window that the pointer is in. If *w* is `InputFocus` is specified, then the destination is the focus window, regardless of pointer position.

If *propagate* is `False`, then the event is sent to every client selecting on the window specified by *w* any of the event types in *event_mask*. If *propagate* is `True` and no clients have been selected on *w* any of the event types in *event_mask*, then the event propagates like any other event.

The event code must be one of the core events, or one of the events defined by a loaded extension, so that the server can correctly byte swap the contents as necessary. The contents of the event are otherwise unaltered and unchecked by the server. The send_event field is in every event type; if `True` it indicates that the event was sent with `XSendEvent( )`.

This function is often used in selection processing. For example, the owner of a selection should use `XSendEvent( )` to send a `SelectionNotify` event to a requestor when a selection has been converted and stored as a property. See Volume One, Chapter 10, *Interclient Communication* for more information.

The status returned by `XSendEvent( )` indicates whether or not the given `XEvent` structure was successfully converted into a wire event. This value is zero on failure, or non-zero on success.

Errors

`BadValue`   Specified event is not a valid core or extension event type, or event mask is invalid.

`BadWindow`

Structures

See Appendix E, *Event Reference*, for the contents of each event structure.

See Also

XQLength(), XAllowEvents(), XCheckIfEvent(), XCheckMaskEvent(), XCheckTypedEvent(), XCheckTypedWindowEvent(), XCheckWindowEvent(), XEventsQueued(), XGetInputFocus(), XGetMotionEvents(), XIfEvent(), XMaskEvent(), XNextEvent(), XPeekEvent(), XPeekIfEvent(), XPending(), XPutBackEvent(), XSelectInput(), XSetInputFocus(), XSynchronize(), XWindowEvent().

XServerVendor

Name

XServerVendor, ServerVendor – return the vendor of connected server.

Synopsis

```
char *XServerVendor(display)
    Display *display;
```

Arguments

display   Specifies a connection to an X server; returned from XOpenDisplay().

Returns

The server vendor's string.

Description

XServerVendor() returns a pointer to a NULL-terminated string that provides some identification of the X server implementation. If the data returned by the server is in the Latin Portable Character Encoding, then the string is in the Host Portable Character Encoding. Otherwise, the contents of the string are implementation-dependent.

This function and XVendorRelease() make it possible to work around bugs in particular server implementations.

The C language macro ServerVendor() is equivalent and slightly more efficient.

Note also that in Release 5, the XlibSpecificationRelease symbol is defined (with the value 5) by Xlib. Before Release 5 this symbol was not defined.

See Also

XVendorRelease().

XSetAccessControl

Name

XSetAccessControl – disable or enable access control.

Synopsis

```
XSetAccessControl(display, mode)
    Display *display;
    int mode;
```

Arguments

display   Specifies a connection to an X server; returned from XOpenDisplay().

mode   Specifies whether you want to enable or disable the access control. Pass one of these constants: EnableAccess or DisableAccess.

Description

XSetAccessControl() specifies whether the server should check the host access list before allowing access to clients running on remote hosts. If the constant used is Disable-Access, clients from any host have access unchallenged.

This routine can only be called from a client running on the same host as the server.

For more information on access control lists, see Volume One, Chapter 13, *Other Programming Techniques*.

Errors

```
BadAccess
BadValue
```

See Also

XAddHost(), XAddHosts(), XDisableAccessControl(), XEnableAccessControl(), XListHosts(), XRemoveHost(), XRemoveHosts().

XSetAfterFunction

Name

XSetAfterFunction – set a function called after all Xlib functions.

Synopsis

```
int (*XSetAfterFunction(display, procedure))()
    Display *display;
    int (*procedure)();
```

Arguments

display Specifies a connection to an X server; returned from `XOpenDisplay()`.

procedure Specifies the user-defined function to be called after each Xlib function. This function is called with one argument, the *display* pointer.

Returns

The previous after function.

Description

All Xlib functions that generate protocol requests call what is known as an *after function* after completing their work (the default after function does nothing). `XSetAfter-Function()` allows you to write a function to be called. `XSetAfterFunction()` returns the previous after function.

`XSynchronize()` sets an after function to make sure that the input and request buffers are flushed after every Xlib routine.

For more information, see Volume One, Chapter 13, *Other Programming Techniques*.

See Also

XDisplayName(), *XGetErrorDatabaseText()*, *XGetErrorText()*, *XSetErrorHandler()*, *XSetIOError-Handler()*, *XSynchronize()*.

XSetArcMode

Name

XSetArcMode – set the arc mode in a graphics context.

Synopsis

```
XSetArcMode(display, gc, arc_mode)
    Display *display;
    GC gc;
    int arc_mode;
```

Arguments

display   Specifies a connection to an X server; returned from XOpenDisplay().

gc   Specifies the graphics context.

arc_mode   Specifies the arc mode for the specified graphics context. Possible values are ArcChord or ArcPieSlice.

Description

XSetArcMode() sets the *arc_mode* component of a GC, which controls filling in the XFillArcs() function. ArcChord specifies that the area between the arc and a line segment joining the endpoints of the arc is filled. ArcPieSlice specifies that the area filled is delimited by the arc and two line segments connecting the ends of the arc to the center point of the rectangle defining the arc.

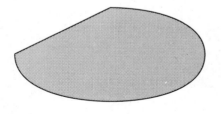

ArcChord

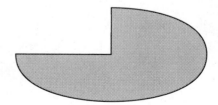

ArcPieSlice

Errors

```
BadAlloc
BadGC
BadValue
```

See Also

XDefaultGC(), XChangeGC(), XCopyGC(), XCreateGC(), XFreeGC(), XGContextFromGC(), XSet-Background(), XSetClipMask(), XSetClipOrigin(), XSetClipRectangles(), XSetDashes(), XSetFillRule(), XSetFillStyle(), XSetForeground(), XSetFunction(), XSetGraphicsExposures(), XSetLineAttributes(), XSetPlaneMask(), XSetState(), XSetStipple(), XSetSubwindowMode(), XSetTSOrigin().

XSetBackground

Name

XSetBackground – set the background pixel value in a graphics context.

Synopsis

```
XSetBackground(display, gc, background)
    Display *display;
    GC gc;
    unsigned long background;
```

Arguments

display   Specifies a connection to an X server; returned from XOpenDisplay().

gc   Specifies the graphics context.

background   Specifies the background component of the GC.

Description

XSetBackground() sets the background pixel value component of a GC. Note that this is different from the background of a window, which can be set with either XSet-WindowBackground() or XSetWindowBackgroundPixmap().

The specified pixel value must be returned by BlackPixel(), WhitePixel(), or one of the routines that allocate colors.

Errors

BadAlloc
BadGC

See Also

XDefaultGC(), XChangeGC(), XCopyGC(), XCreateGC(), XFreeGC(), XGContextFromGC(), XSetArc-Mode(), XSetClipMask(), XSetClipOrigin(), XSetClipRectangles(), XSetDashes(), XSetFillRule(), XSet-FillStyle(), XSetForeground(), XSetFunction(), XSetGraphicsExposures(), XSetLineAttributes(), XSet-PlaneMask(), XSetState(), XSetStipple(), XSetSubwindowMode(), XSetTSOrigin().

XSetClassHint

Name

XSetClassHint – set the XA_WM_CLASS property of a window.

Synopsis

```
XSetClassHint(display, w, class_hints)
    Display *display;
    Window w;
    XClassHint *class_hints;
```

Arguments

display   Specifies a connection to an X server; returned from XOpenDisplay().

w   Specifies the ID of the window for which the class hint is to be set.

class_hints   Specifies the XClassHint structure that is to be used.

Description

XSetClassHint() sets the XA_WM_CLASS property for the specified window. The window manager may (or may not) read this property, and use it to get resource defaults that apply to the window manager's handling of this application. If the strings in class_hints are not in the Host Portable Character Encoding, the result is implementation-dependent.

The XClassHint structure set contains res_class and res_name fields. The res_name field contains the application name, and the res_class field contains the application class. Note that the name set in this property may differ from the name set as WM_NAME. That is, WM_NAME specifies what should be displayed in the title bar and, therefore, can contain temporal information (for example, the name of a file currently in an editor's buffer). On the other hand, the name specified as part of WM_CLASS is the formal name of the application that should be used when retrieving the application's resources from the resource database.

There are several more powerful functions that set XA_WM_CLASS. They include XSet-WMProperties(), and (in R5) XmbSetWMProperties(). These functions read the RESOURCE_NAME environment variable if res_name is NULL, and they use argv[0] stripped of any directory prefixes if RESOURCE_NAME is not set. XSetClassHint() only uses the explicit value of res_name.

For more information, see Volume One, Chapter 10, *Interclient Communication*.

Errors

```
BadAlloc
BadWindow
```

Structures

```
typedef struct {
    char *res_name;
    char *res_class;
} XClassHint;
```

See Also

XAllocClassHint(), XFetchName(), XGetClassHint(), XGetIconName(), XGetIconSizes(), XGetNormal-Hints(), XGetSizeHints(), XGetTransientForHint(), XGetWMHints(), XGetZoomHints(), XSet-Command(), XSetIconName(), XSetIconSizes(), XSetNormalHints(), XSetSizeHints(), XSetTransientFor-Hint(), XSetWMHints(), XSetZoomHints(), XStoreName(), XSetWMProperties().

XSetClipMask

Name

XSetClipMask – set `pixmap` pixmap in a graphics context.

Synopsis

```
XSetClipMask(display, gc, pixmap)
    Display *display;  ˙
    GC gc;
    Pixmap pixmap;
```

Arguments

display   Specifies a connection to an X server; returned from `XOpenDisplay()`.

gc   Specifies the graphics context.

pixmap   Specifies a pixmap of depth 1 to be used as the clip mask. Pass the constant None if no clipping is desired.

Description

`XSetClipMask()` sets the `pixmap` component of a GC to a pixmap. The `pixmap` filters which pixels in the destination are drawn. If `pixmap` is set to None, the pixels are always drawn, regardless of the clip origin. Use `XSetClipRectangles()` to set `pixmap` to a set of rectangles, or `XSetRegion()` to set `pixmap` to a region.

For more information, see Volume One, Chapter 5, *The Graphics Context*.

Errors

```
BadAlloc
BadGC
BadMatch
BadPixmap
```

See Also

XDefaultGC(), XChangeGC(), XCopyGC(), XCreateGC(), XFreeGC(), XGContextFromGC(), XSetArcMode(), XSetBackground(), XSetClipOrigin(), XSetClipRectangles(), XSetDashes(), XSetFillRule(), XSetFillStyle(), XSetForeground(), XSetFunction(), XSetGraphicsExposures(), XSetLineAttributes(), XSetPlaneMask(), XSetState(), XSetStipple(), XSetSubwindowMode(), XSetTSOrigin().

XSetClipOrigin

Name

XSetClipOrigin – set the clip origin in a graphics context.

Synopsis

```
XSetClipOrigin(display, gc, clip_x_origin, clip_y_origin)
    Display *display;
    GC gc;
    int clip_x_origin, clip_y_origin;
```

Arguments

display   Specifies a connection to an X server; returned from XOpen-
                 Display().

gc   Specifies the graphics context.

clip_x_origin   Specify the coordinates of the clip origin (interpreted later relative to
clip_y_origin   the window drawn into with this GC).

Description

XSetClipOrigin() sets the *clip_x_origin* and *clip_y_origin* components of a
GC. The clip origin controls the position of the clip_mask in the GC, which filters which
pixels are drawn in the destination of a drawing request using this GC.

For more information, see Volume One, Chapter 5, *The Graphics Context*.

Errors

BadAlloc
BadGC

See Also

*XDefaultGC(), XChangeGC(), XCopyGC(), XCreateGC(), XFreeGC(), XGContextFromGC(), XSetArc-
Mode(), XSetBackground(), XSetClipMask(), XSetClipRectangles(), XSetDashes(), XSetFillRule(), XSet-
FillStyle(), XSetForeground(), XSetFunction(), XSetGraphicsExposures(), XSetLineAttributes(), XSet-
PlaneMask(), XSetState(), XSetStipple(), XSetSubwindowMode(), XSetTSOrigin().*

XSetClipRectangles

Name

XSetClipRectangles – change `clip_mask` in a graphics context to a list of rectangles.

Synopsis

```
XSetClipRectangles(display, gc, clip_x_origin,
                 clip_y_origin, rectangles, n, ordering)
    Display *display;
    GC gc;
    int clip_x_origin, clip_y_origin;
    XRectangle rectangles[];
    int n;
    int ordering;
```

Arguments

display	Specifies a connection to an X server; returned from `XOpenDisplay()`.
gc	Specifies the graphics context.
clip_x_origin *clip_y_origin*	Specify the x and y coordinates of the clip origin (interpreted later relative to the window drawn into with this GC).
rectangles	Specifies an array of rectangles. These are the rectangles you want drawing clipped to.
n	Specifies the number of rectangles.
ordering	Specifies the ordering relations of the rectangles. Possible values are `Unsorted`, `YSorted`, `YXSorted`, or `YXBanded`.

Description

`XSetClipRectangles()` changes the `clip_mask` component in the specified GC to the specified list of rectangles and sets the clip origin to `clip_x_origin` and `clip_y_origin`. The rectangle coordinates are interpreted relative to the clip origin. The output from drawing requests using that GC are henceforth clipped to remain contained within the rectangles. The rectangles should be nonintersecting, or the graphics results will be undefined. If the list of rectangles is empty, output is effectively disabled as all space is clipped in that GC. This is the opposite of a `clip_mask` of `None` in `XCreateGC()`, `XChangeGC()`, or `XSetClipMask()`.

If known by the client, ordering relations on the rectangles can be specified with the *ordering* argument. This may provide faster operation by the server. If an incorrect ordering is specified, the X server may generate a `BadMatch` error, but it is not required to do so. If no error is generated, the graphics results are undefined. `Unsorted` means the rectangles are in arbitrary order. `YSorted` means that the rectangles are nondecreasing in their y origin. `YXSorted` additionally constrains `YSorted` order in that all rectangles with an equal y origin are nondecreasing in their x origin. YXBanded additionally constrains YXSorted by requiring that, for every possible horizontal y scan line, all rectangles that include that scan line have identical y origins and y extents.

To cancel the effect of this command, so that there is no clipping, pass None as the clip_mask in XChangeGC() or XSetClipMask().

For more information, see Volume One, Chapter 5, *The Graphics Context*.

Structures

```
typedef struct {
    short x,y;
    unsigned short width, height;
} XRectangle;
```

Errors

BadAlloc

BadGC

BadMatch   Incorrect *ordering* (error message server-dependent).

BadValue

See Also

XDefaultGC(), XChangeGC(), XCopyGC(), XCreateGC(), XFreeGC(), XGContextFromGC(), XSetArc-Mode(), XSetBackground(), XSetClipMask(), XSetClipOrigin(), XSetDashes(), XSetFillRule(), XSetFill-Style(), XSetForeground(), XSetFunction(), XSetGraphicsExposures(), XSetLineAttributes(), XSetPlane-Mask(), XSetState(), XSetStipple(), XSetSubwindowMode(), XSetTSOrigin().

XSetCloseDownMode

Xlib – Client Connections

Name

XSetCloseDownMode – change the close down mode of a client.

Synopsis

```
XSetCloseDownMode(display, close_mode)
    Display *display;
    int close_mode;
```

Arguments

display   Specifies a connection to an X server; returned from XOpenDisplay().

close_mode   Specifies the client close down mode you want. Pass one of these constants: DestroyAll, RetainPermanent, or RetainTemporary.

Description

XSetCloseDownMode() defines what will happen to the client's resources at connection close. A connection between a client and the server starts in DestroyAll mode, and all resources associated with that connection will be freed when the client process dies. If the close down mode is RetainTemporary or RetainPermanent when the client dies, its resources live on until a call to XKillClient(). The *resource* argument of XKill-Client() can be used to specify which client to kill, or it may be the constant All-Temporary, in which case XKillClient() kills all resources of all clients that have terminated in RetainTemporary mode.

One use of RetainTemporary or RetainPermanent might be to allow an application to recover from a failure of the network connection to the display server. After restarting, the application would need to be able to identify its own resources and reclaim control of them.

Errors

BadValue

See Also

XKillClient().

676   *Xlib Reference Manual*

XSetCommand

Name

XSetCommand – set the XA_WM_COMMAND atom (command-line arguments).

Synopsis

```
XSetCommand(display, w, argv, argc)
    Display *display;
    Window w;
    char **argv;
    int argc;
```

Arguments

display   Specifies a connection to an X server; returned from XOpenDisplay().

w   Specifies the ID of the window whose atom is to be set.

argv   Specifies a pointer to the command and arguments used to start the application.

argc   Specifies the number of arguments.

Description

XSetCommand() is used by the application to set the XA_WM_COMMAND property for the window manager with the command and its arguments used to invoke the application. If the string is not in the Host Portable Character Encoding, the result is implementation-dependent.

XSetCommand() creates a zero-length property if argc is zero.

Use this command only if not calling XSetStandardProperties() or XSet-WMProperties().

Errors

BadAlloc
BadWindow

See Also

XFetchName(), XGetClassHint(), XGetCommand(), XGetIconName(), XGetIconSizes(), XGetNormal-Hints(), XGetSizeHints(), XGetTransientForHint(), XGetWMHints(), XGetZoomHints(), XSetClassHint(), XSetIconName(), XSetIconSizes(), XSetNormalHints(), XSetSizeHints(), XSetTransientForHint(), XSet-WMHints(), XSetZoomHints(), XStoreName().

XSetDashes

Name

XSetDashes – set a pattern of line dashes in a graphics context.

Synopsis

```
XSetDashes(display, gc, dash_offset, dash_list, n)
    Display *display;
    GC gc;
    int dash_offset;
    char dash_list[];
    int n;
```

Arguments

display   Specifies a connection to an X server; returned from XOpenDisplay().

gc   Specifies the graphics context.

dash_offset Specifies the phase of the pattern for the dashed line style.

dash_list   Specifies the dash list for the dashed line style. An odd-length list is equivalent to the same list concatenated with itself to produce an even-length list.

n   Specifies the length of the dash list argument.

Description

XSetDashes() sets the dashes component of a GC. The initial and alternating elements of the dash_list argument are the dashes, the others are the gaps. All of the elements must be non-zero, with lengths measured in pixels. The dash_offset argument defines the phase of the pattern, specifying how many pixels into the dash_list the pattern should actually begin in the line drawn by the request.

n specifies the length of dash_list. An odd value for n is interpreted as specifying the dash_list concatenated with itself to produce twice as long a list.

Ideally, a dash length is measured along the slope of the line, but server implementors are only required to match this ideal for horizontal and vertical lines. Failing the ideal semantics, it is suggested that the length be measured along the major axis of the line. The major axis is defined as the x axis for lines drawn at an angle of between −45 and +45 degrees or between 315 and 225 degrees from the x axis. For all other lines, the major axis is the y axis.

See Volume One, Chapter 5, *The Graphics Context*, for further information.

Errors

`BadAlloc`

`BadGC`

`BadValue`   No values in *dash_list*.
                    Element in *dash_list* is 0.

See Also

XDefaultGC(), XChangeGC(), XCopyGC(), XCreateGC(), XFreeGC(), XGContextFromGC(), XSetArc-Mode(), XSetBackground(), XSetClipMask(), XSetClipOrigin(), XSetClipRectangles(), XSetFillRule(), XSetFillStyle(), XSetForeground(), XSetFunction(), XSetGraphicsExposures(), XSetLineAttributes(), XSetPlaneMask(), XSetState(), XSetStipple(), XSetSubwindowMode(), XSetTSOrigin().

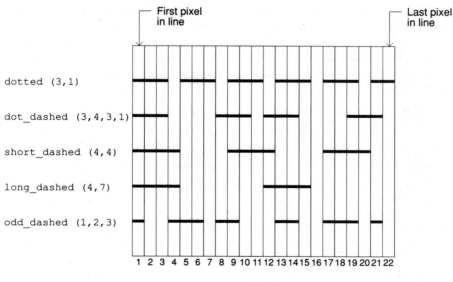

XSetErrorHandler

Name

XSetErrorHandler – set a nonfatal error event handler.

Synopsis

```
int (*XSetErrorHandler(handler))()
    int (* handler)(Display *, XErrorEvent *)
```

Arguments

handler   The user-defined function to be called to handle error events. If a NULL
                 pointer, reinvoke the default handler, which prints a message and exits.

Returns

The previous nonfatal error handler.

Description

The error handler function specified in *handler* will be called by Xlib whenever an XError event is received. These are nonfatal conditions, such as unexpected values for arguments, or a failure in server memory allocation. It is acceptable for this procedure to return, though the default handler simply prints a message and exits. However, the error handler should NOT perform any operations (directly or indirectly) that generate protocol requests or that look for input events.

In Release 4 and Release 5, XSetErrorHandler() returns a pointer to the previous error handler.

The function is called with two arguments: the display variable and a pointer to the XErrorEvent structure. Here is a trivial example of a user-defined error handler:

```
int myhandler (display, myerr)
Display *display;
XErrorEvent *myerr;
{
    char msg[80];
    XGetErrorText(display, myerr->error_code, msg, 80);
    fprintf(stderr, "Error code %s\n", msg);
}
```

This is how the example routine would be used in XSetErrorHandler():

```
XSetErrorHandler(myhandler);
```

Note that XSetErrorHandler() is one of the few routines that does not require a display argument. The routine that calls the error handler gets the display variable from the XErrorEvent structure.

The error handler is not called on BadName errors from OpenFont, LookupColor, and AllocNamedColor protocol requests, or on BadFont errors from a QueryFont protocol request. These errors are all indicated by `Status` return value of zero in the corresponding Xlib routines, which must be caught and handled by the application.

Use `XIOErrorHandler` to provide a handler for I/O errors such as network failures or server host crashes.

In the `XErrorEvent` structure shown below, the `serial` member is the number of requests (starting from 1) sent over the network connection since it was opened. It is the number that was the value of the request sequence number immediately after the failing call was made. The `request_code` member is a protocol representation of the name of the procedure that failed and is defined in *<X11/Xproto.h>*.

For more information, see Volume One, Chapter 3, *Basic Window Program*.

Structures

```
typedef struct {
    int type
    Display *display;            /* display the event was read from */
    XID resourceid;              /* resource ID */
    unsigned long serial;        /* serial number of failed request */
    unsigned char error_code;    /* error code of failed request */
    unsigned char request_code;  /* major opcode of failed request */
    unsigned char minor_code;    /* minor opcode of failed request */
} XErrorEvent;
```

See Also

XDisplayName(), XGetErrorDatabaseText(), XGetErrorText(), XSetAfterFunction(), XSetIOError-Handler(), XSynchronize().

XSetFillRule

Name

XSetFillRule – set the fill rule in a graphics context.

Synopsis

```
XSetFillRule(display, gc, fill_rule)
    Display *display;
    GC gc;
    int fill_rule;
```

Arguments

display   Specifies a connection to an X server; returned from XOpenDisplay().

gc   Specifies the graphics context.

fill_rule   Specifies the fill rule you want to set for the specified graphics context. Possible values are EvenOddRule or WindingRule.

Description

XSetFillRule() sets the *fill_rule* component of a GC. The *fill_rule* member of the GC determines what pixels are drawn in XFillPolygon() requests. Simply put, WindingRule fills overlapping areas of the polygon, while EvenOddRule does not fill areas that overlap an odd number of times. Technically, EvenOddRule means that the point is drawn if an arbitrary ray drawn from the point would cross the path determined by the request an odd number of times. WindingRule indicates that a point is drawn if a point crosses an unequal number of clockwise and counterclockwise path segments, as seen from the point.

A clockwise-directed path segment is one which crosses the ray from left to right as observed from the point. A counterclockwise segment is one which crosses the ray from right to left as observed from the point. The case where a directed line segment is coincident with the ray is uninteresting because you can simply choose a different ray that is not coincident with a segment.

All calculations are performed on infinitely small points, so that if any point within a pixel is considered inside, the entire pixel is drawn. Pixels with centers exactly on boundaries are considered inside only if the filled area is to the right, except that on horizontal boundaries, the pixel is considered inside only if the filled area is below the pixel.

See Volume One, Chapter 5, *The Graphics Context*, for more information.

Errors

```
BadAlloc
BadGC
BadValue
```

See Also

XDefaultGC(), XChangeGC(), XCopyGC(), XCreateGC(), XFreeGC(), XGContextFromGC(), XSetArc-Mode(), XSetBackground(), XSetClipMask(), XSetClipOrigin(), XSetClipRectangles(), XSetDashes(), XSetFillStyle(), XSetForeground(), XSetFunction(), XSetGraphicsExposures(), XSetLineAttributes(), XSetPlaneMask(), XSetState(), XSetStipple(), XSetSubwindowMode(), XSetTSOrigin().

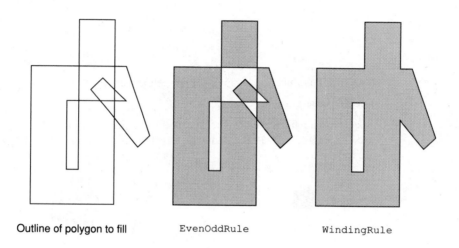

| Outline of polygon to fill | EvenOddRule | WindingRule |

XSetFillStyle

Name

XSetFillStyle – set the fill style in a graphics context.

Synopsis

```
XSetFillStyle(display, gc, fill_style)
    Display *display;
    GC gc;
    int fill_style;
```

Arguments

display   Specifies a connection to an X server; returned from XOpenDisplay().

gc   Specifies the graphics context.

fill_style   Specifies the fill style for the specified graphics context. Possible values
               are FillSolid, FillTiled, FillStippled, or FillOpaque-
               Stippled.

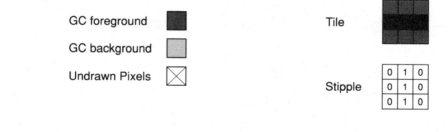

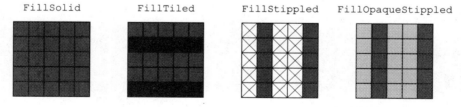

Description

XSetFillStyle() sets the fill_style component of a GC. The fill_style
defines the contents of the source for line, text, and fill requests. FillSolid indicates that
the pixels represented by set bits in the source are drawn in the foreground pixel value,
and unset bits in the source are not drawn. FillTiled uses the tile specified in the GC
to determine the pixel values for set bits in the source. FillOpaqueStippled specifies
that bits set in the stipple are drawn in the foreground pixel value and unset bits are

drawn in the `background`. `FillStippled` draws bits set in the source and set in the stipple in the `foreground` color, and leaves unset bits alone.

For more information, see Volume One, Chapter 5, *The Graphics Context*.

Errors

```
BadAlloc
BadGC
BadValue
```

See Also

XDefaultGC(), XChangeGC(), XCopyGC(), XCreateGC(), XFreeGC(), XGContextFromGC(), XSetArc-Mode(), XSetBackground(), XSetClipMask(), XSetClipOrigin(), XSetClipRectangles(), XSetDashes(), XSetFillRule(), XSetForeground(), XSetFunction(), XSetGraphicsExposures(), XSetLineAttributes(), XSetPlaneMask(), XSetState(), XSetStipple(), XSetSubwindowMode(), XSetTSOrigin().

XSetFont

Name

XSetFont – set the current font in a graphics context.

Synopsis

```
XSetFont(display, gc, font)
    Display *display;
    GC gc;
    Font font;
```

Arguments

display   Specifies a connection to an X server; returned from XOpenDisplay().

gc   Specifies the graphics context.

font   Specifies the ID of the font to be used.

Description

XSetFont() sets the font in the GC. Text drawing requests using this GC will use this font only if the font is loaded. Otherwise, the text will not be drawn.

For more information, see Volume One, Chapter 5, *The Graphics Context*.

Errors

```
BadAlloc
BadFont
BadGC
```

See Also

XCreateFontCursor(), XFreeFont(), XFreeFontInfo(), XFreeFontNames(), XFreeFontPath(), XGetFontPath(), XGetFontProperty(), XListFonts(), XListFontsWithInfo(), XLoadFont(), XLoadQueryFont(), XQueryFont(), XSetFontPath(), XUnloadFont().

XSetFontPath

Name

XSetFontPath – set the font search path.

Synopsis

```
XSetFontPath(display, directories, ndirs)
    Display *display;
    char **directories;
    int ndirs;
```

Arguments

display   Specifies a connection to an X server; returned from XOpenDisplay().

directories Specifies the directory path used to look for the font. Setting the path to the empty list restores the default path defined for the X server.

ndirs   Specifies the number of directories in the path.

Description

XSetFontPath() defines the directory search path for font lookup for all clients. Therefore the user should construct a new directory search path carefully by adding to the old directory search path obtained by XGetFontPath(). Passing an invalid path can result in preventing the server from accessing any fonts. Also avoid restoring the default path, since some other client may have changed the path on purpose.

The interpretation of the strings is operating-system-dependent, but they are intended to specify directories to be searched in the order listed. Also, the contents of these strings are operating system specific and are not intended to be used by client applications.

An X server is permitted to cache font information internally, for example, it might cache an entire font from a file and not check on subsequent opens of that font to see if the underlying font file has changed. However, when the font path is changed the X server is guaranteed to flush all cached information about fonts for which there currently are no explicit resource IDs allocated.

The meaning of errors from this request is implementation-dependent.

Errors

BadValue

See Also

XCreateFontCursor(), XFreeFont(), XFreeFontInfo(), XFreeFontNames(), XFreeFontPath(), XGetFontPath(), XGetFontProperty(), XListFonts(), XListFontsWithInfo(), XLoadFont(), XLoadQueryFont(), XQueryFont(), XSetFont(), XUnloadFont().

XSetForeground

Name

XSetForeground – set the foreground pixel value in a graphics context.

Synopsis

```
XSetForeground(display, gc, foreground)
    Display *display;
    GC gc;
    unsigned long foreground;
```

Arguments

display   Specifies a connection to an X server; returned from XOpenDisplay().

gc   Specifies the graphics context.

foreground   Specifies the foreground pixel value you want for the specified graphics context.

Description

XSetForeground() sets the *foreground* component in a GC. This pixel value is used for set bits in the source according to the fill_style. This pixel value must be returned by BlackPixel, WhitePixel(), or a routine that allocates colors.

See Volume One, Chapter 5, *The Graphics Context*, for more information on the GC.

Errors

```
BadAlloc
BadGC
```

See Also

XDefaultGC(), XChangeGC(), XCopyGC(), XCreateGC(), XFreeGC(), XGContextFromGC(), XSetArcMode(), XSetBackground(), XSetClipMask(), XSetClipOrigin(), XSetClipRectangles(), XSetDashes(), XSetFillRule(), XSetFillStyle(), XSetFunction(), XSetGraphicsExposures(), XSetLineAttributes(), XSetPlaneMask(), XSetState(), XSetStipple(), XSetSubwindowMode(), XSetTSOrigin().

XSetFunction

Name

XSetFunction – set the bitwise logical operation in a graphics context.

Synopsis

```
XSetFunction(display, gc, function)
    Display *display;
    GC gc;
    int function;
```

Arguments

display   Specifies a connection to an X server; returned from XOpenDisplay().

gc   Specifies the graphics context.

function   Specifies the logical operation you want for the specified graphics context.
             See Description for the choices and their meanings.

Description

XSetFunction() sets the logical operation applied between the source pixel values (generated by the drawing request) and existing destination pixel values (already in the window or pixmap) to generate the final destination pixel values in a drawing request (what is actually drawn to the window or pixmap). Of course, the plane_mask and clip_mask in the GC also affect this operation by preventing drawing to planes and pixels respectively. GXcopy, GXinvert, and GXxor are the only logical operations that are commonly used.

See Volume One, Chapter 5, *The Graphics Context*, for more information about the logical function.

The function symbols and their logical definitions are:

Symbol	Bit	Meaning
GXclear	0x0	0
GXand	0x1	src AND dst
GXandReverse	0x2	src AND (NOT dst)
GXcopy	0x3	src
GXandInverted	0x4	(NOT src) AND dst
GXnoop	0x5	dst
GXxor	0x6	src XOR dst
GXor	0x7	src OR dst
GXnor	0x8	(NOT src) AND (NOT dst)
GXequiv	0x9	(NOT src) XOR dst
GXinvert	0xa	(NOT dst)
GXorReverse	0xb	src OR (NOT dst)

Symbol	Bit	Meaning
GXcopyInverted	0xc	(NOT src)
GXorInverted	0xdu	(NOT src)OR dst
GXnand	0xe	(NOT src) OR (NOT dst)
GXset	0xf	1

Errors

BadAlloc
BadGC
BadValue

See Also

XDefaultGC(), XChangeGC(), XCopyGC(), XCreateGC(), XFreeGC(), XGContextFromGC(), XSetArc-Mode(), XSetBackground(), XSetClipMask(), XSetClipOrigin(), XSetClipRectangles(), XSetDashes(), XSetFillRule(), XSetFillStyle(), XSetForeground(), XSetGraphicsExposures(), XSetLineAttributes(), XSetPlaneMask(), XSetState(), XSetStipple(), XSetSubwindowMode(), XSetTSOrigin().

XSetGraphicsExposures

Name

XSetGraphicsExposures – set the `graphics_exposures` component in a graphics context.

Synopsis

```
XSetGraphicsExposures(display, gc, graphics_exposures)
    Display *display;
    GC gc;
    Bool graphics_exposures;
```

Arguments

display   Specifies a connection to an X server; returned from `XOpenDisplay()`.

gc   Specifies the graphics context.

graphics_exposures

Specifies whether you want `GraphicsExpose` and `NoExpose` events when calling `XCopyArea()` and `XCopyPlane()` with this graphics context.

Description

`XSetGraphicsExposure` sets the *graphics_exposures* member of a GC. If *graphics_exposures* is `True`, `GraphicsExpose` events will be generated when `XCopyArea()` and `XCopyPlane()` requests cannot be completely satisfied because a source region is obscured, and `NoExpose` events are generated when they can be completely satisfied. If *graphics_exposures* is `False`, these events are not generated.

These events are not selected in the normal way with `XSelectInput()`. Setting the *graphics_exposures* member of the GC used in the `CopyArea` or `CopyPlane` request is the only way to select these events.

For more information, see Volume One, Chapter 5, *The Graphics Context*.

Errors

```
BadAlloc
BadGC
BadValue
```

See Also

XDefaultGC(), XChangeGC(), XCopyGC(), XCreateGC(), XFreeGC(), XGContextFromGC(), XSetArcMode(), XSetBackground(), XSetClipMask(), XSetClipOrigin(), XSetClipRectangles(), XSetDashes(), XSetFillRule(), XSetFillStyle(), XSetForeground(), XSetFunction(), XSetLineAttributes(), XSetPlaneMask(), XSetState(), XSetStipple(), XSetSubwindowMode(), XSetTSOrigin().

XSetICFocus

Name

XSetICFocus – set input context focus.

Synopsis

```
void XSetICFocus(ic)
    XIC ic;
```

Arguments

ic   Specifies the input context.

Availability

Release 5 and later.

Description

XSetICFocus() allows a client to notify an input method that the focus window attached to the specified input context has received keyboard focus. The input method should take action to provide appropriate feedback.

See Also

XCreateIC(), XSetICValues(), XmbResetIC(), XwcResetIC, XUnsetICFocus().

XSetIconName

Name

XSetIconName – set the name to be displayed in a window's icon.

Synopsis

```
XSetIconName(display, w, icon_name)
    Display *display;
    Window w;
    char *icon_name;
```

Arguments

display   Specifies a connection to an X server; returned from XOpenDisplay().

w   Specifies the ID of the window whose icon name is being set.

icon_name   Specifies the name to be displayed in the window's icon. The name should
              be a NULL-terminated string. This name is returned by any subsequent call
              to XGetIconName(). If the string is not in the Host Portable Character
              Encoding, the result is implementation-dependent.

Description

XSetIconName() is superseded by XSetWMIconName() in Release 4.

XSetIconName() sets the XA_WM_ICON_NAME property for a window. This is usually set
by an application for the window manager. The name should be short, since it is to be
displayed in association with an icon.

XSetStandardProperties() (in Release 4) or XSetWMProperties() (in Release
4) also set this property.

For more information, see Volume One, Chapter 10, *Interclient Communication*.

Errors

```
BadAlloc
BadWindow
```

See Also

XFetchName(), XGetClassHint(), XGetIconName(), XGetIconSizes(), XGetNormalHints(), XGetSize-Hints(), XGetTransientForHint(), XGetWMHints(), XGetZoomHints(), XSetClassHint(), XSet-Command(), XSetIconSizes(), XSetNormalHints(), XSetSizeHints(), XSetTransientForHint(), XSet-WMHints(), XSetZoomHints(), XStoreName().

XSetIconSizes

Name

XSetIconSizes – set the value of the XA_WM_ICON_SIZE property.

Synopsis

```
XSetIconSizes(display, w, size_list, count)
    Display *display;
    Window w;
    XIconSize *size_list;
    int count;
```

Arguments

display	Specifies a connection to an X server; returned from XOpenDisplay().
w	Specifies the ID of the window whose icon size property is to be set. Normally the root window.
size_list	Specifies a pointer to the size list.
count	Specifies the number of items in the size list.

Description

XSetIconSizes() is normally used by a window manager to set the range of preferred icon sizes in the XA_WM_ICON_SIZE property of the root window.

Applications can then read the property with XGetIconSizes().

Structures

```
typedef struct {
    int min_width, min_height;
    int max_width, max_height;
    int width_inc, height_inc;
} XIconSize;
```

Errors

```
BadAlloc
BadWindow
```

See Also

XAllocIconSize(), XFetchName(), XGetClassHint(), XGetIconName(), XGetIconSizes(), XGetNormal-Hints(), XGetSizeHints(), XGetTransientForHint(), XGetWMHints(), XGetZoomHints(), XSetClassHint(), XSetCommand(), XSetIconName(), XSetNormalHints(), XSetSizeHints(), XSetTransientForHint(), XSet-WMHints(), XSetZoomHints(), XStoreName().

XSetICValues

Name

XSetICValues – set input context attributes.

Synopsis

```
char * XSetICValues(ic, ...)
    XIC ic;
```

Arguments

ic   Specifies the input context.

...   Specifies the variable length argument list to set or get XIC values.

Returns

NULL if no error occurred; otherwise, the name of the first attribute that could not be set.

Availability

Release 5 and later.

Description

XSetICValues() sets the values of input context attributes. The first argument is the input context, and it is followed by a NULL-terminated variable-length argument list of attribute name/value pairs. The standard attributes and their types are listed in the tables below.

Input Context Attributes

Name	Type	Notes
XNInputStyle	XIMStyle	Required at IC creation; may not be changed.
XNClientWindow	Window	Must be set before IC use; may not be changed.
XNFocusWindow	Window	Changes may cause geometry negotiation.
XNResourceName	char *	
XNResourceClass	char *	
XNGeometryCallback	XIMCallback *	
XNFilterEvents	unsigned long	Read-only attribute; may not be set.
XNPreeditAttributes	XVaNestedList	See sub-attributes below.
XNStatusAttributes	XVaNestedList	See sub-attributes below.

Preedit and Status Area Sub-attributes

Name	Type	Notes
XNArea	XRectangle *	
XNAreaNeeded	XRectangle *	
XNSpotLocation	XPoint *	Required at IC creation for XIMPreeditPosition style.
XNColormap	Colormap	
XNStdColormap	Atom	
XNForeground	unsigned long	
XNBackground	unsigned long	
XNBackgroundPixmap	Pixmap	
XNFontSet	XFontSet	Required at IC creation; changes may cause geometry negotiation.
XNLineSpacing	int	Changes may cause geometry negotiation.
XNCursor	Cursor	
XNPreeditStartCallback	XIMCallback *	Required at IC creation for XIMPreeditCallbacks style.
XNPreeditDoneCallback	XIMCallback *	Required at IC creation for XIMPreeditCallbacks style.
XNPreeditDrawCallback	XIMCallback *	Required at IC creation for XIMPreeditCallbacks style.
XNPreeditCaretCallback	XIMCallback *	Required at IC creation for XIMPreeditCallbacks style.
XNStatusStartCallback	XIMCallback *	Required at IC creation for XIMStatusCallbacks style.
XNStatusDoneCallback	XIMCallback *	Required at IC creation for XIMStatusCallbacks style.
XNStatusDrawCallback	XIMCallback *	Required at IC creation for XIMStatusCallbacks style.

In addition to the attribute names above, the special name `XNVaNestedList` indicates that the following argument is a `XVaNestedList` of attribute name/value pairs. When a nested list is encountered in an argument list, the contents of the nested list are processed as if they appeared in the original argument list at that point.

XSetICValues() returns NULL if no error occurred; otherwise, it returns the name of the first attribute that could not be set. An attribute could be not set for any of the following reasons:

- A read-only attribute was set (for example, XNFilterEvents).

- The attribute name is not recognized.

- The input method encountered an input method implementation-dependent error.

Each value to be set must match the type of the attribute.

Errors

BadAtom	A value for an Atom argument does not name a defined Atom.
BadColor	A value for a Colormap argument does not name a defined Colormap.
BadCursor	A value for a Cursor argument does not name a defined Cursor.
BadPixmap	A value for a Pixmap argument does not name a defined Pixmap.
BadWindow	A value for a Window argument does not name a defined Window.

See Also

XCreateIC(), XSetICFocus(), XmbResetIC(), XwcResetIC, XGetICValues().

XSetInputFocus

Name

XSetInputFocus – set the keyboard focus window.

Synopsis

```
XSetInputFocus(display, focus, revert_to, time)
    Display *display;
    Window focus;
    int revert_to;
    Time time;
```

Arguments

display   Specifies a connection to an X server; returned from XOpenDisplay().

focus   Specifies the ID of the window you want to be the keyboard focus. Pass the
           window ID, PointerRoot, or None.

revert_to Specifies which window the keyboard focus reverts to if the focus window
           becomes not viewable. Pass one of these constants: RevertToParent,
           RevertToPointerRoot, or RevertToNone. Must not be a window ID.

time   Specifies the time when the focus change should take place. Pass either a
           timestamp, expressed in milliseconds, or the constant CurrentTime. Also
           returns the time of the focus change when CurrentTime is specified.

Description

XSetInputFocus() changes the keyboard focus and the last-focus-change time. The
function has no effect if time is earlier than the current last-focus-change time or later than
the current X server time. Otherwise, the last-focus-change time is set to the specified time,
with CurrentTime replaced by the current X server time.

XSetInputFocus() generates FocusIn and FocusOut events if focus is different
from the current focus.

XSetInputFocus() executes as follows, depending on what value you assign to the
focus argument:

- If you assign None, all keyboard events are discarded until you set a new focus window.
  In this case, revert_to is ignored.

- If you assign a window ID, it becomes the main keyboard's focus window. If a generated
  keyboard event would normally be reported to this window or one of its inferiors, the
  event is reported normally; otherwise, the event is reported to the focus window. The
  specified focus window must be viewable at the time of the request (else a BadMatch
  error). If the focus window later becomes not viewable, the focus window will change to
  the revert_to argument.

- If you assign `PointerRoot`, the focus window is dynamically taken to be the root window of whatever screen the pointer is on at each keyboard event. In this case, *revert_to* is ignored. This is the default keyboard focus setting.

If the focus window later becomes not viewable, `XSetInputFocus()` evaluates the *revert_to* argument to determine the new focus window:

- If you assign `RevertToParent`, the focus reverts to the parent (or the closest viewable ancestor) automatically with a new *revert_to* argument of `RevertToName`.

- If you assign `RevertToPointerRoot` or `RevertToNone`, the focus reverts to that value automatically. `FocusIn` and `FocusOut` events are generated when the focus reverts, but the last focus change time is not affected.

Errors

BadMatch   *focus* window not viewable when `XSetInputFocus()` called.

BadValue

BadWindow

See Also

XQLength(), XAllowEvents(), XCheckIfEvent(), XCheckMaskEvent(), XCheckTypedEvent(), XCheckTypedWindowEvent(), XCheckWindowEvent(), XEventsQueued(), XGetInputFocus(), XGetMotionEvents(), XIfEvent(), XMaskEvent(), XNextEvent(), XPeekEvent(), XPeekIfEvent(), XPending(), XPutBackEvent(), XSelectInput(), XSendEvent(), XSynchronize(), XWindowEvent().

XSetIOErrorHandler

Name

XSetIOErrorHandler – set a nonfatal error event handler.

Synopsis

```
int (*XSetIOErrorHandler(handler))()
    int (* handler)(Display *, XErrorEvent *)
```

Arguments

handler   Specifies user-defined fatal error handling routine. If NULL, reinvoke the default fatal error handler.

Description

XSetIOErrorHandler() specifies a user-defined error handling routine for fatal errors. This error handler will be called by Xlib if any sort of system call error occurs, such as the connection to the server being lost. The called routine should not return. If the I/O error handler does return, the client process will exit.

If handler is a NULL pointer, the default error handler is reinstated. The default I/O error handler prints an error message and exits.

In Release 4 and later, XSetIOErrorHandler() returns a pointer to the previous error handler.

For more information, see Volume One, Chapter 3, *Basic Window Program*.

See Also

XDisplayName(), *XGetErrorDatabaseText()*, *XGetErrorText()*, *XSetAfterFunction()*, *XSetError-Handler()*, *XSynchronize()*.

XSetLineAttributes

Name

XSetLineAttributes – set the line drawing components in a graphics context.

Synopsis

```
XSetLineAttributes(display, gc, line_width, line_style,
                   cap_style, join_style)
    Display *display;
    GC gc;
    unsigned int line_width;
    int line_style;
    int cap_style;
    int join_style;
```

Arguments

display   Specifies a connection to an X server; returned from XOpenDisplay().

gc   Specifies the graphics context.

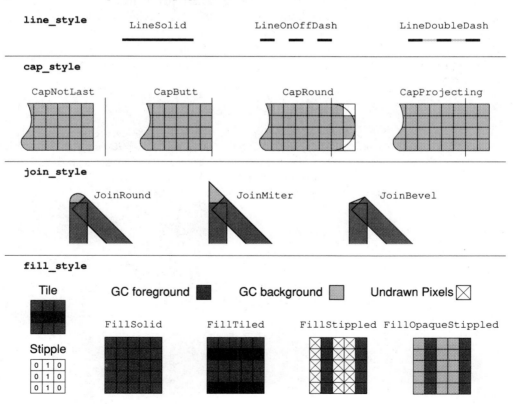

`line_width`	Specifies the line width in the specified graphics context.
`line_style`	Specifies the line style in the specified graphics context. Possible values are `LineSolid`, `LineOnOffDash`, or `LineDoubleDash`.
`cap_style`	Specifies the line and cap style in the specified graphics context. Possible values are `CapNotLast`, `CapButt`, `CapRound`, or `CapProjecting`.
`join_style`	Specifies the line-join style in the specified graphics context. Possible values are `JoinMiter`, `JoinRound`, or `JoinBevel`. If you specify `JoinMitre`, `JoinBevel` is used instead if the angle separating the two lines is less than 11 degrees.

Description

`XSetLineAttributes()` sets four types of line characteristics in the GC: `line_width`, `line_style`, `cap_style`, and `join_style`.

See the description of line and join styles in Volume One, Chapter 5, *The Graphics Context*. See also `XSetDashes()`.

A `line_width` of zero (0) means to use the fastest algorithm for drawing a line of one pixel width. These lines may not meet properly with lines specified as width one or more.

Errors

```
BadAlloc
BadGC
BadValue
```

See Also

XDefaultGC(), XChangeGC(), XCopyGC(), XCreateGC(), XFreeGC(), XGContextFromGC(), XSetArcMode(), XSetBackground(), XSetClipMask(), XSetClipOrigin(), XSetClipRectangles(), XSetDashes(), XSetFillRule(), XSetFillStyle(), XSetForeground(), XSetFunction(), XSetGraphicsExposures(), XSetPlaneMask(), XSetState(), XSetStipple(), XSetSubwindowMode(), XSetTSOrigin().

XSetLocaleModifiers

Name

XSetLocaleModifiers – configure locale modifiers.

Synopsis

```
char *XSetLocaleModifiers(modifier_list)
    char *modifier_list;
```

Arguments

modifier_list Specifies the modifiers.

Returns

The previous locale modifiers on success; NULL on failure.

Availability

Release 5 and later.

Description

XSetLocaleModifiers() sets or queries the X modifiers for the current locale setting. If the *modifier_list* argument is NULL, XSetLocaleModifiers() returns the current settings of the X modifiers without modifying them. Otherwise, the *modifier_list* argument is the empty string or a string of the form "{@*category=value*}", that is, having zero or more concatenated "@*category=value*" entries where *category* is a category name and *value* is the (possibly empty) setting for that category. The values are encoded in the current locale. Category names are restricted to the POSIX Portable Filename Character Set.

The local host X locale modifiers announcer (on POSIX-compliant systems, the XMODIFIERS environment variable) is appended to the *modifier_list* to provide default values on the local host. If a given category appears more than once in the list, the first setting in the list is used. If a given category is not included in the full modifier list, the category is set to an implementation-dependent default for the current locale. An empty value for a category explicitly specifies the implementation-dependent default.

If XSetLocaleModifiers() is successful, it returns a string of the current locale modifiers obtained from the *modifier_list* argument and the XMODIFIERS environment variable. This string is formatted so that it may be passed in a subsequent call to XSetLocale-Modifiers() to restore the state of the X modifiers. When the current modifiers are queried with a NULL *modifier_list* argument, the returned string is also in this format.

If invalid values are given for one or more modifier categories supported by the locale, a NULL pointer is returned, and none of the current modifiers are changed.

At program startup the modifiers that are in effect are unspecified until the first successful call to set them. Whenever the locale is changed, the modifiers that are in effect become unspecified until the next successful call to set them. Clients should always call `XSet-LocaleModifiers()` with a non-`NULL` *modifier_list* after setting the locale, before they call any locale-dependent Xlib routine.

The only standard modifier category currently defined is "im," which identifies the desired input method. The values for this category are not standardized. A single locale may use multiple input methods, switching input method under user control. The modifier may specify the initial input method in effect, or an ordered list of input methods. Multiple input methods may be specified in a single im value string in an implementation-dependent manner.

The returned modifiers string is owned by Xlib and should not be modified or freed by the client. It may be freed by Xlib after the current locale or modifiers is changed. Until freed, it will not be modified by Xlib.

See Also

XSupportsLocale().

XSetModifierMapping

Name

XSetModifierMapping – set keycodes to be used as modifiers (Shift, Control, etc.).

Synopsis

```
int XSetModifierMapping(display, mod_map)
    Display *display;
    XModifierKeymap *mod_map;
```

Arguments

display   Specifies a connection to an X server; returned from XOpenDisplay().

mod_map   Specifies the XModifierKeymap() structure containing the desired modi-
               fier key codes.

Returns

MappingSuccess on success; MappingFailed or MappingBusy on failure.

Description

XSetModifierMapping() is one of two ways to specify the keycodes of the keys that
are to be used as modifiers (like Shift, Control, etc.). XSetModifierMapping() specifies all the keycodes for all the modifiers at once. The other, easier, way is to use perhaps
multiple calls to XInsertModifiermapEntry() and XDeleteModifiermap-
Entry(), which add or delete a single keycode for a single modifier key. XSet-
ModifierMapping() does the work in a single call, but you need to manually set up the
XModifierKeymap() structure pointed to by mod_map. This manual set-up involves
knowing how the XModifierKeymap() structure is defined and organized, as described in
the next three paragraphs.

The XModifierKeymap() structure for the mod_map argument should be created using
XNewModifierMap or XGetModifierMapping(). The max_keypermod element of
the structure specifies the maximum number of keycodes that can be mapped to each modifier. You define this number but there may be an upper limit on a particular server.

The modifiermap element of the structure is an array of keycodes. There are eight by
max_keypermod keycodes in this array: eight because there are eight modifiers, and
max_keypermod because that is the number of keycodes that must be reserved for each
modifier.

The eight modifiers are represented by the constants ShiftMapIndex, LockMapIndex,
ControlMapIndex, Mod1MapIndex, Mod2MapIndex, Mod3MapIndex, Mod4Map-
Index, and Mod5MapIndex. These are not actually used as arguments, but they are convenient for referring to each row in the modifiermap structure while filling it. The definitions of these constants are shown in the "Structures" section below.

Now you can interpret the `modifiermap` array. For each modifier in a given `modifier-map`, the keycodes which correspond are from `modifiermap[index * max_keypermod]` to `modifiermap[((index + 1) * max_keyspermod) -1]` where `index` is the appropriate modifier index definition (`ShiftMapIndex`, `LockMap-Index`, etc.). You must set the `mod_map` array up properly before calling `XSet-ModifierMapping()`. Now you know why `XInsertModifiermapEntry` and `XDeleteModifiermapEntry()` were created!

Zero keycodes are ignored. No keycode may appear twice anywhere in the map (otherwise, a `BadValue` error is generated). In addition, all of the non-zero keycodes must be in the range specified by `min_keycode` and `max_keycode` in the `Display` structure (otherwise a `BadValue` error occurs).

A server can impose restrictions on how modifiers can be changed. For example, certain keys may not generate up transitions in hardware, certain keys may always auto-repeat and therefore be unsuitable for use as modifiers, or multiple modifier keys may not be supported. If a restriction is violated, then the status reply is `MappingFailed`, and none of the modifiers are changed.

`XSetModifierMapping()` can also return `MappingSuccess` or `MappingBusy`. The server generates a `MappingNotify` event on a `MappingSuccess` status. If the new keycodes specified for a modifier differ from those currently defined and any (current or new) keys for that modifier are in the down state, then the status reply is `MappingBusy`, and none of the modifiers are changed.

A value of zero for `modifiermap` indicates that no keys are valid as any modifier.

Structures

```
typedef struct {
    int max_keypermod;         /* server's max # of keys per modifier */
    KeyCode *modifiermap;      /* an 8 by max_keypermod array */
} XModifierKeymap;

/* Modifier name symbols.  Used to build a SetModifierMapping request or
   to read a GetModifierMapping request. */
#define ShiftMapIndex       0
#define LockMapIndex        1
#define ControlMapIndex     2
#define Mod1MapIndex        3
#define Mod2MapIndex        4
#define Mod3MapIndex        5
#define Mod4MapIndex        6
#define Mod5MapIndex        7
```

Errors

BadAlloc

BadValue   Keycode appears twice in the map.

Keycode < *display->*min_keycode or
keycode > *display->max_keycode*.

See Also

*XChangeKeyboardMapping(),   XDeleteModifiermapEntry(),   XDeleteModifiermapEntry(),   XFree-
Modifiermap(),   XGetKeyboardMapping(),   XGetModifierMapping(),   XInsertModifiermapEntry(),
XInsertModifiermapEntry(),   XKeycodeToKeysym(),   XKeysymToKeycode(),   XKeysymToString(),
XLookupKeysym(),   XLookupString(),   XNewModifiermap(),   XQueryKeymap(),   XRebindKeysym(),
XRefreshKeyboardMapping(), XStringToKeysym().*

XSetNormalHints

Name

XSetNormalHints – set the size hints property of a window in normal state (not zoomed or iconified).

Synopsis

```
void XSetNormalHints(display, w, hints)
    Display *display;
    Window w;
    XSizeHints *hints;
```

Arguments

display   Specifies a connection to an X server; returned from XOpenDisplay().

w   Specifies the window ID.

hints   Specifies a pointer to the sizing hints for the window in its normal state.

Description

XSetNormalHints() has been superseded by XSetWMNormalHints() as of Release 4.

XSetNormalHints() sets the XA_WM_NORMAL_HINTS property for the specified window. Applications use XSetNormalHints() to inform the window manager of the size or position desirable for that window. In addition, an application wanting to move or resize itself should call XSetNormalHints() specifying its new desired location and size, in addition to making direct X calls to move or resize. This is because some window managers may redirect window configuration requests, but ignore the resulting events and pay attention to property changes instead.

To set size hints, an application must assign values to the appropriate elements in the hints structure, and also set the flags field of the structure to indicate which members have assigned values and the source of the assignment. These flags are listed in the Structures section below.

For more information on using hints, see Volume One, Chapter 10, *Interclient Communication*.

Structures

```
typedef struct {
    long flags;     /* which fields in structure are defined */
    int x, y;
    int width, height;
    int min_width, min_height;
    int max_width, max_height;
    int width_inc, height_inc;
```

```
struct {
    int x;      /* numerator */
    int y;      /* denominator */
} min_aspect, max_aspect;
int base_width, base_height;
int win_gravity;
} XSizeHints;        /* new fields in R4 here */

#define USPosition      (1L << 0)      /* user specified x, y */
#define USSize          (1L << 1)      /* user specified width, height */

#define PPosition       (1L << 2)      /* program specified position */
#define PSize           (1L << 3)      /* program specified size */
#define PMinSize        (1L << 4)      /* program specified minimum size */
#define PMaxSize        (1L << 5)      /* program specified maximum size */
#define PResizeInc      (1L << 6)      /* program specified resize increments */
#define PAspect         (1L << 7)      /* program specified min/max aspect ratios */
#define PBaseSize       (1L << 8)
#define PWinGravity     (1L << 9)
#define PAllHints (PPosition|PSize|PMinSize|PMaxSize|PResizeInc|PAspect)
```

Errors

```
BadAlloc
BadWindow
```

See Also

XFetchName(), XGetClassHint(), XGetIconName(), XGetIconSizes(), XGetNormalHints(), XGetSize-Hints(), XGetTransientForHint(), XGetWMHints(), XGetZoomHints(), XSetClassHint(), XSet-Command(), XSetIconName(), XSetIconSizes(), XSetSizeHints(), XSetTransientForHint(), XSet-WMHints(), XSetZoomHints(), XStoreName().

XSetPlaneMask

Name

XSetPlaneMask – set the plane mask in a graphics context.

Synopsis

```
XSetPlaneMask(display, gc, plane_mask)
    Display *display;
    GC gc;
    unsigned long plane_mask;
```

Arguments

display   Specifies a connection to an X server; returned from XOpenDisplay().

gc   Specifies the graphics context.

plane_mask Specifies the plane mask. You can use the macro AllPlanes() if desired.

Description

XSetPlaneMask() sets the plane_mask component of the specified GC. The plane_mask determines which planes of the destination drawable are affected by a graphics request.

For more information, see Volume One, Chapter 5, *The Graphics Context*.

Errors

```
BadAlloc
BadGC
```

See Also

XDefaultGC(), XChangeGC(), XCopyGC(), XCreateGC(), XFreeGC(), XGContextFromGC(), XSetArcMode(), XSetBackground(), XSetClipMask(), XSetClipOrigin(), XSetClipRectangles(), XSetDashes(), XSetFillRule(), XSetFillStyle(), XSetForeground(), XSetFunction(), XSetGraphicsExposures(), XSetLineAttributes(), XSetState(), XSetStipple(), XSetSubwindowMode(), XSetTSOrigin().

XSetPointerMapping

Name

XSetPointerMapping – set the pointer button mapping.

Synopsis

```
int XSetPointerMapping(display, map, nmap)
    Display *display;
    unsigned char map[];
    int nmap;
```

Arguments

display   Specifies a connection to an X server; returned from XOpenDisplay().

map   Specifies the mapping list.

nmap   Specifies the number of items in the mapping list.

Returns

MappingSuccess on success; MappingBusy on failure.

Description

XSetPointerMapping() sets the mapping of the pointer buttons. Elements of the map list are indexed starting from 1. The length of the list nmap must be the same as XGet-PointerMapping() returns (you must call that first). The index is a physical button number, and the element of the list defines the effective button number. In other words, if map[2] is set to 1, when the second physical button is pressed, a ButtonPress event will be generated if Button1Mask was selected but not if Button2Mask was selected. The button member in the event will read Button1.

No two elements can have the same non-zero value (else a BadValue error). A value of zero for an element of map disables a button, and values for elements are not restricted in value by the number of physical buttons. If any of the buttons to be altered are currently in the down state, the returned value is MappingBusy and the mapping is not changed.

This function returns either MappingSuccess or MappingBusy. XSetPointer-Mapping() generates a MappingNotify event when it returns MappingSuccess.

Errors

BadValue   Two elements of map[] have same non-zero value.

            nmap not equal to XGetPointerMapping() return value.

See Also

XChangeActivePointerGrab(),   *XChangePointerControl()*,   *XGetPointerControl()*,   *XGetPointer-Mapping()*, *XGrabPointer()*, *XQueryPointer()*, *XUngrabPointer()*, *XWarpPointer()*.

XSetRegion

Name

XSetRegion – set `clip_mask` of the graphics context to the specified region.

Synopsis

```
XSetRegion(display, gc, r)
    Display *display;
    GC gc;
    Region r;
```

Arguments

display   Specifies a connection to an X server; returned from `XOpenDisplay()`.

gc   Specifies the graphics context.

r   Specifies the region.

Description

`XSetRegion()` sets the *clip_mask* component of a GC to the specified region. Thereafter, all drawing made with `gc` will be confined to the area of intersection of the region and the drawable. Once it is set in the GC, the region can be destroyed.

Regions are located using an offset from a point (the *region origin*) which is common to all regions. It is up to the application to interpret the location of the region relative to a drawable. When the region is to be used as a `clip_mask` by calling `XSetRegion()`, the upper-left corner of region relative to the drawable used in the graphics request will be at (`xoffset` + `clip_x_origin`, `yoffset` + `clip_y_origin`), where `xoffset` and `yoffset` are the offset of the region and `clip_x_origin` and `clip_y_origin` are elements of the GC used in the graphics request.

For more information on regions, see Volume One, Chapter 5, *The Graphics Context*, and Chapter 6, *Drawing Graphics and Text*.

Structures

`Region` is a pointer to an opaque structure type.

See Also

XClipBox(), *XCreateRegion()*, *XDestroyRegion()*, *XEmptyRegion()*, *XEqualRegion()*, *XIntersectRegion()*, *XOffsetRegion()*, *XPointInRegion()*, *XPolygonRegion()*, *XRectInRegion()*, *XShrinkRegion()*, *XSubtractRegion()*, *XUnionRectWithRegion()*, *XUnionRegion()*, *XXorRegion()*.

XSetRGBColormaps

Name

XSetRGBColormaps – set an XStandardColormap structure.

Synopsis

```
void XSetRGBColormaps(display, w, std_colormap, count, property)
    Display *display;
    Window w;
    XStandardColormap *std_colormap;
    int count;
    Atom property;
```

Arguments

display   Specifies a connection to an X server; returned from XOpenDisplay().

w   Specifies the window.

std_colormap
                Specifies the XStandardColormap structure to be used.

count   Specifies the number of colormaps.

property   Specifies the property name.

Availability

Release 4 and later.

Description

XSetRGBColormaps() replaces the RGB colormap definition in the specified property on the named window. If the property does not already exist, XSetRGBColormaps() sets the RGB colormap definition in the specified property on the named window. The property is stored with a type of RGB_COLOR_MAP and a format of 32. Note that it is the caller's responsibility to honor the ICCCM restriction that only RGB_DEFAULT_MAP contain more than one definition.

To create a standard colormap, follow this procedure:

1.   Open a new connection to the same server.

2.   Grab the server.

3.   See if *property* is on the property list of the root window for the display, using XGetStandardColormap(). If so, see if the *colormap* field is non-zero. If it is, the colormap already exists.

4.   If the desired property is not present, do the following:

     •   Determine the color capabilities of the display. Choose a visual.

- Create a colormap (not required for XA_RGB_DEFAULT_MAP).
- Call XAllocColorPlanes() or XAllocColorCells() to allocate cells in the colormap.
- Call XStoreColors() to store appropriate color values in the colormap.
- Fill in the descriptive fields in the structure.
- Call XSetRGBColormaps() to set the property on the root window.
- Use XSetCloseDownMode() to make the resource permanent.
- Close the new connection to the server.

5.   Ungrab the server.

6.   XSetRGBColormaps() supersedes XSetStandardColormap().

For more information, see Volume One, Chapter 7, *Color*.

Structures

```
typedef struct {
    Colormap colormap;
    unsigned long red_max;
    unsigned long red_mult;
    unsigned long green_max;
    unsigned long green_mult;
    unsigned long blue_max;
    unsigned long blue_mult;
    unsigned long base_pixel;
    VisualID visualid;              /* added by ICCCM version 1 */
    XID killid;                     /* added by ICCCM version 1 */
} XStandardColormap;
```

Errors

```
BadAlloc
BadAtom
BadWindow
```

See Also

XAllocStandardColormap(), XGetRGBColormaps(), XVisualIDFromVisual().

XSetScreenSaver

Name

XSetScreenSaver – set the parameters of the screen saver.

Synopsis

```
XSetScreenSaver(display, timeout, interval, prefer_blanking,
                 allow_exposures)
    Display *display;
    int timeout, interval;
    int prefer_blanking;
    int allow_exposures;
```

Arguments

display Specifies a connection to an X server; returned from XOpenDisplay().

timeout Specifies the time of inactivity, in seconds, before the screen saver turns on.

interval Specifies the interval, in seconds, between screen saver invocations. This is for intermittent changes to the display, not blanking.

prefer_blanking
Specifies whether to enable screen blanking. Possible values are Dont-PreferBlanking, PreferBlanking, or DefaultBlanking.

allow_exposures
Specifies the current screen saver control values. Possible values are DontAllowExposures, AllowExposures, or Default-Exposures.

Description

XSetScreenSaver() sets the parameters that control the screen saver. *timeout* and *interval* are specified in seconds. A positive *timeout* enables the screen saver. A *timeout* of zero (0) disables the screen saver, while a timeout of −1 restores the default. An *interval* of zero (0) disables the random pattern motion. If no input from devices (keyboard, mouse, etc.) is generated for the specified number of timeout seconds, the screen saver is activated.

For each screen, if blanking is preferred and the hardware supports video blanking, the screen will simply go blank. Otherwise, if either exposures are allowed or the screen can be regenerated without sending exposure events to clients, the screen is tiled with the root window background tile, with a random origin, each *interval* seconds. Otherwise, the state of the screen does not change. All screen states are restored at the next input from a device.

If the server-dependent screen saver method supports periodic change, *interval* serves as a hint about how long the change period should be, and a value of zero (0) hints that no periodic change should be made. Examples of ways to change the screen include scrambling the color map periodically, moving an icon image about the screen periodically, or tiling the screen with the root window background tile, randomly reoriginated periodically.

For more information on the screen saver, see Volume One, Chapter 13, *Other Programming Techniques*.

Errors

BadValue   *timeout* < −1.

See Also

XActivateScreenSaver(), XForceScreenSaver(), XGetScreenSaver(), XResetScreenSaver().

XSetSelectionOwner

Name

XSetSelectionOwner – set the owner of a selection.

Synopsis

```
XSetSelectionOwner(display, selection, owner, time)
    Display *display;
    Atom selection;
    Window owner;
    Time time;
```

Arguments

display   Specifies a connection to an X server; returned from XOpenDisplay().

selection   Specifies the selection atom. Predefined atoms are XA_PRIMARY and XA_SECONDARY.

owner   Specifies the desired owner of the specified selection atom. This value is either a window ID or None.

time   Specifies the time when the selection should take place. Pass either a timestamp, expressed in milliseconds, or the constant CurrentTime.

Description

XSetSelectionOwner() sets the owner and last-change time of a selection property. This should be called by an application that supports cutting and pasting between windows (or at least cutting), when the user has made a selection of any kind of text, graphics, or data. This makes the information available so that other applications can request the data from the new selection owner using XConvertSelection(), which generates a Selection-Request event specifying the desired type and format of the data. Then the selection owner sends a SelectionNotify using XSendEvent(), which notes that the information is stored in the selection property in the desired format or indicates that it couldn't do the conversion to the desired type.

If *owner* is specified as None, then this client is giving up ownership voluntarily. Otherwise, the new owner is the client executing the request.

If the new owner is not the same as the current owner of the selection, and the current owner is a window, then the current owner is sent a SelectionClear event. This indicates to the old owner that the selection should be unhighlighted.

If the selection owner window is later destroyed, the owner of the selection automatically reverts to None.

The value you pass to the *time* argument must be no earlier than the last-change time of the specified selection, and no later than the current time, or the selection is not affected. The new last-change time recorded is the specified time, with CurrentTime replaced by the current server time. If the X server reverts a selection owner to None, the last-change time is not affected.

For more information on selections, see Volume One, Chapter 10, *Interclient Communication*.

Errors

BadAtom
BadWindow

See Also

XConvertSelection(), *XGetSelectionOwner()*.

Name

XSetSizeHints – set the value of any property of type XA_WM_SIZE_HINTS.

Synopsis

```
XSetSizeHints(display, w, hints, property)
    Display *display;
    Window w;
    XSizeHints *hints;
    Atom property;
```

Arguments

display   Specifies a connection to an X server; returned from XOpenDisplay().

w   Specifies the window ID.

hints   Specifies a pointer to the size hints.

property   Specifies the property atom.

Description

XSetSizeHints() has been superseded by XSetWMSizeHints() as of Release 4.

XSetSizeHints() sets the named property on the specified window to the specified XSizeHints structure. This routine is useful if new properties of type XA_WM_SIZE_HINTS are defined. The predefined properties of that type have their own set and get functions, XSetNormalHints() and XSetZoomHints() (XSetWMHints() in Release 4 and later—zoom hints are obsolete).

The flags member of XSizeHints must be set to the OR of the symbols representing each member to be set.

For more information on using hints, see Volume One, Chapter 10, *Interclient Communication*.

Structures

```
typedef struct {
    long flags;    /* which fields in structure are defined */
    int x, y;
    int width, height;
    int min_width, min_height;
    int max_width, max_height;
    int width_inc, height_inc;
    struct {
        int x;     /* numerator */
        int y;     /* denominator */
    } min_aspect, max_aspect;
    int base_width, base_height;
```

```
        int win_gravity;
} XSizeHints;

/* flags argument in size hints */
#define USPosition  (1L << 0)    /* user specified x, y */
#define USSize      (1L << 1)    /* user specified width, height */
#define PPosition   (1L << 2)    /* program specified position */
#define PSize       (1L << 3)    /* program specified size */
#define PMinSize    (1L << 4)    /* program specified minimum size */
#define PMaxSize    (1L << 5)    /* program specified maximum size */
#define PResizeInc  (1L << 6)    /* program specified resize increments */
#define PAspect     (1L << 7)    /* program specified min/max aspect ratios */
#define PBaseSize   (1L << 8)
#define PWinGravity (1L << 9)
#define PAllHints (PPosition|PSize|PMinSize|PMaxSize|PResizeInc|PAspect)
```

Errors

```
BadAlloc
BadAtom
BadWindow
```

See Also

XFetchName(), XGetClassHint(), XGetIconName(), XGetIconSizes(), XGetNormalHints(), XGetSize-Hints(), XGetTransientForHint(), XGetWMHints(), XGetZoomHints(), XSetClassHint(), XSet-Command(), XSetIconName(), XSetIconSizes(), XSetNormalHints(), XSetTransientForHint(), XSet-WMHints(), XSetZoomHints(), XStoreName().

XSetStandardColormap

Name

XSetStandardColormap – change the standard colormap property.

Synopsis

```
void XSetStandardColormap(display, w, cmap_info, property)
    Display *display;
    Window w;
    XStandardColormap *cmap_info;
    Atom property;
```

Arguments

display   Specifies a connection to an X server; returned from XOpenDisplay().

w   Specifies the ID of the window with which this colormap will be associated.

cmap_info Specifies the filled colormap information structure.

property   Specifies the standard colormap property to set. The predefined standard colormaps are: XA_RGB_BEST_MAP, XA_RGB_RED_MAP, XA_RGB_GREEN_ MAP, XA_RGB_BLUE_MAP, XA_RGB_DEFAULT_MAP, and XA_RGB_ GRAY_MAP.

Description

XSetStandardColormap() has been superseded by XSetRGBColormap as of Release 4.

XSetStandardColormap() defines a standard colormap property.

See description of standard colormaps in Volume One, Chapter 7, *Color*.

Errors

```
BadAlloc
BadAtom
BadDrawable
BadWindow
```

Structures

```
typedef struct {
    Colormap colormap;      /* ID of colormap made by XCreateColormap */
    unsigned long red_max;
    unsigned long red_mult;
    unsigned long green_max;
    unsigned long green_mult;
    unsigned long blue_max;
    unsigned long blue_mult;
    unsigned long base_pixel;
```

XSetStandardColormap *(continued)*

```
      Visual ID visualid;
      XID killid;
  } XStandardColormap;      /* new fields in R4 */
```

See Also

XDefaultColormap(), XDisplayCells(), XCopyColormapAndFree(), XCreateColormap(), XFree-Colormap(), XGetStandardColormap(), XInstallColormap(), XListInstalledColormaps(), XSetWindow-Colormap(), XUninstallColormap().

XSetStandardProperties

Name

XSetStandardProperties – set the minimum set of properties for the window manager.

Synopsis

```
XSetStandardProperties(display, w, window_name, icon_name,
                icon_pixmap, argv, argc, hints)
    Display *display;
    Window w;
    char *window_name;
    char *icon_name;
    Pixmap icon_pixmap;
    char **argv;
    int argc;
    XSizeHints *hints
```

Arguments

display	Specifies a connection to an X server; returned from XOpenDisplay().
w	Specifies the window ID.
window_name	Specifies the name of the window. Should be a NULL-terminated string.
icon_name	Specifies the name to be displayed in the window's icon. Should be a NULL-terminated string.
icon_pixmap	Specifies the pixmap that is to be used for the icon, or None. This pixmap must be of depth 1.
argv	Specifies a pointer to the command and arguments used to start the application.
argc	Specifies the number of arguments.
hints	Specifies a pointer to the size hints for the window in its normal state.

Description

XSetStandardProperties() is superseded by XSetWMProperties() in Release 4.

XSetStandardProperties() sets in a single call the most essential properties for a quickie application. XSetStandardProperties() gives a window manager some information about your program's preferences; it probably will not be sufficient for complex programs. If the strings are not in the Host Portable Character Encoding, the result is implementation-dependent.

See Volume One, Chapter 10, *Interclient Communication* for a description of standard properties.

Structures

```
typedef struct {
    long flags;          /* which fields in structure are defined */
    int x, y;
    int width, height;
    int min_width, min_height;
    int max_width, max_height;
    int width_inc, height_inc;
    struct {
        int x;      /* numerator */
        int y;      /* denominator */
    } min_aspect, max_aspect;
    int base_width, base_height;
    int win_gravity;
} XSizeHints;

/* flags argument in size hints */
#define USPosition  (1L << 0)  /* user specified x, y */
#define USSize      (1L << 1)  /* user specified width, height */

#define PPosition   (1L << 2)  /* program specified position */
#define PSize       (1L << 3)  /* program specified size */
#define PMinSize    (1L << 4)  /* program specified minimum size */
#define PMaxSize    (1L << 5)  /* program specified maximum size */
#define PResizeInc  (1L << 6)  /* program specified resize increments */
#define PAspect     (1L << 7)  /* program specified min and max aspect ratios */
#define PBaseSize (1L << 8)
#define PWinGravity (1L << 9)
#define PAllHints (PPosition|PSize|PMinSize|PMaxSize|PResizeInc|PAspect)
```

Errors

```
BadAlloc
BadWindow
```

See Also

XChangeProperty(), XDeleteProperty(), XGetAtomName(), XGetFontProperty(), XGetWindow-Property(), XInternAtom(), XListProperties(), XRotateWindowProperties().

XSetState

Name

XSetState – set the foreground, background, logical function, and plane mask in a graphics context.

Synopsis

```
XSetState(display, gc, foreground, background, function, plane_mask)
    Display *display;
    GC gc;
    unsigned long foreground, background;
    int function;
    unsigned long plane_mask;
```

Arguments

display	Specifies a connection to an X server; returned from XOpenDisplay().
gc	Specifies the graphics context.
foreground	Specifies the foreground for the specified graphics context.
background	Specifies the background for the specified graphics context.
function	Specifies the logical function for the specified graphics context.
plane_mask	Specifies the plane mask for the specified graphics context.

Description

XSetState() sets the foreground and background pixel values, the logical function, and the plane_mask in a GC. See XSetForeground(), XSetBackground(), XSetFunction(), and XSetPlaneMask() for what these members do and appropriate values.

See Volume One, Chapter 5, *The Graphics Context*, for more information.

Errors

```
BadAlloc
BadGC
BadValue
```

See Also

XDefaultGC(), XChangeGC(), XCopyGC(), XCreateGC(), XFreeGC(), XGContextFromGC(), XSetArcMode(), XSetBackground(), XSetClipMask(), XSetClipOrigin(), XSetClipRectangles(), XSetDashes(), XSetFillRule(), XSetFillStyle(), XSetForeground(), XSetFunction(), XSetGraphicsExposures(), XSetLineAttributes(), XSetPlaneMask(), XSetStipple(), XSetSubwindowMode(), XSetTSOrigin().

XSetStipple

Name

XSetStipple – set the stipple in a graphics context.

Synopsis

```
XSetStipple(display, gc, stipple)
    Display *display;
    GC gc;
    Pixmap stipple;
```

Arguments

display   Specifies a connection to an X server; returned from XOpenDisplay().

gc   Specifies the graphics context.

stipple   Specifies the stipple for the specified graphics context.

Description

XSetStipple() sets the stipple component of a GC. The stipple is a pixmap of depth one. It is laid out like a tile. Set bits in the stipple determine which pixels in an area are drawn in the foreground pixel value. Unset bits in the stipple determine which pixels are drawn in the background pixel value if the fill_style is FillOpaque-Stippled. If fill_style is FillStippled, pixels overlain with unset bits in the stipple are not drawn. If fill_style is FillTiled or FillSolid, the stipple is not used.

For more information, see Volume One, Chapter 5, *The Graphics Context*.

Errors

BadAlloc
BadGC
BadMatch
BadPixmap

See Also

XDefaultGC(), *XChangeGC()*, *XCopyGC()*, *XCreateGC()*, *XFreeGC()*, *XGContextFromGC()*, *XSetArc-Mode()*, *XSetBackground()*, *XSetClipMask()*, *XSetClipOrigin()*, *XSetClipRectangles()*, *XSetDashes()*, *XSetFillRule()*, *XSetFillStyle()*, *XSetForeground()*, *XSetFunction()*, *XSetGraphicsExposures()*, *XSet-LineAttributes()*, *XSetPlaneMask()*, *XSetState()*, *XSetSubwindowMode()*, *XSetTSOrigin()*.

XSetSubwindowMode

Name

XSetSubwindowMode – set the subwindow mode in a graphics context.

Synopsis

```
XSetSubwindowMode(display, gc, subwindow_mode)
    Display *display;
    GC gc;
    int subwindow_mode;
```

Arguments

display   Specifies a connection to an X server; returned from XOpenDisplay().

gc   Specifies the graphics context.

subwindow_mode
            Specifies the subwindow mode you want to set for the specified graphics context. Possible values are ClipByChildren or IncludeInferiors.

Description

XSetSubwindowMode() sets the subwindow_mode component of a GC. ClipBy-Children means that graphics requests will be clipped by all viewable children. IncludeInferiors means draw through all subwindows.

For more information, see Volume One, Chapter 5, *The Graphics Context*.

Errors

```
BadAlloc
BadGC
BadValue
```

See Also

XDefaultGC(), XChangeGC(), XCopyGC(), XCreateGC(), XFreeGC(), XGContextFromGC(), XSetArcMode(), XSetBackground(), XSetClipMask(), XSetClipOrigin(), XSetClipRectangles(), XSetDashes(), XSetFillRule(), XSetFillStyle(), XSetForeground(), XSetFunction(), XSetGraphicsExposures(), XSetLineAttributes(), XSetPlaneMask(), XSetState(), XSetStipple(), XSetTSOrigin().

XSetTextProperty

Name

XSetTextProperty – set one of a window's text properties.

Synopsis

```
void XSetTextProperty(display, w, text_prop, property)
    Display *display;
    Window w;
    XTextProperty *text_prop;
    Atom property;
```

Arguments

display   Specifies a connection to an X server; returned from XOpenDisplay().

w   Specifies the window.

text_prop   Specifies the XTextProperty structure to be used.

property   Specifies the property name.

Availability

Release 4 and later.

Description

XSetTextProperty() sets the specified property for the named window with the data, type, format, and number of items determined by the *value* field, the *encoding* field, the *format* field, and the *nitems* field, respectively, of the specified XTextProperty structure.

Structures

```
typedef struct {
    unsigned char *value;          /* same as Property routines */
    Atom encoding;                 /* prop type */
    int format;                    /* prop data format: 8, 16, or 32 */
    unsigned long nitems;          /* number of data items in value */
} XTextProperty;
```

Errors

```
BadAlloc
BadAtom
BadValue
BadWindow
```

See Also

XFreeStringList(), XGetTextProperty(), XStringListToTextProperty(), XTextPropertytoStringList().

XSetTile

Name

XSetTile – set the fill tile in a graphics context.

Synopsis

```
XSetTile(display, gc, tile)
    Display *display;
    GC gc;
    Pixmap tile;
```

Arguments

display   Specifies a connection to an X server; returned from XOpenDisplay().

gc   Specifies the graphics context.

tile   Specifies the desired tile for the specified graphics context.

Description

XSetTile() sets the tile member of the GC. This member of the GC determines the pixmap used to tile areas. The tile must have the same depth as the destination drawable. This tile will only be used in drawing if the fill_style is *FillTiled*.

For more information, see Volume One, Chapter 5, *The Graphics Context*.

Errors

```
BadAlloc
BadGC
BadMatch
BadPixmap
```

See Also

XCreateBitmapFromData(), XCreatePixmap(), XCreatePixmapFromBitmapData(), XFreePixmap(), XQueryBestSize(), XQueryBestStipple(), XQueryBestTile(), XReadBitmapFile(), XSetWindow-BackgroundPixmap(), XSetWindowBorderPixmap(), XWriteBitmapFile().

XSetTransientForHint

Name

XSetTransientForHint – set the XA_WM_TRANSIENT_FOR property for a window.

Synopsis

```
XSetTransientForHint(display, w, prop_window)
    Display *display;
    Window w;
    Window prop_window;
```

Arguments

display   Specifies a connection to an X server; returned from XOpenDisplay().

w   Specifies the window ID, normally of a dialog box popup.

prop_window   Specifies the window ID that the XA_WM_TRANSIENT_FOR property is to be set to. This is usually the main window of the application.

Description

XSetTransientForHint() sets the XA_WM_TRANSIENT_FOR property of the specified window. This should be done when the window w is a temporary child (for example, a dialog box) and the main top-level window of its application is prop_window. Some window managers may use this information to unmap an application's dialog boxes (for example, when the main application window gets iconified).

For more information, see Volume One, Chapter 10, *Interclient Communication*.

Errors

```
BadAlloc
BadWindow
```

See Also

XFetchName(), XGetClassHint(), XGetIconName(), XGetIconSizes(), XGetNormalHints(), XGetSize-Hints(), XGetTransientForHint(), XGetWMHints(), XGetZoomHints(), XSetClassHint(), XSet-Command(), XSetIconName(), XSetIconSizes(), XSetNormalHints(), XSetSizeHints(), XSetWMHints(), XSetZoomHints(), XStoreName().

XSetTSOrigin

Name

XSetTSOrigin – set the tile/stipple origin in a graphics context.

Synopsis

```
XSetTSOrigin(display, gc, ts_x_origin, ts_y_origin)
    Display *display;
    GC gc;
    int ts_x_origin, ts_y_origin;
```

Arguments

display   Specifies a connection to an X server; returned from XOpen-Display().

gc   Specifies the graphics context.

ts_x_origin   Specify the x and y coordinates of the tile/stipple origin.
ts_y_origin

Description

XSetTSOrigin() sets the ts_x_origin and ts_y_origin components in a GC, which are measured relative to the origin of the drawable specified in the drawing request that uses the GC. This controls the placement of the tile or the stipple pattern that patterns an area. To tile or stipple a child so that the pattern matches the parent, you need to subtract the current position of the child window from ts_x_origin and ts_y_origin.

For more information, see Volume One, Chapter 5, *The Graphics Context*.

Errors

```
BadAlloc
BadGC
```

See Also

XDefaultGC(), *XChangeGC()*, *XCopyGC()*, *XCreateGC()*, *XFreeGC()*, *XGContextFromGC()*, *XSetArcMode()*, *XSetBackground()*, *XSetClipMask()*, *XSetClipOrigin()*, *XSetClipRectangles()*, *XSetDashes()*, *XSetFillRule()*, *XSetFillStyle()*, *XSetForeground()*, *XSetFunction()*, *XSetGraphicsExposures()*, *XSetLineAttributes()*, *XSetPlaneMask()*, *XSetState()*, *XSetStipple()*, *XSetSubwindowMode()*.

XSetWindowBackground

Name

XSetWindowBackground – set the background pixel value attribute of a window.

Synopsis

```
XSetWindowBackground(display, w, background_pixel)
    Display *display;
    Window w;
    unsigned long background_pixel;
```

Arguments

display   Specifies a connection to an X server; returned from XOpenDisplay().

w   Specifies the window ID. Must be an InputOutput window.

background_pixel
               Specifies which entry in the colormap is used as the background color. The
               constant CopyFromParent is NOT valid.

Description

XSetWindowBackground() sets the background attribute of a window, setting the
pixel value to be used to fill the background. This overrides any previous call to XSet-
WindowBackground or XSetWindowBackgroundPixmap() on the same window.

XSetWindowBackground() does not change the current window contents immediately.
The background is automatically repainted after Expose events. You can also redraw the
background without Expose events by calling XClearWindow() immediately after.

For more information, see Volume One, Chapter 4, *Window Attributes*.

Errors

BadMatch   Setting background of InputOnly window.

BadWindow

See Also

*XChangeWindowAttributes(), XGetGeometry(), XGetWindowAttributes(), XSetWindowBackground-
Pixmap(), XSetWindowBorder(), XSetWindowBorderPixmap().*

XSetWindowBackgroundPixmap

Name

XSetWindowBackgroundPixmap – change the background tile attribute of a window.

Synopsis

```
XSetWindowBackgroundPixmap(display, w, background_pixmap)
    Display *display;
    Window w;
    Pixmap background_pixmap;
```

Arguments

display   Specifies a connection to an X server; returned from XOpenDisplay().

w   Specifies the window ID. Must be an InputOutput class window.

background_pixmap
                 Specifies a pixmap ID, None or ParentRelative, to be used as a background.

Description

XSetWindowBackgroundPixmap() sets the background_pixmap attribute of a window. This overrides any previous background_pixel or background_pixmap attribute setting set with XSetWindowBackgroundPixmap(), XSetWindow-Background(), or XChangeWindowAttributes(). Drawing into the pixmap that was set as the background pixmap attribute has an undefined effect on the window background. The server may or may not make a copy of the pixmap.

If the background is set to a pixmap, the background is tiled with the pixmap. If the pixmap is not explicitly referenced again, it can be freed, since a copy is maintained in the server. The background of the window will not be redrawn with the new tile until the next Expose event or XClearWindow() call.

If the background is set to None, the window background initially will be invisible and will share the bits of its parent, but only if the background_pixel attribute is not set. When anything is drawn by any client into the area enclosed by the window, the contents will remain until the area is explicitly cleared with XClearWindow(). The background is not automatically refreshed after exposure.

If the background is set to ParentRelative, the parent's background is used, and the origin for tiling is the parent's origin (or the parent's parent if the parent's background_pixmap attribute is also ParentRelative, and so on). The difference between setting ParentRelative and explicitly setting the same pixmap as the parent is the origin of the tiling. The difference between ParentRelative and None is that for Parent-Relative the background is automatically repainted on exposure.

For ParentRelative, the window must have the same depth as the parent, or a Bad-Match error will occur. If the parent has background None, then the window will also have background `None`. The parent's background is re-examined each time the window background is required (when it needs to be redrawn due to mapping or exposure). The window's contents will be lost when the window is moved relative to its parent, and the contents will have to be redrawn.

Changing the `background_pixmap` attribute of the root window to `None` or `Parent-Relative` restores the default.

`XSetWindowBackgroundPixmap()` can only be performed on an `InputOutput` window. A `BadMatch` error will result otherwise.

`XSetWindowBackground()` may be used if a solid color instead of a tile is desired.

For more information, see Volume One, Chapter 4, *Window Attributes*.

Errors

```
BadMatch
BadPixmap
BadWindow
```

See Also

XCreateBitmapFromData(), *XCreatePixmap()*, *XCreatePixmapFromBitmapData()*, *XFreePixmap()*, *XQueryBestSize()*, *XQueryBestStipple()*, *XQueryBestTile()*, *XReadBitmapFile()*, *XSetTile()*, *XSetWindowBorderPixmap()*, *XWriteBitmapFile()*.

XSetWindowBorder

Name

XSetWindowBorder – change a window border pixel value attribute and repaint the border.

Synopsis

```
XSetWindowBorder(display, w, border_pixel)
    Display *display;
    Window w;
    unsigned long border_pixel;
```

Arguments

display   Specifies a connection to an X server; returned from XOpenDisplay().

w   Specifies the window ID. Must be an InputOutput window.

border_pixel
              Specifies the colormap entry with which the server will paint the border.

Description

XSetWindowBorder() sets the border_pixel attribute of window w to a pixel value, and repaints the border. The border is also automatically repainted after Expose events.

Use XSetWindowBorderPixmap() to create a tiled border. On top-level windows, the window manager often resets the border, so applications should not depend on their settings.

For more information, see Volume One, Chapter 4, *Window Attributes*.

Errors

BadMatch   Setting border of InputOnly window.

BadWindow

See Also

XChangeWindowAttributes(), XGetGeometry(), XGetWindowAttributes(), XSetWindowBackground(), XSetWindowBackgroundPixmap(), XSetWindowBorderPixmap().

XSetWindowBorderPixmap

Name

XSetWindowBorderPixmap – change a window border tile attribute and repaint the border.

Synopsis

```
XSetWindowBorderPixmap(display, w, border_pixmap)
    Display *display;
    Window w;
    Pixmap border_pixmap;
```

Arguments

display   Specifies a connection to an X server; returned from `XOpenDisplay()`.

w   Specifies the ID of an `InputOutput` window whose border is to be to a file.

border_pixmap
          Specifies any pixmap or `CopyFromParent`.

Description

`XSetWindowBorderPixmap()` sets the `border_pixmap` attribute of a window and repaints the border. The `border_pixmap` can be freed immediately after the call if no further explicit references to it are to be made. If you specify `CopyFromParent`, a copy of the parent window's border pixmap is used.

This function can only be performed on an `InputOutput` window. On top-level windows, the window manager often resets the border, so applications should not depend on their settings.

Errors

```
BadMatch
BadPixmap
BadWindow
```

See Also

XCreateBitmapFromData(), *XCreatePixmap()*, *XCreatePixmapFromBitmapData()*, *XFreePixmap()*, *XQueryBestSize()*, *XQueryBestStipple()*, *XQueryBestTile()*, *XReadBitmapFile()*, *XSetTile()*, *XSetWindowBackgroundPixmap()*, *XWriteBitmapFile()*.

XSetWindowBorderWidth

Name

XSetWindowBorderWidth – change the border width of a window.

Synopsis

```
XSetWindowBorderWidth(display, w, width)
    Display *display;
    Window w;
    unsigned int width;
```

Arguments

display   Specifies a connection to an X server; returned from XOpenDisplay().

w   Specifies the ID of the window whose border is to be changed.

width   Specifies the width of the window border.

Description

XSetWindowBorderWidth() changes the border width of a window. This request is often used on top-level windows by the window manager as an indication of the current keyboard focus window, so other clients should not depend on the border width of top-level windows.

Errors

BadMatch   Setting border width of an InputOnly window.

BadWindow

See Also

XCirculateSubwindows(), XCirculateSubwindowsDown(), XCirculateSubwindowsUp(), XConfigure-Window(), XLowerWindow(), XMoveResizeWindow(), XMoveWindow(), XQueryTree(), XRaise-Window(), XReparentWindow(), XResizeWindow(), XRestackWindows().

XSetWindowColormap

Name

XSetWindowColormap — set the colormap attribute for a window.

Synopsis

```
XSetWindowColormap(display, w, colormap)
    Display *display;
    Window w;
    Colormap colormap;
```

Arguments

display   Specifies a connection to an X server; returned from XOpenDisplay().

w   Specifies the ID of the window for which you want to set the colormap.

colormap   Specifies the colormap.

Description

XSetWindowColormap() sets the colormap attribute of the specified window. The colormap need not be installed to be set as an attribute. colormap will be used to translate pixel values drawn into this window when colormap is installed in the hardware, which will be taken care of by the window manager.

In Release 3, applications must install their own colormaps if they cannot use the default colormap. In Release 4 and later, they should never do so.

The colormap must have the same visual as the window.

Errors

BadColor   Invalid colormap.

BadMatch

BadWindow

See Also

XChangeWindowAttributes(), XGetGeometry(), XGetWindowAttributes(), XSetWindowBackground(), XSetWindowBackgroundPixmap(), XSetWindowBorder(), XSetWindowBorderPixmap(), XSet-WMColormapWindows().

XSetWMClientMachine

Name

XSetWMClientMachine – set a window's XA_WM_CLIENT_MACHINE property.

Synopsis

```
void XSetWMClientMachine(display, w, text_prop)
    Display *display;
    Window w;
    XTextProperty *text_prop;
```

Arguments

display	Specifies a connection to an X server; returned from XOpenDisplay().
w	Specifies the window.
text_prop	Specifies the XTextProperty structure to be used.

Availability

Release 4 and later.

Description

XSetWMClientMachine() performs an XSetTextProperty() to set the XA_WM_CLIENT_MACHINE property of the specified window. This property should contain the name of the host machine on which this client is being run, as seen from the server.

For more information, see Volume One, Chapter 10, *Interclient Communication*.

Structures

```
typedef struct {
    unsigned char *value;           /* same as Property routines */
    Atom encoding;                  /* prop type */
    int format;                     /* prop data format: 8, 16, or 32 */
    unsigned long nitems;           /* number of data items in value */
} XTextProperty;
```

See Also

XGetWMClientMachine().

XSetWMColormapWindows

Name

XSetWMColormapWindows – set a window's XA_WM_COLORMAP_WINDOWS property.

Synopsis

```
Status XSetWMColormapWindows(display, w, colormap_windows, count)
    Display *display;
    Window w;
    Window *colormap_windows;
    int count;
```

Arguments

display   Specifies a connection to an X server; returned from XOpenDisplay().

w   Specifies the window.

colormap_windows
Specifies the list of windows.

count   Specifies the number of windows in the list.

Returns

Zero on failure, non-zero on success.

Availability

Release 4 and later.

Description

XSetWMColormapWindows() sets the XA_WM_COLORMAP_WINDOWS property on the specified window to the list of windows specified by the *colormap_windows* argument. The property is stored with a type of WINDOW and a format of 32. If it cannot intern the XA_WM_COLORMAP_WINDOWS atom, XSetWMColormapWindows() returns a zero status. Otherwise, it returns a non-zero status.

This property tells the window manager that subwindows of this application need to have their own colormaps installed.

For more information, see Volume One, Chapter 10, *Interclient Communication*.

Errors

```
BadAlloc
BadWindow
```

See Also

XGetWMColormapWindows().

Name

XSetWMHints – set a window manager hints property.

Synopsis

```
XSetWMHints(display, w, wmhints)
    Display *display;
    Window w;
    XWMHints *wmhints;
```

Arguments

display   Specifies a connection to an X server; returned from XOpenDisplay().

w   Specifies the ID for which window manager hints are to be set.

wmhints   Specifies a pointer to the window manager hints.

Description

XSetWMHints() sets the window manager hints that include icon information and location, the initial state of the window, and whether the application relies on the window manager to get keyboard input.

This function is unnecessary in Release 4 and later if you call XSetWMProperties().

See Volume One, Chapter 10, *Interclient Communication*, for a description of each XWMHints structure member.

Structures

```
typedef struct {
    long flags;             /* marks defined fields in structure */
    Bool input;             /* does application need window manager for
                             * keyboard input */
    int initial_state;      /* see below */
    Pixmap icon_pixmap;     /* pixmap to be used as icon */
    Window icon_window;     /* window to be used as icon */
    int icon_x, icon_y;     /* initial position of icon */
    Pixmap icon_mask;       /* icon mask bitmap */
    XID window_group;       /* ID of related window group */
    /* this structure may be extended in the future */
} XWMHints;

/* definitions for the flags field: */
#define InputHint        (1L << 0)
#define StateHint        (1L << 1)
#define IconPixmapHint   (1L << 2)
#define IconWindowHint   (1L << 3)
#define IconPositionHint (1L << 4)
#define IconMaskHint     (1L << 5)
```

```
#define WindowGroupHint  (1L << 6)
#define AllHints (InputHint|StateHint|IconPixmapHint|IconWindowHint| \
   IconPositionHint|IconMaskHint|WindowGroupHint)

/* definitions for the initial state flag: */
#define WithdrawnState   0    /* application would like to be unmapped */
#define NormalState      1    /* most applications want to start this way */
#define IconicState      3    /* application wants to start as an icon */
```

Errors

```
BadAlloc
BadWindow
```

See Also

XAllocWMHints(), XFetchName(), XGetClassHint(), XGetIconName(), XGetIconSizes(), XGetNormal-Hints(), XGetSizeHints(), XGetTransientForHint(), XGetWMHints(), XGetZoomHints(), XSetClassHint(), XSetCommand(). XSetIconName(), XSetIconSizes(), XSetNormalHints(), XSetSizeHints(), XSet-TransientForHint(), XSetZoomHints(), XStoreName(), XSetWMProperties().

XSetWMIconName

Name

XSetWMIconName – set a window's XA_WM_ICON_NAME property.

Synopsis

```
void XSetWMIconName(display, w, text_prop)
    Display *display;
    Window w;
    XTextProperty *text_prop;
```

Arguments

display   Specifies a connection to an X server; returned from XOpenDisplay().

w   Specifies the window.

text_prop   Specifies the XTextProperty structure to be used.

Availability

Release 4 and later.

Description

XSetWMIconName() performs an XSetTextProperty() to set the XA_WM_ICON_NAME property of the specified window. XSetWMIconName() supersedes XSetIconName().

This is usually called by an application to set the property for the window manager. The name should be short, since it is to be displayed in association with an icon.

XSetStandardProperties() (in Release 3) or XSetWMProperties() (in Release 4 and later) also set this property.

For more information, see Volume One, Chapter 10, *Interclient Communication*.

Structures

```
typedef struct {
    unsigned char *value;           /* same as Property routines */
    Atom encoding;                  /* prop type */
    int format;                     /* prop data format: 8, 16, or 32 */
    unsigned long nitems;           /* number of data items in value */
} XTextProperty;
```

See Also

XGetWMIconName(), XGetWMName(), XSetWMName(), XSetWMProperties().

XSetWMName

Name

XSetWMName – set a window's XA_WM_NAME property.

Synopsis

```
void XSetWMName(display, w, text_prop)
    Display *display;
    Window w;
    XTextProperty *text_prop;
```

Arguments

display   Specifies a connection to an X server; returned from XOpenDisplay().

w   Specifies the window.

text_prop   Specifies the XTextProperty structure to be used.

Availability

Release 4 and later.

Description

XSetWMName() performs a XSetTextProperty() to set the XA_WM_NAME property on the specified window. XSetWMName() supersedes XStoreName(). This property can also be set with XSetWMProperties().

XSetWMName() should be used by the application to communicate a string to the window manager. According to current conventions, this string should either:

*   permit the user to identify one of a number of instances of the same client, or

*   provide the user with noncritical state information.

Clients can assume that at least the beginning of this string is visible to the user.

The XA_WM_CLASS property, on the other hand, has two members which should be used to identify the application's instance and class name, for the lookup of resources. See XSet-ClassHint() for details.

For more information, see Volume One, Chapter 10, *Interclient Communication*.

Structures

```
typedef struct {
    unsigned char *value;          /* same as Property routines */
    Atom encoding;                 /* prop type */
    int format;                    /* prop data format: 8, 16, or 32 */
    unsigned long nitems;          /* number of data items in value */
} XTextProperty;
```

See Also

XGetWMIconName(), *XGetWMName()*, *XSetWMIconName()*, *XSetWMProperties()*.

XSetWMNormalHints

Name

XSetWMNormalHints – set a window's XA_WM_NORMAL_HINTS property.

Synopsis

```
void XSetWMNormalHints(display, w, hints)
    Display *display;
    Window w;
    XSizeHints *hints;
```

Arguments

display	Specifies a connection to an X server; returned from XOpenDisplay().
w	Specifies the window.
hints	Specifies the size hints for the window in its normal state.

Availability

Release 4 and later.

Description

XSetWMNormalHints() sets the size hints in the XA_WM_NORMAL_HINTS property on the specified window. The property is stored with a type of WM_SIZE_HINTS and a format of 32. XSetWMNormalHints() supersedes XSetNormalHints(). This property can also be set with XSetWMProperties().

Applications use XSetNormalHints() to inform the window manager of the sizes desirable for that window.

To set size hints, an application must assign values to the appropriate elements in the hints structure, and also set the flags field of the structure to indicate which members have assigned values and the source of the assignment. These flags are listed in the Structures section below.

For more information, see Volume One, Chapter 10, *Interclient Communication*.

Structures

```
typedef struct {
    long flags;          /* marks which fields in this structure */
                         /* are defined */
    int x, y;            /* obsolete for new window mgrs, but clients */
    int width, height;   /* should set so old wm's don't mess up */
    int min_width, min_height;
    int max_width, max_height;
    int width_inc, height_inc;
    struct {
```

```
              int x;  /* numerator */
              int y;  /* denominator */
      } min_aspect, max_aspect;
      int base_width, base_height;        /* added by ICCCM version 1 */
      int win_gravity;                    /* added by ICCCM version 1 */
} XSizeHints;

#define USPosition    (1L << 0)    /* user specified x, y */
#define USSize        (1L << 1)    /* user specified width, height */

#define PPosition     (1L << 2)    /* program specified position
*/
#define PSize         (1L << 3)    /* program specified size */
#define PMinSize      (1L << 4)    /* program specified minimum size */
#define PMaxSize      (1L << 5)    /* program specified maximum size */
#define PResizeInc    (1L << 6)    /* program specified resize increments *
/
#define PAspect       (1L << 7)    /* program specified min/max aspect
ratios */
#define PAllHints (PPosition|PSize|PMinSize|PMaxSize|PResizeInc|PAspect)
#define PBaseSize     (1L << 8)    /* program specified base
                                   * for incrementing */
#define PWinGravity   (1L << 9)    /* program specified window gravity */
```

Errors

```
BadAlloc
BadWindow
```

See Also

XGetWMNormalHints(), XSetWMProperties(), XSetWMSizeHints(), XGetWMSizeHints().

XSetWMProperties

Name

XSetWMProperties – set a window's standard window manager properties.

Synopsis

```
void XSetWMProperties(display, w, window_name, icon_name, argv, argc,
        normal_hints, wm_hints, class_hints)
    Display *display;
    Window w;
    XTextProperty *window_name;
    XTextProperty *icon_name;
    char **argv;
    int argc;
    XSizeHints *normal_hints;
    XWMHints *wm_hints;
    XClassHint *class_hints;
```

Arguments

display   Specifies a connection to an X server; returned from XOpenDisplay().

w   Specifies the window.

window_name   Specifies the window name, which should be a NULL-terminated string.

icon_name   Specifies the icon name, which should be a NULL-terminated string.

argv   Specifies the application's argument list.

argc   Specifies the number of arguments.

normal_hints
                Specifies the size hints for the window in its normal state.

wm_hints   Specifies the XWMHints structure to be used.

class_hints   Specifies the XClassHint structure to be used.

Availability

Release 4 and later.

Description

XSetWMProperties() provides a single programming interface for setting the essential window properties that communicate with window and session managers. XSetWMProperties() supersedes XSetStandardProperties().

If the window_name argument is non-null, XSetWMProperties() calls XSetWMName(), which, in turn, sets the WM_NAME property. If the icon_name argument is non-null, XSetWMProperties() calls XSetWMIconName(), which sets the WM_ICON_NAME property. If the argv argument is non-null, XSetWMProperties()

calls XSetCommand( ), which sets the WM_COMMAND property. Note that an *argc* of 0 is allowed to indicate a zero-length command. XSetWMProperties( ) stores the hostname of this machine using XSetWMClientMachine( ).

If the *normal_hints* argument is non-null, XSetWMProperties( ) calls XSet-WMNormalHints( ), which sets the WM_NORMAL_HINTS property. If the *wm_hints* argument is non-null, XSetWMProperties( ) calls XSetWMHints( ), which sets the WM_HINTS property.

If the *class_hints* argument is non-null, XSetWMProperties( ) calls XSetClass-Hint( ), which sets the WM_CLASS property. If the res_name member in the XClass-Hint structure is set to the null pointer and the RESOURCE_NAME environment variable is set, then value of the environment variable is substituted for res_name. If the res_name member is NULL, and if the environment variable is not set, and if *argv* and *argv[0]* are set, then the value of *argv[0]*, stripped of any directory prefixes, is substituted for res_name.

For more information, see Volume One, Chapter 10, *Interclient Communication*.

Structures

```
typedef struct {
    unsigned char *value;           /* same as Property routines */
    Atom encoding;                  /* prop type */
    int format;                     /* prop data format: 8, 16, or 32 */
    unsigned long nitems;           /* number of data items in value */
} XTextProperty;

typedef struct {
    long flags;             /* marks which fields in this structure */
                            /* are defined */
    int x, y;               /* obsolete for new window mgrs, but clients */
    int width, height;      /* should set so old wm's don't mess up */
    int min_width, min_height;
    int max_width, max_height;
    int width_inc, height_inc;
    struct {
            int x;  /* numerator */
            int y;  /* denominator */
    } min_aspect, max_aspect;
    int base_width, base_height;    /* added by ICCCM version 1 */
    int win_gravity;                /* added by ICCCM version 1 */
} XSizeHints;

/* flags argument in size hints */
#define USPosition (1L << 0)     /* user specified x, y */
#define USSize     (1L << 1)     /* user specified width, height */
#define PPosition  (1L << 2)     /* program specified position */
#define PSize      (1L << 3)     /* program specified size */
```

```
#define PMinSize    (1L << 4)    /* program specified minimum size */
#define PMaxSize    (1L << 5)    /* program specified maximum size */
#define PResizeInc  (1L << 6)    /* program specified resize increments */
#define PAspect     (1L << 7)    /* program specified min/max aspect ratios */
#define PAllHints (PPosition|PSize|PMinSize|PMaxSize|PResizeInc|PAspect)
#define PBaseSize   (1L << 8)    /* program specified base for incrementing */
#define PWinGravity (1L << 9)    /* program specified window gravity */

typedef struct {
    long flags;                  /* marks which fields in this structure */
                                 /* are defined */
    Bool input;                  /* does this application rely on the window */
                                 /* manager to get keyboard input? */
    int initial_state;           /* see below */
    Pixmap icon_pixmap;          /* pixmap to be used as icon */
    Window icon_window;          /* window to be used as icon */
    int icon_x, icon_y;          /* initial position of icon */
    Pixmap icon_mask;            /* icon mask bitmap */
    XID window_group;            /* id of related window group */
    /* this structure may be extended in the future */
} XWMHints;

#define InputHint          (1L << 0)
#define StateHint          (1L << 1)
#define IconPixmapHint     (1L << 2)
#define IconWindowHint     (1L << 3)
#define IconPositionHint   (1L << 4)
#define IconMaskHint       (1L << 5)
#define WindowGroupHint    (1L << 6)

#define AllHints (InputHint|StateHint|IconPixmapHint|IconWindowHint\
    |IconPositionHint|IconMaskHint|WindowGroupHint)
#define PBaseSize   (1L << 8)    /* program specified base for incrementing */
#define PWinGravity (1L << 9)    /* program specified window gravity */

typedef struct {
    char *res_name;
    char *res_class;
} XClassHint;
```

Errors

```
BadAlloc
BadWindow
```

See Also

XGetClassHint(), XGetCommand(), XGetWMHints(), XGetWMIconName(), XGetWMName(), XGet-WMNormalHints(), XSetWMClientMachine(), XSetWMColormapWindows(), XSetWMProtocols().

XSetWMProtocols

Name

XSetWMProtocols – set a window's XA_WM_PROTOCOLS property.

Synopsis

```
Status XSetWMProtocols(display, w, protocols, count)
    Display *display;
    Window w;
    Atom *protocols;
    int count;
```

Arguments

display   Specifies a connection to an X server; returned from XOpenDisplay().

w   Specifies the window.

protocols   Specifies the list of protocols.

count   Specifies the number of protocols in the list.

Returns

Zero on failure, non-zero on success.

Availability

Release 4 and later.

Description

XSetWMProtocols() sets the XA_WM_PROTOCOLS property on the specified window to the list of atoms specified by the protocols argument. The property is stored with a type of ATOM and a format of 32. If it cannot intern the XA_WM_PROTOCOLS atom, XSet-WMProtocols() returns a zero status. Otherwise, it returns a non-zero status.

The list of standard protocols at present is as follows:

WM_TAKE_FOCUS   Assignment of keyboard focus.

WM_SAVE_YOURSELF   Save client state warning.

WM_DELETE_UNKNOWN   Request to delete top-level window.

For more information, see Volume One, Chapter 10, *Interclient Communication*.

Errors

```
BadAlloc
BadWindow
```

See Also

XGetWMProtocols().

XSetWMSizeHints

Name

XSetWMSizeHints – set a window's XA_WM_SIZE_HINTS property.

Synopsis

```
void XSetWMSizeHints(display, w, hints, property)
    Display *display;
    Window w;
    XSizeHints *hints;
    Atom property;
```

Arguments

display   Specifies a connection to an X server; returned from XOpenDisplay().

w   Specifies the window.

hints   Specifies the XSizeHints structure to be used.

property   Specifies the property name.

Availability

Release 4 and later.

Description

XSetWMSizeHints() sets the size hints for the specified property on the named window. The property is stored with a type of XA_WM_SIZE_HINTS and a format of 32. To set a window's normal size hints, you can use the XSetWMNormalHints() function instead. XSetWMSizeHints() supersedes XSetSizeHints().

This routine is useful if new properties of type XA_WM_SIZE_HINTS are defined.

The flags member of XSizeHints must be set to the OR of the symbols representing each member to be set.

For more information, see Volume One, Chapter 10, *Interclient Communication*.

Structures

```
typedef struct {
    long flags;          /* marks which fields in this structure are */
                         /* defined as */
    int x, y;            /* obsolete for new window mgrs, but clients */
    int width, height;   /* should set so old wm's don't mess up */
    int min_width, min_height;
    int max_width, max_height;
    int width_inc, height_inc;
    struct {
            int x;   /* numerator */
```

```
            int y;  /* denominator */
    } min_aspect, max_aspect;
    int base_width, base_height;      /* added by ICCCM version 1 */
    int win_gravity;                  /* added by ICCCM version 1 */
} XSizeHints;

#define USPosition    (1L << 0)    /* user specified x, y */
#define USSize        (1L << 1)    /* user specified width, height */

#define PPosition     (1L << 2)    /* program specified position
*/
#define PSize         (1L << 3)    /* program specified size */
#define PMinSize      (1L << 4)    /* program specified minimum size */
#define PMaxSize      (1L << 5)    /* program specified maximum size */
#define PResizeInc    (1L << 6)    /* program specified resize increments *
/
#define PAspect       (1L << 7)    /* program specified min/max aspect
ratios */
#define PAllHints (PPosition|PSize|PMinSize|PMaxSize|PResizeInc|PAspect)
#define PBaseSize     (1L << 8)    /* program specified base for incrementing */
#define PWinGravity   (1L << 9)    /* program specified window gravity */
```

Errors

```
BadAlloc
BadAtom
BadWindow
```

See Also

XAllocSizeHints(), XGetWMNormalHints(), XGetWMSizeHints(), XSetWMNormalHints().

Name

XSetZoomHints – set the size hints property of a zoomed window.

Synopsis

```
XSetZoomHints(display, w, zhints)
    Display *display;
    Window w;
    XSizeHints *zhints;
```

Arguments

display   Specifies a connection to an X server; returned from `XOpenDisplay()`.

w   Specifies the ID of the window for which zoom hints are to be set.

zhints   Specifies a pointer to the zoom hints.

Description

XSetZoomHints() is no longer used as of Release 3.

XSetZoomHints() sets the XA_WM_ZOOM_HINTS property for an application's top-level window in its zoomed state. Many window managers think of windows in three states: iconified, normal, or zoomed, corresponding to small, medium, and large. Applications use XSetZoomHints() to inform the window manager of the size or position desirable for the zoomed window.

In addition, an application wanting to move or resize its zoomed window should call XSetZoomHints() specifying its new desired location and size, in addition to making direct X calls to move or resize. This is because some window managers may redirect window configuration requests, but ignore the resulting events and pay attention to property changes instead.

To set size hints, an application must assign values to the appropriate elements in the hints structure, and set the flags field of the structure to indicate which members have assigned values and the source of the assignment. These flags are listed in the Structures section below.

For more information on using hints, see Volume One, Chapter 10, *Interclient Communication*.

Structures

```
typedef struct {
    long flags;             /* marks defined fields in structure */
    int x, y;
    int width, height;
    int min_width, min_height;
    int max_width, max_height;
```

```
      int width_inc, height_inc;
      struct {
            int x;      /* numerator */
            int y;      /* denominator */
      } min_aspect, max_aspect;
      int base_width, base_height;
      int win_gravity;
} XSizeHints;

/* flags argument in size hints */
#define USPosition  (1L << 0)    /* user specified x, y */
#define USSize      (1L << 1)    /* user specified width, height */

#define PPosition   (1L << 2)    /* program specified position */
#define PSize       (1L << 3)    /* program specified size */
#define PMinSize    (1L << 4)    /* program specified minimum size */
#define PMaxSize    (1L << 5)    /* program specified maximum size */
#define PResizeInc  (1L << 6)    /* program specified resize increments */
#define PAspect     (1L << 7)    /* program specified min/max aspect ratios */
#define PAllHints (PPosition|PSize|PMinSize|PMaxSize|PResizeInc|PAspect)
#define PBaseSize   (1L << 8)
#define WinGravity  (1L << a
```

Errors

```
BadAlloc
BadWindow
```

See Also

XFetchName(), XGetClassHint(), XGetIconName(), XGetIconSizes(), XGetNormalHints(), XGetSize-Hints(), XGetTransientForHint(), XGetWMHints(), XGetZoomHints(), XSetClassHint(), XSet-Command(), XSetIconName(), XSetIconSizes(), XSetNormalHints(), XSetSizeHints(), XSetTransientFor-Hint(), XSetWMHints(), XStoreName().

XShrinkRegion

Name

XShrinkRegion – reduce or expand the size of a region.

Synopsis

```
XShrinkRegion(r, dx, dy)
    Region r;
    int dx, dy;
```

Arguments

r   Specifies the region.

dx
dy   Specify the amounts by which you want to shrink or expand the specified region. Positive values shrink the region while negative values expand the region.

Description

XShrinkRegion() changes the width and/or height of the specified region. Positive values shrink the region; negative values expand the region. It is legal to expand the region in one dimension at the same time as shrinking it in the other dimension. The offset of the region is changed to keep the center of the resized region near its original position.

The exact amount of shrinkage for a given value for dx or dy is not specified by Xlib.

Structures

Region is a pointer to an opaque structure type.

See Also

XClipBox(), XCreateRegion(), XDestroyRegion(), XEmptyRegion(), XEqualRegion(), XIntersect-Region(), XOffsetRegion(), XPointInRegion(), XPolygonRegion(), XRectInRegion(), XSetRegion(), XSubtractRegion(), XUnionRectWithRegion(), XUnionRegion(), XXorRegion().

XStoreBuffer

Name

XStoreBuffer – store data in a cut buffer.

Synopsis

```
XStoreBuffer(display, bytes, nbytes, buffer)
    Display *display;
    char bytes[];
    int nbytes;
    int buffer;
```

Arguments

display   Specifies a connection to an X server; returned from XOpenDisplay().

bytes   Specifies the string of bytes you want stored. The byte string is not necessarily ASCII or NULL-terminated.

nbytes   Specifies the number of bytes in the string.

buffer   Specifies the cut buffer in which to store the byte string. Must be in the range 0-7.

Description

XStoreBuffer() stores the specified data into any one of the eight cut buffers. All eight buffers must be stored into before they can be circulated with XRotateBuffers(). The cut buffers are numbered 0 through 7. Use XFetchBuffer() to recover data from any cut buffer.

Note that selections are the preferred method of transferring data between applications.

For more information on cut buffers, see Volume One, Chapter 13, *Other Programming Techniques*. For more information on selections, see Volume One, Chapter 10, *Interclient Communication*.

Errors

```
BadAlloc
BadAtom
```

See Also

XFetchBuffer(), *XFetchBytes()*, *XRotateBuffers()*, *XStoreBytes()*.

XStoreBytes

Name

XStoreBytes – store data in cut buffer 0.

Synopsis

```
XStoreBytes(display, bytes, nbytes)
    Display *display;
    char bytes[];
    int nbytes;
```

Arguments

display   Specifies a connection to an X server; returned from XOpenDisplay().

bytes   Specifies the string of bytes to store. The byte string is not necessarily ASCII or NULL-terminated.

nbytes   Specifies the number of bytes to store.

Description

XStoreBytes() stores data in cut buffer 0, usually for reading by another client that already knows the meaning of the contents. Note that the cut buffer's contents need not be text, so null bytes are not special.

The cut buffer's contents may be retrieved later by any client calling XFetchBytes().

Use XStoreBuffer() to store data in buffers 1-7. Note that selections are the preferred method of transferring data between applications.

For more information on cut buffers, see Volume One, Chapter 13, *Other Programming Techniques*. For more information on selections, see Volume One, Chapter 10, *Interclient Communication*.

Errors

BadAlloc

See Also

XFetchBuffer(), XFetchBytes(), XRotateBuffers(), XStoreBuffer().

XStoreColor

Xlib – Color Cells –

Name

XStoreColor – set or change the RGB values of a read/write colormap entry to the closest possible hardware color.

Synopsis

```
XStoreColor(display, cmap, colorcell_def)
    Display *display;
    Colormap cmap;
    XColor *colorcell_def;
```

Arguments

display   Specifies a connection to an X server; returned from XOpen-
               Display().

cmap   Specifies the colormap.

colorcell_def Specifies a pixel value and the desired RGB values.

Description

XStoreColor() changes the RGB values of a colormap entry specified by
colorcell_def.pixel to the closest values possible on the hardware. This pixel value
must be a read/write cell and a valid index into cmap. XStoreColor() changes the red,
green, and/or blue color components in the cell according to the colorcell_def.flags
member, which you set by ORing the constants DoRed, DoGreen, and/or DoBlue.

If the colormap is an installed map for its screen, the changes are visible immediately.

For more information, see Volume One, Chapter 7, Color.

Structures

```
typedef struct {
    unsigned long pixel;
    unsigned short red, green, blue;
    char flags;      /* DoRed, DoGreen, DoBlue */
    char pad;
} XColor;
```

Errors

BadAccess   A specified pixel is unallocated or read-only.

BadColor   Invalid colormap.

BadValue   pixel not valid index into cmap.

762   Xlib Reference Manual

See Also

XBlackPixel(), *XWhitePixel()*, *XAllocColor()*, *XAllocColorCells()*, *XAllocColorPlanes()*, *XAllocNamed-
Color()*, *XFreeColors()*, *XLookupColor()*, *XParseColor()*, *XQueryColor()*, *XQueryColors()*, *XStore-
Colors()*, *XStoreNamedColor()*.

XStoreColors

Name

XStoreColors – set or change the RGB values of read/write colorcells to the closest possible hardware colors.

Synopsis

```
XStoreColors(display, colormap, color, ncolors)
    Display *display;
    Colormap colormap;
    XColor color[ncolors];
    int ncolors;
```

Arguments

display   Specifies a connection to an X server; returned from XOpenDisplay().

colormap   Specifies the colormap.

color   Specifies an array of color definition structures.

ncolors   Specifies the number of XColor structures in color.

Description

XStoreColors() changes the RGB values of each colormap entry specified by color[].pixel to the closest possible hardware colors. Each pixel value must be a read/write cell and a valid index into colormap. XStoreColors() changes the red, green, and/or blue color components in each cell according to the color[].flags member, which you set by ORing the constants DoRed, DoGreen, and/or DoBlue. The specified pixels are changed if they are writable by any client, even if one or more pixels generates an error.

If the colormap is an installed map for its screen, the changes are visible immediately. For more information, see Volume One, Chapter 7, Color.

Structures

```
typedef struct {
    unsigned long pixel;
    unsigned short red, green, blue;
    char flags;     /* DoRed, DoGreen, DoBlue */
    char pad;
} XColor;
```

Errors

BadAccess   A specified pixel is unallocated or read-only.

BadColor   Invalid colormap.

BadValue   A specified pixel is not a valid entry into *colormap*.

See Also

XBlackPixel(), *XWhitePixel()*, *XAllocColor()*, *XAllocColorCells()*, *XAllocColorPlanes()*, *XAllocNamed-Color()*, *XFreeColors()*, *XLookupColor()*, *XParseColor()*, *XQueryColor()*, *XQueryColors()*, *XStore-Color()*, *XStoreNamedColor()*.

XStoreName

Name

XStoreName – assign a name to a window for the window manager.

Synopsis

```
XStoreName(display, w, window_name)
    Display *display;
    Window w;
    char *window_name;
```

Arguments

display   Specifies a connection to an X server; returned from XOpenDisplay().

w   Specifies the ID of the window to which you want to assign a name.

window_name   Specifies the name of the window. The name should be a NULL-terminated
                string. If the string is not in the Host Portable Character Encoding, the
                result is implementation-dependent. This name is returned by any subse-
                quent call to XFetchName().

Description

XStoreName() is superseded in Release 4 by XSetWMName().

XStoreName() sets the XA_WM_NAME property, which should be used by the application to
communicate the following information to the window manager, according to current conventions:

- To permit the user to identify one of a number of instances of the same client.

- To provide the user with noncritical state information.

Clients can assume that at least the beginning of this string is visible to the user.

The XA_WM_CLASS property, on the other hand, has two members which should be used to
identify the application's instance and class name, for the lookup of resources. See XSet-
ClassHint() for details.

For more information, see Volume One, Chapter 10, *Interclient Communication*.

Errors

```
BadAlloc
BadWindow
```

See Also

*XFetchName(), XGetClassHint(), XGetIconName(), XGetIconSizes(), XGetNormalHints(), XGetSize-
Hints(), XGetTransientForHint(), XGetWMHints(), XSetClassHint(), XSetCommand(), XSetIconName(),
XSetNormalHints(), XSetSizeHints(), XSetTransientForHint(), XSetWMHints().*

XStoreNamedColor

Name

XStoreNamedColor – set RGB values of a read/write colorcell by color name.

Synopsis

```
XStoreNamedColor(display, colormap, color, pixel, flags)
    Display *display;
    Colormap colormap;
    char *color;
    unsigned long pixel;
    int flags;
```

Arguments

display   Specifies a connection to an X server; returned from `XOpenDisplay()`.

colormap   Specifies the colormap.

color   Specifies the color name string (for example, "red"). This cannot be in hex format (as used in `XParseColor()`). Uppercase or lowercase is not important. The string should be in ISO LATIN-1 encoding, which means that the first 128 character codes are ASCII, and the second 128 character codes are for special characters needed in western languages other than English.

pixel   Specifies the entry in the colormap to store color in.

flags   Specifies which red, green, and blue indexes are set.

Description

XStoreNamedColor() looks up the named *color* in the database, with respect to the screen associated with *colormap*, then stores the result in the read/write colorcell of *colormap* specified by *pixel*. If the color name is not in the Host Portable Character Encoding, the result is implementation-dependent. Uppercase or lowercase in name does not matter. The *flags* argument, a bitwise OR of the constants DoRed, DoGreen, and Do-Blue, determines which subfields within the pixel value in the cell are written.

For more information, see Volume One, Chapter 7, *Color*.

Errors

BadAccess   *pixel* is unallocated or read-only.

BadColor   Invalid colormap.

BadName   *color* is not in server's color database.

BadValue   *pixel* is not a valid index into *colormap*.

See Also

XDefaultColormap(),   *XDisplayCells()*,   *XCopyColormapAndFree()*,   *XCreateColormap()*,   *XFree-Colormap()*, *XGetStandardColormap()*, *XInstallColormap()*, *XListInstalledColormaps()*, *XSetStandard-Colormap()*, *XSetWindowColormap()*, *XUninstallColormap()*.

XStringListToTextProperty

Name

XStringListToTextProperty – set the specified list of strings to an XTextProperty structure.

Synopsis

```
Status XStringListToTextProperty(list, count, text_prop_return)
    char **list;
    int count;
    XTextProperty *text_prop_return;
```

Arguments

list   Specifies a list of NULL-terminated character strings.

count   Specifies the number of strings.

text_prop_return
                Returns the XTextProperty structure.

Returns

Zero on failure, non-zero on success.

Availability

Release 4 and later.

Description

XStringListToTextProperty() fills the specified XTextProperty structure so that it represents a property of type STRING (format 8) with a value representing the concatenation of the specified list of null-separated character strings. An extra byte containing NULL (which is not included in the nitems member) is stored at the end of the value field of text_prop. The strings are assumed (without verification) to be in the STRING encoding. If insufficient memory is available for the new value string, XStringListToText-Property() does not set any fields in the XTextProperty structure and returns a zero status. Otherwise, it returns a non-zero status. To free the storage for the value field, use XFree().

For more information, see Volume One, Chapter 10, *Interclient Communication*.

Structures

```
typedef struct {
    unsigned char *value;        /* same as Property routines */
    Atom encoding;               /* prop type */
    int format;                  /* prop data format: 8, 16, or 32 */
    unsigned long nitems;        /* number of data items in value */
} XTextProperty;
```

See Also

XSetTextProperty(), *XGetTextProperty()*, *XTextPropertyToStringList()*, *XFreeStringList()*.

XStringToKeysym

Name

XStringToKeysym – convert a keysym name string to a keysym.

Synopsis

```
KeySym XStringToKeysym(string)
    char *string;
```

Arguments

string   Specifies the name of the keysym that is to be converted.

Returns

The keysym.

Description

XStringToKeysym() translates the character string version of a keysym name ("Shift") to the matching keysym which is a constant (XK_Shift). Valid keysym names are listed in *<X11/keysymdef.h>*. If the keysym name is not in the Host Portable Character Encoding, the result is implementation-dependent. If the specified string does not match a valid keysym, XStringToKeysym() returns NoSymbol.

This string is not the string returned in the *buffer* argument of XLookupString(), which can be set with XRebindKeysym(). If that string is used, XStringToKeysym() will return NoSymbol except by coincidence.

In Release 4, XStringToKeysym() can return keysyms that are not defined by the Xlib standard. Note that the set of keysyms that are available in this manner and the mechanisms by which Xlib obtains them is implementation-dependent. (In the MIT sample implementation, the resource file */usr/lib/X11/XKeysymDB* is used starting in Release 4. The keysym name is used as the resource name, and the resource value is the keysym value in uppercase hexadecimal.)

For more information, see Volume One, Chapter 9, *The Keyboard and Pointer*.

See Also

XChangeKeyboardMapping(), XDeleteModifiermapEntry(), XFreeModifiermap(), XGetKeyboard-Mapping(), XGetModifierMapping(), XInsertModifiermapEntry(), XKeycodeToKeysym(), XKeysymTo-Keycode(), XKeysymToString(), XLookupKeysym(), XLookupString(), XNewModifierMap, XQuery-Keymap(), XRebindKeysym(), XRefreshKeyboardMapping(), XSetModifierMapping().

XSubImage

Name

XSubImage – create a subimage from part of an image.

Synopsis

```
XImage *XSubImage(ximage, x, y, subimage_width, subimage_height)
    XImage *ximage;
    int x;y;
    unsigned int subimage_width, subimage_height;
```

Arguments

ximage   Specifies a pointer to the image.

x   Specify the x and y coordinates in the existing image where the
y   subimage will be extracted.

subimage_width
subimage_height   Specify the width and height (in pixels) of the new subimage.

Returns

The created image.

Description

XSubImage() creates a new image that is a subsection of an existing one. It allocates the memory necessary for the new XImage structure and returns a pointer to the new image. The data is copied from the source image, and the rectangle defined by x, y, subimage_width, and subimage_height must by contained in the image.

XSubImage() extracts a subimage from an image, while XGetSubImage() extracts an image from a drawable.

For more information on images, see Volume One, Chapter 6, *Drawing Graphics and Text*.

See Also

XImageByteOrder(), XAddPixel(), XCreateImage(), XDestroyImage(), XGetImage(), XGetPixel(), XGet-SubImage(), XPutImage(), XPutPixel().

XSubtractRegion

Name

XSubtractRegion – subtract one region from another.

Synopsis

```
XSubtractRegion(sra, srb, dr_return)
    Region sra, srb;
    Region dr_return;
```

Arguments

sra
srb
Specify the two regions in which you want to perform the computation.

dr_return   Returns the result of the computation.

Description

XSubtractRegion() calculates the difference between the two regions specified (*sra* – *srb*) and puts the result in *dr_return*.

This function returns a region which contains all parts of *sra* that are not also in *srb*.

For more information on regions, see Volume One, Chapter 6, *Drawing Graphics and Text*.

Structures

Region is a pointer to an opaque structure type.

See Also

XClipBox(), *XCreateRegion()*, *XDestroyRegion()*, *XEmptyRegion()*, *XEqualRegion()*, *XIntersect-Region()*, *XOffsetRegion()*, *XPointInRegion()*, *XPolygonRegion()*, *XRectInRegion()*, *XSetRegion()*, *XShrinkRegion()*, *XUnionRectWithRegion()*, *XUnionRegion()*, *XXorRegion()*.

XSupportsLocale

Name

XSupportsLocale – determine locale support.

Synopsis

```
Bool XSupportsLocale( )
```

Returns

True if supported, else False.

Availability

Release 5 and later.

Description

XSupportsLocale( ) returns True if Xlib functions are capable of operating under the current locale. If XSupportsLocale( ) returns False, the client should usually switch to a supported locale or exit. When the current locale is not supported, some Xlib routines will return the status XLocaleNotSupported, and others will silently operate in the default C locale.

See Also

XSetLocaleModifiers().

XSync

Name

XSync – flush the request buffer and wait for all events and errors to be processed by the server.

Synopsis

```
XSync(display, discard)
    Display *display;
    int discard;
```

Arguments

display   Specifies a connection to an X server; returned from XOpenDisplay().

discard   Specifies whether XSync() discards all events on the input queue. This argument is either True or False.

Description

XSync() flushes the request buffer, then waits until all events and errors resulting from previous calls have been received and processed by the X server. Events are placed on the input queue. The client's XError routine is called once for each error received.

If discard is True, XSync() discards all events on the input queue (including those events that were on the queue before XSync() was called).

XSync() is sometimes used with window manipulation functions (by the window manager) to wait for all resulting exposure events. Very few clients need to use this function.

See Also

XFlush().

XSynchronize

Name

XSynchronize – enable or disable synchronization for debugging.

Synopsis

```
int (*XSync*()
    Display *display;
    Bool onoff;
```

Arguments

display   Specifies a connection to an X server; returned from XOpenDisplay().

onoff   Specifies whether to enable or disable synchronization. You can pass
            False (normal asynchronous mode) or True (enable synchronization for
            debugging).

Returns

The previous after function.

Description

XSynchronize() turns on or off synchronous mode for debugging. If onoff is True, it
turns on synchronous behavior; False resets the state to normal mode.

When events are synchronized, they are reported as they occur instead of at some later time,
but server performance is many times slower. This can be useful for debugging complex
event handling routines. Under UNIX, the same result can be achieved without hardcoding
by setting the global variable _Xdebug to True from within a debugger.

XSynchronize() returns the previous after function.

For more information, see Volume One, Chapter 3, *Basic Window Program*.

See Also

XQLength(), XAllowEvents(), XCheckIfEvent(), XCheckMaskEvent(), XCheckTypedEvent(), XCheck-
TypedWindowEvent(), XCheckWindowEvent(), XEventsQueued(), XGetInputFocus(), XGetMotion-
Events(), XIfEvent(), XMaskEvent(), XNextEvent(), XPeekEvent(), XPeekIfEvent(), XPending(), XPut-
BackEvent(), XSelectInput(), XSendEvent(), XSetInputFocus(), XWindowEvent().

XTextExtents

Name

XTextExtents – get string and font metrics locally.

Synopsis

```
XTextExtents(font_struct, string, nchars, direction_return,
                  font_ascent_return, font_descent_return, overall_return)
    XFontStruct *font_struct;
    char *string;
    int nchars;
    int *direction_return;
    int *font_ascent_return, *font_descent_return;
    XCharStruct *overall_return;
```

Arguments

font_struct   Specifies a connection to an XFontStruct structure.

string   Specifies the character string for which metrics are to be returned.

nchars   Specifies the number of characters in the character string.

direction_return
              Returns the value of the direction element of the XFontStruct. Either
              FontRightToLeft or FontLeftToRight.

font_ascent_return
              Returns the font ascent element of the XFontStruct. This is the overall
              maximum ascent for the font.

font_descent_return
              Returns the font descent element of the XFontStruct. This is the over-
              all maximum descent for the font.

overall_return
              Returns the overall characteristics of the string. These are the sum of the
              width   measurements   for   each   character,   the   maximum
              font_ascent_return and font_descent_return, the minimum
              lbearing added to the width of all characters up to the character with the
              smallest lbearing, and the maximum rbearing added to the width of
              all characters up to the character with the largest rbearing.

Description

XTextExtents() returns the dimensions in pixels that specify the bounding box of the
specified string of characters in the named font, and the maximum ascent and descent for the
entire font. This function performs the size computation locally and, thereby, avoids the
roundtrip overhead of XQueryTextExtents(), but it requires a filled XFontStruct.

font_ascent_return and font_descent_return return information about the
font, while overall_return returns information about the given string. The returned

font_ascent_return and *font_descent_return* should usually be used to calculate the line spacing, while the width, rbearing, and lbearing members of *overall_return* should be used for horizontal measures. The total height of the bounding rectangle, good for any string in this font, is *font_ascent_return* + *font_descent_return*.

overall_return.ascent is the maximum of the ascent metrics of all characters in the string. The *overall_return.descent* is the maximum of the descent metrics. The *overall_return.width* is the sum of the character-width metrics of all characters in the string. The *overall_return.lbearing* is the lbearing of the character in the string with the smallest lbearing plus the width of all the characters up to but not including that character. The *overall_return.rbearing* is the rbearing of the character in the string with the largest rbearing plus the width of all the characters up to but not including that character. If the font has no defined default character, undefined characters in the string are taken to have all zero metrics.

For more information on drawing text, see Volume One, Chapter 6, *Drawing Graphics and Text*.

Structures

```
typedef struct {
    XExtData *ext_data;          /* hook for extension to hang data */
    Font fid;                    /* font ID for this font */
    unsigned direction;          /* hint about direction the font is painted */
    unsigned min_char_or_byte2;  /* first character */
    unsigned max_char_or_byte2;  /* last character */
    unsigned min_byte1;          /* first row that exists */
    unsigned max_byte1;          /* last row that exists */
    Bool all_chars_exist;        /* flag if all characters have non-zero size */
    unsigned default_char;       /* char to print for undefined character */
    int n_properties;            /* how many properties there are */
    XFontProp *properties;       /* pointer to array of additional properties */
    XCharStruct min_bounds;      /* minimum bounds over all existing char */
    XCharStruct max_bounds;      /* minimum bounds over all existing char */
    XCharStruct *per_char;       /* first_char to last_char information */
    int ascent;             /* logical extent above baseline for spacing */
    int descent;            /* logical descent below baseline for spacing */
} XFontStruct;

typedef struct {
    short lbearing;              /* origin to left edge of character */
    short rbearing;              /* origin to right edge of character */
    short width;                 /* advance to next char's origin */
    short ascent;                /* baseline to top edge of character */
    short descent;               /* baseline to bottom edge of character */
    unsigned short attributes;   /* per char flags (not predefined) */
} XCharStruct;
```

See Also

XDrawImageString(), *XDrawImageString16()*, *XDrawString()*, *XDrawString16()*, *XDrawText()*, *XDraw-Text16()*, *XQueryTextExtents()*, *XQueryTextExtents16()*, *XTextExtents16()*, *XTextWidth()*, *XText-Width16()*.

XTextExtents16

Name

XTextExtents16 – get string and font metrics of a 16-bit character string, locally.

Synopsis

```
XTextExtents16(font_struct, string, nchars, direction_return,
        font_ascent_return, font_descent_return, overall_return)
    XFontStruct *font_struct;
    XChar2b *string;
    int nchars;
    int *direction_return;
    int *font_ascent_return, *font_descent_return;
    XCharStruct *overall_return;
```

Arguments

font_struct   Specifies an XFontStruct structure.

string   Specifies the character string made up of XChar2b structures.

nchars   Specifies the number of characters in the character string.

direction_return
               Returns the value of the direction element of the XFontStruct. Font-
               RightToLeft of FontLeftToRight.

font_ascent_return
               Returns the font ascent element of the XFontStruct. This is the overall
               maximum ascent for the font.

font_descent_return
               Returns the font descent element of the XFontStruct. This is the over-
               all maximum descent for the font.

overall_return
               Returns the overall characteristics of the string. These are the sum of the
               width measurements for each character, the maximum
               font_ascent_return and font_descent_return, the minimum
               lbearing added to the width of all characters up to the character with the
               smallest lbearing, and the maximum rbearing added to the width of
               all characters up to the character with the largest rbearing.

Description

XTextExtents16() returns the dimensions in pixels that specify the bounding box of the
specified string of characters in the named font, and the maximum ascent and descent for the
entire font. This function performs the size computation locally and, thereby, avoids the
roundtrip overhead of XQueryTextExtents16(), but it requires a filled XFont-
Struct.

font_ascent_return and *font_descent_return* return information about the font, while *overall_return* returns information about the given string. The returned *font_ascent_return* and *font_descent_return* should usually be used to calculate the line spacing, while the width, rbearing, and lbearing members of *overall_return* should be used for horizontal measures. The total height of the bounding rectangle, good for any string in this font, is *font_ascent_return* + *font_descent_return*.

overall_return.ascent is the maximum of the ascent metrics of all characters in the string. The *overall_return.descent* is the maximum of the descent metrics. The *overall_return.width* is the sum of the character-width metrics of all characters in the string. The *overall_return.lbearing* is the lbearing of the character in the string with the smallest lbearing plus the width of all the characters up to but not including that character. The *overall_return.rbearing* is the rbearing of the character in the string with the largest rbearing plus the width of all the characters up to but not including that character.

For fonts defined with linear indexing rather than 2-byte matrix indexing, each XChar2b structure is interpretd as a 16-bit number with byte1 as the most-significant byte. If the font has no defined default character, undefined characters in the string are taken to have all zero metrics. For more information on drawing text, see Volume One, Chapter 6, *Drawing Graphics and Text*.

Structures

```
typedef struct {
    short lbearing;              /* origin to left edge of character */
    short rbearing;              /* origin to right edge of character */
    short width;                 /* advance to next char's origin */
    short ascent;                /* baseline to top edge of character */
    short descent;               /* baseline to bottom edge of character */
    unsigned short attributes;   /* per char flags (not predefined) */
} XCharStruct;

typedef struct {
    XExtData *ext_data;             /* hook for extension to hang data */
    Font fid;                       /* font ID for this font */
    unsigned direction;             /* hint about direction the font is painted */
    unsigned min_char_or_byte2;     /* first character */
    unsigned max_char_or_byte2;     /* last character */
    unsigned min_byte1;             /* first row that exists */
    unsigned max_byte1;             /* last row that exists */
    Bool all_chars_exist;           /* flag if all characters have non-zero size*/
    unsigned default_char;          /* char to print for undefined character */
    int n_properties;               /* how many properties there are */
    XFontProp *properties;          /* pointer to array of additional properties*/
    XCharStruct min_bounds;         /* minimum bounds over all existing char*/
    XCharStruct max_bounds;         /* minimum bounds over all existing char*/
```

```
    XCharStruct *per_char;        /* first_char to last_char information */
    int ascent;      /* logical extent above baseline for spacing */
    int descent;     /* logical descent below baseline for spacing */
} XFontStruct;

typedef struct {    /* normal 16 bit characters are two bytes */
    unsigned char byte1;
    unsigned char byte2;
} XChar2b;
```

See Also

XDrawImageString(), *XDrawImageString16()*, *XDrawString()*, *XDrawString16()*, *XDrawText()*, *XDraw-Text16()*, *XQueryTextExtents()*, *XQueryTextExtents16()*, *XTextExtents()*, *XTextWidth()*, *XTextWidth16()*.

XTextPropertyToStringList

Name

XTextPropertyToStringList – obtain a list of strings from a specified `XTextProperty` structure.

Synopsis

```
Status XTextPropertyToStringList(text_prop, list_return, count_return)
    XTextProperty *text_prop;
    char ***list_return;
    int *count_return;
```

Arguments

text_prop   Specifies the `XTextProperty` structure to be used.

list_return   Returns a list of NULL-terminated character strings.

count_return   Returns the number of strings.

Returns

Zero on failure, non-zero on success.

Availability

Release 4 and later.

Description

`XTextPropertyToStringList()` returns a list of strings representing the null-separated elements of the specified `XTextProperty` structure. The data in `text_prop` must be of type STRING and format 8. Multiple elements of the property (for example, the strings in a disjoint text selection) are separated by a NULL (encoding 0). The contents of the property are not NULL-terminated. If insufficient memory is available for the list and its elements, `XTextPropertyToStringList()` sets no return values and returns a zero status. Otherwise, it returns a non-zero status. To free the storage for the list and its contents, use `XFreeStringList()`.

For more information, see Volume One, Chapter 10, *Interclient Communication*.

Structures

```
typedef struct {
    unsigned char *value;          /* same as Property routines */
    Atom encoding;                 /* prop type */
```

```
    int format;              /* prop data format: 8, 16, or 32 */
    unsigned long nitems;    /* number of data items in value */
} XTextProperty;
```

See Also

XFreeStringList(), XGetTextProperty(), XSetTextProperty(), XStringListToTextProperty().

Name

XTextWidth – get the width in pixels of an 8-bit character string, locally.

Synopsis

```
int XTextWidth(font_struct, string, count)
    XFontStruct *font_struct;
    char *string;
    int count;
```

Arguments

font_struct   Specifies the font description structure of the font in which you want to draw the string.

string   Specifies the character string whose width is to be returned.

count   Specifies the character count in string.

Returns

The width in pixels.

Description

XTextWidth() returns the width in pixels of the specified string using the specified font. This is the sum of the XCharStruct.width for each character in the string. This is also equivalent to the value of overall.width returned by XQueryTextExtents() or XTextExtents(). The calculation is done assuming 8-bit font indexing.

For more information on drawing text, see Volume One, Chapter 6, *Drawing Graphics and Text*.

Structures

```
typedef struct {
    XExtData *ext_data;            /* hook for extension to hang data */
    Font fid;                      /* font ID for this font */
    unsigned direction;            /* hint about direction the font is painted */
    unsigned min_char_or_byte2;    /* first character */
    unsigned max_char_or_byte2;    /* last character */
    unsigned min_byte1;            /* first row that exists */
    unsigned max_byte1;            /* last row that exists */
    Bool all_chars_exist;          /* flag if all characters have non-zero size*/
    unsigned default_char;         /* char to print for undefined character */
    int n_properties;              /* how many properties there are */
    XFontProp *properties;         /* pointer to array of additional properties*/
    XCharStruct min_bounds;        /* minimum bounds over all existing char*/
    XCharStruct max_bounds;        /* minimum bounds over all existing char*/
```

```
      XCharStruct *per_char;     /* first_char to last_char information */
      int ascent;                /* logical extent above baseline for spacing */
      int descent;               /* logical descent below baseline for spacing */
} XFontStruct;
```

See Also

XDrawImageString(), XDrawImageString16(), XDrawString(), XDrawString16(), XDrawText(), XDraw-Text16(), XQueryTextExtents(), XQueryTextExtents16(), XTextExtents(), XTextExtents16(), XText-Width16().

XTextWidth16

Name

XTextWidth16 – get the width in pixels of a 16-bit character string, locally.

Synopsis

```
int XTextWidth16(font_struct, string, count)
    XFontStruct *font_struct;
    XChar2b *string;
    int count;
```

Arguments

font_struct   Specifies the font description structure of the font in which you want to draw the string.

string   Specifies a character string made up of XChar2b structures.

count   Specifies the character count in string.

Returns

The width in pixels.

Description

XTextWidth16() returns the width in pixels of the specified string using the specified font. This is the sum of the XCharStruct.width for each character in the string. This is also equivalent to the value of overall.width returned by XQueryText-Extents16() or XTextExtents16().

The calculation is done assuming 16-bit font indexing.

For more information on drawing text, see Volume One, Chapter 6, *Drawing Graphics and Text*.

Structures

```
typedef struct {
    XExtData *ext_data;              /* hook for extension to hang data */
    Font fid;                       /* font ID for this font */
    unsigned direction;             /* hint about direction the font is painted */
    unsigned min_char_or_byte2;     /* first character */
    unsigned max_char_or_byte2;     /* last character */
    unsigned min_byte1;             /* first row that exists */
    unsigned max_byte1;             /* last row that exists */
    Bool all_chars_exist;           /* flag if all characters have non-zero size */
    unsigned default_char;          /* char to print for undefined character */
    int n_properties;               /* how many properties there are */
    XFontProp *properties;          /* pointer to array of additional properties*/
    XCharStruct min_bounds;         /* minimum bounds over all existing char*/
```

```
    XCharStruct max_bounds;       /* minimum bounds over all existing char*/
    XCharStruct ·*per_char;       /* first_char to last_char information */
    int ascent;      /* logical extent above baseline for spacing */
    int descent;     /* logical descent below baseline for spacing */
} XFontStruct;
```

See Also

XDrawImageString(), XDrawImageString16(), XDrawString(), XDrawString16(), XDrawText(), XDraw-
Text16(), XQueryTextExtents(), XQueryTextExtents16(), XTextExtents(), XTextExtents16(), XTextWidth().

XTranslateCoordinates

Name

XTranslateCoordinates – change the coordinate system from one window to another.

Synopsis

```
Bool XTranslateCoordinates(display, src_w, dest_w, src_x, src_y,
      dest_x_return, dest_y_return, child_return)
   Display *display;
   Window src_w, dest_w;
   int src_x, src_y;
   int *dest_x_return, *dest_y_return;
   Window *child_return;
```

Arguments

display   Specifies a connection to an X server; returned from XOpen-Display().

src_w   Specifies the ID of the source window.

dest_w   Specifies the ID of the frame of reference window.

src_x
src_y   Specify the x and y coordinates within the source window.

dest_x_return
dest_y_return   Return the translated x and y coordinates within the frame of reference window.

child   If the point is contained in a mapped child of the destination window, then that child ID is returned in *child*.

Returns

True if the two windows are on the same screen, else False.

Description

XTranslateCoordinates() translates coordinates from the frame of reference of one window to another.

XTranslateCoordinates() returns False and *dest_x_return* and *dest_y_return* are set to zero if src_w and dest_w are on different screens. In addition, if the coordinates are contained in a mapped child of dest_w, then that child is returned in the *child_return* argument. When src_w and frame_y are on the same screen, XTranslateCoordinates() returns True, sets *dest_x_return* and *dest_y_return* to the location of the point relative to dest_w, and sets *child_return* to None.

This function should be avoided in most applications since it requires a roundtrip request to the server. Most applications benefit from the window-based coordinate system anyway and don't need global coordinates. Window managers often need to perform a coordinate transformation from the coordinate space of one window to another, or unambiguously determine which subwindow a coordinate lies in. `XTranslateCoordinates()` fulfills this need, while avoiding any race conditions by asking the server to perform this operation.

Errors

```
BadWindow
```

See Also

XGeometry, *XParseGeometry()*.

XUndefineCursor

Name

XUndefineCursor – disassociate a cursor from a window.

Synopsis

```
XUndefineCursor(display, w)
    Display *display;
    Window w;
```

Arguments

display   Specifies a connection to an X server; returned from XOpenDisplay().

w   Specifies the ID of the window whose cursor is to be undefined.

Description

XUndefineCursor() sets the cursor attribute for a window to its parent's cursor, undoing the effect of a previous XDefineCursor() for this window. On the root window the default cursor is restored.

Errors

BadWindow

See Also

XCreateFontCursor(), XCreateGlyphCursor(), XCreatePixmapCursor(), XDefineCursor(), XFreeCursor(), XQueryBestCursor(), XQueryBestSize(), XRecolorCursor().

XUngrabButton

Name

XUngrabButton – release a button from a passive grab.

Synopsis

```
XUngrabButton(display, button, modifiers, grab_window)
    Display *display;
    unsigned int button;
    unsigned int modifiers;
    Window grab_window;
```

Arguments

display	Specifies a connection to an X server; returned from XOpenDisplay().
button	Specifies the mouse button to be released from grab. Specify Button1, Button2, Button3, Button4, Button5, or the constant AnyButton, which is equivalent to issuing the ungrab request for all possible buttons.
modifiers	Specifies a set of keymasks. This is a bitwise OR of one or more of the following symbols: ShiftMask, LockMask, ControlMask, Mod1Mask, Mod2Mask, Mod3Mask, Mod4Mask, Mod5Mask, or AnyModifier. AnyModifier is equivalent to issuing the ungrab button request for all possible modifier combinations (including no modifiers).
grab_window	Specifies the ID of the window you want to release the button grab.

Description

XUngrabButton() cancels the passive grab on a button/key combination on the specified window if it was grabbed by this client. A *modifiers* of AnyModifier is equivalent to issuing the ungrab request for all possible modifier combinations (including the combination of no modifiers). A *button* of AnyButton is equivalent to issuing the request for all possible buttons. This call has no effect on an active grab.

For more information, see Volume One, Chapter 9, *The Keyboard and Pointer*.

Errors

BadWindow
BadValue   Invalid *button* or *modifiers* mask.

See Also

XChangeActivePointerGrab(), XGrabButton(), XGrabKey(), XGrabKeyboard(), XGrabPointer(), XGrabServer(), XUngrabKey(), XUngrabKeyboard(), XUngrabPointer(), XUngrabServer().

XUngrabKey

Name

XUngrabKey – release a key from a passive grab.

Synopsis

```
XUngrabKey(display, keycode, modifiers, grab_window)
    Display *display;
    int keycode;
    unsigned int modifiers;
    Window grab_window;
```

Arguments

display   Specifies a connection to an X server; returned from XOpenDisplay().

keycode   Specifies the keycode. This keycode maps to the specific key you want to ungrab. Pass either a keycode or AnyKey.

modifiers   Specifies a set of keymasks. This is a bitwise OR of one or more of the following symbols: ShiftMask, LockMask, ControlMask, Mod1Mask, Mod2Mask, Mod3Mask, Mod4Mask, Mod5Mask, or AnyModifier. AnyModifier is equivalent to issuing the ungrab key request for all possible modifier combinations (including no modifiers).

grab_window   Specifies the ID of the window for which you want to ungrab the specified keys.

Description

XUngrabKey() cancels the passive grab on the key combination on the specified window if it was grabbed by this client. A *modifiers* of AnyModifier is equivalent to issuing the request for all possible modifier combinations (including the combination of no modifiers). A *keycode* of AnyKey is equivalent to issuing the request for all possible nonmodifier key codes. This call has no effect on an active grab.

For more information, see Volume One, Chapter 9, *The Keyboard and Pointer*.

Errors

BadWindow   Invalid *keycode* or *modifiers* mask.
BadValue

See Also

XChangeActivePointerGrab(), *XGrabButton()*, *XGrabKey()*, *XGrabKeyboard()*, *XGrabPointer()*, *XGrabServer()*, *XUngrabButton()*, *XUngrabKeyboard()*, *XUngrabPointer()*, *XUngrabServer()*.

XUngrabKeyboard

Name

XUngrabKeyboard – release the keyboard from an active grab.

Synopsis

```
XUngrabKeyboard(display, time)
    Display *display;
    Time time;
```

Arguments

display   Specifies a connection to an X server; returned from XOpenDisplay().

time   Specifies the time. Pass either a timestamp, expressed in milliseconds, or the constant CurrentTime. If this time is earlier than the last-keyboard-grab time or later than the current server time, the keyboard will not be ungrabbed.

Description

XUngrabKeyboard() releases any active grab on the keyboard by this client. It executes as follows:

- Releases the keyboard and any queued events if this client has it actively grabbed from either XGrabKeyboard() or XGrabKey().

- Does not release the keyboard and any queued events if *time* is earlier than the last-keyboard-grab time or is later than the current X server time.

- Generates FocusIn and FocusOut events.

The X server automatically performs an UngrabKeyboard if the *grab_window* (argument to XGrabKey() and XGrabKeyboard()) becomes unviewable.

For more information, see Volume One, Chapter 9, *The Keyboard and Pointer*.

See Also

XChangeActivePointerGrab(), XGrabButton(), XGrabKey(), XGrabKeyboard(), XGrabPointer(), XGrabServer(), XUngrabButton(), XUngrabKey(), XUngrabPointer(), XUngrabServer().

XUngrabPointer

Name

XUngrabPointer – release the pointer from an active grab.

Synopsis

```
XUngrabPointer(display, time)
    Display *display;
    Time time;
```

Arguments

display Specifies a connection to an X server; returned from XOpenDisplay().

time   Specifies the time when the grab should take place. Pass either a times-tamp, expressed in milliseconds, or the constant CurrentTime. If this time is earlier than the last-pointer-grab time or later than current server time, the pointer will not be grabbed.

Description

XUngrabPointer() releases an active grab on the pointer by the calling client. It executes as follows:

- Releases the pointer and any queued events, if this client has actively grabbed the pointer from XGrabPointer(), XGrabButton(), or from a normal button press.

- Does not release the pointer if the specified time is earlier than the last-pointer-grab time or is later than the current X server time.

- Generates EnterNotify and LeaveNotify events.

The X server performs an XUngrabPointer() automatically if the *event_window* or *confine_to* window (arguments of XGrabButton() and XGrabPointer()) becomes not viewable, or if the confine_to window is moved completely outside the root window.

For more information, see Volume One, Chapter 9, *The Keyboard and Pointer*.

See Also

XChangeActivePointerGrab(), XChangePointerControl(), XGetPointerControl(), XGetPointer-Mapping(), XGrabPointer(), XQueryPointer(), XSetPointerMapping(), XWarpPointer().

XUngrabServer

Name

XUngrabServer – release the server from grab.

Synopsis

```
XUngrabServer(display)
    Display *display;
```

Arguments

display   Specifies a connection to an X server; returned from XOpenDisplay().

Description

XUngrabServer() releases the grabbed server, and begins execution of all the requests queued during the grab. XUngrabServer() is called automatically when a client closes its connection.

For more information, see Volume One, Chapter 9, *The Keyboard and Pointer*.

See Also

XChangeActivePointerGrab(), XGrabButton(), XGrabKey(), XGrabKeyboard(), XGrabPointer(), XGrabServer(), XUngrabButton(), XUngrabKey(), XUngrabKeyboard(), XUngrabPointer().

XUninstallColormap

Name

XUninstallColormap – uninstall a colormap; install default if not already installed.

Synopsis

```
XUninstallColormap(display, colormap)
    Display *display;
    Colormap colormap;
```

Arguments

display   Specifies a connection to an X server; returned from XOpenDisplay().

colormap   Specifies the colormap to be uninstalled.

Description

If colormap is an installed map for its screen, it is uninstalled. If the screen's default colormap is not installed, it is installed.

If colormap is an installed map, a ColormapNotify event is generated on every window having this colormap as an attribute. If a colormap is installed as a result of the uninstall, a ColormapNotify event is generated on every window having that colormap as an attribute.

At any time, there is a subset of the installed colormaps, viewed as an ordered list, called the *required list*. The length of the required list is at most the min_maps specified for each screen in the Display structure. When a colormap is installed with XInstall-Colormap() it is added to the head of the required list and the last colormap in the list is removed if necessary to keep the length of the list at min_maps. When a colormap is uninstalled with XUninstallColormap() and it is in the required list, it is removed from the list. No other actions by the server or the client change the required list. It is important to realize that on all but high-performance workstations, min_maps is likely to be one.

For more information on installing and uninstalling colormaps, see Volume One, Chapter 7, *Color*.

Errors

BadColor   Invalid colormap.

See Also

XDefaultColormap(), XDisplayCells(), XCopyColormapAndFree(), XCreateColormap(), XFreeColormap(), XGetStandardColormap(), XInstallColormap(), XListInstalledColormaps(), XSetStandardColormap(), XSetWindowColormap().

XUnionRectWithRegion

Name

XUnionRectWithRegion – add a rectangle to a region.

Synopsis

```
XUnionRectWithRegion(rectangle, src_region, dest_region_return)
    XRectangle *rectangle;
    Region src_region;
    Region dest_region_return;
```

Arguments

rectangle   Specifies the rectangle to add to the region.

src_region   Specifies the source region to be used.

dest_region_return

        Specifies the resulting region. May be the same as src_region.

Description

XUnionRectWithRegion() computes the destination region from a union of the specified rectangle and the specified source region. The source and destination regions may be the same.

One common application of this function is to simplify the combining of the rectangles specified in contiguous Expose events into a clip_mask in the GC, thus restricting the redrawn areas to the exposed rectangles. Use XUnionRectWithRegion() to combine the rectangle in each Expose event into a region, then call XSetRegion(). XSetRegion() sets the clip_mask in a GC to the region. In this case, src_region and dest_region_return would be the same region.

If src_region and dest_region_return are not the same region, src_region is copied to dest_region_return before the rectangle is added to dest_region_return.

For more information on regions, see Volume One, Chapter 6, *Drawing Graphics and Text*.

Structures

```
typedef struct {
    short x, y;
    unsigned short width, height;
} XRectangle;
```

Region is a pointer to an opaque data type.

See Also

XClipBox(), XDestroyRegion(), XEmptyRegion(), XEqualRegion(), XIntersectRegion(), XOffsetRegion(), XPointInRegion(), XPolygonRegion(), XRectInRegion(), XSetRegion(), XShrinkRegion(), XSubtract-Region(), XUnionRegion(), XXorRegion().

XUnionRegion

Name

XUnionRegion – compute the union of two regions.

Synopsis

```
XUnionRegion(sra, srb, dr_return)
    Region sra, srb;
    Region dr_return;
```

Arguments

sra   Specify the two regions in which you want to perform the computation.
srb

dr_return   Returns the result of the computation.

Description

XUnionRegion() computes the union of two regions and places the result in dr_return. The resulting region will contain all the area of both the source regions.

For more information on regions, see Volume One, Chapter 6, *Drawing Graphics and Text*.

Structures

Region is a pointer to an opaque structure type.

See Also

XClipBox(), *XCreateRegion()*, *XDestroyRegion()*, *XEmptyRegion()*, *XEqualRegion()*, *XIntersectRegion()*, *XOffsetRegion()*, *XPointInRegion()*, *XPolygonRegion()*, *XRectInRegion()*, *XSetRegion()*, *XShrinkRegion()*, *XSubtractRegion()*, *XUnionRectWithRegion()*, *XXorRegion()*.

XUniqueContext

Name

XUniqueContext – create a new context ID (not graphics context).

Synopsis

```
XContext XUniqueContext()
```

Returns

The context ID.

Description

The context manager allows association of arbitrary data with a resource ID. This call creates a unique ID that can be used in subsequent calls to XFindContext(), XDelete-Context(), and XSaveContext().

For more information on the context manager, see Volume One, Chapter 13, *Other Programming Techniques*.

Structures

```
typedef int XContext;
```

See Also

XDeleteContext(), *XFindContext()*, *XSaveContext()*.

XUnloadFont

Name

XUnloadFont – unload a font.

Synopsis

```
XUnloadFont(display, font)
    Display *display;
    Font font;
```

Arguments

display   Specifies a connection to an X server; returned from XOpenDisplay().

font   Specifies the ID of the font to be unloaded.

Description

XUnloadFont() indicates to the server that this client no longer needs the specified font. The font may be unloaded on the X server if this is the last client that needs the font. In any case, the font should never again be referenced by this client because Xlib destroys the resource ID.

For more information on loading and unloading fonts, see Volume One, Chapter 6, *Drawing Graphics and Text*.

Errors

BadFont

See Also

XCreateFontCursor(), XFreeFont(), XFreeFontInfo(), XFreeFontNames(), XFreeFontPath(), XGet-FontPath(), XGetFontProperty(), XListFonts(), XListFontsWithInfo(), XLoadFont(), XLoadQueryFont(), XQueryFont(), XSetFont(), XSetFontPath().

XUnmapSubwindows

Name

XUnmapSubwindows – unmap all subwindows of a given window.

Synopsis

```
XUnmapSubwindows(display, w)
    Display *display;
    Window w;
```

Arguments

display   Specifies a connection to an X server; returned from XOpenDisplay().

w   Specifies the ID of the window whose subwindows are to be unmapped.

Description

XUnmapSubwindows() performs an XUnmapWindow() on all mapped children of *w*, in bottom to top stacking order. (It does not unmap subwindows of subwindows.)

XUnmapSubwindows() also generates an UnmapNotify event on each subwindow and generates exposure events on formerly obscured windows. This function is much more efficient than unmapping many subwindows one at a time, since much of the work need only be performed once for all of the subwindows rather than for each subwindow.

For more information on window mapping, see Volume One, Chapter 2, *X Concepts*.

Errors

BadWindow

See Also

XMapRaised(), XMapSubwindows(), XMapWindow(), XUnmapWindow().

XUnmapWindow

Name

XUnmapWindow – unmap a window.

Synopsis

```
XUnmapWindow(display, w)
    Display *display;
    Window w;
```

Arguments

display   Specifies a connection to an X server; returned from XOpenDisplay().

w   Specifies the window ID.

Description

XUnmapWindow() removes *w* and all its descendants from the screen (but does not unmap the descendents). If *w* is already unmapped, XUnmapWindow() has no effect. Otherwise, *w* is unmapped and an UnmapNotify event is generated. Normal exposure processing on formerly obscured windows is performed.

Descendants of *w* will not be visible until *w* is mapped again. In other words, the subwindows are still mapped, but are not visible because *w* is unmapped. Unmapping a window will generate exposure events on windows that were formerly obscured by *w*.

For more information on window mapping, see Volume One, Chapter 2, *X Concepts*.

Errors

BadWindow

See Also

XMapRaised(), XMapSubwindows(), XMapWindow(), XUnmapSubwindows().

XUnsetICFocus

Name

XUnsetICFocus – unset input context focus.

Synopsis

```
void XUnsetICFocus(ic)
    XIC ic;
```

Arguments

ic   Specifies the input context.

Availability

Release 5 and later.

Description

XUnsetICFocus() allows a client to notify an input method that the specified input context has lost the keyboard focus and that no more input is expected on the focus window attached to that input context. The input method should take action to provide appropriate feedback.

See Also

XCreateIC(), XSetICValues(), XmbResetIC(), XwcResetIC, XSetICFocus().

XVaCreateNestedList

Name

XVaCreateNestedList – allocate a nested variable argument list.

Synopsis

```
XVaNestedList XVaCreateNestedList(dummy, ...)
    int dummy;
```

Arguments

dummy   Unused argument (required by ANSI C).

. . .   Specifies the variable length argument list.

Returns

The variable-length argument list.

Availability

Release 5 and later.

Description

XVaCreateNestedList() creates a nested argument list of type XVaNestedList. The first argument is an integer value which is unused but required because ANSI-C does not allow variable-length argument lists which do not have any "non-variable" arguments. This first argument is followed by a NULL-terminated variable-length argument list. Generally, the arguments will be input method or input context attribute name/value pairs.

Nested lists created in this way may be used in any of the input method and input context functions which require a variable-length argument list. Also, the XNPreedit-Attributes and XNStatusAttributes input context attributes are of this type XVa-NestedList.

XVaCreateNestedList() allocates memory and copies its arguments into a single list pointer which may be used as value for arguments requiring a list value. Any entries are copied as specified. Data passed by reference is not copied; the caller must ensure that data remains valid for the lifetime of the nested list. The list should be freed using XFree() when it is no longer needed.

See Also

XCreateIC(), XSetICValues(), XGetICValues().

XVendorRelease

Name

XVendorRelease, VendorRelease – return vendor release number.

Synopsis

```
int XVendorRelease(display)
      Display *display;
```

Arguments

display   Specifies a connection to an X server; returned from XOpenDisplay().

Returns

The vendor release number.

Description

XVendorRelease() return a number related to a vendor's release of the X server.

The C language macro VendorRelease() is equivalent and slightly more efficient.

Note also that in Release 5, the XlibSpecificationRelease symbol is defined (with the value 5) by Xlib. Before Release 5 this symbol was not defined.

See Also

XServerVendor().

XVisualIDFromVisual

——Xlib – Window Manager Hints—

Name

XVisualIDFromVisual – obtain the visual ID from a `Visual`.

Synopsis

```
VisualID XVisualIDFromVisual(visual)
    Visual *visual;
```

Arguments

visual   Specifies the visual type.

Returns

The visual ID.

Description

`XVisualIDFromVisual()` returns the visual ID for the specified visual. This is needed when filling an `XVisualInfo` structure template before calling `XGetVisualInfo()`.

For more information, see Volume One, Chapter 10, *Interclient Communication*.

See Also

XGetVisualInfo().

808   Xlib Reference Manual

XVisualIDFromVisual

Name

XVisualIDFromVisual – returns the visual ID for the specified visual structure.

Synopsis

```
VisualID XVisualIDFromVisual(visual)
      Visual *visual;
```

Arguments

visual   Specifies the visual structure.

Returns

The visual ID.

Description

XVisualIDFromVisual() returns the visual ID for the specified visual structure. It simply extracts a field from the XVisualInfo structure.

The visual ID is occasionally useful in association with standard colormap structures and in matching or selecting visuals.

There is no macro called VisualIDFromVisual().

XWarpPointer

Name

XWarpPointer – move the pointer to another point on the screen.

Synopsis

```
XWarpPointer(display, src_w, dest_w, src_x, src_y, src_width, src_height,
        dest_x, dest_y)
    Display *display;
    Window src_w, dest_w;
    int src_x, src_y;
    unsigned int src_width, src_height;
    int dest_x, dest_y;
```

Arguments

display	Specifies a connection to an X server; returned from XOpen-Display().
src_w	Specifies the ID of the source window. You can also pass None.
dest_w	Specifies the ID of the destination window. You can also pass None.
src_x src_y	Specify the x and y coordinates within the source window. These are used with src_width and src_height to determine the rectangle the pointer must be in in order to be moved. They are not the present pointer position. If src_w is None, these coordinates are relative to the root window of src_w.
src_width src_height	Specify the width and height in pixels of the source area. Used with src_x and src_y.
dest_x dest_y	Specify the destination x and y coordinates within the destination window. If dest_w is None, these coordinates are relative to the root window of dest_w.

Description

XWarpPointer() moves the pointer suddenly from one point on the screen to another.

If dest_w is a window, XWarpPointer() moves the pointer to [dest_x, dest_y] relative to the destination window's origin. If dest_w is None, XWarpPointer() moves the pointer according to the offsets [dest_x, dest_y] relative to the current position of the pointer.

If src_w is None, the move is independent of the current cursor position (dest_x and dest_y use global coordinates). If the source window is not None, the move only takes place if the pointer is currently contained in a visible portion of the rectangle of the source window (including its inferiors) specified by src_x, src_y, src_width and

src_height. If src_width is zero (0), the pointer must be between src_x and the right edge of the window to be moved. If src_height is zero (0), the pointer must be between src_y and the bottom edge of the window to be moved.

XWarpPointer() cannot be used to move the pointer outside the confine_to window of an active pointer grab. If such an attempt is made, the pointer is moved to the point on the border of the confine_to window nearest the requested destination.

XWarpPointer() generates events as if the user had (instantaneously) moved the pointer.

This function should not be used unless absolutely necessary, and then only in tightly controlled, predictable situations. It has the potential to confuse the user.

Errors

BadWindow

See Also

XChangeActivePointerGrab(), XChangePointerControl(), XGetPointerControl(), XGetPointer-Mapping(), XGrabPointer(), XQueryPointer(), XSetPointerMapping(), XUngrabPointer().

XwcDrawImageString

Name

XwcDrawImageString – draw internationalized wide-character image text.

Synopsis

```
void XwcDrawImageString(display, drawable, font_set, gc, x, y, string,
        num_wchars)
    Display *display;
    Drawable drawable;
    XFontSet font_set;
    GC gc;
    int x, y;
    wchar_t *string;
    int num_wchars;
```

Arguments

display	Specifies the connection to the X server.
drawable	Specifies the drawable.
font_set	Specifies the font set.
gc	Specifies the graphics context.
x, y	Specifies the starting position and baseline of the text, relative to the origin of the specified drawable.
string	Specifies the character string.
num_wchars	Specifies the number of characters in the string argument.

Availability

Release 5 and later.

Description

XwcDrawImageString() fills a destination rectangle with the background pixel defined in the GC and then paints the specified wide-character text with the foreground pixel. The filled rectangle is the rectangle returned to *overall_logical_return* by XmbText-Extents() or XwcTextExtents() for the same text and XFontSet.

When the XFontSet has missing charsets, each unavailable character is drawn with the default string returned by XCreateFontSet(). The behavior for an invalid codepoint is undefined.

XwcDrawImageString() draws with fonts from the font set rather than the font of the GC. For this reason, it may modify the font value of the GC. Except for the font, it uses the same GC components as its pre-X11R5 analog XDrawImageString().

See Also

XDrawImageString(), *XDrawString()*, *XDrawText()*, *XwcDrawString()*, *XwcDrawText()*, *XmbDraw-ImageString()*.

XwcDrawString

Name

XwcDrawString – draw internationalized wide-character text.

Synopsis

```
void XwcDrawString(display, drawable, font_set, gc, x, y, string,
        num_wchars)
    Display *display;
    Drawable drawable;
    XFontSet font_set;
    GC gc;
    int x, y;
    wchar_t *string;
    int num_wchars;
```

Arguments

display	Specifies the connection to the X server.
drawable	Specifies the drawable.
font_set	Specifies the font set.
gc	Specifies the graphics context.
x, y	Specifies the starting position and baseline of the text, relative to the origin of the specified drawable.
string	Specifies the character string.
num_wchars	Specifies the number of characters in the string argument.

Availability

Release 5 and later.

Description

XwcDrawString() draws the specified wide-character text with the foreground pixel. When the XFontSet has missing charsets, each unavailable character is drawn with the default string returned by XCreateFontSet(). The behavior for an invalid codepoint is undefined.

XwcDrawString() draws with fonts from the font set rather than the font of the GC. For this reason, it may modify the font value of the GC. Except for the font, it uses the same GC components as its pre-X11R5 analog XDrawString().

See Also

XDrawImageString(), *XDrawString()*, *XDrawText()*, *XwcDrawImageString()*, *XwcDrawText()*, *Xmb-DrawString()*.

XwcDrawText

Name

XwcDrawText – draw internationalized wide-character text using multiple font sets.

Synopsis

```
void XwcDrawText(display, drawable, gc, x, y, items, nitems)
    Display *display;
    Drawable drawable;
    GC gc;
    int x, y;
    XwcTextItem *items;
    int nitems;
```

Arguments

display	Specifies the connection to the X server.
drawable	Specifies the drawable.
gc	Specifies the graphics context.
x, y	Specifies the starting position and baseline of the text, relative to the origin of the specified drawable.
items	Specifies an array of text items.
nitems	Specifies the number of text items in the array.

Availability

Release 5 and later.

Description

XwcDrawText() allows complex spacing and font set shifts between wide-character text strings. Each text item is processed in turn, with the origin of a text element advanced in the primary draw direction by the escapement of the previous text item. A text item delta specifies an additional escapement of the text item drawing origin in the primary draw direction. A font_set member other than None in an item causes the font set to be used for this and subsequent text items in the items list. Leading text items with font_set member set to None will not be drawn.

XwcDrawText() does not perform any context-dependent rendering between text segments. Clients may compute the drawing metrics by passing each text segment to XwcTextExtents() or XmbTextPerCharExtents(). When the XFontSet has missing charsets, each unavailable character is drawn with the default string returned by XCreateFontSet(). The behavior for an invalid codepoint is undefined.

XwcDrawText() draws with fonts from the font sets of the *items* list rather than the font of the GC. For this reason, it may modify the font value of the GC. Except for the font, it uses the same GC components as its pre-X11R5 analog XDrawText().

Structures

The XwcTextItem structure contains:

```
typedef struct {
    wchar_t *chars;         /* pointer to wide char string */
    int nchars;             /* number of wide characters */
    int delta;              /* pixel delta between strings */
    XFontSet font_set;      /* fonts, None means don't change */
} XwcTextItem;
```

See Also

XDrawImageString(), *XDrawString()*, *XDrawText()*, *XwcDrawImageString()*, *XwcDrawString()*, *XmbDrawText()*.

XwcFreeStringList

Name

XwcFreeStringList – free memory allocated by XwcTextPropertyToTextList.

Synopsis

```
void XwcFreeStringList(list)
    wchar_t **list;
```

Arguments

list   Specifies the list of strings to be freed.

Availability

Release 5 and later.

Description

XwcFreeStringList() frees the string list and component strings allocated by Xwc-
TextPropertyToTextList().

See Also

XwcTextPropertyToTextList().

XwcLookupString

Name

XwcLookupString – obtain composed wide-character input from an input method.

Synopsis

```
int XwcLookupString(ic, event, buffer_return, bytes_buffer,
        keysym_return, status_return)
    XIC ic;
    XKeyPressedEvent *event;
    wchar_t *buffer_return;
    int wchars_buffer;
    KeySym *keysym_return;
    Status *status_return;
```

Arguments

ic	Specifies the input context.
event	Specifies the keypress event to be used.
buffer_return	Returns a wide-character string (if any) from the input method.
wchars_buffer	Specifies the number of wide-characters in return buffer.
keysym_return	Returns the KeySym computed from the event if this argument is not NULL.
status_return	Returns a value indicating what kind of data is returned.

Returns

The length, in wide characters, of the string returned in *buffer_return*, if any.

Availability

Release 5 and later.

Description

XwcLookupString() passes a KeyPress event to an input context, returns composed text in the encoding of the locale of the input context if any is ready, and may return a keysym corresponding to the KeyPress event as well.

There are several possible results of a call to XwcLookupString(), and a client should check the value returned in the *status_return* argument to determine which has occured. The possible values are:

XBufferOverflow
> The input string to be returned is too large for the supplied *buffer_return*. The required size in wide characters is returned as the value of the function, and the contents of *buffer_return* and *keysym_return* are not modified.

The client should re-call the function with the same event and a buffer of adequate size in order to obtain the string.

`XLookupNone`

No consistent input has been composed so far. The contents of *buffer_return* and *keysym_return* are not modified, and the function returns zero.

`XLookupChars`

Some input characters have been composed. They are placed in the *buffer_return* argument, and the string length in wide characters is returned as the value of the function. The string is encoded in the locale bound to the input context. The contents of the *keysym_return* argument is not modified.

`XLookupKeySym`

A KeySym has been returned instead of a string and is returned in *keysym_return*. The contents of the *buffer_return* argument is not modified, and the function returns zero.

`XLookupBoth`

Both a KeySym and a string are returned; `XLookupChars` and `XLookupKeySym` occur simultaneously.

When `XwcLookupString()` returns a string, the return value of the function is the length, in wide characters, of that string. The returned string is a wide-character string in the encoding of the locale of the input context. If that encoding is state-dependent, the string begins in the initial state of the encoding.

When both a keysym and a string are returned, the string does not necessarily correspond to the keysym. An application that is not interested in return keysyms can pass a NULL *keysym_return*

Note that only `KeyPress` events should be passed to `XwcLookupString()`. When `KeyRelease` events are passed, the resulting behavior is undefined. It does not make any difference if the input context passed as an argument to `XmbLookupString()` and `XwcLookupString()` is the one currently in possession of the focus or not. Input may have been composed within an input context before it lost the focus, and that input may be returned on subsequent calls to `XmbLookupString()` or `XwcLookupString()`, even though it no longer has any more keyboard focus.

See Also

XLookupKeysym(), XmbLookupString().

XwcResetIC

Name

XwcResetIC – reset the state of an input context.

Synopsis

```
wchar_t * XwcResetIC(ic)
    XIC ic;
```

Arguments

ic   Specifies the input context.

Returns

Availability

Release 5 and later. Implementation-dependent - see the "Description" section.

Description

XwcResetIC resets an input context to its initial state. Any input pending on that context is deleted. The input method is required to clear the Preedit area, if any, and update the Status area accordingly. Calling this function does not change the input context focus.

The return value of XwcResetIC is implementation-dependent. If there was input pending on the input context, XwcResetIC may return composed wide-character text in the encoding of the locale of the input context, or it may return NULL. If any string is returned, the client is responsible for freeing it by calling XFree().

See Also

XCreateIC(), XSetICFocus(), XSetICValues(), XmbResetIC().

XwcTextEscapement

Name

XwcTextEscapement – obtain the width of internationalized wide-character text.

Synopsis

```
int XwcTextEscapement(font_set, string, num_wchars)
    XFontSet font_set;
    wchar_t *string;
    int num_wchars;
```

Arguments

font_set   Specifies the font set.

string   Specifies the character string.

num_wchars   Specifies the number of characters in the string argument.

Returns

The escapement in pixels.

Availability

Release 5 and later.

Description

XwcTextEscapement() returns the escapement in pixels of the specified wide-character string using the fonts loaded for the specified font set. The escapement is the distance in pixels in the primary draw direction from the drawing origin to the origin of the next character to be drawn, assuming that the rendering of the next character is not dependent on the supplied string.

The escapement is always positive, regardless of the character-rendering order.

See Also

XwcTextExtents(), *XwcTextPerCharExtents()*, *XmbTextEscapement()*.

XwcTextExtents

Name

XwcTextExtents – compute the extents of internationalized wide-character text.

Synopsis

```
int XwcTextExtents(font_set, string, num_wchars, overall_ink_return,
        overall_logical_return)
    XFontSet font_set;
    wchar_t *string;
    int num_wchars;
    XRectangle *overall_ink_return;
    XRectangle *overall_logical_return;
```

Arguments

font_set   Specifies the font set.

string   Specifies the character string.

num_wchars   Specifies the number of characters in the string argument.

overall_ink_return
                    Returns the overall ink dimensions.

overall_logical_return
                    Returns the overall logical dimensions.

Returns

The escapement in pixels.

Availability

Release 5 and later.

Description

XwcTextExtents() sets the components of the specified *overall_ink_return* and *overall_logical_return* arguments to the overall bounding box of the string's image, and the overall logical bounding box of the string's image plus inter-line and inter-character spacing. It returns the value returned by XwcTextEscapement(). The returned metrics are relative to the drawing origin of the string, using the fonts loaded for the specified font set.

If the *overall_ink_return* argument is non-NULL, it is set to the bounding box of the string's character ink. Note that the *overall_ink_return* for a non-descending horizontally drawn Latin character is conventionally entirely above the baseline, that is, *overall_ink_return.height* <= -*overall_ink_return.y*. The *overall_ink_return* for a nonkerned character is entirely at and to the right of the origin, that is, *overall_ink_return.x* >= 0. A character consisting of a single pixel at the origin would have *overall_ink_return* fields $y = 0$, $x = 0$, *width* = 1, and *height* = 1.

If the *overall_logical_return* argument is non-NULL, it is set to the bounding box which provides minimum spacing to other graphical features for the string. Other graphical features, for example, a border surrounding the text, should not intersect this rectangle.

When the XFontSet has missing charsets, metrics for each unavailable character are taken from the default string returned by XCreateFontSet() so that the metrics represent the text as it will actually be drawn. The behavior for an invalid codepoint is undefined.

Structures

```
typedef struct {
    short x, y;
    unsigned short width, height;
} XRectangle;
```

See Also

XwcTextEscapement(), XwcTextPerCharExtents(), XmbTextExtents().

Name

XwcTextListToTextProperty – convert an internationalized wide-character text list to a text property structure.

Synopsis

```
int XwcTextListToTextProperty(display, list, count, style,
        text_prop_return)
    Display *display;
    wchar_t **list;
    int count;
    XICCEncodingStyle style;
    XTextProperty *text_prop_return;
```

Arguments

display   Specifies the connection to the X server.

list   Specifies an array of NULL-terminated wide-character strings.

count   Specifies the number of strings specified.

style   Specifies the manner in which the property is encoded.

text_prop_return
                  Returns the XTextProperty structure.

Returns

Success on success; The number of unconvertible characters, XLocaleNotSupported, or XNoMemory on failure.

Availability

Release 5 and later.

Description

XwcTextListToTextProperty() sets the specified XTextProperty value to a set of null-separated elements representing the concatenation of the specified list of NULL-terminated text strings. A final terminating null is stored at the end of the *value* field of *text_prop_return* but is not included in the *nitems* field.

XwcTextListToTextProperty() sets the encoding field of *text_prop_return* to an Atom (for the specified display), which names the encoding specified by *style*, and converts the specified text list to this encoding for storage in the value field of *text_prop_return*. If the style XStringStyle or XCompoundTextStyle is specified, this encoding is STRING or COMPOUND_TEXT, respectively. If the style XTextStyle is specified, this encoding is the encoding of the current locale. If the style XStdICCText-

Style is specified, this encoding is STRING if the text is fully convertible to STRING, otherwise it is COMPOUND_TEXT.

If insufficient memory is available for the new value string, XwcTextListToText-Property() returns XNoMemory. If the current locale is not supported, it returns XLocaleNotSupported. In both of these error cases, it does not set *text_prop_return*. XmbTextListToTextProperty() will not return XLocale-NotSupported if XSupportsLocale() has returned True for the current locale.

To determine if the functions are guaranteed not to return XLocaleNotSupported, use XSupportsLocale().

If the supplied text is not fully convertible to the specified encoding, XwcTextListTo-TextProperty() returns the number of unconvertible characters. Each unconvertible character is converted to an implementation-defined and encoding-specific default string. If the text is fully convertible, XwcTextListToTextProperty() returns Success. Note that full convertibility to all styles except XStringStyle is guaranteed. If the supplied text contains bytes that are not valid characters in the encoding of the locale ("invalid codepoints"), the result is undefined.

XwcTextListToTextProperty() allocates memory for the *value* field of the XTextProperty. The client is responsible for freeing this memory by calling XFree().

Structures

The XTextProperty structure contains:

```
typedef struct   {
    unsigned char *value;          /* property data */
    Atom encoding;                 /* type of property */
    int format;                    /* 8, 16, or 32 */
    unsigned long nitems;          /* number of items in value */
} XTextProperty;
```

The XICCEncodingStyle type has the following values:

```
typedef enum    {
    XStringStyle,                  /* STRING */
    XCompoundTextStyle,            /* COMPOUND_TEXT */
    XTextStyle,                    /* text in owner's encoding (current locale) */
    XStdICCTextStyle               /* STRING, else COMPOUND_TEXT */
} XICCEncodingStyle;
```

The possible return values of this function are as follows:

```
#define    XNoMemory                 −1
#define    XLocaleNotSupported       −2
#define    XConverterNotFound        −3
#define    XConverterNotFound        −3
```

See Also

XSetTextProperty(), XStringListToTextProperty(), XDefaultString(), XmbTextListToTextProperty(), Xmb-TextPropertyToTextList(), XwcTextPropertyToTextList(), XwcFreeStringList().

XwcTextPerCharExtents

Name

XwcTextPerCharExtents – obtain per-character measurements of an internationalized wide-character text string.

Synopsis

```
Status XwcTextPerCharExtents(font_set, string, num_wchars,
        ink_array_return, logical_array_return, array_size,
        num_chars_return, overall_ink_return, overall_logical_return)
    XFontSet font_set;
    wchar_t *string;
    int num_wchars;
    XRectangle *ink_array_return;
    XRectangle *logical_array_return;
    int array_size;
    int *num_chars_return;
    XRectangle *overall_ink_return;
    XRectangle *overall_logical_return;
```

Arguments

font_set   Specifies the font set.

string   Specifies the character string.

num_wchars   Specifies the number of characters in the string argument.

ink_array_return
                Returns the ink dimensions for each character.

logical_array_return
                Returns the logical dimensions for each character.

array_size   Specifies the size of ink_array_return and the size of logical_array_return. The caller must pass in arrays of this size.

num_chars_return
                Returns the number characters in the string argument.

overall_ink_return
                Returns the overall ink extents of the entire string.

overall_logical_return
                Returns the overall logical extents of the entire string.

Returns

Zero on failure, non-zero on success.

Availability

Release 5 and later.

Description

XwcTextPerCharExtents() returns the text dimensions of each character of the specified text, using the fonts loaded for the specified font set. Each element of *ink_array_return* and *logical_array_return* is set to the corresponding character's drawn metrics, relative to the drawing origin of the string. The number of elements of *ink_array_return* and *logical_array_return* that have been set is returned in *num_chars_return*.

Each element of *ink_array_return* is set to the bounding box of the corresponding character's drawn foreground color. Each element of *logical_array_return* is set to the bounding box which provides minimum spacing to other graphical features for the corresponding character. Other graphical features should not intersect any of the *logical_array_return* rectangles.

Note that an XRectangle represents the effective drawing dimensions of the character, regardless of the number of font glyphs that are used to draw the character, or the direction in which the character is drawn. If multiple characters map to a single character glyph, the dimensions of all the XRectangles of those characters are the same.

When the XFontSet has missing charsets, metrics for each unavailable character are taken from the default string returned by XCreateFontSet(), so that the metrics represent the text as it will actually be drawn. The behavior for an invalid codepoint is undefined.

If the *array_size* is too small for the number of characters in the supplied text, the function returns zero and *num_chars_return* is set to the number of rectangles required. Otherwise, it returns a non-zero value.

If the *overall_ink_return* or *overall_logical_return* argument is non-NULL, XwcTextPerCharExtents() returns the maximum extent of the string's metrics to *overall_ink_return* or *overall_logical_return*, as is done by XwcTextExtents().

Structures

```
typedef struct {
    short x, y;
    unsigned short width, height;
} XRectangle;
```

See Also

XwcTextEscapement(), XwcTextExtents(), XmbTextPerCharExtents().

XwcTextPropertyToTextList

Name

XwcTextPropertyToTextList – convert an internationalized text property to a list of wide-character strings.

Synopsis

```
int XwcTextPropertyToTextList(display, text_prop, list_return,
        count_return)
    Display *display;
    XTextProperty *text_prop;
    wchar_t ***list_return;
    int *count_return;
```

Arguments

display	Specifies the connection to the X server.
text_prop	Specifies the XTextProperty structure to be used.
list_return	Returns a list of NULL-terminated character strings.
count_return	Returns the number of strings.

Returns

Success on success. XNoMemory, XLocaleNotSupported, or XConverterNot-Found on failure. The number of unconvertible characters on partial success.

Availability

Release 5 and later.

Description

XwcTextPropertyToTextList() return a list of wide-character text strings encoded in the current locale representing the null-separated elements of the specified XText-Property structure. The data in text_prop must be format 8.

Multiple elements of the property (for example, the strings in a disjoint text selection) are separated by a null byte. The contents of the property are not required to be NULL-terminated; any terminating null should not be included in text_prop.nitems.

If insufficient memory is available for the list and its elements, XwcTextPropertyTo-TextList() returns XNoMemory. If the current locale is not supported, it returns XLocaleNotSupported. If the encoding field of text_prop is not convertible to the encoding of the current locale, it returns XConverterNotFound. For supported locales, existence of a converter from COMPOUND_TEXT, STRING, or the encoding of the current locale is guaranteed although the actual text may contain unconvertible characters. Conversion of other encodings is implementation-dependent. In all of these error cases, the function does not set any return values.

Otherwise, `XwcTextPropertyToTextList()` returns the list of NULL-terminated text strings to *list_return*, and the number of text strings to *count_return*.

If the value field of *text_prop* is not fully convertible to the encoding of the current locale, the functions return the number of unconvertible characters. Each unconvertible character is converted to a string in the current locale that is specific to the current locale. To obtain the value of this string, use `XDefaultString()`. If all characters are convertible, `XwcTextPropertyToTextList()` returns `Success`. If the text property contains "invalid codepoints" or bytes that are not valid characters in the encoding of the property, the result is undefined.

Structures

The `XTextProperty` structure contains:

```
typedef struct          {
    unsigned char *value;          /* property data */
    Atom encoding;                 /* type of property */
    int format;                    /* 8, 16, or 32 */
    unsigned long nitems;          /* number of items in value */
} XTextProperty;
```

The possible return values of this function are as follows:

```
#define    XNoMemory               -1
#define    XLocaleNotSupported     -2
#define    XConverterNotFound      -3
```

See Also

XSetTextProperty(), *XStringListToTextProperty()*, *XDefaultString()*, *XmbTextListToTextProperty()*, *XmbTextPropertyToTextList()*, *XwcFreeStringList()*, *XwcTextListToTextProperty()*.

XWhitePixel*

Name

XWhitePixel, XWhitePixelOfScreen, WhitePixel, WhitePixelOfScreen – get the white pixel value.

Synopsis

```
unsigned long XWhitePixel(display, screen_number)
      Display *display;
      int screen_number;

unsigned long XWhitePixelOfScreen(screen)
      Screen *screen;
```

Arguments

display   Specifies a connection to an X server; returned from XOpenDisplay().

screen_number
         Specifies the appropriate screen number on the server, as returned by XDefaultScreen*() or the DefaultScreen() macro.

screen   Specifies the appropriate Screen structure, as returned by XDefault-ScreenOfDisplay() or XScreenOfDisplay(), or the Default-ScreenOfDisplay() or ScreenOfDisplay() macros.

Returns

The pixel value.

Description

Each screen has a default colormap which has pixel values for white and white already allocated. These functions return the white pixel value. Note that this pixel value only represents white in a screen's default colormap.

XWhitePixel() and XWhitePixelOfScreen() are equivalent except that they require different arguments. One requires a pointer to a Screen structure, while the other requires a screen number. Unless you already have the pointer to a Screen structure in a variable, XWhitePixel*() is more convenient.

The C language macros WhitePixel() and WhitePixelOfScreen() are equivalent and slightly more efficient.

See Also

XBlackPixel(), *XBlackPixelOfScreen*(), *XDefaultColormap*().

XWidth*OfScreen

Name

XWidthOfScreen, XWidthMMOfScreen, WidthOfScreen, WidthMMOfScreen – get width of screen in pixels or millimeters

Synopsis

```
int XWidthOfScreen(screen)
    Screen *screen;

int XWidthMMOfScreen(screen)
    Screen *screen;
```

Arguments

screen   Specifies the appropriate Screen structure.

Returns

The width in pixels or millimeters.

Description

XWidthOfScreen() returns the width of the specified screen in pixels. XWidth-MMOfScreen() returns the width of the specified screen in millimeters.

The C language macros WidthOfScreen() and WidthMMOfScreen() are equivalent and slightly more efficient.

These functions are equivalent to XDisplayWidth*() and XDisplayWidthMM() except that they take different arguments.

See Also

XDisplayHeight(), XDisplayHeightMM().

XWindowEvent

Name

XWindowEvent – remove the next event that matches the specified mask and window.

Synopsis

```
XWindowEvent(display, w, event_mask, event_return)
    Display *display;
    Window w;
    long event_mask;
    XEvent *event_return;
```

Arguments

display   Specifies a connection to an X server; returned from XOpenDisplay().

w   Specifies the ID of the window whose next matching event you want.

event_mask   Specifies the event mask. See XSelectInput() for a complete list of event masks.

event_return
               Returns the event removed from the input queue.

Description

XWindowEvent removes the next event in the queue which matches both the passed window and the passed mask. The event is copied into an XEvent structure supplied by the caller. Other events in the queue are not discarded. If no such event has been queued, XWindowEvent flushes the request buffer and waits until one is received.

Structures

See individual event structures described in Volume One, Chapter 8, *Events*, and Appendix F, *Structure Reference*, in this volume.

See Also

XQLength(), XAllowEvents(), XCheckIfEvent(), XCheckMaskEvent(), XCheckTypedEvent(), XCheck-TypedWindowEvent(), XCheckWindowEvent(), XEventsQueued(), XGetInputFocus(), XGetMotion-Events(), XIfEvent(), XMaskEvent(), XNextEvent(), XPeekEvent(), XPeekIfEvent(), XPending(), XPut-BackEvent(), XSelectInput(), XSendEvent(), XSetInputFocus(), XSynchronize().

XWithdrawWindow

Name

XWithdrawWindow – request that a top-level window be withdrawn.

Synopsis

```
Status XWithdrawWindow(display, w, screen_number)
    Display *display;
    Window w;
    int screen_number;
```

Arguments

display   Specifies a connection to an X server; returned from `XOpenDisplay()`.

w   Specifies the window.

screen_number
                Specifies the appropriate screen number on the server.

Returns

Zero on failure, non-zero on success.

Availability

Release 4 and later.

Description

XWithdrawWindow() informs the window manager that the specified window and its icon should be unmapped. It unmaps the specified window and sends a synthetic `UnmapNotify` event to the root window of the specified screen. Window managers may elect to receive this message and may treat it as a request to change the window's state to withdrawn. When a window is in the withdrawn state, neither its normal nor its iconic representation is visible. XWithdrawWindow() returns a non-zero status if the `UnmapNotify` event is successfully sent; otherwise, it returns a zero status.

For more information, see Volume One, Chapter 10, *Interclient Communication*.

Errors

`BadWindow`

See Also

XIconifyWindow(), *XReconfigureWMWindow()*.

XWMGeometry

Name

XWMGeometry – obtain a window's geometry information.

Synopsis

```
int XWMGeometry(display, screen, user_geom, def_geom, bwidth_return,
        hints, x_return, y_return, width_return, height_return, grav-
        ity_return)
    Display *display;
    int screen;
    char *user_geom;
    char *def_geom;
    unsigned int bwidth_return;
    XSizeHints *hints;
    int *x_return, *y_return;
    int *width, *height_return;
    int *gravity_return;
```

Arguments

display   Specifies a connection to an X server; returned from XOpenDisplay().

screen   Specifies the screen.

user_geom   Specifies the user-specified geometry or NULL.

def_geom   Specifies the application's default geometry or NULL.

bwidth   Specifies the border width.

hints   Specifies the size hints for the window in its normal state.

x_return
y_return   Return the x and y offsets.

width
height_return
               Return the width and height determined.

gravity_return
               Returns the window gravity.

Availability

Release 4 and later. A mask - see the "Description" section.

Description

XWMGeometry combines possibly incomplete or nonexistent geometry information (given in the format used by XParseGeometry()) specified by the user and by the calling program with complete program-supplied default size hints (usually the ones to be stored in WM_NORMAL_HINTS) and returns the position, size, and gravity (NorthWestGravity, NorthEastGravity, SouthEastGravity or SouthWestGravity) that describe the window. If the base size is not set in the XSizeHints structure, the minimum size is used if set. Otherwise, a base size of zero is assumed. If no minimum size is set in the hints structure, the base size is used. A mask (in the form returned by XParseGeometry()) that describes which values came from the user and whether or not the position coordinates are relative to the right and bottom edges is returned (which will have already been accounted for in the x_return and y values).

Note that invalid user geometry specifications can cause a width or height of zero to be returned. The caller may pass the address of the win_gravity field of the *hints* argument as the *gravity_return* argument.

For more information, see Volume One, Chapter 10, *Interclient Communication*.

Structures

```
typedef struct {
        long flags;            /* marks which fields in this structure are
                               /* defined */
        int x, y;              /* obsolete for new window mgrs, but clients */
        int width, height; /* should set so old wm's don't mess up */
        int min_width, min_height;
        int max_width, max_height;
        int width_inc, height_inc;
        struct {
                int x;     /* numerator */
                int y;     /* denominator */
        } min_aspect, max_aspect;
        int base_width, base_height;   /* added by ICCCM version 1 */
        int win_gravity;               /* added by ICCCM version 1 */
} XSizeHints
```

See Also

XChangeWindowAttributes(), XParseGeometry(), XSetWMProperties().

XWriteBitmapFile

Name

XWriteBitmapFile – write a bitmap to a file.

Synopsis

```
int XWriteBitmapFile(display, filename, bitmap, width, height, x_hot,
        y_hot)
    Display *display;
    char *filename;
    Pixmap bitmap;
    unsigned int width, height;
    int x_hot, y_hot;
```

Arguments

display	Specifies a connection to an X server; returned from XOpenDisplay().
filename	Specifies the filename to use. The format of the filename is operating system specific.
bitmap	Specifies the bitmap to be written.
width height	Specify the width and height in pixels of the bitmap to be written.
x_hot y_hot	Specify where to place the hotspot coordinates (or –1,–1 if none present) in the file.

Returns

BitmapSuccess on success. BitmapOpenFailed or BitmapNoMemory on failure.

Description

XWriteBitmapFile() writes a bitmap to a file. The file is written out in X version 11 bitmap file format, shown below. The file is written in the encoding of the current locale.

If the file cannot be opened for writing, XWriteBitmapFile() returns BitmapOpenFailed. If insufficient memory is allocated XWriteBitmapFile() returns BitmapNoMemory. Otherwise, on no error, XWriteBitmapFile() returns BitmapSuccess.

If x_hot and y_hot are not –1, –1, then XWriteBitmapFile() writes them out as the hotspot coordinates for the bitmap.

The following is an example of the contents of a bitmap file created. The name used ("gray" in this example) is the portion of filename after the last "/".

```
#define gray_width 16
#define gray_height 16
#define gray_x_hot 8
#define gray_y_hot 8
static char gray_bits[] = {
    0xf8, 0x1f, 0xe3, 0xc7, 0xcf, 0xf3, 0x9f, 0xf9, 0xbf, 0xfd, 0x33, 0xcc,
    0x7f, 0xfe, 0x7f, 0xfe, 0x7e, 0x7e, 0x7f, 0xfe, 0x37, 0xec, 0xbb, 0xdd,
    0x9c, 0x39, 0xcf, 0xf3, 0xe3, 0xc7, 0xf8, 0x1f};
```

For more information on bitmaps, see Volume One, Chapter 6, *Drawing Graphics and Text.*

Errors

BadAlloc

BadDrawable

BadMatch   The specified *width* and *height* did not match dimensions of the speci-
                  fied *bitmap*.

See Also

XCreateBitmapFromData(), XCreatePixmap(), XCreatePixmapFromBitmapData(), XFreePixmap(), XQueryBestSize(), XQueryBestStipple(), XQueryBestTile(), XReadBitmapFile(), XSetTile(), XSetWindowBackgroundPixmap(), XSetWindowBorderPixmap().

XXorRegion

Name

XXorRegion – calculate the difference between the union and intersection of two regions.

Synopsis

```
XXorRegion(sra, srb, dr_return)
    Region sra, srb;
    Region dr_return;
```

Arguments

sra   Specify the two regions on which you want to perform the computation.
srb

dr_return   Returns the result of the computation.

Description

XXorRegion() calculates the union minus the intersection of two regions, and places it in *dr_return*. Xor is short for "Exclusive OR", meaning that a pixel is included in *dr_return* if it is set in either *sra* or *srb* but not in both.

For more information on regions, see Volume One, Chapter 6, *Drawing Graphics and Text*.

Structures

Region is a pointer to an opaque structure type.

See Also

XClipBox(), XCreateRegion(), XDestroyRegion(), XEmptyRegion(), XEqualRegion(), XIntersect-Region(), XOffsetRegion(), XPointInRegion(), XPolygonRegion(), XRectInRegion(), XSetRegion(), XShrinkRegion(), XSubtractRegion(), XUnionRectWithRegion(), XUnionRegion().

Appendices

In The Appendices:

A
Function Group Summary

This quick reference is intended to help you find and use the right function for a particular task. It supplies two lists:

- Listing of Functions by Groups

- Alphabetical Listing of Functions

Both functions and macros are listed in all the groups in which they belong. Therefore, several of them are listed more than once.

Remember that Xlib functions begin with the letter "X"; macros do not.

A.1 Group Listing with Brief Descriptions

Association Tables

XCreateAssocTable	Create a new association table (X10).
XDeleteAssoc	Delete an entry from an association table.
XDestroyAssocTable	Free the memory allocated for an association table.
XLookUpAssoc	Obtain data from an association table.
XMakeAssoc	Create an entry in an association table.

Buffers

XStoreBuffer	Store data in a cut buffer.
XStoreBytes	Store data in cut buffer 0.
XFetchBuffer	Return data from a cut buffer.
XFetchBytes	Return data from cut buffer 0.
XRotateBuffers	Rotate the cut buffers.

Client Connections

XKillClient	Destroy a client or its remaining resources.
XSetCloseDownMode	Change the close down mode of a client.

Color (Device-Independent)

ClientWhitePointOfCCC	Return the client white point of the screen associated with a Color Conversion Context.
DisplayOfCCC	Return the display associated with a Color Conversion Context.
ScreenNumberOfCCC	Return screen number associated with the specified Color Conversion Context.
ScreenWhitePointOfCCC	Return the white point of the screen associated with a specified Color Conversion Context.
VisualOfCCC	Return the visual associated with a specified Color Conversion Context.
XcmsAddColorSpace	Add a device-independent color space.
XcmsAddFunctionSet	Add a Color Characterization function set.
XcmsAllocColor	Allocate a color specified in device-independent or device-dependent form.
XcmsAllocNamedColor	Allocate a color specified as a string.
XcmsCCCOfColormap	Get the Color Conversion Context of a colormap.
XcmsCIELabQueryMaxC	Obtain the maximum Chroma for a given Hue and Lightness within the screen's color gamut in terms of CIE L*a*b* coordinates.
XcmsCIELabQueryMaxL	Obtain the maximum Lightness for a given Hue and Chroma within the screen's color gamut in terms of CIE L*a*b* coordinates.
XcmsCIELabQueryMaxLC	Obtain the maximum Chroma for a given Hue within the screen's color gamut in terms of CIE L*a*b* coordinates.
XcmsCIELabQueryMinL	Obtain the minimum Lightness for a given Hue and Chroma within the screen's color gamut in terms of CIE L*a*b* coordinates.
XcmsCIELuvQueryMaxC	Obtain the maximum Chroma for a given Hue and Lightness within the screen's color gamut in terms of CIE L*u*v* coordinates.
XcmsCIELuvQueryMaxL	Obtain the maximum Lightness for a given Hue and Chroma within the screen's color gamut in terms of CIE L*u*v* coordinates.
XcmsCIELuvQueryMaxLC	Obtain the maximum Chroma for a given Hue within the screen's color gamut in terms of CIE L*u*v* coordinates.
XcmsCIELuvQueryMinL	Obtain the minimum Lightness for a given Hue and Chroma within the screen's color gamut in terms of CIE L*u*v* coordinates.

XcmsClientWhitePointOfCCC	Return the client white point associated with the specified Color Conversion Context.
XcmsColor	Xcms color structure.
XcmsColorSpace	Xcms color space structure.
XcmsCompressionProc	Interface definition for gamut compression procedure.
XcmsConversionProc	Interface definition for the procedure for color conversion between device-independent color spaces.
XcmsConvertColors	Convert color specifications in XcmsColor structures to another color-space-specific encoding.
XcmsCreateCCC	Create a Color Conversion Context.
XcmsDefaultCCC	Get the default Color Conversion Context for a screen.
XcmsDisplayOfCCC	Return the display associated with a Color Conversion Context.
DisplayOfCCC	Return the display associated with a Color Conversion Context.
XcmsFormatOfPrefix	Obtain the format ID of the color space associated with a specified color string prefix.
XcmsFreeCCC	Free a Color Conversion Context.
XcmsFunctionSet	Xcms Color Characterization Function Set structure.
XcmsLookupColor	Obtain color values from a string.
XcmsParseStringProc	Interface definition for color string parsing procedure.
XcmsPrefixOfFormat	Obtain the color string prefix associated with the color space specified by a color format.
XcmsQueryBlack	Obtain a color specification for screen black.
XcmsQueryBlue	Obtain a color specification for screen blue.
XcmsQueryColor	Obtain the color specification of a specified color-cell.
XcmsQueryColors	Obtain the color specifications of the specified color-cells.
XcmsQueryGreen	Obtain a color specification for screen green.
XcmsQueryRed	Obtain a color specification for screen red.
XcmsQueryWhite	Obtain a color specification for screen white.
XcmsScreenFreeProc	Interface definition for the Function Set routine that frees the per-screen data.
XcmsScreenInitProc	Interface specification for the Function Set routine that obtains and initializes per-screen information.
XcmsScreenNumberOfCCC	Screen number associated with the specified Color Conversion Context.
ScreenNumberOfCCC	Screen number associated with the specified Color Conversion Context.
XcmsScreenWhitePointOfCCC	Obtain the white point of the screen associated with a specified Color Conversion Context.

ScreenWhitePointOfCCC	Obtain the white point of the screen associated with a specified Color Conversion Context.
XcmsSetCCCOfColormap	Change the Color Conversion Context associated with a colormap.
XcmsSetCompressionProc	Change the gamut compression procedure in a specified Color Conversion Context.
XcmsSetWhiteAdjustProc	Change the white point adjustment procedure in a specified Color Conversion Context.
XcmsSetWhitePoint	Set the Client White Point of a Color Conversion Context.
XcmsStoreColor	Store a specified color into a read/write colormap cell.
XcmsStoreColors	Store the specified colors in read/write colormap cells.
XcmsTekHVCQueryMaxC	Find the maximum Chroma for a given TekHVC Hue and Value.
XcmsTekHVCQueryMaxV	Find the maximum Value for a given TekHVC Hue and Chroma.
XcmsTekHVCQueryMaxVC	Find the maximum Chroma and the Value at which it occurs.
XcmsTekHVCQueryMaxVSamples	Return the boundaries of the TekHVC gamut for a given Hue.
XcmsTekHVCQueryMinV	Find the minimum Value for a given TekHVC Hue and Chroma.
XcmsVisualOfCCC	Return the visual associated with a specified Color Conversion Context.
VisualOfCCC	Return the visual associated with a specified Color Conversion Context.
XcmsWhiteAdjustProc	Interface definition for the white point adjustment procedure.

Colorcells

XAllocColor	Allocate a read-only colormap cell with closest hardware-supported color.
XAllocColorCells	Allocate read/write (nonshared) colorcells.
XAllocColorPlanes	Allocate read/write (nonshareable) color planes.
XAllocNamedColor	Allocate a read-only colorcell from color name.
XLookupColor	Get Database RGB values and closest hardware-supported RGB values from color name.
XParseColor	Look up or translate RGB values from color name or hexadecimal value.
XQueryColor	Obtain the RGB values for a specified pixel value.

Colorcells (continued)

XQueryColors	Obtain RGB values and flags for each specified pixel value.
XStoreColor	Set or change a read/write entry of a colormap to the closest available hardware color.
XStoreColors	Set or change read/write colorcells to the closest available hardware colors.
XStoreNamedColor	Allocate a read/write colorcell by English color name.
XFreeColors	Free colormap cells or planes.
BlackPixel	Return a black pixel value on the default colormap of screen.
WhitePixel	Return a pixel value representing white in default colormap.

Colormaps

XCopyColormapAndFree	Copy a colormap and return a new colormap ID.
XCreateColormap	Create a colormap.
XFreeColormap	Delete a colormap and install the default colormap.
XGetStandardColormap	Get the standard colormap property.
XSetStandardColormap	Change the standard colormap property.
XSetWindowColormap	Set the colormap for a specified window.
XInstallColormap	Install a colormap.
XUninstallColormap	Uninstall a colormap; install default if not already installed.
XListInstalledColormaps	Get a list of installed colormaps.
DefaultColormap	Return the default colormap on the default screen.
DefaultColormapOfScreen	Return the default colormap on the specified screen.
DisplayCells	Return the maximum number of colormap cells on the connected display.

Context Manager

XDeleteContext	Delete a context entry for a given window and type.
XFindContext	Get data from the context manager (not graphics context).
XSaveContext	Save a data value corresponding to a window and context type (not graphics context).
XUniqueContext	Create a new context ID (not graphics context).

Cursors

XDefineCursor	Assign a cursor to a window.
XUndefineCursor	Disassociate a cursor from a window.
XCreateFontCursor	Create a cursor from the standard cursor font.
XCreateGlyphCursor	Create a cursor from font glyphs.
XCreatePixmapCursor	Create a cursor from two bitmaps.
XFreeCursor	Destroy a cursor.
XRecolorCursor	Change the color of a cursor.
XQueryBestCursor	Get the closest supported cursor sizes.
XQueryBestSize	Obtain the "best" supported cursor, tile, or stipple size.

Device-Independent Color

(*see Color (Device-Independent)*)

Display Specifications

DefaultColormap	Return the default colormap on the specified screen.
DefaultDepth	Return the depth of the default root window for a screen.
DefaultGC	Return the default graphics context for the root window of a screen.
DefaultScreen	Return the screen integer; i.e., the last segment of a string passed to **XOpenDisplay()**, or the DISPLAY environment variable if **NULL** was used.
DefaultVisual	Return the default visual structure for a screen.
DisplayCells	Return the maximum number of colormap cells on the connected display.
DisplayHeight	Return an integer that describes the height of the screen in pixels.
DisplayHeightMM	Return the height of the specified screen in millimeters.
DisplayPlanes	Return the number of planes on the connected display.
DisplayString	Return the string that was passed to **XOpenDisplay()** or if that was **NULL**, the DISPLAY variable.
DisplayWidth	Return the width of the screen in pixels.
DisplayWidthMM	Return the width of the specified screen in millimeters.
RootWindow	Return the ID of the root window.
ScreenCount	Return the number of available screens.
XDisplayMotionBufferSize	Return size of server's motion history buffer.
XListDepths	Return a list of the depths supported on this server.

Display Specifications (continued)

`XListPixmapFormats`	Return a list of the pixmap formats supported on this server.
`XMaxRequestSize`	Return maximum request size allowed on this server.
`XResourceManagerString`	Return string containing user's resource database.

Drawing Primitives

`XDraw`	Draw a polyline or curve between vertex list (from X10).
`XDrawArc`	Draw an arc fitting inside a rectangle.
`XDrawArcs`	Draw multiple arcs.
`XDrawFilled`	Draw a filled polygon or curve from vertex list (from X10).
`XDrawLine`	Draw a line between two points.
`XDrawLines`	Draw multiple connected lines.
`XDrawPoint`	Draw a point.
`XDrawPoints`	Draw multiple points.
`XDrawRectangle`	Draw an outline of a rectangle.
`XDrawRectangles`	Draw the outlines of multiple rectangles.
`XDrawSegments`	Draw multiple disjoint lines.
`XCopyArea`	Copy an area of a drawable.
`XCopyPlane`	Copy a single plane of a drawable into a drawable with depth, applying pixel values.
`XFillArc`	Fill an arc.
`XFillArcs`	Fill multiple arcs.
`XFillPolygon`	Fill a polygon.
`XFillRectangle`	Fill a rectangular area.
`XFillRectangles`	Fill multiple rectangular areas.
`XClearArea`	Clear a rectangular area in a window.
`XClearWindow`	Clear an entire window.

Errors

`XGetErrorDatabaseText`	Obtain error messages from the error database.
`XGetErrorText`	Obtain a description of error code.
`XSetErrorHandler`	Set a nonfatal error event handler.
`XSetIOErrorHandler`	Handle fatal I/O errors.
`XDisplayName`	Report the display name when connection to a display fails.
`XSetAfterFunction`	Set a function called after all Xlib functions.
`XSynchronize`	Enable or disable synchronization for debugging.

Function Group

Events

XSelectInput	Select the event types to be sent to a window.
XSendEvent	Send an event.
XSetInputFocus	Set the keyboard focus window.
XGetInputFocus	Return the current keyboard focus window.
XWindowEvent	Remove the next event that matches mask and window.
XCheckWindowEvent	Remove the next event that matches both passed window and passed mask; don't wait.
XCheckTypedEvent	Return the next event in queue that matches event type; don't wait.
XCheckTypedWindowEvent	Return the next event in queue that matches type and window.
XMaskEvent	Remove the next event that matches mask.
XCheckMaskEvent	Remove the next event that matches mask; don't wait.
XIfEvent	Wait for matching event.
XCheckIfEvent	Check the event queue for a matching event.
XPeekEvent	Get an event without removing it from the queue.
XPeekIfEvent	Get an event without recovering it from the queue; don't wait.
XAllowEvents	Control the behavior of keyboard and pointer events when these resources are grabbed.
XGetMotionEvents	Get pointer motion events.
XDisplayMotionBufferSize	Return size of server's motion history buffer.
XNextEvent	Get the next event of any type or window.
XPutBackEvent	Push an event back on the input queue.
XEventsQueued	Check the number of events in the event queue.
XPending	Flush the request buffer and return the number of pending input events.
XSynchronize	Enable or disable synchronization for debugging.
QLength	Return the current length of the input queue on the connected display.

Extensions

XFreeExtensionList	Free memory allocated for a list of installed extensions to X.
XListExtensions	Return a list of all extensions to X supported by the server.
XQueryExtension	Get extension information.

Extension Writing

`LockDisplay`	Lock display structure for multi-threaded access to connection.
`UnlockDisplay`	Lock display structure for multi-threaded access to connection.
`XAddExtension`	Add an extension.
`XAddToExtensionList`	Add an extension to Xlib's extension list.
`XAllocID`	Allocate a resource ID; used only in extension writing.
`XFlushGC`	Force cached GC changes to be sent to the server.
`XFindOnExtensionList`	Find an extension on Xlib's extension list.
`XInitExtension`	Initialize an extension.

Fonts

`XLoadFont`	Load a font if not already loaded; get font ID.
`XUnloadFont`	Unload a font.
`XFreeFont`	Unload a font and free storage for the font structure.
`XFreeFontInfo`	Free multiple font information arrays.
`XFreeFontNames`	Free the font name array.
`XFreeFontPath`	Free the memory allocated by **`XGetFontPath()`**.
`XListFonts`	Return a list of the available font names.
`XListFontsWithInfo`	Obtain the names and information about loaded fonts.
`XQueryFont`	Return information about a loaded font.
`XSetFont`	Set the current font in a graphics context.
`XSetFontPath`	Set the font search path.
`XGetFontPath`	Get the current font search path.
`XGetFontProperty`	Get a font property given its atom.
`XCreateFontCursor`	Create a cursor from the standard cursor font.

Grabbing

`XGrabKey`	Grab a key.
`XUngrabKey`	Release a key from grab.
`XGrabKeyboard`	Grab the keyboard.
`XUngrabKeyboard`	Release the keyboard from grab.
`XGrabButton`	Grab a pointer button.
`XUngrabButton`	Release a button from grab.
`XGrabPointer`	Grab the pointer.
`XUngrabPointer`	Release the pointer from grab.
`XGrabServer`	Grab the server grab.
`XUngrabServer`	Release the server from grab.
`XChangeActivePointerGrab`	Change the parameters of an active pointer grab.

Graphics Context

XCreateGC	Create a new graphics context for a given screen with the depth of the specified drawable.
XChangeGC	Change the components of a given graphics context.
XCopyGC	Copy a graphics context.
XFlushGC	Force cached GC changes to be sent to the server.
XFreeGC	Free a graphics context.
XGContextFromGC	Obtain the **GContext** (resource ID) associated with the specified graphics context.
XGetGCValues	Get GC component values from Xlib's GC cache.
XSetArcMode	Set the arc mode in a graphics context.
XSetClipMask	Set `clip_mask` pixmap in a graphics context.
XSetClipOrigin	Set the clip origin in a graphics context.
XSetClipRectangles	Set `clip_mask` in a graphics context to the list of rectangles.
XSetRegion	Set `clip_mask` of the graphics context to the specified region.
XSetDashes	Set `dash_offset` and `dashes` (for lines) in a graphics context.
XSetLineAttributes	Set the line drawing components in a graphics context.
XSetFillRule	Set the fill rule in a graphics context.
XSetFillStyle	Set the fill style in a graphics context.
XSetTile	Set the fill tile in a graphics context.
XSetStipple	Set the stipple in a graphics context.
XSetTSOrigin	Set the tile/stipple origin in a graphics context.
XSetGraphicsExposures	Set `graphics_exposures` in a graphics context.
XSetForeground	Set the foreground pixel value in a graphics context.
XSetBackground	Set the background pixel value in a graphics context.
XSetFunction	Set the bitwise logical operation in a graphics context.
XSetPlaneMask	Set the plane mask in a graphics context.
XSetState	Set the foreground, background, logical function and plane mask in a graphics context.
XSetSubwindowMode	Set the subwindow mode in a graphics context.
DefaultGC	Return the default graphics context for the root window of a screen.

Host Access

XAddHost	Add a host to the access control list.
XAddHosts	Add multiple hosts to the access control list.
XListHosts	Obtain a list of hosts having access to this display.
XRemoveHost	Remove a host from the access control list.
XRemoveHosts	Remove multiple hosts from the access control list.

Host Access (continued)

XDisableAccessControl	Allow access from any host.
XEnableAccessControl	Use access control list to allow or deny connection requests.
XSetAccessControl	Disable or enable access control.

HouseKeeping

XFree	Free specified in-memory data created by an Xlib function.
XOpenDisplay	Connect a client program to an X server.
XCloseDisplay	Disconnect a client program from an X server and display.
XNoOp	Send a NoOp to exercise connection with the server.

Images

BitmapBitOrder	Query the bitmap format of a display.
BitmapPad	Query the bitmap format of a display.
BitmapUnit	Query the bitmap format of a display.
XCreateImage	Allocate memory for an **XImage** structure.
XDestroyImage	Deallocate memory associated with an image.
XPutImage	Draw a rectangular image on a window or pixmap.
XSubImage	Create a subimage from part of an image.
XGetImage	Place contents of a rectangle from drawable into an image.
XGetSubImage	Copy a rectangle in drawable to a location within the pre-existing image.
XAddPixel	Add a constant value to every pixel value in an image.
XPutPixel	Set a pixel value in an image.
XGetPixel	Obtain a single pixel value from an image.
ImageByteOrder	Specify the required byte order for images for each scan line unit in **XYFormat** (bitmap) or for each pixel value in **ZFormat**. Returns either **LSBFirst** or **MSBFirst**.
XBitmapBitOrder	Query the bitmap format of a display.
XBitmapPad	Query the bitmap format of a display.
XBitmapUnit	Query the bitmap format of a display.

Interclient Communication

(see Window Manager Hints, Selections, and Cut Buffers)

Function Group

Internationalized Text Input

XCloseIM	Close an input method.
XCreateIC	Create an input context.
XDefaultString	Return the default string used for text conversion.
XDestroyIC	Destroy an input context.
XDisplayOfIM	Get the display of an input method.
XFilterEvent	Filter X events for an input method.
XGetICValues	Get input context attributes.
XGetIMValues	Obtain input method information.
XIMOfIC	Obtain the input method of an input context.
XLocaleOfIM	Get the locale of an input method.
XmbLookupString	Obtain composed multi-byte input from an input method.
XmbResetIC	Reset the state of an input context.
XmbTextListToTextProperty	Convert an internationalized multi-byte text list to a text property structure.
XmbTextPropertyToTextList	Convert an internationalized text property to a list of multi-byte strings.
XOpenIM	Open input method.
XSetICFocus	Set input context focus.
XSetICValues	Set input context attributes.
XSetLocaleModifiers	Configure locale modifiers.
XSupportsLocale	Determine locale support.
XUnsetICFocus	Set and unset input context focus.
XwcFreeStringList	Free memory allocated by **XwcTextPropertyToTextList**.
XwcLookupString	Obtain composed wide-character input from an input method.
XwcResetIC	Reset the state of an input context.
XwcTextListToTextProperty	Convert an internationalized wide-character text list to a text property structure.
XwcTextPropertyToTextList	Convert an internationalized text property to a list of wide-character strings.
XVaCreateNestedList	Allocate a nested variable argument list.

Internationalized Text Output

XBaseFontNameListOfFontSet	Get the base font list of a font set.
XContextDependentDrawing	Get a hint about context dependencies in the text of the locale.
XCreateFontSet	Create a font set.
XExtentsOfFontSet	Obtain the maximum extents structure for a font set.
XFontsOfFontSet	Get the list of fonts used by a font set.
XFreeFontSet	Free a font set.
XLocaleOfFontSet	Get the locale of a font set.

Internationalized Text Output (continued)

XmbDrawImageString	Draw internationalized multi-byte image text.
XmbDrawString	Draw internationalized multi-byte text.
XmbDrawText	Draw internationalized multi-byte text using multiple font sets.
XmbTextEscapement	Obtain the width of internationalized multi-byte text.
XmbTextExtents	Compute the extents of internationalized multi-byte text.
XmbTextPerCharExtents	Obtain per-character measurements of an internationalized multi-byte text string.
XwcDrawImageString	Draw internationalized wide-character image text.
XwcDrawString	Draw internationalized wide-character text.
XwcDrawText	Draw internationalized wide-character text using multiple font sets.
XwcTextEscapement	Obtain the width of internationalized wide-character text.
XwcTextExtents	Compute the extents of internationalized wide-character text.
XwcTextPerCharExtents	Obtain per-character measurements of an internationalized wide-character text string.

Keyboard

XKeycodeToKeysym	Convert a keycode to a keysym.
XKeysymToKeycode	Convert a keysym to the appropriate keycode.
XKeysymToString	Convert a keysym symbol to a string.
XStringToKeysym	Convert a keysym name string to a keysym.
XLookupKeysym	Get the keysym corresponding to a keycode in a structure.
XRebindKeysym	Rebind a keysym to a string for client.
XLookupString	Map a key event to ASCII string, keysym, and ComposeStatus.
XQueryKeymap	Obtain a bit vector for the current state of the keyboard.
XGetKeyboardMapping	Return symbols for keycodes.
XChangeKeyboardMapping	Change the keyboard mapping.
XRefreshKeyboardMapping	Update the stored modifier and keymap information.
XSetModifierMapping	Set keycodes to be used as modifiers (Shift, Control, etc.).
XGetModifierMapping	Obtain modifier key mapping (Shift, Control, etc.).
XDeleteModifiermapEntry	Delete an entry from an **XModifierKeymap** structure.
XInsertModifiermapEntry	Add a new entry to an **XModifierKeymap** structure.

Keyboard (continued)

XNewModifiermap	Create a keyboard modifier mapping structure.
XFreeModifiermap	Destroy and free a keyboard modifier mapping structure.
XDisplayKeycodes	Returns range of keycodes used by server.

Macros, Display

AllPlanes	Return an unsigned long value with all bits set.
BlackPixel	Return a black pixel value on the default colormap of screen.
BlackPixelOfScreen	Return the black pixel value in the default colormap of the specified screen.
CellsOfScreen	Return the number of colormap cells of the specified screen.
ConnectionNumber	Return the connection number (file descriptor on UNIX system).
DefaultColormap	Return the default colormap on the specified screen.
DefaultColormapOfScreen	Return the default colormap of the specified screen.
DefaultDepth	Return the depth of the default root window for a screen.
DefaultDepthOfScreen	Return the default depth of the specified screen.
DefaultGC	Return the default graphics context for the root window of a screen.
DefaultGCOfScreen	Return the default graphics context of the specified screen.
DefaultRootWindow	Return the root window for the default screen.
DefaultScreen	Return the screen integer; the last segment of a string passed to **XOpenDisplay,** or the DISPLAY environment variable if **NULL** was used.
DefaultScreenOfDisplay	Return the default screen of the specified display.
DefaultVisual	Return the default visual structure for a screen.
DefaultVisualOfScreen	Return the default visual of the specified screen.
DisplayCells	Return the maximum number of colormap cells on the connected display.
DisplayHeight	Return an integer that describes the height of the screen in pixels.
DisplayHeightMM	Return the height of the specified screen in millimeters.
DisplayOfScreen	Return the display of the specified screen.
DisplayPlanes	Return the number of planes on the connected display.
DisplayString	Return the string that was passed to **XOpenDisplay** or if that was **NULL,** the DISPLAY variable.
DisplayType	Return the connected display manufacturer, as defined in *<X11/Xvendors.h>*.

DisplayWidth	Return the width of the screen in pixels.
DisplayWidthMM	Return the width of the specified screen in millimeters.
DoesBackingStore	Return a value indicating whether the screen supports backing stores. Return one of **WhenMapped**, **NotUseful**, or **Always**.
DoesSaveUnders	Return whether the screen supports save unders. **True** or **False**.
dpyno	Return the file descriptor of the connected display.
EventMaskOfScreen	Return the initial root event mask for the specified screen.
HeightOfScreen	Return the height of the specified screen.
HeightMMOfScreen	Return the height of the specified screen in millimeters.
Keyboard	Return the device ID for the main keyboard connected to the display.
LastKnownRequestProcessed	Return the serial ID of the last known protocol request to have been issued.
MaxCmapsOfScreen	Return the maximum number of colormaps supported by a screen.
MinCmapsOfScreen	Return the minimum number of colormaps supported by a screen.
NextRequest	Return the serial ID of the next protocol request to be issued.
PlanesOfScreen	Return the number of planes in a screen.
ProtocolRevision	Return the minor protocol revision number of the X server.
ProtocolVersion	Return the version number of the X protocol on the connected display.
QLength	Return the current length of the input queue on the connected display.
RootWindow	Return the ID of the root window.
RootWindowOfScreen	Return the root window of the specified screen.
ScreenCount	Return the number of available screens.
XScreenNumberOfScreen	Return the integer corresponding to the specified pointer to a **Screen** structure.
ScreenOfDisplay	Return the specified screen of the specified display.
ServerVendor	Return a pointer to a **NULL**-terminated string giving some identification of the maker of the X server implementation.
VendorRelease	Return a number related to the release of the X server by the vendor.
WhitePixel	Return a pixel value representing white in default colormap.

Function Group

Macros, Display (continued)

`WhitePixelOfScreen`	Return the white pixel value in the default colormap of the specified screen.
`WidthOfScreen`	Return the width of the specified screen.
`WidthMMOfScreen`	Return the width of the specified screen in millimeters.
`XDisplayMotionBufferSize`	Return size of server's motion history buffer.
`XListDepths`	Return a list of the depths supported on this server.
`XListPixmapFormats`	Return a list of the pixmap formats supported on this server.
`XMaxRequestSize`	Return maximum request size allowed on this server.
`XResourceManagerString`	Return string containing user's resource database.

Macros, Image Format

`BitmapBitOrder`	Return `LeastSignificant` or `MostSignificant`. Indicates the bit order in `BitmapUnit`.
`BitmapPad`	Each scan line is padded to a multiple of bits specified by the value returned by this macro.
`BitmapUnit`	The scan line is quantized (calculated) in multiples of this value.
`ByteOrder`	Return the required byte order for images for each scan line unit in XYFormat (bitmap) or for each pixel value in ZFormat. Possible values are `LSBFirst` or `MSBFirst`.
`ImageByteOrder`	Return the required byte order for images for each scan line unit in XYFormat (bitmap) or for each pixel value in `ZFormat`. Return either `LSBFirst` or `MSBFirst`.

Macros, Keysym Classification

`IsCursorKey`	Return `True` if the keysym is on the cursor key.
`IsFunctionKey`	Return `True` if the keysym is on the function keys.
`IsKeypadKey`	Return `True` if the keysym is on the key pad.
`IsMiscFunctionKey`	Return `True` if the keysym is on the miscellaneous function keys.
`IsModifierKey`	Return `True` if the keysym is on the modifier keys.
`IsPFKey`	Return `True` if the keysym is on the PF keys. (*see Window Mapping, Keyboard, or Pointer*)
`XFlush`	Flush the request buffer.
`XSync`	Flush the request buffer and wait for all events to be processed by the server.

Pointers

XQueryPointer	Get the current pointer location.
XWarpPointer	Move the pointer to another point on the screen.
XGrabPointer	Grab the pointer.
XUngrabPointer	Release the pointer from grab.
XGetPointerMapping	Get the pointer button mapping.
XSetPointerMapping	Set the pointer button mapping.
XGetPointerControl	Get the current pointer preferences.
XChangePointerControl	Change the pointer preferences.
XChangeActivePointerGrab	Change the parameters of an active pointer grab.

Properties

XListProperties	Get the property list for a window.
XDeleteProperty	Delete a window property.
XChangeProperty	Change a property associated with a window.
XSetStandardProperties	Set the minimum set of properties for the window manager.
XRotateWindowProperties	Rotate properties in the properties array.
XGetAtomName	Get a name for a given atom.
XGetFontProperty	Get a font property given its atom.
XGetWindowProperty	Obtain the atom type and property format for a window.
XInternAtom	Return an atom for a given name string.
XGetTextProperty	Read a TEXT property.
XSetTextProperty	Write a TEXT property.
XStringListToTextProperty	Convert a list of strings to an **XTextProperty** structure.
XTextPropertyToStringList	Convert an **XTextProperty** to a list of strings.
XFreeStringList	Free memory allocated by **XTextPropertyToStringList( )**.

Regions

XCreateRegion	Create a new empty region.
XDestroyRegion	Deallocate storage associated with a region.
XEmptyRegion	Determine if a region is empty.
XPolygonRegion	Generate a region from points.
XPointInRegion	Determine if a point resides in a region.
XRectInRegion	Determine if a rectangle resides in a region.
XUnionRectWithRegion	Add a rectangle to a region.
XClipBox	Generate the smallest rectangle enclosing a region.
XOffsetRegion	Change offset of a region.
XShrinkRegion	Reduce the size of a region.
XEqualRegion	Determine if two regions have the same size, offset, and space.

Regions (continued)

XSetRegion	Set `clip_mask` of the graphics context to the specified region.
XSubtractRegion	Subtract one region from another.
XIntersectRegion	Compute the intersection of two regions.
XUnionRegion	Compute the union of two regions.
XXorRegion	Calculate the difference between the union and intersection of 2 regions.

Resource Manager

Xpermalloc	Allocate memory never to be freed.
XResourceManagerString	Get user's database set with *xrdb* from **Display** structure.
XrmClassToString	Convert **XrmClass** to string. Same as **XrmQuarkToString()**.
XrmCombineDatabase	Combine the contents of two resource databases.
XrmCombineFileDatabase	Combine the contents of a resource file and a resource database.
XrmDestroyDatabase	Destroy a resource database.
XrmEnumerateDatabase	Enumerate resource database entries.
XrmGetDatabase	Retrieve the resource database associated with a display.
XrmGetFileDatabase	Retrieve a database from a file.
XrmGetResource	Get a resource from name and class as strings.
XrmGetStringDatabase	Retrieve and store resource databases.
XrmInitialize	Initialize the resource manager.
XrmLocaleOfDatabase	Return the locale of a resource database.
XrmMergeDatabases	Merge the contents of one database with another.
XrmNameToString	Convert **XrmName** to string. Same as **XrmQuarkToString()**.
XrmParseCommand	Load a resource database from command-line arguments.
XrmPermStringToQuark	Convert a string to a quark.
XrmPutFileDatabase	Retrieve and store resource databases.
XrmPutLineResource	Add a resource entry given as a string of name and value.
XrmPutResource	Store a resource into a database.
XrmPutStringResource	Add a resource that is specified as a string.
XrmQGetResource	Get a resource from name and class as quarks.
XrmQGetSearchList	Return a list of database levels.
XrmQGetSearchResource	Search resource database levels for a given resource.
XrmQPutResource	Store a resource into a database using quarks.
XrmQPutStringResource	Add a string resource value to a database using quarks.
XrmQuarkToString	Convert a quark to a string.

Resource Manager (continued)

XrmRepresentationToString	Convert **XrmRepresentation** to string. Same as **XrmQuarkToString( )**.
XrmSetDatabase	Associate a resource database with a display.
XrmStringToBinding- QuarkList	Convert a key string to a binding list and a quark list.
XrmStringToClass	Convert string to **XrmClass**. Same as **XrmStringToQuark( )**.
XrmStringToName	Convert string to **XrmName**. Same as **XrmStringToQuark( )**.
XrmStringToQuarkList	Convert a key string to a quark list.
XrmStringToQuark	Convert a string to a quark.
XrmStringToRepresentation	Convert string to **XrmRepresentation**. Same as **XrmStringToQuark( )**.
XrmUniqueQuark	Allocate a new quark.
XScreenResourceString	Obtain server resource properties.

Save Set

XAddToSaveSet	Add a window to the client's save-set.
XRemoveFromSaveSet	Remove a window from the client's save-set.
XChangeSaveSet	Add or remove a window to or from the client's save-set.

Screen Saver

XActivateScreenSaver	Activate screen blanking.
XForceScreenSaver	Turn the screen saver on or off.
XResetScreenSaver	Reset the screen saver.
XGetScreenSaver	Get the current screen saver parameters.
XSetScreenSaver	Set the parameters of the screen saver.

Selections

XGetSelectionOwner	Return the owner of a selection.
XSetSelectionOwner	Set the owner of a selection.
XConvertSelection	Use the value of a selection.

Server Specifications

(*see Display Specifications*)

Standard Geometry

XGeometry	Calculate window geometry given user geometry string and default geometry. Superseded in R4 by **XWMGeometry**.
XWMGeometry	Calculate window geometry given user geometry string and default geometry.
XParseGeometry	Generate position and size from standard window geometry string.
XTranslateCoordinates	Change the coordinate system from one window to another.

Text

XDrawImageString	Draw 8-bit image text characters.
XDrawImageString16	Draw 16-bit image text characters.
XDrawString	Draw an 8-bit text string, foreground only.
XDrawString16	Draw two-byte text strings.
XDrawText	Draw 8-bit polytext strings.
XDrawText16	Draw 16-bit polytext strings.
XQueryTextExtents	Query the server for string and font metrics.
XQueryTextExtents16	Query the server for string and font metrics of a 16-bit character string.
XTextExtents	Get string and font metrics.
XTextExtents16	Get string and font metrics of a 16-bit character string.
XTextWidth	Get the width in pixels of an 8-bit character string.
XTextWidth16	Get the width in pixels of a 16-bit character string.

Tile, Pixmap, Stipple and Bitmap

XCreatePixmap	Create a pixmap.
XFreePixmap	Free a pixmap ID.
XQueryBestSize	Obtain the "best" supported cursor, tile, or stipple size.
XQueryBestStipple	Obtain the best supported stipple shape.
XQueryBestTile	Obtain the best supported fill tile shape.
XSetTile	Set the fill tile in a graphics context.
XSetWindowBorderPixmap	Change a window border tile attribute and repaint the border.
XSetWindowBackgroundPixmap	Change the background tile attribute of a window.
XReadBitmapFile	Read a bitmap from disk.
XWriteBitmapFile	Write a bitmap to a file.
XCreateBitmapFromData	Create a bitmap from X11 bitmap format data.
XCreatePixmapFromBitmapData	Create a pixmap with depth from bitmap data.
XListPixmapFormats	Read supported pixmap formats from **Display** structure.

User Preferences

XAutoRepeatOff	Turn off the keyboard auto-repeat keys.
XAutoRepeatOn	Turn on the keyboard auto-repeat keys.
XBell	Ring the bell (Control G).
XGetDefault	Scan the user preferences for program name and options.
XGetPointerControl	Get the current pointer preferences.
XGetKeyboardControl	Obtain a list of the current keyboard preferences.
XChangeKeyboardControl	Change the keyboard preferences.

Visuals

XGetVisualInfo	Find a visual information structure that matches the specified template.
XMatchVisualInfo	Obtain the visual information that matches the desired depth and class.
DefaultVisual	Return the default visual structure for a screen.
XVisualIDFromVisual	Get resource ID from a visual structure.

Window Attributes

XGetWindowAttributes	Obtain the current attributes of window.
XChangeWindowAttributes	Set window attributes.
XSetWindowBackground	Set the background pixel attribute of a window.
XSetWindowBackgroundPixmap	Change the background tile attribute of a window.
XSetWindowBorder	Change a window border attribute to the specified pixel value and repaint the border.
XSetWindowBorderPixmap	Change a window border tile attribute and repaint the border.
XSetWindowColormap	Set the colormap for a specified window.
XDefineCursor	Assign a cursor to a window.
XGetGeometry	Obtain the current geometry of drawable.
XSelectInput	Select the event types to be sent to a window.

Window Configuration

XMoveWindow	Move a window.
XResizeWindow	Change a window's size.
XMoveResizeWindow	Change the size and position of a window.
XSetWindowBorderWidth	Change the border width of a window.
XRestackWindows	Change the stacking order of siblings.
XConfigureWindow	Change the window position, size, border width, or stacking order.

Window Configuration (continued)

XGetGeometry	Obtain the current geometry of drawable.
XReconfigureWMWindow	Change top-level window position, size, border width, or stacking order.

Window Existence

XCreateSimpleWindow	Create an unmapped **InputOutput** subwindow.
XCreateWindow	Create a window and set attributes.
XDestroySubwindows	Destroy all subwindows of a window.
XDestroyWindow	Unmap and destroy a window and all subwindows.

Window Manager Hints

XAllocClassHint	Allocate and zero fields in **XClassHint** structure.
XAllocIconSize	Allocate and zero fields in **XIconSize** structure.
XAllocSizeHints	Allocate and zero fields in **XSizeHints** structure.
XAllocStandardColormap	Allocate and zero fields in **XStandardColormap** structure.
XAllocWMHints	Allocate and zero fields in **XWMHints** structure.
XGetClassHint	Get the **XA_WM_CLASS** property of a window. Obsolete in R4.
XSetClassHint	Set the **XA_WM_CLASS** property of a window. Obsolete in R4.
XGetCommand	Get the **XA_WM_COMMAND** property (command-line arguments).
XSetCommand	Set the **XA_WM_COMMAND** property (command-line arguments). Obsolete in R4.
XGetNormalHints	Get the size hints property of a window in normal state (not zoomed or iconified). Obsolete in R4.
XSetNormalHints	Set the size hints property of a window in normal state (not zoomed or iconified). Obsolete in R4.
XGetSizeHints	Read any property of type **XA_WM_SIZE_HINTS**. Obsolete in R4.
XSetSizeHints	Set the value of any property of type **XA_WM_SIZE_HINTS**. Obsolete in R4.
XGetTransientForHint	Get the **XA_WM_TRANSIENT_FOR** property of a window.
XSetTransientForHint	Set the **XA_WM_TRANSIENT_FOR** property of a window.
XGetWMHints	Read a window manager hints property.
XSetWMHints	Set a window manager hints property.
XGetZoomHints	Read the size hints property of a zoomed window. Obsolete in R4.
XSetZoomHints	Set the size hints property of a zoomed window. Obsolete in R4.

Window Manager Hints (continued)

`XFetchName`	Get a window's name (**XA_WM_NAME** property). Obsolete in R4.
`XStoreName`	Assign a name to a window for the window manager. Obsolete in R4.
`XGetIconName`	Get the name to be displayed in an icon. Obsolete in R4.
`XSetIconName`	Set the name to be displayed in a window's icon. Obsolete in R4.
`XGetIconSizes`	Get preferred icon sizes.
`XSetIconSizes`	Set the value of the **XA_WM_ICON_SIZE** property.
`XGetRGBColormaps`	Read standard colormap property. Replaces `XGetStandardColormap`.
`XSetRGBColormaps`	Write standard colormap property. Replaces `XSetStandardColormap`.
`XGetWMClientMachine`	Read **WM_CLIENT_MACHINE** property.
`XSetWMClientMachine`	Write **WM_CLIENT_MACHINE** property.
`XGetWMIconName`	Read **XA_WM_ICON_NAME** property. Replaces `XGetIconName`.
`XSetWMIconName`	Write **XA_WM_ICON_NAME** property. Replaces `XSetIconName`.
`XGetWMProtocols`	Read **WM_PROTOCOLS** property.
`XSetWMProtocols`	Write **WM_PROTOCOLS** property.
`XGetWMNormalHints`	Read **XA_WM_NORMAL_HINTS** property. Replaces `XGetNormalHints`.
`XSetWMNormalHints`	Write **XA_WM_NORMAL_HINTS** property. Replaces `XSetNormalHints`.
`XSetWMSizeHints`	Write **XA_WM_SIZE_HINTS** property. Replaces `XSetSizeHints`.
`XSetWMColormapWindows`	Write **WM_COLORMAP_WINDOWS** property.
`XGetWMColormapWindows`	Read **WM_COLORMAP_WINDOWS** property.
`XSetWMProperties`	Write all standard properties. Replaces `XSetStandardProperties`.
`XSetWMName`	Write **XA_WM_NAME** property. Replaces `XStoreName`.
`XGetWMName`	Read **XA_WM_NAME** property. Replaces `XFetchName`.

Window Manipulation

`XLowerWindow`	Lower a window in the stacking order.
`XRaiseWindow`	Raise a window to the top of the stacking order.
`XCirculateSubwindows`	Circulate the stacking order of children up or down.
`XCirculateSubwindowsDown`	Circulate the bottom child to the top of the stacking order.

Window Manipulation (continued)

XCirculateSubwindowsUp	Circulate the top child to the bottom of the stacking order.
XQueryTree	Return a list of children, parent, and root.
XReparentWindow	Change a window's parent.
XMoveWindow	Move a window.
XResizeWindow	Change a window's size.
XMoveResizeWindow	Change the size and position of a window.
XSetWindowBorderWidth	Change the border width of a window.
XRestackWindows	Change the stacking order of siblings.
XConfigureWindow	Change the window position, size, border width, or stacking order.
XIconifyWindow	Inform window manager that a top-level window should be iconified.
XWithdrawWindow	Inform window manager that a top-level window should be unmapped.
XReconfigureWMWindow	Reconfigure a top-level window.

Window Mapping

XMapRaised	Map a window on top of its siblings.
XMapSubwindows	Map all subwindows.
XMapWindow	Map a window.
XUnmapSubwindows	Unmap all subwindows of a given window.
XUnmapWindow	Unmap a window.
XIconifyWindow	Inform window manager that a top-level window should be iconified.
XWithdrawWindow	Inform window manager that a top-level window should be unmapped.

A.2 Alphabetical Listing of Functions and Macros

Table A-1. Alphabetical Listing of Functions and Macros

Routine	Description
AllPlanes	Return a value with all bits set to 1 suitable for plane argument.
BitmapBitOrder	Query the bitmap format of a display.
BitmapPad	Query the bitmap format of a display.
BitmapUnit	Query the bitmap format of a display.
BlackPixel	Get the black pixel value.
BlackPixelOfScreen	Get the black pixel value.
CellsOfScreen	Return size of default colormap.

Routine	Description
ClientWhitePointOfCCC	Return the client white point from a Color Conversion Context.
ConnectionNumber	Get connection number or file descriptor.
DefaultColormap	Get screen's default colormap.
DefaultColormapOfScreen	Get screen's default colormap.
DefaultDepth	Get screen's default depth.
DefaultDepthOfScreen	Get screen's default depth.
DefaultGC	Get screen's default GC.
DefaultGCOfScreen	Get screen's default GC.
DefaultRootWindow	Get screen's default root window.
DefaultScreen	Get screen number of default screen.
DefaultScreenOfDisplay	Get Screen structure of default screen.
DefaultVisual	Get screen's default visual structure.
DefaultVisualOfScreen	Get screen's default visual structure.
DisplayCells	Query number of cells in default colormap of screen.
DisplayHeight	Query height of screen in pixels.
DisplayHeightMM	Query height of screen in millimeters.
DisplayOfCCC	Return the display associated with a Color Conversion Context.
DisplayOfScreen	Get Display structure of specified Screen structure.
DisplayPlanes	Get number of planes of specified screen.
DisplayString	Get string passed to **XOpenDisplay()**.
DisplayWidth	Query width of screen in pixels.
DisplayWidthMM	Query width of screen in millimeters.
DoesBackingStore	Query server support for backing store or save unders.
DoesSaveUnders	query server support for backing store or save unders.
EventMaskOfScreen	Get initial root window event mask.
FlushGC	Force cached GC changes to the server.
HeightMMOfScreen	Get height of screen in millimeters.
HeightOfScreen	Get height of screen in pixels.
ImageByteOrder	Get server's byte order.
IsCursorKey	Determine if keysym is a cursor key.
IsFunctionKey	determine if keysym is a function key.
IsKeypadKey	Determine if keysym is a keypad key.
IsMiscFunctionKey	Determine if keysym is a miscellaneous function key.
IsModifierKey	Determine if keysym is a modifier key.
IsPFKey	Determine if keysym is a PF key.
LastKnownRequestProcessed	Get serial number of last request processed by server.
LockDisplay	Lock display structure for multi-threaded access to connection.

Function Group

Routine	Description
MaxCmapsOfScreen	Get maximum number of installed colormaps supported by a screen.
MinCmapsOfScreen	Get minimum number of installed colormaps supported by a screen.
NextRequest	Return serial number of next request.
PlanesOfScreen	Return the depth of a root window.
ProtocolRevision	Return protocol revision number.
ProtocolVersion	Return protocol version number (currently 11).
QLength	Return the number of events on the queue.
RootWindow	Return root window ID.
RootWindowOfScreen	Return root window ID.
ScreenCount	Get screen information.
ScreenNumberOfCCC	Screen number associated with the specified Color Conversion Context.
ScreenOfDisplay	Get screen information.
ScreenWhitePointOfCCC	Obtain the white point of the screen associated with a specified Color Conversion Context.
ServerVendor	Return the vendor of connected server.
UnlockDisplay	Lock display structure for multi-threaded access to connection.
VendorRelease	Return vendor release number.
VisualOfCCC	Return the visual associated with a specified Color Conversion Context.
WhitePixel	Get the white pixel value.
WhitePixelOfScreen	Get the white pixel value.
WidthMMOfScreen	Get width of screen in millimeters.
WidthOfScreen	Get width of screen in pixels.
XActivateScreenSaver	Activate screen blanking.
XAddExtension	Add an extension.
XAddHost	Add a host to the access control list.
XAddHosts	Add multiple hosts to the access control list.
XAddPixel	Add a constant value to every pixel value in an image.
XAddToExtensionList	Add an extension to Xlib's extension list.
XAddToSaveSet	Add a window to the client's save-set.
XAllocClassHint	Allocate and zero fields in **XClassHint** structure.
XAllocColor	Allocate a read-only colormap cell with closest hardware-supported color.
XAllocColorCells	Allocate read/write (nonshared) colorcells.
XAllocColorPlanes	Allocate read/write (nonshareable) color planes.
XAllocIconSize	Allocate and zero fields in **XIconSize** structure.
XAllocID	Allocate a resource ID; used only in extension writing.

Routine	Description
XAllocNamedColor	Allocate a read-only colorcell from color name.
XAllocSizeHints	Allocate and zero fields in **XSizeHints** structure.
XAllocStandardColormap	Allocate and zero fields in **XStandardColormap** structure.
XAllocWMHints	Allocate and zero fields in **XWMHints** structure.
XAllowEvents	Control the behavior of keyboard and pointer events when these resources are grabbed.
XAllPlanes	Return a value with all bits set to 1 suitable for plane argument.
XAutoRepeatOff	Turn off the keyboard auto-repeat keys.
XAutoRepeatOn	Turn on the keyboard auto-repeat keys.
XBaseFontNameListOfFontSet	Get the base font list of a font set.
XBell	Ring the bell (Control G).
XBitmapBitOrder	Query the bitmap format of a display.
XBitmapPad	Query the bitmap format of a display.
XBitmapUnit	Query the bitmap format of a display.
XBlackPixel	Get the black pixel value.
XBlackPixelOfScreen	Get the black pixel value.
XCellsOfScreen	Return size of default colormap.
XChangeActivePointerGrab	Change the parameters of an active pointer grab.
XChangeGC	Change the components of a given graphics context.
XChangeKeyboardControl	Change the keyboard preferences such as key click.
XChangeKeyboardMapping	Change the keyboard mapping.
XChangePointerControl	Change the pointer preferences.
XChangeProperty	Change a property associated with a window.
XChangeSaveSet	Add or remove a window to or from the client's save-set.
XChangeWindowAttributes	Set window attributes.
XCheckIfEvent	Check the event queue for a matching event.
XCheckMaskEvent	Remove the next event that matches mask; don't wait.
XCheckTypedEvent	Return the next event in queue that matches event type; don't wait.
XCheckTypedWindowEvent	Return the next event in queue matching type and window.
XCheckWindowEvent	Remove the next event matching both passed window and passed mask; don't wait.
XCirculateSubwindows	Circulate the stacking order of children up or down.
XCirculateSubwindowsDown	Circulate the bottom child to the top of the stacking order.
XCirculateSubwindowsUp	Circulate the top child to the bottom of the stacking order.
XClearArea	Clear a rectangular area in a window.

Function Group

Routine	Description
XClearWindow	Clear an entire window.
XClipBox	Generate the smallest rectangle enclosing a region.
XCloseDisplay	Disconnect a client program from an X server and display.
XCloseIM	Close an input method.
XcmsAddColorSpace	Add a device-independent color space.
XcmsAddFunctionSet	Add a Color Characterization function set.
XcmsAllocColor	Allocate a color specified in device-independent or device-dependent form.
XcmsAllocNamedColor	Allocate a color specified as a string.
XcmsCCCOfColormap	Get the Color Conversion Context of a colormap.
XcmsCIELabQueryMaxC	Obtain the maximum Chroma for a given Hue and Lightness within the screen's color gamut in terms of CIE L*a*b* coordinates.
XcmsCIELabQueryMaxL	Obtain the maximum Lightness for a given Hue and Chroma within the screen's color gamut in terms of CIE L*a*b* coordinates.
XcmsCIELabQueryMaxLC	Obtain the maximum Chroma for a given Hue within the screen's color gamut in terms of CIE L*a*b* coordinates.
XcmsCIELabQueryMinL	Obtain the minimum Lightness for a given Hue and Chroma within the screen's color gamut in terms of CIE L*a*b* coordinates.
XcmsCIELuvQueryMaxC	Obtain the maximum Chroma for a given Hue and Lightness within the screen's color gamut in terms of CIE L*u*v* coordinates.
XcmsCIELuvQueryMaxL	Obtain the maximum Lightness for a given Hue and Chroma within the screen's color gamut in terms of CIE L*u*v* coordinates.
XcmsCIELuvQueryMaxLC	Obtain the maximum Chroma for a given Hue within the screen's color gamut in terms of CIE L*u*v* coordinates.
XcmsCIELuvQueryMinL	Obtain the minimum Lightness for a given Hue and Chroma within the screen's color gamut in terms of CIE L*u*v* coordinates.
XcmsClientWhitePointOfCCC	Return the client white point associated with the specified Color Conversion Context.
XcmsColor	xcms color structure.
XcmsColorSpace	xcms color space structure.
XcmsCompressionProc	Interface definition for gamut compression procedure.
XcmsConversionProc	Interface definition for the procedure for color conversion between device-independent color spaces.

Routine	Description
XcmsConvertColors	Convert color specifications in XcmsColor structures to another color space specific encoding.
XcmsCreateCCC	Create a Color Conversion Context.
XcmsDefaultCCC	Get the default Color Conversion Context for a screen.
XcmsDisplayOfCCC	Return the display associated with a Color Conversion Context.
XcmsFormatOfPrefix	Obtain the format ID of the color space associated with a specified color string prefix.
XcmsFreeCCC	Free a Color Conversion Context.
XcmsFunctionSet	xcms Color Characterization Function Set structure.
XcmsLookupColor	Obtain color values from a string.
XcmsParseStringProc	Interface definition for color string parsing procedure.
XcmsPrefixOfFormat	Obtain the color string prefix associated with the color space specified by a color format.
XcmsQueryBlack	Obtain a color specification for screen black.
XcmsQueryBlue	Obtain a color specification for screen blue.
XcmsQueryColor	Obtain the color specification of a specified color-cell.
XcmsQueryColors	Obtain the color specifications of the specified color-cells.
XcmsQueryGreen	Obtain a color specification for screen green.
XcmsQueryRed	Obtain a color specification for screen red.
XcmsQueryWhite	Obtain a color specification for screen white.
XcmsScreenFreeProc	Interface definition for the Function Set routine that frees the per-screen data.
XcmsScreenInitProc	Interface specification for the Function Set routine that obtains and initializes per-screen information.
XcmsScreenNumberOfCCC	Screen number associated with the specified Color Conversion Context.
XcmsScreenWhitePointOfCCC	Obtain the white point of the screen associated with a specified Color Conversion Context.
XcmsSetCCCOfColormap	Change the Color Conversion Context associated with a colormap.
XcmsSetCompressionProc	Change the gamut compression procedure in a specified Color Conversion Context.
XcmsSetWhiteAdjustProc	Change the white point adjustment procedure in a specified Color Conversion Context.
XcmsSetWhitePoint	Set the Client White Point of a Color Conversion Context.
XcmsStoreColor	Store a specified color into a read/write colormap cell.

Function Group

Routine	Description
XcmsStoreColors	Store the specified colors in read/write colormap cells.
XcmsTekHVCQueryMaxC	Find the maximum Chroma for a given TekHVC Hue and Value.
XcmsTekHVCQueryMaxV	Find the maximum Value for a given TekHVC Hue and Chroma.
XcmsTekHVCQueryMaxVC	Find the maximum Chroma and the Value at which it occurs.
XcmsTekHVCQueryMaxVSamples	Return the boundaries of the TekHVC gamut for a given Hue.
XcmsTekHVCQueryMinV	Find the minimum Value for a given TekHVC Hue and Chroma.
XcmsVisualOfCCC	Return the visual associated with a specified Color Conversion Context.
XcmsWhiteAdjustProc	Interface definition for the white point adjustment procedure.
XConfigureWindow	Change the window position, size, border width, or stacking order.
XConnectionNumber	Get connection number or file descriptor.
XContextDependentDrawing	Get a hint about context dependencies in the text of the locale.
XConvertSelection	Use the value of a selection.
XCopyArea	Copy an area of a drawable.
XCopyColormapAndFree	Copy a colormap and return a new colormap ID.
XCopyGC	Copy a graphics context.
XCopyPlane	Copy a single plane of a drawable into a drawable with depth, applying pixel values.
XCreateAssocTable	Create a new association table (X10).
XCreateBitmapFromData	Create a bitmap from X11 bitmap format data.
XCreateColormap	Create a colormap.
XCreateFontCursor	Create a cursor from the standard cursor font.
XCreateFontSet	Create a font set.
XCreateGC	Create a new graphics context for a given screen with the depth of the specified drawable.
XCreateGlyphCursor	Create a cursor from font glyphs.
XCreateIC	Create an input context.
XCreateImage	Allocate memory for an **XImage** structure.
XCreatePixmap	Create a pixmap.
XCreatePixmapCursor	Create a cursor from two bitmaps.
XCreatePixmapFromBitmapData	Create a pixmap with depth from bitmap data.
XCreateRegion	Create a new empty region.
XCreateSimpleWindow	Create an unmapped **InputOutput** window.

Routine	Description
`XCreateWindow`	Create a window and set attributes.
`XDefaultColormap`	Get screen's default colormap.
`XDefaultColormapOfScreen`	Get screen's default colormap.
`XDefaultDepth`	Get screen's default depth.
`XDefaultDepthOfScreen`	Get screen's default depth.
`XDefaultGC`	Get screen's default GC.
`XDefaultGCOfScreen`	Get screen's default GC.
`XDefaultRootWindow`	Get screen's default root window.
`XDefaultScreen`	Get screen number of default screen.
`XDefaultScreenOfDisplay`	Get Screen structure of default screen.
`XDefaultString`	Return the default string used for text conversion.
`XDefaultVisual`	Get screen's default visual structure.
`XDefaultVisualOfScreen`	Get screen's default visual structure.
`XDefineCursor`	Assign a cursor to a window.
`XDeleteAssoc`	Delete an entry from an association table.
`XDeleteContext`	Delete a context entry for a given window and type.
`XDeleteModifiermapEntry`	Delete an entry from an **XModifierKeymap** structure.
`XDeleteProperty`	Delete a window property.
`XDestroyAssocTable`	Free the memory allocated for an association table.
`XDestroyIC`	Destroy an input context.
`XDestroyImage`	Deallocate memory associated with an image.
`XDestroyRegion`	Deallocate storage associated with a region.
`XDestroySubwindows`	Destroy all subwindows of a window.
`XDestroyWindow`	Unmap and destroy a window and all subwindows.
`XDisableAccessControl`	Allow access from any host.
`XDisplayCells`	Query number of cells in default colormap of screen.
`XDisplayHeight`	Query height of screen in pixels.
`XDisplayHeightMM`	Query height of screen in millimeters.
`XDisplayKeycodes`	Returns range of keycodes used by server.
`XDisplayMotionBufferSize`	Return size of server's motion history buffer.
`XDisplayName`	Report the display name when connection to a display fails.
`XDisplayOfIM`	Get the display of an input method.
`XDisplayOfScreen`	Get Display structure of specified Screen structure.
`XDisplayPlanes`	Get number of planes of specified screen.
`XDisplayString`	Get string passed to **XOpenDisplay()**.
`XDisplayWidth`	Query width of screen in pixels.
`XDisplayWidthMM`	Query width of screen in millimeters.
`XDoesBackingStore`	Query server support for backing store or save unders.
`XDoesSaveUnders`	Query server support for backing store or save unders.

Routine	Description
XDraw	Draw a polyline or curve between vertex list (from X10).
XDrawArc	Draw an arc fitting inside a rectangle.
XDrawArcs	Draw multiple arcs.
XDrawFilled	Draw a filled polygon or curve from vertex list (from X10).
XDrawImageString	Draw 8-bit image text characters.
XDrawImageString16	Draw 16-bit image text characters.
XDrawLine	Draw a line between two points.
XDrawLines	Draw multiple connected lines.
XDrawPoint	Draw a point.
XDrawPoints	Draw multiple points.
XDrawRectangle	Draw an outline of a rectangle.
XDrawRectangles	Draw the outlines of multiple rectangles.
XDrawSegments	Draw multiple disjoint lines.
XDrawString	Draw an 8-bit text string, foreground only.
XDrawString16	Draw two-byte text strings.
XDrawText	Draw 8-bit polytext strings.
XDrawText16	Draw 16-bit polytext strings.
XEmptyRegion	Determine if a region is empty.
XEnableAccessControl	Use access control list to allow or deny connection requests.
XEqualRegion	Determine if two regions have the same size, offset, and shape.
XEventMaskOfScreen	Get initial root window event mask.
XEventsQueued	Check the number of events in the event queue.
XExtentsOfFontSet	Obtain the maximum extents structure for a font set.
XFetchBuffer	Return data from a cut buffer.
XFetchBytes	Return data from cut buffer 0.
XFetchName	Get a window's name (**XA_WM_NAME** property).
XFillArc	Fill an arc.
XFillArcs	Fill multiple arcs.
XFillPolygon	Fill a polygon.
XFillRectangle	Fill a rectangular area.
XFillRectangles	Fill multiple rectangular areas.
XFilterEvent	Filter X events for an input method.
XFindContext	Get data from the context manager (not graphics context).
XFindOnExtensionList	Find an extension on Xlib's extension list.
XFlush	Flush the request buffer (display all queued requests).
XFlushGC	Force cached GC changes to the server.
XFontSetExtents	XFontSetExtents structure.

Routine	Description
XFontsOfFontSet	Get the list of fonts used by a font set.
XForceScreenSaver	Turn the screen saver on or off.
XFree	Free specified in-memory data created by an Xlib function.
XFreeColormap	Delete a colormap and install the default colormap.
XFreeColors	Free colormap cells or planes.
XFreeCursor	Destroy a cursor.
XFreeExtensionList	Free memory allocated for a list of installed extensions to X.
XFreeFont	Unload a font and free storage for the font structure.
XFreeFontInfo	Free multiple font information arrays.
XFreeFontNames	Free the font name array.
XFreeFontPath	Free the memory allocated by **XGetFontPath()**.
XFreeFontSet	Free a font set.
XFreeGC	Free a graphics context.
XFreeModifiermap	Destroy and free a keyboard modifier mapping structure.
XFreePixmap	Free a pixmap ID.
XFreeStringList	Free memory allocated by **XTextPropertyToStringList**.
XGContextFromGC	Obtain the **GContext** (resource ID) associated with the specified graphics context.
XGeometry	Calculate window geometry given user geometry string and default geometry.
XGetAtomName	Get a name for a given atom.
XGetClassHint	Get the **XA_WM_CLASS** property of a window.
XGetCommand	Get the **XA_WM_COMMAND** property (command-line arguments).
XGetDefault	Scan the user preferences for program name and options.
XGetErrorDatabaseText	Obtain error messages from the error database.
XGetErrorText	Obtain a description of error code.
XGetFontPath	Get the current font search path.
XGetFontProperty	Get a font property given its atom.
XGetGCValues	Get GC component values from Xlib's GC cache.
XGetGeometry	Obtain the current geometry of drawable.
XGetIconName	Get the name to be displayed in an icon.
XGetIconSizes	Get preferred icon sizes.
XGetICValues	Get input context attributes.
XGetImage	Place contents of a rectangle from drawable into an image.
XGetIMValues	Obtain input method information.
XGetInputFocus	Return the current keyboard focus window.

Function Group

Routine	Description
XGetKeyboardControl	Obtain a list of the current keyboard preferences.
XGetKeyboardMapping	Return symbols for keycodes.
XGetModifierMapping	Obtain a mapping of modifier keys (Shift, Control, etc.).
XGetMotionEvents	Get pointer motion events.
XGetNormalHints	Get the size hints property of a window in normal state (not zoomed or iconified).
XGetPixel	Obtain a single pixel value from an image.
XGetPointerControl	Get the current pointer preferences.
XGetPointerMapping	Get the pointer button mapping.
XGetRGBColormaps	Read standard colormap property. Replaces **XGetStandardColormap**.
XGetScreenSaver	Get the current screen saver parameters.
XGetSelectionOwner	Return the owner of a selection.
XGetSizeHints	Read any property of type **XA_WM_SIZE_HINTS**.
XGetStandardColormap	Get the standard colormap property.
XGetSubImage	Copy a rectangle in drawable to a location within the pre-existing image.
XGetTextProperty	Read a TEXT property.
XGetTransientForHint	Get the **XA_WM_TRANSIENT_FOR** property of a window.
XGetVisualInfo	Find a visual information structure that matches the specified template.
XGetWindowAttributes	Obtain the current attributes of window.
XGetWindowProperty	Obtain the atom type and property format for a window.
XGetWMClientMachine	Read **WM_CLIENT_MACHINE** property.
XGetWMColormapWindows	Read **WM_COLORMAP_WINDOWS** property.
XGetWMHints	Read a window manager hints property.
XGetWMIconName	Read **XA_WM_ICON_NAME** property. Replaces **XGetIconName**.
XGetWMName	Read **XA_WM_NAME** property. Replaces **XFetchName**.
XGetWMNormalHints	Read **XA_WM_NORMAL_HINTS** property. Replaces **XGetNormalHints**.
XGetWMProtocols	Read **WM_PROTOCOLS** property.
XGetWMSizeHints	Read **XA_WM_SIZE_HINTS** property. Replaces **XGetSizeHints**.
XGetZoomHints	Read the size hints property of a zoomed window.
XGrabButton	Grab a pointer button.
XGrabKey	Grab a key.
XGrabKeyboard	Grab the keyboard.
XGrabPointer	Grab the pointer.

Routine	Description
XGrabServer	Grab the server.
XHeightMMOfScreen	Get height of screen in millimeters.
XHeightOfScreen	Get height of screen in pixels.
XIconifyWindow	Inform window manager that a top-level window should be iconified.
XIfEvent	Wait for matching event.
XImageByteOrder	Get server's byte order.
XIMOfIC	Obtain the input method of an input context.
XInitExtension	Initialize an extension.
XInsertModifiermapEntry	Add a new entry to an **XModifierKeymap** structure.
XInstallColormap	Install a colormap.
XInternAtom	Return an atom for a given name string.
XIntersectRegion	Compute the intersection of two regions.
XKeycodeToKeysym	Convert a keycode to a keysym.
XKeysymToKeycode	Convert a keysym to the appropriate keycode.
XKeysymToString	Convert a keysym symbol to a string.
XKillClient	Destroy a client or its remaining resources.
XLastKnownRequestProcessed	Get serial number of last request processed by server.
XListDepths	Return a list of the depths supported on this server.
XListExtensions	Return a list of all extensions to X supported by the server.
XListFonts	Return a list of the available font names.
XListFontsWithInfo	Obtain the names and information about loaded fonts.
XListHosts	Obtain a list of hosts having access to this display.
XListInstalledColormaps	Get a list of installed colormaps.
XListPixmapFormats	Return a list of the pixmap formats supported on this server.
XListProperties	Get the property list for a window.
XLoadFont	Load a font if not already loaded; get font ID.
XLoadQueryFont	Load a font and fill information structure.
XLocaleOfFontSet	Get the locale of a font set.
XLocaleOfIM	Get the locale of an input method.
XLookUpAssoc	Obtain data from an association table.
XLookupColor	Get database RGB values and closest hardware-- supported RGB values from color name.
XLookupKeysym	Get the keysym corresponding to a keycode in structure.
XLookupString	Map a key event to ASCII string, keysym, and **ComposeStatus**.
XLowerWindow	Lower a window in the stacking order.
XMakeAssoc	Create an entry in an association table.

Function Group

Routine	Description
XMapRaised	Map a window on top of its siblings.
XMapSubwindows	Map all subwindows.
XMapWindow	Map a window.
XMaskEvent	Remove the next event that matches mask.
XMatchVisualInfo	Obtain the visual information that matches the desired depth and class.
XMaxCmapsOfScreen	Get maximum number of installed colormaps supported by a screen.
XMaxRequestSize	Get maximum request size supported by server.
XmbDrawImageString	Draw internationalized multi-byte image text.
XmbDrawString	Draw internationalized multi-byte text.
XmbDrawText	Draw internationalized multi-byte text using multiple font sets.
XmbLookupString	Obtain composed multi-byte input from an input method.
XmbResetIC	Reset the state of an input context.
XmbSetWMProperties	Set window manager properties with multi-byte text.
XmbTextEscapement	Obtain the width of internationalized multi-byte text.
XmbTextExtents	Compute the extents of internationalized multi-byte text.
XmbTextListToTextProperty	Convert an internationalized multi-byte text list to a text property structure.
XmbTextPerCharExtents	Obtain per-character measurements of an internationalized multi-byte text string.
XmbTextPropertyToTextList	Convert an internationalized text property to a list of multi-byte strings.
XMinCmapsOfScreen	Get minimum number of installed colormaps supported by a screen.
XMoveResizeWindow	Change the size and position of a window.
XMoveWindow	Move a window.
XNewModifiermap	Create a keyboard modifier mapping structure.
XNextEvent	Get the next event of any type or window.
XNextRequest	Return serial number of next request.
XNoOp	Send a NoOp to exercise connection with the server.
XOffsetRegion	Change offset of a region.
XOpenDisplay	Connect a client program to an X server.
XOpenIM	Open input method.
XParseColor	Look up or translate RGB values from ASCII color name or hexadecimal value.
XParseGeometry	Generate position and size from standard window geometry string.
XPeekEvent	Get an event without removing it from the queue.

Routine	Description
XPeekIfEvent	Get an event without removing it from the queue; do not wait.
XPending	Flush the request buffer and return the number of pending input events.
Xpermalloc	Allocate memory never to be freed.
XPlanesOfScreen	Return the depth of a root window.
XPointInRegion	determine if a point is inside a region.
XPolygonRegion	generate a region from points.
XProtocolRevision	Return protocol revision number.
XProtocolVersion	Return protocol version number (currently 11).
XPutBackEvent	Push an event back on the input queue.
XPutImage	Draw a rectangular image on a window or pixmap.
XPutPixel	Set a pixel value in an image.
XQLength	Return the number of events on the queue.
XQueryBestCursor	Get the closest supported cursor sizes.
XQueryBestSize	Obtain the "best" supported cursor, tile, or stipple size.
XQueryBestStipple	Obtain the best supported stipple shape.
XQueryBestTile	Obtain the best supported fill tile shape.
XQueryColor	Obtain the RGB values and flags for a specified pixel value.
XQueryColors	Obtain RGB values for an array of pixel values.
XQueryExtension	Get extension information.
XQueryFont	Return information about a loaded font.
XQueryKeymap	Obtain a bit vector for the current state of the keyboard.
XQueryPointer	Get the current pointer location.
XQueryTextExtents	Query the server for string and font metrics.
XQueryTextExtents16	Query the server for string and font metrics of a 16-bit character string.
XQueryTree	Return a list of children, parent, and root.
XRaiseWindow	Raise a window to the top of the stacking order.
XReadBitmapFile	Read a bitmap from disk.
XRebindKeysym	Rebind a keysym to a string for client.
XRecolorCursor	Change the color of a cursor.
XReconfigureWMWindow	Change top-level window position, size, border width, or stacking order.
XRectInRegion	Determine if a rectangle resides in a region.
XRefreshKeyboardMapping	Update the stored modifier and keymap information.
XRemoveFromSaveSet	Remove a window from the client's save-set.
XRemoveHost	Remove a host from the access control list.
XRemoveHosts	Remove multiple hosts from the access control list.
XReparentWindow	Change a window's parent.

Function Group

Routine	Description
`XResetScreenSaver`	Reset the screen saver.
`XResizeWindow`	Change a window's size.
`XResourceManagerString`	Return string containing user's resource database.
`XRestackWindows`	Change the stacking order of siblings.
`XrmClassToString`	Convert `XrmClass` to string. Same as `XrmQuarkToString()`.
`XrmCombineDatabase`	Combine the contents of two resource databases.
`XrmCombineFileDatabase`	Combine the contents of a resource file and a resource database.
`XrmDestroyDatabase`	Destroy a resource database.
`XrmEnumerateDatabase`	Enumerate resource database entries.
`XrmGetDatabase`	Retrieve the resource database associated with a display.
`XrmGetFileDatabase`	Retrieve a database from a file.
`XrmGetResource`	Get a resource from name and class as strings.
`XrmGetStringDatabase`	Retrieve and store resource databases.
`XrmInitialize`	Initialize the resource manager.
`XrmLocaleOfDatabase`	Return the locale of a resource database.
`XrmMergeDatabases`	Merge the contents of one database with another.
`XrmNameToString`	Convert `XrmName` to string. Same as `XrmQuarkToString()`.
`XrmParseCommand`	Load a resource database from command-line arguments.
`XrmPermStringToQuark`	Convert a string to a quark.
`XrmPutFileDatabase`	Retrieve and store resource databases.
`XrmPutLineResource`	Add a resource entry given as a string of name and value.
`XrmPutResource`	Store a resource into a database.
`XrmPutStringResource`	Add a resource that is specified as a string.
`XrmQGetResource`	Get a resource from name and class as quarks.
`XrmQGetSearchList`	Return a list of database levels.
`XrmQGetSearchResource`	Search resource database levels for a given resource.
`XrmQPutResource`	Store a resource into a database using quarks.
`XrmQPutStringResource`	Add a string resource value to a database using quarks.
`XrmQuarkToString`	Convert a quark to a string.
`XrmRepresentationToString`	Convert `XrmRepresentation` to string. Same as `XrmQuarkToString()`.
`XrmSetDatabase`	Associate a resource database with a display.
`XrmStringToBindingQuarkList`	Convert a key string to a binding list and a quark list.
`XrmStringToClass`	Convert string to `XrmClass`. Same as `XrmStringToQuark()`.

Routine	Description
XrmStringToName	Convert string to **XrmName**. Same as **XrmStringToQuark()**.
XrmStringToQuark	Convert a string to a quark.
XrmStringToQuarkList	Convert a key string to a quark list.
XrmStringToRepresentation	Convert string to **XrmRepresentation**. Same as **XrmStringToQuark()**.
XrmUniqueQuark	Allocate a new quark.
XRootWindow	Return root window ID.
XRootWindowOfScreen	Return root window ID.
XRotateBuffers	Rotate the cut buffers.
XRotateWindowProperties	Rotate properties in the properties array.
XSaveContext	Save a data value corresponding to a window and context type (not graphics context).
XScreenCount	Get screen information.
XScreenNumberOfScreen	Get screen information.
XScreenOfDisplay	Get screen information.
XScreenResourceString	Returns the SCREEN_RESOURCES property of the specified screen.
XSelectInput	Select the event types to be sent to a window.
XSendEvent	Send an event.
XServerVendor	Return the vendor of connected server.
XSetAccessControl	Disable or enable access control.
XSetAfterFunction	Set a function called after all Xlib functions.
XSetArcMode	Set the arc mode in a graphics context.
XSetBackground	Set the background pixel value in a graphics context.
XSetClassHint	Set the **XA_WM_CLASS** property of a window.
XSetClipMask	Set **clip_mask** pixmap in a graphics context.
XSetClipOrigin	Set the clip origin in a graphics context.
XSetClipRectangles	Change **clip_mask** in a graphics context to the list of rectangles.
XSetCloseDownMode	Change the close down mode of a client.
XSetCommand	Set the **XA_WM_COMMAND** atom (command-line arguments).
XSetDashes	Set **dash_offset** and **dashes** (for lines) in a graphics context.
XSetErrorHandler	Set a nonfatal error event handler.
XSetFillRule	Set the fill rule in a graphics context.
XSetFillStyle	Set the fill style in a graphics context.
XSetFont	Set the current font in a graphics context.
XSetFontPath	Set the font search path.
XSetForeground	Set the foreground pixel value in a graphics context.
XSetFunction	Set the bitwise logical operation in a graphics context.

Function Group

Routine	Description
XSetGraphicsExposures	Set `graphics_exposures` in a graphics context.
XSetICFocus	Set input context focus.
XSetIconName	Set the name to be displayed in a window's icon.
XSetIconSizes	Set the value of the **XA_WM_ICON_SIZE** property.
XSetICValues	Set input context attributes.
XSetInputFocus	Set the keyboard focus window.
XSetIOErrorHandler	Handle fatal I/O errors.
XSetLineAttributes	Set the line drawing components in a graphics context.
XSetLocaleModifiers	Configure locale modifiers.
xSetModifierMapping	Set keycodes to be used as modifiers (Shift, Control, etc.).
XSetNormalHints	Set the size hints property of a window in normal state (not zoomed or iconified).
XSetPlaneMask	Set the plane mask in a graphics context.
XSetPointerMapping	Set the pointer button mapping.
XSetRegion	Set `clip_mask` of the graphics context to the specified region.
XSetRGBColormaps	Write standard colormap property. Replaces **XSetStandardColormap**.
XSetScreenSaver	Set the parameters of the screen saver.
XSetSelectionOwner	Set the owner of a selection.
XSetSizeHints	Set the value of any property of type **XA_WM_SIZE_HINTS**.
XSetStandardColormap	Change the standard colormap property.
XSetStandardProperties	Set the minimum set of properties for the window manager.
XSetState	Set the foreground, background, logical function, and plane mask in a graphics context.
xSetStipple	Set the stipple in a graphics context.
xSetSubwindowMode	Set the subwindow mode in a graphics context.
XSetTextProperty	Write a TEXT property using **XTextProperty** structure.
XSetTile	Set the fill tile in a graphics context.
XSetTransientForHint	Set the **XA_WM_TRANSIENT_FOR** property of a window.
XSetTSOrigin	Set the tile/stipple origin in a graphics context.
XSetWindowBackground	Set the background pixel attribute of a window.
XSetWindowBackgroundPixmap	Change the background tile attribute of a window.
XSetWindowBorder	Change a window border attribute to the specified pixel value and repaint the border.

Routine	Description
XSetWindowBorderPixmap	Change a window border tile attribute and repaint the border.
XSetWindowBorderWidth	Change the border width of a window.
XSetWindowColormap	Set the colormap for a specified window.
XSetWMClientMachine	Write **WM_CLIENT_MACHINE** property.
XSetWMColormapWindows	Write **WM_COLORMAP_WINDOWS** property.
XSetWMHints	Set a window manager hints property.
XSetWMIconName	Write **XA_WM_ICON_NAME** property. Replaces **XSetIconName**.
XSetWMName	Write **XA_WM_NAME** property. Replaces **XStoreName**.
XSetWMNormalHints	Write **XA_WM_NORMAL_HINTS** property. Replaces **XSetNormalHints**.
XSetWMProperties	Write all standard properties. Replaces **XSetStandardProperties**.
XSetWMProtocols	Write **WM_PROTOCOLS** property.
XSetWMSizeHints	Write **XA_WM_SIZE_HINTS** property. Replaces **XSetSizeHints**.
XSetZoomHints	Set the size hints property of a zoomed window.
XShrinkRegion	Reduce or expand the size of a region.
XStoreBuffer	Store data in a cut buffer.
XStoreBytes	Store data in cut buffer 0.
XStoreColor	Set or change a read/write entry of a colormap to the closest available hardware color.
XStoreColors	Set or change read/write colorcells to the closest available hardware colors.
XStoreName	Assign a name to a window for the window manager.
XStoreNamedColor	Allocate a read/write colorcell by English color name.
XStringListToTextProperty	Convert a list of strings to an **XTextProperty** structure.
XStringToKeysym	Convert a keysym name string to a keysym.
XSubImage	Create a subimage from part of an image.
XSubtractRegion	Subtract one region from another.
XSupportsLocale	Determine locale support.
XSync	Flush the request buffer and wait for all events and errors to be processed by the server.
XSynchronize	Enable or disable synchronization for debugging.
XTextExtents	Get string and font metrics.
XTextExtents16	Get string and font metrics of a 16-bit character string.
XTextPropertyToStringList	Obtain a list of strings from a **XTextProperty** structure.

Function Group

Routine	Description
XTextWidth	Get the width in pixels of an 8-bit character string.
XTextWidth16	Get the width in pixels of a 16-bit character string.
XTranslateCoordinates	Change the coordinate system from one window to another.
XUndefineCursor	Disassociate a cursor from a window.
XUngrabButton	Release a button from grab.
XUngrabKey	Release a key from grab.
XUngrabKeyboard	Release the keyboard from grab.
XUngrabPointer	Release the pointer from grab.
XUngrabServer	Release the server from grab.
XUninstallColormap	Uninstall a colormap; install default if not already installed.
XUnionRectWithRegion	Add a rectangle to a region.
XUnionRegion	Compute the union of two regions.
XUniqueContext	Create a new context ID (not graphics context).
XUnloadFont	Unload a font.
XUnmapSubwindows	Unmap all subwindows of a given window.
XUnmapWindow	Unmap a window.
XUnsetICFocus	Set and unset input context focus.
XVaCreateNestedList	Allocate a nested variable argument list.
XVendorRelease	Return vendor release number.
XVisualIDFromVisual	Returns the visual ID for the specified visual structure.
XWarpPointer	Move the pointer to another point on the screen.
XwcDrawImageString	Draw internationalized wide-character image text.
XwcDrawString	Draw internationalized wide-character text.
XwcDrawText	Draw internationalized wide-character text using multiple font sets.
XwcFreeStringList	Free memory allocated by **XwcTextPropertyToTextList( )**.
XwcLookupString	Obtain composed wide-character input from an input method.
XwcResetIC	Reset the state of an input context.
XwcTextEscapement	Obtain the width of internationalized wide-character text.
XwcTextExtents	Compute the extents of internationalized wide-character text.
XwcTextListToTextProperty	Convert an internationalized wide-character text list to a text property structure.
XwcTextPerCharExtents	Obtain per-character measurements of an internationalized wide-character text string.
XwcTextPropertyToTextList	Convert an internationalized text property to a list of wide-character strings.

Routine	Description
XWhitePixel	Get the white pixel value.
XWhitePixelOfScreen	Get the white pixel value.
XWidthMMOfScreen	Get width of screen in millimeters.
XWidthOfScreen	Get width of screen in pixels.
XWindowEvent	Remove the next event matching mask and window.
XWithdrawWindow	Request that window manager unmap a top-level window.
XWMGeometry	Calculate window geometry given user geometry string and default geometry.
XWriteBitmapFile	Write a bitmap to a file.
XXorRegion	Calculate the difference between the union and intersection of two regions.

Function Group

Error Messages and Protocol Requests

This appendix contains two tables: Table B-1 describes the standard error codes (the `error_code` member of `XErrorEvent`) and what causes them, and Table B-2 describes the mapping between protocol requests and Xlib functions. Each reference page in this volume describes in more detail the errors that may occur because of that Xlib routine. Volume One, Chapter 3, *Basic Window Program*, describes the handling of errors in general. Volume Zero, *X Protocol Reference Manual*, provides detailed reference pages for each protocol request. Volume Zero also provides a list of Xlib functions and the protocol requests they generate, the opposite table to the one provided here.

A protocol request is the actual network message that is sent from Xlib to the server. Many convenience functions are provided in Xlib to make programs easier to write and more readable. When any one of several convenience routines is called it will be translated into one type of protocol request. For example, `XMoveWindow()` and `XResizeWindow()` are convenience routines for the more general `XConfigureWindow()`. Both of these Xlib routines use the protocol request ConfigureWindow. The protocol request that causes an error, along with other information about the error is printed to the standard error output by the default error handlers. In order to find out where in your code the error occurred, you will need to know what Xlib function to look for. Use Table B-2 to find this function.

Xlib functions that do not appear in Table B-2 do not generate protocol requests. They perform their function without affecting the display and without requiring information from the server. If errors can occur in them, the errors are reported in the returned value.

Table B-1. Error Messages

Error Code	Possible Cause
BadAccess	Specifies that the client attempted to grab a key/button combination that is already grabbed by another client; free a colormap entry that is not allocated by the client; free a colormap entry in a colormap that was created with all entries writable (`AllocAll`); store into a read-only or unallocated colormap entry; modify the access control list from other than the local (or otherwise authorized) host; or select an event type that only one client can select at a time, when another client has already selected it.

Error Code	Possible Cause
BadAlloc	Specifies that the server failed to allocate the requested resource. Note that the server can generate `BadAlloc` on any request.
BadAtom	Specifies that a value for an `Atom` argument does not name a defined `Atom`.
BadColor	Specifies that a value for a `Colormap` argument does not name a defined `Colormap`.
BadCursor	Specifies that a value for a `Cursor` argument does not name a defined `Cursor`.
BadDrawable	Specifies that a value for a `Drawable` argument does not name a defined `Window` or `Pixmap`.
BadFont	Specifies that a value for a font argument does not name a defined `Font`, or in some cases a defined `GContext`.
BadGC	Specifies that a value for a `GContext` argument does not name a defined `GContext`.
BadIDChoice	Specifies that the value chosen for a resource identifier either is not included in the range assigned to the client or is already in use. This is an internal Xlib or server error.
BadImplementation	Specifies that the server does not implement some aspect of the request. A server that generates this error for a core request is deficient. Clients should be prepared to receive such errors and either handle or discard them.
BadLength	Specifies that the length of a request exceeds the maximum length accepted by the server, or that the length of a request is shorter or longer than that required to contain the arguments. The latter is an internal Xlib or server error.
BadMatch	Specifies that the root and depth of the GC in a graphics request does not match that of the drawable, or that an `InputOnly` window is used as a `Drawable` or lacks the attribute being set, or that some argument (or pair of arguments) has the correct type and range but fails to ''match'' in some other way required by the request.
BadName	Specifies that a font or color of the specified name does not exist.
BadPixmap	Specifies that a value for a `Pixmap` argument does not name a defined `Pixmap`.
BadRequest	Specifies that the major or minor opcode does not specify a valid request. This is usually an internal Xlib or server error.

Table B-1. Error Messages (continued)

Error Code	Possible Cause
BadValue	Specifies that some numeric value falls outside the range of values accepted by the request. Unless a specific range is specified for an argument, the full range defined by the argument's type is accepted. Any argument defined as a set of alternatives can generate this error.
BadWindow	Specifies that a value for a `Window` argument does not name a defined `Window`.

The `BadAtom`, `BadColor`, `BadCursor`, `BadDrawable`, `BadFont`, `BadGC`, `Bad-Pixmap`, and `BadWindow` errors are also used when the argument type should be among a set of fixed alternatives (for example, a window ID, `PointerRoot`, or `None`) and some other constant or variable is used.

Table B-2. Protocol Requests to Xlib Functions

Protocol Request	Xlib Function
AllocColor	`XAllocColor` `XcmsAllocColor`
AllocColorCells	`XAllocColorCells`
AllocColorPlanes	`XAllocColorPlanes`
AllocNamedColor	`XAllocNamedColor` `XcmsAllocNamedColor`
AllowEvents	`XAllowEvents`
Bell	`XBell`
ChangeActivePointerGrab	`XChangeActivePointerGrab`

ChangeGC	`XChangeGC`
	`XFlushGC` (triggers)
	`XSetArcMode`
	`XSetBackground`
	`XSetClipMask`
	`XSetClipOrigin`
	`XSetFillRule`
	`XSetFillStyle`
	`XSetFont`
	`XSetForeground`
	`XSetFunction`
	`XSetGraphicsExposures`
	`XSetLineAttributes`
	`XSetPlaneMask`
	`XSetState`
	`XSetStipple`
	`XSetSubwindowMode`

Errors

Protocol Request	Xlib Function
	`XSetTile`
	`XSetTSOrigin`
ChangeHosts	`XAddHost`
	`XAddHosts`
	`XRemoveHost`
	`XRemoveHosts`
ChangeKeyboardControl	`XAutoRepeatOff`
	`XAutoRepeatOn`
	`XChangeKeyboardControl`
ChangeKeyboardMapping	`XChangeKeyboardMapping`
ChangePointerControl	`XChangePointerControl`
ChangeProperty	`XChangeProperty`
	`XmbSetWMProperties`
	`XSetClassHint`
	`XSetCommand`
	`XSetIconName`
	`XSetIconSizes`
	`XSetNormalHints`
	`XSetRGBColormaps`
	`XSetSizeHints`
	`XSetStandardProperties`
	`XSetTextProperty`
	`XSetTransientForHint`
	`XSetWMProperties`
	`XSetWMClientMachine`
	`XSetWMColormapWindows`
	`XSetWMIconName`
	`XSetWMName`
	`XSetWMNormalHints`
	`XSetWMProtocols`
	`XSetWMSizeHints`
	`XSetWMHints`
	`XSetZoomHints`
	`XStoreBuffer`
	`XStoreBytes`
	`XStoreName`
ChangeSaveSet	`XAddToSaveSet`
	`XChangeSaveSet`
	`XRemoveFromSaveSet`
ChangeWindowAttributes	`XChangeWindowAttributes`
	`XDefineCursor`
	`XSelectInput`
	`XSetWindowBackground`
	`XSetWindowBackgroundPixmap`
	`XSetWindowBorder`

Protocol Request	Xlib Function

	`XSetWindowBorderPixmap`
	`XSetWindowColormap`
	`XUndefineCursor`

CirculateWindow	`XCirculateSubwindows`
	`XCirculateSubwindowsDown`
	`XCirculateSubwindowsUp`

ClearArea	`XClearArea` `XClearWindow`
CloseFont	`XFreeFont` `XUnloadFont`

ConfigureWindow	`XConfigureWindow`
	`XLowerWindow`
	`XMapRaised`
	`XMoveResizeWindow`
	`XMoveWindow`
	`XRaiseWindow`
	`XReconfigureWMWindow`
	`XResizeWindow`
	`XRestackWindows`
	`XSetWindowBorderWidth`

ConvertSelection	`XConvertSelection`
CopyArea	`XCopyArea`
CopyColormapAndFree	`XCopyColormapAndFree`
CopyGC	`XCopyGC`
CopyPlane	`XCopyPlane`
CreateColormap	`XCreateColormap`
CreateCursor	`XCreatePixmapCursor`
CreateGC	`XCreateGC` `XOpenDisplay`
CreateGlyphCursor	`XCreateFontCursor` `XCreateGlyphCursor`
CreatePixmap	`XCreatePixmap`
CreateWindow	`XCreateSimpleWindow` `XCreateWindow`
DeleteProperty	`XDeleteProperty`
DestroySubwindows	`XDestroySubwindows`
DestroyWindow	`XDestroyWindow`
FillPoly	`XFillPolygon`

Errors

Protocol Request	Xlib Function

ForceScreenSaver	`XActivateScreenSaver`
	`XForceScreenSaver`
	`XResetScreenSaver`

FreeColormap	`XFreeColormap`
FreeColors	`XFreeColors`
FreeCursor	`XFreeCursor`
FreeGC	`XFreeGC`
FreePixmap	`XFreePixmap`
GetAtomName	`XGetAtomName`
GetFontPath	`XGetFontPath`
GetGeometry	`XGetGeometry` `XGetWindowAttributes`
GetImage	`XGetImage`

GetInputFocus	`XGetInputFocus`
	`XSync`
	`XSynchronize`

GetKeyboardControl	`XGetKeyboardControl`
GetKeyboardMapping	`XGetKeyboardMapping`
GetModifierMapping	`XGetModifierMapping`
GetMotionEvents	`XGetMotionEvents`
GetPointerControl	`XGetPointerControl`
GetPointerMapping	`XGetPonterMapping`

GetProperty	`XFetchBytes`
	`XFetchName`
	`XGetClassHint`
	`XGetIconName`
	`XGetIconSizes`
	`XGetNormalHints`
	`XGetRGBColormaps`
	`XGetSizeHints`
	`XGetTextProperty`
	`XGetTransientForHint`
	`XGetWindowProperty`
	`XGetWMClientMachine`
	`XGetWMColormapWindows`
	`XGetWMHints`
	`XGetWMIconName`
	`XGetWMName`
	`XGetWMNormalHints`

Protocol Request	Xlib Function
	`XGetWMProtocols`
	`XGetWMProperties`
	`XGetWMSizeHints`
	`XGetZoomHints`
GetScreenSaver	`XGetScreenSaver`
GetSelectionOwner	`XGetSelectionOwner`
GetWindowAttributes	`XGetWindowAttributes`
GrabButton	`XGrabButton`
GrabKey	`XGrabKey`
GrabKeyboard	`XGrabKeyboard`
GrabPointer	`XGrabPointer`
GrabServer	`XGrabServer`
ImageText8	`XDrawImageString`
	`XmbDrawImageString`
	`XwcDrawImageString`
ImageText16	`XDrawImageString16`
InstallColormap	`XInstallColormap`
InternAtom	`XInternAtom`
	`XGetWMProtocols`
	`XGetWMColormapWindows`
	`XIconifyWindow`
	`XSetWMProtocols`
	`XSetWMColormapWindows`
KillClient	`XKillClient`
ListExtensions	`XListExtensions`
ListFonts	`XListFonts`
ListFontsWithInfo	`XListFontsWithInfo`
ListHosts	`XListHosts`
ListInstalledColormaps	`XListInstalledColormaps`
ListProperties	`XListProperties`
LookupColor	`XLookupColor`
	`XcmsLookupColor`
	`XParseColor`
MapSubwindows	`XMapSubwindows`
MapWindow	`XMapRaised`
	`XMapWindow`

Errors

Protocol Request	Xlib Function
NoOperation	`XNoOp`
OpenFont	`XLoadFont` `XLoadQueryFont`
PolyArc	`XDrawArc` `XDrawArcs`
PolyFillArc	`XFillArc` `XFillArcs`
PolyFillRectangle	`XFillRectangle` `XFillRectangles`
PolyLine	`XDrawLines`
PolyPoint	`XDrawPoint` `XDrawPoints`
PolyRectangle	`XDrawRectangle` `XDrawRectangles`
PolySegment	`XDrawLine` `XDrawSegments`

PolyText8	`XDrawString`
	`XDrawText`
	`XmbDrawString`
	`XmbDrawText`
	`XwcDrawString`
	`XwcDrawText`

PolyText16	`XDrawString16` `XDrawText16`
PutImage	`XPutImage`

QueryBestSize	`XQueryBestCursor`
	`XQueryBestSize`
	`XQueryBestStipple`
	`XQueryBestTile`

QueryColors	`XQueryColor`
	`XQueryColors`
	`XcmsQueryColor`
	`XcmsQueryColors`

QueryExtension	`XInitExtension` `XQueryExtension`
QueryFont	`XLoadQueryFont`
QueryKeymap	`XQueryKeymap`
QueryPointer	`XQueryPointer`
QueryTextExtents	`XQueryTextExtents`

Protocol Request	Xlib Function
	`XQueryTextExtents16`
QueryTree	`XQueryTree`
RecolorCursor	`XRecolorCursor`
ReparentWindow	`XReparentWindow`
RotateProperties	`XRotateBuffers` `XRotateWindowProperties`

SendEvent	`XSendEvent`
	`XIconifyWindow`
	`XReconfigureWMWindow`
	`XWithdrawWindow`

SetAccessControl	`XDisableAccessControl`
	`XEnableAccessControl`
	`XSetAccessControl`

SetClipRectangles	`XSetClipRectangles`
SetCloseDownMode	`XSetCloseDownMode`
SetDashes	`XSetDashes`
SetFontPath	`XSetFontPath`
SetInputFocus	`XSetInputFocus`
SetModifierMapping	`XSetModifierMapping`
SetPointerMapping	`XSetPointerMapping`
SetScreenSaver	`XSetScreenSaver`
SetSelectionOwner	`XSetSelectionOwner`

StoreColors	`XStoreColor`
	`XStoreColors`
	`XcmsStoreColor`
	`XcmsStoreColors`

StoreNamedColor	`XStoreNamedColor`
TranslateCoords	`XTranslateCoordinates`
UngrabButton	`XUngrabButton`
UngrabKey	`XUngrabKey`
UngrabKeyboard	`XUngrabKeyboard`
UngrabPointer	`XUngrabPointer`
UngrabServer	`XUngrabServer`
UninstallColormap	`XUninstallColormap`
UnmapSubwindows	`XUnmapSubWindows`

Errors

Protocol Request	Xlib Function
UnmapWindow	`XUnmapWindow`
	`XWithdrawWindow`
WarpPointer	`XWarpPointer`

C
Macros

Once you have successfully connected your application to an X server, you can obtain data from the **Display**, **Screen**, and **Visual** structures associated with that display. The Xlib interface provides a number of useful C language macros which return data from these structures.

Xlib provides function versions of the **Display**, **Screen**, and **Visual** macros, primarily for use with language bindings other than C; they have the same names as the macros except that the function versions begin with the letter "X." These functions have reference pages in the main part of this book (sometimes several functions on one page). The macros and equivalent functions use the same arguments. Using the macro versions is slightly more efficient in C because it eliminates function call overhead.

Note that some macros (and their corresponding functions) take as arguments an integer screen number (*scr_num*) while others take a pointer to a **Screen** structure (*scr_ptr*). *scr_num* is returned by the **DefaultScreen()** macro and *scr_ptr* is returned by the **DefaultScreenOfDisplay()** macro. It's easy to provide the wrong one, and that can cause a core dump.

A few Xlib functions access **Display** and **Visual** structure members, and are simple enough to have macro versions, but macro versions are not defined in the Xlib standard. These are **XDisplayMotionBufferSize()**, **XResourceManagerString()**, **XDisplayKeycodes()**, **XMaxRequestSize()**, **XScreenNumberOfScreen()**, **XListDepths()**, **XListPixmapFormats()**, and **XVisualIDFromVisual()**.

Xlib also provides macros for interpreting keycodes, returning the an image's format, converting between various resource manager types, flushing the GC, and accessing various Color Conversion Context values. For the purposes of this appendix, the macros are divided into five categories: Display macros, Image Format macros, Keysym Classification macros, Resource Manager macros, and Miscellaneous macros. The macros are listed alphabetically within each category.

C.1 Display Macros

`AllPlanes()`   Return a value with all bits set suitable for use as a plane mask argument.

`BlackPixel()`*(display,scr_num)*
>   Return the black pixel value in the default colormap that is created by `XOpenDisplay()`.

`BlackPixelOfScreen()`*(scr_ptr)*
>   Return the black pixel value in the default colormap of the specified screen.

`CellsOfScreen()`*(scr_ptr)*
>   Return the number of colormap cells in the default colormap of the specified screen.

`ConnectionNumber()`*(display)*
>   Return a connection number for the specified display. On a UNIX system, this is the file descriptor of the connection.

`DefaultColormap()`*(display,scr_num)*
>   Return the default colormap for the specified screen. Most routine allocations of color should be made out of this colormap.

`DefaultColormapOfScreen()`*(scr_ptr)*
>   Return the default colormap of the specified screen.

`DefaultDepth()`*(display,scr_num)*
>   Return the depth (number of planes) of the root window for the specified screen. Other depths may also be supported on this screen. See Volume One, Chapter 7, *Color*, or the reference pages for `XMatchVisual-Info()` and `XGetVisualInfo()` to find out how to determine what depths are available.

`DefaultDepthOfScreen()`*(scr_ptr)*
>   Return the default depth of the specified screen.

`DefaultGC()`*(display,scr_num)*
>   Return the default graphics context for the specified screen.

`DefaultGCOfScreen()`*(scr_ptr)*
>   Return the default graphics context (GC) of the specified screen.

`DefaultRootWindow()`*(display)*
>   Return the ID of the root window on the default screen. Most applications should use `RootWindow()` instead so that screen selection is supported.

`DefaultScreen()`*(display)*
>   Return the integer that was specified in the last segment of the string passed to `XOpenDisplay()` or from the DISPLAY environment variable if NULL was used. For example, if the DISPLAY environment were `Ogre:0.1`, then `DefaultScreen()` would return 1.

`DefaultScreenOfDisplay()`(*display*)

> Return the default screen of the specified display.

`DefaultVisual()`(*display,scr_num*)

> Return a pointer to the default visual structure for the specified screen.

`DefaultVisualOfScreen()`(*scr_ptr*)

> Return the default visual of the specified screen.

`DisplayCells()`(*display,scr_num*)

> Return the maximum possible number of colormap cells on the specified screen. This macro is misnamed: it should have been **ScreenCells**.

`DisplayHeight()`(*display,scr_num*)

> Return the height in pixels of the screen. This macro is misnamed: it should have been **ScreenHeight**.

`DisplayHeightMM()`(*display,scr_num*)

> Return the height in millimeters of the specified screen. This macro is misnamed: it should have been **ScreenHeightMM**.

`DisplayOfScreen()`(*scr_ptr*)

> Return the display associated with the specified screen.

`DisplayPlanes()`(*display,scr_num*)

> Return the number of planes on the specified screen. This macro is misnamed: it should have been **ScreenPlanes**.

`DisplayString()`(*display*)

> Return the string that was passed to **XOpenDisplay()** when the current display was opened (or, if that was **NULL**, the value of the DISPLAY environment variable). This macro is useful in applications which invoke the fork system call and want to open a new connection to the same display from the child process.

`DisplayWidth()`(*display,scr_num*)

> Return the width in pixels of the screen. This macro is misnamed: it should have been **ScreenWidth**.

`DisplayWidthMM()`(*display,scr_num*)

> Return the width in millimeters of the specified screen. This macro is misnamed: it should have been **ScreenWidthMM**.

`DoesBackingStore()`(*scr_ptr*)

> Return a value indicating whether the screen supports backing stores. Values are **WhenMapped**, **NotUseful**, or **Always**. See Volume One for a discussion of the backing store.

`DoesSaveUnders()`(*scr_ptr*)

> Return a Boolean value indicating whether the screen supports save unders. If **True**, the screen supports save unders. If **False**, the screen does not support save unders. See Volume One for a discussion of the save under.

Macros

dpyno(*display*)
> Return the file descriptor of the connected display. On a UNIX system, you can then pass this returned file descriptor to the *select*(3) system call when your application program is driving more than one display at a time.

EventMaskOfScreen()(*scr_ptr*)
> Return the initial event mask for the root window of the specified screen.

HeightOfScreen()(*scr_ptr*)
> Return the height in pixels of the specified screen.

HeightMMOfScreen()(*scr_ptr*)
> Return the height in millimeters of the specified screen.

Keyboard(*display*)
> Return the device ID for the main keyboard connected to the display.

LastKnownRequestProcessed()(*display*)
> Return the serial ID of the last known protocol request to have been issued. This can be useful in processing errors, since the serial number of failing requests are provided in the **XErrorEvent** structure.

MaxCmapsOfScreen()(*scr_ptr*)
> Return the maximum number of installed (hardware) colormaps supported by the specified screen.

MinCmapsOfScreen()(*scr_ptr*)
> Return the minimum number of installed (hardware) colormaps supported by the specified screen.

NextRequest()(*display*)
> Return the serial ID of the next protocol request to be issued. This can be useful in processing errors, since the serial number of failing requests are provided in the **XErrorEvent** structure.

PlanesOfScreen()(*scr_ptr*)
> Return the number of planes in the specified screen.

ProtocolRevision()(*display*)
> Return the minor protocol revision number of the X server.

ProtocolVersion()(*display*)
> Return the version number of the X protocol associated with the connected display. This is currently 11.

QLength()(*display*)
> Return the number of events that can be queued by the specified display.

RootWindow()(*display,scr_num*)
> Return the ID of the root window. This macro is necessary for routines that reference the root window or create a top-level window for an application.

RootWindowOfScreen()(*scr_ptr*)
> Return the ID of the root window of the specified screen.

`ScreenCount()`(*display*)

>Return the number of available screens on a specified display.

`ScreenOfDisplay()`(*display,scr_num*)

>Return the specified screen of the specified display.

`ServerVendor()`(*display*)

>Return a pointer to a null terminated string giving some identification of the owner of the X server implementation.

`VendorRelease()`(*display*)

>Return a number related to the release of the X server by the vendor.

`WhitePixel()`(*display,scr_num*)

>Return the white pixel value in the default colormap that is created by **XOpenDisplay()**.

`WhitePixelOfScreen()`(*scr_ptr*)

>Return the white pixel value in the default colormap of the specified screen.

`WidthOfScreen()`(*scr_ptr*)

>Return the width of the specified screen.

`WidthMMOfScreen()`(*scr_ptr*)

>Return the width of the specified screen in millimeters.

`XDisplayMotionBufferSize()`(*display*)

>Return an **unsigned long** value containing the size of the motion buffer on the server. If this function returns zero, the server has no motion history buffer.

`XMaxRequestSize()`(*display*)

>Return a **long** value containing the maximum size of a protocol request for the specified server, in units of four bytes.

`XScreenNumberOfScreen()`(*scr_ptr*)

>Return the integer screen number corresponding to the specified pointer to a Screen structure.

`XVisualIDFromVisual()`(*visual*)

>Returns the ID of the server resource associated with a visual structure. This is useful when storing standard colormap properties.

C.2 Image Format Macros

BitmapBitOrder()(*display*)

> Within each **BitmapUnit()**, the leftmost bit in the bitmap as displayed on the screen is either the least or the most significant bit in the unit. Returns **LSBFirst** or **MSBFirst**.

BitmapPad()(*display*)

> Each scan line must be padded to a multiple of bits specified by the value returned by this macro.

BitmapUnit()(*display*)

> Returns the size of a bitmap's unit. The scan line is quantized (calculated) in multiples of this value.

ImageByteOrder()(*display*)

> Returns the byte order for images required by the server for each scan line unit in XY format (bitmap) or for each pixel value in Z format. Values are **LSBFirst** or **MSBFirst**.

C.3 Keysym Classification Macros

You may want to test if a keysym of the defined set (XK_MISCELLANY) is, for example, on the key pad or the function keys. You can use the keysym macros to perform the following tests:

IsCursorKey()(*keysym*)

> Return **True** if the keysym represents a cursor key.

IsFunctionKey()(*keysym*)

> Return **True** if the keysym represents a function key.

IsKeypadKey()(*keysym*)

> Return **True** if the keysym represents a key pad.

IsMiscFunctionKey()(*keysym*)

> Return **True** if the keysym represents a miscellaneous function key.

IsModifierKey()(*keysym*)

> Return **True** if the keysym represents a modifier key.

IsPFKey()(*keysym*)

> Return **True** if the keysym represents a PF key.

C.4 Resource Manager Macros

These macros convert from strings to quarks and quarks to strings. They are used by the resource manager. Note that they do not follow the normal naming conventions for macros, since they begin with an X.

`XrmStringToName(string)`

Convert string to **XrmName**. Same as **XrmStringToQuark( )**.

`XrmStringToClass(string)`

Convert string to **XrmClass**. Same as **XrmStringToQuark( )**.

`XrmStringToRepresentation (string)`

Convert string to **XrmRepresentation**. Same as **XrmString-ToQuark( )**.

`XrmNameToString(name)`

Convert **XrmName** to string. Same as **XrmQuarkToString( )**.

`XrmClassToString(class)`

Convert **XrmClass** to string. Same as **XrmQuarkToString( )**.

`XrmRepresentationToString (type)`

Convert **XrmRepresentation** to string. Same as **XrmQuark-ToString( )**.

`XResourceManagerString( ) display)`

Return a pointer to the resource database string stored in the **Display** structure. This string is read from the RESOURCE_MANAGER property on the root window; this property is normally set by the *xrdb* client.

C.5 Miscellaneous Macros

`FlushGC( )(display, gc)`

Force cached GC changes to the server. Used mostly in extension writing.

`ClientWhitePointOfCCC( )(ccc)`

Returns the client white point of a Color Conversion Context.

`DisplayOfCCC( )(ccc)`

Returns the display of a Color Conversion Context.

`ScreenNumberOfCCC( )(ccc)`

Returns the screen number of a Color Conversion Context.

`ScreenWhitePointOfCCC( )(ccc)`

Returns the white point of the screen associated with a Color Conversion Context.

`VisualOfCCC( )(ccc)`

Returns the visual of a Color Conversion Context.

D
The Server-side Color Database

The server-side color database is used by the server to translate color name strings into RGB values. It is used by `XParseColor()`, `XLookupColor()`, and `XStoreNamed-Color()`. These routines make it easier to allow the user to specify color names. Use of these names for routine color allocation of read-only colorcells is encouraged since this increases the chance of sharing colorcells and thereby makes the colormap go further before running out of colorcells. The location in the file system of the text version of the color database is an implementation detail, but by default on a UNIX system it is */usr/lib/X11/rgb.txt*.

It should be noted that while a sample color database is provided with the standard X11 distribution, it is not specified as an X Consortium standard and is not part of the X Protocol or Xlib. Therefore, it is permissible for server vendors to change the color names, although they will probably only add color names. Furthermore, hardware vendors are intended to change the RGB values for each display hardware to achieve the proper "gamma correction" so that the colors described by the name really generate that color. But few of them actually do so, so the colors you get might not be what you expect.

The RGB values in the Release 3 database were originally tuned for the DEC VT240 display. The color that appears on our Sun system given these RGB values for "pink," for example, looks more like light burgundy. In Release 4, a new RGB color database is provided, which provides many more color names and provides values that generate colors that match their names on more monitors. We are listing only the Release 4 color database here, since few people are still using Release 3.

In Release 5, the X Color Management System was introduced. This is a device-independent color system that provides identical colors on all screens and output devices, if they are properly calibrated. Xcms provides its own databases of color names and their device-independent color values, kept on the client side, in addition to the RGB color database kept by the server. The Xcms color database is not standardized and so we cannot list what colors will be defined on the systems you use. Check your Xlib vendor's documentation for details.

Each color name in the database may be used in the form shown or in mixed case, with initial capitals and all spaces eliminated. Table D-1 (see next page) shows the Release 4 database.

Table D-1. The R4 Color Database

English Words	Red	Green	Blue	English Words	Red	Green	Blue
snow	255	250	250	black	0	0	0
ghost white	248	248	255	dark slate gray	47	79	79
GhostWhite	248	248	255	DarkSlateGray	47	79	79
white smoke	245	245	245	dark slate grey	47	79	79
WhiteSmoke	245	245	245	DarkSlateGrey	47	79	79
gainsboro	220	220	220	dim gray	105	105	105
floral white	255	250	240	DimGray	105	105	105
FloralWhite	255	250	240	dim grey	105	105	105
old lace	253	245	230	DimGrey	105	105	105
OldLace	253	245	230	slate gray	112	128	144
linen	250	240	230	SlateGray	112	128	144
antique white	250	235	215	slate grey	112	128	144
AntiqueWhite	250	235	215	SlateGrey	112	128	144
papaya whip	255	239	213	light slate gray	119	136	153
PapayaWhip	255	239	213	LightSlateGray	119	136	153
blanched almond	255	235	205	light slate grey	119	136	153
BlanchedAlmond	255	235	205	LightSlateGrey	119	136	153
bisque	255	228	196	gray	192	192	192
peach puff	255	218	185	grey	192	192	192
PeachPuff	255	218	185	light grey	211	211	211
navajo white	255	222	173	LightGrey	211	211	211
NavajoWhite	255	222	173	light gray	211	211	211
moccasin	255	228	181	LightGray	211	211	211
cornsilk	255	248	220	midnight blue	25	25	112
ivory	255	255	240	MidnightBlue	25	25	112
lemon chiffon	255	250	205	navy	0	0	128
LemonChiffon	255	250	205	navy blue	0	0	128
seashell	255	245	238	NavyBlue	0	0	128
honeydew	240	255	240	cornflower blue	100	149	237
mint cream	245	255	250	CornflowerBlue	100	149	237
MintCream	245	255	250	dark slate blue	72	61	139
azure	240	255	255	DarkSlateBlue	72	61	139
alice blue	240	248	255	slate blue	106	90	205
AliceBlue	240	248	255	SlateBlue	106	90	205
lavender	230	230	250	medium slate blue	123	104	238
lavender blush	255	240	245	MediumSlateBlue	123	104	238
LavenderBlush	255	240	245	light slate blue	132	112	255
misty rose	255	228	225	LightSlateBlue	132	112	255
MistyRose	255	228	225	medium blue	0	0	205
white	255	255	255	MediumBlue	0	0	205

English Words	Red	Green	Blue	English Words	Red	Green	Blue
royal blue	65	105	225	sea green	46	139	87
RoyalBlue	65	105	225	SeaGreen	46	139	87
blue	0	0	255	medium sea green	60	179	113
dodger blue	30	144	255	MediumSeaGreen	60	179	113
DodgerBlue	30	144	255	light sea green	32	178	170
deep sky blue	0	191	255	LightSeaGreen	32	178	170
DeepSkyBlue	0	191	255	pale green	152	251	152
sky blue	135	206	235	PaleGreen	152	251	152
SkyBlue	135	206	235	spring green	0	255	127
light sky blue	135	206	250	SpringGreen	0	255	127
LightSkyBlue	135	206	250	lawn green	124	252	0
steel blue	70	130	180	LawnGreen	124	252	0
SteelBlue	70	130	180	green	0	255	0
light steel blue	176	196	222	chartreuse	127	255	0
LightSteelBlue	176	196	222	medium spring green	0	250	154
light blue	173	216	230	MediumSpringGreen	0	250	154
LightBlue	173	216	230	green yellow	173	255	47
powder blue	176	224	230	GreenYellow	173	255	47
PowderBlue	176	224	230	lime green	50	205	50
pale turquoise	175	238	238	LimeGreen	50	205	50
PaleTurquoise	175	238	238	yellow green	154	205	50
dark turquoise	0	206	209	YellowGreen	154	205	50
DarkTurquoise	0	206	209	forest green	34	139	34
medium turquoise	72	209	204	ForestGreen	34	139	34
MediumTurquoise	72	209	204	olive drab	107	142	35
turquoise	64	224	208	OliveDrab	107	142	35
cyan	0	255	255	dark khaki	189	183	107
light cyan	224	255	255	DarkKhaki	189	183	107
LightCyan	224	255	255	khaki	240	230	140
cadet blue	95	158	160	pale goldenrod	238	232	170
CadetBlue	95	158	160	PaleGoldenrod	238	232	170
medium aquamarine	102	205	170	light goldenrod yellow	250	250	210
MediumAquamarine	102	205	170	LightGoldenrodYellow	250	250	210
aquamarine	127	255	212	light yellow	255	255	224
dark green	0	100	0	LightYellow	255	255	224
DarkGreen	0	100	0	yellow	255	255	0
dark olive green	85	107	47	gold	255	215	0
DarkOliveGreen	85	107	47	light goldenrod	238	221	130
dark sea green	143	188	143	LightGoldenrod	238	221	130
DarkSeaGreen	143	188	143	goldenrod	218	165	32

English Words	Red	Green	Blue	English Words	Red	Green	Blue
dark goldenrod	184	134	11	LightPink	255	182	193
DarkGoldenrod	184	134	11	pale violet red	219	112	147
rosy brown	188	143	143	PaleVioletRed	219	112	147
RosyBrown	188	143	143	maroon	176	48	96
indian red	205	92	92	medium violet red	199	21	133
IndianRed	205	92	92	MediumVioletRed	199	21	133
saddle brown	139	69	19	violet red	208	32	144
SaddleBrown	139	69	19	VioletRed	208	32	144
sienna	160	82	45	magenta	255	0	255
peru	205	133	63	violet	238	130	238
burlywood	222	184	135	plum	221	160	221
beige	245	245	220	orchid	218	112	214
wheat	245	222	179	medium orchid	186	85	211
sandy brown	244	164	96	MediumOrchid	186	85	211
SandyBrown	244	164	96	dark orchid	153	50	204
tan	210	180	140	DarkOrchid	153	50	204
chocolate	210	105	30	dark violet	148	0	211
firebrick	178	34	34	DarkViolet	148	0	211
brown	165	42	42	blue violet	138	43	226
dark salmon	233	150	122	BlueViolet	138	43	226
DarkSalmon	233	150	122	purple	160	32	240
salmon	250	128	114	medium purple	147	112	219
light salmon	255	160	122	MediumPurple	147	112	219
LightSalmon	255	160	122	thistle	216	191	216
orange	255	165	0	snow1	255	250	250
dark orange	255	140	0	snow2	238	233	233
DarkOrange	255	140	0	snow3	205	201	201
coral	255	127	80	snow4	139	137	137
light coral	240	128	128	seashell1	255	245	238
LightCoral	240	128	128	seashell2	238	229	222
tomato	255	99	71	seashell3	205	197	191
orange red	255	69	0	seashell4	139	134	130
OrangeRed	255	69	0	AntiqueWhite1	255	239	219
red	255	0	0	AntiqueWhite2	238	223	204
hot pink	255	105	180	AntiqueWhite3	205	192	176
HotPink	255	105	180	AntiqueWhite4	139	131	120
deep pink	255	20	147	bisque1	255	228	196
DeepPink	255	20	147	bisque2	238	213	183
pink	255	192	203	bisque3	205	183	158
light pink	255	182	193	bisque4	139	125	107

English Words	Red	Green	Blue	English Words	Red	Green	Blue
PeachPuff1	255	218	185	RoyalBlue1	72	118	255
PeachPuff2	238	203	173	RoyalBlue2	67	110	238
PeachPuff3	205	175	149	RoyalBlue3	58	95	205
PeachPuff4	139	119	101	RoyalBlue4	39	64	139
NavajoWhite1	255	222	173	blue1	0	0	255
NavajoWhite2	238	207	161	blue2	0	0	238
NavajoWhite3	205	179	139	blue3	0	0	205
NavajoWhite4	139	121	94	blue4	0	0	139
LemonChiffon1	255	250	205	DodgerBlue1	30	144	255
LemonChiffon2	238	233	191	DodgerBlue2	28	134	238
LemonChiffon3	205	201	165	DodgerBlue3	24	116	205
LemonChiffon4	139	137	112	DodgerBlue4	16	78	139
cornsilk1	255	248	220	SteelBlue1	99	184	255
cornsilk2	238	232	205	SteelBlue2	92	172	238
cornsilk3	205	200	177	SteelBlue3	79	148	205
cornsilk4	139	136	120	SteelBlue4	54	100	139
ivory1	255	255	240	DeepSkyBlue1	0	191	255
ivory2	238	238	224	DeepSkyBlue2	0	178	238
ivory3	205	205	193	DeepSkyBlue3	0	154	205
ivory4	139	139	131	DeepSkyBlue4	0	104	139
honeydew1	240	255	240	SkyBlue1	135	206	255
honeydew2	224	238	224	SkyBlue2	126	192	238
honeydew3	193	205	193	SkyBlue3	108	166	205
honeydew4	131	139	131	SkyBlue4	74	112	139
LavenderBlush1	255	240	245	LightSkyBlue1	176	226	255
LavenderBlush2	238	224	229	LightSkyBlue2	164	211	238
LavenderBlush3	205	193	197	LightSkyBlue3	141	182	205
LavenderBlush4	139	131	134	LightSkyBlue4	96	123	139
MistyRose1	255	228	225	SlateGray1	198	226	255
MistyRose2	238	213	210	SlateGray2	185	211	238
MistyRose3	205	183	181	SlateGray3	159	182	205
MistyRose4	139	125	123	SlateGray4	108	123	139
azure1	240	255	255	LightSteelBlue1	202	225	255
azure2	224	238	238	LightSteelBlue2	188	210	238
azure3	193	205	205	LightSteelBlue3	162	181	205
azure4	131	139	139	LightSteelBlue4	110	123	139
SlateBlue1	131	111	255	LightBlue1	191	239	255
SlateBlue2	122	103	238	LightBlue2	178	223	238
SlateBlue3	105	89	205	LightBlue3	154	192	205
SlateBlue4	71	60	139	LightBlue4	104	131	139

English Words	Red	Green	Blue	English Words	Red	Green	Blue
LightCyan1	224	255	255	SpringGreen1	0	255	127
LightCyan2	209	238	238	SpringGreen2	0	238	118
LightCyan3	180	205	205	SpringGreen3	0	205	102
LightCyan4	122	139	139	SpringGreen4	0	139	69
PaleTurquoise1	187	255	255	green1	0	255	0
PaleTurquoise2	174	238	238	green2	0	238	0
PaleTurquoise3	150	205	205	green3	0	205	0
PaleTurquoise4	102	139	139	green4	0	139	0
CadetBlue1	152	245	255	chartreuse1	127	255	0
CadetBlue2	142	229	238	chartreuse2	118	238	0
CadetBlue3	122	197	205	chartreuse3	102	205	0
CadetBlue4	83	134	139	chartreuse4	69	139	0
turquoise1	0	245	255	OliveDrab1	192	255	62
turquoise2	0	229	238	OliveDrab2	179	238	58
turquoise3	0	197	205	OliveDrab3	154	205	50
turquoise4	0	134	139	OliveDrab4	105	139	34
cyan1	0	255	255	DarkOliveGreen1	202	255	112
cyan2	0	238	238	DarkOliveGreen2	188	238	104
cyan3	0	205	205	DarkOliveGreen3	162	205	90
cyan4	0	139	139	DarkOliveGreen4	110	139	61
DarkSlateGray1	151	255	255	khaki1	255	246	143
DarkSlateGray2	141	238	238	khaki2	238	230	133
DarkSlateGray3	121	205	205	khaki3	205	198	115
DarkSlateGray4	82	139	139	khaki4	139	134	78
aquamarine1	127	255	212	LightGoldenrod1	255	236	139
aquamarine2	118	238	198	LightGoldenrod2	238	220	130
aquamarine3	102	205	170	LightGoldenrod3	205	190	112
aquamarine4	69	139	116	LightGoldenrod4	139	129	76
DarkSeaGreen1	193	255	193	LightYellow1	255	255	224
DarkSeaGreen2	180	238	180	LightYellow2	238	238	209
DarkSeaGreen3	155	205	155	LightYellow3	205	205	180
DarkSeaGreen4	105	139	105	LightYellow4	139	139	122
SeaGreen1	84	255	159	yellow1	255	255	0
SeaGreen2	78	238	148	yellow2	238	238	0
SeaGreen3	67	205	128	yellow3	205	205	0
SeaGreen4	46	139	87	yellow4	139	139	0
PaleGreen1	154	255	154	gold1	255	215	0
PaleGreen2	144	238	144	gold2	238	201	0
PaleGreen3	124	205	124	gold3	205	173	0
PaleGreen4	84	139	84	gold4	139	117	0

English Words	Red	Green	Blue	English Words	Red	Green	Blue
goldenrod1	255	193	37	brown1	255	64	64
goldenrod2	238	180	34	brown2	238	59	59
goldenrod3	205	155	29	brown3	205	51	51
goldenrod4	139	105	20	brown4	139	35	35
DarkGoldenrod1	255	185	15	salmon1	255	140	105
DarkGoldenrod2	238	173	14	salmon2	238	130	98
DarkGoldenrod3	205	149	12	salmon3	205	112	84
DarkGoldenrod4	139	101	8	salmon4	139	76	57
RosyBrown1	255	193	193	LightSalmon1	255	160	122
RosyBrown2	238	180	180	LightSalmon2	238	149	114
RosyBrown3	205	155	155	LightSalmon3	205	129	98
RosyBrown4	139	105	105	LightSalmon4	139	87	66
IndianRed1	255	106	106	orange1	255	165	0
IndianRed2	238	99	99	orange2	238	154	0
IndianRed3	205	85	85	orange3	205	133	0
IndianRed4	139	58	58	orange4	139	90	0
sienna1	255	130	71	DarkOrange1	255	127	0
sienna2	238	121	66	DarkOrange2	238	118	0
sienna3	205	104	57	DarkOrange3	205	102	0
sienna4	139	71	38	DarkOrange4	139	69	0
burlywood1	255	211	155	coral1	255	114	86
burlywood2	238	197	145	coral2	238	106	80
burlywood3	205	170	125	coral3	205	91	69
burlywood4	139	115	85	coral4	139	62	47
wheat1	255	231	186	tomato1	255	99	71
wheat2	238	216	174	tomato2	238	92	66
wheat3	205	186	150	tomato3	205	79	57
wheat4	139	126	102	tomato4	139	54	38
tan1	255	165	79	OrangeRed1	255	69	0
tan2	238	154	73	OrangeRed2	238	64	0
tan3	205	133	63	OrangeRed3	205	55	0
tan4	139	90	43	OrangeRed4	139	37	0
chocolate1	255	127	36	red1	255	0	0
chocolate2	238	118	33	red2	238	0	0
chocolate3	205	102	29	red3	205	0	0
chocolate4	139	69	19	red4	139	0	0
firebrick1	255	48	48	DeepPink1	255	20	147
firebrick2	238	44	44	DeepPink2	238	18	137
firebrick3	205	38	38	DeepPink3	205	16	118
firebrick4	139	26	26	DeepPink4	139	10	80

English Words	Red	Green	Blue	English Words	Red	Green	Blue
HotPink1	255	110	180	DarkOrchid1	191	62	255
HotPink2	238	106	167	DarkOrchid2	178	58	238
HotPink3	205	96	144	DarkOrchid3	154	50	205
HotPink4	139	58	98	DarkOrchid4	104	34	139
pink1	255	181	197	purple1	155	48	255
pink2	238	169	184	purple2	145	44	238
pink3	205	145	158	purple3	125	38	205
pink4	139	99	108	purple4	85	26	139
LightPink1	255	174	185	MediumPurple1	171	130	255
LightPink2	238	162	173	MediumPurple2	159	121	238
LightPink3	205	140	149	MediumPurple3	137	104	205
LightPink4	139	95	101	MediumPurple4	93	71	139
PaleVioletRed1	255	130	171	thistle1	255	225	255
PaleVioletRed2	238	121	159	thistle2	238	210	238
PaleVioletRed3	205	104	137	thistle3	205	181	205
PaleVioletRed4	139	71	93	thistle4	139	123	139*
maroon1	255	52	179				
maroon2	238	48	167				
maroon3	205	41	144				
maroon4	139	28	98				
VioletRed1	255	62	150				
VioletRed2	238	58	140				
VioletRed3	205	50	120				
VioletRed4	139	34	82				
magenta1	255	0	255				
magenta2	238	0	238				
magenta3	205	0	205				
magenta4	139	0	139				
orchid1	255	131	250				
orchid2	238	122	233				
orchid3	205	105	201				
orchid4	139	71	137				
plum1	255	187	255				
plum2	238	174	238				
plum3	205	150	205				
plum4	139	102	139				
MediumOrchid1	224	102	255				
MediumOrchid2	209	95	238				
MediumOrchid3	180	82	205				
MediumOrchid4	122	55	139				

---

*Also defined are the color names "gray0" through "gray 100", spelled with an "e" or an "a". "gray0" is black and "gray100" is white.

E
Event Reference

This appendix describes each event structure in detail and briefly shows how each event type is used. It covers the most common uses of each event type, the information contained in each event structure, how the event is selected, and the side effects of the event, if any. Each event is described on a separate reference page.

Table E-1 lists each event mask, its associated event types, and the associated structure definition. See Chapter 8, *Events*, of Volume One, *Xlib Programming Manual*, for more information on events.

Table E-1. Event Masks, Event Types, and Event Structures

Event Mask	Event Type	Structure
KeyPressMask	KeyPress	XKeyPressedEvent
KeyReleaseMask	KeyRelease	XKeyReleasedEvent
ButtonPressMask	ButtonPress	XButtonPressedEvent
ButtonReleaseMask	ButtonRelease	XButtonReleasedEvent
OwnerGrabButtonMask	n/a	n/a
KeymapStateMask	KeymapNotify	XKeymapEvent
PointerMotionMask PointerMotionHintMask ButtonMotionMask Button1MotionMask Button2MotionMask Button3MotionMask Button4MotionMask Button5MotionMask	MotionNotify	XPointerMovedEvent
EnterWindowMask	EnterNotify	XEnterWindowEvent
LeaveWindowMask	LeaveNotify	XLeaveWindowEvent
FocusChangeMask	FocusIn FocusOut	XFocusInEvent XFocusOutEvent

Event Mask	Event Type	Structure
`ExposureMask`	`Expose`	`XExposeEvent`
selected in GC by `graphics_expose` member	`GraphicsExpose` `NoExpose`	`XGraphicsExposeEvent` `XNoExposeEvent`
`ColormapChangeMask`	`ColormapNotify`	`XColormapEvent`
`PropertyChangeMask`	`PropertyNotify`	`XPropertyEvent`
`VisibilityChangeMask`	`VisibilityNotify`	`XVisibilityEvent`
`ResizeRedirectMask`	`ResizeRequest`	`XResizeRequestEvent`
`StructureNotifyMask`	`CirculateNotify` `ConfigureNotify` `DestroyNotify` `GravityNotify` `MapNotify` `ReparentNotify` `UnmapNotify`	`XCirculateEvent` `XConfigureEvent` `XDestroyWindowEvent` `XGravityEvent` `XMapEvent` `XReparentEvent` `XUnmapEvent`
`SubstructureNotifyMask`	`CirculateNotify` `ConfigureNotify` `CreateNotify` `DestroyNotify` `GravityNotify` `MapNotify` `ReparentNotify` `UnmapNotify`	`XCirculateEvent` `XConfigureEvent` `XCreateWindowEvent` `XDestroyWindowEvent` `XGravityEvent` `XMapEvent` `XReparentEvent` `XUnmapEvent`
`SubstructureRedirectMask`	`CirculateRequest` `ConfigureRequest` `MapRequest`	`XCirculateRequestEvent` `XConfigureRequestEvent` `XMapRequestEvent`
(always selected)	`MappingNotify`	`XMappingEvent`
(always selected)	`ClientMessage`	`XClientMessageEvent`
(always selected)	`SelectionClear`	`XSetSelectClearEvent`
(always selected)	`SelectionNotify`	`XSelectionEvent`
(always selected)	`SelectionRequest`	`XSelectionRequestEvent`

E.1 Meaning of Common Structure Elements

Example E-1 shows the **XEvent** union and a simple event structure that is one member of the union. Several of the members of this structure are present in nearly every event structure. They are described here before we go into the event-specific members (see also Section 8.2.2 of Volume One, *Xlib Programming Manual*).

Example E-1. XEvent union and XAnyEvent structure

```
typedef union _XEvent {
        int type;                       /* Must not be changed; first member */
        XAnyEvent xany;
        XButtonEvent xbutton;
        XCirculateEvent xcirculate;
        XCirculateRequestEvent xcirculaterequest;
        XClientMessageEvent xclient;
        XColormapEvent xcolormap;
        XConfigureEvent xconfigure;
        XConfigureRequestEvent xconfigurerequest;
        XCreateWindowEvent xcreatewindow;
        XDestroyWindowEvent xdestroywindow;
        XCrossingEvent xcrossing;
        XExposeEvent xexpose;
        XFocusChangeEvent xfocus;
        XNoExposeEvent xnoexpose;
        XGraphicsExposeEvent xgraphicsexpose;
        XGravityEvent xgravity;
        XKeymapEvent xkeymap;
        XKeyEvent xkey;
        XMapEvent xmap;
        XUnmapEvent xunmap;
        XMappingEvent xmapping;
        XMapRequestEvent xmaprequest;
        XMotionEvent xmotion;
        XPropertyEvent xproperty;
        XReparentEvent xreparent;
        XResizeRequestEvent xresizerequest;
        XSelectionClearEvent xselectionclear;
        XSelectionEvent xselection;
        XSelectionRequestEvent xselectionrequest;
        XVisibilityEvent xvisibility;
} XEvent;

typedef struct {
        int type;
        unsigned long serial;     /* # of last request processed by server */
        Bool send_event;          /* True if this came from SendEvent
                                   * request */
        Display *display;         /* Display the event was read from */
        Window window;            /* window on which event was requested
                                   * in event mask */
} XAnyEvent;
```

The first member of the **XEvent** union is the type of event. When an event is received (with **XNextEvent()**, for example), the application checks the **type** member in the **XEvent** union. Then the specific event type is known and the specific event structure (such as **xbutton**) is used to access information specific to that event type.

Before the branching depending on the event type, only the **XEvent** union is used. After the branching, only the event structure which contains the specific information for each event type should be used in each branch. For example, if the **XEvent** union were called **report**, the **report.xexpose** structure should be used within the branch for **Expose** events.

You will notice that each event structure also begins with a **type** member. This member is rarely used, since it is an identical copy of the **type** member in the **XEvent** union.

Most event structures also have a **window** member. The only ones that do not are selection events (**SelectionClear**, **SelectionNotify**, and **SelectionRequest**) and events selected by the **graphics_exposures** member of the GC (**GraphicsExpose** and **NoExpose**). The **window** member indicates the event window that selected and received the event. This is the window where the event arrives if it has propagated through the hierarchy as described in Section 8.3.2, of Volume One, *Xlib Programming Manual*. One event type may have two different meanings to an application, depending on which window it appears in.

Many of the event structures also have a **display** and/or **root** member. The **display** member identifies the connection to the server that is active. The **root** member indicates which screen the window that received the event is linked to in the hierarchy. Most programs only use a single screen and therefore do not need to worry about the **root** member. The **display** member can be useful, since you can pass the display variable into routines by simply passing a pointer to the event structure, eliminating the need for a separate display argument.

All event structures include a **serial** member that gives the number of the last protocol request processed by the server. This is useful in debugging, since an error can be detected by the server but not reported to the user (or programmer) until the next routine that gets an event. That means several routines may execute successfully after the error occurs. The last request processed will often indicate the request that contained the error.

All event structures also include a **send_event** flag, which, if **True**, indicates that the event was sent by **XSendEvent()** (i.e., by another client rather than by the server).

The following pages describe each event type in detail. The events are presented in alphabetical order, each on a separate page. Each page describes the circumstances under which the event is generated, the mask used to select it, the structure itself, its members, and useful programming notes. Note that the description of the structure members does not include those members common to many structures. If you need more information on these members, please refer to this introductory section.

ButtonPress, ButtonRelease

When Generated

There are two types of pointer button events: `ButtonPress` and `ButtonRelease`. Both contain the same information.

Select With

May be selected separately, using `ButtonPressMask` and `ButtonReleaseMask`.

XEvent Structure Name

```
typedef union _XEvent {
    . . .
    XButtonEvent xbutton;
    . . .
} XEvent;
```

Event Structure

```
typedef struct {
int type;                    /* of event */
unsigned long serial;        /* # of last request processed by server */
Bool send_event;             /* True if this came from a SendEvent request */
Display *display;            /* Display the event was read from */
Window window;               /* event window it is reported relative to */
Window root;                 /* root window that the event occurred under */
Window subwindow;            /* child window */
Time time;                   /* when event occurred, in milliseconds */
int x, y;                    /* pointer coordinates relative to receiving
                              * window */
int x_root, y_root;          /* coordinates relative to root */
unsigned int state;          /* mask of all buttons and modifier keys */
unsigned int button;         /* button that triggered event */
Bool same_screen;            /* same screen flag */
} XButtonEvent;
typedef XButtonEvent XButtonPressedEvent;
typedef XButtonEvent XButtonReleasedEvent;
```

Event Structure Members

subwindow   If the source window is the child of the receiving window, then the `subwindow` member is set to the ID of that child.

time   The server time when the button event occurred, in milliseconds. `Time` is declared as `unsigned long`, so it wraps around when it reaches the maximum value of a 32-bit number (every 49.7 days).

x, y   If the receiving window is on the same screen as the root window specified by `root`, then `x` and `y` are the pointer coordinates relative to the receiving window's origin. Otherwise, x and y are zero.

When active button grabs and pointer grabs are in effect (see Section 9.4 of Volume One, *Xlib Programming Manual*), the coordinates relative to the receiving window may not be within the window (they may be negative or greater than window height or width).

x_root, y_root   The pointer coordinates relative to the root window which is an ancestor of the event window. If the pointer was on a different screen, these are zero.

state   The state of all the buttons and modifier keys just before the event, represented by a mask of the button and modifier key symbols: Button1Mask, Button2Mask, Button3Mask, Button4Mask, Button5Mask, ControlMask, LockMask, Mod1Mask, Mod2-Mask, Mod3Mask, Mod4Mask, Mod5Mask, and ShiftMask. If a modifier key is pressed and released when no other modifier keys are held, the ButtonPress will have a state member of 0 and the ButtonRelease will have a non-zero state member indicating that itself was held just before the event.

button   A value indicating which button changed state to trigger this event. One of the constants: Button1, Button2, Button3, Button4, or Button5.

same_screen   Indicates whether the pointer is currently on the same screen as this window. This is always True unless the pointer was actively grabbed before the automatic grab could take place.

Notes

Unless an active grab already exists or a passive grab on the button combination that was pressed already exists at a higher level in the hierarchy than where the ButtonPress occurred, an automatic active grab of the pointer takes place when a ButtonPress occurs. Because of the automatic grab, the matching ButtonRelease is sent to the same application that received the ButtonPress event. If OwnerGrabButtonMask has been selected, the ButtonRelease event is delivered to the window which contained the pointer when the button was released, as long as that window belongs to the same client as the window in which the ButtonPress event occurred. If the ButtonRelease occurs outside of the client's windows or OwnerGrabButtonMask was not selected, the ButtonRelease is delivered to the window in which the ButtonPress occurred. The grab is terminated when all buttons are released. During the grab, the cursor associated with the grabbing window will track the pointer anywhere on the screen.

If the application has invoked a passive button grab on an ancestor of the window in which the ButtonPress event occurs, then that grab takes precedence over the automatic grab, and the ButtonRelease will go to that window, or it will be handled normally by that client depending on the owner_events flag in the XGrabButton call.

CirculateNotify

When Generated

A `CirculateNotify` event reports a call to change the stacking order, and it includes whether the final position is on the top or on the bottom. This event is generated by `XCirculateSubwindows()`, `XCirculateSubwindowsDown()`, or `XCirculate-SubwindowsUp()`. See also the `CirculateRequest` and `ConfigureNotify` reference pages.

Select With

This event is selected with `StructureNotifyMask` in the `XSelectInput` call for the window to be moved or with `SubstructureNotifyMask` for the parent of the window to be moved.

XEvent Structure Name

```
typedef union _XEvent {
    . . .
    XCirculateEvent xcirculate;
    . . .
} XEvent;
```

Event Structure

```
typedef struct {
    int type;
    unsigned long serial;    /* # of last request processed by server */
    Bool send_event;         /* True if this came from SendEvent request */
    Display *display;        /* Display the event was read from */
    Window event;
    Window window;
    int place;               /* PlaceOnTop, PlaceOnBottom */
} XCirculateEvent;
```

Event Structure Members

event   The window receiving the event. If the event was selected by `Structure-NotifyMask`, event will be the same as window. If the event was selected by `SubstructureNotifyMask`, event will be the parent of window.

window   The window that was restacked.

place   Either `PlaceOnTop` or `PlaceOnBottom`. Indicates whether the window was raised to the top or bottom of the stack.

CirculateRequest

When Generated

A `CirculateRequest` event reports when `XCirculateSubwindows`, `XCirculate-SubwindowsDown()`, `XCirculateSubwindowsUp()`, or `XRestackWindows()` is called to change the stacking order of a group of children.

This event differs from `CirculateNotify` in that it delivers the parameters of the request before it is carried out. This gives the client that selects this event (usually the window manager) the opportunity to review the request in the light of its window management policy before executing the circulate request itself or to deny the request. (`CirculateNotify` indicates the final outcome of the request.)

Select With

This event is selected for the parent window with `SubstructureRedirectMask`.

XEvent Structure Name

```
typedef union _XEvent {
    ...
    XCirculateRequestEvent xcirculaterequest;
    ...
} XEvent;
```

Event Structure

```
typedef struct {
    int type;
    unsigned long serial;      /* # of last request processed by server */
    Bool send_event;           /* True if this came from SendEvent request */
    Display *display;          /* Display the event was read from */
    Window parent;
    Window window;
    int place;                 /* PlaceOnTop, PlaceOnBottom */
} XCirculateRequestEvent;
```

Event Structure Members

parent   The parent of the window that was restacked. This is the window that selected the event.

window   The window being restacked.

place   `PlaceOnTop` or `PlaceOnBottom`. Indicates whether the window was to be placed on the top or on the bottom of the stacking order.

ClientMessage

When Generated

A ClientMessage event is sent as a result of a call to XSendEvent() by a client to a particular window. Any type of event can be sent with XSendEvent(), but it will be distinguished from normal events by the send_event member being set to True. If your program wants to be able to treat events sent with XSendEvent() as different from normal events, you can read this member.

Select With

There is no event mask for ClientMessage events, and they are not selected with XSelectInput. Instead XSendEvent directs them to a specific window, which is given as a window ID: the PointerWindow or the InputFocus.

XEvent Structure Name

```
typedef union _XEvent {
    . . .
    XClientMessageEvent xclient;
    . . .
} XEvent;
```

Event Structure

```
typedef struct {
    int type;
    unsigned long serial;     /* # of last request processed by server */
    Bool send_event;          /* True if this came from SendEvent request */
    Display *display;         /* Display the event was read from */
    Window window;
    Atom message_type;
    int format;
    union {
        char b[20];
        short s[10];
        long l[5];
    } data;
} XClientMessageEvent;
```

Event Structure Members

message_type   An atom that specifies how the data is to be interpreted by the receiving client. The X server places no interpretation on the type or the data, but it must be a list of 8-bit, 16-bit, or 32-bit quantities, so that the X server can correctly swap bytes as necessary. The data always consists of twenty 8-bit values, ten 16-bit values, or five 32-bit values, although each particular message might not make use of all of these values.

format   Specifies the format of the property specified by `message_type`. This will be on of the values 8, 16, or 32.

ColormapNotify

When Generated

A `ColormapNotify` event reports when the colormap attribute of a window changes or when the colormap specified by the attribute is installed, uninstalled, or freed. This event is generated by `XChangeWindowAttributes()`, `XFreeColormap()`, `XInstall-Colormap()`, and `XUninstallColormap()`.

Select With

This event is selected with `ColormapChangeMask`.

XEvent Structure Name

```
typedef union _XEvent {
    ...
    XColormapEvent xcolormap;
    ...
} XEvent;
```

Event Structure

```
typedef struct {
    int type;
    unsigned long serial;       /* # of last request processed by server */
    Bool send_event;            /* True if this came from SendEvent request */
    Display *display;           /* Display the event was read from */
    Window window;
    Colormap colormap;          /* a colormap or None */
    Bool new;
    int state;                  /* ColormapInstalled, ColormapUninstalled */
} XColormapEvent;
```

Event Structure Members

window   The window whose associated colormap or attribute changes.

colormap   The colormap associated with the window, either a colormap ID or the constant None. It will be None only if this event was generated due to an `XFreeColormap` call.

new   True when the colormap attribute has been changed, or **False** when the colormap is installed or uninstalled.

state   Either `ColormapInstalled` or `ColormapUninstalled`; it indicates whether the colormap is installed or uninstalled.

ConfigureNotify

When Generated

A `ConfigureNotify` event announces actual changes to a window's configuration (size, position, border, and stacking order). See also the `CirculateRequest` reference page.

Select With

This event is selected for a single window by specifying the window ID of that window with `StructureNotifyMask`. To receive this event for all children of a window, specify the parent window ID with `SubstructureNotifyMask`.

XEvent Structure Name

```
typedef union _XEvent {
    ...
    XConfigureEvent xconfigure;
    ...
} XEvent;
```

Event Structure

```
typedef struct {
    int type;
    unsigned long serial;      /* # of last request processed by server */
    Bool send_event;           /* True if this came from SendEvent request */
    Display *display;          /* Display the event was read from */
    Window event;
    Window window;
    int x, y;
    int width, height;
    int border_width;
    Window above;
    Bool override_redirect;
} XConfigureEvent;
```

Event Structure Members

event	The window that selected the event. The `event` and `window` members are identical if the event was selected with `StructureNotifyMask`.
window	The window whose configuration was changed.
x, y	The final coordinates of the reconfigured window relative to its parent.
width, height	The width and height in pixels of the window after reconfiguration.

`border_width`   The width in pixels of the border after reconfiguration.

`above`   If this member is None, then the window is on the bottom of the stack with respect to its siblings. Otherwise, the window is immediately on top of the specified sibling window.

`override_redirect` The `override_redirect` attribute of the reconfigured window. If True, it indicates that the client wants this window to be immune to interception by the window manager of configuration requests. Window managers normally should ignore this event if `override_redirect` is True.

Event Reference

ConfigureRequest

When Generated

A `ConfigureRequest` event reports when another client attempts to change a window's size, position, border, and/or stacking order.

This event differs from `ConfigureNotify` in that it delivers the parameters of the request before it is carried out. This gives the client that selects this event (usually the window manager) the opportunity to revise the requested configuration before executing the `XConfigureWindow()` request itself or to deny the request. (`ConfigureNotify` indicates the final outcome of the request.)

Select With

This event is selected for any window in a group of children by specifying the parent window with `SubstructureRedirectMask`.

XEvent Structure Name

```
typedef union _XEvent {
    ...
    XConfigureRequestEvent xconfigurerequest;
    ...
} XEvent;
```

Event Structure

```
typedef struct {
    int type;
    unsigned long serial;      /* # of last request processed by server */
    Bool send_event;           /* True if this came from SendEvent request */
    Display *display;          /* Display the event was read from */
    Window parent;
    Window window;
    int x, y;
    int width, height;
    int border_width;
    Window above;
    int detail;                /* Above, Below, BottomIf, TopIf, Opposite */
    unsigned long value_mask;
} XConfigureRequestEvent;
```

Event Structure Members

parent   The window that selected the event. This is the parent of the window being configured.

window   The window that is being configured.

x, y   The requested position for the upper-left pixel of the window's border relative to the origin of the parent window.

width, height   The requested width and height in pixels for the window.

border_width   The requested border width for the window.

above   The sibling specified in the XConfigureWindow call, or Above if no sibling was specified.

detail   None, Above, Below, TopIf, BottomIf, or Opposite. Specifies the sibling window on top of which the specified window should be placed. If this member has the constant None, then the specified window should be placed on the bottom.

value_mask   A bit mask representing which elements of configuration are to be changed.

Notes

The geometry is derived from the XConfigureWindow request that triggered the event.

CreateNotify

When Generated

A `CreateNotify` event reports when a window is created.

Select With

This event is selected on children of a window by specifying the parent window ID with `SubstructureNotifyMask`. (Note that this event type cannot be selected by `StructureNotifyMask`.)

XEvent Structure Name

```
typedef union _XEvent {
    ...
    XCreateWindowEvent xcreatewindow;
    ...
} XEvent;
```

Event Structure

```
typedef struct {
    int type;
    unsigned long serial;        /* # of last request processed by server */
    Bool send_event;             /* True if this came from SendEvent
                                  * request */
    Display *display;            /* Display the event was read from */
    Window parent;               /* parent of the window */
    Window window;               /* window ID of window created */
    int x, y;                    /* window location */
    int width, height;           /* size of window */
    int border_width;            /* border width */
    Bool override_redirect;      /* creation should be overridden */
} XCreateWindowEvent;
```

Event Structure Members

`parent`	The ID of the created window's parent.
`window`	The ID of the created window.
`x, y`	The coordinates of the created window relative to its parent.
`width, height`	The width and height in pixels of the created window.
`border_width`	The width in pixels of the border of the created window.

override_redirect The override_redirect attribute of the created window. If
                   True, it indicates that the client wants this window to be immune
                   to interception by the window manager of configuration requests.
                   Window managers normally should ignore this event if
                   override_redirect is True.

Notes

For descriptions of these members, see the XCreateWindow function and the XSet-
WindowAttributes structure.

Event Reference

DestroyNotify

When Generated

A `DestroyNotify` event reports that a window has been destroyed.

Select With

To receive this event type on children of a window, specify the parent window ID and pass `SubstructureNotifyMask` as part of the `event_mask` argument to `XSelectInput`. This event type cannot be selected with `StructureNotifyMask`.

XEvent Structure Name

```
typedef union _XEvent {
    . . .
    XDestroyWindowEvent xdestroywindow;
    . . .
} XEvent;
```

Event Structure

```
typedef struct {
    int type;
    unsigned long serial;       /* # of last request processed by server */
    Bool send_event;            /* True if this came from SendEvent request */
    Display *display;           /* Display the event was read from */
    Window event;
    Window window;
} XDestroyWindowEvent;
```

Event Structure Members

event   The window that selected the event.

window   The window that was destroyed.

EnterNotify, LeaveNotify

When Generated

EnterNotify and LeaveNotify events occur when the pointer enters or leaves a window.

When the pointer crosses a window border, a LeaveNotify event occurs in the window being left and an EnterNotify event occurs in the window being entered. Whether or not each event is queued for any application depends on whether any application selected the right event on the window in which it occurred.

In addition, EnterNotify and LeaveNotify events are delivered to windows that are *virtually crossed*. These are windows that are between the origin and destination windows in the hierarchy but not necessarily on the screen. Further explanation of virtual crossing is provided two pages following.

Select With

Each of these events can be selected separately with XEnterWindowMask and XLeave-WindowMask.

XEvent Structure Name

```
typedef union _XEvent {
    ...
    XCrossingEvent xcrossing;
    ...
} XEvent;
```

Event Structure

```
typedef struct {
    int type;                   /* of event */
    unsigned long serial;       /* # of last request processed by server */
    Bool send_event;            /* True if this came from SendEvent request */
    Display *display;           /* Display the event was read from */
    Window window;              /* event window it is reported relative to */
    Window root;                /* root window that the event occurred on */
    Window subwindow;           /* child window */
    Time time;                  /* milliseconds */
    int x, y;                   /* pointer x,y coordinates in receiving
                                 * window */
    int x_root, y_root;         /* coordinates relative to root */
    int mode;                   /* NotifyNormal, NotifyGrab, NotifyUngrab */
    int detail;                 /* NotifyAncestor, NotifyInferior,
                                 * NotifyNonLinear, NotifyNonLinearVirtual,
                                 * NotifyVirtual */
    Bool same_screen;           /* same screen flag */
    Bool focus;                 /* boolean focus */
```

Event Reference

```
        unsigned int state;      /* key or button mask */
} XCrossingEvent;
typedef XCrossingEvent XEnterWindowEvent;
typedef XCrossingEvent XLeaveWindowEvent;
```

Event Structure Members

The following list describes the members of the `XCrossingEvent` structure.

subwindow
: In a `LeaveNotify` event, if the pointer began in a child of the receiving window, then the `child` member is set to the window ID of the child. Otherwise, it is set to `None`. For an `EnterNotify` event, if the pointer ends up in a child of the receiving window, then the `child` member is set to the window ID of the child. Otherwise, it is set to `None`.

time
: The server time when the crossing event occurred, in milliseconds. `Time` is declared as `unsigned long`, so it wraps around when it reaches the maximum value of a 32-bit number (every 49.7 days).

x, y
: The point of entry or exit of the pointer relative to the event window.

x_root, y_root
: The point of entry or exit of the pointer relative to the root window.

mode
: Normal crossing events or those caused by pointer warps have mode `NotifyNormal`, events caused by a grab have mode `NotifyGrab`, and events caused by a released grab have mode `NotifyUngrab`.

detail
: The value of the `detail` member depends on the hierarchical relationship between the origin and destination windows and the direction of pointer transfer. Determining which windows receive events and with which `detail` members is quite complicated. This topic is described in the next section.

same_screen
: Indicates whether the pointer is currently on the same screen as this window. This is always `True` unless the pointer was actively grabbed before the automatic grab could take place.

focus
: If the receiving window is the focus window or a descendant of the focus window, the `focus` member is `True`; otherwise, it is `False`.

state
: The state of all the buttons and modifier keys just before the event, represented by a mask of the button and modifier key symbols: `Button1Mask`, `Button2Mask`, `Button3Mask`, `Button4Mask`, `Button5Mask`, `ControlMask`, `LockMask`, `Mod1Mask`, `Mod2Mask`, `Mod3Mask`, `Mod4Mask`, `Mod5Mask`, and `ShiftMask`.

Virtual Crossing and the detail Member

Virtual crossing occurs when the pointer moves between two windows that do not have a parent-child relationship. Windows between the origin and destination windows in the hierarchy receive EnterNotify and LeaveNotify events. The detail member of each of these events depends on the hierarchical relationship of the origin and destination windows and the direction of pointer transfer.

Virtual crossing is an advanced topic that you should not spend time figuring out unless you have an important reason to use it. We have never seen an application that uses this feature, and we know of no reason for its extreme complexity. With that word of warning, proceed.

Let's say the pointer has moved from one window, the origin, to another, the destination. First, we'll specify what types of events each window gets and then the detail member of each of those events.

The window of origin receives a LeaveNotify event and the destination window receives an EnterNotify event, if they have requested this type of event. If one is an inferior of the other, the detail member of the event received by the inferior is NotifyAncestor and the detail of the event received by the superior is NotifyInferior. If the crossing is between parent and child, these are the only events generated.

However, if the origin and destination windows are not parent and child, other windows are *virtually crossed* and also receive events. If neither window is an ancestor of the other, ancestors of each window, up to but not including the least common ancestor, receive LeaveNotify events, if they are in the same branch of the hierarchy as the origin, and EnterNotify events, if they are in the same branch as the destination. These events can be used to track the motion of the pointer through the hierarchy.

- In the case of a crossing between a parent and a child of a child, the middle child receives a LeaveNotify with detail NotifyVirtual.

- In the case of a crossing between a child and the parent of its parent, the middle child receives an EnterNotify with detail NotifyVirtual.

- In a crossing between windows whose least common ancestor is two or more windows away, both the origin and destination windows receive events with detail Notify-Nonlinear. The windows between the origin and the destination in the hierarchy, up to but not including their least common ancestor, receive events with detail Notify-NonlinearVirtual. The least common ancestor is the lowest window from which both are descendants.

- If the origin and destination windows are on separate screens, the events and details generated are the same as for two windows not parent and child, except that the root windows of the two screens are considered the least common ancestor. Both root windows also receive events.

Table E-1 shows the event types generated by a pointer crossing from window A to window B when window C is the least common ancestor of A and B.

Table E-1. Border Crossing Events and Window Relationship

LeaveNotify	EnterNotify
Origin window (A).	Destination window (B).
Windows between A and B, exclusive, if A is inferior.	Windows between A and B, exclusive, if B is inferior.
Windows between A and C, exclusive.	Windows between B and C, exclusive.
Root window on screen of origin if different from screen of destination.	Root window on screen of destination if different from screen of origin.

Table E-2 lists the `detail` members in events generated by a pointer crossing from window A to window B.

Table E-2. Event detail Member and Window Relationship

detail Flag	Window Delivered To
NotifyAncestor	Origin or destination when either is descendant.
NotifyInferior	Origin or destination when either is ancestor.
NotifyVirtual	Windows between A and B, exclusive, if either is descendant.
NotifyNonlinear	Origin and destination when A and B are two or more windows distant from least common ancestor C.
NotifyNonlinearVirtual	Windows between A and C, exclusive, and between B and C, exclusive, when A and B have least common ancestor C; also on both root windows if A and B are on different screens.

For example, Figure E-1 shows the events that are generated by a movement from a window (window *A*) to a child (window *B1*) of a sibling (window *B*). This would generate three events: a LeaveNotify with detail NotifyNonlinear for the window *A*, an Enter-Notify with detail NotifyNonlinearVirtual for its sibling window *B*, and an EnterNotify with detail NotifyNonlinear for the child (window *B1*).

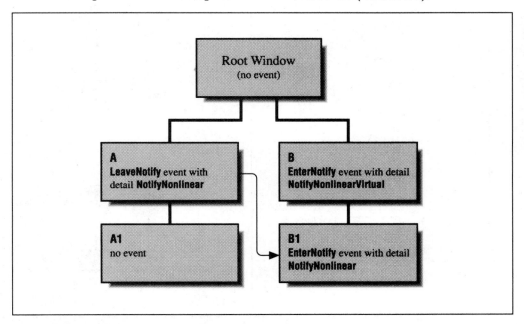

Figure E-1. Events generated by a move between windows

EnterNotify and LeaveNotify events are also generated when the pointer is grabbed, if the pointer was not already inside the grabbing window. In this case, the grabbing window receives an EnterNotify and the window containing the pointer receives a Leave-Notify event, both with mode NotifyUngrab. The pointer position in both events is the position before the grab. The result when the grab is released is exactly the same, except that the two windows receive EnterNotify instead of LeaveNotify and vice versa.

Figure E-2 demonstrates the events and details caused by various pointer transitions, indicated by heavy arrows.

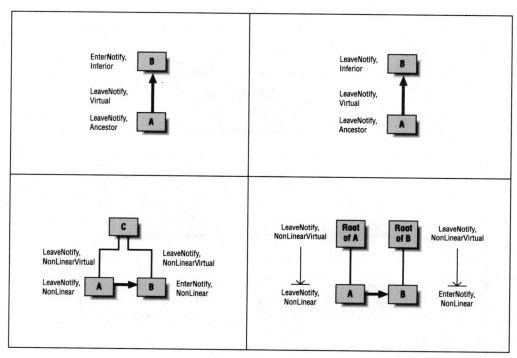

Figure E-2. Border crossing events and detail member for pointer movement from window A to window B, for various window relationships

Expose

When Generated

An Expose event is generated when a window becomes visible or a previously invisible part of a window becomes visible. Only InputOutput windows generate or need to respond to Expose events; InputOnly windows never generate or need to respond to them. The Expose event provides the position and size of the exposed area within the window and a rough count of the number of remaining exposure events for the current window.

Select With

This event is selected with ExposureMask.

XEvent Structure Name

```
typedef union _XEvent {
    ...
    XExposeEvent xexpose;
    ...
} XEvent;
```

Event Structure

```
typedef struct {
    int type;
    unsigned long serial;    /* # of last request processed by server */
    Bool send_event;         /* True if this came from SendEvent request */
    Display *display;        /* Display the event was read from */
    Window window;
    int x, y;
    int width, height;
    int count;               /* If nonzero, at least this many more */
} XExposeEvent;
```

Event Structure Members

x, y The coordinates of the upper-left corner of the exposed region relative to the origin of the window.

width, height The width and height in pixels of the exposed region.

count The approximate number of remaining contiguous Expose events that were generated as a result of a single function call.

Notes

A single action such as a window movement or a function call can generate several exposure events on one window or on several windows. The server guarantees that all exposure events generated from a single action will be sent contiguously, so that they can all be handled before moving on to other event types. This allows an application to keep track of the rectangles specified in contiguous Expose events, set the clip_mask in a GC to the areas specified in the rectangle using XSetRegion or XSetClipRectangles, and then finally redraw the window clipped with the GC in a single operation after all the Expose events have arrived. The last event to arrive is indicated by a count of 0. In Release 2, XUnion-RectWithRegion can be used to add the rectangle in Expose events to a region before calling XSetRegion.

If your application is able to redraw partial windows, you can also read each exposure event in turn and redraw each area.

FocusIn, FocusOut

When Generated

FocusIn and FocusOut events occur when the keyboard focus window changes as a result of an XSetInputFocus() call. They are much like EnterNotify and Leave-Notify events except that they track the focus rather than the pointer.

When a focus change occurs, a FocusOut event is delivered to the old focus window and a FocusIn event to the window which receives the focus. In addition, windows in between these two windows in the window hierarchy are virtually crossed and receive focus change events, as described below. Some or all of the windows between the window containing the pointer at the time of the focus change and the root window also receive focus change events, as described below.

Select With

FocusIn and FocusOut events are selected with FocusChangeMask. They cannot be selected separately.

XEvent Structure Name

```
typedef union _XEvent {
    . . .
    XFocusChangeEvent xfocus;
    . . .
} XEvent;
```

Event Structure

```
typedef struct {
    int type;                /* FocusIn or FocusOut */
    unsigned long serial;    /* # of last request processed by server */
    Bool send_event;         /* True if this came from SendEvent request */
    Display *display;        /* Display the event was read from */
    Window window;           /* Window of event */
    int mode;                /* NotifyNormal, NotifyGrab, NotifyUngrab */
    int detail;              /* NotifyAncestor, NotifyDetailNone,
                                NotifyInferior, NotifyNonLinear,
                                NotifyNonLinearVirtual, NotifyPointer,
                                NotifyPointerRoot, NotifyVirtual */
} XFocusChangeEvent;
typedef XFocusChangeEvent XFocusInEvent;
typedef XFocusChangeEvent XFocusOutEvent;
```

Event Structure Members

mode   For events generated when the keyboard is not grabbed, `mode` is `Notify-Normal`; when the keyboard is grabbed, `mode` is `NotifyGrab`; and when a keyboard is ungrabbed, `mode` is `NotifyUngrab`.

detail   The `detail` member identifies the relationship between the window that receives the event and the origin and destination windows. It will be described in detail after the description of which windows get what types of events.

Notes

The *keyboard focus* is a window that has been designated as the one to receive all keyboard input irrespective of the pointer position. Only the keyboard focus window and its descendants receive keyboard events. By default, the focus window is the root window. Since all windows are descendants of the root, the pointer controls the window that receives input.

Most window managers allow the user to set a focus window to avoid the problem where the pointer sometimes gets bumped into the wrong window and your typing does not go to the intended window. If the pointer is pointing at the root window, all typing is usually lost, since there is no application for this input to propagate to. Some applications may set the keyboard focus so that they can get all keyboard input for a given period of time, but this practice is not encouraged.

Focus events are used when an application wants to act differently when the keyboard focus is set to another window or to itself. `FocusChangeMask` is used to select `FocusIn` and `FocusOut` events.

When a focus change occurs, a `FocusOut` event is delivered to the old focus window and a `FocusIn` event is delivered to the window which receives the focus. Windows in between in the hierarchy are virtually crossed and receive one focus change event each depending on the relationship and direction of transfer between the origin and destination windows. Some or all of the windows between the window containing the pointer at the time of the focus change and that window's root window can also receive focus change events. By checking the `detail` member of `FocusIn` and `FocusOut` events, an application can tell which of its windows can receive input.

The `detail` member gives clues about the relationship of the event receiving window to the origin and destination of the focus. The `detail` member of `FocusIn` and `FocusOut` events is analogous to the `detail` member of `EnterNotify` and `LeaveNotify` events but with even more permutations to make life complicated.

Virtual Focus Crossing and the detail Member

We will now embark on specifying the types of events sent to each window and the `detail` member in each event, depending on the relative position in the hierarchy of the origin window (old focus), destination window (new focus), and the pointer window (window containing pointer at time of focus change). Don't even try to figure this out unless you have to.

Table E-3 shows the event types generated by a focus transition from window A to window B when window C is the least common ancestor of A and B. This table includes most of the events generated, but not all of them. It is quite possible for a single window to receive more than one focus change event from a single focus change.

Table E-3. FocusIn and FocusOut Events and Window Relationship

FocusOut	FocusIn
Origin window (*A*)	Destination window (*B*)
Windows between *A* and *B*, exclusive, if *A* is inferior.	Windows between *A* and *B*, exclusive, if *B* is inferior.
Windows between *A* and *C*, exclusive.	Windows between *B* and *C*, exclusive.
Root window on screen of origin if different from screen of destination.	Root window on screen of destination if different from screen of origin.
Pointer window up to but not including origin window if pointer window is descendant of origin.	Pointer window up to but not including destination window if pointer window is descendant of destination.
Pointer window up to and including pointer window's root if transfer was from `PointerRoot`.	Pointer window up to and including pointer window's root if transfer was to `PointerRoot`.

Table E-4 lists the `detail` members in events generated by a focus transition from window *A* to window *B* when window *C* is the least common ancestor of *A* and *B*, with *P* being the window containing the pointer.

Table E-4. Event detail Member and Window Relationship

`detail` Flag	Window Delivered To
`NotifyAncestor`	Origin or destination when either is descendant.
`NotifyInferior`	Origin or destination when either is ancestor.
`NotifyVirtual`	Windows between *A* and *B*, exclusive, if either is descendant.
`NotifyNonlinear`	Origin and destination when *A* and *B* are two or more windows distant from least common ancestor *C*.
`NotifyNonlinearVirtual`	Windows between *A* and *C*, exclusive, and between *B* and *C*, exclusive, when *A* and *B* have least common ancestor *C*; also on both root windows if *A* and *B* are on different screens.
`NotifyPointer`	Window *P* and windows up to but not including the origin or destination windows.
`NotifyPointerRoot`	Window *P* and all windows up to its root, and all other roots, when focus is set to or from `PointerRoot`.
`NotifyDetailNone`	All roots, when focus is set to or from `None`.

Figure E-3 shows all the possible combinations of focus transitions and of origin, destination, and pointer windows and shows the types of events that are generated and their `detail` member. Solid lines indicate branches of the hierarchy. Dotted arrows indicate the direction of transition of the focus. At each end of this arrow are the origin and destination windows, windows *A* to *B*. Arrows ending in a bar indicate that the event type and detail described are delivered to all windows up to the bar.

In any branch, there may be windows that are not shown. Windows in a single branch between two boxes shown will get the event types and details shown beside the branch.

Event Reference

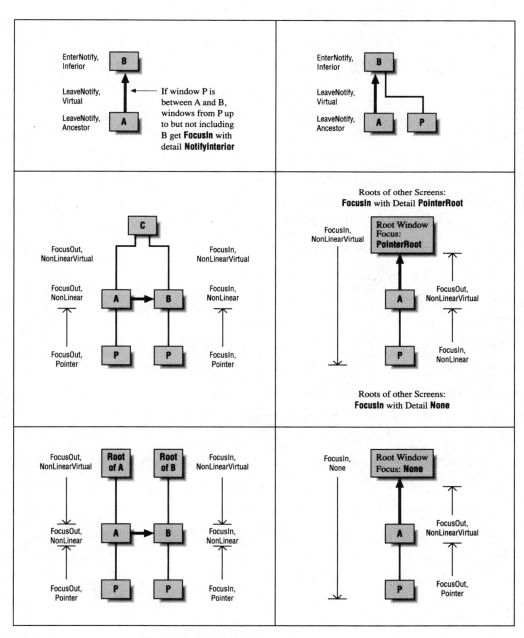

Figure E-3. FocusIn and FocusOut event schematics

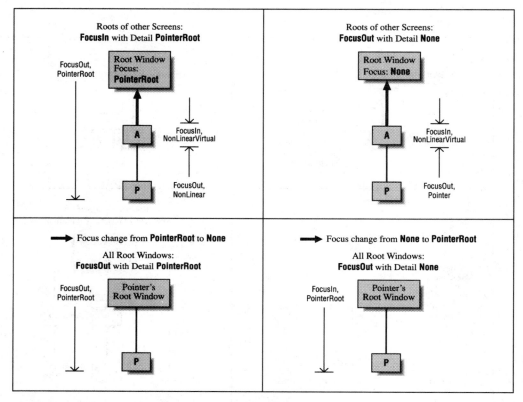

Figure E-3. FocusIn and FocusOut event schematics (cont'd)

`FocusIn` and `FocusOut` events are also generated when the keyboard is grabbed, if the focus was not already assigned to the grabbing window. In this case, all windows receive events as if the focus was set from the current focus to the grab window. When the grab is released, the events generated are just as if the focus was set back.

GraphicsExpose, NoExpose

When Generated

GraphicsExpose events indicate that the source area for a XCopyArea() or XCopy-Plane() request was not available because it was outside the source window or obscured by a window. NoExpose events indicate that the source region was completely available.

Select With

These events are not selected with XSelectInput but are sent if the GC in the XCopyArea or XCopyPlane request had its graphics_exposures flag set to True. If graphics_exposures is True in the GC used for the copy, either one NoExpose event or one or more GraphicsExpose events will be generated for every XCopyArea or XCopyPlane call made.

XEvent Structure Name

```
typedef union _XEvent {
    . . .
    XNoExposeEvent xnoexpose;
    XGraphicsExposeEvent xgraphicsexpose;
    . . .
} XEvent;
```

Event Structure

```
typedef struct {
    int type;
    unsigned long serial;       /* # of last request processed by server */
    Bool send_event;            /* True if this came from SendEvent request */
    Display *display;           /* Display the event was read from */
    Drawable drawable;
    int x, y;
    int width, height;
    int count;                  /* if nonzero, at least this many more */
    int major_code;             /* core is X_CopyArea or X_CopyPlane */
    int minor_code;             /* not defined in the core */
} XGraphicsExposeEvent;

typedef struct {
    int type;
    unsigned long serial;       /* # of last request processed by server */
    Bool send_event;            /* True if this came from SendEvent request */
    Display *display;           /* Display the event was read from */
    Drawable drawable;
    int major_code;             /* core is X_CopyArea or X_CopyPlane */
    int minor_code;             /* not defined in the core */
} XNoExposeEvent;
```

Event Structure Members

`drawable`	A window or an off-screen pixmap. This specifies the destination of the graphics request that generated the event.
`x, y`	The coordinates of the upper-left corner of the exposed region relative to the origin of the window.
`width, height`	The width and height in pixels of the exposed region.
`count`	The approximate number of remaining contiguous `Graphics-Expose` events that were generated as a result of the `XCopyArea` or `XCopyPlane` call.
`major_code`	The graphics request used. This may be one of the symbols `Copy-Area` or `CopyPlane` or a symbol defined by a loaded extension.
`minor_code`	Zero unless the request is part of an extension.

Notes

`Expose` events and `GraphicsExpose` events both indicate the region of a window that was actually exposed (`x`, `y`, `width`, and `height`). Therefore, they can often be handled similarly. The symbols `X_CopyPlane` and `X_CopyArea` are defined in *<X11/Xproto.h>*. These symbols are used to determine whether a `GraphicsExpose` or `NoExpose` event occurred because of an `XCopyArea` call or an `XCopyPlane` call.

GravityNotify

When Generated

A GravityNotify event reports when a window is moved because of a change in the size of its parent. This happens when the win_gravity attribute of the child window is something other than StaticGravity or UnmapGravity.

Select With

This event is selected for a single window by specifying the window ID of that window with StructureNotifyMask. To receive notification of movement due to gravity for a group of siblings, specify the parent window ID with SubstructureNotifyMask.

XEvent Structure Name

```
typedef union _XEvent {
    ...
    XGravityEvent xgravity;
    ...
} XEvent;
```

Event Structure

```
typedef struct {
    int type;
    unsigned long serial;       /* # of last request processed by server */
    Bool send_event;            /* True if this came from SendEvent request */
    Display *display;           /* Display the event was read from */
    Window event;
    Window window;
    int x, y;
} XGravityEvent;
```

Event Structure Members

event   The window that selected the event.

window   The window that was moved.

x, y   The new coordinates of the window relative to its parent.

KeyPress, KeyRelease

When Generated

KeyPress and KeyRelease events are generated for all keys, even those mapped to modifier keys such as Shift or Control.

Select With

Each type of keyboard event may be selected separately with KeyPressMask and Key-ReleaseMask.

XEvent Structure Name

```
typedef union _XEvent {
    ...
    XKeyEvent xkey;
    ...
} XEvent;
```

Event Structure

```
typedef struct {
    int type;                  /* of event */
    unsigned long serial;      /* # of last request processed by server */
    Bool send_event;           /* True if this came from SendEvent request */
    Display *display;          /* Display the event was read from */
    Window window;             /* event window it is reported relative to */
    Window root;               /* root window that the event occurred on */
    Window subwindow;          /* child window */
    Time time;                 /* milliseconds */
    int x, y;                  /* pointer coordinates relative to receiving
                                                window */
    int x_root, y_root;        /* coordinates relative to root */
    unsigned int state;        /* modifier key and button mask */
    unsigned int keycode;      /* server-dependent code for key */
    Bool same_screen;          /* same screen flag */
} XKeyEvent;
typedef XKeyEvent XKeyPressedEvent;
typedef XKeyEvent XKeyReleasedEvent;
```

Event Structure Members

subwindow   If the source window is the child of the receiving window, then the subwindow member is set to the ID of that child.

time   The server time when the button event occurred, in milliseconds. Time is declared as unsigned long, so it wraps around when it reaches the maximum value of a 32-bit number (every 49.7 days).

x, y	If the receiving window is on the same screen as the root window specified by root, then x and y are the pointer coordinates relative to the receiving window's origin. Otherwise, x and y are zero.
	When active button grabs and pointer grabs are in effect (see Section 9.4 of Volume One, *Xlib Programming Manual*), the coordinates relative to the receiving window may not be within the window (they may be negative or greater than window height or width).
x_root, y_root	The pointer coordinates relative to the root window which is an ancestor of the event window. If the pointer was on a different screen, these are zero.
state	The state of all the buttons and modifier keys just before the event, represented by a mask of the button and modifier key symbols: Button1Mask, Button2Mask, Button3Mask, Button4Mask, Button5Mask, ControlMask, LockMask, Mod1Mask, Mod2-Mask, Mod3Mask, Mod4Mask, Mod5Mask, and ShiftMask.
keycode	The keycode member contains a server-dependent code for the key that changed state. As such, it should be translated into the portable symbol called a keysym before being used. It can also be converted directly into ASCII with XLookupString. For a description and examples of how to translate keycodes, see Volume One, Section 9.1.1.

Notes

Remember that not all hardware is capable of generating release events and that only the main keyboard (a-z, A-Z, 0-9), Shift, and Control keys are always found.

Keyboard events are analogous to button events, though, of course, there are many more keys than buttons and the keyboard is not automatically grabbed between press and release.

All the structure members have the same meaning as described for ButtonPress and ButtonRelease events, except that button is replaced by keycode.

KeymapNotify

When Generated

A `KeymapNotify` event reports the state of the keyboard and occurs when the pointer or keyboard focus enters a window. `KeymapNotify` events are reported immediately after `EnterNotify` or `FocusIn` events. This is a way for the application to read the keyboard state as the application is "woken up," since the two triggering events usually indicate that the application is about to receive user input.

Select With

This event is selected with `KeymapStateMask`.

XEvent Structure Name

```
typedef union _XEvent {
    ...
    XKeymapEvent xkeymap;
    ...
} XEvent;
```

Event Structure

```
typedef struct {
    int type;
    unsigned long serial;      /* # of last request processed by server */
    Bool send_event;           /* True if this came from SendEvent request */
    Display *display;          /* Display the event was read from */
    Window window;
    char key_vector[32];
} XKeymapEvent;
```

Event Structure Members

window
: Reports the window which was reported in the `window` member of the preceding `EnterNotify` or `FocusIn` event.

key_vector
: A bit vector or mask, each bit representing one physical key, with a total of 256 bits. For a given key, its keycode is its position in the keyboard vector. You can also get this bit vector by calling `XQueryKeymap`.

Notes

The `serial` member of `KeymapNotify` does not contain the serial number of the most recent protocol request processed, because this event always follows immediately after `EnterNotify` or `FocusIn` events in which the `serial` member is valid.

MapNotify, UnmapNotify

When Generated

The X server generates `MapNotify` and `UnmapNotify` events when a window changes state from unmapped to mapped or vice versa.

Select With

To receive these events on a single window, use `StructureNotifyMask` in the call to `XSelectInput` for the window. To receive these events for all children of a particular parent, specify the parent window ID and use `SubstructureNotifyMask`.

XEvent Structure Name

```
typedef union _XEvent {
    ...
    XMapEvent xmap;
    XUnmapEvent xunmap;
    ...
} XEvent;
```

Event Structure

```
typedef struct {
    int type;
    unsigned long serial;       /* # of last request processed by server */
    Bool send_event;            /* True if this came from SendEvent request */
    Display *display;           /* Display the event was read from */
    Window event;
    Window window;
    Bool override_redirect;     /* boolean, is override set */
} XMapEvent;

typedef struct {
    int type;
    unsigned long serial;       /* # of last request processed by server */
    Bool send_event;            /* True if this came from SendEvent request */
    Display *display;           /* Display the event was read from */
    Window event;
    Window window;
    Bool from_configure;
} XUnmapEvent;
```

Event Structure Members

event   The window that selected this event.

window   The window that was just mapped or unmapped.

override_redirect (XMapEvent only)

>   True or False. The value of the override_redirect attribute of the window that was just mapped.

from_configure (XUnmapEvent only)

>   True if the event was generated as a result of a resizing of the window's parent when the window itself had a win_gravity of UnmapGravity. See the description of the win_gravity attribute in Section 4.3.4 of Volume One, *Xlib Programming Manual*. False otherwise.

MapRequest

When Generated

A `MapRequest` event occurs when the functions `XMapRaised()` and `XMapWindow()` are called.

This event differs from `MapNotify` in that it delivers the parameters of the request before it is carried out. This gives the client that selects this event (usually the window manager) the opportunity to revise the size or position of the window before executing the map request itself or to deny the request. (`MapNotify` indicates the final outcome of the request.)

Select With

This event is selected by specifying the window ID of the parent of the receiving window with `SubstructureRedirectMask`. (In addition, the `override_redirect` member of the `XSetWindowAttributes` structure for the specified window must be `False`.)

XEvent Structure Name

```
typedef union _XEvent {
    ...
    XMapRequestEvent xmaprequest;
    ...
} XEvent;
```

Event Structure

```
typedef struct {
    int type;
    unsigned long serial;       /* # of last request processed by server */
    Bool send_event;            /* True if this came from SendEvent request */
    Display *display;           /* Display the event was read from */
    Window parent;
    Window window;
} XMapRequestEvent;
```

Event Structure Members

parent   The ID of the parent of the window being mapped.

window   The ID of the window being mapped.

MappingNotify

When Generated

A `MappingNotify` event is sent when any of the following is changed by another client: the mapping between physical keyboard keys (keycodes) and keysyms, the mapping between modifier keys and logical modifiers, or the mapping between physical and logical pointer buttons. These events are triggered by a call to `XSetModifierMapping()` or `XSet-PointerMapping()`, if the return status is `MappingSuccess`, or by any call to `XChangeKeyboardMapping()`.

This event type should not be confused with the event that occurs when a window is mapped; that is a `MapNotify` event. Nor should it be confused with the `KeymapNotify` event, which reports the state of the keyboard as a mask instead of as a keycode.

Select With

The X server sends `MappingNotify` events to all clients. It is never selected and cannot be masked with the window attributes.

XEvent Structure Name

```
typedef union _XEvent {
    ...
    XMappingEvent xmapping;
    ...
} XEvent;
```

Event Structure

```
typedef struct {
    int type;
    unsigned long serial;    /* # of last request processed by server */
    Bool send_event;         /* True if this came from SendEvent request */
    Display *display;        /* Display the event was read from */
    Window window;           /* unused */
    int request;             /* one of MappingMapping, MappingKeyboard,
                              * MappingPointer */
    int first_keycode;       /* first keycode */
    int count;               /* range of change with first_keycode*/
} XMappingEvent;
```

Event Structure Members

request   The kind of mapping change that occurred: `MappingModifier` for a successful `XSetModifierMapping` (keyboard Shift, Lock, Control, Meta keys), `MappingKeyboard` for a successful `XChange-KeyboardMapping` (other keys), and `MappingPointer` for a successful `XSetPointerMapping` (pointer button numbers).

first_keycode   If the `request` member is `MappingKeyboard` or `Mapping-Modifier`, then `first_keycode` indicates the first in a range of keycodes with altered mappings. Otherwise, it is not set.

count   If the `request` member is `MappingKeyboard` or `Mapping-Modifier`, then `count` indicates the number of keycodes with altered mappings. Otherwise, it is not set.

Notes

If the `request` member is `MappingKeyboard`, clients should call `XRefresh-KeyboardMapping`.

The normal response to a `request` member of `MappingPointer` or `Mapping-Modifier` is no action. This is because the clients should use the logical mapping of the buttons and modifiers to allow the user to customize the keyboard if desired. If the application requires a particular mapping regardless of the user's preferences, it should call `XGet-ModifierMapping` or `XGetPointerMapping` to find out about the new mapping.

MotionNotify

When Generated

A `MotionNotify` event reports that the user moved the pointer or that a program warped the pointer to a new position within a single window.

Select With

This event is selected with `ButtonMotionMask`, `Button1MotionMask`, `Button2-MotionMask`, `Button3MotionMask`, `Button4MotionMask`, `Button5Motion-Mask`, `PointerMotionHintMask`, and `PointerMotionMask`. These masks determine the specific conditions under which the event is generated.

See Section 8.3.3.3 of Volume One, *Xlib Programming Manual*, for a description of selecting button events.

XEvent Structure Name

```
typedef union _XEvent {
    ...
    XMotionEvent xmotion;
    ...
} XEvent;
```

Event Structure

```
typedef struct {
    int type;                  /* of event */
    unsigned long serial;      /* # of last request processed by server */
    Bool send_event;           /* True if this came from SendEvent request */
    Display *display;          /* Display the event was read from */
    Window window;             /* event window it is reported relative to */
    Window root;               /* root window that the event occurred on */
    Window subwindow;          /* child window */
    Time time;                 /* milliseconds */
    int x, y;                  /* pointer coordinates relative to receiving
                                           window */
    int x_root, y_root;        /* coordinates relative to root */
    unsigned int state;        /* button and modifier key mask */
    char is_hint;              /* is this a motion hint */
    Bool same_screen;          /* same screen flag */
} XMotionEvent;
typedef XMotionEvent XPointerMovedEvent;
```

Event Structure Members

subwindow   If the source window is the child of the receiving window, then the
             `subwindow` member is set to the ID of that child.

time

The server time when the button event occurred, in milliseconds. Time is declared as unsigned long, so it wraps around when it reaches the maximum value of a 32-bit number (every 49.7 days).

x, y

If the receiving window is on the same screen as the root window specified by root, then x and y are the pointer coordinates relative to the receiving window's origin. Otherwise, x and y are zero. When active button grabs and pointer grabs are in effect (see Volume One, Section 9.4), the coordinates relative to the receiving window may not be within the window (they may be negative or greater than window height or width).

x_root, y_root

The pointer coordinates relative to the root window which is an ancestor of the event window. If the pointer was on a different screen, these are zero.

state

The state of all the buttons and modifier keys just before the event, represented by a mask of the button and modifier key symbols: Button1Mask, Button2Mask, Button3Mask, Button4Mask, Button5Mask, ControlMask, LockMask, Mod1Mask, Mod2-Mask, Mod3Mask, Mod4Mask, Mod5Mask, and ShiftMask.

is_hint

Either the constant NotifyNormal or NotifyHint. Notify-Hint indicates that the PointerMotionHintMask was selected. In this case, just one event is sent when the mouse moves, and the current position can be found by calling XQueryPointer or by examining the motion history buffer with XGetMotionEvents, if a motion history buffer is available on the server. NotifyNormal indicates that the event is real, but it may not be up to date, since there may be many more later motion events on the queue.

same_screen

Indicates whether the pointer is currently on the same screen as this window. This is always True unless the pointer was actively grabbed before the automatic grab could take place.

Notes

If the processing you have to do for every motion event is fast, you can probably handle all of them without requiring motion hints. However, if you have extensive processing to do for each one, you might be better off using the hints and calling XQueryPointer or using the history buffer if it exists. XQueryPointer is a round-trip request, so it can be slow.

EnterNotify and LeaveNotify events are generated instead of MotionEvents if the pointer starts and stops in different windows.

PropertyNotify

When Generated

A `PropertyNotify` event indicates that a property of a window has changed or been deleted. This event can also be used to get the current server time (by appending zero-length data to a property). `PropertyNotify` events are generated by `XChangeProperty()`, `XDeleteProperty()`, `XGetWindowProperty()`, or `XRotateWindow-Properties()`.

Select With

This event is selected with `PropertyChangeMask`.

XEvent Structure Name

```
typedef union _XEvent {
    ...
    XPropertyEvent xproperty;
    ...
} XEvent;
```

Event Structure

```
typedef struct {
    int type;
    unsigned long serial;     /* # of last request processed by server */
    Bool send_event;          /* True if this came from SendEvent request */
    Display *display;         /* Display the event was read from */
    Window window;
    Atom atom;
    Time time;
    int state;                /* PropertyNewValue, PropertyDeleted */
} XPropertyEvent;
```

Event Structure Members

window   The window whose property was changed, not the window that selected the event.

atom   The property that was changed.

state   Either `PropertyNewValue` or `PropertyDeleted`. Whether the property was changed to a new value or deleted.

time   The `time` member specifies the server time when the property was changed.

ReparentNotify

When Generated

A ReparentNotify event reports when a client successfully reparents a window.

Select With

This event is selected with SubstructureNotifyMask by specifying the window ID of the old or the new parent window or with StructureNotifyMask by specifying the window ID.

XEvent Structure Name

```
typedef union _XEvent {
    ...
    XReparentEvent xreparent;
    ...
} XEvent;
```

Event Structure

```
typedef struct {
    int type;
    unsigned long serial;    /* # of last request processed by server */
    Bool send_event;         /* True if this came from SendEvent request */
    Display *display;        /* Display the event was read from */
    Window event;
    Window window;
    Window parent;
    int x, y;
    Bool override_redirect;
} XReparentEvent;
```

Event Structure Members

window   The window whose parent window was changed.

parent   The new parent of the window.

x, y   The coordinates of the upper-left pixel of the window's border relative to the new parent window's origin.

override_redirect   The override_redirect attribute of the reparented window. If True, it indicates that the client wants this window to be immune to meddling by the window manager. Window managers normally should not have reparented this window to begin with.

ResizeRequest

When Generated

A `ResizeRequest` event reports another client's attempt to change the size of a window. The X server generates this event type when another client calls `XConfigureWindow()`, `XMoveResizeWindow()`, or `XResizeWindow()`. If this event type is selected, the window is not resized. This gives the client that selects this event (usually the window manager) the opportunity to revise the new size of the window before executing the resize request or to deny the request itself.

Select With

To receive this event type, specify a window ID and pass `ResizeRedirectMask` as part of the `event_mask` argument to `XSelectInput`. Only one client can select this event on a particular window. When selected, this event is triggered instead of resizing the window.

XEvent Structure Name

```
typedef union _XEvent {
    ...
    XResizeRequestEvent xresizerequest;
    ...
} XEvent;
```

Event Structure

```
typedef struct {
    int type;
    unsigned long serial;      /* # of last request processed by server */
    Bool send_event;           /* True if this came from SendEvent request */
    Display *display;          /* Display the event was read from */
    Window window;
    int width, height;
} XResizeRequestEvent;
```

Event Structure Members

window   The window whose size another client attempted to change.

width, height   The requested size of the window, not including its border.

SelectionClear

When Generated

A `SelectionClear` event reports to the current owner of a selection that a new owner is being defined.

Select With

This event is not selected. It is sent to the previous selection owner when another client calls `XSetSelectionOwner` for the same selection.

XEvent Structure Name

```
typedef union _XEvent {
    ...
    XSelectionClearEvent xselectionclear;
    ...
} XEvent;
```

Event Structure

```
typedef struct {
    int type;
    unsigned long serial;       /* # of last request processed by server */
    Bool send_event;            /* True if this came from SendEvent request */
    Display *display;           /* Display the event was read from */
    Window window;
    Atom selection;
    Time time;
} XSelectionClearEvent;
```

Event Structure Members

window   The window that is receiving the event and losing the selection.

selection   The selection atom specifying the selection that is changing ownership.

time   The last-change time recorded for the selection.

SelectionNotify

When Generated

A SelectionNotify event is sent only by clients, not by the server, by calling XSend-Event(). The owner of a selection sends this event to a requestor (a client that calls XConvertSelection() for a given property) when a selection has been converted and stored as a property or when a selection conversion could not be performed (indicated with property None).

Select With

There is no event mask for SelectionNotify events, and they are not selected with XSelectInput. Instead XSendEvent directs the event to a specific window, which is given as a window ID: PointerWindow, which identifies the window the pointer is in, or InputFocus, which identifies the focus window.

XEvent Structure Name

```
typedef union _XEvent {
    ...
    XSelectionEvent xselection;
    ...
} XEvent;
```

Event Structure

```
typedef struct {
    int type;
    unsigned long serial;    /* # of last request processed by server */
    Bool send_event;         /* True if this came from SendEvent request */
    Display *display;        /* Display the event was read from */
    Window requestor;
    Atom selection;
    Atom target;
    Atom property;           /* Atom or None */
    Time time;
} XSelectionEvent;
```

Event Structure Members

The members of this structure have the values specified in the XConvertSelection call that triggers the selection owner to send this event, except that the property member either will return the atom specifying a property on the requestor window with the data type specified in target or will return None, which indicates that the data could not be converted into the target type.

SelectionRequest

When Generated

A SelectionRequest event is sent to the owner of a selection when another client requests the selection by calling XConvertSelection().

Select With

There is no event mask for SelectionRequest events, and they are not selected with XSelectInput.

XEvent Structure Name

```
typedef union _XEvent {
    ...
    XSelectionRequestEvent xselectionrequest;
    ...
} XEvent;
```

Event Structure

```
typedef struct {
    int type;
    unsigned long serial;       /* # of last request processed by server */
    Bool send_event;            /* True if this came from SendEvent request */
    Display *display;           /* Display the event was read from */
    Window owner;
    Window requestor;
    Atom selection;
    Atom target;
    Atom property;
    Time time;
} XSelectionRequestEvent;
```

Event Structure Members

The members of this structure have the values specified in the XConvertSelection call that triggers this event.

The owner should convert the selection based on the specified target type, if possible. If a property is specified, the owner should store the result as that property on the requestor window and then send a SelectionNotify event to the requestor by calling XSendEvent. If the selection cannot be converted as requested, the owner should send a Selection-Notify event with property set to the constant None.

Event Reference

VisibilityNotify

xvisibility—

When Generated

A `VisibilityNotify` event reports any change in the visibility of the specified window. This event type is never generated on windows whose class is `InputOnly`. All of the window's subwindows are ignored when calculating the visibility of the window.

Select With

This event is selected with `VisibilityChangeMask`.

XEvent Structure Name

```
typedef union _XEvent {
    ...
    XVisibilityEvent xvisibility;
    ...
} XEvent;
```

Event Structure

```
typedef struct {
    int type;
    unsigned long serial;    /* # of last request processed by server */
    Bool send_event;         /* True if this came from SendEvent request */
    Display *display;        /* Display the event was read from */
    Window window;
    int state;               /* VisibilityFullyObscured,
                                VisibilityPartiallyObscured,
                                VisibilityUnobscured */
} XVisibilityEvent;
```

Event Structure Members

state   A symbol indicating the final visibility status of the window: `Visibility-FullyObscured`, `VisibilityPartiallyObscured`, or `VisibilityUnobscured`.

Notes

Table E-5 lists the transitions that generate `VisibilityNotify` events and the corresponding `state` member of the `XVisibilityEvent` structure.

Table E-5. State Element of the XVisibilityEvent Structure

Visibility Status Before	Visibility Status After	State Member
Partially obscured, fully obscured, or not viewable.	Viewable and completely unobscured.	`VisibilityUnobscured`
Viewable and completely unobscured, viewable and fully obscured, or not viewable.	Viewable and partially obscured.	`VisibilityPartially-Obscured`
Viewable and completely unobscured, viewable and partially obscured, or not viewable.	Viewable and partially obscured.	`VisibilityPartially-Obscured`

F
Structure Reference

This appendix summarizes the contents of the include files for Xlib and presents each structure in alphabetical order.

F.1 Description of Header Files

All include files are normally located in */usr/include/X11*. All Xlib programs require *<X11/Xlib.h>*, which includes *<X11/X.h>*. *<X11/Xlib.h>* contains most of the structure declarations, while *<X11/X.h>* contains most of the defined constants. Virtually all programs will also require *<X11/Xutil.h>*, which include structure types and declarations applicable to window manager hints, colors, visuals, regions, standard geometry strings, and images.

Here is a summary of the contents of the include files:

<X11/Xlib.h>	Structure declarations for core Xlib functions.
<X11/X.h>	Constant definitions for Xlib functions.
<X11/Xutil.h>	Additional structure types and constant definitions for miscellaneous Xlib functions.
<X11/Xatom.h>	The predefined atoms for properties, types, and font characteristics.
<X11/cursorfont.h>	The constants used to select a cursor shape from the standard cursor font.
<X11/keysym.h>	Predefined key symbols corresponding to keycodes. It includes *<X11/keysymdef.h>*.
<X11/Xresource.h>	Resource manager structure definitions and function declarations.

F.2 Resource Types

The following types are defined in *<X11/X.h>*:

```
unsigned long XID
XID Colormap
XID Cursor
XID Drawable
XID Font
XID GContext
XID KeySym
XID Pixmap
XID Window
unsigned long Atom
unsigned char KeyCode
unsigned long Mask
unsigned long Time
unsigned long VisualID
```

F.3 Structure Definitions

This section lists all public Xlib structure definitions in `Xlib.h` and `Xutil.h`, in alphabet-ical order, except the event structures, which are listed on the reference page for each event in Appendix E, *Event Reference*.

Before each structure is a description of what the structure is used for and a list of the Xlib routines that use the structure.

Opaque structures, such as `Display`, `Screen`, and `XFontSet` are not listed here, either because they should be treated as IDs and their contents never referenced, or their contents should only be accessed through the macros listed in Appendix C, or the functions mentioned there.

F.3.1 XArc

`XArc` specifies the bounding box for an arc and two angles indicating the extent of the arc within the box. A list of these structures is used in `XDrawArcs()` and `XFillArcs()`.

```
typedef struct {
    short x, y;
    unsigned short width, height;
    short angle1, angle2;
} XArc;
```

F.3.2 XChar2b

XChar2b specifies a character in a two-byte font. A list of structures of this type is an argument to **XDrawImageString16()**, **XDrawString16()**, **XDrawText16()**, **XQueryTextExtents16()**, **XTextExtents16()**, and **XTextWidth16()**. The only two-byte font currently available is Kanji (Japanese).

```
typedef struct {                        /* normal 16 bit characters are two bytes */
    unsigned char byte1;
    unsigned char byte2;
} XChar2b;
```

F.3.3 XCharStruct

XCharStruct describes the metrics of a single character in a font or the overall characteristics of a font. This structure is the type of several of members of **XFontStruct** and is used to return the overall characteristics of a string in **XQueryTextExtents*()** and **XTextExtents*()**.

```
typedef struct {
    short lbearing;                 /* origin to left edge of raster */
    short rbearing;                 /* origin to right edge of raster */
    short width;                    /* advance to next char's origin */
    short ascent;                   /* baseline to top edge of raster */
    short descent;                  /* baseline to bottom edge of raster */
    unsigned short attributes;      /* per char flags (not predefined) */
} XCharStruct;
```

F.3.4 XClassHint

XClassHint is used to set or get the **XA_WM_CLASS_HINT** property for an application's top-level window, as arguments to **XSetClassHint()** or **XGetClassHint()**.

```
typedef struct {
    char *res_name;
    char *res_class;
} XClassHint;
```

F.3.5 XcmsColor

See the **XcmsColor** reference page for information on this structure and the **XcmsRGB**, **XcmsRGBi**, **XcmsCIEXYZ**, **XcmsCIEuvY**, **XcmsCIExyY**, **XcmsCIELab**, **Xcms-CIELuv**, and **XcmsTekHVC** structures. All these structures are used by the color allocation and colorcell setting in functions such as **XcmsAllocColor()** and **XcmsStore-Color()**.

F.3.6 XColor

XColor describes a single colorcell. This structure is used to specify and return the pixel value and RGB values for a colorcell. The flags indicate which of the RGB values should be changed when used in **XStoreColors( )**, **XAllocNamedColor( )**, or **XAlloc-Color( )**. Also used in **XCreateGlyphCursor( )**, **XCreatePixmapCursor( )**, **XLookupColor( )**, **XParseColor( )**, **XQueryColor**, **XQueryColors( )**, and **XRecolorCursor( )**.

```
typedef struct {
    unsigned long pixel;
    unsigned short red, green, blue;
    char flags;                          /* DoRed, DoGreen, DoBlue */
    char pad;
} XColor;
```

F.3.7 XComposeStatus

XComposeStatus describes the current state of a multikey character sequence. Used in calling **XLookupString( )**. This processing is not implemented in the MIT sample servers.

```
typedef struct _XComposeStatus {
    char *compose_ptr;                   /* state table pointer */
    int chars_matched;                   /* match state */
} XComposeStatus;
```

F.3.8 XExtCodes

XExtCodes is a structure used by the extension mechanism. This structure is returned by **XInitExtension( )** which is not a standard Xlib routine but should be called within the extension code. Its contents are not normally accessible to the application.

```
typedef struct {                         /* public to extension, cannot be changed */
    int extension;                       /* extension number */
    int major_opcode;                    /* major opcode assigned by server */
    int first_event;                     /* first event number for the extension */
    int first_error;                     /* first error number for the extension.*/
} XExtCodes;
```

F.3.9 XExtData

XExtData provides a way for extensions to attach private data to the existing structure types GC, **Visual**, **Screen**, **Display**, and **XFontStruct**. This structure is not used in normal Xlib programming.

```
typedef struct _XExtData {
    int number;                  /* number returned by XRegisterExtension */
    struct _XExtData *next;      /* next item on list of data for structure */
    int (*free_private)();       /* called to free private storage */
    char *private_data;          /* data private to this extension */
} XExtData;
```

F.3.10 XFontProp

XFontProp is used in **XFontStruct**. This structure allows the application to find out the names of additional font properties beyond the predefined set, so that they too can be accessed with **XGetFontProperty()**. This structure is not used as an argument or return value for any core Xlib function.

```
typedef struct {
    Atom name;
    unsigned long card32;
} XFontProp;
```

F.3.11 XFontSetExtents()

The **XFontSetExtents()** structure is returned by **XExtentsOfFontSet()**. New in Release 5.

```
typedef struct {
    XRectangle max_ink_extent;       /* over all drawable characters */
    XRectangle max_logical_extent;   /* over all drawable characters */
} XFontSetExtents;
```

F.3.12 XFontStruct

XFontStruct specifies metric information for an entire font. This structure is filled with the **XLoadQueryFont()** and **XQueryFont()** routines. **ListFontsWithInfo** also fills it but with metric information for the entire font only, not for each character. A pointer to this structure is used in the routines **XFreeFont**, **XFreeFontInfo()**, **XGetFont-Prop**, **XTextExtents*()**, and **XTextWidth*()**.

```
typedef struct {
    XExtData *ext_data;          /* hook for extension to hang data */
```

```
        Font fid;                    /* font ID for this font */
        unsigned direction;          /* direction the font is painted */
        unsigned min_char_or_byte2;  /* first character */
        unsigned max_char_or_byte2;  /* last character */
        unsigned min_byte1;          /* first row that exists */
        unsigned max_byte1;          /* last row that exists */
        Bool all_chars_exist;        /* flag if all characters have nonzero size*/
        unsigned default_char;       /* char to print for undefined character */
        int n_properties;            /* how many properties there are */
        XFontProp *properties;       /* pointer to array of additional properties*/
        XCharStruct min_bounds;      /* minimum bounds over all existing char*/
        XCharStruct max_bounds;      /* maximum bounds over all existing char*/
        XCharStruct *per_char;       /* first_char to last_char information */
        int ascent;                  /* logical extent above baseline for spacing */
        int descent;                 /* logical descent below baseline for spacing */
} XFontStruct;
```

F.3.13 XGCValues

XGCValues is used to set or change members of the GC by the routines **XCreateGC()**
and **XChangeGC()**.

```
typedef struct {
        int function;                    /* logical operation */
        unsigned long plane_mask;        /* plane mask */
        unsigned long foreground;        /* foreground pixel */
        unsigned long background;        /* background pixel */
        int line_width;                  /* line width */
        int line_style;                  /* LineSolid, LineOnOffDash, LineDoubleDash */
        int cap_style;                   /* CapNotLast, CapButt, CapRound, CapProjecting */
        int join_style;                  /* JoinMiter, JoinRound, JoinBevel */
        int fill_style;                  /* FillSolid, FillTiled, FillStippled */
        int fill_rule;                   /* EvenOddRule, WindingRule */
        int arc_mode;                    /* ArcPieSlice, ArcChord */
        Pixmap tile;                     /* tile pixmap for tiling operations */
        Pixmap stipple;                  /* stipple 1 plane pixmap for stippling */
        int ts_x_origin;                 /* offset for tile or stipple operations */
        int ts_y_origin;
        Font font;                       /* default text font for text operations */
        int subwindow_mode;              /* ClipByChildren, IncludeInferiors */
        Bool graphics_exposures;         /* Boolean, should exposures be generated */
        int clip_x_origin;               /* origin for clipping */
        int clip_y_origin;
        Pixmap clip_mask;                /* bitmap clipping; other calls for rects */
        int dash_offset;                 /* patterned/dashed line information */
        char dashes;
} XGCValues;
```

F.3.14 XHostAddress

XHostAddress specifies the address of a host machine that is to be added or removed from the host access list for a server. Used in **XAddHost**, **XAddHosts()**, **XListHosts()**, **XRemoveHost**, and **XRemoveHosts()**.

```
typedef struct {
    int family;                    /* for example FAMILY_INTERNET */
    int length;                    /* length of address, in bytes */
    char *address;                 /* pointer to where to find the bytes */
} XHostAddress;
```

F.3.15 XIconSize

XIconSize is Used to set or read the **XA_WM_ICON_SIZE** property. This is normally set by the window manager with **XSetIconSizes()** and read by each application with **XGetIconSizes()**.

```
typedef struct {
    int min_width, min_height;
    int max_width, max_height;
    int width_inc, height_inc;
} XIconSize;
```

F.3.16 XImage

XImage describes an area of the screen; is used in **XCreateImage()**, **XDestroyImage()**, **XGetPixel()**, **XPutPixel()**, **XSubImage()**, **XAddPixel()**, **XGetImage()**, **XGetSubImage()**, and **XPutImage()**.

```
typedef struct _XImage {
    int width, height;             /* size of image */
    int xoffset;                   /* number of pixels offset in X direction */
    int format;                    /* XYBitmap, XYPixmap, ZPixmap */
    char *data;                    /* pointer to image data */
    int byte_order;                /* data byte order, LSBFirst, MSBFirst */
    int bitmap_unit;               /* quant. of scan line 8, 16, 32 */
    int bitmap_bit_order;          /* LSBFirst, MSBFirst */
    int bitmap_pad;                /* 8, 16, 32 either XY or ZPixmap */
    int depth;                     /* depth of image */
    int bytes_per_line;            /* accelerator to next line */
    int bits_per_pixel;            /* bits per pixel (ZPixmap) */
    unsigned long red_mask;        /* bits in z arrangement */
    unsigned long green_mask;
    unsigned long blue_mask;
    char *obdata;                  /* hook for the object routines to hang on */
    struct funcs {                 /* image manipulation routines */
    struct _XImage *(*create_image)();
    int (*destroy_image)();
```

```
        unsigned long (*get_pixel)();
        int (*put_pixel)();
        struct _XImage *(*sub_image)();
        int (*add_pixel)();
        } f;
    } XImage;
```

F.3.17 XIMPreeditCaretCallbackStruct

`XIMPreeditCaretCallbackStruct` is an argument of the `PreeditCaret-Callback` prototype procedure you might need to write for internationalization. New in Release 5.

```
typedef struct _XIMPreeditCaretCallbackStruct {
    int position;    /* Caret offset within preedit string */
    XIMCaretDirection direction;    /* Caret moves direction */
    XIMCaretStyle style;    /* Feedback of the caret */
} XIMPreeditCaretCallbackStruct;
```

F.3.18 XIMPreeditDrawCallbackStruct

`XIMPreeditDrawCallbackStruct` is an argument of the `PreeditDraw-Callback` prototype procedure you might need to write for internationalization. New in Release 5.

```
typedef struct _XIMPreeditDrawCallbackStruct {
    int caret;    /* Cursor offset within preedit string */
    int chg_first;    /* Starting change position */
    int chg_length;    /* Length of the change in character count */
    XIMText *text;
} XIMPreeditDrawCallbackStruct;
```

F.3.19 XIMStatusDrawCallbackStruct

`XIMStatusDrawCallbackStruct` is an argument of the `StatusDrawCallback` prototype procedure you might need to write for internationalization. New in Release 5.

```
typedef enum {
    XIMTextType,
    XIMBitmapType,
} XIMStatusDataType;

typedef struct _XIMStatusDrawCallbackStruct {
    XIMStatusDataType type;
    union {
        XIMText *text;
```

```
        Pixmap  bitmap;
    } data;
} XIMStatusDrawCallbackStruct;
```

F.3.20 XIMText

The **XIMText** structure is used in the **XIMPreeditDrawCallbackStruct** which in turn is an argument of the **PreeditDrawCallback** function you might need to write for internationalization. New in Release 5.

```
typedef struct _XIMText {
    unsigned short length;
    XIMFeedback * feedback;
    Bool encoding_is_wchar;
    union {
        char * multi_byte;
        wchar_t * wide_char;
        } string;
} XIMText;
```

F.3.21 XIMStyles

The **XIMStyles** structure is returned by **XGetIMValues()**. New in Release 5.

```
typedef struct {
    unsigned short count_styles;
    XIMStyle * supported_styles;
} XIMStyles;
```

F.3.22 XKeyboardControl()

XKeyboardControl() is used to set user preferences with **XChangeKeyboard-Control()**.

```
typedef struct {
    int key_click_percent;
    int bell_percent;
    int bell_pitch;
    int bell_duration;
    int led;
    int led_mode;
    int key;
    int auto_repeat_mode;        /* AutoRepeatModeOn, AutoRepeatModeOff,
                                  * AutoRepeatModeDefault */
} XKeyboardControl;
```

F.3.23 XKeyboardState()

XKeyboardState() is used to return the current settings of user preferences with **XGet-KeyboardControl()**.

```
typedef struct {
    int key_click_percent;
    int bell_percent;
    unsigned int bell_pitch, bell_duration;
    unsigned long led_mask;
    int global_auto_repeat;
    char auto_repeats[32];
} XKeyboardState;
```

F.3.24 XmbTextItem()

XmbTextItem() is the structure that holds multi-byte text items for internationalized text drawing. New in Release 5.

```
typedef struct {
    char        *chars;
    int          nchars;
    int          delta;
    XFontSet     font_set;
} XmbTextItem;
```

F.3.25 XModifierKeymap()

XModifierKeymap() specifies which physical keys are mapped to modifier functions. This structure is returned by **XGetModifierMapping()** and is an argument to **XDeleteModifiermapEntry()**, **XFreeModifiermap()**, **XInsertModifiermapEntry()**, **XNewModifiermap()**, and **XSetModifierMapping()**.

```
typedef struct {
    int max_keypermod;      /* server's max # of keys per modifier */
    KeyCode *modifiermap;   /* an 8 by max_keypermod array of modifiers */
} XModifierKeymap;
```

F.3.26 XPixmapFormatValues

XPixmapFormatValues describes one pixmap format that is supported on the server. A list of these structures is returned by **XListPixmapFormats()**.

```
typedef struct {
    int depth;
    int bits_per_pixel;
    int scanline_pad;
} XPixmapFormatValues;
```

F.3.27 XPoint

XPoint specifies the coordinates of a point. Used in **XDrawPoints()**, **XDrawLines()**, **XFillPolygon()**, and **XPolygonRegion()**.

```
typedef struct {
    short x, y;
} XPoint;
```

F.3.28 XRectangle

XRectangle specifies a rectangle. Used in **XClipBox()**, **XDrawRectangles()**, **XFillRectangles()**, **XSetClipRectangles()**, and **XUnionRectWithRegion()**.

```
typedef struct {
    short x, y;
    unsigned short width, height;
} XRectangle;
```

F.3.29 XSegment

XSegment specifies two points. Used in **XDrawSegments()**.

```
typedef struct {
    short x1, y1, x2, y2;
} XSegment;
```

F.3.30 XSetWindowAttributes

XSetWindowAttributes contains all the attributes that can be set without window manager intervention. Used in **XChangeWindowAttributes()** and **XCreateWindow()**.

```
typedef struct {
    Pixmap background_pixmap;          /* background or None or ParentRelative */
    unsigned long background_pixel;    /* background pixel */
    Pixmap border_pixmap;              /* border of the window */
    unsigned long border_pixel;        /* border pixel value */
    int bit_gravity;                   /* one of bit gravity values */
    int win_gravity;                   /* one of the window gravity values */
    int backing_store;                 /* NotUseful, WhenMapped, Always */
    unsigned long backing_planes;      /* planes to be preserved if possible */
    unsigned long backing_pixel;       /* value to use in restoring planes */
    Bool save_under;                   /* should bits under be saved? (popups) */
    long event_mask;                   /* set of events that should be saved */
    long do_not_propagate_mask;        /* set of events that should not */
                                        * propagate */

    Bool override_redirect;            /* Boolean value for override-redirect */
    Colormap colormap;                 /* colormap to be associated with window */
    Cursor cursor;                     /* cursor to be displayed (or None) */
} XSetWindowAttributes;
```

F.3.31 XSizeHints

XSizeHints describes a range of preferred sizes and aspect ratios. Used to set the XA_WM_NORMAL_HINTS and XA_WM_ZOOM_HINTS properties for the window manager with **XSetStandardProperties()**, **XSetNormalHints()**, **XSetSizeHints()**, or **XSetZoomHints()** in R3, and **XSetWMProperties()**, **XSetWMNormalHints()**, and **XSetWMSizeHints()** in R4. Also used in reading these properties with **XGetNormalHints()**, **XGetSizeHints()**, or **XGetZoomHints()** in R3, and **XGetWMNormalHints()** and **XGetWMSizeHints()**.

```
typedef struct {
    long flags;                        /* marks defined fields in structure */
    int x, y;                          /* obsolete in R4 */
    int width, height;                 /* obsolete in R4 */
    int min_width, min_height;
    int max_width, max_height;
    int width_inc, height_inc;
    struct {
        int x;                         /* numerator */
        int y;                         /* denominator */
    } min_aspect, max_aspect;
    int base_width, base_height;       /* Added in R4 */
    int win_gravity;                   /* Added in R4 */
} XSizeHints;
```

F.3.32 XStandardColormap

XStandardColormap describes a standard colormap, giving its ID and its color characteristics. This is the format of the standard colormap properties set on the root window, which can be changed with **XSetRGBColormaps()** (**XSetStandardProperties()** in R3) and read with **XGetRGBColormaps()** (**XGetStandardProperties** in R3).

```
typedef struct {
    Colormap colormap;
    unsigned long red_max;
    unsigned long red_mult;
    unsigned long green_max;
    unsigned long green_mult;
    unsigned long blue_max;
    unsigned long blue_mult;
    unsigned long base_pixel;
    VisualID visualid;              /* added in R4 */
    XID killid;                     /* added in R4 */
} XStandardColormap;
```

F.3.33 XTextItem

XTextItem describes a string, the font to print it in, and the horizontal offset from the previous string drawn or from the location specified by the drawing command. Used in **XDrawText()**.

```
typedef struct {
    char *chars;              /* pointer to string */
    int nchars;              /* number of characters */
    int delta;              /* delta between strings */
    Font font;              /* font to print it in, None don't change */
} XTextItem;
```

F.3.34 XTextItem16

XTextItem16 describes a string in a two-byte font, the font to print it in, and the horizontal offset from the previous string drawn or from the location specified by the drawing command. Used in **XDrawText16()**.

```
typedef struct {
    XChar2b *chars;              /* two-byte characters */
    int nchars;              /* number of characters */
    int delta;              /* delta between strings */
    Font font;              /* font to print it in, None don't change */
} XTextItem16;
```

F.3.35 XTextProperty

XTextProperty holds the information necessary to write or read a TEXT property, which contains a list of strings. This structure is used by many of the R4 routines that write and read window manager hints that are in string format. The purpose of this structure is to allow these properties to be processed in non-european languages where more than 8 bits might be needed. These structures are also used in **XGetTextProperty()**, **XSetText-Property()**, **XStringListToTextProperty()**, and **XTextProperty-ToStringList()**.

```
typedef struct {
    unsigned char *value;          /* same as Property routines */
    Atom encoding;                 /* prop type */
    int format;                    /* prop data format: 8, 16, or 32 */
    unsigned long nitems;          /* number of data items in value */
} XTextProperty;
```

F.3.36 XTimeCoord

XTimeCoord specifies a time and position pair, for use in tracking the pointer with **XGet-MotionEvents()**. This routine is not supported on all systems.

```
typedef struct {
    Time time;
    short x, y;
} XTimeCoord;
```

F.3.37 XVisualInfo

XVisualInfo contains all the information about a particular visual. It is used in **XGet-VisualInfo()** and **XMatchVisualInfo()** to specify the desired visual type. The visual member of **XVisualInfo** is used for the *visual* argument of **XCreate-Colormap()** or **XCreateWindow()**.

```
typedef struct {
    Visual *visual;
    VisualID visualid;
    int screen;
    unsigned int depth;
    int class;
    unsigned long red_mask;
    unsigned long green_mask;
    unsigned long blue_mask;
    int colormap_size;
    int bits_per_rgb;
} XVisualInfo;
```

F.3.38 XwcTextItem()

`XwcTextItem()` is the structure that holds wide character text items for internationalized text drawing. New in Release 5.

```
typedef struct {
    wchar_t          *chars;
    int              nchars;
    int              delta;
    XFontSet         font_set;
} XwcTextItem;
```

F.3.39 XWindowAttributes

`XWindowAttributes` describes the complete set of window attributes, including those that cannot be set without window manager interaction. This structure is returned by `XGet-WindowAttributes()`. It is *not* used by `XChangeWindowAttributes()` or `XCreateWindow()`.

```
typedef struct {
    int x, y;                           /* location of window */
    int width, height;                  /* width and height of window */
    int border_width;                   /* border width of window */
    int depth;                          /* depth of window */
    Visual *visual;                     /* the associated visual structure */
    Window root;                        /* root of screen containing window */
    int class;                          /* InputOutput, InputOnly*/
    int bit_gravity;                    /* one of bit gravity values */
    int win_gravity;                    /* one of the window gravity values */
    int backing_store;                  /* NotUseful, WhenMapped, Always */
    unsigned long backing_planes;       /* planes to be preserved if possible */
    unsigned long backing_pixel;        /* value to be used when restoring planes */
    Bool save_under;                    /* Boolean, should bits under be saved */
    Colormap colormap;                  /* colormap to be associated with window */
    Bool map_installed;                 /* Boolean, is colormap currently installed*/
    int map_state;                      /* IsUnmapped, IsUnviewable, IsViewable */
    long all_event_masks;               /* events all people have interest in*/
    long your_event_mask;               /* my event mask */
    long do_not_propagate_mask;         /* set of events that should not propagate */
    Bool override_redirect;             /* Boolean value for override-redirect */
    Screen *screen;
} XWindowAttributes;
```

F.3.40 XWindowChanges

XWindowChanges describes a configuration for a window. Used in **XConfigure-Window( )**, which can change the screen layout and therefore can be intercepted by the window manager. This sets some of the remaining members of **XWindowAttributes** that cannot be set with **XChangeWindowAttributes( )** or **XCreateWindow( )**.

```
typedef struct {
    int x, y;
    int width, height;
    int border_width;
    Window sibling;
    int stack_mode;
} XWindowChanges;
```

F.3.41 XWMHints

XWMHints describes various application preferences for communication to the window manager via the **XA_WM_HINTS** property. Used in **XSetWMHints( )** and **XGet-WMHints( )**.

```
typedef struct {
    long flags;                        /* marks defined fields in structure */
    Bool input;                        /* does application need window manager for
                                        * keyboard input */

    int initial_state;                 /* see below */
    Pixmap icon_pixmap;                /* pixmap to be used as icon */
    Window icon_window;                /* window to be used as icon */
    int icon_x, icon_y;                /* initial position of icon */
    Pixmap icon_mask;                  /* icon mask bitmap */
    XID window_group;                  /* ID of related window group */
    /* this structure may be extended in the future */
} XWMHints;
```

G
Symbol Reference

This appendix presents an alphabetical listing of the symbols used in Xlib. The routines in parentheses following the descriptions indicate the routines associated with those symbols.

A

Above	Specifies that the indicated window is placed above the indicated sibling window. (**XConfigureWindow()**)
AllHints	**XA_WM_HINTS** property, stores optional information for the window manager. If **AllHints** is set, all members of **XA_WM_HINTS** are set. (**XGetWMHints()**, **XSetWMHints()**)
AllocAll	Creates a colormap and allocates all of its entries. Available for the **DirectColor**, **GrayScale**, and **PseudoColor** visual classes only. (**XCreateColormap()**)
AllocNone	Creates a colormap and allocates none of its entries. (**XCreateColormap()**)
AllowExposures	Specifies that exposures are generated when the screen is restored after blanking. (**XGetScreenSaver()**, **XSetScreenSaver()**)
AllTemporary	Specifies that the resources of all clients that have terminated in **RetainTemporary** (see **XSetCloseDownMode()**) should be killed. (**XKillClient()**)
AllValues	Mask used by **XParseGeometry()**; returns those set by user.
AlreadyGrabbed	Specifies that the pointer or keyboard is actively grabbed by another client. (**XGrabKeyboard()**, **XGrabPointer()**)
Always	Advises the server to maintain contents even when the window is unmapped. (**XChangeWindowAttributes()**, **XCreateWindow()**)
AnyButton	Specifies that any button is to be grabbed (**XGrabButton()**) or ungrabbed (**XUngrabButton()**) or that any button will trigger a **ButtonPress** or **ButtonRelease** event.
AnyKey	Specifies that any key is to be grabbed or ungrabbed. (**XGrabKey**, **XUngrabKey()**)
AnyModifier	Specifies a modifier keymask for **XGrabButton()**, **XGrabKey()**, and **XUngrabKey()**, and for the results of **XQueryPointer()**.

AnyPropertyType	Specifies that the property from a specified window should be returned regardless of its type. (`XGetWindowProperty()`)
ArcChord	Value of the `arc_mode` member of the GC: specifies that the area between the arc and a line segment joining the endpoints of the arc is filled. (`XSetArcMode()`)
ArcPieSlice	Value of the `arc_mode` member of the GC: specifies that the area filled is delineated by the arc and two line segments connecting the ends of the arc to the center point of the rectangle defining the arc. (`XSetArcMode()`)
AsyncBoth	Specifies that pointer and keyboard event processing resume normally if both the pointer and the keyboard are frozen by the client when `XAllowEvents()` is called with `AsyncBoth`. (`XAllowEvents()`)
AsyncKeyboard	Specifies that keyboard event processing resumes normally if the keyboard is frozen by the client when `XAllowEvents()` is called with `AsyncPointer`. (`XAllowEvents()`)
AsyncPointer	Specifies that pointer event processing resumes normally if the pointer is frozen by the client when `XAllowEvents()` is called with `AsyncPointer`. (`XAllowEvents()`)
AutoRepeatModeDefault	Value of `auto_repeat_mode`: specifies that the key or keyboard is set to the default setting for the server. (`XChangeKeyboardControl()`, `XGetKeyboardControl()`)
AutoRepeatModeOff	Value of `auto_repeat_mode`: specifies that no keys will repeat. (`XChangeKeyboardControl()`, `XGetKeyboardControl()`)
AutoRepeatModeOn	Value of `auto_repeat_mode`: specifies that keys that are set to `auto_repeat` will do so. (`XChangeKeyboardControl()`, `XGetKeyboardControl()`)

B

BadAccess	Used by non-fatal error handlers only, meaning depends on context.
BadAlloc	Used by non-fatal error handlers only, insufficient resources.
BadAtom	Used by non-fatal error handlers only, parameter not an `Atom`.
BadColor	Used by non-fatal error handlers only, no such colormap.
BadCursor	Used by non-fatal error handlers only, parameter not a `Cursor`.
BadDrawable	Used by non-fatal error handlers only, parameter not a `Pixmap` or `Window`.
BadFont	Used by non-fatal error handlers only, parameter not a `Font`.
BadGC	Used by non-fatal error handlers only, parameter not a `GC`.
BadIDChoice	Used by non-fatal error handlers only, choice not in range or already used.
BadImplementation	Used by non-fatal error handlers only, server is defective.
BadLength	Used by non-fatal error handlers only, request length incorrect.
BadMatch	Used by non-fatal error handlers only, parameter mismatch.

BadName	Used by non-fatal error handlers only, font or color name does not exist.
BadPixmap	Used by non-fatal error handlers only, parameter not a Pixmap.
BadRequest	Used by non-fatal error handlers only, bad request code.
BadValue	Used by non-fatal error handlers only, integer parameter out of range.
BadWindow	Used by non-fatal error handlers only, parameter not a Window.
Below	Specifies that the indicated window is placed below the indicated sibling window. (XConfigureWindow())
BitmapFileInvalid	Specifies that a file does not contain valid bitmap data. (XReadBitmapFile(), XWriteBitmapFile())
BitmapNoMemory	Specifies that insufficient working storage is allocated. (XReadBitmapFile(), XWriteBitmapFile())
BitmapOpenFailed	Specifies that a file cannot be opened. (XReadBitmapFile(), XWriteBitmapFile())
BitmapSuccess	Specifies that a file is readable and valid. (XReadBitmapFile(), XWriteBitmapFile())
BottomIf	Specifies that the indicated window is placed at the bottom of the stack if it is obscured by the indicated sibling window. (XConfigureWindow())
Button1	Specifies that button1 is to be grabbed (XGrabButton()) or ungrabbed (XUngrabButton()).
Button1Mask	Returns the current state of button1. (XQueryPointer())
Button1MotionMask	Specifies that any button1 MotionNotify events are to be selected for this window. A MotionNotify event reports pointer movement. (XSelectInput())
Button2	Specifies that button2 is to be grabbed (XGrabButton()) or ungrabbed (XUngrabButton()).
Button2Mask	Returns the current state of button2. (XQueryPointer())
Button2MotionMask	Specifies that any button2 MotionNotify events are to be selected for this window. A MotionNotify event reports pointer movement. (XSelectInput())
Button3	Specifies that button3 is to be grabbed (XGrabButton()) or ungrabbed (XUngrabButton()).
Button3Mask	Returns the current state of button3. (XQueryPointer())
Button3MotionMask	Specifies that any button3 MotionNotify events are to be selected for this window. A MotionNotify event reports pointer movement. (XSelectInput())
Button4	Specifies that button4 is to be grabbed (XGrabButton()) or ungrabbed (XUngrabButton()).
Button4Mask	Returns the current state of button4. (XQueryPointer())

Button4MotionMask	Specifies that any button4 MotionNotify events are to be selected for this window. A MotionNotify event reports pointer movement. (XSelectInput())
Button5	Specifies that button5 is to be grabbed (XGrabButton()) or ungrabbed (XUngrabButton()).
Button5Mask	Returns the current state of button5. (XQueryPointer())
Button5MotionMask	Specifies that any button5 MotionNotify events are to be selected for this window. A MotionNotify event reports pointer movement. (XSelectInput())
ButtonMotionMask	Specifies that any button MotionNotify events are to be selected for this window. A MotionNotify event reports pointer movement. (XSelectInput())
ButtonPress	Event type.
ButtonPressMask	Specifies that any ButtonPress events are to be selected for this window. A ButtonPress event reports that a pointing device button has been pressed. (XSelectInput())
ButtonRelease	Event type.
ButtonReleaseMask	Specifies that any ButtonRelease events are to be selected for this window. A ButtonRelease event reports that a pointing device button has been released. (XSelectInput())

C

CapButt	Value of the cap_style member of a GC: specifies that lines will be square at the endpoint with no projection beyond. (XSetLineAttributes())
CapNotLast	Value of the cap_style member of a GC: equivalent to CapButt except that, for a line_width of 0 or 1, the final endpoint is not drawn. (XSetLineAttributes())
CapProjecting	Value of the cap_style member of a GC: specifies that lines will be square at the end but with the path continuing beyond the endpoint for a distance equal to half the line_width. (XSetLineAttributes())
CapRound	Value of the cap_style member of a GC: specifies that lines will be terminated by a circular arc. (XSetLineAttributes())
CenterGravity	When a window is resized, specifies the new location of the contents or the children of the window. (XChangeWindowAttributes(), XCreateWindow())
CirculateNotify	Event type.
CirculateRequest	Event type.
ClientIconState	Indicates that the client wants its icon_window to be visible. If an icon_window is not available, it wants its top-level window visible. (Value for initial_state member of XWMHints.)
ClientMessage	Event type.

ClipByChildren	Value of the `subwindow_mode` member of the GC: specifies that graphics requests will not draw through viewable children. (`XSetSubwindowMode()`)
ColormapChangeMask	Specifies that `ColormapNotify` events are to be selected for the window. A `ColormapNotify` event reports colormap changes. (`XSelectInput()`)
ColormapInstalled	In a `ColormapNotify` event, specifies that the colormap is installed.
ColormapNotify	Event type.
ColormapUninstalled	In a `ColormapNotify` event, specifies that the colormap is uninstalled.
Complex	Specifies that paths may self-intersect in polygon shapes. (`XFillPolygon()`)
ConfigureNotify	Event type.
ConfigureRequest	Event type.
ControlMapIndex	Identifies one of eight modifiers to which keycodes can be mapped. (`XDeleteModifiermapEntry()`, `XGetModifierMapping()`, `XInsertModifiermapEntry()`, `XLookupKeysym()`, `XSetModifierMapping()`)
ControlMask	Specifies a modifier keymask for `XGrabButton()`, `XGrabKey()`, `XUngrabButton()`, and `XUngrabKey()`, and for the results of `XQueryPointer()`.
Convex	Specifies that a polygon's path is wholly convex. (`XFillPolygon()`)
CoordModeOrigin	Specifies that all coordinates are relative to the origin of the drawable. (`XDrawLines()`, `XDrawPoints()`, `XFillPolygon()`)
CoordModePrevious	Specifies that all coordinates are relative to the previous point (the first point is relative to the origin). (`XDrawLines()`, `XDrawPoints()`, `XFillPolygon()`)
CopyFromParent	Specifies that a window's border pixmap, visual ID, or class should be copied from the window's parent. (`XChangeWindowAttributes()`, `XCreateWindow()`)
CreateNotify	Event type.
CurrentTime	Specifies time in most time arguments.
CursorShape	Specifies the "best" supported cursor size available on the display hardware. (`XQueryBestSize()`)
CWBackingPixel	Mask to set the `backing_pixel` window attribute. (`XChangeWindowAttributes()`, `XCreateWindow()`)
CWBackingPlanes	Mask to set the `backing_planes` window attribute. (`XChangeWindowAttributes()`, `XCreateWindow()`)
CWBackingStore	Mask to set the `backing_store` window attribute. (`XChangeWindowAttributes()`, `XCreateWindow()`)
CWBackPixel	Mask to set the `background_pixel` window attribute. (`XChangeWindowAttributes()`, `XCreateWindow()`)

Symbol Reference

CWBackPixmap	Mask to set the `background_pixmap` window attribute. (`XChangeWindowAttributes()`, `XCreateWindow()`)
CWBitGravity	Mask to set the `bit_gravity` window attribute.
CWBorderPixel	Mask to set the `border_pixel` window attribute.
CWBorderPixmap	Mask to set the `border_pixmap` window attribute.
CWBorderWidth	Mask to set a new width for the window's border. (`XConfigureWindow()`)
CWColormap	Mask to set the `colormap` window attribute. (`XChangeWindowAttributes()`, `XCreateWindow()`)
CWCursor	Mask to set the `cursor` window attribute. (`XChangeWindowAttributes()`, `XCreateWindow()`)
CWDontPropagate	Mask to set the `do_not_propagate_mask` window attribute. (`XChangeWindowAttributes()`, `XCreateWindow()`)
CWEventMask	Mask to set the `event_mask` window attribute. (`XChangeWindowAttributes()`, `XCreateWindow()`)
CWHeight	Mask to set a new height for the window. (`XConfigureWindow()`)
CWOverrideRedirect	Mask to set the `override_redirect` window attribute. (`XChangeWindowAttributes()`, `XCreateWindow()`)
CWSaveUnder	Mask to set the `save_under` window attribute. (`XChangeWindowAttributes()`, `XCreateWindow()`)
CWSibling	Mask to specify a sibling of the window, used in stacking operations. (`XConfigureWindow()`)
CWStackMode	Mask to set a new stack mode for the window. (`XConfigureWindow()`)
CWWidth	Mask to set a new width for the window. (`XConfigureWindow()`)
CWWinGravity	Mask to set the `win_gravity` window attribute. (`XChangeWindowAttributes()`, `XCreateWindow()`)
CWX	Mask to set a new X value for the window's position. (`XConfigureWindow()`)
CWY	Mask to set a new Y value for the window's position. (`XConfigureWindow()`)

DEF

DefaultBlanking	Specifies default screen saver screen blanking. (`XGetScreenSaver()`, `XSetScreenSaver()`)
DefaultExposures	Specifies that the default will govern whether or not exposures are generated when the screen is restored after blanking. (`XGetScreenSaver()`, `XSetScreenSaver()`)
DestroyAll	Specifies that all resources associated with a client/server connection will be freed when the client process dies. (`XSetCloseDownMode()`)
DestroyNotify	Event type.

DirectColor	Visual class, read/write. (**XGetVisualInfo()**, **XMatch-VisualInfo()**)
DisableAccess	Specifies that clients from any host have access unchallenged (access control is disabled). (**XSetAccessControl()**)
DisableScreenInterval	Internal to Xlib.
DisableScreenSaver	Internal to Xlib.
DoBlue	Sets or changes the read/write colormap cell that corresponds to the specified pixel value to the hardware color that most closely matches the specified blue value. (**XStoreColor, XStoreColors()**, **XStoreNamedColor()**)
DoGreen	Sets or changes the read/write colormap cell that corresponds to the specified pixel value to the hardware color that most closely matches the specified green value. (**XStoreColor, XStoreColors()**, **XStoreNamedColor()**)
DontAllowExposures	Specifies that exposures are not generated when the screen is restored after blanking. (**XGetScreenSaver()**, **XSet-ScreenSaver()**)
DontCareState	Indicates that the client does not know or care what the initial state of the client is when the top-level window is mapped. Obsolete in R4. (Value for **initial_state** member of **XWMHints**.)
DontPreferBlanking	Specifies no screen saver screen blanking. (**XGetScreen-Saver()**, **XSetScreenSaver()**)
DoRed	Sets or changes the read/write colormap cell that corresponds to the specified pixel value to the hardware color that most closely matches the specified red value. (**XStoreColor, XStoreColors()**, **XStoreNamedColor()**)
EastGravity	When a window is resized, specifies the new location of the contents or the children of the window. (**XChangeWindow-Attributes()**, **XCreateWindow()**)
EnableAccess	Specifies that the host access list should be checked before allowing access to clients running on remote hosts (access control is enabled). (**XSetAccessControl()**)
EnterNotify	Event type.
EnterWindowMask	Specifies that any **EnterNotify** events are to be selected for this window. An **EnterNotify** event reports pointer window entry. (**XSelectInput()**)
EvenOddRule	Value of the **fill_rule** member of a GC: specifies that areas overlapping an odd number of times should not be part of the region. (**XPolygonRegion()**, **XSetFillRule()**)
Expose	Event type.
ExposureMask	Specifies that any exposure event except **GraphicsExpose** or **NoExpose** is to be selected for the window. An **Expose** event reports when a window or a previously invisible part of a window becomes visible. (**XSelectInput()**)
FamilyChaos	Specifies an address in the ChaosNet network. (**XAddHost()**)
FamilyDECnet	Specifies an address in the DECnet network. (**XAddHost()**)

Symbol Reference

FamilyInternet	Specifies an address in the Internet network. (XAddHost())
FillOpaqueStippled	Value of the fill_style member of a GC: specifies that graphics should be drawn using stipple, using the foreground pixel value for set bits in stipple and the background pixel value for unset bits in pixel. (XSetFillStyle())
FillSolid	Value of the fill_style member of a GC: specifies that graphics should be drawn using the foreground pixel value. (XSetFillStyle())
FillStippled	Value of the fill_style member of a GC: specifies that graphics should be drawn using the foreground pixel value masked by stipple. (XSetFillStyle())
FillTiled	Value of the fill_style member of a GC: specifies that graphics should be drawn using the tile pixmap. (XSetFillStyle())
FirstExtensionError	Use if writing extension.
FocusChangeMask	Specifies that any FocusIn and FocusOut events are to be selected for this window. FocusIn and FocusOut events report changes in keyboard focus. (XSelectInput())
FocusIn	Event type.
FocusOut	Event type.
FontChange	Internal to Xlib.
FontLeftToRight	Reports that, using the specified font, the string would be drawn left to right. (XQueryFont(), XQueryTextExtents, XQueryTextExtents16(), XTextExtents, XTextExtents16())
FontRightToLeft	Reports that, using the specified font, the string would be drawn right to left. (XQueryFont(), XQueryTextExtents, XQueryTextExtents16(), XTextExtents, XTextExtents16())
ForgetGravity	Specifies that window contents should always be discarded after a size change. (XChangeWindowAttributes(), XCreateWindow())

G

GCArcMode	Mask to set the arc_mode component of a GC. (XChangeGC(), XCopyGC(), XCreateGC())
GCBackground	Mask to set the background component of a GC. (XChangeGC(), XCopyGC(), XCreateGC())
GCCapStyle	Mask to set the cap_style component of a GC. (XChangeGC(), XCopyGC(), XCreateGC())
GCClipMask	Mask to set the clip_mask component of a GC. (XChangeGC(), XCopyGC(), XCreateGC())
GCClipXOrigin	Mask to set the clip_x_origin of the clip_mask. (XChangeGC(), XCopyGC(), XCreateGC())
GCClipYOrigin	Mask to set the clip_y_origin of the clip_mask. (XChangeGC(), XCopyGC(), XCreateGC())

GCDashList	Mask to set the dashes component of a GC. (XChangeGC( ), XCopyGC( ), XCreateGC( ))
GCDashOffset	Mask to set the dash_offset component of a GC. (XChangeGC( ), XCopyGC( ), XCreateGC( ))
GCFillRule	Mask to set the fill_rule component of a GC. (XChangeGC( ), XCopyGC( ), XCreateGC( ))
GCFillStyle	Mask to set the fill_style component of a GC. (XChangeGC( ), XCopyGC( ), XCreateGC( ))
GCFont	Mask to set the font component of a GC. (XChangeGC( ), XCopyGC( ), XCreateGC( ))
GCForeground	Mask to set the foreground component of a GC. (XChangeGC( ), XCopyGC( ), XCreateGC( ))
GCFunction	Mask to set the function component of a GC. (XChangeGC( ), XCopyGC( ), XCreateGC( ))
GCGraphicsExposures	Mask to set the graphics_exposures component of a GC. (XChangeGC( ), XCopyGC( ), XCreateGC( ))
GCJoinStyle	Mask to set the join_style component of a GC. (XChangeGC( ), XCopyGC( ), XCreateGC( ))
GCLastBit	Higher than last GC mask value.
GCLineStyle	Mask to set the line_style component of a GC. (XChangeGC( ), XCopyGC( ), XCreateGC( ))
GCLineWidth	Mask to set the line_width component of a GC. (XChangeGC( ), XCopyGC( ), XCreateGC( ))
GCPlaneMask	Mask to set the plane_mask component of a GC. (XChangeGC( ), XCopyGC( ), XCreateGC( ))
GCStipple	Mask to set the stipple component of a GC. (XChangeGC( ), XCopyGC( ), XCreateGC( ))
GCSubwindowMode	Mask to set the subwindow_mode component of a GC. (XChangeGC( ), XCopyGC( ), XCreateGC( ))
GCTile	Mask to set the tile component of a GC. (XChangeGC( ), XCopyGC( ), XCreateGC( ))
GCTileStipXOrigin	Mask to set the ts_x_origin component of a GC. (XChangeGC( ), XCopyGC( ), XCreateGC( ))
GCTileStipYOrigin	Mask to set the ts_y_origin component of a GC. (XChangeGC( ), XCopyGC( ), XCreateGC( ))
GrabFrozen	Specifies that the pointer is frozen by an active grab of another client. (XGrabKeyboard( ), XGrabPointer( ))
GrabInvalidTime	Specifies that the indicated grab time is involved (earlier than the last keyboard grab time or later than the current server time). (XGrabKeyboard( ), XGrabPointer( ))
GrabModeAsync	Specifies the pointer or keyboard mode. (XGrabButton( ), XGrabKey, XGrabKeyboard( ), XGrabPointer( ))
GrabModeSync	Specifies the pointer or keyboard mode. (XGrabButton( ), XGrabKey, XGrabKeyboard( ), XGrabPointer( ))

GrabNotViewable	Specifies that the grab_window is not viewable. (XGrabKeyboard(), XGrabPointer())
GrabSuccess	Specifies a successful pointer or keyboard grab. (XGrabKeyboard(), XGrabPointer())
GraphicsExpose	Event type.
GravityNotify	Event type.
GrayScale	Visual class, read/write. (XGetVisualInfo(), XMatchVisualInfo())
GXand	Value of the function member of the GC: used with source and destination pixels to generate final destination pixel values: src AND dst. (XChangeGC(), XCreateGC(), XSetFunction())
GXandInverted	(NOT src) AND dst. (XChangeGC(), XCreateGC(), XSetFunction())
GXandReverse	src AND (NOT dst). (XChangeGC(), XCreateGC(), XSetFunction())
GXclear	Set dst to 0. (XChangeGC(), XCreateGC(), XSetFunction())
GXcopy	src. (XChangeGC(), XCreateGC(), XSetFunction())
GXcopyInverted	(NOT src). (XChangeGC(), XCreateGC(), XSetFunction())
GXequiv	(NOT src) XOR dst. (XChangeGC(), XCreateGC(), XSetFunction())
GXinvert	(NOT dst). (XChangeGC(), XCreateGC(), XSetFunction())
GXnand	(NOT src) OR (NOT dst). (XChangeGC(), XCreateGC(), XSetFunction())
GXnoop	dst. (XChangeGC(), XCreateGC(), XSetFunction())
GXnor	(NOT src) AND (NOT dst). (XChangeGC(), XCreateGC(), XSetFunction())
GXor	src OR dst. (XChangeGC(), XCreateGC(), XSetFunction())
GXorInverted	(NOT src) OR dst. (XChangeGC(), XCreateGC(), XSetFunction())
GXorReverse	src OR (NOT dst). (XChangeGC(), XCreateGC(), XSetFunction())
GXset	set pixel. (XChangeGC(), XCreateGC(), XSetFunction())
GXxor	src XOR dst. (XChangeGC(), XCreateGC(), XSetFunction())

HIJ

HeightValue	Represents a user-specified window height in the standard window geometry string. (XParseGeometry())

HostDelete	Used internally to distinguish **XAddHost** and **XRemove-Host( )**.
HostInsert	Used internally to distinguish **XAddHost** and **XRemove-Host( )**.
IconicState	Indicates that the client wants to be iconified when the top-level window is mapped. (Value for **initial_state** member of **XWMHints**.)
IconMaskHint	In the **XA_WM_HINTS** property, the icon pixmap mask mask communicates to the window manager a bitmap that determines which pixels in **icon_pixmap** are drawn on the icon window. (**XGetWMHints( )**, **XSetWMHints( )**)
IconPixmapHint	In the **XA_WM_HINTS** property, the icon pixmap mask communicates to the window manager the pattern used to distinguish this icon from other clients. (**XGetWMHints( )**, **XSetWMHints( )**)
IconPositionHint	In the **XA_WM_HINTS** property, the position mask communicates to the window manager the preferred initial position of the icon. (**XGetWMHints( )**, **XSetWMHints( )**)
IconWindowHint	In the **XA_WM_HINTS** property, the icon window mask communicates to the window manager that **icon_window** contains a window that should be used instead of creating a new one. (**XGetWMHints( )**, **XSetWMHints( )**)
IgnoreState	Indicates that the client wants the window manager to ignore this window. (Value for **initial_state** member of **XWMHints**.)
InactiveState	Indicates that the client wants to be inactive when the top-level window is mapped. Obsolete in R4. (Value for **initial_state** member of **XWMHints**.)
IncludeInferiors	Value of the **subwindow_mode** member of the GC: specifies that graphics requests will draw through viewable children. (**XSetSubwindowMode( )**)
InputFocus	Specifies that the event will be sent to the focus window, regardless of the position of the pointer. (**XSendEvent( )**)
InputHint	In the **XA_WM_HINTS** property, the input member mask communicates to the window manager the keyboard focus model used by the application. (**XGetWMHints( )**, **XSetWMHints( )**)
InputOnly	**InputOnly** is a window class in which windows may receive input but may not be used to display output. (**XCreate-Window( )**)
InputOutput	**InputOutput** is a window class in which windows may receive input and may be used to display output. (**XCreate-Window( )**)
IsCursorKey( )	Keysym class macro.
IsFunctionKey( )	Keysym class macro.
IsKeypadKey( )	Keysym class macro.
IsMiscFunctionKey( )	Keysym class macro.

IsModifierKey()	Keysym class macro.
IsPFKey()	Keysym class macro.
IsUnmapped	Means that the window is unmapped. (XGetWindow-Attributes())
IsUnviewable	Means that the window is mapped but is unviewable because some ancestor is unmapped. (XGetWindowAttributes())
IsViewable	Means that the window is currently viewable. (XGetWindow-Attributes())
JoinBevel	Value of the join_style member of a GC: specifies Cap-Butt endpoint styles, with the triangular notch filled. (XSet-LineAttributes())
JoinMiter	Value of the join_style member of a GC: specifies that the outer edges of the two lines should extend to meet at an angle. (XSetLineAttributes())
JoinRound	Value of the join_style member of a GC: specifies that the lines should be joined by a circular arc with diameter equal to the line_width, centered on the join point. (XSetLine-Attributes())

KL

KBAutoRepeatMode	Mask to specify keyboard auto-repeat preferences. (XChangeKeyboardControl(), XGetKeyboard-Control())
KBBellDuration	Mask to specify keyboard bell-duration preferences. (XChangeKeyboardControl(), XGetKeyboard-Control())
KBBellPercent	Mask to specify keyboard base-volume preferences. (XChangeKeyboardControl(), XGetKeyboard-Control())
KBBellPitch	Mask to specify keyboard bell-pitch preferences. (XChange-KeyboardControl(), XGetKeyboardControl())
KBKey	Mask to specify the keycode of the key whose auto-repeat status will be changed to the setting specified by auto_repeat_mode. (XChangeKeyboardControl(), XGetKeyboardControl())
KBKeyClickPercent	Mask to set keyboard key click-volume preferences. (XChangeKeyboardControl(), XGetKeyboard-Control())
KBLed	Mask to specify keyboard led preferences. (XChange-KeyboardControl(), XGetKeyboardControl())
KBLedMode	Mask to specify keyboard led_mode preferences. (XChange-KeyboardControl(), XGetKeyboardControl())
KeymapNotify	Event type.
KeymapStateMask	Specifies that any KeymapNotify events are to be selected for this window. A KeymapNotify event notifies the client about the state of the keyboard when the pointer or keyboard focus enters a window. (XSelectInput())

KeyPress	Event type.
KeyPressMask	Specifies that any KeyPress events are to be selected for this window. A KeyPress event reports that a keyboard key has been pressed. (XSelectInput())
KeyRelease	Event type.
KeyReleaseMask	Specifies that any KeyRelease events are to be selected for this window. A KeyRelease event reports that a keyboard key has been released. (XSelectInput())
LASTEvent	Bigger than any event type value. For extensions.
LastExtensionError	Use if writing extension.
LeaveNotify	Event type.
LeaveWindowMask	Specifies that any LeaveNotify events are to be selected for this window. A LeaveNotify event reports when the pointer leaves the window. (XSelectInput())
LedModeOff	Value of led_mode: specifies that the states of all the lights are not changed. (XChangeKeyboardControl(), XGet-KeyboardControl())
LedModeOn	Value of led_mode: specifies that the states of all the lights are changed. (XChangeKeyboardControl(), XGet-KeyboardControl())
LineDoubleDash	Value of the line_style member of a GC: specifies that dashes are drawn with the foreground pixel value and gaps with the background pixel value. (XSetLineAttributes())
LineOnOffDash	Value of the line_style member of a GC: specifies that only the dashes are drawn with the foreground pixel value, and cap_style applies to each dash. (XSetLine-Attributes())
LineSolid	Value of the line_style member of a GC: specifies that the full path of the line is drawn using the foreground pixel value. (XSetLineAttributes())
LockMapIndex	Identifies one of eight modifiers to which keycodes can be mapped. (XDeleteModifiermapEntry(), XGet-ModifierMapping(), XInsertModifiermapEntry(), XLookupKeysym(), XSetModifierMapping())
LockMask	Specifies a modifier keymask for XGrabButton(), XGrab-Key(), XUngrabButton(), and XUngrabKey(), and for the results of XQueryPointer().
LowerHighest	Specifies that the stacking order of children should be circulated down. (XCirculateSubwindows())
LSBFirst	In image structure, specifies the byte order used by VAXes. (XCreateImage())

M

MapNotify	Event type.
MappingBusy	Specifies that, in pointer or modifier mapping, no modifiers were changed because new keycodes for a modifier differ from those currently defined and any (current or new) keys for that

	modifier are in a down state. (**XSetModifierMapping()**, **XSetPointerMapping()**)
MappingFailed	Specifies that pointer or modifier mapping failed. (**XSetModifierMapping()**, **XSetPointerMapping()**)
MappingKeyboard	In a **MappingNotify** event, reports that keyboard mapping was changed.
MappingModifier	In a **MappingNotify** event, reports that keycodes were set to be used as modifiers.
MappingNotify	Event type.
MappingPointer	In a **MappingNotify** event, reports that pointer button mapping was set.
MappingSuccess	Specifies that pointer or modifier mapping succeeded. (**XSetModifierMapping()**, **XSetPointerMapping()**)
MapRequest	Event type.
MessageHint	In the **XA_WM_HINTS** property, the message member mask communicates to the window manager the obsolete mask for setting the **XA_WM_HINTS(s+ property** (**XGetWMHints()**, **XSetWMHints()**)
Mod1MapIndex	Identifies one of eight modifiers to which keycodes can be mapped. (**XDeleteModifiermapEntry()**, **XGetModifierMapping()**, **XInsertModifiermapEntry()**, **XLookupKeysym()**, **XSetModifierMapping()**)
Mod1Mask	Specifies a modifier keymask for **XGrabButton()**, **XGrabKey()**, **XUngrabButton()**, and **XUngrabKey()**, and for the results of **XQueryPointer()**.
Mod2MapIndex	Identifies one of eight modifiers to which keycodes can be mapped. (**XDeleteModifiermapEntry()**, **XGetModifierMapping()**, **XInsertModifiermapEntry()**, **XLookupKeysym()**, **XSetModifierMapping()**)
Mod2Mask	Specifies a modifier keymask for **XGrabButton()**, **XGrabKey()**, **XUngrabButton()**, and **XUngrabKey()**, and for the results of **XQueryPointer()**.
Mod3MapIndex	Identifies one of eight modifiers to which keycodes can be mapped. (**XDeleteModifiermapEntry()**, **XGetModifierMapping()**, **XInsertModifiermapEntry()**, **XLookupKeysym()**, **XSetModifierMapping()**)
Mod3Mask	Specifies a modifier keymask for **XGrabButton()**, **XGrabKey()**, **XUngrabButton()**, and **XUngrabKey()**, and for the results of **XQueryPointer()**.
Mod4MapIndex	Identifies one of eight modifiers to which keycodes can be mapped. (**XDeleteModifiermapEntry()**, **XGetModifierMapping()**, **XInsertModifiermapEntry()**, **XLookupKeysym()**, **XSetModifierMapping()**)
Mod4Mask	Specifies a modifier keymask for **XGrabButton()**, **XGrabKey()**, **XUngrabButton()**, and **XUngrabKey()**, and for the results of **XQueryPointer()**.

Mod5MapIndex	Identifies one of eight modifiers to which keycodes can be mapped. (XDeleteModifiermapEntry(), XGet-ModifierMapping(), XInsertModifiermapEntry(), XLookupKeysym(), XSetModifierMapping())
Mod5Mask	Specifies a modifier keymask for XGrabButton(), XGrab-Key(), XUngrabButton(), and XUngrabKey(), and for the results of XQueryPointer().
MotionNotify	Event type.
MSBFirst	In image structure, specifies the byte order used by 68000-family systems. (XCreateImage())

N

NoEventMask	Specifies that no events are to be selected for this window. (XSelectInput())
NoExpose	Event type.
Nonconvex	Specifies that a polygon's path does not self-intersect but that the polygon is not wholly convex. (XFillPolygon())
None	Specifies a universal NULL resource or NULL atom.
NormalState	Indicates that the client wants its top-level window visible. (Value for initial_state member of XWMHints.)
NorthEastGravity	When a window is resized, specifies the new location of the contents or the children of the window. (XChangeWindow-Attributes(), XCreateWindow())
NorthGravity	When a window is resized, specifies the new location of the contents or the children of the window. (XChangeWindow-Attributes(), XCreateWindow())
NorthWestGravity	When a window is resized, specifies the new location of the contents or the children of the window. (XChangeWindow-Attributes(), XCreateWindow())
NoSymbol	Specifies the keysym for no symbol.
NotifyAncestor	In EnterNotify, FocusIn, FocusOut, and LeaveNotify events, specifies the hierarchical relationship of the origin and destination windows.
NotifyDetailNone	In EnterNotify, FocusIn, FocusOut, and LeaveNotify events, specifies the hierarchical relationship of the origin and destination windows.
NotifyGrab	In EnterNotify, FocusIn, FocusOut, and LeaveNotify events, specifies that the keyboard or pointer was grabbed.
NotifyHint	In a MotionNotify event, a hint that specifies that PointerMotionHintMask was selected.
NotifyInferior	In EnterNotify, FocusIn, FocusOut, and LeaveNotify events, specifies the hierarchical relationship of the origin and destination windows.
NotifyNone	In EnterNotify, FocusIn, FocusOut, and LeaveNotify events, specifies the hierarchical relationship of the origin and destination windows.

NotifyNonlinear	In `EnterNotify`, `FocusIn`, `FocusOut`, and `LeaveNotify` events, specifies the hierarchical relationship of the origin and destination windows.
NotifyNonlinear- Virtual	In `EnterNotify`, `FocusIn`, `FocusOut`, and `LeaveNotify` events, specifies the hierarchical relationship of the origin and destination windows.
NotifyNormal	In a `MotionNotify` event, a hint that specifies that the event is real but may not be up to date since there may be many more later motion events on the queue. In `EnterNotify`, `FocusIn`, `FocusOut`, and `LeaveNotify` events, specifies that the keyboard was not grabbed at the time the event was generated.
NotifyPointer	In `FocusIn` and `FocusOut` events, specifies the hierarchical relationship of the origin and destination windows.
NotifyPointerRoot	In `FocusIn` and `FocusOut` events, specifies the hierarchical relationship of the origin and destination windows.
NotifyUngrab	In `EnterNotify`, `FocusIn`, `FocusOut`, and `LeaveNotify` events, specifies that the keyboard or pointer was ungrabbed.
NotifyVirtual	In `EnterNotify`, `FocusIn`, `FocusOut`, and `LeaveNotify` events, specifies the hierarchical relationship of the origin and destination windows.
NotifyWhileGrabbed	`EnterNotify`, `FocusIn`, `FocusOut`, `LeaveNotify` mode.
NotUseful	Specifies that maintaining the contents of an unmapped window is unnecessary. (`XChangeWindowAttributes()`, `XCreateWindow()`)
NoValue	Mask used by `XParseGeometry()`; returns those set by user.

OP

Opposite	Specifies that, if the indicated sibling occludes the indicated window, the window is placed at the top of the stack; if the window occludes the sibling, the window is placed at the bottom of the stack. (`XConfigureWindow()`)
OwnerGrabButtonMask	Controls the distribution of button events to a client between `ButtonPress` and `ButtonRelease` events. (`XSelect-Input()`)
PAllHints	Specifies that the program determined the window hints. (`XGetNormalHints()`, `XSetNormalHints()`)
ParentRelative	Specifies that a window's background will be repainted when it is moved. (`XSetWindowBackgroundPixmap()`)
PAspect	Specifies that the program determined the min and max aspect ratio. (`XGetNormalHints()`, `XSetNormalHints()`)
PBaseSize	Specifies that the program determined the base window size. (`XGetNormalHints()`, `XSetNormalHints()`)
PlaceOnBottom	In a `CirculateNotify` event, specifies that the window will be placed on the bottom of the stack.

PlaceOnTop	In a `CirculateNotify` event, specifies that the window will be placed on the top of the stack.
PMaxSize	Specifies that the program determined the maximum desired window size. (`XGetNormalHints()`, `XSetNormalHints()`)
PMinSize	Specifies that the program determined the minimum desired window size. (`XGetNormalHints()`, `XSetNormalHints()`)
PointerMotionHintMask	Specifies that the server should send only one `MotionNotify` event when the pointer moves. Used in concert with other pointer motion masks to reduce the number of events generated. (`XSelectInput()`)
PointerMotionMask	Specifies that any pointer `MotionNotify` events are to be selected for this window. A `MotionNotify` event reports pointer movement. (`XSelectInput()`)
PointerRoot	Specifies the ID of the window that is the current keyboard focus. (`XGetInputFocus()`, `XSetInputFocus()`)
PointerWindow	Specifies that the event will be sent to the window that the pointer is in. (`XSendEvent()`)
PPosition	Specifies that the program determined the window position. (`XGetNormalHints()`, `XSetNormalHints()`)
PreferBlanking	Specifies screen saver screen blanking. (`XGetScreenSaver()`, `XSetScreenSaver()`)
PResizeInc	Specifies that the program determined the window resize increments. (`XGetNormalHints()`, `XSetNormalHints()`)
PropertyChangeMask	Specifies that any `PropertyNotify` events are to be selected for this window. A `PropertyNotify` event indicates that a property of a certain window was changed or deleted. (`XSelectInput()`)
PropertyDelete	In a `PropertyNotify` event, specifies that a property of a window was deleted.
PropertyNewValue	In a `PropertyNotify` event, specifies that a property of a window was changed.
PropertyNotify	Event type.
PropModeAppend	Appends the data onto the end of the existing data. (`XChangeProperty()`)
PropModePrepend	Inserts the data before the beginning of the existing data. (`XChangeProperty()`)
PropModeReplace	Discards the previous property and stores the new data. (`XChangeProperty()`)
PseudoColor	Visual class, read/write. (`XGetVisualInfo()`, `XMatchVisualInfo()`)
PSize	Specifies that the program determined the window size. (`XGetNormalHints()`, `XSetNormalHints()`)
PWinGravity	Specifies that the program determined the window gravity. (`XGetNormalHints()`, `XSetNormalHints()`)

Symbol Reference

Q

QueuedAlready	Return code for **XEventsQueued()**.
QueuedAfterReading	Return code for **XEventsQueued()**.
QueuedAfterFlush	Return code for **XEventsQueued()**.

R

RaiseLowest — Specifies that the stacking order of children should be circulated up. (**XCirculateSubwindows()**)

RectangleIn — Specifies that the rectangle is inside the region. (**XRectInRegion()**)

RectangleOut — Specifies that the rectangle is completely outside the region. (**XRectInRegion()**)

RectanglePart — Specifies that the rectangle is partly inside the region. (**XRectInRegion()**)

ReleaseByFreeing Colormap — Value for the **killid** field of **XStandardColormap**. (**XSetRGBColormap** and **XGetRGBColormap**)

ReparentNotify — Event type.

ReplayKeyboard — Specifies the conditions under which queued events are released: **ReplayKeyboard** has an effect only if the keyboard is grabbed by the client and thereby frozen as the result of an event. (**XAllowEvents()**)

ReplayPointer — Specifies the conditions under which queued events are released: **ReplayPointer** has an effect only if the pointer is grabbed by the client and thereby frozen as the result of an event. (**XAllowEvents()**)

ResizeRedirectMask — Specifies that any **ResizeRequest** events should be selected for this window when some other client (usually the window manager) attempts to resize the window on which this mask is selected. (**XSelectInput()**)

ResizeRequest — Event type.

RetainPermanent — Specifies that resources associated with a client/server connection live on after the client exits until a call to **XKillClient()**. To destroy these resources, pass a resource ID from the client to **XKillClient()**s+. (**XSetCloseDownMode()**)

RetainTemporary — Specifies that resources associated with a client/server connection live on until a call to **XKillClient()**. If **AllTemporary** is specified in **XKillClient()**, the resources of all clients that have terminated in **RetainTemporary** are destroyed. (**XSetCloseDownMode()**)

RevertToNone — Specifies that there is no backup keyboard focus window. (**XGetInputFocus()**, **XSetInputFocus()**)

RevertToParent	Specifies that the backup keyboard focus window is the parent window. (`XGetInputFocus()`, `XSetInputFocus()`)
RevertToPointerRoot	Specifies that the backup keyboard focus window is the pointer root window. (`XGetInputFocus()`, `XSetInputFocus()`)

S

ScreenSaverActive	Specifies that the screen saver is to be activated. (`XForceScreenSaver()`)
ScreenSaverReset	Specifies that the screen saver is to be turned off. (`XForceScreenSaver()`)
SelectionClear	Event type.
SelectionNotify	Event type.
SelectionRequest	Event type.
SetModeDelete	Specifies that a subwindow is to be deleted from the client's save-set. (`XChangeSaveSet()`)
SetModeInsert	Specifies that a subwindow is to be added to the client's save-set. (`XChangeSaveSet()`)
ShiftMapIndex	Identifies one of eight modifiers to which keycodes can be mapped. (`XDeleteModifiermapEntry()`, `XGetModifierMapping()`, `XInsertModifiermapEntry()`, `XLookupKeysym()`, `XSetModifierMapping()`)
ShiftMask	Specifies a modifier keymask for `XGrabButton()`, `XGrabKey()`, `XUngrabButton()`, and `XUngrabKey()`, and for the results of `XQueryPointer()`.
SouthEastGravity	When a window is resized, specifies the new location of the contents or the children of the window. (`XChangeWindowAttributes()`, `XCreateWindow()`)
SouthGravity	When a window is resized, specifies the new location of the contents or the children of the window. (`XChangeWindowAttributes()`, `XCreateWindow()`)
SouthWestGravity	When a window is resized, specifies the new location of the contents or the children of the window. (`XChangeWindowAttributes()`, `XCreateWindow()`)
StateHint	In the `XA_WM_HINTS` property, the window state mask communicates to the window manager whether the client prefers to be in iconified, zoomed, normal, or inactive state. (`XGetWMHints()`, `XSetWMHints()`)
StaticColor	Visual class, read-only. (`XGetVisualInfo()`, `XMatchVisualInfo()`)
StaticGravity	Specifies that window contents should not move relative to the origin of the root window. (`XChangeWindowAttribute`, `XCreateWindow()`)
StaticGray	Visual class, read-only. (`XGetVisualInfo()`, `XMatchVisualInfo()`)
StippleShape	Specifies the "best" supported stipple size available on the display hardware. (`XQueryBestSize()`)

Symbol Reference

StructureNotifyMask	Selects a group of event types (`CirculateNotify`, `ConfigureNotify`, `DestroyNotify`, `GravityNotify`, `MapNotify`, `ReparentNotify`, `UnmapNotify`) that report when the state of a window has changed. (`XSelectInput()`)
SubstructureNotify- Mask	Selects a group of event types (`CirculateNotify`, `ConfigureNotify`, `DestroyNotify`, `GravityNotify`, `MapNotify`, `ReparentNotify`, `UnmapNotify`) that report when the state of a window has changed, plus an event that indicates that a window has been created. It monitors all the subwindows of the window specified in the `XSelectInput()` call that used this mask.
SubstructureRedirect- Mask	The three event types selected by this mask (`Circulate-Request`, `ConfigureRequest`, and `MapRequest`) can be used by the window manager to intercept and cancel window-configuration-changing requests made by other clients. (`XSelectInput()`)
Success	Indicates that everything is okay.
SyncBoth	Specifies that pointer and keyboard event processing resumes normally, until the next `ButtonPress`, `ButtonRelease`, `KeyPress`, or `KeyRelease` event, if the pointer and the keyboard are both frozen by the client when `XAllowEvents()` is called with `SyncBoth`. (`XAllowEvents()`)
SyncKeyboard	Specifies that key event processing resumes normally, until the next `ButtonPress` or `ButtonRelease` event, if the keyboard is frozen by the client when `XAllowEvents()` is called with `SyncPointer`. (`XAllowEvents()`)
SyncPointer	Specifies that pointer event processing resumes normally, until the next `ButtonPress` or `ButtonRelease` event, if the pointer is frozen by the client when `XAllowEvents()` is called with `SyncPointer`. (`XAllowEvents()`)

TU

TileShape	Specifies the "best" supported tile size available on the display hardware. (`XQueryBestSize()`)
TopIf	Specifies that the indicated window is placed on top of the stack if it is obscured by the indicated sibling window. (`XConfigureWindow()`)
TrueColor	Visual class, read-only. (`XGetVisualInfo()`, `XMatch-VisualInfo()`)
UnmapGravity	Specifies that the child is unmapped when the parent is resized and an `UnmapNotify` event is generated. (`XChangeWindow-Attributes()`, `XCreateWindow()`)
UnmapNotify	Event type.
Unsorted	Specifies that the ordering of rectangles specified for a particular GC is arbitrary. (`XSetClipRectangles()`)
USPosition	Specifies that the user provided a position value for the window. (`XGetNormalHints()`, `XSetNormalHints()`)

USSize	Specifies that the user provided a size value for the window. (XGetNormalHints(), XSetNormalHints())

VW

VisibilityChangeMask	Specifies that any VisibilityNotify events are to be selected for this window, except when the window becomes not viewable. A VisibilityNotify event reports any changes in the window's visibility. (XSelectInput())
VisibilityFully-Obscured	In a VisibilityNotify event, specifies that the window is fully obscured.
VisibilityNotify	Event type.
VisibilityPartially-Obscured	In a VisibilityNotify event, specifies that the window is partially obscured.
VisibilityUnobscured	In a VisibilityNotify event, specifies that the window is unobscured.
VisualAllMask	Determines which elements in a template are to be matched. (XGetVisualInfo(), XMatchVisualInfo())
VisualBitsPerRGBMask	Determines which elements in a template are to be matched. (XGetVisualInfo(), XMatchVisualInfo())
VisualBlueMaskMask	Determines which elements in a template are to be matched. (XGetVisualInfo(), XMatchVisualInfo())
VisualClassMask	Determines which elements in a template are to be matched. (XGetVisualInfo(), XMatchVisualInfo())
VisualColormapSize-Mask	Determines which elements in a template are to be matched. (XGetVisualInfo(), XMatchVisualInfo())
VisualDepthMask	Determines which elements in a template are to be matched. (XGetVisualInfo(), XMatchVisualInfo())
VisualGreenMaskMask	Determines which elements in a template are to be matched. (XGetVisualInfo(), XMatchVisualInfo())
VisualIDMask	Determines which elements in a template are to be matched. (XGetVisualInfo(), XMatchVisualInfo())
VisualNoMask	Determines which elements in a template are to be matched. (XGetVisualInfo(), XMatchVisualInfo())
VisualRedMaskMask	Determines which elements in a template are to be matched. (XGetVisualInfo(), XMatchVisualInfo())
VisualScreenMask	Determines which elements in a template are to be matched. (XGetVisualInfo(), XMatchVisualInfo())
WestGravity	When a window is resized, specifies the new location of the contents or the children of the window. (XChangeWindow-Attributes(), XCreateWindow())
WhenMapped	Advises the server to maintain contents of obscured regions when the window is unmapped. (XChangeWindow-Attributes(), XCreateWindow())

Symbol Reference

WidthValue	Represents a user-specified window width in the standard window geometry string. (`XParseGeometry()`)
WindingRule	Value of the `fill_rule` member of a GC: specifies that areas overlapping an odd number of times should be part of the region. (`XPolygonRegion()`, `XSetFillRule()`)
WindowGroupHint	In the `XA_WM_HINTS` property, the group property mask communicates to the window manager that the client has multiple top-level windows. (`XGetWMHints()`, `XSetWMHints()`)
WithdrawnState	Indicates that the client wants neither its top-level nor its icon visible. (Value for `initial_state` member of `XWMHints`.)

X

XA_ARC	Specifies the atom of the type property that specifies the desired format for the data. (`XConvertSelection()`)
XA_ATOM	Specifies the atom of the type property that specifies the desired format for the data. (`XConvertSelection()`)
XA_BITMAP	Specifies the atom of the type property that specifies the desired format for the data. (`XConvertSelection()`)
XA_CAP_HEIGHT	Predefined type atom.
XA_CARDINAL	Specifies the atom of the type property that specifies the desired format for the data. (`XConvertSelection()`)
XA_COLORMAP	Specifies the atom of the type property that specifies the desired format for the data. (`XConvertSelection()`)
XA_COPYRIGHT	Predefined font atom.
XA_CURSOR	Specifies the atom of the type property that specifies the desired format for the data. (`XConvertSelection()`)
XA_CUT_BUFFER0	Represents a predefined cut buffer atom.
XA_CUT_BUFFER1	Represents a predefined cut buffer atom.
XA_CUT_BUFFER2	Represents a predefined cut buffer atom.
XA_CUT_BUFFER3	Represents a predefined cut buffer atom.
XA_CUT_BUFFER4	Represents a predefined cut buffer atom.
XA_CUT_BUFFER5	Represents a predefined cut buffer atom.
XA_CUT_BUFFER6	Represents a predefined cut buffer atom.
XA_CUT_BUFFER7	Represents a predefined cut buffer atom.
XA_DRAWABLE	Specifies the atom of the type property that specifies the desired format for the data. (`XConvertSelection()`)
XA_END_SPACE	Specifies the additional spacing at the end of sentences.
XA_FAMILY_NAME	Predefined font atom.
XA_FONT	Specifies the atom of the type property that specifies the desired format for the data. (`XConvertSelection()`)
XA_FONT_NAME	Predefined font atom.
XA_FULL_NAME	Predefined font atom.
XA_INTEGER	Specifies the atom of the type property that specifies the desired format for the data. (`XConvertSelection()`)

XA_ITALIC_ANGLE	Specifies the angle of the dominant staffs of characters in the font.
XA_LAST_PREDEFINED	Predefined font atom.
XA_MAX_SPACE	Specifies the maximum interword spacing.
XA_MIN_SPACE	Specifies the minimum interword spacing.
XA_NORM_SPACE	Specifies the normal interword spacing.
XA_NOTICE	Predefined font atom.
XA_PIXMAP	Specifies the atom of the type property that specifies the desired format for the data. (XConvertSelection())
XA_POINT	Specifies the atom of the type property that specifies the desired format for the data. (XConvertSelection())
XA_POINT_SIZE	Specifies the point size of this font at the ideal resolution, expressed in tenths of a point.
XA_PRIMARY	Specifies the primary built-in selection atom used in transferring data between clients.
XA_QUAD_WIDTH	"1 em" as in TeX but expressed in units of pixels. The width of an *m* in the current font and point size.
XA_RECTANGLE	Specifies the atom of the type property that specifies the desired format for the data. (XConvertSelection())
XA_RESOLUTION	Specifies the number of pixels per point at which this font was created.
XA_RESOURCE_MANAGER	Specifies a predefined resource manager property containing default values for user preferences.
XA_RGB_BEST_MAP	Specifies a predefined colormap atom that defines the "best" RGB colormap available on the display.
XA_RGB_BLUE_MAP	Specifies a predefined colormap atom that defines an all-blue colormap.
XA_RGB_COLOR_MAP	Specifies the atom of the type property that specifies the desired format for the data. (XConvertSelection())
XA_RGB_DEFAULT_MAP	Specifies a predefined colormap atom that defines part of the system default colormap.
XA_RGB_GRAY_MAP	Specifies a predefined colormap atom that defines the "best" gray-scale colormap available on the display.
XA_RGB_GREEN_MAP	Specifies a predefined colormap atom that defines an all-green colormap.
XA_RGB_RED_MAP	Specifies a predefined colormap atom that defines an all-red colormap.
XA_SECONDARY	Specifies the secondary built-in selection atom used in transferring data between clients.
XA_STRIKEOUT_ASCENT	Specifies the vertical extents (in pixels) for boxing or voiding characters.
XA_STRIKEOUT_DESCENT	Specifies the vertical extents (in pixels) for boxing or voiding characters.
XA_STRING	Specifies the atom of the type property that specifies the desired format for the data. (XConvertSelection())

Symbol Reference

`XA_SUBSCRIPT_X`	Specifies the X offset (in pixels) from the character origin where subscripts should begin.
`XA_SUBSCRIPT_Y`	Specifies the Y offset (in pixels) from the character origin where subscripts should begin.
`XA_SUPERSCRIPT_X`	Specifies the X offset (in pixels) from the character origin where superscripts should begin.
`XA_SUPERSCRIPT_Y`	Specifies the Y offset (in pixels) from the character origin where superscripts should begin.
`XA_UNDERLINE_POSITION`	Specifies the Y offset (in pixels) from the baseline to the top of the underline.
`XA_UNDERLINE_` `THICKNESS`	Specifies the thickness (in pixels) from the baseline to the top of the underline.
`XA_VISUALID`	Specifies the atom of the type property that specifies the desired format for the data. (`XConvertSelection()`)
`XA_WEIGHT`	Specifies the weight or boldness of the font, expressed as a value between 0 and 1000.
`XA_WINDOW`	Specifies the atom of the type property that specifies the desired format for the data. (`XConvertSelection()`)
`XA_WM_CLASS`	The `XA_WM_CLASS` property is a string containing two **NULL**-separated elements, `res_class` and `res_name`, that are meant to be used by clients both as a means of permanent identification and as the handles by which both the client and the window manager obtain resources related to the window.
`XA_WM_CLIENT_MACHINE`	The `XA_WM_CLIENT_MACHINE` property is a string forming the name of the machine running the client, as seen from the machine running the server.
`XA_WM_COMMAND`	The `XA_WM_COMMAND` property stores the shell command and arguments used to invoke the application.
`XA_WM_HINTS`	The `XA_WM_HINTS` property contains hints stored by the window manager that provide a means of communicating optional information from the client to the window manager.
`XA_WM_ICON_NAME`	The `XA_WM_ICON_NAME` property is an uninterpreted string that the client wishes displayed in association with the window when it is iconified (for example, in an icon label).
`XA_WM_ICON_SIZE`	The window manager may set the `XA_WM_ICON_SIZE` property on the root window to specify the icon sizes it allows.
`XA_WM_NAME`	The `XA_WM_NAME` property is an uninterpreted string that the client wishes displayed in association with the window (for example, a window headline bar).
`XA_WM_NORMAL_HINTS`	The `XA_WM_NORMAL_HINTS` property is an `XSizeHints` structure describing the desired position and range of sizes that are preferable for each top-level window in normal state.
`XA_WM_SIZE_HINTS`	The `XA_WM_SIZE_HINTS` property contains hints stored..
`XA_WM_TRANSIENT_FOR`	The `XA_WM_TRANSIENT_FOR` property is the ID of another top-level window.

XA_WM_ZOOM_HINTS	The **XA_WM_ZOOM_HINTS** property is an **XSizeHints** structure describing the desired position and range of sizes that are preferable for each top-level window in a zoomed state.
XA_X_HEIGHT	"1 ex" as in TeX but expressed in units of pixels, often the height of lower case *x*.
XBufferOverflow	Value for **status_return** argument of **XwcLookup-String()** and **XmbLookupString()**. New in Release 5.
XcmsFailure	Status return for Xcms functions where gamut mapping may occur. New in Release 5.
XcmsCIELabFormat	Status return for **XcmsLookupColor()** indicates format of returned color values. New in Release 5.
XcmsCIELuvFormat	Status return for **XcmsLookupColor()** indicates format of returned color values. New in Release 5.
XcmsCIEuvYFormat	Status return for **XcmsLookupColor()** indicates format of returned color values. New in Release 5.
XcmsCIExyYFormat	Status return for **XcmsLookupColor()** indicates format of returned color values. New in Release 5.
XcmsCIEXYZFormat	Status return for **XcmsLookupColor()** indicates format of returned color values.
XcmsInitNone	Value for member of **XcmsPerScrnInfo** structure, used for initialization of user-defined function set. New in Release 5.
XcmsInitSuccess	Value for member of **XcmsPerScrnInfo** structure, used for initialization of user-defined function set. New in Release 5.
XcmsInitDefault	Value for member of **XcmsPerScrnInfo** structure, used for initialization of user-defined function set. New in Release 5.
XcmsRGBFormat	Status return for **XcmsLookupColor()** indicates format of returned color values. New in Release 5.
XcmsRGBiFormat	Status return for **XcmsLookupColor()** indicates format of returned color values. New in Release 5.
XcmsSuccess	Status return for Xcms functions where gamut mapping may occur. New in Release 5.
XcmsSuccessWith-Compression	Status return for Xcms functions where gamut mapping may occur. New in Release 5.
XcmsTekHVCFormat	Status return for **XcmsLookupColor()** indicates format of returned color values. New in Release 5.
XcmsUndefinedFormat	Status return for **XcmsLookupColor()** indicates format of returned color values. New in Release 5.
XCNOENT	Association table lookup return codes, No entry in table.
XCNOMEM	Association table lookup return codes, Out of memory.
XCSUCCESS	Association table lookup return codes, No error.
XIMHighlight	**XIMFeedback** value used in **XIMText** structure.
XIMPreeditArea	Input method style masks. New in Release 5.
XIMPreeditPosition	Input method style masks. New in Release 5.
XIMPreeditCallbacks	Input method style masks. New in Release 5.

XIMPreeditNothing	Input method style masks. New in Release 5.
XIMPreeditNone	Input method style masks. New in Release 5.
XIMPrimary	**XIMFeedback** value used in **XIMText** structure.
XIMReverse	**XIMFeedback** value used in **XIMText** structure.
XIMSecondary	**XIMFeedback** value used in **XIMText** structure.
XIMStatusArea	Input method style masks. New in Release 5.
XIMStatusCallbacks	Input method style masks. New in Release 5.
XIMStatusNothing	Input method style masks. New in Release 5.
XIMStatusNone	Input method style masks. New in Release 5.
XIMTertiary	**XIMFeedback** value used in **XIMText** structure.
XIMUnderline	**XIMFeedback** value used in **XIMText** structure.
XlibSpecification-Release	Xlib release number: currently 5. New in Release 5.
XLookupNone	Value for **status_return** argument of **XwcLookupString()** and **XmbLookupString()**. New in Release 5.
XLookupChars	Value for **status_return** argument of **XwcLookupString()** and **XmbLookupString()**. New in Release 5.
XLookupKeysym()	Value for **status_return** argument of **XwcLookupString()** and **XmbLookupString()**. New in Release 5.
XLookupBoth	Value for **status_return** argument of **XwcLookupString()** and **XmbLookupString()**. New in Release 5.
XK_*	Keysyms, see Appendix H, *Keysym Reference*.
XNegative	Represents a user-specified negative X offset in the standard window geometry string. (**XParseGeometry()**)
XN*	Input context strings. New in Release 5. The complete list is: **XNVaNestedList, XNQueryInputStyle, XNClientWindow, XNInputStyle, XNFocusWindow, XNResourceName, XNResourceClass, XNGeometryCallback, XNFilterEvents, XNPreeditStartCallback, XNPreeditDoneCallback, XNPreeditDrawCallback, XNPreeditCaretCallback, XNPreeditAttributes, XNStatusStartCallback, XNStatusDoneCallback, XNStatusDrawCallback, XNStatusAttributes, XNArea, XNAreaNeeded, XNSpotLocation, XNColormap, XNStdColormap, XNForeground, XNBackground, XNBackgroundPixmap, XNFontSet, XNLineSpace**, and **XNCursor**.
XValue	Represents a user-specified positive X offset in the standard window geometry string. (**XParseGeometry()**)
XYBitmap	**XYBitmap** specified the format for an image. The data for an image is said to be in **XYBitmap** format if the bitmap is

represented in scan line order, with each scan line made up of multiples of the `bitmap_unit` and padded with meaningless bits. (`XGetImage()`, `XPutImage()`)

XYPixmap	Depth == drawable depth. (`XGetImage()`, `XPutImage()`)
X_PROTOCOL	Current protocol version.
X_PROTOCOL_REVISION	Current minor revision.

YZ

YNegative	Represents a user-specified negative Y offset in the standard window geometry string. (`XParseGeometry()`)
YSorted	Specifies that rectangles specified for a particular GC are non-decreasing in their Y origin. (`XSetClipRectangles()`)
YValue	Represents a user-specified positive Y offset in the standard window geometry string. (`XParseGeometry()`)
YXBanded	Specifies that, in addition to the constraints of `YXSorted`, for every possible horizontal Y scan line, all rectangles that include that scan line have identical Y origins and X extents. (`XSetClipRectangles()`)
YXSorted	Specifies that rectangles specified for a particular GC are non-decreasing in their Y origin and that all rectangles with an equal Y origin are nondecreasing in their X origin. (`XSetClipRectangles()`)
ZoomState	Indicates that the client wants to be in zoomed state when the top-level window is mapped. Obsolete in R4. (Value for `initial_state` member of `XWMHints`.)
ZPixmap	Depth == drawable depth. (`XGetImage()`, `XPutImage()`)

Symbol Reference

This appendix provides a list of keysyms and a brief description of each keysym. Keysyms, as you may remember, are the portable representation of the symbols on the caps of keys.

The normal way to process a keyboard event is to use **XLookupKeysym()** to determine the keysym or, if the application allows remapping of keys to strings, it may use **XLookup-String()** to get the ASCII string mapped to the key or keys pressed. This allows the application to treat keys in a simple and portable manner, and places the responsibility of tailoring the mapping between keys and keysyms on the server vendor.* There are also internationalized versions of **XLookupString()** called **XmbLookupString()** and **XwcLookup-String()**.

Many keysyms do not have obvious counterparts on the keyboard, but may be generated with certain key combinations. You will need a table for each particular model of hardware you intend the program to work on, to tell you what key combination results in each keysym that is not present on the caps of the keyboard. For real portability, you will want to use only the keysyms that are supported on all vendors equipment you intend the program to be displayed on.

The keysyms are defined in two standard include files: *<X11/keysym.h>* and *<X11/keysymdef.h>*. There are several families of keysyms defined in *<X11/keysymdef.h>*; LATIN1, LATIN2, LATIN3, LATIN4, KATAKANA, ARABIC, CYRILLIC, GREEK, TECHNICAL, SPECIAL, PUBLISHING, APL, HEBREW, and MISCELLANY. Preprocessor symbols **XK_** followed by the family name determine which families are enabled. By default, only the LATIN1, LATIN2, LATIN3, LATIN4, GREEK, and MISCELLANY families are enabled in the standard *<X11/keysym.h>* file, probably because some compilers have an upper limit on the number of defined symbols that are allowed.

The X Protocol defines a set of Keysyms called the Keyboard set, which contains miscellaneous common keyboard keys, some not covered in other sets. However, no C symbols for these Keysyms have been defined in Xlib as of Release 5.

The developers of X at MIT say that to the best of their knowledge the Latin, Kana, Arabic, Cyrillic, Greek, Technical, APL, and Hebrew keysym sets are from the appropriate ISO (International Standards Organization) and/or ECMA international standards. There are no

Technical, Special nor Publishing international standards, so these sets are based on Digital Equipment Corporation standards.*

Keysyms are four byte long values. In the standard keysyms, the least significant 8 bits indicate a particular character within a set. and the next 8 bits indicate a particular keysym set. The order of the sets is important since not all the sets are complete. Each character set contains gaps where codes have been removed that were duplicates with codes in previous (that is, with lesser keysym set) character sets.

The 94 and 96 character code sets have been moved to occupy the right-hand quadrant (decimal 129 – 256), so the ASCII subset has a unique encoding across the least significant byte which corresponds to the ASCII character code. However, this cannot be guaranteed in the keysym sets of future releases and does not apply to all of the Keyboard set.

As far as possible, keysym codes are the same as the character code. In the LATIN1 to LATIN4 sets, all duplicate glyphs occupy the same position. However, duplicates between GREEK and TECHNICAL do not occupy the same code position. Thus, applications wishing to use the TECHNICAL character set must transform the keysym using an array.

The MISCELLANY set is a miscellaneous collection of commonly occurring keys on keyboards. Within this set, the keypad symbols are generally duplicates of symbols found on keys on the alphanumeric part of the keyboard but are distinguished here because they often have distinguishable keycodes associated with them.

There is a difference between European and US usage of the names Pilcrow, Paragraph, and Section, as shown in Table H-1.

Table H-1. European vs. US usage of Pilcrow, Paragraph, and Section symbol names

US name	European name	Keysym in LATIN1	Symbol
Section sign	Paragraph sign	XK_section	§
Paragraph sign	Pilcrow sign	XK_paragraph	¶

X has adopted the names used by both the ISO and ECMA standards. Thus, **XK_paragraph** is what Europeans call the pilcrow sign, and **XK_section** is what they would call the paragraph sign. This favors the US usage.

---

* While keycode information is not necessary for normal application programming, it may be necessary for writing certain programs that change the keycode to keysym mapping. If you are writing such an application, you will need to obtain a list of keycodes and their normal mappings from the server manufacturer. Any program that uses this mapping is not fully portable.

H.1 Keysyms and Description

Tables H-2 through H-7 list the six commonly available sets of keysyms (MISCELLANY, LATIN1 through LATIN4, and GREEK) and describe each keysym briefly. When necessary and possible, these tables show a representative character or characters that might appear on the cap of the key or on the screen when the key or keys corresponding to the keysym were typed.

Table H-2. MISCELLANY

Keysym	Description
XK_BackSpace	Backspace, Back Space, Back Char
XK_Tab	Tab
XK_Linefeed	Linefeed, LF
XK_Clear	Clear
XK_Return	Return, Enter
XK_Pause	Pause, Hold, Scroll Lock
XK_Escape	Escape
XK_Delete	Delete, Rubout
XK_Multi_key	Multi-key character preface
XK_Kanji	Kanji, Kanji convert
XK_Home	Home
XK_Left	Left, move left, left arrow
XK_Up	Up, move up, up arrow
XK_Right	Right, move right, right arrow
XK_Down	Down, move down, down arrow
XK_Prior	Prior, previous
XK_Next	Next
XK_End	End, EOL
XK_Begin	Begin, BOL
XK_Select	Select, mark
XK_Print	Print
XK_Execute	Execute, run, do
XK_Insert	Insert, insert here
XK_Undo	Undo, oops
XK_Redo	Redo, again
XK_Menu	Menu
XK_Find	Find, search
XK_Cancel	Cancel, stop, abort, exit
XK_Help	Help, question mark
XK_Break	Break
XK_Mode_switch	Mode switch, script switch, character set switch
XK_script_switch	Alias for mode switch, script switch, character set switch
XK_Num_Lock	Num Lock
XK_KP_Space	Keypad Space

Keysym	Description
XK_KP_Tab	Keypad Tab
XK_KP_Enter	Keypad Enter
XK_KP_F1	Keypad F1, PF1, a
XK_KP_F2	Keypad F2, PF2, b
XK_KP_F3	Keypad F3, PF3, c
XK_KP_F4	Keypad F4, PF4, d
XK_KP_Equal	Keypad equals sign
XK_KP_Multiply	Keypad multiplication sign, asterisk
XK_KP_Add	Keypad plus sign
XK_KP_Separator	Keypad separator, comma
XK_KP_Subtract	Keypad minus sign, hyphen
XK_KP_Decimal	Keypad decimal point, full stop
XK_KP_Divide	Keypad division sign, solidus
XK_KP_0	Keypad digit zero
XK_KP_1	Keypad digit one
XK_KP_2	Keypad digit two
XK_KP_3	Keypad digit three
XK_KP_4	Keypad digit four
XK_KP_5	Keypad digit five
XK_KP_6	Keypad digit six
XK_KP_7	Keypad digit seven
XK_KP_8	Keypad digit eight
XK_KP_9	Keypad digit nine
XK_F1	F1 function key
XK_F2	F2 function key
XK_F3	F3 function key
XK_F4	F4 function key
XK_F5	F5 function key
XK_F6	F6 function key
XK_F7	F7 function key
XK_F8	F8 function key
XK_F9	F9 function key
XK_F10	F10 function key
XK_F11	F11 function key
XK_L1	L1 function key
XK_F12	F12 function key
XK_L2	L2 function key
XK_F13	F13 function key
XK_L3	L3 function key
XK_F14	F14 function key
XK_L4	L4 function key
XK_F15	F15 function key
XK_L5	L5 function key
XK_F16	F16 function key
XK_L6	L6 function key

Keysym	Description
XK_F17	F17 function key
XK_L7	L7 function key
XK_F18	F18 function key
XK_L8	L8 function key
XK_F19	F19 function key
XK_L9	L9 function key
XK_F20	F20 function key
XK_L10	L10 function key
XK_F21	F21 function key
XK_R1	R1 function key
XK_F22	F22 function key
XK_R2	R2 function key
XK_F23	F23 function key
XK_R3	R3 function key
XK_F24	F24 function key
XK_R4	R4 function key
XK_F25	F25 function key
XK_R5	R5 function key
XK_F26	F26 function key
XK_R6	R6 function key
XK_F27	F27 function key
XK_R7	R7 function key
XK_F28	F28 function key
XK_R8	R8 function key
XK_F29	F29 function key
XK_R9	R9 function key
XK_F30	F30 function key
XK_R10	R10 function key
XK_F31	F31 function key
XK_R11	R11 function key
XK_F32	F32 function key
XK_R12	R12 function key
XK_R13	F33 function key
XK_F33	R13 function key
XK_F34	F34 function key
XK_R14	R14 function key
XK_F35	F35 function key
XK_R15	R15 function key
XK_Shift_L	Left Shift
XK_Shift_R	Right Shift
XK_Control_L	Left Control
XK_Control_R	Right Control
XK_Caps_Lock	Caps Lock
XK_Shift_Lock	Shift Lock
XK_Meta_L	Left Meta

Keysym	Description
XK_Meta_R	Right Meta
XK_Alt_L	Left Alt
XK_Alt_R	Right Alt
XK_Super_L	Left Super
XK_Super_R	Right Super
XK_Hyper_L	Left Hyper
XK_Hyper_R	Right Hyper

Table H-3. LATIN1

Keysym	Description	Character
XK_space	Space	
XK_exclam	Exclamation point	!
XK_quotedbl	Quotation mark	"
XK_numbersign	Number sign	#
XK_dollar	Dollar sign	$
XK_percent	Percent sign	%
XK_ampersand	Ampersand	&
XK_quoteright	Apostrophe	'
XK_parenleft	Left parenthesis	(
XK_parenright	Right parenthesis	)
XK_asterisk	Asterisk	*
XK_plus	Plus sign	+
XK_comma	Comma	,
XK_minus	Hyphen, minus sign	−
XK_period	Full stop	.
XK_slash	Solidus	/
XK_0	Digit zero	0
XK_1	Digit one	1
XK_2	Digit two	2
XK_3	Digit three	3
XK_4	Digit four	4
XK_5	Digit five	5
XK_6	Digit six	6
XK_7	Digit seven	7
XK_8	Digit eight	8
XK_9	Digit nine	9

Keysym	Description	Character
XK_colon	Colon	:
XK_semicolon	Semicolon	;
XK_less	Less than sign	<
XK_equal	Equals sign	=
XK_greater	Greater than sign	>
XK_question	Question mark	?
XK_at	Commercial at	@
XK_A	Latin capital A	A
XK_B	Latin capital B	B
XK_C	Latin capital C	C
XK_D	Latin capital D	D
XK_E	Latin capital E	E
XK_F	Latin capital F	F
XK_G	Latin capital G	G
XK_H	Latin capital H	H
XK_I	Latin capital I	I
XK_J	Latin capital J	J
XK_K	Latin capital K	K
XK_L	Latin capital L	L
XK_M	Latin capital M	M
XK_N	Latin capital N	N
XK_O	Latin capital O	O
XK_P	Latin capital P	P
XK_Q	Latin capital Q	Q
XK_R	Latin capital R	R
XK_S	Latin capital S	S
XK_T	Latin capital T	T
XK_U	Latin capital U	U
XK_V	Latin capital V	V
XK_W	Latin capital W	W
XK_X	Latin capital X	X
XK_Y	Latin capital Y	Y
XK_Z	Latin capital Z	Z
XK_bracketleft	Left square bracket	[
XK_backslash	Reverse solidus	\
XK_bracketright	Right square bracket	]
XK_asciicircum	Circumflex accent	^

Keysym Reference

Keysym	Description	Character
XK_underscore	Low line	_
XK_quoteleft	Grave accent	`
XK_a	Latin small a	a
XK_b	Latin small b	b
XK_c	Latin small c	c
XK_d	Latin small d	d
XK_e	Latin small e	e
XK_f	Latin small f	f
XK_g	Latin small g	g
XK_h	Latin small h	h
XK_i	Latin small i	i
XK_j	Latin small j	j
XK_k	Latin small k	k
XK_l	Latin small l	l
XK_m	Latin small m	m
XK_n	Latin small n	n
XK_o	Latin small o	o
XK_p	Latin small p	p
XK_q	Latin small q	q
XK_r	Latin small r	r
XK_s	Latin small s	s
XK_t	Latin small t	t
XK_u	Latin small u	u
XK_v	Latin small v	v
XK_w	Latin small w	w
XK_x	Latin small x	x
XK_y	Latin small y	y
XK_z	Latin small z	z
XK_braceleft	Left brace	{
XK_bar	Vertical line	|
XK_braceright	Right brace	}
XK_asciitilde	Tilde	~
XK_nobreakspace	No-break space	
XK_exclamdown	Inverted exclamation mark	¡
XK_cent	Cent sign	¢
XK_sterling	Pound sign	£
XK_currency	Currency sign	

Keysym	Description	Character
XK_yen	Yen sign	¥
XK_brokenbar	Broken vertical bar	¦
XK_section	Paragraph sign, section sign	§
XK_diaeresis	Diaeresis	¨
XK_copyright	Copyright sign	©
XK_ordfeminine	Feminine ordinal indicator	ª
XK_guillemotleft	Left angle quotation mark	«
XK_notsign	Not sign	¬
XK_hyphen	Short horizontal hyphen	-
XK_registered	Registered trade mark sign	®
XK_macron	Macron	¯
XK_degree	Degree sign, ring above	°
XK_plusminus	Plus-minus sign	±
XK_twosuperior	Superscript two	²
XK_threesuperior	Superscript three	³
XK_acute	Acute accent	´
XK_mu	Micro sign	µ
XK_paragraph	Pilcrow sign	¶
XK_periodcentered	Middle dot	·
XK_cedilla	Cedilla	¸
XK_onesuperior	Superscript one	¹
XK_masculine	Masculine ordinal indicator	º
XK_guillemotright	Right angle quotation mark	»
XK_onequarter	Vulgar fraction one quarter	¼
XK_onehalf	Vulgar fraction one half	½
XK_threequarters	Vulgar fraction three quarters	¾
XK_questiondown	Inverted question mark	¿
XK_Agrave	Latin capital A with grave accent	À
XK_Aacute	Latin capital A with acute accent	Á
XK_Acircumflex	Latin capital A with circumflex accent	Â
XK_Atilde	Latin capital A with tilde	Ã
XK_Adiaeresis	Latin capital A with diaeresis	Ä
XK_Aring	Latin capital A with ring above	Å
XK_AE	Latin capital diphthong AE	Æ
XK_Ccedilla	Latin capital C with cedilla	Ç
XK_Egrave	Latin capital E with grave accent	È
XK_Eacute	Latin capital E with acute accent	É

Keysym	Description	Character
XK_Ecircumflex	Latin capital E with circumflex accent	Ê
XK_Ediaeresis	Latin capital E with diaeresis	Ë
XK_Igrave	Latin capital I with grave accent	Ì
XK_Iacute	Latin capital I with acute accent	Í
XK_Icircumflex	Latin capital I with circumflex accent	Î
XK_Idiaeresis	Latin capital I with diaeresis	Ï
XK_Eth	Icelandic capital ETH	
XK_Ntilde	Latin capital N with tilde	Ñ
XK_Ograve	Latin capital O with grave accent	Ò
XK_Oacute	Latin capital O with acute accent	Ó
XK_Ocircumflex	Latin capital O with circumflex accent	Ô
XK_Otilde	Latin capital O with tilde	Õ
XK_Odiaeresis	Latin capital O with diaeresis	Ö
XK_multiply	Multiplication sign	×
XK_Ooblique	Latin capital O with oblique stroke	Ø
XK_Ugrave	Latin capital U with grave accent	Ù
XK_Uacute	Latin capital U with acute accent	Ú
XK_Ucircumflex	Latin capital U with circumflex accent	Û
XK_Udiaeresis	Latin capital U with diaeresis	Ü
XK_Yacute	Latin capital Y with acute accent	Ý
XK_Thorn	Icelandic capital THORN	
XK_ssharp	German small sharp s	
XK_agrave	Latin small a with grave accent	à
XK_aacute	Latin small a with acute accent	á
XK_acircumflex	Latin small a with circumflex accent	â
XK_atilde	Latin small a with tilde	ã
XK_adiaeresis	Latin small a with diaeresis	ä
XK_aring	Latin small a with ring above	å
XK_ae	Latin small diphthong ae	æ
XK_ccedilla	Latin small c with cedilla	ç
XK_egrave	Latin small e with grave accent	è
XK_eacute	Latin small e with acute accent	é
XK_ecircumflex	Latin small e with circumflex accent	ê
XK_ediaeresis	Latin small e with diaeresis	ë
XK_igrave	Latin small i with grave accent	ì
XK_iacute	Latin small i with acute accent	í
XK_icircumflex	Latin small i with circumflex accent	î

Keysym	Description	Character
XK_idiaeresis	Latin small i with diaeresis	ï
XK_eth	Icelandic small eth	
XK_ntilde	Latin small n with tilde	ñ
XK_ograve	Latin small o with grave accent	ò
XK_oacute	Latin small o with acute accent	ó
XK_ocircumflex	Latin small o with circumflex accent	ô
XK_otilde	Latin small o with tilde	õ
XK_odiaeresis	Latin small o with diaeresis	ö
XK_division	Division sign	÷
XK_oslash	Latin small o with oblique stroke	ø
XK_ugrave	Latin small u with grave accent	ù
XK_uacute	Latin small u with acute accent	ú
XK_ucircumflex	Latin small u with circumflex accent	û
XK_udiaeresis	Latin small u with diaeresis	ü
XK_yacute	Latin small y with acute accent	ý
XK_thorn	Icelandic small thorn	
XK_ydiaeresis	Latin small y with diaeresis	ÿ

Keysym	Description	Character
XK_Aogonek	Latin capital A with ogonek	A
XK_breve	Breve	˘
XK_Lstroke	Latin capital L with stroke	Ł
XK_Lcaron	Latin capital L with caron	Ľ
XK_Sacute	Latin capital S with acute accent	Ś
XK_Scaron	Latin capital S with caron	Š
XK_Scedilla	Latin capital S with cedilla	Ş
XK_Tcaron	Latin capital T with caron	Ť
XK_Zacute	Latin capital Z with acute accent	Ź
XK_Zcaron	Latin capital Z with caron	Ž
XK_Zabovedot	Latin capital Z with dot above	Ż
XK_aogonek	Latin small a with ogonek	a
XK_ogonek	Ogonek	˛
XK_lstroke	Latin small l with stroke	ł
XK_lcaron	Latin small l with caron	ľ
XK_sacute	Latin small s with acute accent	ś
XK_caron	Caron	˘
XK_scaron	Latin small s with caron	š
XK_scedilla	Latin small s with cedilla	ş
XK_tcaron	Latin small t with caron	ť
XK_zacute	Latin small z with acute accent	ź
XK_doubleacute	Double acute accent	˝
XK_zcaron	Latin small z with caron	ž
XK_zabovedot	Latin small z with dot above	ż
XK_Racute	Latin capital R with acute accent	Ŕ
XK_Abreve	Latin capital A with breve	Ă
XK_Cacute	Latin capital C with acute accent	Ć
XK_Ccaron	Latin capital C with caron	Č
XK_Eogonek	Latin capital E with ogonek	E
XK_Ecaron	Latin capital E with caron	Ě
XK_Dcaron	Latin capital D with caron	Ď
XK_Nacute	Latin capital N with acute accent	Ń
XK_Ncaron	Latin capital N with caron	Ň
XK_Odoubleacute	Latin capital O with double acute accent	Ő
XK_Rcaron	Latin capital R with caron	Ř
XK_Uring	Latin capital U with ring above	Ů
XK_Udoubleacute	Latin capital U with double acute accent	Ű

Keysym	Description	Character
XK_Tcedilla	Latin capital T with cedilla	Ţ
XK_racute	Latin small r with acute accent	ŕ
XK_abreve	Latin small a with breve	ă
XK_cacute	Latin small c with acute accent	ć
XK_ccaron	Latin small c with caron	č
XK_eogonek	Latin small e with ogonek	ę
XK_ecaron	Latin small e with caron	ě
XK_dcaron	Latin small d with caron	ď
XK_nacute	Latin small n with acute accent	ń
XK_ncaron	Latin small n with caron	ň
XK_odoubleacute	Latin small o with double acute accent	ő
XK_rcaron	Latin small r with caron	ř
XK_uring	Latin small u with ring above	ů
XK_udoubleacute	Latin small u with double acute accent	ű
XK_tcedilla	Latin small t with cedilla	ţ
XK_abovedot	Dot above	·

Keysym	Description	Character
XK_Hstroke	Latin capital H with stroke	
XK_Hcircumflex	Latin capital H with circumflex accent	Ĥ
XK_Iabovedot	Latin capital I with dot above	İ
XK_Gbreve	Latin capital G with breve	Ğ
XK_Jcircumflex	Latin capital J with circumflex accent	Ĵ
XK_hstroke	Latin small h with stroke	
XK_hcircumflex	Latin small h with circumflex accent	ĥ
XK_idotless	Small dotless i	ı
XK_gbreve	Latin small g with breve	ğ
XK_jcircumflex	Latin small j with circumflex accent	ĵ
XK_Cabovedot	Latin capital C with dot above	Ċ
XK_Ccircumflex	Latin capital C with circumflex accent	Ĉ
XK_Gabovedot	Latin capital G with dot above	Ġ
XK_Gcircumflex	Latin capital G with circumflex accent	Ĝ
XK_Ubreve	Latin capital U with breve	Ŭ
XK_Scircumflex	Latin capital S with circumflex accent	Ŝ
XK_cabovedot	Latin small c with dot above	ċ
XK_ccircumflex	Latin small c with circumflex accent	ĉ
XK_gabovedot	Latin small g with dot above	ġ
XK_gcircumflex	Latin small g with circumflex accent	ĝ
XK_ubreve	Latin small u with breve	ŭ
XK_scircumflex	Latin small s with circumflex accent	ŝ

Keysym	Description	Character
XK_kappa	Latin small kappa	
XK_Rcedilla	Latin capital R with cedilla	Ŗ
XK_Itilde	Latin capital I with tilde	Ĩ
XK_Lcedilla	Latin capital L with cedilla	Ļ
XK_Emacron	Latin capital E with macron	Ē
XK_Gcedilla	Latin capital G with cedilla	Ģ
XK_Tslash	Latin capital T with oblique stroke	
XK_rcedilla	Latin small r with cedilla	ŗ
XK_itilde	Latin small i with tilde	ĩ
XK_lcedilla	Latin small l with cedilla	ļ
XK_emacron	Latin small e with macron	ē
XK_gacute	Latin small g with acute accent	ǵ
XK_tslash	Latin small t with oblique stroke	
XK_ENG	Lappish capital ENG	
XK_eng	Lappish small eng	
XK_Amacron	Latin capital A with macron	Ā
XK_Iogonek	Latin capital I with ogonek	I
XK_Eabovedot	Latin capital E with dot above	Ė
XK_Imacron	Latin capital I with macron	Ī
XK_Ncedilla	Latin capital N with cedilla	ŋ
XK_Omacron	Latin capital O with macron	Ō
XK_Kcedilla	Latin capital K with cedilla	Ķ
XK_Uogonek	Latin capital U with ogonek	U
XK_Utilde	Latin capital U with tilde	Ũ
XK_Umacron	Latin capital U with macron	Ū
XK_amacron	Latin small a with macron	ā
XK_iogonek	Latin small i with ogonek	i
XK_eabovedot	Latin small e with dot above	ė
XK_imacron	Latin small i with macron	ī
XK_ncedilla	Latin small n with cedilla	ŋ
XK_omacron	Latin small o with macron	ō
XK_kcedilla	Latin small k with cedilla	ķ
XK_uogonek	Latin small u with ogonek	u
XK_utilde	Latin small u with tilde	ũ
XK_umacron	Latin small u with macron	ū

Table H-7. GREEK

Keysym	Description	Character
XK_Greek_ALPHAaccent	Greek capital alpha with accent	Ά
XK_Greek_EPSILONaccent	Greek capital epsilon with accent	Έ
XK_Greek_ETAaccent	Greek capital eta with accent	Ή
XK_Greek_IOTAaccent	Greek capital iota with accent	Ί
XK_Greek_IOTAdiaeresis	Greek capital iota with diaeresis	Ϊ
XK_Greek_IOTAaccentdiaeresis	Greek capital iota with accent+dieresis	Ϊ́
XK_Greek_OMICRONaccent	Greek capital omicron with accent	Ό
XK_Greek_UPSILONaccent	Greek capital upsilon with accent	Ύ
XK_Greek_UPSILONdieresis	Greek capital upsilon with dieresis	Ϋ
XK_Greek_UPSILONaccentdieresis	Greek capital upsilon with accent+dieresis	Ϋ́
XK_Greek_OMEGAaccent	Greek capital omega with accent	Ώ
XK_Greek_alphaaccent	Greek small alpha with accent	ά
XK_Greek_epsilonaccent	Greek small epsilon with accent	έ
XK_Greek_etaaccent	Greek small eta with accent	ή
XK_Greek_iotaaccent	Greek small iota with accent	ί
XK_Greek_iotadieresis	Greek small iota with dieresis	ϊ
XK_Greek_iotaaccentdieresis	Greek small iota with accent+dieresis	ΐ
XK_Greek_omicronaccent	Greek small omicron with accent	ό
XK_Greek_upsilonaccent	Greek small upsilon with accent	ύ
XK_Greek_upsilondieresis	Greek small upsilon with dieresis	ϋ
XK_Greek_upsilonaccentdieresis	Greek small upsilon with accent+dieresis	ΰ
XK_Greek_omegaaccent	Greek small omega with accent	ώ
XK_Greek_ALPHA	Greek capital alpha	A
XK_Greek_BETA	Greek capital beta	B
XK_Greek_GAMMA	Greek capital gamma	Γ
XK_Greek_DELTA	Greek capital delta	Δ
XK_Greek_EPSILON	Greek capital epsilon	E
XK_Greek_ZETA	Greek capital zeta	Z
XK_Greek_ETA	Greek capital eta	H
XK_Greek_THETA	Greek capital theta	Θ
XK_Greek_IOTA	Greek capital iota	I
XK_Greek_KAPPA	Greek capital kappa	K
XK_Greek_LAMBDA	Greek capital lambda	Λ
XK_Greek_MU	Greek capital mu	M
XK_Greek_NU	Greek capital nu	N
XK_Greek_XI	Greek capital xi	Ξ
XK_Greek_OMICRON	Greek capital omicron	O

Keysym	Description	Character
XK_Greek_PI	Greek capital pi	Π
XK_Greek_RHO	Greek capital rho	P
XK_Greek_SIGMA	Greek capital sigma	Σ
XK_Greek_TAU	Greek capital tau	T
XK_Greek_UPSILON	Greek capital upsilon	Y
XK_Greek_PHI	Greek capital phi	Φ
XK_Greek_CHI	Greek capital chi	X
XK_Greek_PSI	Greek capital psi	Ψ
XK_Greek_OMEGA	Greek capital omega	Ω
XK_Greek_alpha	Greek small alpha	α
XK_Greek_beta	Greek small beta	β
XK_Greek_gamma	Greek small gamma	γ
XK_Greek_delta	Greek small delta	δ
XK_Greek_epsilon	Greek small epsilon	ε
XK_Greek_zeta	Greek small zeta	ζ
XK_Greek_eta	Greek small eta	η
XK_Greek_theta	Greek small theta	θ
XK_Greek_iota	Greek small iota	ι
XK_Greek_kappa	Greek small kappa	κ
XK_Greek_lambda	Greek small lambda	λ
XK_Greek_mu	Greek small mu	μ
XK_Greek_nu	Greek small nu	ν
XK_Greek_xi	Greek small xi	ξ
XK_Greek_omicron	Greek small omicron	o
XK_Greek_pi	Greek small pi	π
XK_Greek_rho	Greek small rho	ϱ
XK_Greek_sigma	Greek small sigma	σ
XK_Greek_finalsmallsigma	Greek small final small sigma	ς
XK_Greek_tau	Greek small tau	τ
XK_Greek_upsilon	Greek small upsilon	υ
XK_Greek_phi	Greek small phi	φ
XK_Greek_chi	Greek small chi	χ
XK_Greek_psi	Greek small psi	ψ
XK_Greek_omega	Greek small omega	ω
XK_Greek_switch	Switch to Greek set	

The Cursor Font

A standard font consisting of a number of cursor shapes is available. This font is loaded automatically when **XCreateFontCursor()**, the routine used to create a standard cursor, is called. To specify a cursor shape from the standard font, use one of the symbols defined in the file *<X11/cursorfont.h>*, by including it in your source code. The symbols for the available cursors and an illustration of their shapes is provided here. The technique used for creating a cursor is described in Volume One, Section 6.6.

The standard cursor shapes, along with the corresponding symbol definitions from *<X11/cursorfont.h>* are shown in Figure I-1.

✖	XC_X_cursor	◯	XC_circle	▨	XC_draped_box
➚	XC_arrow	⊞	XC_clock	⇆	XC_exchange
⊤	XC_based_arrow_down	⊟	XC_coffee_mug	✛	XC_fleur
⊥	XC_based_arrow_up	✚	XC_cross		XC_gobbler
⇨	XC_boat	✳	XC_cross_reverse		XC_gumby
⊞	XC_bogosity	✛	XC_crosshair		XC_hand1
⌎	XC_bottom_left_corner	⊕	XC_diamond_cross		XC_hand2
⌐	XC_bottom_right_corner	●	XC_dot	♡	XC_heart
↓	XC_bottom_side	⊡	XC_dotbox	▢	XC_icon
⊥	XC_bottom_tee	↕	XC_double_arrow	✖	XC_iron_cross
▣	XC_box_spiral	➚	XC_draft_large	➤	XC_left_ptr
↟	XC_center_ptr	➚	XC_draft_small	⊩	XC_left_side

Figure I-1. The Standard Cursors ☞

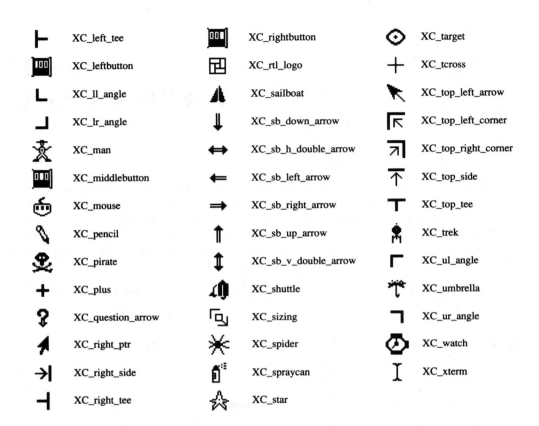

⊢	XC_left_tee	▥	XC_rightbutton	⊙	XC_target
▦	XC_leftbutton	⊞	XC_rtl_logo	+	XC_tcross
L	XC_ll_angle	▲	XC_sailboat	↖	XC_top_left_arrow
⅃	XC_lr_angle	⇓	XC_sb_down_arrow	⌜	XC_top_left_corner
⚐	XC_man	⬌	XC_sb_h_double_arrow	⬈	XC_top_right_corner
▥	XC_middlebutton	⬅	XC_sb_left_arrow	⬆	XC_top_side
⚏	XC_mouse	⇒	XC_sb_right_arrow	⊤	XC_top_tee
✎	XC_pencil	⇑	XC_sb_up_arrow	⚑	XC_trek
☠	XC_pirate	⇕	XC_sb_v_double_arrow	⌐	XC_ul_angle
+	XC_plus	⛴	XC_shuttle	☂	XC_umbrella
⸮	XC_question_arrow	⌐	XC_sizing	⌐	XC_ur_angle
◀	XC_right_ptr	✳	XC_spider	⊘	XC_watch
→‖	XC_right_side	⬗	XC_spraycan	I	XC_xterm
⊣	XC_right_tee	☆	XC_star		

Figure I-1. The Standard Cursors (continued)

The Xmu Library is a collection of miscellaneous utility functions that have been useful in building various applications and Xt toolkit widgets. Though not defined by any X consortium standard, this library is written and supported by MIT in the core distribution, and therefore should be available on most machines.

This appendix presents reference pages for each Xmu function available in Release 4 and Release 5. For a summary of the contents of Xmu, see Volume One, Appendix F, *The Xmu Library*. At each release the number and variety of functions in this library has increased dramatically. In Release 5, the new Xlib-related functions are `XmuDistinguishable-Colors()`, `XmuDistinguishablePixels()`, and `XmuLocatePixmapFile()`. (The Xt-related Xmu functions are documented in Volume Five, *X Toolkit Intrinsics Reference Manual*.)

Each group of Xmu functions designed around a particular task has its own header file, listed in the Synopsis section of each reference page. Note that the location of the header files of Xmu has changed in R4. In R3 and earlier, the header files for all X libraries were stored in */usr/include/X11*. In R4, the header files for Xmu and Xaw are located in subdirectories of this directory, named after each library. In other words, the Xmu header files are now located (by default, on UNIX-based systems) in */usr/include/X11/Xmu*.

XmuAddCloseDisplayHook

Name

XmuAddCloseDisplayHook – add callback function to be called when display connection is
closed.

Synopsis

```
#include <X11/Xmu/CloseHook.h>
CloseHook XmuAddCloseDisplayHook(display, func, arg)
    Display *display;
    int(*func)();
    caddr_t arg;
```

Arguments

display   Specifies a connection to an X server; returned from XOpenDisplay().

func   Specifies the function to call at display close.

arg   Specifies arbitrary data to pass to func.

Description

XmuAddCloseDisplayHook registers a callback for the given display. When the display
is closed, the given function will be called with the given display and argument as:

    (*func)(display, arg)

The function is declared to return int even though the value is ignored, because some compilers have problems with functions returning void.

This routine returns NULL if it was unable to add the callback, otherwise it returns an opaque
handle that can be used to remove or lookup the callback.

See Also

XmuAddCloseDisplayHook, *XmuLookupCloseDisplayHook*, *XmuRemoveCloseDisplayHook*.

XmuAllStandardColormaps

Name

XmuAllStandardColormaps – create all supported standard colormaps and set standard color-map properties.

Synopsis

```
#include <X11/Xmu/StdCmap.h>
Status XmuAllStandardColormaps(display)
   Display *display;
```

Arguments

display   Specifies a connection to an X server; returned from XOpenDisplay().

Description

XmuAllStandardColormaps creates all of the appropriate standard colormaps for every visual of every screen on a given display.

XmuAllStandardColormaps defines and retains as permanent resources all these standard colormaps. It returns zero on failure, non-zero on success. If the property of any standard colormap is already defined, this function will redefine it.

This function is intended to be used by window managers or a special client at the start of a session.

The standard colormaps of a screen are defined by properties associated with the screen's root window. The property names of standard colormaps are predefined, and each property name except RGB_DEFAULT_MAP may describe at most one colormap.

The standard colormaps are: RGB_BEST_MAP, RGB_RED_MAP, RGB_GREEN_MAP, RGB_BLUE_MAP, RGB_DEFAULT_MAP, and RGB_GRAY_MAP. Therefore a screen may have at most 6 standard colormap properties defined.

A standard colormap is associated with a particular visual of the screen. A screen may have multiple visuals defined, including visuals of the same class at different depths. Note that a visual ID might be repeated for more than one depth, so the visual ID and the depth of a visual identify the visual. The characteristics of the visual will determine which standard colormaps are meaningful under that visual, and will determine how the standard colormap is defined. Because a standard colormap is associated with a specific visual, there must be a method of determining which visuals take precedence in defining standard colormaps.

The method used here is: for the visual of greatest depth, define all standard colormaps meaningful to that visual class, according to this order of (descending) precedence: Direct-Color; PseudoColor; TrueColor; and GrayScale; and finally StaticColor and StaticGray.

Xmu Library

This function allows success on a per screen basis. For example, if a map on screen 1 fails, the maps on screen 0, created earlier, will remain. However, none on screen 1 will remain. If a map on screen 0 fails, none will remain.

See Also

XmuCreateColormap, XmuDeleteStandardColormap, XmuGetColormapAllocation, XmuLookupStd-Cmp, XmuStandardColormap, XmuVisualStandardColormaps.

XmuClientWindow

Name

XmuClientWindow – find a window which has a WM_STATE property.

Synopsis

```
#include <X11/Xmu/WinUtil.h>
Window XmuClientWindow(display, win)
   Display *display;
   Window win;
```

Arguments

display   Specifies a connection to an X server; returned from XOpenDisplay().

win   Specifies the window.

Description

XmuClientWindow finds a window, at or below the specified window, which has a WM_STATE property. If such a window is found, it is returned, otherwise the argument window is returned.

See Also

XmuScreenOfWindow, XmuUpdateMapHints.

XmuCompareISOLatin1

Name

XmuCompareISOLatin1 – compare and determine order of two strings, ignoring case.

Synopsis

```
#include <X11/Xmu/CharSet.h>
int XmuCompareISOLatin1(first, second)
   char *first, *second;
```

Arguments

first   Specifies a string to compare.

second   Specifies a string to compare.

Description

XmuCompareISOLatin1 compares two NULL terminated Latin-1 strings, ignoring case differences, and returns an integer greater than, equal to, or less than zero, according to whether first is lexicographically greater than, equal to, or less than second. The two strings are assumed to be encoded using ISO 8859-1 (Latin-1).

See Also

XmuCopyISOLatin1Lowered, *XmuCopyISOLatin1Uppered*, *XmuLookup*.

XmuCopyISOLatin1Lowered

Name

XmuCopyISOLatin1Lowered – copy string, changing uppercase to lowercase.

Synopsis

```
#include <X11/Xmu/CharSet.h>
void XmuCopyISOLatin1Lowered(dst, src)
    char *dst, *src;
```

Arguments

dst   Returns the string copy.

src   Specifies the string to copy.

Description

XmuCopyISOLatin1Lowered copies a NULL-terminated string from *src* to *dst* (including the NULL), changing all Latin-1 uppercase letters to lowercase. The string is assumed to be encoded using ISO 8859-1 (Latin-1).

See Also

XmuCompareISOLatin1, *XmuCopyISOLatin1Uppered*, *XmuLookup*.

XmuCopyISOLatin1Uppered

Name

XmuCopyISOLatin1Uppered – copy string, changing lowercase to uppercase.

Synopsis

```
#include <X11/Xmu/CharSet.h>
void XmuCopyISOLatin1Uppered(dst, src)
    char *dst, *src;
```

Arguments

dst   Returns the string copy.

src   Specifies the string to copy.

Description

XmuCopyISOLatin1Uppered copies a NULL-terminated string from *src* to *dst* (including the NULL), changing all Latin-1 lowercase letters to uppercase. The string is assumed to be encoded using ISO 8859-1 (Latin-1).

See Also

XmuCompareISOLatin1, *XmuCopyISOLatin1Lowered*, *XmuLookup*.

XmuCreateColormap

Name

XmuCreateColormap – create a standard colormap from information in an XStandard-Colormap structure.

Synopsis

```
#include <X11/Xmu/StdCmap.h>
Status XmuCreateColormap(display, colormap)
  Display *display;
  XStandardColormap *colormap;
```

Arguments

display   Specifies the connection under which the map is created.

colormap   Specifies the map to be created.

Description

XmuCreateColormap creates any one colormap which is described by an XStandard-Colormap structure.

XmuCreateColormap returns zero on failure, and non-zero on success. The base_pixel field of the XStandardColormap structure is set on success. Resources created by this function are not made permanent. No argument error checking is provided; use at your own risk.

All colormaps are created with read-only allocations, with the exception of read-only allocations of colors which fail to return the expected pixel value, and these are individually defined as read/write allocations. This is done so that all the cells defined in the colormap are contiguous, for use in image processing. This typically happens with White and Black in the default map.

Colormaps of static visuals are considered to be successfully created if the map of the static visual matches the definition given in the standard colormap structure.

See Also

XmuAllStandardColormaps, XmuDeleteStandardColormap, XmuGetColormapAllocation, XmuLookup-StdCmp, XmuStandardColormap, XmuVisualStandardColormaps.

XmuCreatePixmapFromBitmap

Name

XmuCreatePixmapFromBitmap – create multi-plane pixmap and copy data from one-plane pixmap.

Synopsis

```
#include <X11/Xmu/Drawing.h>
Pixmap XmuCreatePixmapFromBitmap(display, d, bitmap, width, height,
       depth, fore, back)
 Display *display;
 Drawable d;
 Pixmap bitmap;
 unsigned int width, height;
 unsigned int depth;
 unsigned long fore, back;
```

Arguments

display   Specifies a connection to an X server; returned from XOpenDisplay().

d   Specifies the screen the pixmap is created on.

bitmap   Specifies the bitmap source.

width   Specifies the width of the pixmap.

height   Specifies the height of the pixmap.

depth   Specifies the depth of the pixmap.

fore   Specifies the foreground pixel value.

back   Specifies the background pixel value.

Description

XmuCreatePixmapFromBitmap creates a pixmap of the specified width, height, and depth, on the same screen as the specified drawable, and then performs an XCopyPlane() from the specified bitmap to the pixmap, using the specified foreground and background pixel values. The created pixmap is returned. The original bitmap is not destroyed.

See Also

XmuCreateStippledPixmap, XmuDrawLogo, XmuDrawRoundedRectangle, XmuFillRoundedRectangle, XmuLocateBitmapFile, XmuReadBitmapData, XmuReadBitmapDataFromFile, XmuReleaseStippled-Pixmap.

XmuCreateStippledPixmap

Name

XmuCreateStippledPixmap – create two pixel by two pixel gray pixmap.

Synopsis

```
#include <X11/Xmu/Drawing.h>
Pixmap XmuCreateStippledPixmap(screen, fore, back, depth)
    Screen *screen;
    Pixel fore, back;
    unsigned int depth;
```

Arguments

screen   Specifies the screen the pixmap is created on.

fore   Specifies the foreground pixel value.

back   Specifies the background pixel value.

depth   Specifies the depth of the pixmap.

Description

XmuCreateStippledPixmap creates a two pixel by two pixel stippled pixmap of specified depth on the specified screen. The pixmap is cached so that multiple requests share the
same pixmap. The pixmap should be freed with XmuReleaseStippledPixmap to maintain correct reference counts.

See Also

*XmuCreatePixmapFromBitmap, XmuDrawLogo, XmuDrawRoundedRectangle, XmuFillRounded-
Rectangle, XmuLocateBitmapFile, XmuReadBitmapData, XmuReadBitmapDataFromFile, XmuRelease-
StippledPixmap.*

XctCreate

Name

XctCreate – create a XctData structure for parsing a Compound Text string.

Synopsis

```
#include <X11/Xmu/Xct.h>
XctData XctCreate(string, length, flags)
   XctString string;
   int length;
   XctFlags flags;
```

Arguments

string   Specifies the Compound Text string.

length   Specifies the number of bytes in string.

flags   Specifies parsing control flags.

Description

XctCreate creates an XctData structure for parsing a Compound Text string. The string need not be NULL-terminated. The following flags are defined to control parsing of the string:

XctSingleSetSegments

This means that returned segments should contain characters from only one set (C0, C1, GL, GR). When this is requested, XctSegment is never returned by XctNextItem, instead XctC0Segment, XctC1Segment, XctGlSegment, and XctGRSegment are returned. C0 and C1 segments are always returned as singleton characters.

XctProvideExtensions

This means that if the Compound Text string is from a higher version than this code is implemented to, then syntactically correct but unknown control sequences should be returned as XctExtension items by XctNextItem. If this flag is not set, and the Compound Text string version indicates that extensions cannot be ignored, then each unknown control sequence will be reported as an XctError.

XctAcceptC0Extensions

This means that if the Compound Text string is from a higher version than this code is implemented to, then unknown C0 characters should be treated as if they were legal, and returned as C0 characters (regardless of how XctProvideExtensions is set) by XctNextItem. If this flag is not set, then all unknown C0 characters are treated according to XctProvideExtensions.

XctAcceptC1Extensions

This means that if the Compound Text string is from a higher version than this code is implemented to, then unknown C1 characters should be treated as if they were legal, and returned as C1 characters (regardless of how XctProvideExtensions is set) by

XctNextItem. If this flag is not set, then all unknown C1 characters are treated according to XctProvideExtensions.

XctHideDirection

This means that horizontal direction changes should be reported as XctHorizontal items by XctNextItem. If this flag is not set, then direction changes are not returned as items, but the current direction is still maintained and reported for other items. The current direction is given as an enumeration, with the values XctUnspecified, XctLeftToRight, and XctRightToLeft.

XctFreeString

This means that XctFree should free the Compound Text string that is passed to XctCreate. If this flag is not set, the string is not freed.

XctShiftMultiGRToGL

This means that XctNextItem should translate GR segments on-the-fly into GL segments for the GR sets: GB2312.1980-1, JISX0208.1983-1, and KSC5601.1987-1.

See Also

XctFree, XctNextItem, XctReset.

XctFree

Name

XctFree – free an `XctData` structure.

Synopsis

```
#include <X11/Xmu/Xct.h>
void XctFree(data )
   XctData data;
```

Arguments

data   Specifies the Compound Text structure.

Description

`XctFree` frees all data associated with the `XctData` structure.

See Also

XctNextItem, *XctReset*.

XctNextItem

Name

XctNextItem – parse the next item in a Compound Text string.

Synopsis

```
#include <X11/Xmu/Xct.h>
XctResult XctNextItem(data)
    XctData data;
```

Arguments

data   Specifies the Compound Text structure.

Description

XctNextItem parses the next item in the Compound Text string. The return value indicates what kind of item is returned. The item itself, it's length, and the current contextual state, are reported as components of the XctData structure. XctResult is an enumeration, with the following values:

XctSegment
> The item contains some mixture of C0, GL, GR, and C1 characters.

XctC0Segment
> The item contains only C0 characters.

XctGLSegment
> The item contains only GL characters.

XctC1Segment
> the item contains only C1 characters.

XctGRSegment
> the item contains only GR characters.

XctExtendedSegment
> The item contains an extended segment.

XctExtension
> The item is an unknown extension control sequence.

XctHorizontal
> The item indicates a change in horizontal direction or depth. The new direction and depth are recorded in the XctData structure.

XctEndOfText
> The end of the Compound Text string has been reached.

XctError
> The string contains a syntactic or semantic error; no further parsing should be performed.

Structures

```
typedef struct {
    XctString item;                /* the action item */
    int item_length;               /* the length of item in bytes */
    int char_size;                 /* the number of bytes per character in
                                    * item, with zero meaning variable */
    char *encoding;                /* the XLFD encoding name for item */
    XctHDirection horizontal;      /* the direction of item */
    int horz_depth;                /* the current direction nesting depth */
    char *GL;                      /* the "{I} F" string for the current GL */
    char *GL_encoding;             /* the XLFD encoding name for the current GL */
    int GL_set_size;               /* 94 or 96 */
    int GL_char_size;              /* the number of bytes per GL character */
    char *GR;                      /* the "{I} F" string for the current GR */
    char *GR_encoding;             /* the XLFD encoding name the for current GR */
    int GR_set_size;               /* 94 or 96 */
    int GR_char_size;              /* the number of bytes per GR character */
    char *GLGR_encoding;           /* the XLFD encoding name for the current
                                    * GL+GR, if known */
        .
        .
        .
} XctData;
```

See Also

XctCreate, XctFree, XctReset.

XctReset

Name

XctReset – reset an XctData structure for reparsing a Compound Text string.

Synopsis

```
#include <X11/Xmu/Xct.h>
void XctReset(data)
    XctData data;
```

Arguments

data   Specifies the Compound Text structure.

Description

XctReset resets the XctData structure to reparse the Compound Text string from the beginning.

See Also

XctCreate, XctFree, XctNextItem.

XmuCursorNameToIndex

Name

XmuCursorNameToIndex – return index in cursor font given string name.

Synopsis

```
#include <X11/Xmu/CurUtil.h>
int XmuCursorNameToIndex(name)
   char *name;
```

Arguments

name   Specifies the name of the cursor.

Description

XmuCursorNameToIndex takes the name of a standard cursor and returns its index in the standard cursor font. The cursor names are formed by removing the XC_ prefix from the cursor defines listed in Appendix I, *The Cursor Font*.

XmuDeleteStandardColormap

Name

XmuDeleteStandardColormap – remove any standard colormap property.

Synopsis

```
void XmuDeleteStandardColormap(display, screen, property)
    Display *display;
    int screen;
    Atom property;
```

Arguments

display   Specifies a connection to an X server; returned from XOpenDisplay().

screen   Specifies the screen of the display.

property Specifies the standard colormap property.

Description

XmuDeleteStandardColormap will remove the specified property from the specified screen, releasing any resources used by the colormap(s) of the property, if possible.

See Also

XmuAllStandardColormaps, XmuCreateColormap, XmuGetColormapAllocation, XmuLookupStdCmp, XmuStandardColormap, XmuVisualStandardColormaps.

XmuDistinguishableColors

Name

XmuDistinguishableColors – determine if colors are visibly different.

Synopsis

```
Bool XmuDistinguishableColors(colors, count)
    XColor *colors;
    int count;
```

Arguments

colors   An array of XColor structures to be tested for distinguishability.

count   The number of elements in the colors array.

Availability

Release 5 and later.

Description

This function returns True if and only if all the colors in the passed array are "distinguishable" from one another. There is no formal definition for "distinguishable," and this function does not make use of device independent color, so the algorithm used is somewhat arbitrary. Note that there is no Xmu header file that declares this function, so the declaration should be done explictly.

See Also

XmuDistinguishablePixels.

XmuDistinguishablePixels

Name

XmuDistinguishablePixels – determine if colormap cells contain visibly different colors.

Synopsis

```
Bool XmuDistinguishablePixels(dpy, cmap, pixels, count)
    Display *dpy;
    Colormap cmap;
    unsigned long *pixels;
    int count;
```

Arguments

dpy	Specifies the display.
cmap	Specifies the colormap.
pixels	An array of colormap cells to be tested for distinguishablity.
count	The number of cells in the pixels array.

Availability

Release 5 and later.

Description

This function returns True if and only if the colors in the colormap cells specified by the pixels array are "distinguishable" from one another. There is no formal definition for "distinguishable," and this function does not make use of device independent color, so the algorithm used is somewhat arbitrary. Note that there is no Xmu header file that declares this function, so the declaration should be done explictly.

See Also

XmuDistinguishableColors.

XmuDQAddDisplay

Name

XmuDQAddDisplay – add a display connection to a display queue.

Synopsis

```
#include <X11/Xmu/DisplayQue.h>
XmuDisplayQueueEntry *XmuDQAddDisplay(q, display, data)
   XmuDisplayQueue *q;
   Display *display;
   caddr_t data;
```

Arguments

q   Specifies the queue.

display   Specifies the display connection to add.

data   Specifies private data for the free callback function.

Description

XmuDQAddDisplay adds the specified display to the queue. If successful, the queue entry is returned, otherwise NULL is returned. The data value is simply stored in the queue entry for use by the queue's free callback. This function does not attempt to prevent duplicate entries in the queue; the caller should use XmuDQLookupDisplay to determine if a display has already been added to a queue.

See Also

XmuDQCreate, XmuDQDestroy, XmuDQLookupDisplay, XmuDQNDisplays, XmuDQRemoveDisplay.

XmuDQCreate

Name

XmuDQCreate – creates an empty display queue.

Synopsis

```
#include <X11/Xmu/DisplayQue.h>
XmuDisplayQueue *XmuDQCreate(closefunc, freefunc, data)
    int(*closefunc)();
    int(*freefunc)();
    caddr_t data;
```

Arguments

closefunc   Specifies the close function.

freefunc   Specifies the free function.

data   Specifies private data for the functions.

Description

XmuDQCreate creates and returns an empty XmuDisplayQueue (which is really just a set of displays, but is called a queue for historical reasons). The queue is initially empty, but displays can be added using XmuAddDisplay. The data value is simply stored in the queue for use by the display close and free callbacks. Whenever a display in the queue is closed using XCloseDisplay(), the display close callback (if non-NULL) is called with the queue and the display's XmuDisplayQueueEntry as follows:

```
(*closefunc)(queue, entry)
```

The free callback (if non-NULL) is called whenever the last display in the queue is closed, as follows:

```
(*freefunc)(queue)
```

The application is responsible for actually freeing the queue, by calling XmuDQDestroy.

See Also

XmuDQAddDisplay, XmuDQDestroy, XmuDQLookupDisplay, XmuDQNDisplays, XmuDQRemoveDisplay.

XmuDQDestroy

Name

XmuDQDestroy – destroy a display queue, and optionally call callbacks.

Synopsis

```
#include <X11/Xmu/DisplayQue.h>
Bool XmuDQDestroy(q, docallbacks)
  XmuDisplayQueue *q;
  Bool docallbacks;
```

Arguments

q   Specifies the queue to destroy.

docallbacks Specifies whether the close callback functions should be called.

Description

XmuDQDestroy releases all memory associated with the specified queue. If *docallbacks* is True, then the queue's close callback (if non-NULL) is first called for each display in the queue, even though XCloseDisplay() is not called on the display.

See Also

XmuDQAddDisplay, *XmuDQCreate*, *XmuDQLookupDisplay*, *XmuDQNDisplays*, *XmuDQRemoveDisplay*.

XmuDQLookupDisplay

Name

XmuDQLookupDisplay – determine display queue entry for specified display connection.

Synopsis

```
#include <X11/Xmu/DisplayQue.h>
XmuDisplayQueueEntry *XmuDQLookupDisplay(q, display)
    XmuDisplayQueue *q;
    Display *display;
```

Arguments

q   Specifies the queue.

display   Specifies the display to lookup.

Description

XmuDQLookupDisplay returns the queue entry for the specified display, or NULL if the display is not in the queue.

See Also

XmuDQAddDisplay, *XmuDQCreate*, *XmuDQDestroy*, *XmuDQNDisplays*, *XmuDQRemoveDisplay*.

XmuDQNDisplays

Name

XmuDQNDisplays – return the number of display connections in a display queue.

Synopsis

```
#include <X11/Xmu/DisplayQue.h>
XmuDQNDisplays(q)
```

Description

XmuDQNDisplays returns the number of displays in the specified queue.

See Also

XmuDQAddDisplay, XmuDQCreate, XmuDQDestroy, XmuDQLookupDisplay, XmuDQRemoveDisplay.

XmuDQRemoveDisplay

Name

XmuDQRemoveDisplay – remove a display connection from a display queue.

Synopsis

```
#include <X11/Xmu/DisplayQue.h>
Bool XmuDQRemoveDisplay(q, display)
  XmuDisplayQueue *q;
  Display *display;
```

Arguments

q   Specifies the queue.

display   Specifies the display to remove.

Description

XmuDQNDisplays removes the specified display connection from the specified queue. No callbacks are performed. If the display is not found in the queue, False is returned, otherwise True is returned.

See Also

XmuDQAddDisplay, XmuDQCreate, XmuDQDestroy, XmuDQLookupDisplay, XmuDQNDisplays.

Xmu Library

XmuDrawLogo

Xmu – Graphics Functions

Name

XmuDrawLogo – draws the standard X logo.

Synopsis

```
#include <X11/Xmu/Drawing.h>
XmuDrawLogo(display, drawable, gcFore, gcBack, x, y, width, height)
    Display *display;
    Drawable drawable;
    GC gcFore, gcBack;
    int x, y;
    unsigned int width, height;
```

Arguments

display	Specifies a connection to an X server; returned from `XOpenDisplay()`.
drawable	Specifies the drawable.
gcFore	Specifies the foreground GC.
gcBack	Specifies the background GC.
x	Specifies the upper-left x coordinate.
y	Specifies the upper-left y coordinate.
width	Specifies the logo width.
height	Specifies the logo height.

Description

XmuDrawLogo draws the "official" X Window System logo. The bounding box of the logo in the drawable is given by *x*, *y*, *width*, and *height* . The logo itself is filled using *gcFore*, and the rest of the rectangle is filled using *gcBack*.

See Also

XmuCreatePixmapFromBitmap, *XmuCreateStippledPixmap*, *XmuDrawRoundedRectangle*, *XmuFillRoundedRectangle*, *XmuLocateBitmapFile*, *XmuReadBitmapData*, *XmuReadBitmapDataFromFile*, *XmuReleaseStippledPixmap*.

1058   *Xlib Reference Manual*

Name

XmuDrawRoundedRectangle – draws a rectangle with rounded corners.

Synopsis

```
#include <X11/Xmu/Drawing.h>
void XmuDrawRoundedRectangle(display, draw, gc, x, y, w, h, ew, eh)
   Display *display;
   Drawable draw;
   GC gc;
   int x, y, w, h, ew, eh;
```

Arguments

display	Specifies a connection to an X server; returned from `XOpenDisplay()`.
draw	Specifies the drawable.
gc	Specifies the GC.
x	Specifies the upper-left x coordinate.
y	Specifies the upper-left y coordinate.
w	Specifies the rectangle width.
h	Specifies the rectangle height.
ew	Specifies the corner width.
eh	Specifies the corner height.

Description

XmuDrawRoundedRectangle draws a rounded rectangle, where *x*, *y*, *w*, *h* are the dimensions of the overall rectangle, and *ew* and *eh* are the sizes of a bounding box that the corners are drawn inside of; *ew* should be no more than half of *w*, and *eh* should be no more than half of *h*. The current GC line attributes control all attributes of the line.

See Also

XmuCreatePixmapFromBitmap, *XmuCreateStippledPixmap*, *XmuDrawLogo*, *XmuFillRounded-Rectangle*, *XmuLocateBitmapFile*, *XmuReadBitmapData*, *XmuReadBitmapDataFromFile*, *XmuRelease-StippledPixmap*.

XmuFillRoundedRectangle

Name

XmuFillRoundedRectangle – fill a rectangle with rounded corners.

Synopsis

```
#include <X11/Xmu/Drawing.h>
void XmuFillRoundedRectangle(display, draw, gc, x, y, w, h, ew, eh)
    Display *display;
    Drawable draw;
    GC gc;
    int x, y, w, h, ew, eh;
```

Arguments

display	Specifies a connection to an X server; returned from `XOpenDisplay()`.
draw	Specifies the drawable.
gc	Specifies the GC.
x	Specifies the upper-left x coordinate.
y	Specifies the upper-left y coordinate.
w	Specifies the rectangle width.
h	Specifies the rectangle height.
ew	Specifies the corner width.
eh	Specifies the corner height.

Description

`XmuFillRoundedRectangle` draws a filled rounded rectangle, where *x*, *y*, *w*, *h* are the dimensions of the overall rectangle, and *ew* and *eh* are the sizes of a bounding box that the corners are drawn inside of; *ew* should be no more than half of *w*, and *eh* should be no more than half of *h*. The current GC fill settings control all attributes of the fill contents.

See Also

XmuCreatePixmapFromBitmap, XmuCreateStippledPixmap, XmuDrawLogo, XmuDrawRounded-Rectangle, XmuLocateBitmapFile, XmuReadBitmapData, XmuReadBitmapDataFromFile, XmuRelease-StippledPixmap.

XmuGetAtomName

Name

XmuGetAtomName – returns the property name string corresponding to the specified atom.

Synopsis

```
#include <X11/Xmu/Atoms.h>
char *XmuGetAtomName(d, atom)
    Display *d;
    Atom atom;
```

Arguments

d
: Specifies a connection to an X server; returned from XOpenDisplay().

atom
: Specifies the atom whose name is desired.

Description

XmuGetAtomName returns the property name string corresponding to the specified atom. The result is cached, such that subsequent requests do not cause another round-trip to the server. If the atom is zero, XmuGetAtomName returns "(BadAtom)".

See Also

XmuInternAtom, XmuInternStrings, XmuMakeAtom, XmuNameofAtom.

Xmu Library

XmuGetColormapAllocation

Name

XmuGetColormapAllocation – determine best allocation of reds, greens, and blues in a standard colormap.

Synopsis

```
#include <X11/Xmu/StdCmap.h>
Status XmuGetColormapAllocation(vinfo, property, red_max, green_max,
        blue_max)
    XVisualInfo *vinfo;
    Atom property;
    unsigned long *red_max, *green_max, *blue_max;
```

Arguments

vinfo	Specifies visual information for a chosen visual.
property	Specifies one of the standard colormap property names.
red_max	Returns maximum red value.
green_max	Returns maximum green value.
blue_max	Returns maximum blue value.

Description

`XmuGetColormapAllocation` determines the best allocation of reds, greens, and blues in a standard colormap.

`XmuGetColormapAllocation` returns zero on failure, non-zero on success. It is assumed that the visual is appropriate for the colormap property.

See Also

XmuAllStandardColormaps, XmuCreateColormap, XmuDeleteStandardColormap, XmuLookupStdCmp, XmuStandardColormap, XmuVisualStandardColormaps.

XmuGetHostname

Name

XmuGetHostname – operating system independent routine to get machine name.

Synopsis

```
#include <X11/Xmu/SysUtil.h>
int XmuGetHostname(buf, maxlen)
   char *buf;
   int maxlen;
```

Arguments

buf   Returns the host name.

maxlen   Specifies the length of buf.

Description

XmuGetHostname stores the NULL-terminated name of the local host in buf, and returns the length of the name. This function hides operating system differences, such as whether to call gethostname or uname.

Xmu Library

XmuInternAtom

Name

XmuInternAtom – get an atom from the server and load it into an `AtomPtr`.

Synopsis

```
Atom XmuInternAtom(d, atom_ptr)
    Display *d;
    AtomPtr atom_ptr;
```

Arguments

d   Specifies a connection to an X server; returned from `XOpenDisplay()`.

atom_ptr   Specifies the `AtomPtr`.

Description

`XmuInternAtom` gets an atom from the server (for the string stored in `AtomPtr`) and stores the atom in the specified `AtomPtr`. The atom is cached such that subsequent requests do not cause another round-trip to the server.

See Also

XmuGetAtomName, XmuInternStrings, XmuMakeAtom, XmuNameofAtom.

XmuInternStrings

Name

XmuInternStrings – get the atoms for several property name strings.

Synopsis

```
#include <X11/Xmu/Atoms.h>
void XmuInternStrings(d, names, count, atoms)
   Display *d;
   String *names;
   Cardinal count;
   Atom *atoms;
```

Arguments

d	Specifies a connection to an X server; returned from `XOpenDisplay()`.
names	Specifies the strings to intern.
count	Specifies the number of strings.
atoms	Returns the list of Atoms value.

Description

`XmuInternStrings` converts a list of property name strings into a list of atoms, possibly by querying the server. The results are cached, such that subsequent requests do not cause further round-trips to the server. The caller is responsible for preallocating the array of atoms.

See Also

XmuGetAtomName, XmuInternAtom, XmuMakeAtom, XmuNameofAtom.

Xmu Library

XmuLocateBitmapFile

Name

XmuLocateBitmapFile – creates a one-plane pixmap from a bitmap file in a standard location.

Synopsis

```
#include <X11/Xmu/Drawing.h>
XmuLocateBitmapFile(screen, name, srcname, srcnamelen, widthp,
        heightp, xhotp, yhotp)
 Screen *screen;
 char *name;
 char *srcname;
 int srcnamelen;
 int *widthp, *heightp, *xhotp, *yhotp;
```

Arguments

screen	Specifies the appropriate Screen structure.
name	Specifies the file to read from.
srcname	Returns the full filename of the bitmap.
srcnamelen	Specifies the length of the srcname buffer.
width	Returns the width of the bitmap.
height	Returns the height of the bitmap.
xhotp	Returns the x coordinate of the hotspot.
yhotp	Returns the y coordinate of the hotspot.

Description

XmuLocateBitmapFile reads a file in standard bitmap file format, using XRead-BitmapFile(), and returns the created bitmap. The filename may be absolute, or relative to the global resource named *bitmapFilePath* with class *BitmapFilePath*. If the resource is not defined, the default value is the build symbol BITMAPDIR, which is typically */usr/include/X11/bitmaps*. If srcnamelen is greater than zero and srcname is not NULL, the NULL-terminated filename will be copied into srcname. The size and hotspot of the bitmap are also returned.

See Also

XmuCreatePixmapFromBitmap, XmuCreatePixmapFromBitmap, XmuCreateStippledPixmap, XmuCreateStippledPixmap, XmuDrawLogo, XmuDrawLogo, XmuDrawRoundedRectangle, XmuDrawRoundedRectangle, XmuFillRoundedRectangle, XmuFillRoundedRectangle, XmuReadBitmapData, XmuReadBitmapData, XmuReadBitmapDataFromFile, XmuReadBitmapDataFromFile, XmuReleaseStippledPixmap.

XmuLocatePixmapFile

Name

XmuLocatePixmapFile – create a pixmap from a file in a standard location.

Synopsis

```
#include <X11/Xmu/Drawing.h>
Pixmap XmuLocatePixmapFile (screen, name, fore, back, depth, srcname,
        srcnamelen, widthp, heightp, xhotp, yhotp)
    Screen *screen;
    char *name;
    unsigned long fore, back;
    unsigned int depth;
    char *srcname;
    int srcnamelen;
    int *widthp, *heightp, *xhotp, *yhotp;
```

Arguments

screen	Specifies the screen.
name	Specifies the pixmap filename.
fore, back	Specify the foreground and background colors of the pixmap.
depth	Specifies the depth of the pixmap.
srcname	Returns the absolute filename of the pixmap.
srcnamelen	Specifies the length of the srcname buffer.
widthp, heightp	Return the width and height of the pixmap.
xhotp, yhotp	Return the x and y coordinates of the pixmap hotspot.

Availability

Release 5 and later.

Description

This function reads a file in standard bitmap file format, using XmuReadBitmapData-FromFile and creates a pixmap with the specified foreground and background colors and specified depth using XCreatePixmapFromBitmapData(). The filename may be absolute, or relative to the global resource named bitmapFilePath with class BitmapFile-Path. If the resource is not defined, the default value is /usr/include/X11/bitmaps. If srcnamelen is greater than zero and srcname is not NULL, the NULL-terminated filename will be copied into srcname. The size and hotspot of the bitmap are also returned.

See Also

XmuLocateBitmapFile, XmuCreatePixmapFromBitmap, XmuReadBitmapData, XmuReadBitmapData-FromFile, XCreatePixmapFromBitmapData().

Name

XmuLookup* – translate a key event into a keysym and string, using various keysym sets.

Synopsis

```
#include <X11/Xmu/CharSet.h>
int XmuLookupLatin1(event, buffer, nbytes, keysym, status)
int XmuLookupLatin2(event, buffer, nbytes, keysym, status)
int XmuLookupLatin3(event, buffer, nbytes, keysym, status)
int XmuLookupLatin4(event, buffer, nbytes, keysym, status)
int XmuLookupKana(event, buffer, nbytes, keysym, status)
int XmuLookupJISX0201(event, buffer, nbytes, keysym, status)
int XmuLookupArabic(event, buffer, nbytes, keysym, status)
int XmuLookupCyrillic(event, buffer, nbytes, keysym, status)
int XmuLookupGreek(event, buffer, nbytes, keysym, status)
int XmuLookupHebrew(event, buffer, nbytes, keysym, status)
int XmuLookupAPL(event, buffer, nbytes, keysym, status)
   XKeyEvent *event;
   char *buffer;
   int nbytes;
   KeySym *keysym;
   XComposeStatus *status;
```

Arguments

event	Specifies the key event.
buffer	Returns the translated characters.
nbytes	Specifies the length of the buffer.
keysym	Returns the computed KeySym, or None.
status	Specifies or returns the compose state.

Description

These functions translate a key event into a keysym and string, using a keysym set other than Latin-1, as shown in the following table.

Function	Converts To
XmuLookupLatin1	Latin-1 (ISO 8859-1), or ASCII control (Synonym for XLookupString).
XmuLookupLatin2	Latin-2 (ISO 8859-2), or ASCII control.
XmuLookupLatin3	Latin-3 (ISO 8859-3), or ASCII control.
XmuLookupLatin4	Latin-4 (ISO 8859-4), or ASCII control.
XmuLookupKana	Latin-1 (ISO 8859-1) and ASCII control in the Graphics Left half (values 0 to 127), and Katakana in the Graphics Right half (values 128 to 255), using the values from JIS X201-1976.
XmuLookupJISX0201	JIS X0201-1976 encoding, including ASCII control.
XmuLookupArabic	Latin/Arabic (ISO 8859-6), or ASCII control.
XmuLookupCyrillic	Latin/Cyrillic (ISO 8859-5), or ASCII control.
XmuLookupGreek	Latin/Greek (ISO 8859-7), or ASCII control.
XmuLookupHebrew	Latin/Hebrew (ISO 8859-8), or ASCII control string.
XmuLookupAPL	APL string.

XmuLookupLatin1 is identical to XLookupString(), and exists only for naming symmetry with other functions covered on this page.

See Also

XmuCompareISOLatin1, XmuCopyISOLatin1Lowered, XmuCopyISOLatin1Uppered.

XmuLookupCloseDisplayHook

Name

XmuLookupCloseDisplayHook – get currently registered close display callback function.

Synopsis

```
#include <X11/Xmu/CloseHook.h>
Bool XmuLookupCloseDisplayHook(display, handle, func, arg)
    Display *display;
    CloseHook handle;
    int(*func)();
    caddr_t arg;
```

Xmu Library

Arguments

display   Specifies a connection to an X server; returned from XOpenDisplay().

handle   Specifies the callback by ID, or NULL.

func   Specifies the callback by function.

arg   Specifies the function data to match.

Description

XmuLookupCloseDisplayHook determines if a callback is registered. If *handle* is not NULL, it specifies the callback to look for, and the *func* and *arg* parameters are ignored. If handle is NULL, the function will look for any callback that matches the specified *func* and *arg*. This function returns True if a matching callback exists, or otherwise False.

See Also

XmuAddCloseDisplayHook, *XmuRemoveCloseDisplayHook*.

XmuLookupStandardColormap

Name

XmuLookupStandardColormap – create a standard colormap if not already created.

Synopsis

```
#include <X11/Xmu/StdCmap.h>
XmuLookupStandardColormap(display, screen, visualid, depth, property,
        replace, retain)
   Display *display;
   int screen;
   VisualID visualid;
   unsigned int depth;
   Atom property;
   Bool replace;
   Bool retain;
```

Arguments

display	Specifies a connection to an X server; returned from XOpenDisplay().
screen	Specifies the screen of the display.
visualid	Specifies the visual type.
depth	Specifies the visual depth.
property	Specifies the standard colormap property.
replace	Specifies whether or not to replace.
retain	Specifies whether or not to retain.

Description

XmuLookupStandardColormap creates a standard colormap if one does not currently exist, or replaces the currently existing standard colormap.

Given a screen, a visual, and a property, this function will determine the best allocation for the property under the specified visual, and determine whether to create a new colormap or to use the default colormap of the screen.

If *replace* is True, any previous definition of the property will be replaced. If *retain* is True, the property and the colormap will be made permanent for the duration of the server session. However, pre-existing property definitions which are not replaced cannot be made permanent by a call to this function; a request to retain resources pertains to newly created resources.

XmuLookupStandardColormap returns zero on failure, non-zero on success. A request to create a standard colormap upon a visual which cannot support such a map is considered a failure. An example of this would be requesting any standard colormap property on a monochrome visual, or, requesting an RGB_BEST_MAP on a display whose colormap size is 16.

See Also

XmuAllStandardColormaps, *XmuCreateColormap*, *XmuDeleteStandardColormap*, *XmuGetColormap-Allocation*, *XmuStandardColormap*, *XmuVisualStandardColormaps*.

XmuMakeAtom

Name

XmuMakeAtom – create `AtomPtr` to hold atom list for a property name string.

Synopsis

```
#include <X11/Xmu/Atoms.h>
AtomPtr XmuMakeAtom(name)
    char* name;
```

Arguments

name   Specifies the atom name.

Description

`XmuMakeAtom` creates and initializes an `AtomPtr`, which is an opaque object that contains a property name string and a list of atoms for that string—one for each display. `Xmu-InternAtom` is used to fill in the atom for each display.

See Also

XmuGetAtomName, XmuInternAtom, XmuInternStrings, XmuNameofAtom.

XmuNameOfAtom

Name

XmuNameOfAtom – return property name string represented by an `AtomPtr`.

Synopsis

```
#include <X11/Xmu/Atoms.h>
char *XmuNameOfAtom(atom_ptr)
   AtomPtr atom_ptr;
```

Arguments

atom_ptr   Specifies the `AtomPtr`.

Description

XmuNameOfAtom returns the property name string represented by the specified `AtomPtr`.

See Also

XmuGetAtomName, XmuInternAtom, XmuInternStrings, XmuMakeAtom.

XmuPrintDefaultErrorMessage

Name

XmuPrintDefaultErrorMessage – print the standard protocol error message.

Synopsis

```
#include <X11/Xmu/Error.h>
int XmuPrintDefaultErrorMessage(display, event, fp)
    Display *display;
    XErrorEvent *event;
    FILE *fp;
```

Arguments

display   Specifies a connection to an X server; returned from `XOpenDisplay()`.

event   Specifies the error event whose contents will be printed.

fp   Specifies where to print the error message.

Description

`XmuPrintDefaultErrorMessage` prints an error message, equivalent to Xlib's default error message for protocol errors. It returns a non-zero value if the caller should consider exiting, otherwise it returns zero. This function can be used when you need to write your own error handler, but need to print out an error from within that handler.

See Also

XmuSimpleErrorHandler.

XmuReadBitmapData

Name

XmuReadBitmapData – read and check bitmap data from any stream source.

Synopsis

```
#include <X11/Xmu/Drawing.h>
int XmuReadBitmapData(fstream, width, height, datap, x_hot, y_hot)
  FILE *fstream;
  unsigned int *width, *height;
  unsigned char **datap;
  int *x_hot, *y_hot;
```

Arguments

stream	Specifies the stream to read from.
width	Returns the width of the bitmap.
height	Returns the height of the bitmap.
datap	Returns the parsed bitmap data.
x_hot	Returns the x coordinate of the hotspot.
y_hot	Returns the y coordinate of the hotspot.

Description

XmuReadBitmapData reads a standard bitmap file description from the specified stream, and returns the parsed data in a format suitable for passing to XCreatePixmapFrom-BitmapData(). The return value of the function has the same meaning as the return value for XReadBitmapFile().

XmuReadBitmapData is equivalent to XReadBitmapFile(), except that this routine processes any type of stream input, and it does not create a pixmap containing the resulting data. This is useful when you want to create a multi-plane pixmap from the data, and don't want to create an intermediate one-plane pixmap.

See Also

XmuCreatePixmapFromBitmap, XmuCreateStippledPixmap, XmuDrawLogo, XmuDrawRounded-Rectangle, XmuFillRoundedRectangle, XmuLocateBitmapFile, XmuReadBitmapDataFromFile, XmuReleaseStippledPixmap.

XmuReadBitmapDataFromFile

Name

XmuReadBitmapDataFromFile – read and check bitmap data from a file.

Synopsis

```
#include <X11/Xmu/Drawing.h>
int XmuReadBitmapDataFromFile(filename, width, height, datap, x_hot,
        y_hot)
  char *filename;
  unsigned int *width, *height;
  unsigned char **datap;
  int *x_hot, *y_hot;
```

Arguments

filename   Specifies the file to read from.

width   Returns the width of the bitmap.

height   Returns the height of the bitmap.

datap   Returns the parsed bitmap data.

x_hot   Returns the x coordinate of the hotspot.

y_hot   Returns the y coordinate of the hotspot.

Description

XmuReadBitmapDataFromFile reads a standard bitmap file description from the specified file, and returns the parsed data in a format suitable for passing to XCreatePixmap-FromBitmapData( ). The return value of the function has the same meaning as the return value for XReadBitmapFile( ).

Unlike XReadBitmapFile( ), this function does not create a pixmap. This function is useful when you want to create a multi-plane pixmap without creating an intermediate one-plane pixmap.

See Also

XmuCreatePixmapFromBitmap, *XmuCreateStippledPixmap*, *XmuDrawLogo*, *XmuDrawRounded-Rectangle*, *XmuFillRoundedRectangle*, *XmuLocateBitmapFile*, *XmuReadBitmapData*, *XmuRelease-StippledPixmap*.

XmuReleaseStippledPixmap

Name

XmuReleaseStippledPixmap – release pixmap created with `XmuCreateStippledPixmap`.

Synopsis

```
#include <X11/Xmu/Drawing.h>
void XmuReleaseStippledPixmap(screen, pixmap)
   Screen *screen;
   Pixmap pixmap;
```

Arguments

screen   Specifies the screen the pixmap was created on.

pixmap   Specifies the pixmap to free.

Description

`XmuReleaseStippledPixmap` frees a pixmap created with `XmuCreateStippledPixmap`, to maintain correct cache reference counts.

See Also

XmuCreatePixmapFromBitmap, XmuCreateStippledPixmap, XmuDrawLogo, XmuDrawRoundedRectangle, XmuFillRoundedRectangle, XmuLocateBitmapFile, XmuReadBitmapData, XmuReadBitmapDataFromFile.

XmuRemoveCloseDisplayHook

Xmu – CloseDisplay Hook —

Name

XmuRemoveCloseDisplayHook – remove registered close display callback function.

Synopsis

```
#include <X11/Xmu/CloseHook.h>
Bool XmuRemoveCloseDisplayHook(display, handle, func, arg)
    Display *display;
    CloseHook handle;
    int(*func)();
    caddr_t arg;
```

Arguments

display   Specifies a connection to an X server; returned from XOpenDisplay().

handle   Specifies the callback by ID, or NULL.

func   Specifies the callback by function.

arg   Specifies the function data to match.

Description

XmuRemoveCloseDisplayHook unregisters a callback that has been registered with XmuAddCloseDisplayHook. If handle is not NULL, it specifies the ID of the callback to remove, and the *func* and *arg* parameters are ignored. If handle is NULL, the first callback found to match the specified *func* and *arg* will be removed. Returns True if a callback was removed, else returns False.

See Also

XmuAddCloseDisplayHook, XmuLookupCloseDisplayHook.

XmuScreenOfWindow

Name

XmuScreenOfWindow – returns a pointer to the `Screen` structure for the specified window.

Synopsis

```
#include <X11/Xmu/WinUtil.h>
Screen *XmuScreenOfWindow(display, w)
   Display *display;
   Window w;
```

Arguments

display   Specifies a connection to an X server; returned from `XOpenDisplay()`.

w   Specifies the window.

Description

`XmuScreenOfWindow` returns a pointer to the `Screen` structure that describes the screen on which the specified window was created.

See Also

XmuClientWindow, *XmuUpdateMapHints*.

XmuSimpleErrorHandler

Name

XmuSimpleErrorHandler – an error handler that ignores certain errors.

Synopsis

```
#include <X11/Xmu/Error.h>
int XmuSimpleErrorHandler(display, error)
  Display *display;
  XErrorEvent *error;
```

Arguments

display   Specifies a connection to an X server; returned from `XOpenDisplay()`.

error   Specifies the error event.

Description

`XmuSimpleErrorHandler` ignores `BadWindow` errors for `XQueryTree()` and `XGetWindowAttributes()`, and ignores `BadDrawable` errors for `XGet-Geometry()`; it returns zero in those cases. Otherwise, it prints the default error message, and returns a non-zero value if the caller should consider exiting, and zero if the caller should not exit.

See Also

XmuPrintDefaultErrorMessage.

XmuStandardColormap

Name

XmuStandardColormap – create one standard colormap.

Synopsis

```
#include <X11/Xmu/StdCmap.h>
XmuStandardColormap(display, screen, visualid, depth, property, cmap,
        red_max, green_max, blue_max)
    Display display;
    int screen;
    VisualID visualid;
    unsigned int depth;
    Atom property;
    Colormap cmap;
    unsigned long red_max, green_max, blue_max;
```

Arguments

display	Specifies a connection to an X server; returned from XOpenDisplay().
screen	Specifies the screen of the display.
visualid	Specifies the visual type.
depth	Specifies the visual depth.
property	Specifies the standard colormap property.
cmap	Specifies the colormap ID, or None.
red_max	Specifies the red allocation.
green_max	Specifies the green allocation.
blue_max	Specifies the blue allocation.

Description

XmuStandardColormap creates one standard colormap for the given screen, visualid, and visual depth, with the given red, green, and blue maximum values, with the given standard property name. Upon success, it returns a pointer to an XStandardColormap structure which describes the newly created colormap. Upon failure, it returns NULL. If cmap is the default colormap of the screen, the standard colormap will be defined on the default colormap; otherwise a new colormap is created.

Resources created by this function are not made permanent; that is the caller's responsibility.

See Also

XmuAllStandardColormaps, XmuCreateColormap, XmuDeleteStandardColormap, XmuGetColormapAllocation, XmuLookupStdCmp, XmuVisualStandardColormaps.

XmuUpdateMapHints

Name

XmuUpdateMapHints – set WM_HINTS flags to USSize and USPosition.

Synopsis

```
#include <X11/Xmu/WinUtil.h>
Bool XmuUpdateMapHints(display, w, hints)
    Display *display;
    Window w;
    XSizeHints *hints;
```

Arguments

display   Specifies a connection to an X server; returned from XOpenDisplay().

win   Specifies the window.

hints   Specifies the new hints, or NULL.

Description

XmuUpdateMapHints clears the PPosition and PSize flags and sets the USPosition and USSize flags in the hints structure, and then stores the hints for the window using
XSetWMNormalHints() and returns True. If NULL is passed for the hints structure, then
the current hints are read back from the window using XGetWMNormalHints() the flags
are set as described above, the property is reset, and True is returned. XmuUpdateMap-
Hints returns False if it was unable to allocate memory or, when NULL is passed, if the
existing hints could not be read.

See Also

XmuClientWindow, *XmuScreenOfWindow*.

XmuVisualStandardColormaps

Name

XmuVisualStandardColormaps – create all standard colormaps for given visual and screen.

Synopsis

```
#include <X11/Xmu/StdCmap.h>
XmuVisualStandardColormaps(display, screen, visualid, depth, replace,
        retain)
    Display *display;
    int screen;
    VisualID visualid;
    unsigned int depth;
    Bool replace;
    Bool retain;
```

Arguments

display	Specifies a connection to an X server; returned from XOpenDisplay().
screen	Specifies the screen of the display.
visualid	Specifies the visual type.
depth	Specifies the visual depth.
replace	Specifies whether or not to replace the standard colormap property.
retain	Specifies whether or not to retain the colormap resource permanently.

Description

XmuVisualStandardColormaps creates all of the appropriate standard colormaps for a given visual on a given screen, and optionally redefines the corresponding standard colormap properties.

If replace is True, any previous definition will be removed. If retain is True, new properties will be retained for the duration of the server session. This function returns zero on failure, non-zero on success. On failure, no new properties will be defined, but old ones may have been removed if replace was True.

Not all standard colormaps are meaningful to all visual classes. This routine will check and define the following properties for the following classes, provided that the size of the colormap is not too small. For DirectColor and PseudoColor: RGB_DEFAULT_MAP, RGB_BEST_MAP, RGB_RED_MAP, RGB_GREEN_MAP, RGB_BLUE_MAP, and RGB_GRAY_MAP. For TrueColor and StaticColor: RGB_BEST_MAP. For GrayScale and Static-Gray: RGB_GRAY_MAP.

See Also

XmuAllStandardColormaps, XmuCreateColormap, XmuDeleteStandardColormap, XmuGetColormap-Allocation, XmuLookupStdCmp, XmuStandardColormap.

K
Character Sets and Encodings

Some of the Xlib functions make reference to specific character sets and character encodings. The following ones are the most common:

X Portable Character Set

A basic set of 97 characters which are assumed to exist in all locales supported by Xlib. This set contains the following characters:

```
a..z A..Z 0..9
!"#$%&'()*+,-./:;<=>?@[\\]^_'{|}~
<space>, <tab>, and <newline>
```

This is the left/lower half of the graphic character set of ISO8859-1 plus <space>, <tab>, and <newline>. It is also the set of graphic characters in 7-bit ASCII plus the same three control characters. The actual encoding of these characters on the host is system dependent.

Host Portable Character Encoding

The encoding of the X Portable Character Set on the host. The encoding itself is not defined by this standard, but the encoding must be the same in all locales supported by Xlib on the host. If a string is said to be in the Host Portable Character Encoding, then it only contains characters from the X Portable Character Set, in the host encoding.

Latin-1

The coded character set defined by the ISO8859-1 standard.

STRING encoding

Latin-1, plus tab and newline.

POSIX Portable Filename Character Set

The set of 65 characters which can be used in naming files on a POSIX-compliant host that are correctly processed in all locales. The set is:

```
a..z A..Z 0..9 ._-
```

Index

Index

F

Index

Index

Index

Index

Index

USPosition flag, 999
USSize flag, 1000

V

Value, finding maximum Chroma for, 187
variable argument lists, nested, 806
vendor release number, 807
VendorRelease macro, 807, 900
virtual crossing, 932
VisibilityChangeMask event mask, 1000
VisibilityFully event state, 1000
VisibilityNotify event, 963, 1000
VisibilityPartially event state, 1000
VisibilityUnobscured event state, 1000
visual ID, obtaining from a visual, 808
    returning, 809
VisualAllMask, 1000
VisualBitsPerRGBMask, 1000
VisualBlueMaskMask, 1000
VisualClassMask, 1000
VisualColormapSize mask, 1000
VisualDepthMask, 1000
VisualGreenMaskMask, 1000
VisualIDMask, 1000
VisualNoMask, 1000
VisualOfCCC, 197
VisualRedMaskMask, 1000
visuals, 419
    associated with CCC, 197
    returning visual information for, 504
    visual structures, returning list of, 418
    (see also XVisualInfo structure)
VisualScreenMask, 1000

W

WestGravity mode, 1000
WhenMapped value, 1000
white pixel values, 831
white point, 146
    adjustment procedure, 198
    changing, 180

obtaining, 176
    setting, 182
WhitePixel macro, 831, 900
WhitePixelOfScreen macro, 831, 900
wide-character input, obtaining, 818
WidthMMOfScreen macro, 832, 900
WidthOfScreen macro, 832, 900
WidthValue mask, 1001
WindingRule, 553, 682, 1001
window attributes, obtaining, 420
    setting, 111
window management, 119
window manager, 428
    client machines, 426
    colormap windows, 428
    hints property, 430
    icon names, 432
    names, 434
    normal hints, 436
    properties, 516;
        hints, 744;
        setting, 751;
        setting minimum set for, 724
    protocols, 438
    size hints, 440
    WM_CLIENT_MACHINE property, 426
    WM_COLORMAP_WINDOWS property, 428
    WM_PROTOCOLS property, 438
    XA_WM_CLASS property, 364
    XA_WM_HINTS property, 430
    XA_WM_ICON_NAME property, 432
    XA_WM_NAME property, 434
    XA_WM_NORMAL_HINTS property, 436
    XA_WM_SIZE_HINTS property, 440
    XA_WM_TRANSIENT_FOR property, 417
    (see also WM_ properties)
WindowGroupHint, 1001
windows, background attributes, 734
    background_pixmap attribute, 735

Index

Index

Window Attributes at a Glance - 1

Member	Values / Default	Mask	Convenience Function
Pixmap background_pixmap;	pixmap (depth of window), ParentRelative / **None**	CWBackPixmap	XSetWindowBackgroundPixmap
unsigned long background_pixel;	pixelvalue / **undefined**	CWBackPixel	XSetWindowBackground
Pixmap border_pixmap;	pixmap (depth of window), None / **CopyFromParent**	CWBorderPixmap	XSetWindowBorderPixmap
unsigned long border_pixel;	pixel value / **undefined**	CWBorderPixel	XSetWindowBorder
int bit_gravity;	StaticGravity, NorthWestGravity, NorthGravity, NorthEastGravity, WestGravity, CenterGravity, SouthWestGravity, SouthGravity, EastGravity, SouthEastGravity / **ForgetGravity**	CWBitGravity	none
int win_gravity;	same as above, UnmapGravity / **NorthWestGravity**	CWWinGravity	none
int backing_store;	WhenMapped, Always/ **NotUseful**	CWBackingStore	none
unsigned long backing_planes;	bit mask / **AllPlanes**	CWBackingPlanes	none
unsigned long backing_pixel;	pixel value / **0**	CWBackingPixel	none
Bool save_under;	True / **False**	CWOverrideRedirect	none
long event_mask,	OR of event mask symbols * / **0**	CWSaveUnder	XSelectInput
long do_not_propagate_mask;	OR of event mask symbols * / **0**	CWEventMask	none
Bool override_redirect;	True / **False**	CWDontPropagate	none
Colormap colormap;	colormap ID, None / **CopyFromParent**	CWColormap	XSetWindowColormap
Cursor cursor;	cursor ID / **None** (copy from parent)	CWCursor	XDefineCursor, XUndefineCursor

All attributes can be set with XCreateWindow or XChangeWindowAttributes.

* The event_mask symbols are:

NoEventMask, KeyPressMask, KeyReleaseMask, ButtonPressMask, ButtonReleaseMask, EnterWindowMask, LeaveWindowMask, PointerMotionMask, PointerMotionHintMask, Button1MotionMask, Button2MotionMask, Button3MotionMask, Button4MotionMask, Button5MotionMask, ButtonMotionMask, KeymapStateMask, ExposureMask, VisibilityChangeMask, StructureNotifyMask, ResizeRedirectMask, SubstructureNotifyMask, SubstructureRedirectMask, FocusChangeMask, PropertyChangeMask, ColormapChangeMask, OwnerGrabButtonMask.

The GC at a Glance - 2

Member	Values / Default	Mask	Convenience Function
int function;	GXclear, GXand, GXandReverse, GXandInverted, GXnoop, GXxor, GXor, GXnor, GXequiv, GXinvert, GXorReverse, GXset, GXcopyInverted, GXorInverted, GXnand / **GXcopy**	GCFunction	XSetFunction
unsigned long plane_mask;	bit for each plane / all 1's	GCPlaneMask	XSetPlaneMask
unsigned long foreground;	pixel value / 0	GCForeground	XSetForeground
unsigned long background;	pixel value / 1	GCBackground	XSetBackground
int line_width;	in pixels / 0	GCLineWidth	XSetLineAttributes
int line_style;	LineOnOffDash, LineDoubleDash / **LineSolid**	GCLineStyle	XSetLineAttributes
int cap_style;	CapNotLast, CapRound, CapProjecting / **CapButt**	GCCapStyle	XSetLineAttributes
int join_style;	JoinRound, JoinBevel / **JoinMiter**	GCJoinStyle	XSetLineAttributes
int fill_style;	FillTiled, FillStippled, FillOpaqueStippled / **FillSolid**	GCFillStyle	XSetFillStyle
int fill_rule;	WindingRule / **EvenOddRule**	GCFillRule	XSetFillRule
int arc_mode;	ArcChord / **ArcPieSlice**	GCArcMode	XSetArcMode
Pixmap tile;	depth of destination / filled with **foreground**	GCTile	XSetTile
Pixmap stipple;	depth 1 / **all 1's**	GCStipple	XSetStipple
int ts_x_origin;	from drawable origin / 0	GCTileStipXOrigin	XSetTSOrigin
int ts_y_origin;	from drawable origin / 0	GCTileStipYOrigin	XSetTSOrigin
Font font;	ID, not necessarily loaded / **server-dependent**	GCFont	XSetFont
int subwindow_mode;	IncludeInferiors / **ClipByChildren**	GCSubwindowMode	XSetSubwindowMode
Bool graphics_exposures;	False / **True**	GCGraphicsExposures	XSetGraphicsExposures
int clip_x_origin;	from drawable origin / 0	GCClipXOrigin	XSetClipOrigin
int clip_y_origin;	from drawable origin / 0	GCClipYOrigin	XSetClipOrigin
Pixmap clip_mask;	depth 1 / **None**	GCClipMask	XSetClipMask, XSetClipRectangles, XSetRegion
int dash_offset;	in pixels / 0	GCDashOffset	XSetDashes
char dashes;	lengths of dashes / **4**	GCDashList	XSetDashes

The GC at a Glance - 3

line_style

LineSolid   LineOnOffDash   LineDoubleDash

cap_style

CapNotLast   CapButt   CapRound   CapProjecting

join_style

JoinRound   JoinMiter   JoinBevel

fill_style

Tile

GC foreground   GC background   Undrawn Pixels

Stipple

0	1	0
0	1	0
0	1	0

FillSolid   FillTiled   FillStippled   FillOpaqueStippled

fill_rule

Outline of polygon to fill   EvenOddRule   WindingRule

arc_mode

ArcChord   ArcPieSlice

subwindow_mode

IncludeInferiors — Graphics drawn with this setting will appear through all mapped subwindows, but not through siblings.

ClipByChildren — Graphics drawn will not draw through any other window that has a background.

graphics_exposures

True — Generate GraphicsExpose or NoExpose events when XCopyArea or XCopyPlane is called with this GC.

False — Don't generate GraphicsExpose or NoExpose events.

The GC at a Glance - 4

	arc_mode	background	cap_style	clip_mask	clip_x_origin	clip_y_origin	dashes	dash_offset	fill_rule	fill_style	font	foreground	function	graphics_exposures	join_style	line_style	line_width	plane_mask	tile	stipple	subwindow_mode	ts_x_origin	ts_y_origin
xClearArea																							
XClearWindow																							
XCopyArea				■	■	■							■	■				■			■		
XCopyPlane		■		■	■	■						■	■	■				■			■		
XDrawArc		□	■	■	□	□	□	□		■		□	■			■	■	■	□	□	■	□	□
XDrawArcs		□	■	■	□	□	□	□		■		□	■			■	■	■	□	□	■	□	□
XDrawImageString		■		■	□	□					■	■						■			■		
XDrawImageString16		■		■	□	□					■	■						■			■		
XDrawLine		□	■	■	□	□	□	□		■		□	■		■	■	■	■	□	□	■	□	□
XDrawLines		□	■	■	□	□	□	□		■		□	■		■	■	■	■	□	□	■	□	□
XDrawPoint		□		■	□	□				■		□	■					■	□	□	■	□	□
XDrawPoints		□		■	□	□				■		□	■					■	□	□	■	□	□
XDrawSegments		□	■	■	□	□	□	□		■		□	■		■	■	■	■	□	□	■	□	□
XDrawString		□		■	□	□				■	■	□	■					■	□	□	■	□	□
XDrawString16		□		■	□	□				■	■	□	■					■	□	□	■	□	□
XDrawText		□		■	□	□				■	■	□	■					■	□	□	■	□	□
XDrawText16		□		■	□	□				■	■	□	■					■	□	□	■	□	□
XDrawRectangle		□	■	■	□	□	□	□		■		□	■		■	■	■	■	□	□	■	□	□
XDrawRectangles		□	■	■	□	□	□	□		■		□	■		■	■	■	■	□	□	■	□	□
XFillArc	■	□		■	□	□				■		□	■					■	□	□	■	□	□
XFillArcs	■	□		■	□	□				■		□	■					■	□	□	■	□	□
XFillPolygon		□		■	□	□			■	■		□	■					■	□	□	■	□	□
XFillRectangle		□		■	□	□				■		□	■					■	□	□	■	□	□
XFillRectangles		□		■	□	□				■		□	■					■	□	□	■	□	□
XGetImage																		■					
XPutImage		▨		■	□	□						▨	■					■			■		

Legend:

□ - foreground, background, tile or stipple are used depending on setting of fill_style, dash_offset and dashes may be used depending on the setting of line_style.

■ - component always used.

▨ - used only if image is XYBitmap format.

About the Editor

Adrian Nye is a senior technical writer at O'Reilly & Associates. In addition to the X Window System programming manuals, he has written user's manuals for data acquisition products, and customized UNIX documentation for Sun Microsystems and Prime. Adrian has also worked as a programmer writing educational software in C, and as a mechanical engineer designing offshore oilspill cleanup equipment. He has long-term interests in using his technical writing skills to promote recycling and other environmentally-sound technologies. He graduated from the Massachusetts Institute of Technology in 1984 with a B.S. in Mechanical Engineering.

DEMCO

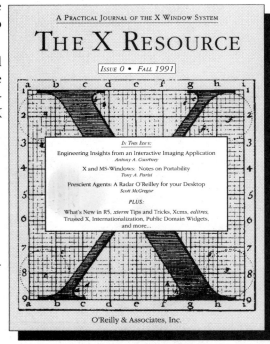